D1780258

# THESES
# IN
# AMERICAN LITERATURE
# 1896-1971

# THESES
# IN
# AMERICAN LITERATURE
# 1896-1971

Compiled and Edited
by
**PATSY C. HOWARD**
Abilene Christian College

THE PIERIAN PRESS
Ann Arbor, Michigan
1973

Library of Congress Catalog Card Number 74-172775
ISBN 0-87650-022-X

©Copyright 1973, The Pierian Press
All Rights Reserved

THE PIERIAN PRESS
P.O. Box 1808
Ann Arbor, MI. 48106

*To Barbara and Dave*

*Debby, Karen, Brian,*

*Jimmy, Diane and*

*Kathleen*

## FOREWORD

This bibliography of unpublished baccalaureate and masters' theses is drawn primarily from listings made by the compiler who personally collected the material at many southwestern, southern and eastern colleges and universities during the summer of 1970. The collection is necessarily incomplete. It serves as the beginning of a series whose goal is to make a complete, easily accessible listing of theses in literature throughout the world.

The purposes of this compilation are: 1) to indicate which fields of research have received noticeable attention; 2) to indicate those areas of research generally unexplored by graduate students; and 3) to provide convenient bibliographies on highly specialized topics for those students presently engaged in bibliographic scholarship.

The entries in this volume are arranged alphabetically by the most commonly used name for each American writer. Under each classification the theses and essays are alphabetized by thesis author. Each title is numbered, and cross references, if any, are indicated by these numbers. A cumulative thesis author index as well as a limited subject index is provided at the end of the bibliography. A list of participating institutions is also provided immediately following this Foreword.

As to the form taken by the bibliography, the editors feel it is the most useful one in view of the thesis series far-reaching scope. Along with the usually accepted abbreviations, we decided to shorten State (St), College (Coll) and University (Univ). The designation of the degree was also abbreviated: MA for Master of Arts, M Phil for Master of Philosophy, M Ed for Master of Education, MS for Master of Science, M Litt for Master of Literature, MFA for Master of Fine Arts, BA for Bachelor of Arts, B Litt for Bachelor of Literature and BS for Bachelor of Science.

In this first volume of American literature theses the basis for the selection of the bibliographic entries has been one of availability. The response from librarians has been overwhelming. Those contacted have been very gracious and most enthusiastic. The compiler wishes to thank the numerous reference librarians, department heads and personal friends for their contributions to this work. Contributions from the following are gratefully acknowledged:

Charles Adams, Sister Albina-Marie, C M Baker, Cheryl Bandy, Patty Barker, Carolynne Barnes, Harry Bergholz, Edmund Bojarski, Laura Boyer, Luther Brown, Randy Brown, Charles E Butler, John K Cameron, Myrtle Carroll, Beverly Carter, Richard R Chamberlin, Marcy Chambers, Antoinette Ciolli, Dorothy H Claybourne, William Cook Jr, Kathleen Creech, Joyce A Crenshaw, Barna Csuros, J H Deardoff, Frieda Dickson, Sister Laura Dillon, Elva Love Dobson, Don and Nancy Donham, Evelyn Ehrlich, C M Ellis, Charlotte Engelhardt, Teri Falls, Obion W Feagin, Sue Findley, Ezra C Fitch, Kathyrn Forbes, Thomas Frazier, A C Garvin, Dennis Gibson, Paula Gillen, Eleanor Goehring, Sara Lou Goff, Martha Graham, Beth Granichen, Rebecca Green, S B Gribble, Arthur Goldzweig, Bernadette Gualtieri, Willie D Halsell, Helen Haney, Trena Harlan, Mary Harlow, Betty Hartbank, Lois Harzfeld, Thomas Havins, Dorothy Heicke, Millicent Hering, Ruth V Hewlett, Ann T Hinckley, Beryl Hoskin, Lillian Howard, Monty Howard, I Isaacson, the Edgar Jacksons, Jennifer Jacques, Katherine Jaffe, Jane Ann Jenkins, Ruth Johnson, Barbara Jones, Martha Jones, Margaret A Joseph, Minnie S Kallam, Margaret J Keefe, Charles H Kemp, Edith Keys, Floreine Kibler, Margaret J Kyle, Evelyn Lightfoot, Bob and Judy McCourt, John MacEachern, Mary A McKenzie, Edmund Maloney, Sister Mary Marguerite, Larry May, Floyd S Merritt, William Messenger, Eleanor Mitchell, Dorothy Moore, Margaret Moseley, Judith Mowery, A M Mumper, Janet H Murphy, M G Nelson, Roberto Pasqualato, Angela Paulos, Beth Petty, Sandy Pinsker, Sara and Franz Pittman, Mary Lynn Potts, Helen J Poulton, James Pula, Linda Rabon, Dianne Rabun, Diane Reynolds, Frances D Rhome, Charity M Roth, Deborah Rudloff, Anna Loe Russell, Shirley Sailors, Orlan Sawey, Sara Sawey, Elizabeth B Scott, Rita Scott, P O Selby,

John H Sharpe, Donald Siefker, Henry L Simmons, Charles Small, Lee Smith, Dolores Smittle, Mildred D Southwick, W A Stanton, Elizabeth Steele, Alice Steger, Marion Stein, Jocelyn E Stevens, Joan Stewart, Ken Swearingen, Sharon Swindle, Bruce Teets, Juanita Terry, Dan R Thorson, Elaine M Tieman, Anne L Turner, Margaret D Uridge, Dean Waddell, Arnold S Wajenberg, Mary Lou and Wayne Walden, Jim Walter, Nancy A Whitman, Marvin E Wiggins, Geneva Williams, Robert Williams, Harold Williamson, Henry W Wingate, Marian H Withington, Anne Womeldorf, and Beverly Woodward.

The following bibliographies have been most helpful: Paul F Friesner's *Bibliography of Masters' Theses at Fort Hays Kansas State College 1930-1962;* Clyde H Cantrell and Walton R Patrick's *Southern Literary Culture: A Bibliography of Masters' and Doctors' Theses;* S J Sackett's *Masters' Theses in Literature (1964-1966).*

PATSY C HOWARD
Abilene Christian College

LIST OF INSTITUTIONS

ALABAMA

Auburn University (Auburn); Birmingham-Southern College (Birmingham); University of Alabama (University)

ALASKA

University of Alaska (College)

ARIZONA

Arizona State College (Flagstaff); Arizona State University (Tempe); Northern Arizona University (Flagstaff); University of Arizona (Tucson)

ARKANSAS

Arkansas State College (Conway); Henderson State College (Arkadelphia); University of Arkansas (Fayetteville)

CALIFORNIA

California State College at Long Beach (Long Beach); Catholic University at San Rafael (San Rafael); Chico State College (Chico); Claremont Graduate School (Claremont); College of the Holy Names at Oakland (Oakland); Dominican College of San Rafael (San Rafael); Fresno State College (Fresno); La Verne College (La Verne); Occidental College (Los Angeles); Pepperdine College (Los Angeles); Sacramento State College (Sacramento); San Diego College for Women (San Diego); San Diego State College (San Diego); San Jose State College (San Jose); Stanford University (Palo Alto); University of California at Berkeley (Berkeley); University of California at Los Angeles (Los Angeles); University of California at Riverside (Riverside); University of California at Santa Barbara (Santa Barbara); University of Pacific (Stockton); University of Redlands (Redlands); University of San Diego (San Diego); University of Santa Clara (Santa Clara); University of Southern California (Los Angeles); Whittier College (Whittier)

COLORADO

Adams State College (Alamosa); Colorado College (Colorado Springs); Colorado State College (Greeley); Colorado State University (Fort Collins); University of Colorado (Boulder); University of Denver (Denver); Western State College of Colorado (Gunnison)

CONNECTICUT

Central Connecticut State College (New Britain); Connecticut College (New London); St Joseph College (West Hartford); Southern Connecticut State College (New Haven); Trinity College (Hartford); University of Connecticut (Storrs); Wesleyan University (Middletown); Yale University (New Haven)

DELAWARE

University of Delaware (Newark)

DISTRICT OF COLUMBIA

American University (Washington, D C); Catholic University of America (Washington, D C); Georgetown University (Washington, D C); George Washington University (Washington, D C); Howard University (Washington, D C)

FLORIDA

Barry College (Miami); Florida State University (Tallahassee); Stetson University (Deland); University of Florida (Gainesville); University of Miami (Coral Gables)

GEORGIA

Atlanta University (Atlanta); Emory University (Atlanta); Oglethorpe University (Atlanta); University of Georgia (Athens)

HAWAII

University of Hawaii (Honolulu)

IDAHO

Idaho State University (Pocatello); University of Idaho (Moscow)

ILLINOIS

DePaul University (Chicago); Eastern Illinois University (Charleston); Illinois State University (Normal); Loyola University at Chicago (Chicago); Northern Illinois University (Dekalb); Northwestern University (Evanston); Roosevelt University at Chicago (Chicago); Southern Illinois University at Carbondale (Carbondale); University of Chicago (Chicago); University of Illinois at Chicago Circle (Chicago); University of Illinois at Urbana (Urbana); Western Illinois University (Macomb)

INDIANA

Ball State University (Muncie); Butler University (Indianapolis); DePauw University (Greencastle); Indiana University (Bloomington); Purdue University (Lafayette); University of Notre Dame (Notre Dame)

IOWA

Drake University (Des Moines); State College of Iowa (Cedar Falls); University of Iowa (Iowa City)

KANSAS

Fort Hays Kansas State College (Hays); Kansas State College at Pittsburg (Pittsburg); Kansas State Teachers College (Emporia); Kansas State University (Manhattan); University of Kansas (Lawrence); Wichita State University (Wichita)

KENTUCKY

Eastern Kentucky University (Richmond); Morehead State University (Morehead); University of Kentucky (Lexington); University of Louisville (Louisville); Western Kentucky University (Bowling Green)

LOUISIANA

Louisiana Technological University (Ruston); Louisiana State University (Baton Rouge); Loyola University (New Orleans); McNeese State University (Lake Charles); Northeast Louisiana University (Monroe); Northwestern Louisiana State College (Natchitoches); Tulane University (New Orleans); University of Southwestern Louisiana (Lafayette); Xavier University of Louisiana (New Orleans)

MAINE

University of Maine (Orono)

MARYLAND

Johns Hopkins University (Baltimore); St Joseph College (Emmitsburg); University of Maryland (College Park)

MASSACHUSETTS

Amherst College (Amherst); Boston College (Boston); Boston University (Boston); Clark University (Worcester); Harvard University (Cambridge); Mount Holyoke College (South Hadley); Smith College (Northampton); State College at Fitchburg (Fitchburg); Tufts University (Medford); University of Massachusetts (Amherst); Williams College (Williamstown)

MICHIGAN

Aquinas College (Grand Rapids); Central Michigan University (Mount Pleasant); Michigan State University (East Lansing); Siena Heights College (Adrian); Wayne State University (Detroit)

MINNESOTA

Bemidji State College (Bemidji); Mankato State College (Mankato); Moorhead State College (Moorhead); St Cloud State College (St Cloud); St John's University (Collegeville); University of Minnesota (Minneapolis)

MISSOURI

Northeast Missouri State College (Kirksville); St Louis University (St Louis); University of Missouri (Columbia); Washington University of St Louis (St Louis)

MISSISSIPPI

Mississippi College (Clinton); Mississippi State University (State College); University of Mississippi (University); University of Southern Mississippi (Hattiesburg)

MONTANA

University of Montana (Missoula)

NEBRASKA

Creighton University (Omaha); Kearney State College (Kearney); Municipal University of Omaha (Omaha); University of Nebraska (Lincoln); University of Omaha (Omaha); Wayne State College (Wayne)

NEVADA

University of Nevada (Reno)

NEW HAMPSHIRE

Plymouth State College (Plymouth); Rivier College (Nashua); University of New Hampshire (Durham)

NEW JERSEY

Fairleigh Dickinson University (Rutherford); Rutgers State University (New

Brunswick); Seton Hall University (South Orange)

NEW MEXICO

Eastern New Mexico University (Portales); New Mexico Highlands University (Las Vegas); University of New Mexico (Albuquerque); Western New Mexico University (Silver City)

NEW YORK

Adelphi University (Garden City); Brooklyn College of the City University of New York (Brooklyn); City College of the City University of New York (New York); Colgate University (Hamilton); Columbia University (New York); Cornell University (Ithaca); C W Post College (Brookville, Long Island); Fordham University (New York); Hunter College of the City University of New York (New York); Long Island University (Brooklyn); Manhattan College (Bronx); New York State Teachers College (New York); New York University (New York); Niagara University (Niagara); St Bonaventure University (St Bonaventure); St John's University (Jamaica); Sarah Lawrence College (Bronxville); Siena College (Loudonville); State University of New York at Albany (Albany); State University of New York at Buffalo (Buffalo); Syracuse University (Syracuse); University of Rochester (Rochester); Wagner College (Staten Island)

NORTH CAROLINA

Duke University (Durham); East Carolina University (Greenville); North Carolina Central University (Durham); University of North Carolina at Chapel Hill (Chapel Hill); University of North Carolina at Greensboro (Greensboro); University of North Carolina at Raleigh (Raleigh); Wake Forest University (Winston-Salem); Western Carolina University (Cullowhee); North Carolina State University at Raleigh (Raleigh)

NORTH DAKOTA

University of North Dakota (Grand Forks)

OHIO

Bowling Green State University (Bowling Green); John Carroll University (Cleveland); Kent State University (Kent); Miami University (Oxford); Ohio State University (Columbus); Ohio University (Athens); University of Cincinnati (Cincinnati); University of Toledo (Toledo); Wittenberg University (Springfield)

OKLAHOMA

Oklahoma State University (Stillwater); University of Oklahoma (Norman); University of Tulsa (Tulsa)

OREGON

Pacific University (Forest Grove); Reed College (Portland); University of Oregon (Eugene); University of Portland (Portland)

PENNSYLVANIA

Bucknell University (Lewisburg); Carnegie-Mellon University (Pittsburgh); Duquesne University (Pittsburgh); Indiana University of Pennsylvania (Indiana); Lehigh University (Bethlehem); Pennsylvania State University (University Park); Shippensburg State College (Shippensburg); Slippery Rock State College (Slippery Rock); Swarthmore College (Swarthmore); Temple University

(Philadelphia); University of Pennsylvania (Philadelphia); University of Pittsburgh (Pittsburgh); University of Scranton (Scranton); Villanova University (Villanova); West Chester State College (West Chester); Westminister College (New Wilmington)

RHODE ISLAND

Brown University (Providence); University of Rhode Island (Kingston)

SOUTH CAROLINA

Clemson University (Clemson); Furman University (Greenville); University of South Carolina (Columbia); Winthrop College (Rock Hill); Wofford College (Spartanburg)

SOUTH DAKOTA

South Dakota State University (Brookings); University of South Dakota (Vermillion)

TENNESSEE

East Tennessee State University (Johnson City); Fisk University (Nashville); George Peabody College for Teachers (Nashville); Memphis State University (Memphis); Middle Tennessee State University (Murfreesboro); Siena College (Memphis); University of Tennessee (Knoxville); Vanderbilt University (Nashville)

TEXAS

Austin College (Sherman); Baylor University (Waco); East Texas State University (Commerce); Hardin-Simmons University (Abilene); Howard Payne College (Brownwood); Lamar Technological University (Beaumont); Midwestern University (Wichita Falls); North Texas State University (Denton); Rice University (Houston); St Mary's University (San Antonio); Sam Houston State College (Huntsville); Southern Methodist University (Dallas); Southwest Texas State University (San Marcos); Southwestern University (Georgetown); Stephen F Austin State University (Nacogdoches); Sul Ross State College (Alpine); Texas Agricultural and Mechanical University (College Station); Texas Arts and Industries University (Kingsville); Texas Christian University (Fort Worth); Texas Technological University (Lubbock); Texas Woman's University (Denton); Trinity University at San Antonio (San Antonio); University of Houston (Houston); University of Texas at Arlington (Arlington); University of Texas at Austin (Austin); University of Texas at El Paso (El Paso); West Texas State University (Canyon)

UTAH

Brigham Young University (Provo); University of Utah (Salt Lake City); Utah State University at Logan (Logan)

VERMONT

University of Vermont (Burlington)

VIRGINIA

Longwood College (Farmville); University of Richmond (Richmond); University of Virginia (Charlottesville); Virginia State College (Petersburg); Washington and Lee University (Lexington); William and Mary College (Williamsburg)

WASHINGTON

Central Washington State College at Ellensburg (Ellensburg); Gonzaga University (Spokane); Western Washington State College (Bellingham); University of Puget Sound (Tacoma); University of Washington (Seattle); Washington State University at Pullman (Pullman)

WEST VIRGINIA

Marshall University (Huntington); West Virginia University (Morgantown)

WISCONSIN

Marquette University (Milwaukee); University of Wisconsin (Madison)

WYOMING

University of Wyoming (Laramie)

FOREIGN COLLEGES AND UNIVERSITIES

Acadia University (Wolfville, Nova Scotia, Canada); Ca Foscari Institute (Venice, Italy); Cambridge University (Cambridge, England); Carleton University (Ottawa, Ontario, Canada); Dalhousie University (Halifax, Nova Scotia, Canada); Leeds University (Leeds, England); McGill University (Montreal, Quebec, Canada); McMaster University (Hamilton, Ontario, Canada); Memorial University of Newfoundland (St John's, Newfoundland, Canada); Mount Allison University (Sackville, New Brunswick, Canada); Queen's University (Kingston, Ontario, Canada); Saint Mary's University (Halifax, Nova Scotia, Canada); University of Alberta (Edmonton, Alberta, Canada); University of British Columbia (Vancouver, British Columbia, Canada); University of London (London, England); University of Manitoba (Winnipeg, Manitoba, Canada); University of Montreal (Montreal, Quebec, Canada); University of New Brunswick (Fredericton, New Brunswick, Canada); University of Ottawa (Ottawa, Canada); Saskatchewan University (Saskatoon, Saskatchewan, Canada); University of Toronto (Toronto, Ontario, Canada); University of Western Ontario (London, Ontario, Canada); University of Windsor (Windsor, Ontario, Canada)

## TABLE OF CONTENTS

| | |
|---|---|
| FOREWORD | vii |
| LIST OF INSTITUTIONS | ix |
| INDIVIDUAL AUTHORS | |
|   Jacob Abbott | 1-2 |
|   Andy Adams | 3-5 |
|   Henry Adams | 6-26 |
|   John Adams | 27-31 |
|   James Agee | 32-42 |
|   Conrad Aiken | 43-53 |
|   Edward Albee | 54-84 |
|   The Alcotts | 85-94 |
|   James Lane Allen | 95-107 |
|   Washington Allston | 108-110 |
|   Maxwell Anderson | 111-157 |
|   Sherwood Anderson | 158-191 |
|   Gertrude Franklin Atherton | 192-196 |
|   Mary Hunter Austin | 197-202 |
|   Irving Babbitt | 203-212 |
|   George Pierce Baker | 213-214 |
|   James Baldwin | 215-228 |
|   Joel Barlow | 229-230 |
|   Djuna Barnes | 231-232 |
|   Philip Barry | 233-241 |
|   John Barth | 242-252 |
|   S N Behrman | 253-355 |
|   Edward Bellamy | 256-262 |
|   Saul Bellow | 263-298 |
|   Stephen Vincent Benet | 299-314 |
|   Thomas Hart Benton | 315-316 |
|   Ambrose Bierce | 317-337 |
|   Robert Montgomery Bird | 338-340 |
|   George Henry Boker | 341-343 |
|   Gamaliel Bradford | 344-346 |
|   Roark Bradford | 347-349 |
|   William Bradford | 350-351 |
|   Anne Bradstreet | 352-353 |
|   Cleanth Brooks | 354-355 |
|   Van Wyck Brooks | 356-357 |
|   Charles Brockden Brown | 358-383 |
|   Orestes Augustus Brownson | 384-389 |
|   William Cullen Bryant | 390-407 |
|   Pearl S Buck | 408-414 |
|   H C Bunner | 415-417 |
|   John Burroughs | 418-419 |
|   William Byrd | 420-425 |
|   James Branch Cabell | 426-447 |
|   George Washington Cable | 448-485 |
|   Erskine Caldwell | 486-490 |
|   Truman Capote | 491-499 |
|   Willa Cather | 500-624 |
|   Madison Cawein | 625-629 |
|   The Channings | 630-634 |
|   Charles W Chestnutt | 635-636 |
|   Thomas Holley Chivers | 637-638 |
|   Kate Chopin | 639-641 |
|   Winston Churchill | 642-645 |
|   Walter Van Tilburg Clark | 646-653 |
|   Henry Clay | 654-656 |
|   Irvin S Cobb | 657-659 |
|   Robert P Coffin | 660-661 |

| | |
|---|---|
| Rose Terry Cooke | 662 664 |
| James Fenimore Cooper | 665-721 |
| James Gould Cozzens | 722-732 |
| Christopher Pearse Cranch | 733-735 |
| Hart Crane | 736-763 |
| Stephen Crane | 764-865 |
| Frances Marion Crawford | 866-873 |
| Davy Crockett | 874-881 |
| E E Cummings | 882-916 |
| George William Curtis | 917-918 |
| The Danas | 919-920 |
| Donald Davidson | 921-922 |
| Rebecca Harding Davis | 923-924 |
| John William DeForest | 925-933 |
| Margaret Deland | 934-938 |
| Joseph Dennie | 939-941 |
| Bernard DeVoto | 942-943 |
| Emily Dickinson | 944-1082 |
| Thomas Dixon | 1083-1084 |
| J Frank Dobie | 1085-1087 |
| Hilda Doolittle | 1088-1091 |
| John Dos Passos | 1092-1121 |
| Theodore Dreiser | 1122-1175 |
| Paul Laurence Dunbar | 1176-1177 |
| Finley Peter Dunne | 1178-1179 |
| Bob Dylan | 1180-1182 |
| Jonathan Edwards | 1183-1195 |
| Edward Eggleston | 1196-1205 |
| T S Eliot | 1206-1378 |
| Ralph Ellison | 1379-1386 |
| Ralph Waldo Emerson | 1387-1538 |
| John Erskine | 1539-1540 |
| W C Falkner | 1541-1543 |
| James T Farrell | 1544-1554 |
| William Faulkner | 1555-1885 |
| Eugene Field | 1886-1889 |
| Dorothy Canfield Fisher | 1890-1895 |
| Vardis Fisher | 1896-1899 |
| Clyde Fitch | 1900-1904 |
| F Scott Fitzgerald | 1905-1989 |
| George Fitzhugh | 1990-1991 |
| John Gould Fletcher | 1992-1996 |
| Stephen C Foster | 1997-1999 |
| John Fox Jr | 2000-2003 |
| Waldo Frank | 2004-2005 |
| Benjamin Franklin | 2006-2013 |
| Harold Frederic | 2014-2025 |
| Mary E Wilkins Freeman | 2026-2039 |
| Alice French | 2040-2042 |
| Philip Freneau | 2043-2052 |
| Robert Frost | 2053-2183 |
| Henry Blake Fuller | 2184-2188 |
| Margaret Fuller | 2189-2209 |
| Lucy Furman | 2210-2211 |
| Hamlin Garland | 2212-2246 |
| Ellen Glasgow | 2247-2328 |
| Caroling Gordon | 2329-2331 |
| Horace Greeley | 2332-2333 |
| Julian Green | 2334-2337 |
| Paul Green | 2338-2356 |
| Louise Imogen Guiney | 2357-2361 |
| Corra Harris | 2362-2364 |

| | |
|---|---|
| George Washington Harris | 2365-2370 |
| Joel Chandler Harris | 2371-2395 |
| Bret Harte | 2396-2425 |
| Nathaniel Hawthorne | 2426-2755 |
| Paul Hamilton Hayne | 2756-2762 |
| Lafcadio Hearn | 2763-2800 |
| Joseph Heller | 2801-2804 |
| Lillian Hellman | 2805-2815 |
| Ernest Hemingway | 2816-3017 |
| Caroline Lee Hentz | 3018-3023 |
| James A Herne | 3024-3027 |
| Robert Herrick | 3028-3031 |
| John Hersey | 3032-3033 |
| DuBose Heyward | 3034-3037 |
| Marietta Holley | 3038-3039 |
| Oliver Wendell Holmes | 3040-3055 |
| Sam Houston | 3056-3058 |
| Sidney Howard | 3059-3065 |
| E W Howe | 3066-3070 |
| William Dean Howells | 3071-3160 |
| Langston Hughes | 3161-3168 |
| James Gibbons Huneker | 3169-3170 |
| Joseph Holt Ingraham | 3171-3172 |
| Washington Irving | 3173-3219 |
| Shirley Jackson | 3220-3221 |
| Henry James | 3222-3447 |
| William James | 3448-3452 |
| Randall Jarrell | 3453-3461 |
| Robinson Jeffers | 3462-3504 |
| Thomas Jefferson | 3505-3513 |
| Sarah Orne Jewett | 3514-3536 |
| James Weldon Johnson | 3537-3541 |
| Mary Johnston | 3542-3545 |
| Richard Malcolm Johnston | 3546-3552 |
| James Jones | 3553-3554 |
| Leroi Jones | 3555-3556 |
| Sylvester Judd | 3557-3558 |
| John Pendleton Kennedy | 3559-3566 |
| Jack Kerouac | 3567-3569 |
| Grace Elizabeth King | 3570-3572 |
| Martin Luther King Jr | 3573-3574 |
| Caroline Kirkland | 3575-3576 |
| Joseph Wood Krutch | 3577-3578 |
| Oliver LaFarge | 3579-3582 |
| Sidney Lanier | 3583-3659 |
| Ring Lardner | 3660-3663 |
| Hugh Swinton Legare | 3664-3665 |
| Alfred Henry Lewis | 3666-3667 |
| Sinclair Lewis | 3668-3721 |
| Abraham Lincoln | 3722-3731 |
| Vachel Lindsay | 3732-3745 |
| Walter Lippmann | 3746-3749 |
| Ross Lockridge | 3750-3753 |
| Jack London | 3754-3774 |
| Henry Wadsworth Longfellow | 3775-3802 |
| Augusta Baldwin Longstreet | 3803-3807 |
| Robert Loveman | 3808-3809 |
| The Lowells | 3810-3869 |
| Charles Fletcher Lummis | 3870-3871 |
| Mary McCarthy | 3872-3873 |
| Carson McCullers | 3874-3909 |
| James Steele MacKaye | 3910-3911 |

| | |
|---|---|
| Archibald MacLeish | 3912-3927 |
| Norman Mailer | 3928-3933 |
| Bernard Malamud | 3934-3943 |
| Walter Malone | 3944-3945 |
| Edwin Markham | 3946-3949 |
| John P Marquand | 3950-3952 |
| Edgar Lee Masters | 3953-3959 |
| Cotton Mather | 3960-3962 |
| Herman Melville | 3963-4216 |
| H L Mencken | 4217-4232 |
| Adah Isaacs Menken | 4233-4235 |
| James Michener | 4236-4237 |
| Edna St Vincent Millay | 4238-4259 |
| Arthur Miller | 4260-4297 |
| Henry Miller | 4298-4307 |
| Joaquin Miller | 4308-4309 |
| Silas Weir Mitchell | 4310-4311 |
| Harriet Monroe | 4312-4314 |
| William Vaughn Moody | 4315-4322 |
| Marianne Moore | 4323-4326 |
| Paul Elmer More | 4327-4328 |
| Gouverneur Morris | 4329-4330 |
| John Muir | 4331-4332 |
| Mary Noailles Murfree | 4333-4348 |
| George Jean Nathan | 4349-4352 |
| Robert Nathan | 4353-5355 |
| John G Neihardt | 4356-4358 |
| Frank Norris | 4359-4407 |
| Flannery O'Connor | 4408-4446 |
| Clifford Odets | 4447-4459 |
| John O'Hara | 4460-4467 |
| O Henry | 4468-4499 |
| Eugene O'Neill | 4500-4697 |
| James Oppenheim | 4698-4699 |
| Thomas Nelson Page | 4700-4711 |
| Walter Hines Page | 4712-4714 |
| Thomas Paine | 4715-4726 |
| Theodore Parker | 4727-4728 |
| Francis Parkman | 4729-4731 |
| James Kirke Paulding | 4732-4737 |
| William Alexander Percy | 4738-4739 |
| Julia Peterkin | 4740-4741 |
| David Graham Phillips | 4742-4744 |
| Edgar Allan Poe | 4745-5014 |
| Katherine Anne Porter | 5015-5057 |
| Ezra Pound | 5058-5084 |
| James Farl Powers | 5085-5086 |
| Ayn Rand | 5087-5088 |
| John Crowe Ransom | 5089-5113 |
| Marjorie Kinnan Rawlings | 5114-5120 |
| Opie Read | 5121-5122 |
| Lizette Woodworth Reese | 5123-5126 |
| Agnes Reppelier | 5127-5129 |
| Cale Young Rice | 5130-5132 |
| Elmer Rice | 5133-5136 |
| Conrad Richter | 5137-5139 |
| Lynn Riggs | 5140-5142 |
| James Whitcomb Riley | 5143-5147 |
| Elizabeth Madox Roberts | 5148-5158 |
| Edwin Arlington Robinson | 5159-5251 |
| Theodore Roethke | 5252-5259 |
| Will Rogers | 5260-5261 |

| | |
|---|---|
| Ole E Rolvaag | 5262-5272 |
| Philip Roth | 5273-5276 |
| Irwin Russell | 5277-5282 |
| Father Ryan | 5283-5284 |
| J D Salinger | 5285-5323 |
| Carl Sandburg | 5324-5347 |
| George Santayana | 5348-5366 |
| William Saroyan | 5367-5372 |
| Dorothy Scarborough | 5373-5382 |
| Karl Shapiro | 5383-5389 |
| Charles M Sheldon | 5390-5391 |
| Stuart Pratt Sherman | 5392-5397 |
| William Gilmore Simms | 5398-5441 |
| Upton Sinclair | 5442-5448 |
| Sol Smith | 5449-5450 |
| Frank L Stanton | 5451-5453 |
| Wilbur Daniel Steele | 5454-5457 |
| Wallace Stegner | 5458-5459 |
| Gertrude Stein | 5460-5468 |
| John Steinbeck | 5469-5561 |
| Wallace Stevens | 5562-5621 |
| Trumbull Stickney | 5622-5623 |
| Frank Stockton | 5624-5627 |
| Harriet Beecher Stowe | 5628-5642 |
| James Street | 5643-5644 |
| T S Stribling | 5645-5651 |
| Jesse Stuart | 5652-5660 |
| Ruth McEnery Stuart | 5661-5663 |
| William Styron | 5664-5672 |
| Father Tabb | 5673-5681 |
| Booth Tarkington | 5682-5690 |
| Allen Tate | 5691-5697 |
| Bayard Taylor | 5698-5702 |
| Edward Taylor | 5703-5718 |
| Sara Teasdale | 5719-5726 |
| Henry David Thoreau | 5727-5832 |
| James Thurber | 5833-5843 |
| Frances O Ticknor | 5844-5846 |
| Henry Timrod | 5847-5858 |
| Ridgely Torrence | 5859-5861 |
| Lionel Trilling | 5862-5863 |
| Mark Twain | 5864-6269 |
| John Updike | 6270-6289 |
| Jones Very | 6290-6294 |
| Artemus Ward | 6295-6296 |
| Mercy Otis Warren | 6297-6298 |
| Robert Penn Warren | 6299-6331 |
| Booker T Washington | 6332-6333 |
| George Washington | 6334-6335 |
| Henry Watterson | 6336-6337 |
| Noah Webster | 6338-6340 |
| Eudora Welty | 6341-6364 |
| Glenway Wescott | 6365-6368 |
| Nathanael West | 6369-6389 |
| Edith Wharton | 6390-6456 |
| Stewart Edward White | 6457-6458 |
| Walt Whitman | 6459-6648 |
| John Greenleaf Whittier | 6649-6676 |
| Richard Wilbur | 6677-6679 |
| Thornton Wilder | 6680-6704 |
| Roger Williams | 6705-6709 |
| Tennessee Williams | 6710-6789 |

| | |
|---|---|
| William Carlos Williams | 6790-6822 |
| Augusta Evans Wilson | 6823-6825 |
| Edmund Wilson | 6826-6828 |
| Woodrow Wilson | 6829-6830 |
| Owen Wister | 6831-6834 |
| Thomas Wolfe | 6835-6949 |
| Constance Fennimore Woolson | 6950-6951 |
| Richard Wright | 6952-6971 |
| Elinor Wylie | 6972-6981 |
| Frank Yerby | 6982-6984 |
| Stark Young | 6985-7000 |

GENERAL INDEX
THESIS AUTHOR INDEX

### JACOB ABBOTT

1. LEAVITT Charles L  The Contribution of Jacob Abbott to American Literature Through the Rollo Books  MA Boston Univ 1947
2. SILVER Rollo G  A Bibliography of Jacob Abbott with a Biographical and Critical Introduction  MA Boston Univ 1941

### ANDY ADAMS

3. HENRY Jean S  Andy Adams  MA Texas Christian Univ 1938  126 p
4. NEWTON Margaret E  The Texas Cowboy and Argentine Gaucho in Literature, as Found in Andy Adams' Novels, Badger Clark's Poetry, Ricardo Guiraldes' *Don Segundo Sombra* and Jose Hernandez' *Martin Fierro*  MA Univ of Texas at Austin 1942
5. SMITH Maudie M  Andy Adams: Cowboy Chronicler  MA Texas Technological Univ 1950

### HENRY ADAMS

6. AXTON William F  Architecture and Scientific Pessimism in Henry Adams' Philosophy  MA Univ of Louisville 1950
7. BREAN Judith A  Like Rome in the Year 300: Henry Adams' Concept of Doom  MA Columbia Univ 1962  127 p
8. CULLINAN John T  Henry Adams' Novels  MA Columbia Univ 1965  40 p
9. FISHER Neil H  Henry Adams and the Art of Narrative  MA Univ of New Brunswick (Canada) 1963
10. GARNER Robert H  The Growth of Henry Adams' Concept of Woman as a Cultural Force  MA Mississippi St Univ 1964  67 p
11. GUILLORY Terrell A  Henry Adams and the Problem of Multiplicity  MA Univ of Texas at Austin 1957  130 p
12. KARAZINCIR Tuge  Henry Adams and William Dean Howells: Two Critics of the "Gilded Age"  MA St Univ of New York at Buffalo 1966
13. LEE Joseph B  Coherent Descriptions of Historical Reality in Two Biographies of Henry Adams  MA Univ of Maryland at College Park 1969  72 p
14. MacLEAN Robert A  The Novels of Henry Adams: The Puritan Dispossessed  MA Columbia Univ 1950
15. NERNEY James K  Henry Adams and Sherwood Anderson: Art and Woman in America  MA Boston Coll 1962
16. RAWLINS Vivian M  The Influence of Brooks Adams' *The Law of Civilization and Decay* on Henry Adams' *Mont-Saint-Michel and Chartres* and *The Education of Henry Adams*  MA Univ of Kentucky 1933
17. RODMAN John R  Masculine and Feminine Force Dramatized in the Novels of Henry Adams  MA Univ of Maryland at College Park 1968  60 p
18. SAKOWITZ Norman  *Democracy* and *The Breadwinners*: Novels of Henry Adams and John Hay  MA Columbia Univ 1954  233 p
19. SAULS Barbara A  Women as a Symbol of Force in Selected Works of Henry Adams  MA Duke Univ 1965
20. STELLER Robert E  A Structural Study of *The Education of Henry Adams*: Patterns of Image and Symbol  MA Bowling Green St Univ 1961
21. STEPHENS Glynda S  Henry Adams and the Art of the Novel  MA Univ of North Carolina at Chapel Hill 1965
22. STEVENSON Sara E  Commentary on Chapters II, XI and XVIII of *The Education of Henry Adams*  MA Univ of Kansas 1960
23. SVITAK Vladimir J  A Historical Analysis of the Ideas of Henry Adams, as Viewed in His *Mont-Saint-Michel and Chartres*, Regarding the Spirit of the Middle Ages, in Comparison with Modern Times  MA Columbia Univ 1935
24. TETZEL George P  Henry Adams and Aspects of Culture  MA Columbia Univ 1953  61 p

25  WHITAKER Teresa R  Woman as Portrayed in the Works of Henry Adams  MA Oklahoma St Univ 1968  136 p
26  WRIGHT Thomas F  The "Failure" of Henry Adams  MA Univ of North Carolina at Chapel Hill 1963
See also 6210

## JOHN ADAMS

27  McDONALD Lena C  John Quincy Adams' Application of His Cultural Background to Conditions in America  MA Univ of Iowa 1931
28  PARKS John S  "Aristocracy" in the Political Thought of John Adams  BA Amherst Coll 1961
29  REYNOLDS Adoline  John Quincy Adams' Services to Education and the Advancement of Learning  M Ed Univ of Texas at Austin 1939  136 p
30  SNODDY Rowena L  The Classical Bases of John Quincy Adams' Theory of Rhetorical Arrangement  MA Univ of Oklahoma 1948
31  WHITE Howard H  The Road to Democracy: An Introduction to the Letters of John Adams and Thomas Jefferson, 1812-1826  MA Oklahoma St Univ 1945  48 p

## JAMES AGEE

32  ALLEN Sr Margaret L  Structural Context in the Art of James Agee  MA Boston Coll 1965
33  BROWN Ruth E  James Agee: The Man and His Work  MA Lamar Technological Univ 1963  131 p
34  GARRY Joseph J  *Permit Me Voyage*: A Study and a Dramatic Adaptation of the Works of James Agee  MA Ohio St Univ 1965  75 p
35  GOAR Thomas T  *A Death in the Family* and *All the Way Home*: Agee's Novel, Mosel's Play, Reisman's Screenplay  MA Univ of Texas at Austin 1966  88 p
36  HAYNE Kathleen M  An Analysis of the Imagery in James Agee's *A Death in the Family*  MA Southern Connecticut St Coll 1965
37  KRAMER Victor A  James Agee's "Dissonant Prologue": A Study of *Let Us Now Praise Famous Men*  MA Univ of Texas at Austin 1963  91 p
38  McCAY Mary A  The Scenarios of James Agee  MA Boston Coll 1966
39  MORROW Jere L  Poetic Realism in the Novels of James Agee  MA Ohio St Univ 1966  60 p
40  OETKEN Judy  The White Sharecropper, Tenant and Migrant During the Great Depression as Seen Through the Eyes of James Agee, Erskine Caldwell and John Steinbeck  MA Texas Arts and Industries Univ 1968
41  POLLARD Patrick H  A Critical Study of James Agee's *A Death in the Family*  MA Univ of Texas at Austin 1963  133 p
42  SWOBODA Robert J  James Agee's New Prose  MA Kansas St Teachers Coll 1964

## CONRAD AIKEN

43  CARPENTER Thomas P  The Element of Psychoanalysis in the Writings of Conrad Aiken  MA Stanford Univ 1939
44  CHAPIN Henry B  Conrad Aiken's *Preludes for Memnon*: A Thematic Analysis  MA Univ of New Mexico 1961
45  CONNELLY Maureen A  Aiken and His Critics  MA Boston Coll 1965
46  CREAGH Nelda  A Critical Study of Conrad Aiken's Fiction  MA American Univ 1966
47  MINTZ Grafton K  A Study of Conrad Aiken's *The Divine Pilgrim*  MA Ohio St Univ 1953
48  RANKIN David L  Musical Parallels in the Early Poetry of Conrad Aiken  MA West Virginia Univ 1969  70 p
49  RICKLEFS Margery C  The Whirling You Unknown: Conrad Aiken's Aesthetic Study of the Unconscious  MA Univ of Vermont 1959  86 p

50  STEPHENS Geraldine M  Conrad Aiken and the Critics  MA Mississippi St Univ 1968  75 p
51  STOBART John F  Form in the Fiction of Conrad Aiken  MA Southern Illinois Univ at Carbondale 1961  107 p
52  WALLACE Virginia  The Function of Music in the Poetry and Prose of Conrad Aiken  MA Univ of Louisville 1949
53  WEST Maudie V  A Study in Conrad Aiken's Poetry  MA Univ of Texas at Austin 1943  92 p
See also 1289

## EDWARD ALBEE

54  BLANKENSHIP Jayne  Devaluation of Language in the Theatre of Pinter and Albee  MA Univ of North Carolina at Chapel Hill 1968
55  BOROS Donald M  *Tiny Alice* by Edward Albee: A Production Record and Analysis with Emphasis on Dynamic Theatrical Symbolism  MA St Cloud St Coll 1967  406 p
56  CAVAROZZI Joyce P  An Analysis of the Plays of Edward Albee  MA Ohio St Univ 1963  63 p
57  COGNARD Roger A  Albee's Enigmatic *Alice*: Its Background, Meaning and Significance  MA Texas Christian Univ 1969  83 p
58  DALEY Ronald E  Heroes and Antiheroes in the Plays of Edward Albee  MA Roosevelt Univ at Chicago 1968
59  DRUGGE Herman  A Study of the Themes and Techniques in the Plays of Edward Albee  MA Univ of Maine 1967  74 p
60  EDMONDSON Doris E  Edward Albee: The Playwright's Protest Against Enslavement in Contemporary American Society  MA Ohio St Univ 1969  80 p
61  FLETCHER William D  An Analysis of the Women Characters in Six of Edward Albee's Plays  MA Indiana Univ 1967
62  FRIEDLI Max  Another American Dream: A Study of Edward Albee's One Act Play, *The American Dream*  MA Gonzaga Univ at Spokane 1967
63  GONTARSKI Stanley E  Albee and the Absurd  MA Long Island Univ 1967  77 p
64  HUBERTH Jonathan C  A Production of Edward Albee's *The American Dream*  BA Amherst Coll 1966
65  JENKINS J A  Social Comment in the Plays of Edward Albee  MA Univ of Texas at Arlington 1969
66  KEATING William P  Edward Albee: His Answers to Female Aggressiveness  MA Colorado St Univ 1967
67  KELLEY Edward G  Dominant Recurring Themes in the Published Plays of Edward Albee  MA Kent St Univ 1966
68  LALLAMANT Robert J  Edward Albee: The American Dream and the American Reality  MA Boston Coll 1964
69  L'HEUREUX John C  Edward Albee and the Theatre of the Absurd  MA Boston Coll 1964
70  McALESTER Constance A  Eugene Ionesco et Edward Albee: Duex Dramaturges Contemporains  MA Southern Connecticut St Coll 1966
71  MacFARLAND David  Imitations of Existentialism: Analogies to Religion in Three of Edward Albee's Plays  MA Stetson Univ 1966
72  MANTEL Myrna G  A Structural Analysis of Edward Albee's *Who's Afraid of Virginia Woolf?*  MA Ohio St Univ 1963  56 p
73  MAYS James L  Edward Albee's Women: Myth Versus Reality  MA Ball St Univ 1968  60 p
74  MEYER B Ruth  Language: Truth and Illusion in *Who's Afraid of Virginia Woolf?*  MA Wichita St Univ 1966
75  OI Judith T  The American Nightmare: An Analysis of Six Plays by Edward Albee  MA Columbia Univ 1964  99 p
76  OLLINGTON Marcus H  Edward Albee and the Theatre of the Absurd  MA Univ of North Carolina at Chapel Hill 1967

77 RITCHER Geraldine  Ionesco, Albee, Pinter and Beckett:  Absurd Partisans of the Self  MA Chico St Coll 1968  55 p
78 ROHLEDER Patricia J  Albee's American Dream  MA Univ of Tulsa 1967  40 p
79 RUSS Carla E  The Absurdity of Edward Albee  MA Fairleigh Dickinson Univ 1969  115 p
80 SMITH Sr Gertrude  Fantasy in Edward Albee and Thornton Wilder  MA Boston Coll 1968
81 SOMOZA Joseph M  Edward Albee and Modern European Dark Comedy:  A Study of Albee's Humor in Perspective  MA Roosevelt Univ at Chicago 1966
82 STACE Ann C  An Analysis and Criticism of the Work of Edward Albee  MA Miami Univ at Oxford 1964
83 SWAN Mary B  Attitudes Towards the American Dream in Selected Plays of Edward Albee and Arthur Miller  MA Univ of Rhode Island 1965  83 p
84 TOWNLEY Raymond D  Monsters to Martyrs:  The Women of Edward Albee  MA Hunter Coll 1968
See also 4539

## THE ALCOTTS

85 ANDERSON Sallie P  The Transcendentalism of Amos Bronson Alcott as a Cause of the Pragmatism of Louisa May Alcott  MA Univ of North Carolina at Chapel Hill 1963
86 COLEMAN Beulah  The Educational Ideas of Louisa May Alcott  MA George Peabody Coll for Teachers 1930
87 DAUER Jean E  Louisa May Alcott:  A Psychograph  MA Boston Univ 1949
88 DISQUE J C  The Literary Criticism of Amos Bronson Alcott  MA Univ of North Carolina at Chapel Hill 1944
89 HATCH Shirley M  Alcott's Philosophy of Education, Sources and Methods  MA Univ of New Hampshire 1950  88 p
90 HINRICHSEN Edna  Amos Bronson Alcott Viewed in the Light of Emerson's *Journals*  MA Univ of Iowa 1933
91 JANNEY Edith H  The Real Little Women  MA George Peabody Coll for Teachers 1930
92 MATHER Merrilee  Realistic American Fiction for Girls from Louisa Alcott to the Present Day  MA Boston Univ 1943
93 SCHILLER Sidney M  Amos Bronson Alcott's Schools  MA Brooklyn Coll of City Univ of New York 1938  60 p
94 WILLIAMS Helen W  Amos Bronson Alcott:  A Study in Development  MA Columbia Univ 1936
See also 1405, 1446

## JAMES LANE ALLEN

95 BRADLEY Eustace U  Kentucky Literature and James Lane Allen  MA Columbia Univ 1919
96 GRUVER Marian A  The Life and Writings of James Lane Allen  MA Univ of Toledo 1926
97 HOLMES J Welford  James Lane Allen: His Literary Theories  MA Univ of Pittsburgh 1931
98 HUNTER Lucy E  James Lane Allen:  The Man and His Works  MA Univ of Kansas 1927
99 HYNES Kenneth N  Sentimentalism in James Lane Allen  MA Tufts Univ 1935
100 IVEY Bessie B  The Kentucky Novels of James Lane Allen  MA Western Kentucky Univ 1935
101 IVEY Burnett S  What James Lane Allen Has to Say for Himself  MA Columbia Univ 1923
102 JENNINGS Ellen L  James Lane Allen's Theories and Practices in Fiction  MA Univ of Virginia 1927
103 McCREADY John D  The Collected Works of James Lane Allen  MA Columbia Univ 1923

104  PURVIS George G  A Study of Nature in Two Novels of James Lane Allen
     MA Texas Christian Univ 1967  61 p
105  TUCKER Ruth E  Kentucky as Portrayed in the Fiction of James Lane Allen
     MA George Peabody Coll for Teachers 1930
106  WELLS Pauline  A Study of the Technique of James Lane Allen's Fiction
     MA Miami Univ at Oxford 1943
107  WHITE Rata R  The Interrelationship to the Life and Work of
     James Lane Allen  MA Ohio St Univ 1942
See also 338, 4340, 6999

## WASHINGTON ALLSTON

108  LEWIS Judith L  The Writings of Washington Allston  MA Columbia Univ
     1961  72 p
109  MURPHY Phillip J  The Writings and Literary Contacts of Washington Allston
     MA Univ of North Carolina at Chapel Hill 1950  106 p
110  QUATTLEBAUM Marvin  Washington Allston  MA Univ of South Carolina 1932

## MAXWELL ANDERSON

111  BARTLETT Patricia A  The Use of History in the Plays of Maxwell Anderson
     MA Univ of Idaho 1957
112  BAY Marjorie C  Idealism in the Writings of Maxwell Anderson  MA Baylor
     Univ 1964  123 p
113  BELL Joanna A  Themes in the Plays of Maxwell Anderson  MA Baylor Univ
     1953  104 p
114  BELL Raynal  The Love Motif in the Plays of Maxwell Anderson  MA Texas
     Christian Univ 1959  85 p
115  BERGLAND Maurine  A Critical Study of the Plays of Maxwell Anderson
     MA Ft Hays Kansas St Coll 1941  220 p
116  BOURQUE Joseph H  Maxwell Anderson's Political Philosophy: A Reeval-
     uation  MA Washington St Univ at Pullman 1968
117  CHAMBERS Mary L  The Plays of Maxwell Anderson, 1923-1936  MA Washington
     Univ at St Louis 1939
118  CHASE Marion C  An Analysis and Production Book of *High Tor* by
     Maxwell Anderson  MA Ohio St Univ 1951
119  DWELLE Ronald  The Politics of Maxwell Anderson  MA Univ of Kansas 1962
120  DYKES Charlotte J  Maxwell Anderson's Theory of Tragedy  MA Oklahoma
     St Univ 1957  100 p
121  GRAVES Eleanore  Maxwell Anderson  MA St Univ of New York at Buffalo 1939
122  GROSS James R  Maxwell Anderson and the Renascence of Verse Drama
     MA Univ of North Carolina at Chapel Hill 1960
123  HARRIS Kenneth E  Maxwell Anderson's Critical Theories and Their
     Application to His Verse Dramas  MA Univ of Pittsburgh 1948
124  HOBSON Henry E  An Essay on Character Portrayal, Style and Technique
     of Writing in Maxwell Anderson's Biographical Plays in Verse
     MA Univ of Pacific 1942  110 p
125  LANCASTER Ray H  Irony in Maxwell Anderson's *Elizabeth the Queen, Mary of
     Scotland* and *Anne of the Thousand Days*  MA Univ of North Carolina at
     Chapel Hill 1966
126  LANDAUER A  Maxwell Anderson: Defeatist or Man of Vision?  MA Univ of
     Connecticut 1940
127  LARRABEE Ruth  Maxwell Anderson's Theory and Practice of Tragedy in
     Relation to the Aristotelian Tradition  MA Fresno St Coll 1951  54 p
128  LEWIS Mary P  The Free Spirit: Some Aspects of the Concept of Man in
     Maxwell Anderson  MA Univ of San Diego 1963
129  LEWIS Wesley L  The Complete Design for a Production of Maxwell Anderson's
     *Journey to Jerusalem*, Together with a Critical Essay upon the
     Problems of Interpretation and Production  MA Whittier Coll nd
130  McCARTY Mary  Maxwell Anderson's Poetic Tragedies  MA Univ of Texas at

El Paso 1946   147 p
131  MAIK Anna J   A Study of the Tragic Vision in Maxwell Anderson's Plays
     MA Univ of Oklahoma 1964
132  MALONEY Martin J   Maxwell Anderson's Debt to Shakespeare   MA Univ of
     Kansas 1937
133  MARLEY Mary C   Study of Maxwell Anderson's Theory and Practice of
     Making Blank Verse:  Drama   MA Boston Coll 1939
134  MEYER Marilyn G   Maxwell Anderson's Dramatic Conception of the
     Historical Personage   MA Texas Christian Univ 1960   120 p
135  MITCHELL Roger E   Maxwell Anderson and His Critics   MA Univ of Maine
     1954   182 p
136  NEWLAND Paul D   *Joan of Lorraine*: A Play in Two Acts by
     Maxwell Anderson   MA Ohio St Univ 1947
137  NORGRESS Ben   Maxwell Anderson as a Dramatic Poet   MA Louisiana St Univ
     1941
138  PAXTON Patricia M   An Analysis of the American Criticism of
     Maxwell Anderson as Playwright and Poet   MA Washington St Univ at
     Pullman 1960
139  PINCKNEY Elizabeth R   The Theme of War in the Plays of Maxwell Anderson
     MA Univ of North Carolina at Chapel Hill 1946   109 p
140  PLOUFFE J B   The Poetic Drama of Maxwell Anderson   MA Boston Univ 1941
141  POTTER Marian L   Protest and Criticism in the Plays of Maxwell Anderson
     MA Univ of Rhode Island nd   149 p
142  ROBBINS Buren   A Prompt Book and Production of Maxwell Anderson's
     *Saturday's Children*   MA Univ of Iowa 1935
143  ROBINSON Doris M   Maxwell Anderson's Tragedies:  A Study in Theory
     and Practice   MA Univ of Arkansas 1951
144  SCHMERL Rudolf B   An Examination of the Social, Political and Economic
     Content in the Plays of Maxwell Anderson   MA Univ of Toledo 1952
145  SCHOOLEY Bill J   Production Notebook for Maxwell Anderson's *Elizabeth
     the Queen*   MFA Univ of Oklahoma 1968
146  SHEILDS James C   Dramatic Irony, an Essential Supplement of
     Maxwell Anderson's Views on Recognition in Tragedy   MA Univ of
     Pittsburgh 1951
147  SHELTON John   A Study of Maxwell Anderson's Conception of Tragedy
     MA Univ of Texas at Austin 1941   258 p
148  SHULAR Mary   The Development of Maxwell Anderson as a Dramatist
     MS Kansas St Coll at Pittsburg 1944
149  SIEGEL Gerald   The Individual as Idealist in Maxwell Anderson's Plays
     MA Texas Christian Univ 1966   109 p
150  SOLLNER William J   Modern Playwrights on Dramatic Theory:  Anderson,
     Eliot and Fry   MA Univ of Kansas 1951
151  STANLEY Aurora M   Maxwell Anderson as a Historical Dramatist
     MA Univ of Texas at Austin 1941   147 p
152  THOMAS Harriett K   Maxwell Anderson's Concept of Men   MA Baylor Univ
     1955   87 p
153  TIDWELL Lois G   Theme of Social Justice in the Dramas of Maxwell Anderson
     MA Texas Arts and Industries Univ 1952
154  TORAN William B   A Study of Maxwell Anderson's Theory of Drama as
     Found in His Own Criticism and the Practice of It as Found in His
     Poetic Plays on Contemporary Themes   MA Univ of Kentucky 1947
155  TOUT Dorothy J   Maxwell Anderson:  His Theories and His Plays
     MA West Texas St Univ 1950   125 p
156  WEINMAN Richard J   "The Core of Belief" of Maxwell Anderson and the
     Structure of His Tragedies   MA Indiana Univ 1965
157  WESHINSKY Roy K   Maxwell Anderson's Application of His Own Theory of
     Verse Tragedy; 1930-1939   MA Southern Illinois Univ at Carbondale
     1950   79 p
See also 4570, 5528

## SHERWOOD ANDERSON

158 AARNES Jane  Sexual Fulfillment in Anderson's Women Characters: Theme and Variations  MA Bowling Green St Univ 1963
159 ANDERSON Judith V  The Egg Versus the Machine in Sherwood Anderson's *Triumph of the Egg*  MA Colorado St Univ 1967
160 CARR Edward F  Sherwood Anderson: Champion of Woman  MA Univ of Pittsburgh 1946
161 COCKRAN Virginia R  Welcome to Winesburg: A Dramatic Reading of Two Stories from *Winesburg, Ohio* by Sherwood Anderson  MA Ball St Univ 1965  64 p
162 DAVENPORT Kenneth  Sherwood Anderson: An Appreciation of His Life and Fiction  MA Ft Hays Kansas St Coll 1937  55 p
163 DAVIS Dale W  A Thematic Study of *Winesburg, Ohio*: The Conflict Between Material and Human Values  MA Univ of Oklahoma 1963
164 DEFOE Jeanne A  Sherwood Anderson's Critical Theory and Literary Practice  MA Oklahoma St Univ 1968  81 p
165 DEICH Frances  The Inverse Moralism of Sherwood Anderson  MA Univ of Oregon 1937
166 ERICKSON Beverly A  Syntactic Patterns in the Writing of Sherwood Anderson and Sinclair Lewis  MA San Diego St Coll 1964  91 p
167 HAYNES Aldameda S  Small Town Life in the Writings of Sherwood Anderson  MA George Peabody Coll for Teachers 1946
168 HIGGS Robert J  Sports and the Athlete in the Works of Sherwood Anderson, Ring Lardner and F Scott Fitzgerald  MA Univ of Tennessee 1964
169 HUGHES Donald F  A Study of Mysticism in the Writings of Sherwood Anderson  MA Syracuse Univ 1950  57 p
170 HUGHES Robert L  The Flight and the Search: The Quest for Creativity in the Novels of Sherwood Anderson  MA Univ of Oklahoma 1956
171 HUMPHREYS David M  *Winesburg, Ohio*: The Struggle for Dignity  MA Bucknell Univ 1969
172 JOHNSON JoAnn  The Search for a New Society for Old Visions: A Comparison of the Grotesques in Sherwood Anderson's *Winesburg, Ohio* with the Grotesques in Maxwell Bodenheim's Novels  MA Univ of Kansas 1963
173 KINTNER Evelyn  Sherwood Anderson: Small Town Man; a Study of the Growth, Revolt and Reconciliation of a Small Town Man  MA Bowling Green St Univ 1942
174 KIRK Gene C  The Short Fiction of Sherwood Anderson  MA Western Illinois Univ 1966
175 LEWIN Lois S  Social Theory in the Work of Sherwood Anderson  MA Univ of Pittsburgh 1960
176 LEWIS Jane K  Sherwood Anderson's Concept of Art and the Artist: Its Influence on the Style and Form of His Novels  MA Univ of Texas at Austin 1963  109 p
177 MOORE Anne G  Sherwood Anderson: The Artist  MA Univ of Mississippi 1959  91 p
178 PALMIERI Anthony F  Sherwood Anderson and Ernest Hemingway: Literary Relationships  MA Univ of Maryland at College Park 1966  112 p
179 PERRONE Maureen B  Alienation in Sherwood Anderson's Fiction  MA Univ of Maryland at College Park 1967  81 p
180 RENALDS Brenda H  Sherwood Anderson: Dramatist  MA Univ of Richmond 1967  81 p
181 RESER James A  Sherwood Anderson: County Newspaper Editor-Owner-Publisher  MA East Tennessee St Univ 1964
182 RHINESMITH Susan C  Artistry and Form in Sherwood Anderson's Short Stories, 1914-1926  MA Stanford Univ 1965
183 ROGERS Albert A  The Small Town in American Literature: A Study of the Small Town in America as Illustrated Particularly by the Stories of Sherwood Anderson  MA Auburn Univ 1931

184  SABUKEWICZ Charles J   A Study of Sherwood Anderson's Use of Myth in
       *Winesburg, Ohio* and *Poor White*   MA Univ of Rhode Island 1965
185  SKEELS George   Sherwood Anderson:   False Gods in Modern American
       Society   MA Univ of Idaho 1951
186  SOLARI Rosetta   Sherwood Anderson   MA Ca Foscari (Italy) 1946
187  STALLARD Charles K   Sherwood Anderson's Criticism of American Writers
       MA East Tennessee St Univ 1968
188  SZUBERLA Guy A   Sherwood Anderson's Influence on Ernest Hemingway
       MA Roosevelt Univ at Chicago 1965
189  WATKINS Jane M   Everyman's Loneliness:   A Study of Loneliness as a
       Theme in the Writings of Sherwood Anderson   MA Univ of Mississippi
       1962   139 p
190  WOOD Marilee M   Structure and Unity in the Novels of Sherwood Anderson
       MA Rice Univ 1964
191  WOODFIN James D   Sherwood Anderson:   Critic of the Machine Age
       MA Auburn Univ 1953   100 p
See also 15, 1144, 1646, 3003, 4460, 4970, 5957

## GERTRUDE FRANKLIN ATHERTON

192  COACCI Romilda   The Works of Gertrude Franklin Atherton   MA Ca Foscari
       (Italy) 1941
193  CRAIG S H   A Comparative Study of the Novels, Dealing with the South-
       west, of Gertrude Atherton and Mary Austin   MA Ohio St Univ 1933
194  EVANS Virgie   The Novels of Gertrude Atherton   MA Louisiana St Univ 1942
195  PETERSON Charlotte S   A Study in Gertrude Atherton   MA San Diego St Coll
       1966   121 p
196  ROMANELLI Lidia   Notes on a Personality in Modern American Fiction:
       Gertrude Franklin Atherton   MA Ca Foscari (Italy) 1933

## MARY HUNTER AUSTIN

197  ATTANE Almira L   A Study of the Short Stories of Mary Austin
       MA George Peabody Coll for Teachers 1948
198  CRAIG Neal A   The Quest for Cosmic Harmony:   Mary Austin and Neoprimi-
       tivism; and the Importance of Point of View or Angle of Narration
       in William Faulkner   MA Univ of Texas at Austin 1967
199  FRITZ William F   Mary Austin:   Interpreter of the Southwest   MA Univ
       of Texas at Austin 1938   145 p
200  FRYE Mary M   The American Indian in the Writings of Mary Austin
       MA Univ of Oklahoma 1949
201  McKINNEY Viola W   Mary Hunter Austin:   Interpreter of the Southwest
       MA Texas Arts and Industries Univ 1950
202  WILSON C M   Mary Austin's Contribution to the Culture of the South
       MA North Texas St Univ 1946
See also 193, 5051

## IRVING BABBITT

203  FITZGERALD J F   Irving Babbitt and Eugene O'Neill:   A Contrast
       MA Boston Coll 1938
204  GOLDMAN Ellen E   The Humanism of Irving Babbitt   MA Univ of Mississippi
       1960   169 p
205  GRANT Gerard G   The Critical Principles of Irving Babbitt   MA St Louis
       Univ 1934   122 p
206  GREEN Charles H   Irving Babbitt and Paul Elmer More on the English
       Romantic Poets   MA Oklahoma St Univ 1942
207  LYON Geraldine M   Irving Babbitt:   A Study of Critical Principles He
       Offers for a Modern Literature   MA Univ of Kentucky 1930
208  McCOID Carrie B   The New Humanistic Criticism of Irving Babbitt

MA Ft Hays Kansas St Coll 1945   95 p
209  PILKINGTON Mary A   New Humanism in America:  Irving Babbitt as Its Exponent   MA George Peabody Coll for Teachers 1933
210  REYNOLDS Verne E   Aristotelian Influence on Irving Babbitt's Humanism   MA Boston Univ 1935
211  TRAPANI Rose M   The Controversy Centering About the Critical Theories of Irving Babbitt; or, the New Humanism Controversy from 1908-1932   MA Brooklyn Coll of City Univ of New York 1936   70 p
212  WYCKOFF Gregory J   The Literary Criticism of Irving Babbitt:  An Interpretation and an Evaluation   MA Columbia Univ 1940

GEORGE PIERCE BAKER

213  HOFFMAN Judith A   George Pierce Baker and the Harvard 47 Workshop (Edward Sheldon, Eugene O'Neill, Philip Barry, John Dos Passos, S N Behrman, Sidney Howard and Thomas Wolfe)   MA Univ of Maine 1965   82 p
214  KILGORE Anna B   George Pierce Baker and the Harvard 47 Workshop (Edward Sheldon, Eugene O'Neill, Philip Barry, John Dos Passos, S N Behrman, Sidney Howard and Thomas Wolfe)   MA Univ of Tennessee 1948

JAMES BALDWIN

215  BROBST Delbert E   Baldwin's Quest Into the Self   MA St Cloud St Coll 1969   67 p
216  CASTLE Rosemary G   James Baldwin's *Another Country* as Language of Alienation   MA Morehead St Univ 1968   107 p
217  COLLINS G Brent   The Technical Deterioration in James Baldwin's First Three Novels   MA Ft Hays Kansas St Coll 1966
218  DeHART Virginia M   "And My Profit On't Is I Know How to Curse":  Some of the Inconsistencies in the Writings of James Baldwin   MA Brigham Young Univ 1966   101 p
219  DOMINIQUE Br Dale   James Baldwin and the Conflict of the Races   MA Univ of Southwest Louisiana 1968   153 p
220  DUKE E A   The Racial Attitudes of the White Person Toward the Black Person as Represented in Selected Works of James Baldwin   MA North Texas St Univ 1968
221  EASTON Peter A   James Baldwin's Involvement in Civil Rights   BA Amherst Coll 1964
222  HAUCH Dale C   James Baldwin:  A Study of His Works   MA Mankato St Coll 1966   66 p
223  JOHNSON Anne S   The Commitment of the Negro Writer:  An Analysis of the Writings of James Baldwin   MA Utah St Univ 1965
224  ORGAIN Marian M   Use of the Bible in James Baldwin's Creative Works   MA Univ of Houston 1966   117 p
225  PATTERSON Jean M   James Baldwin's Portrait of the Black Artist   MA Univ of Massachusetts 1969   50 p
226  RABY Tina N   The Struggle for Artistic Achievement as a Metaphor for the Identity Quest in the Fiction of James Baldwin   MA Univ of Tennessee 1969   106 p
227  SAYRE Robert W   Narcissism and the Failure of Love in the Works of James Baldwin   MA Columbia Univ 1966   102 p
228  SMITH Beulah   James Baldwin:  A Social Critic   MA North Carolina Central Univ 1965   70 p
See also 1379, 1382, 1930, 6952

JOEL BARLOW

229  MATZNER Chester   Joel Barlow's Cosmopolitan Views   MA Brooklyn Coll of

City Univ of New York 1951  58 p
230  TAYLOR Robert M  The Poetic Reputation of Joel Barlow  MA Univ of North Carolina at Chapel Hill 1960

## DJUNA BARNES

231  FLORY Sheldon  The Writings of Djuna Barnes  MA Columbia Univ 1952  230 p
232  NOER Philip G  Mandala Symbolism and Thematic Sequence in the Shorter Works of Djuna Barnes  MA Univ of Louisville 1967  172 p

## PHILIP BARRY

233  BRAY Lloyd B Jr  Philip Barry: Moralist of High Society  MA Univ of North Carolina at Chapel Hill 1968
234  BRINING Elinor L  A Critical Evaluation of Philip Barry's Plays  MA Ft Hays Kansas St Coll 1947  58 p
235  DeSHONG Charles T  Philip Barry and the Comedy of Manners  MA Univ of Oklahoma 1962
236  FRENCH Carol A  The Lightning Bug: A Study of Seven Plays by Philip Barry  MA Univ of Kansas 1966
237  LARSEN Barbara F  An Analysis of the Plays of Philip Barry  MA Boston Coll 1947
238  McCALL Velma  A Prompt Book and Production of *Holiday* by Philip Barry  MA Univ of Iowa 1935
239  MANGANO James V  Philip Barry: Grace and Regeneration in Three Philosophic Plays; the Conflict of Flesh and Spirit in Two Plays on Divorce  MA Brooklyn Coll of City Univ of New York 1967  66 p
240  STEINMETZ Elizabeth M  Philip Barry: Marriage and the Comedy of Manners  MA Columbia Univ 1954  50 p
241  TOMMASULO Br Aquinas  Discontentment as a Theme in the Selected Plays of Philip Barry  MA Boston Coll 1951
See also 213, 214

## JOHN BARTH

242  ALDRICH Terence O  Dialectic and Demonstration in Black Humor: The Novels of John Barth and Terry Southern  MA Univ of Iowa 1966
243  BOWKER Stanley H  John Barth and the Literature of Exhaustion  MA Boston Coll 1969
244  CHAISON Sharon D  A Survey of John Barth's Narrative Art  MA Lamar Technological Univ 1969
245  CLARK Mary L  John Barth: From Antihero to Hero  MA Temple Univ 1967  53 p
246  GREENE Michael T  Agony in the Essence Chamber: John Barth's Three Novels  MA Boston Coll 1968
247  HICKS Walter J  John Barth's Early Novels  MA Univ of North Carolina at Chapel Hill 1967
248  KALTER Marjorie H  The Use of Metaphor in the Novels and Short Fiction of John Barth  MA Univ of Delaware 1969  64 p
249  LEONARD Lionel R  A Study of John Barth's *Giles Goat-Boy* as an "Anatomy"  MA Chico St Coll 1968  92 p
250  POWERS Dennis A  The Themes of Identity Through Value in John Barth's Novels  MA Univ of Idaho 1970
251  SHORE William A  John Barth: A Contemporary Satirist  MA Clemson Univ 1969
252  YOUNG Raymond C  The Unanswered Man: A Comparative Study of John Barth, *End of the Road*; Samuel Beckett, *Molloy*; Albert Camus, *The Stranger*; Hermann Hesse, *Steppenwolf*; and Eugene O'Neill, *The Iceman Cometh*  MA Fairleigh Dickinson Univ 1965  74 p

## S N BEHRMAN

253 LONG Terry L  The Comic Method of S N Behrman  MA Univ of Houston 1963  77 p
254 MILLS John A  The Comic Spirit in Retreat: An Analysis of Thought in the Comedies of S N Behrman  MA Indiana Univ 1960
255 TURNQUIST Susan E  The Conflict Between Involvement and the Comic Virtues in the Plays of S N Behrman  MA Univ of Kansas 1966
See also 213, 214

## EDWARD BELLAMY

256 DeBARD Robert  A Comparative Study of Edward Bellamy's *Looking Backward* and Upton Sinclair's *The Jungle*  MA Bowling Green St Univ 1968
257 DIJKSTRA Abraham J  The Utopian Novels of Edward Bellamy and William Dean Howells  MA Ohio St Univ 1962  73 p
258 ESSARY William H  A Comparison of Bellamy's *Looking Backward* and Morris' *News from Nowhere*  MA George Peabody Coll for Teachers 1953
259 ILES Robert L  Limitations on Individualism in the Utopias of Bellamy and Howells  MA Bowling Green St Univ 1960
260 SMITH Walter A  The Religion of Edward Bellamy  MA Columbia Univ 1937
261 THOMPSON Laverne S  The Literary Influence of Edward Bellamy's *Looking Backward*  MA Univ of Texas at Austin 1949  78 p
262 WARNICK Betty J  Edward Bellamy's Criticism of American Society as Found in Two Novels  MA Univ of Kentucky 1949  85 p

## SAUL BELLOW

263 ADAMS R Brittain  World and Self in the Novels of Saul Bellow  MA Univ of Oklahoma 1962
264 ANDERSEN Marilyn R  The Changing Significance of Death and Death Symbolism in the Works of Saul Bellow  MA Brooklyn Coll of City Univ of New York 1965  67 p
265 ARNOLD Leta F  The Quest for Authenticity by Saul Bellow's Heroes  MA Univ of Houston 1967  106 p
266 BECK Barbara J  The Menagerie of the Grotesque: A Study of Saul Bellow's Novels  MA St Cloud St Coll 1969  83 p
267 BENNETT Henry R  A Study of the Characters of Saul Bellow  MA Univ of Arizona 1966
268 BRAZINA Marcia L  Reality and the Imagination in Contemporary Fiction: A Study of Five Novels by Saul Bellow  MA Ohio St Univ 1964  79 p
269 CALLARD Robert W  The Uses of Imagery in Saul Bellow's Novel *Seize the Day*  MA Marshall Univ 1965
270 CRAIG Sally K  Saul Bellow: A Negative Look at the Horatio Alger Myth  MA Univ of Maryland at College Park 1969  78 p
271 CRASK Rose M  A Thematic Study of the Bellovian Hero: The Novels of Saul Bellow  MA Univ of Louisville 1967  114 p
272 FISCHER Hans C  The Problem of Self-realization in Saul Bellow and Max Frisch  MA Univ of Iowa 1965
273 GABRYS Robert E  Alienation: A Positive Value in the Novels of Saul Bellow  MA Univ of Maryland at College Park 1969  83 p
274 GUTHEIL Robert  Man and Money, Love and Death in the Novels of Saul Bellow  MA Columbia Univ 1964  164 p
275 HARK Richard D  Saul Bellow: Five Characters in Search of Themselves  MA Ohio St Univ 1963  58 p
276 HOLDER Stephen C  Alienation and Philosophical Estrangement in Selected Works of Saul Bellow and Nathanael West  MA Central Michigan Univ 1966

277  HOROWITZ Judith A  Saul Bellow:  The Positive Power of Death  MA Syracuse Univ 1963  89 p
278  HUBER Geneieve  The Use of Anthropological Sources in *Henderson the Rain King*  MA Univ of Maryland at College Park 1967  65 p
279  IZZO Frances M  A Study in the Peripheral Characters in Six Novels of Saul Bellow  MA Univ of Alaska 1970  114 p
280  KRUPAT Arnold  The Saintly Hero:  A Study of *On the Road* and *Henderson the Rain King*  MA Columbia Univ 1964  156 p
281  LACKEY Angela D  The Search for the Soul:  The Novels of Saul Bellow  MA East Carolina Univ 1968
282  LEVINE James A  The Presumptuous Heroes of Saul Bellow  BA Amherst Coll 1967
283  McKITTERICK Thomas M  Encounters with Society:  A Study of the Confidence Men of Saul Bellow  MA Univ of Iowa 1966
284  MARBLESTONE Robert A  Complaint and Comedy in the Novels of Saul Bellow  BA Amherst Coll 1969
285  MARTIN Donald F  The Anti-heroic Encounter in the Short Novels of Saul Bellow  MA Auburn Univ 1966
286  MYERS Alice M  The Essays of Saul Bellow as an Approach to His Novels  MA Univ of Maryland at College Park 1963  83 p
287  NESS Robert W  Isolation and Involvement in Saul Bellow's Novels  MA Washington St Univ at Pullman 1967
288  QUAYLE Thomas D  Saul Bellow's Concept of Self  MA Illinois St Univ at Normal 1967
289  RANSON Rose E  Saul Bellow:  The Search for Identity  MA Trinity Univ of San Antonio 1966
290  ROTHMAN Anita  A Study of the Influence of Judaism on Saul Bellow's Novels  MA Univ of Louisville 1968  118 p
291  SEEDYKE William C  Saul Bellow's Advancement with the Naturalistic Technique  MA Villanova Univ 1965
292  STERN Susan  Saul Bellow's *The Adventures of Augie March*:  A Critical Analysis  MA Columbia Univ 1966  80 p
293  TAFFE Betty J  The Quest of the Hero in the Novels of Saul Bellow  MA Texas Technological Univ 1966  107 p
294  THOMPSON Sharon M  Augie March, Eugene Henderson and Moses Herzog:  Contemporary Romantic Protagonists  MA Wichita St Univ 1966
295  VENETTOZZI Victor  Existential Process in the Novelistic Art of Saul Bellow  MA Morehead St Univ 1968  71 p
296  VITACCO Patrick  The Rhetoric of Saul Bellow  MA Columbia Univ 1963  112 p
297  WIETING Molly S  The Novels of Saul Bellow  MA Univ of Texas at Austin 1963  182 p
298  WILLIAMSON Julian M  Mutations of the Holy Fool:  A Study of the Hero in the Novels of Saul Bellow  MA Columbia Univ 1963  70 p

## STEPHEN VINCENT BENET

299  BEACOM John B  An Examination of Theme in the Novels and Selected Short Stories of Stephen Vincent Benet  MA Oklahoma St Univ 1958
300  BRIER Carl J  Dream, Disillusion and Hope:  A Study of the Life and Works of Stephen Vincent Benet  MA C W Post Coll nd  48 p
301  BRYANT Wilma C  A Study of John Brown in History and in Stephen Vincent Benet's Epic *John Brown's Body*  MA North Carolina Central Univ at Durham 1963  56 p
302  COCKRILL Mary H  Stephen Vincent Benet and His Poetry  MA George Peabody Coll for Teachers 1934
303  DONALDSON Jeanne C  The American Mind:  A Study of the Poetry of Stephen Vincent Benet  MA Univ of Idaho 1948
304  GARBY Helen  Stephen Vincent Benet:  Preparation for Propaganda  MA Columbia Univ 1951

305  GREEN Betty J  Stephen Vincent Benet: His Democratic Ideals as Depicted Through His Literary Portraits  MA Howard Univ 1958  69 p
306  MAXWELL Estele  Stephen Vincent Benet as a Political Propagandist  MA Univ of Texas at El Paso 1965  73 p
307  PETERIE Pearl  Stephen Vincent Benet: The Spirit of Patriotism in His Poetry  MA Ft Hays Kansas St Coll 1959  90 p
308  RAYMOND Elizabeth  Stephen Vincent Benet's Portrayal of the American "Thing" in *John Brown's Body* and Other Works  MA Univ of Kansas 1941
309  ROBINSON P A  Stephen Vincent Benet and the American Dream  MA Univ of Texas at El Paso 1950  98 p
310  ROYALS Bettie J  A Study of Stephen Vincent Benet's Development of Characters in *John Brown's Body* and *Western Star*  MA Univ of Mississippi 1962  187 p
311  SAMPLES Bill T  A Production Thesis of *John Brown's Body*  MA Ft Hays Kansas St Coll 1961
312  SPIVEY Sophia A  Americanism in Stephen Vincent Benet  MA Texas Arts and Industries Univ 1946
313  VERNON Dodd  An Analysis of the Use of Folk Materials in the Works of Stephen Vincent Benet  MA Univ of New Mexico 1949
314  WALKER Carl E  Some Tendencies and Drifts in Modern American Literature with a First Collection of Biographical Fact on Stephen Vincent Benet  MA Univ of Kentucky 1945  118 p

## THOMAS HART BENTON

315  MILLER Florence-Rita A  Thomas Hart Benton and the Oregon Territory  MA Columbia Univ 1942
316  SELKEN Mary A  Thomas Hart Benton and His Influence on the Development of the West  MA Univ of Oklahoma 1935

## AMBROSE BIERCE

317  BRADDY Haldeen  The Life and Art of Ambrose Bierce  MA Univ of Texas at Austin 1929
318  BROOKS Velma M  An Analysis of the Short Stories of Ambrose Bierce  MA George Peabody Coll for Teachers 1932
319  CARMAN Jane D  The Critical Theories of Ambrose Bierce  MA Univ of Maryland at College Park 1948  94 p
320  CLARESON Thomas D  Ambrose Bierce: "Shadow-maker"  MA Indiana Univ 1950
321  CLARKE Peter P  Ambrose Bierce: Style and Point of View in Selected Short Stories  MA Univ of Massachusetts 1967
322  EMMEL Gayle J  Death in Ambrose Bierce's *In the Midst of Life*  MA Auburn Univ 1967
323  FEELEY Br Michael  The Short Stories of Ambrose Bierce and Their Failure to Endure  MA Boston Coll 1950
324  FOLTS Phyllis A  The Use of Color Words in the Major Short Stories of Ambrose Bierce  MA Bowling Green St Univ 1950
325  GRAY Ansel E  A Revaluation of the Literary Reputation of Ambrose Bierce  MA Univ of Houston 1950  114 p
326  GRIFFITH Kathleen S  Ambrose Bierce as a Satirist  MA Indiana Univ 1950
327  LEES Nelson C  Ambrose Bierce: An Analytical Examination of the Short Stories  MA Columbia Univ 1954  138 p
328  LEWIS Charles A  Ambrose Bierce's Use of Irony as a Literary Technique  MA Long Island Univ 1966  64 p
329  MILLIKEN Eugene R  Ambrose Bierce: A Study of His Short Stories  MA Univ of Maine 1966  73 p
330  MOREY James F  Theme and Style in the Civil War Tales of Ambrose Bierce  MA Univ of North Carolina at Chapel Hill 1967
331  SIRE James W  Ambrose Bierce: His Concept and Use of Time  MA Washington St Univ at Pullman 1958

332  SOWA Edward S   An Investigation of the Fiction of Ambrose G Bierce   MA Univ of Rhode Island 1965   70 p
333  STEADMAN Mark S   Ambrose Bierce: Epigram Maker   MA Florida St Univ 1956
334  SWEDA Mary K   Ambrose Bierce's Use of the Occult   MA Univ of Houston 1969   70 p
335  TAPLEY P A   Horror in the Fiction of Ambrose Bierce   MA North Texas St Univ 1962
336  WAGSTAFF Shirley D   Bierce and Mencken as Critics of Their Times   MA Univ of Montana 1931   84 p
337  WITT Robert E   The Critical Theories of Ambrose Bierce   MA Univ of Arkansas 1935
See also 4911

### ROBERT MONTGOMERY BIRD

338  BOYD Jimmye T   The Early Kentucky Frontier as Represented in Novels by Robert Montgomery Bird, James Lane Allen, Winston Churchill and Elizabeth Madox Roberts   MA Texas Christian Univ 1962   125 p
339  GOFFE Lewis C   The Novels of Robert Montgomery Bird   MA Univ of New Hampshire 1946   121 p
340  ROGERS Mildred L   Life and Works of Robert M Bird   MA Columbia Univ 1924
See also 682

### GEORGE HENRY BOKER

341  MORILLO Marvin   George Henry Boker's *Francesca da Rimini*: A Textual Study   MA Univ of North Carolina at Chapel Hill 1948   473 p
342  SITTA Enrica   George Henry Boker: *Francesca da Rimini*   MA Ca Foscari (Italy) 1958
343  THOMPSON Richard F   George Henry Boker: A Literary Anachronism   MA Univ of Pittsburgh 1932

### GAMALIEL BRADFORD

344  FISHLYN Samuel   Gamaliel Bradford: A Literary Miniaturist   MA Tufts Univ 1934
345  MURPHY A F   Gamaliel Bradford: Psychographer   MA Boston Coll 1937
346  SMEDLEY Elizabeth A   Gamaliel Bradford: A Study of Psychography   MA Univ of Idaho 1947

### ROARK BRADFORD

347  ADAMS Marjorie   Roark Bradford's Negro Characters   MA Univ of Texas at Austin 1948   109 p
348  FOLSOM Sarah B   Roark Bradford: His Life and Works   MA Auburn Univ 1941
349  RICHARDSON Rupert N   Roark Bradford: An Analysis of His Works and Technique   MA Univ of Texas at Austin 1941   189 p

### WILLIAM BRADFORD

350  FISLER G W   The First American Historian: William Bradford   MA Boston Univ 1926
351  STANLEY Edith E   William Bradford as a Journalist; Standards of His Own Age   MA Univ of Iowa 1932

### ANNE BRADSTREET

352  CURTIS Anna M   The Changing Attitude Toward Anne Bradstreet   MA Brigham Young Univ 1970   122 p
353  SCHMITT Evelyn L   The Sources of Anne Bradstreet's Imagery   MA Columbia

Univ 1955   70 p

## CLEANTH BROOKS

354   ITNYRE Terry F   Cleanth Brooks:  His Theory of Poetry   MA Mankato St Coll 1958   47 p
355   PROWSE Walter F   The Poetic Theory of Cleanth Brooks   MA Ohio St Univ 1950

## VAN WYCK BROOKS

356   SCHEIN Donald E   The Influence of Van Wyck Brooks on Subsequent Critics of Mark Twain   MA Boston Univ 1943
357   SCHUELLER Thomas G   Van Wyck Brooks:  His Early Critical Theories   BA Amherst Coll 1958

## CHARLES BROCKDEN BROWN

358   BELL Raymond C   The Relationship of Charles Brockden Brown's Novel to Contemporary German Romance   MA Univ of Pittsburgh 1953
359   BRANDON Beth T   The American Scene in the Novels of Charles Brockden Brown   MA Univ of Texas at Austin 1940   154 p
360   BRAZEAU Peter A   Imagination and Reason in the Novels of Charles Brockden Brown   MA Purdue Univ 1967   123 p
361   CANNON W J   The Gothic Element in the Novels of Charles Brockden Brown   MA North Texas St Univ 1950
362   COOPER Jeanette   Charles Brockden Brown:  A Jeffersonian-American Author   MA Brooklyn Coll of City Univ of New York 1967   228 p
363   DAMERST William A   Some Aspects of Imagination and Fancy in Selected Novels of Charles Brockden Brown and Nathaniel Hawthorne   MA Univ of Massachusetts 1955
364   DICKSTEIN Edward L   The Contributions of Charles Brockden Brown to the Gothic Novel in English   M Ed Temple Univ 1934   247 p
365   GINTHER Mary L   Charles Brockden Brown as a Novelist:  His Type, Style and Influence upon Cooper, Hawthorne and Poe   M Ed Henderson St Coll nd
366   GOOCH Charles E   Charles Brockden Brown and the Gothic Tradition   MA Univ of Mississippi 1967
367   GREENWOOD Jessie L   Charles Brockden Brown's Contributions to the Development of Fiction   MA Univ of Idaho 1927
368   IZZARD Gaye G   The Making of *Wieland*:  A Reconsideration of Brockden Brown as a Literary Artist   MA Columbia Univ 1962   111 p
369   JONES Donald R   The Villains of Charles Brockden Brown:  A Study of the Author's Rejection of Liberalism   MA Butler Univ 1969
370   KENNEDY Janice H   Charles Brockden Brown's "Henrietta" Letters   MA Columbia Univ 1960   59 p
371   LONGEST George C   A Survey of the Novels of Charles Brockden Brown   MA Univ of Richmond 1961   83 p
372   MORRIS Mabel M   The Democratic Influence in Charles Brockden Brown's Treatment of the Indian   MA Univ of Iowa 1926
373   NOURSE Archie B   The American Scene Portrayed by Charles Brockden Brown   MA Univ of Iowa 1925
374   RILEY Br Julian   Charles Brockden Brown and His Contribution to the Development of the Novel in America   MA Boston Coll 1949
375   ROSE Alan D   Curiosity as Motivation in the Major Novels of Charles Brockden Brown   MA Chico St Coll 1967   76 p
376   RUBIN Joel   A Study of Charles Brockden Brown and the Gothic Novel   MA C W Post Coll 1962   101 p
377   SOWDERS Barbara E   The Serious Artistic Purpose of Charles Brockden Brown:  Four Novels of Psychological Investigation   MA Eastern Kentucky Univ 1967   139 p

378　VILAS Martin S　Charles Brockden Brown: A Study of Early American Fiction　MA Univ of Vermont 1899　59 p
379　WALTERSDORF Howard L　Charles Brockden Brown and the Sentimental Tradition: Seduction, Suicide and Sensibility　MA Univ of South Dakota 1966
380　WILCOX Earl Jr　Moral Themes in the Novels of Charles Brockden Brown　MA Univ of Texas at Austin 1959　121 p
381　WOODDELL William C　A Study of the Life and Works of Charles Brockden Brown　MA Ohio St Univ 1935
382　WORTHY John　Brockden Brown's *Wieland*: A Critical Interpretation　MA Univ of Florida 1964
383　YUENGERT John L　Charles Brockden Brown: *Yellow Fever*, a Study in Realism　M Ed Slippery Rock St Coll 1965　90 p

## ORESTES AUGUSTUS BROWNSON

384　CARR Harold M　Brownson: The Product of His Childhood　MA Boston Coll 1949
385　COLLIER Sr Mary B　The Educational Principles of Orestes Augustus Brownson　MA Dominican Coll of San Rafael 1946
386　ROLAND Eleanor E　Brownson's Canons of Literary and Aesthetic Criticism as Revealed in His *Quarterly Reviews*　MA Columbia Univ 1936
387　SPRULL J C　Political Ideas of Orestes A Brownson　MA Univ of North Carolina at Chapel Hill 1923
388　SUBY Erik H　Orestes Brownson's *The Boston Quarterly Review*: An Index　MA Columbia Univ 1965　48 p
389　VALASTRO George J　Orestes A Brownson's Contribution to and Subsequent Analysis of the Transcendentalist Movement in Nineteenth-Century America　MA Columbia Univ 1966　67 p

## WILLIAM CULLEN BRYANT

390　BERNARD Edward G　The Unpublished Letters of William Cullen Bryant to Richard Henry Dana Sr　MA Columbia Univ 1936
391　CALLOW James T　William Cullen Bryant: Literary Critic　MA Univ of Toledo 1952
392　CAMERON Stanley D　The Sources of William Cullen Bryant's Critical Ideas　MA Washington St Univ at Pullman 1953
393　CRUMP Sr Aurelia　The Nature Poetry of William Cullen Bryant as a Reflection of Early Nineteenth Century American Literature　MA Boston Coll 1950
394　FISHER Linnie O　An Analysis of Bryant's Poetic Imagery　MA Univ of Texas at Austin 1939　91 p
395　HALLISEY Mildred L　The Sources of Inspiration of Bryant's "Thanatopsis"　MA Univ of New Hampshire 1949　47 p
396　HUDSON W P　The Literary Theory and Critical Practice of William Cullen Bryant　MA Univ of North Carolina at Chapel Hill 1939
397　LITTLEJOHN J J　Nature in William Cullen Bryant's Poetry　MA North Texas St Univ 1943
398　LOGUE Hanchey　How William Cullen Bryant Misread the Mind of the South　MA Auburn Univ 1968
399　MARSHALL Carl L　William Cullen Bryant's Literary Criticism　MA Ohio St Univ 1947
400　MIRANDA Jochebed C　A Comparative Study of the Nature Poetry of William Cullen Bryant and William Wordsworth　MA North Carolina Central Univ 1952　67 p
401　MYERS Carlene　The American Elements in the Work of William Cullen Bryant　MA Univ of Mississippi 1960　116 p

402  SANDERSON Ada B  A Study of William Cullen Bryant's Travel Letters  MA Univ of Texas at Austin 1946  84 p
403  SMITH Violet  Bryant's Critics: A Study in American Literary Criticism, 1821-1850  MA Hunter Coll 1938
404  TYLER Sylvia L  A Study of William Cullen Bryant's Place in Early American Literary Criticism with an Analysis of His Critical Principles  MA Syracuse Univ 1947  95 p
405  UPDEGRAFF Ruth F  The Development of Certain Philosophical Ideas in the Poetry of William Cullen Bryant  MA Univ of Oklahoma 1940
406  WESTERMAN Alma  William Cullen Bryant's Theory and Practice of Journalism  MA Univ of Texas at Austin 1939  112 p
407  WILLS G S  William Cullen Bryant as a Poet  MA Univ of North Carolina at Chapel Hill 1896
See also 666, 696, 704, 4916

## PEARL S BUCK

408  GARRISON Margaret W  Plot, Characters and Style in *The Good Earth*  MA Univ of North Carolina at Chapel Hill 1968
409  LOWTHER Amanda L  The Life and Works of Pearl S Buck  MA George Peabody Coll for Teachers 1933
410  POTTS Shirley M  Pearl Buck: Interpreter of China to Americans  MA Boston Univ 1947
411  SANTARELLI Mirella  East and West in the Works of Pearl S Buck  MA Ca Foscari (Italy) 1950
412  TAKESHITA Setsuko  Pearl Buck's Concept of the Oriental Woman  MA Mankato St Coll 1963  118 p
413  TENN Emma E  A Comparative Study of Pearl S Buck's Treatment of Oriental and Western Characters  MA Univ of Hawaii 1937  117 p
414  THORNTON Ruby M  Pearl Buck's Fiction on Chinese Life  MA Howard Univ 1956  110 p

## H C BUNNER

415  BROOKS Ina B  Henry Cuyler Bunner: A Critical Study of His Works  MA Univ of Kansas 1950
416  FULBOAM Elsie G  The Life and Works of Henry Cuyler Bunner  MA Columbia Univ 1937
417  WINTER Frederick  H C Bunner: A Survey  MA Univ of New Hampshire 1950  119 p

## JOHN BURROUGHS

418  HUGHES Henry J Jr  John Burroughs' Contributions to the Development of the Nature Essay in America  MA Marshall Univ 1965
419  THOMPSON Mary I  John Burroughs as a Literary Critic  MA Univ of Iowa 1930
See also 5802, 6463

## WILLIAM BYRD

420  BOREN Dorothy J  William Byrd of Virginia: Gentleman of Letters  MA Texas Christian Univ 1963  206 p
421  EWING Verma L  William Byrd: Symbol of His Era  M Ed Henderson St Coll nd
422  McEWEN Ruth E  The Vocabulary of William Byrd's *A Journey to the Land of Eden*  MA Univ of Virginia 1933
423  McQUEEN W B Jr  The Literary Background of Colonel William Byrd  MA Univ of North Carolina at Chapel Hill 1932

424 NORTH N C  A Study of William Byrd's *Journal*, His *Secret History* and His *History of the Dividing Line*  MA Univ of North Carolina at Chapel Hill 1935
425 WILLOUGHBY Joe D  Literary Individualism of the Colonial William Byrd of Westover  M Ed Henderson St Coll nd

## JAMES BRANCH CABELL

426 DALEY Bernard J  The Significance of Satire and Romance in the Works of James Branch Cabell  MA Univ of Pittsburgh 1953
427 DAVIS Charles L  The Biography of Dom Manuel: A Study of the Art of James Branch Cabell  MA Univ of Virginia 1926
428 GAY William T  A Study of the Works of James Branch Cabell  MA Univ of Alabama 1928
429 HALBMEIER E V  An Informative Index to the Biography of Manuel of James Branch Cabell  MA New York Univ 1935
430 HAMBLIN James B  James Branch Cabell and the Jurgen Controversy: 1919-1922  MA Ohio St Univ 1969  195 p
431 HENDERLITE Claude E  James Branch Cabell's Philosophy of Romance  MA Univ of Washington at Seattle 1925
432 HODGSON Mary F  James Branch Cabell: Allegorist  MA Univ of Delaware 1968  109 p
433 HUEBSCH George V  The Literary Philosophy and Artistic Method of James Branch Cabell  MA Marquette Univ 1939
434 JERNIGAN Jack J  James Branch Cabell's "Working Code of Romance"  MA Univ of Mississippi 1949  95 p
435 LAPPIN Carol A  A Comparative Analysis of the Lives and Writings of James Branch Cabell and Ellen Glasgow  MA Whittier Coll nd
436 MYERS Walter E  Mr James Branch Cabell's Accomplishment as Judged by His Own Theory of Romance  MA Univ of Kansas 1930
437 OWENS Betsy K  James Branch Cabell as a Critic of American Literature Between 1920 and 1930  MA Univ of Tennessee 1964
438 PALMER Joseph H  The Influences of Chivalry and Gallantry upon James Branch Cabell  MA Univ of Kentucky 1928
439 REVELISE Max  Cabell the Allegorist  MA Univ of South Carolina 1942
440 ROTHE Charles E  James Branch Cabell: Romantic Idealist  MA Univ of Texas at Austin 1937  216 p
441 ROTHMAN Julius L  James Branch Cabell: Satirist  MA Columbia Univ 1947
442 SCOTT Gwendolyn  James Branch Cabell: A Rediscovery  MA East Texas St Univ 1940
443 SHEA Jerome P  Cabell's Three-Foaled Nightmare  MA Colorado St Univ 1966
444 STEVENSON Ruth M  Cabell's Rational Morality as Expressed Through the Dream-Vision Technique in *Jurgen*  MA Univ of Richmond 1962  133 p
445 TOWERS Tom  The Intellectual Identity of James Branch Cabell  MA Univ of New Mexico 1958
446 VILLARREAL Jesse J  The Idea of Creative Evolution in James Branch Cabell  MA Univ of Texas at Austin 1937  131 p
447 WOODWELL Virginia L  James Branch Cabell: A Study of His Cynicism and Its Contribution to His Failure as a Literary Artist  MA Univ of Maine 1964  71 p
See also 3710, 6996

## GEORGE WASHINGTON CABLE

448 ARNAUD Henri A  L'Element Francais dans l'Oeuvre de Georges Washington Cable  MA Louisiana St Univ 1936
449 ASBAHI Muneer  The Potential Drama in the Works of George Washington Cable  MA Bowling Green St Univ 1969
450 BACOATS Irene B  Race Problems in the Fiction of George Washington Cable  MA Univ of Iowa 1943

451 BAUGH Harvey F III  The Placement of the Creoles of Louisiana in American Literature Through the Novels and Short Stories of George Washington Cable, Kate Chopin and Grace Elizabeth King  MA Univ of Virginia 1930
452 BERTHELOT Mary C  Cable's Creoles from a New Angle  MA Louisiana St Univ 1928
453 BONFOEY Winifred L  George W Cable's Treatment of the Negro  MA Duke Univ 1937
454 BRANDWEIN Lillian  Cable and the Quadroons  MA Columbia Univ 1966  106 p
455 BRUBAKER Bill R  George W Cable:  The Writer as Social Conscience  MA Southern Illinois Univ at Carbondale 1956  84 p
456 BUTCHER Charles P  George Washington Cable:  Early Realist of Negro Life  MA Howard Univ 1947  178 p
457 CLEMAN John L  A Study of Atmosphere in Three Works by George Washington Cable  MA Washington St Univ at Pullman 1967
458 CUNNINGHAM Barbara E  George Washington Cable in the *Century Magazine*  MA Fairleigh Dickinson Univ 1969  59 p
459 DeMOTTE Grace M  The Creoles in the Romances of George Washington Cable  MA Univ of Oklahoma 1925
460 DONNELLY W M  George Washington Cable as a Critic of the South  MA North Texas St Univ 1949
461 DOWNEY Thomas H  George Washington Cable  MA Louisiana St Univ 1930
462 FROTSCHER Lydia E  George Cable and His Louisiana Studies  MA Tulane Univ 1907
463 GREGG Dorothy  A Linguistic Study of G W Cable's Novel *The Grandissimes*  MA Univ of Kansas 1930
464 HALL Louise H  Literary Battle Between George W Cable and Grace King  MA Univ of Kansas 1927
465 HANIFORD C M  The Treatment of the Creoles in the Fiction of George Washington Cable, Grace Elizabeth King and Kate Chopin  MA Univ of North Carolina at Chapel Hill 1945
466 HEISSENBUTTEL Ernest G  George Washington Cable:  The History of His Literary Reputation  MA Columbia Univ 1930
467 HOOD Carolyn G  George Washington Cable and His New Orleans Contemporaries  MA Univ of South Carolina 1941
468 HUDSON Florence  Two Interpreters of the Creole Country:  A Comparison of the Materials and Methods of George Washington Cable and Grace Elizabeth King  MA Univ of Missouri 1947
469 JOYAL Sr Marie  Identity in *The Grandissimes* of George Washington Cable  MA Boston Coll 1965
470 JUHAN Norma D  A Critical Study of George Washington Cable's Fiction  MA Univ of Georgia 1940
471 KENDRICK Juanita  George W Cable's Concern with Social Problems in His Fiction  MA Louisiana St Univ 1943
472 LANE Tommy D  Cable's Southerners  MA Texas Christian Univ 1967  75 p
473 LIPANI David J  George W Cable:  Movement into Realism  MA Bowling Green St Univ 1968
474 MORELAND Mary E  A Comparison of Cable's and Twain's Treatment of the Negro Question in *The Grandissimes* and *Pudd'nhead Wilson*  MA Columbia Univ 1962  76 p
475 NIX Rosary V  Creole Versus Cable, or Creoles of Louisiana and George Washington Cable  MA Columbia Univ 1937
476 OLENICK Monte  Albion W Tourgee, George W Cable and Charles W Chestnutt on the South:  1865-1905  MA Brooklyn Coll of City Univ of New York 1958  106 p
477 PALLEZ Mildred A  Cable's Treatment of the Creoles  MA Fordham Univ 1939
478 ROACH Mary L  George W Cable's Literary Career  MA Univ of Texas at El Paso 1963  142 p
479 ROBERTS Mary R  The Southern Atmosphere in the Works of George Washington Cable  M Ed Henderson St Coll nd

480 SCARBORO Louise  George W Cable's New Orleans with Special Reference to *Old Creole Days* and *The Grandissimes*  MA Duke Univ 1944
481 SMITH Anna G  Creole Men in the Works of George Washington Cable  MA George Peabody Coll for Teachers 1936
482 SPITZ Judith D  Social Criticism in the Early Fiction and the Essays of George Washington Cable  MA Hunter Coll 1965
483 SUETTERLIN Etta M  George Washington Cable's Contribution to the Local Color Movement  MA Univ of Missouri 1934
484 WILSON Sally W  Creole Tropes: A Study of the Functions and Biographical Significance of George Washington Cable's Imagery  MA Univ of Mississippi 1955  71 p
485 WINGO Eleanor R  George Washington Cable and the Race Question: His Writings and Their Reception  MA Univ of Texas at Austin 1946  112 p
See also 2036, 4704, 6999

## ERSKINE CALDWELL

486 BENNINGTON Joseph W  *Tobacco Road*: The Comic Characters of Erskine Caldwell  MS Illinois St Univ at Normal 1964
487 FENNELL Cornelia E  Some Naturalistic Patterns of Erskine Caldwell  MA North Carolina Central Univ at Durham 1952  119 p
488 MYERS Cecile R  Erskine Caldwell's Portrait of the South  MA Howard Univ 1956  101 p
489 SUTPHIN Katherine T  Erskine Caldwell as Humorist  MA Howard Univ 1962  61 p
490 WHITEHEAD Kenneth  A Comparative Study of Characterization in the Short Stories of Erskine Caldwell and Flannery O'Connor  MA East Tennessee St Univ 1962
See also 40, 1114, 1882, 3562, 6986

## TRUMAN CAPOTE

491 CLAYTON G N Jr  Truman Capote: Evil and Innocence  MA North Texas St Univ 1968
492 FREY Sharen N  A Study of Truman Capote's Personality as Reflected in His Writing  MA Washington St Univ at Pullman 1967
493 GERETY Robert  Truman Capote and the Delta School  MA Hunter Coll 1958
494 GOAD Craig M  Form as Content in the Works of Truman Capote  MA Kansas St Teachers Coll 1966
495 MOORE James K  Truman Capote's Fiction: Encounters with Evil  MA Univ of North Carolina at Chapel Hill 1965
496 RELKIN Henrietta J  Truman Capote and Man's Search for Values  MA Butler Univ 1968
497 TAYLOR Richard L  The Frozen Palace: The Gothic Mood in Truman Capote's *Other Voices, Other Rooms*  MA Univ of Louisville 1964
498 VINTSCHGER Franz E  The Searching Adolescent: A Study of Character in Truman Capote  MA Boston Coll 1966
499 WARREN Clifford C  The Development of the Theme of Alienation in the Writings of Truman Capote  MA Syracuse Univ 1966  143 p
See also 5511

## WILLA CATHER

500 ABBOTT Rosalie  Imagery and Theme in Willa Cather's Catholic Novels  MA Univ of North Carolina at Chapel Hill 1964
501 ADAMS Hazel M  The Origins of Willa Cather's Novels  MA Univ of Texas at Austin 1936
502 ADAMS Robert M  A Study of the Sensitive Characters in Five Novels by Willa Cather  MA Auburn Univ 1961
503 ALLEN Ann M  A Study of the Influence Exerted by the 1920's on the Works of Willa Cather, Zona Gale and Edna St Vincent Millay

MA Pacific Univ 1967
504 ANKENBRAND Hazel H  Willa Cather: Interpreter of the American Scene  M Ed Temple Univ 1936  125 p
505 ARCHER Jack H  Willa Cather and Her Two Cultures  MA Univ of Texas at Austin 1966
506 ATKINSON James H  Willa Cather's Theories of Education as Revealed in Her Fiction  MA Texas Technological Univ 1953
507 AUSTIN Sr Mary  The Function of Music in Selected Short Stories and Novels of Willa Cather  MA Boston Coll 1960
508 BARBEE Pattye L  Willa Cather: A Critical Study  MA Univ of Oklahoma 1966
509 BEAUJON Ruby J  An Analysis of Representative Novels by Willa Cather According to "The Novel Demeuble"  MA Oklahoma St Univ 1959  65 p
510 BECKELMAN Irene A  Anti-intellectual Tendencies in Willa Cather's Major Novels  MA Texas Christian Univ 1969  111 p
511 BENDOSKI Lawrence  The Theme of Cultural Values in the Novels of Willa Cather  MA Fresno St Coll 1960  99 p
512 BENNER Jean K  The Relation of the Narrator and the Substance of Willa Cather's Prairie Writings  MA Univ of Arkansas 1962
513 BRADLEY E M  The Analysis of Character in Willa Cather's Novels  MA Boston Univ 1941
514 BROWN Ann E  A Comparison-contrast Study of the Land as Force in Willa Cather's *O Pioneers!* and Ellen Glasgow's *Barren Ground*  MA Bowling Green St Univ 1963
515 BURROW Evelyn  Willa Cather's Use of Sources in *Death Comes for the Archbishop*  MA Univ of Texas at Austin 1940  85 p
516 CALHOUN Ruth H  Willa Cather and a Technologically Oriented, Urbanized America: Encounter and Retreat  MA Texas Agricultural and Mechanical Univ 1968  142 p
517 CANDENHEAD Martina  Development of the Women Characters in Willa Cather's Novels  MA Univ of North Carolina at Raleigh 1951  116 p
518 CHELSOM Elinor C  Willa Cather and the Search for Identity  MA Saskatchewan Univ (Canada) 1966
519 CHILDERS Neva J  Willa Cather's Similes  MA Oklahoma St Univ 1954  35 p
520 COHEN Carolyn C  Willa Cather's Debt to Gustave Flaubert  MA Univ of Colorado 1966
521 CORNELIUS Elizabeth J  Through the Eyes of Strangers: The Criticism of American Standards in Willa Cather's Short Stories and Novels of the Immigrant Farmer in the Midwest  MA Univ of Alaska 1966  70 p
522 CORNISH Joel I  Willa Cather as the Artist  MA Univ of Texas at Austin 1957  77 p
523 CUNNINGHAM Inez  Willa Cather as a Novelist of Character  MS Kansas St Coll at Pittsburg 1936
524 CURRY Grace M  A Study of Willa Cather: Her Novels and Short Stories  MA Butler Univ 1949
525 DANIELE Rev Anthony J  Willa Cather: The Vision of Belief  MA Boston Coll 1963
526 DAVIS Madge  The Evolution of Willa Cather's Art  MA Univ of Texas at Austin 1934
527 DENBOSKE Shirley  The Maturing Art of Willa Cather  MA Fairleigh Dickinson Univ 1966
528 DEVLIN Margaret J  A Literary Artist: Willa Cather  M Ed Temple Univ 1932  61 p
529 DINWIDDIE Shirley W  A Study of the Critical Attitudes Towards the Novels of Willa Cather  MA Univ of Maryland at College Park 1950  89 p
530 DOLAN Sr Mary C  Pioneer Characters as Found in the Novels of Willa Cather  MA Boston Coll 1950
531 DOLAN Patricia A  Willa Cather and Ellen Glasgow: Interpreters of the American Past  MA Univ of Illinois at Urbana 1948
532 DOUTHIT Marjorie H  Willa Cather's Symbolic Use of the Land

MA Kansas St Teachers Coll 1965
533 DUNKER Jeanne  Critical Evaluation of Willa Cather  MA Northern Illinois Univ 1965
534 EAGAN Marie G  Willa Cather's Exiles: The Historical Novels  MA Stanford Univ 1966
535 ELEY Margery  Willa Cather: Reflections of Her Life in Selected Works  M Ed Henderson St Coll nd
536 FELKER Dorothy D  Willa Cather and Edith Wharton: The West and the East  MA Sul Ross St Coll 1965
537 FIGGINS Robert H  The Concept of the Prairie in Willa Cather's Early Novels  MA Colorado St Univ 1961
538 FINKEN Elmira P  A Study of the Strength of the Pioneer Character in Willa Cather's Novels  MA Univ of Houston 1956  74 p
539 FOOTE Norma E  The Relationship of the Individual to His Environment in Selected Novels of Willa Cather  MA Bowling Green St Univ 1965
540 FOWLE Patricia N  Willa Cather's Pastoralism  MA Univ of Maryland at College Park 1969  57 p
541 FUNK Fifine Z  The Novels of Willa Sibert Cather with the Emphasis on Character  MA Indiana Univ 1935
542 GALLAHER Mabel E  Willa Cather's Sympathetic Attitude Toward Her Characters  M Ed Henderson St Coll nd
543 GIBBONS Eileen  Tone: Its Sources and Implications in Willa Cather's *Death Comes for the Archbishop*; Techniques Toward Dramatic Intensity in Katherine Mansfield's "The Daughters of the Late Colonel"; and "The Children", "Salt Water Sunday", "When Phil Jones Died", Three Original Short Stories  MA Brigham Young Univ 1959  119 p
544 GRABER Kay E  Willa Cather: The Conscious Artist  MA Univ of Kansas 1965
545 GUNNELL Earl L  Willa Cather and the Value of Struggle  MA Brigham Young Univ 1964  125 p
546 HAMMOND Charles M  Willa Cather and the West: An Analysis of Six Novels  MA Syracuse Univ 1965  97 p
547 HARDEN E S  Willa Cather's Concept of the Frontier as Revealed in Certain Novels and Short Stories  MA Texas Technological Univ 1952
548 HARPER Irma  A Critical Interpretation of Selected Short Stories by Willa Cather  M Ed Henderson St Coll nd
549 HAYES Georgianna C  Willa Cather's Retreat from Reality: An Historical Treatment of Her Novels Showing the Development of Her Essential Asceticism  MA Boston Univ 1934
550 HERN M A  The Pioneer Spirit in the Novels of Willa Cather  MA Boston Coll 1948
551 HEYECK Patricia R  Willa Cather's *The Song of the Lark*: The 1937 Revisions and Their Significance  MA Stanford Univ 1966
552 HOLLADAY Pauline  A Comparison of the Women in the Novels of Willa Cather with Those in the Novels of Ellen Glasgow  MA Univ of Mississippi 1956  124 p
553 HONEYCUTT Ann  Willa Cather's Childhood Memories as Reflected in Selected Works  M Ed Henderson St Coll nd
554 HONOR Sr Maura  An Examination of the Narrative Techniques in the Fiction of Willa Cather  MA Univ of Scranton 1965
555 HORN Katheryn A  The Types of Character in the Works of Willa Cather  MA Univ of Texas at Austin 1942  134 p
556 HUETER Betty A  Gaudy Extravaganza: Willa Cather's Western Trilogy  MA Boston Univ 1949
557 HUFF Marjorie N  Willa Cather's Theme of the Land in Her Plains Novels  MA Texas Arts and Industries Univ 1968
558 HUGHES Eugene E  The Pioneer and the Artist: Two Approaches to Creativity in the Fiction of Willa Cather  MA Univ of Oklahoma 1960
559 HURSEY Roberta L  Willa Cather's European Immigrants: The Conflict

of Old and New World Values  MA Texas Agricultural and Mechanical Univ 1966  133 p
560 IVERSON M  Willa Cather's Interest in the Southwest  MA Univ of Texas at El Paso 1949  86 p
561 JACKSON Imogene  Idealism Versus Materialism as Exemplified by Willa Cather's Masculine Characters  MA Univ of Mississippi 1951  94 p
562 JACKSON Lambert B  The Pioneer, the Artist and the Second Generation: A Study of Willa Cather's Novels and Major Short Stories  BA Univ of Delaware 1964  100 p
563 JAMISON Ruth  The Literary Principles of Willa Cather  MA Univ of Oklahoma 1949
564 JANCEK Camilla  A Study of Characterization in Eight Major Novels of Willa Cather  MA Columbia Univ 1963  99 p
565 JOHNSEN Alice  A Study of the Antimaterialistic Themes in Willa Cather's Major Novels  MA Univ of Houston 1954  59 p
566 JOHNSON Lois  A Study of Willa Cather's Novels of the Middle West  MA Univ of North Carolina at Chapel Hill 1933
567 JOHNSTON W W  Music in the Fiction of Willa Cather  MA North Texas St Univ 1953
568 KALMER Charles A  Willa Cather's Study of Man and His Endeavors  MA Univ of Louisville 1962
569 KERICH Sr Irene M  Psychological Adjustment of the Foreign-born Characters in Willa Cather's Fiction  MA Univ of New Mexico 1956
570 KIBER Mary W  The Critical Theories of Willa Cather as Related to Her Life and Writings  MA Texas Christian Univ 1942  138 p
571 LAGORIO Valerie M  Willa Cather: Critic of American Society  MA Stanford Univ 1964
572 LEE Patricia F  The Ideal Life in Six Willa Cather Novels  MA Brigham Young Univ 1967  94 p
573 LEONARD Wilma M  The Frontier Themes of Willa Cather  MA Baylor Univ 1962  138 p
574 LUCAS Meda F  Willa Sibert Cather as Interpreter of the American Scene  MA Univ of Hawaii 1934  90 p
575 LYONS J R  Autobiographical Reflexes in Willa Cather's Novels  MA Boston Coll 1937
576 McCAUSLAND Irma R  The Influence of the Western Country and Town on the Philosophies of the Major Characters in the Novels and Stories of Willa Cather  MA Whittier Coll nd
577 McGINNES Jeannette H  The Treatment of Religion in the Novels of Willa Cather  MA Baylor Univ 1965  123 p
578 McQUARIE Eugenia  The Sense of Form in the Novels of Willa Cather  MA Oklahoma St Univ 1947
579 MAQUIRE John T  Place-spirit in the Works of Willa Sibert Cather  MA Univ of Idaho 1948
580 MARSH Marilyn M  Willa Cather and Eugene O'Neill: A Bond of Tragedy  MA Municipal Univ of Omaha nd
581 MARTIN Joan F  Qualities in Willa Cather's Admirable Characters  MA Southern Illinois Univ at Carbondale 1960  177 p
582 MATSUMOTO Fusae  Willa Cather as Seen by the Critics Since 1920  MA Baylor Univ 1960  158 p
583 MERRITT Jane  The Heroines in Willa Cather's Novels: The Theme of Harmony  MA Texas Technological Univ 1963  58 p
584 MILLER Norma G  Willa Cather and Catholicism  MA Southern Illinois Univ at Carbondale 1952  78 p
585 MOUDY Lella F  Uses of Nature in the Writings of Willa Cather  MA West Texas St Univ 1951  140 p
586 MULLIN A B  Artistry of Willa Cather  MA Boston Coll 1934
587 NABERS Martha L  Cather's Nest in the Cleft  MA Mississippi St Univ 1970  86 p
588 NOBLE Robert V  The Significance of Nature in the Early Novels of

Willa Cather  MA Univ of Florida  nd
589 NORE Betsy  Willa Cather's Pessimism and Her Search for Value  MA Columbia Univ 1966  59 p
590 ORMSBEE Eleanor  An Interpretation of the Principal Characters in the Novels of Willa Cather  MA Ft Hays Kansas St Coll 1953  80 p
591 OWENS Mildred  Individualism in Willa Cather's Novels  MA Univ of Kentucky 1937
592 PARKS Augusta J  A Comparison of Willa Cather's Obscure Destinies with Gustave Flaubert's *Trois Contes*  MA Oklahoma St Univ 1965  72 p
593 PIERSON Alma N  Social Backgrounds of the Characters in Willa Cather's Novels  MA North Texas St Univ 1938
594 PRENDERGAST Arline F  The Home in the Fiction of Willa Cather  MA Univ of Pittsburgh 1962
595 REXROAT Ruth  A Critical Analysis of Willa Cather's *Death Comes for the Archbishop*  MA Univ of Texas at Austin 1948  117 p
596 RICHARD Sr Rita  Moral Values in Willa Cather's Novels  MA Rivier Coll 1959
597 RICHARDS Lucy R  Figurative Language and Theme in the Novels of Willa Cather  MA Auburn Univ 1954
598 ROSS Robert L  The Frontier Novels of Willa Cather and Conrad Richter: Realization of Purpose Through Technique  MA Texas Christian Univ 1963  85 p
599 ROSSARD Janice A  A Study of Willa Cather's Women Characters in Her Major Novels  MA Bowling Green St Univ 1949
600 ROYE Ellen R  Agrarianism in the Works of Willa Cather  MA Texas Christian Univ 1950  82 p
601 SALTZ K W  Relation of the Life of Willa Cather to Her Works  MA Ohio St Univ 1933
602 SATOMI Hiroko  A Study of Willa Cather's Portraiture of Non-English Characters in Her Fiction  MA Oklahoma St Univ 1959  85 p
603 SCHAEFER Sr Mary R  Pioneer Life Portrayed by Willa Cather and Hamlin Garland  MA George Peabody Coll for Teachers 1936
604 SCHMITT Mary C  Willa Cather: Apostle of the Good Life  MA Univ of Kansas 1948
605 SEWELL Ila  Willa Cather: Her Interest in Different Backgrounds in Her Short Stories  MA Univ of Texas at El Paso 1949  107 p
606 SHAW June L  A Study of Willa Cather's Themes  MA Univ of Tulsa 1964  64 p
607 SIGNOR Lois H  Backgrounds in the Novels of Willa Cather  MA Columbia Univ 1951
608 SMILEY Celia  Willa Cather's Interpretation of the West  MA Louisiana St Univ 1940
609 SMITH Nancy W  Willa Cather's Art of Fiction  MA Florida St Univ 1954
610 SNODDY Anna L  Willa Cather's Preoccupation with Foreign Culture in America  MA Oklahoma St Univ 1940  82 p
611 STALLINGS Evelyn  Willa Cather and the American Frontier  MA Univ of Texas at Austin 1940  147 p
612 STANLEY Sr M Charlotte  Willa Cather's Treatment of the Southwest  MA Villanova Univ 1965
613 STEINHAGEN Carol T  The Relationship of Man and Nature in the Novels of Willa Cather  MA Univ of Maryland at College Park 1967  81 p
614 THEISS Nina L  Music in the Work of Willa Cather  MA Southern Illinois Univ at Carbondale 1950  116 p
615 TORRENCE Audrey  Willa Cather: Her Influence and Limitations as an Author  MA Louisiana St Univ 1939
616 TOWNSEND Howard W  The Tragic Element in Willa Cather's Novels  MA Univ of Texas at Austin 1939  161 p
617 UNTEREINER Marie A  Willa Cather's Attitude Towards the French and Their Culture with Special Reference to the Author's Novels and Short Stories  MA Southern Illinois Univ at Carbondale 1954  106 p

618 VEALE Temperance G  Willa Cather's Novels  MA Boston Univ 1934
619 VOYLES Jimmy P  Proverbs in Willa Cather's Novels  MA Florida St Univ 1964
620 WAGONER Richard D  Willa Cather and Her Use of the American Theme  MA Columbia Univ 1951
621 WEST Fayrene  The Symbolism of the Land and Its Effect on Character in Eight of Willa Cather's Novels  MA Univ of Mississippi 1959  125 p
622 WORLINE Bonnie B  The Art Technique of Willa Cather's Fiction  MA Univ of Pittsburgh 1946
623 YORK Ernest C  Willa Cather's Philosophy of Art with Illustrations from Some of Her Works  MA Univ of Texas at Austin 1948  73 p
624 YOUNG M O  The Problem of the Individual in the Fiction of Willa Cather  MA Ohio St Univ 1949
See also 1816, 2256, 2321, 3387, 4340, 5268

## MADISON CAWEIN

625 DAVIS Frank J  Madison Cawein and His Poetry  MA Univ of Virginia 1935
626 FERGUSON D E  An Appraisal of the Life and Work of Madison Cawein  MA Ohio St Univ 1934
627 HARRISON Richard C  Studies in the Poetry of Madison Cawein  MA Univ of Texas at Austin 1917
628 KING Julia C  Some Aspects of the Poetry of Madison Cawein  MA Univ of Louisville 1916
629 SWANK Albert L  Madison Cawein: A Poet of Kentucky  MA Univ of Pittsburgh 1933
See also 3863, 6996, 6998

## THE CHANNINGS

630 JOYCE Davis D  Edward Channing and the Great Work  MA Univ of Oklahoma 1968  391 p
631 McANDREW A J  William Ellery Channing, the Younger: His Life and Poetry  MA Boston Univ 1938
632 NEWMAN Betty P  The Political Theory of William Ellery Channing  MA Univ of Oklahoma 1951
633 THACHER Archibald G Jr  William Henry Channing and the Spirit of the Age  MA Columbia Univ 1941
634 TRACY Francis X  The Effect of Channing's Unitarianism on New England's Romanticism  MA Boston Coll 1947

## CHARLES W CHESTNUTT

635 HUBERT Julia M  *The Marrow of Tradition*: Studies in the Fiction of Charles W Chestnutt  MA Ohio St Univ 1948
636 MASON Cynthia R  Charles W Chestnutt: His Life and Works  MA Howard Univ 1947  116 p
See also 476, 6964

## THOMAS HOLLEY CHIVERS

637 WALKER William E  A Critical Study of Thomas Holley Chivers  MA Columbia Univ 1948
638 WILSON Edna A  Thomas Holley Chivers, M D: A Forgotten Romantic Poet of Georgia (1809-1838)  MA Auburn Univ 1941

## KATE CHOPIN

639 BRADSHAW Margaret A  Kate Chopin: *The Awakening*  MA Columbia Univ 1960  68 p

640  JORDAN Merle M   Kate Chopin: Social Critic   MA Univ of Texas at Austin 1959   95 p
641  TAGGART Amy E   Mrs Kate O'Flaherty Chopin: Her Life and Her Writing   MA Tulane Univ 1928
See also 451, 465

## WINSTON CHURCHILL

642  CARROLL Mary E   The Theatre as Reflected in Churchill's *Rosciad* and *Apology*   MA Louisiana St Univ 1940
643  FLETCHER Marie   The Novels of Winston Churchill   MA Louisiana St Univ 1944
644  SCHRABER Carl G Jr   The Dichotomy of Romance and Reform in the Novels of Winston Churchill, American   MA Texas Christian Univ 1961   127 p
645  SIMMONS Samuel C   The Early Winston Churchill: A Re-evaluation   MA Univ of Mississippi 1962   206 p
See also 338

## WALTER VAN TILBURG CLARK

646  CHADDON Mary H   Walter Van Tilburg Clark: Allegory and the Traditional West   MA Univ of Alaska 1964   87 p
647  CHRISTIAN Aubry D   Nature and Dream: The Symbolic Mode of Walter Van Tilburg Clark   MA Univ of Texas at Austin 1965
648  HAGGERTY John P   The Gothic Tradition and Walter Van Tilburg Clark   MA Syracuse Univ 1953   149 p
649  POWELL William D   Walter Van Tilburg Clark and *The Watchful Gods*   MA New Mexico Highlands Univ 1965
650  ROEHL Ruth   Psychological Aspects of the Novels of Walter Van Tilburg Clark   MA Mankato St Coll 1967   50 p
651  SLICK Richard D   Sustained Imagery in the Novels of Walter Van Tilburg Clark   MA Indiana Univ of Pennsylvania nd
652  STOTT Nolan G   Authorial Presence in the Three Novels of Walter Van Tilburg Clark   MA Brigham Young Univ 1967   92 p
653  WHITE Judith H   A Study of Walter Van Tilburg Clark: A Vision Fictionalized   MA Univ of Pittsburgh 1960

## HENRY CLAY

654  KINEAVY John F   The Pan-Americanism of Henry Clay   MA Boston Coll 1948
655  SCHREEVEN William J   The Social Philosophy of Henry Clay   MA Univ of Iowa 1933
656  SMITH Mary B   An Analysis of Henry Clay's Speech on the Compromise Resolutions of 1850 by Aristotelian Standards   MA Univ of Iowa 1935

## IRVIN S COBB

657  HALPERN Beulah R   The Place of Irvin S Cobb in the Development of the American Short Story   MA Univ of Texas at Austin 1938   194 p
658  LOGSDON Katherine   Irvin S Cobb and His Judge Priest Stories   MA Western Kentucky Univ 1936
659  PICKARD Lessie D   An Appreciation of the Life and Writings of Irvin S Cobb   MA George Peabody Coll for Teachers 1938
See also 6996

## ROBERT P COFFIN

660  JONES Frangcon L   Strange Wholeness: The Writings of Robert P Tristram Coffin, Citizen of Maine and the Universe; a Regional Reconnaissance   MA Univ of New Hampshire 1947   126 p
661  NAUGLER Frances W   Robert P Tristram Coffin and His Critics (1924-1955)

MA Univ of Maine 1958  92 p
See also 2116

## ROSE TERRY COOKE

662 BOYD Margaret A  Rose Terry Cooke:  New England Traits and Characters in Her Prose Fiction  MA Univ of Pittsburgh 1929
663 HODGSON Georgie C  A Study of Rose Terry Cooke and Her Works  MA George Peabody Coll for Teachers 1929
664 KOONTZ Hilda E  Rose Terry Cooke:  A Pioneer in Realism in the American Short Story  MA George Washington Univ 1965

## JAMES FENIMORE COOPER

665 ASLINGER Annabel  Customs and Characteristics of the Leatherstocking Tales  MA George Peabody Coll for Teachers 1931
666 AVANZI William A  The Bread and Cheese Club  MA Columbia Univ 1936
667 BERTONE Robert E  The Development of the Hero-type in Fenimore Cooper's Works  MA Boston Coll 1965
668 BLAKE Margaret M  The Noble Indian of James Fenimore Cooper  MA Boston Coll 1951
669 BOAKE Mary L  The Development of Cooper's Political and Social Ideas in Relation to the Structure of His Novels  MA Univ of Oklahoma 1939
670 BOROWSKY Anton G  Social Content in Cooper's Sea Novels  MA Univ of North Carolina at Chapel Hill 1964
671 BRADLEY Viola M  The Contrast of Cooper's *The Last of the Mohicans* and Simms' *The Yemassee*  MA Auburn Univ 1944
672 BROWNLEE Carole G  James Fenimore Cooper and Herman Melville: Voyagers on the Same Sea?  MA Univ of Maryland at College Park 1968  50 p
673 BURKE Martin  Cooper as an Exponent of American Romanticism  MA Louisiana St Univ 1935
674 BUSH C W  The Treatment of Religion and Religious Character in the Nineteenth Century American Novel Through Selected Fiction by Cooper, Hawthorne, Melville, Harriet Beecher Stowe, Oliver Wendell Holmes and Mark Twain  M Phil Univ of London 1967
675 CANNON Evelyn  Cooper as a Social Critic  MA Southern Methodist Univ 1930
676 COHEN Barbara K  Plot and Characters in the Novels of James Fenimore Cooper:  The First Decade  MA Rutgers St Univ 1957
677 CONBOY Lawrence J  Social Criticism in the Writings of James Fenimore Cooper  MA Brooklyn Coll of City Univ of New York 1942  139 p
678 DARKENWALD Gordon G  The Evolution of Archetypes in Cooper's Leatherstocking Tales  MA Hunter Coll 1966
679 DUNN Sr M V  Nature as the Primary Teacher of Man in Cooper's Novels  MA Boston Coll 1950
680 ERWIN Mary E  Cooper's Novels on the Adelphi Stage, 1825-1835  MA Columbia Univ 1937
681 FAULKNER Forrest W  James Fenimore Cooper's *The Monikins* Edited by Forrest Wilford Faulkner  MA Univ of Texas at Austin 1965  248 p
682 FIELDS Nadine E  Portraiture of the American Indian in the Novels of Cooper, Bird and Simms  MA Oklahoma St Univ 1957  69 p
683 FIORELLI Edward A  The American Hero:  Natty Bumppo and Mythology of America  MA Brooklyn Coll of City Univ of New York 1967  49 p
684 FRANKS Winifred M  Social Criticism and Literary Artistry in James Fenimore Cooper's Littlepage Trilogy  MA Univ of New Mexico 1966
685 FRENCH Florence  The Use of Proverbs in Selected Novels of James Fenimore Cooper  MA Texas Technological Univ 1967

686 GRUNINGER Hans-Werner  James Fenimore Cooper and Switzerland  MA Southern Illinois Univ at Carbondale 1955  93 p
687 HAAS Inge M  Two Interpretations of Democracy:  A Comparison of Political Views of James Fenimore Cooper and Hugh Henry Brackenridge  MA Smith Coll 1934
688 HARMS Tina C  Dictionary of Characters in Cooper's Leatherstocking Tales  MA Univ of Kansas 1927
689 HARRIS Laura V  A Biographical Character Analysis of Nathaniel Bumppo and Other Characters of the Leatherstocking Series  MA Auburn Univ 1944
690 HAYWOOD Ralph S  James Fenimore Cooper:  Critic of American Society  MA Univ of Texas at El Paso 1959  88 p
691 HOYT George L  Religious Aspects of Cooper's Sea Stories  MA Univ of Iowa 1965
692 JAFFE Mary F  James Fenimore Cooper:  The Pioneer Portrayer of the American Spirit as Revealed by His Major Works  M Ed Temple Univ 1937  248 p
693 JORDAN Howell H Jr  The Changing Character of Natty Bumppo in the Leatherstocking Tales  MA Columbia Univ 1966  103 p
694 JORNS Effie E  Uncas, Red Cloud and Laughing Boy:  The American Indian as Portrayed by the Romanticist Cooper, the Scholar-poet Neihardt and the Anthropologist LaFarge  MA Oklahoma St Univ 1930
695 KNIGHT Mabel T  J F Cooper and the Anti-rent Controversy  MA Univ of Oklahoma 1942
696 KOEHNLINE Phyllis G  The Theory of the Picturesque as Seen in Landscape Art and in the Works of Cooper, Irving and Bryant  MA Ohio St Univ 1952
697 LAMB Susan R  James Fenimore Cooper and His Uses of Quotations  MA Columbia Univ 1936
698 LINDSTRUM June L  A Comparison of Two Novels by James Fenimore Cooper: *The Pioneers* and *Satanstoe*  MA La Verne Coll 1967  79 p
699 McAFEE Annie K  Cooper's Characterization of American Life  MA George Peabody Coll for Teachers 1937
700 McNEER Marietta W  The Boy as a Character in American Fiction by Standard Authors from Cooper to Twain  MA Univ of North Carolina at Chapel Hill 1934
701 MANESS E M  The Indian Figure in James Fenimore Cooper's *The Last of the Mohicans* and William Gilmore Simms' *The Yemassee*  MA North Texas St Univ 1969
702 MILLER Paul A  James Fenimore Cooper and the South Seas  MA Univ of North Dakota 1930  99 p
703 MINOR Dennis E  The Epic Qualities of the Early American Frontier Novel:  Cooper's Leatherstocking Tales  MA Texas Agricultural and Mechanical Univ 1968  98 p
704 MISHLER Craig W  The Prairie:  A Study in Romantic American Landscape as Reflected in the Writings of Cooper, Bryant, Irving, Melville and Whitman, 1827-1888  MA Washington St Univ at Pullman 1967
705 MOONEY D N  Social Principles and Criticism in the Novels of James Fenimore Cooper After 1830  MA Ohio St Univ 1940
706 MURRAY Hazel G  James Fenimore Cooper's Literary Treatment of the American Negro  MA Univ of Tennessee 1956  99 p
707 NICHOLSON Virginia  Cooper's Novels as Source Material for the History of American Culture  MA Texas Woman's Univ 1938
708 OWENS Sarah C  A Study of Three of Cooper's Controversial Novels: *The Monikins*, *Homeward Bound* and *Home As Found*  MA Univ of Kentucky 1936
709 PATES Adaline S  Social Theory in the Fiction of Cooper and Melville  MA Smith Coll 1935
710 PROUTY James W  An Analysis of *The Last of the Mohicans* and *The Way West* for Their Contribution to the Learning Process in a High School

Classroom  MA Chico St Coll 1958  51 p
711 RAWE Lucy R  The Ambiguities of James Fenimore Cooper's Doctrine of Gifts and Its Effects upon the Literary Success of the Leatherstocking Tales  MA St Louis Univ 1967  100 p
712 SCAPIN Maria  Fenimore Cooper's Littlepage Manuscripts  MA Ca Foscari (Italy) 1957
713 SHARP Herbert  Dialect and Colloquialisms in *The Prairie* by James Fenimore Cooper  MA Univ of Kansas 1928
714 SMITH Burley G  An Analysis of the Female Characters in Cooper's Leatherstocking Tales  MA Bowling Green St Univ 1960
715 STENGER Lorna  American Manners and Customs as Shown by the Novels of James Fenimore Cooper  MA Univ of Tulsa 1940
716 SULLIVAN Cecille G  The Indian as Treated by Cooper and Simms  MA Yale Univ 1925
717 TURNER Betty D  Frontier Characters in Writings of Cooper  M Ed Henderson St Coll nd
718 WADE Beatrice G  Cooper's Leatherstocking Tales: The American Epic  MA Boston Univ 1947
719 WEBSTER Clara M  Agrarianism of James Fenimore Cooper  MA Boston Univ 1952
720 WHITE Clara M  A Study of James Fenimore Cooper's Social Teachings on American Democratic Culture  MA Texas Arts and Industries Univ 1946
721 WILLIAMS Owen D  James Fenimore Cooper's "Bad" Indians: A Study of Magua, Mahtoree and Wyandotte  MA Univ of North Carolina at Greensboro 1970

See also 365, 3199, 3783

## JAMES GOULD COZZENS

722 CRADDOCK William B  The Development of the Man of Reason in the Novels of James Gould Cozzens  MA Univ of Texas at Austin 1962  92 p
723 CRAINE Dan T  The Problem of Communication in the Cozzens Novel  MA Syracuse Univ 1960  170 p
724 DAVIS Joyce M  James Gould Cozzens: A View of Man and Society  MA Univ of Mississippi 1970
725 FEATHER George K  The Literary Reputation of James Gould Cozzens  MA Baylor Univ 1963  126 p
726 GOURLEY Dorothy W  James Gould Cozzens: Aristotelian Humanist  MA Indiana Univ of Pennsylvania 1965  104 p
727 HAIRSTON Maxine C  James Gould Cozzens' *By Love Possessed*  MA Univ of Texas at Austin 1958  146 p
728 ISENBERG Byron C  The Art of James Gould Cozzens  MA Univ of Louisville 1957
729 KOSOVE Joseph A  James Gould Cozzens: A Study in Themes and Perspectives  MA Columbia Univ 1959  160 p
730 McGRIFF Ruth C  Puritan Concepts of Morality in the Novels of James Gould Cozzens  MA Auburn Univ 1967
731 PENA Jose A  James Gould Cozzens and the Rational Life: A Study of His Major Novels  MA Columbia Univ 1951
732 RODEWALD Frederick A  Moral Ambiguity as a Theme in the Novels of James Gould Cozzens  MA Univ of Oklahoma 1968  226 p

## CHRISTOPHER PEARSE CRANCH

733 GOLDMAN Philip L  The Work of Christopher Pearse Cranch  MA Columbia Univ 1935
734 MOWRY Vera L  Christopher Pearse Cranch: Transcendental Poet  MA Univ of Pittsburgh 1940
735 WHITNEY R M  The Life of Christopher Pearse Cranch  MA Univ of

New Hampshire 1940 79 p

## HART CRANE

736 ABBOT Craig S  Hart Crane's Attitude Toward Technology  MA Texas Agricultural and Mechanical Univ 1966  69 p
737 BAIN Mary J  Art as Affirmation:  A Study of Hart Crane's "Atlantis"  MA Univ of Massachusetts 1967  62 p
738 BIGELOW Margaret F  An Evaluation of Hart Crane (with Reference to the Munson Correspondence)  MA Ohio St Univ 1936
739 BOND Richard W  Orpheus and Hart Crane:  An Archetypal Summary and an Application  MA Univ of Texas at Austin 1967  135 p
740 BRINEY John  Hart Crane and Walt Whitman:  A Comparison  MA Univ of Louisville 1960
741 CAMPBELL Albert J  Water as a Symbolic Image in Poetry of Hart Crane  MA Univ of Maine 1968  84 p
742 CARPENTER Judith A  Hart Crane's Voyages:  The Logic of Metaphor  MA Temple Univ 1964  66 p
743 FAISON Theodore C  Hart Crane's *The Bridge*:  A First Attempt at an American Epic  MA Fairleigh Dickinson Univ 1963  77 p
744 FESLER Edward E  Hart Crane and the Machine  MA Washington Univ at St Louis 1951
745 FLEMING John W  A Study of the Poetic Imagery of Hart Crane  MA Bowling Green St Univ 1950
746 GIBSON Rosalynde V  Hart Crane's *The Bridge*:  A Critical Study  MA Univ of North Carolina at Chapel Hill 1961
747 KINNELL Galway M  *The Bridge* of Hart Crane:  A Poetic Affirmation in the Twentieth Century  MA Univ of Rochester 1949  136 p
748 LYONS Mary P  A Consideration of the American Myth in Hart Crane's *The Bridge* and William Carlos Williams' *Paterson*  MA Univ of Rhode Island 1966  172 p
749 MALYSZ Thaddeus K  The Poetics of Hart Crane  MA Boston Coll 1952
750 O'BRIEN Michael  The Development of the Language of Hart Crane in *White Buildings*  MA Columbia Univ 1963  93 p
751 PEMBERTON Vivian H  Some Family Figures Behind Hart Crane  MA Kent St Univ 1966
752 PUTNAM Robert E  Hart Crane's Path to Unity:  A Study of the Death and Rebirth Theme in *The Bridge*  MA Roosevelt Univ at Chicago 1969
753 ROWAN Stephanie R  Make My Dark Poem Light, and Light:  A Study of Hart Crane's Manuscripts  MA Columbia Univ 1966  240 p
754 SCHULZ Max F  The Idiom of Hart Crane's *White Buildings*  MA Univ of Pittsburgh 1950
755 SCHWAB Sarah V  Some Uses of Tradition in the Poetry of Hart Crane  MA Univ of Pittsburgh 1958
756 SCHWARTZ Alan H  No Trophies of the Sun:  The Poetry of Hart Crane  MA Columbia Univ 1960  67 p
757 STEWART Albert F  Hart Crane:  A Study in Modern Poetry  MA Univ of Kentucky 1942  190 p
758 TRUSCOTT Robert B  Hart Crane's *White Buildings* and the Extension of Metaphysical Tradition  BA Rutgers St Univ 1966  88 p
759 TUCK Dorothy J  The Problem of Unity in the Poetry of Hart Crane  MA Columbia Univ 1961  113 p
760 VOGT Marilyn E  *White Buildings*:  Hart Crane and the Poetic Experience  MA Ohio St Univ 1964  63 p
761 WALL Van C  Hart Crane:  An Explanation of His Poems  MA Univ of Richmond 1964  88 p
762 WINTERS Anne K  The Influence of Arthur Rimbaud on Hart Crane  MA Columbia Univ 1963  74 p
763 WOOD David B  Hart Crane:  A Study of *The Bridge*  MA McMaster Univ

(Canada) 1966
See also 6627

## STEPHEN CRANE

764 ALDERMAN Taylor  A Comparison of the Short Stories of Stephen Crane and Ernest Hemingway  MA Univ of Wyoming 1965
765 ALTER Lynn E  An Analysis of the Use of Color in Selected Works of Stephen Crane  MA Indiana Univ of Pennsylvania 1967  49 p
766 ARMSTRONG Sara E  Stephen Crane: Naturalism Revaluated  MA Miami Univ at Oxford 1965
767 ARNOLD Hans S  Stephen Crane's War Fiction  MA Univ of Maryland at College Park 1956  225 p
768 BEACH Robert C  An Analysis of Imagery in the Short Stories of Stephen Crane  MA Mankato St Coll 1964  91 p
769 BLAZEK Edward  The Key Ideational Value in Selected Poetry of Stephen Crane  M Ed Henderson St Coll nd
770 BOOTY Don V  The Irony of Stephen Crane  MA Ball St Univ 1969  70 p
771 BREWER Nancy C  The Critical Theories of Stephen Crane  MA Univ of Mississippi 1967
772 BUCHANAN Linda C  The Philosophical Poetry of Stephen Crane  MA Louisiana Technological Univ 1970  78 p
773 BUTLER Judith  The Criticism of *The Red Badge of Courage*  MA Univ of North Carolina at Greensboro 1966
774 COFFIN Arthur B  The Imagery in the Work of Stephen Crane  MA Boston Coll 1958
775 CONERLY M S  Naturalism in the Work of Stephen Crane  MA North Texas St Univ nd
776 COX Charles M  Color Symbolism in *The Red Badge of Courage*  MA East Tennessee St Univ 1969
777 CRAWLEY Sr Mary M  Religious Symbolism in *The Red Badge of Courage*  MA Boston Coll 1966
778 CREECH Esther C  The Naturalistic Tendencies of Stephen Crane as Revealed in Selected Works  M Ed Henderson St Coll nd
779 CUNNINGHAM Sr Shirley A  The Significance of Nature and Animals in Stephen Crane's Prose  MA Ohio St Univ 1968  81 p
780 DABNEY Louise P  Stephen Crane as a Critic of Society  MA Howard Univ 1953  152 p
781 DAMERON John L  The Poetry of Stephen Crane  MA Univ of North Carolina at Chapel Hill 1952  91 p
782 DELL William R  The Characters of Stephen Crane  MA Univ of Idaho 1950
783 DE SOUZA Alfred  *The Red Badge of Courage* and *A Farewell to Arms*: Two Statements on War  MA Columbia Univ 1965  137 p
784 DRUM Charlotte J  A Comparison of the Prose and Poetry of Stephen Crane in Terms of Sentence Structure  MA California St Coll at Long Beach 1966
785 ELDER Owen C Jr  The Significance of Environment in Selected Works of Stephen Crane  MA Bowling Green St Univ 1960
786 FALSON Margaret B  Stephen Crane's Man in War  MA Univ of North Carolina at Greensboro 1969
787 FLAHERTY Douglas E  Stephen Crane: Beyond Literary Parallel to Originality  MA Univ of Massachusetts 1963
788 FREZZA Luciana  Stephen Crane: From Naturalism to Expressionism  MA Ca Foscari (Italy) nd
789 FUCHS David C  Imagery in *The Red Badge of Courage*  MA Univ of Rochester 1951  97 p
790 FULTZ James R Jr  Patterns of Imagery in *The Red Badge of Courage*  MS Kansas St Coll at Pittsburg 1965
791 GARDNER Delbert R  "The More Ambitious Effort": The Search for Meaning in Stephen Crane's Poetry  MA Syracuse Univ 1955  63 p

792  GARDNER Helen   The Relationship Between Man and Nature in Stephen Crane   MA Hunter Coll 1965
793  GOETH Rolf A   Irony in the Works of Stephen Crane   MA Univ of Texas at Austin 1955
794  GOLDBERG Helen W   Techniques and Attitudes in the Fiction of Stephen Crane   MA Columbia Univ 1953   123 p
795  GREGORY Donald L   A Comparative Study of the Prose and Poetry of Stephen Crane   MA Ohio St Univ 1962   110 p
796  HALLIBURTON Juanita G   Variations in Perspective:  A Major Source of Irony in the Fiction of Stephen Crane   MA San Diego St Coll 1965   138 p
797  HANNON Ella M   A Study of the Literary Technique of Stephen Crane as a Naturalist   MA North Carolina Central Univ at Durham 1952   94 p
798  HARVEY Nellie C   Paradox in Stephen Crane   MA Mississippi St Univ 1964   63 p
799  HASSINGER Elizabeth C   The Significance of Stephen Crane in American Fiction   MA Univ of Pittsburgh 1940
800  HAYNES Nina B   Stephen Crane's Poetry:  Its Reception and Philosophy   MA Univ of North Carolina at Chapel Hill 1963
801  HERSHOW Sheila J   Stephen Crane and Ernest Hemingway:  A Comparison   MA Columbia 1966   117 p
802  HILL Onan A   Stephen Crane as a Social Critic   MA Univ of Oklahoma 1950
803  HILT Kathyrn F   Stephen Crane and Women:  A Biographical Study   MA Univ of Maryland at College Park 1964   97 p
804  HOULIHAN Elena S   Stephen Crane's *Whilomville Stories* and the Tradition of Boy Literature   MA DePauw Univ 1968   101 p
805  HUGHES Donna M   Stephen Crane, Journalist:  A Prismatic Career in the Gilded Age   M Ed Central Washington St Coll at Ellensburg 1964   229 p
806  JOHNSON Arnold B   *Maggie:  A Girl of the Streets* as the Archetype of American Naturalistic Heroines   MA Columbia Univ 1955   49 p
807  JOHNSON Greg S   Stephen Crane's Last Novel, *The O'Ruddy*   MA La Verne Coll 1967   104 p
808  JONES Gary E   Stephen Crane's *The Black Riders*:  A Profile in Christian Existentialism   MA Bowling Green St Univ 1969
809  JORDAN J W   A Comparison of Stephen Crane's *The Red Badge of Courage* and Ernest Hemingway's *A Farewell to Arms* as Literary Propaganda   MA Ohio St Univ 1940
810  KEIM Ann M   Structure and Theme in the Fiction of Stephen Crane:  A Study of the Ironic Mode   MA La Verne Coll 1967   132 p
811  KILLINGER John R Jr   Stephen Crane:  Fifty Years of Reviews and Critical Studies in American Magazines (1893-1943)   MA Univ of Kentucky 1954   98 p
812  KIRBY John E   Stephen Crane at War   MA San Diego St Coll 1961   81 p
813  LADD Mary E   A Critical Study of the Poetry of Stephen Crane to Determine His Conception of Man's Place in Nature   MA Bowling Green St Univ 1959
814  LANE David G   Setting in the Western Stories of Stephen Crane   MA Washington St Univ at Pullman 1969
815  LEE Robert E   A Study of the Poetry of Stephen Crane   MA Univ of North Carolina at Greensboro 1954
816  LINDQUEST Robert M   Stephen Crane; with Particular Emphasis upon His Prose and Poetry   MA Univ of New Hampshire 1950   66 p
817  LOGAN Barry L   Stephen Crane's Orphic Vision:  *The Red Badge of Courage*   MA Syracuse Univ 1956   96 p
818  MACHADO Judith   Stephen Crane:  His Critics and His Fictions   MA Univ of California at Riverside 1959
819  McLEAN Robert C   The Reception of Stephen Crane in England   MA Indiana Univ 1955
820  MANNING Gerald F   Stephen Crane:  Impressionist and Ironist   MA Alberta Univ (Canada) 1966

821 MARTIN Terence J  A Study of Dialogue in the Fiction of Stephen Crane  MA Ohio St Univ 1950
822 MERCIER John D  The Unconventional Stephen Crane and His Impact on American Letters  MA Niagara Univ 1965
823 MICKLESON Vernon  Social Ideas in the Writings of Stephen Crane  MA Univ of Montana 1932  47 p
824 MITCHELL Betty L  The Literary Reputation of Stephen Crane  MA Southern Illinois Univ at Carbondale 1950  110 p
825 MIURA Akira  A Study of Stephen Crane's *Maggie: A Girl of the Streets*  MA Columbia Univ 1962  91 p
826 MORRISON Jane T  Evidence of Martial Conflict in the Life and Selected Works of Stephen Crane  MA La Verne Coll 1970  110 p
827 MORRISSEY William R  The *Whilomville Stories* of Stephen Crane  MA Ohio St Univ 1968  86 p
828 MURPHY Clare  Stephen Crane: The Rebel  MA Univ of Texas at El Paso 1957  89 p
829 MURRAY H F  Symbolism of Stephen Crane and Ernest Hemingway  MA Western St Coll of Colorado 1966  172 p
830 NEAL Audrey H  Stephen Crane: The Emergence of Naturalism in American Literature  MA Univ of Houston 1954  98 p
831 NELSON Harland S  Form and Idea in the Poetry of Stephen Crane  MA Washington St Univ at Pullman 1951
832 NELSON John R  Some Aspects of the Philosophy of Stephen Crane  MA Univ of Maine 1962  123 p
833 NISNEWITZ Freda  "The Spectral Image": An Analysis of Stephen Crane's "The Open Boat" and "The Blue Hotel" in Terms of Color Imagery  MA Columbia Univ 1962  67 p
834 OBERPARLEITER Lee G  An Analysis of Stephen Crane's Poetry, Tracing the Development of His Concept of God  MA Univ of Maine 1967  97 p
835 O'DONNELL Thomas F  An Analysis of the Poetry of Stephen Crane  MA Syracuse Univ 1947  67 p
836 O'KEEFE Irene M  Existentialism in Stephen Crane's *The Red Badge of Courage*  MA Central Connecticut St Coll 1965
837 PARK Ruth  Stephen Crane: Genre Painter  MA Texas Arts and Industries Univ 1950
838 PRENGEL Roger D  A Comparative Study of *The Red Badge of Courage, All Quiet on the Western Front* and *April Morning*  MA Brigham Young Univ 1970  107 p
839 RAMSEY Emily S  Stephen Crane's Indictment of Society in His Prose Works  MA Mississippi St Univ 1964  93 p
840 REEVES Elizabeth W  Stephen Crane: Forerunner of American Naturalism  MA Howard Univ 1943  135 p
841 ROGERS Ralph R  Stephen Crane's Narrative Technique  MA Columbia Univ 1954  119 p
842 ROSENER Ann  Stephen Crane: A Study in Individualism  MA Columbia Univ 1937
843 ROSS Frances A  Literary Naturalism in Stephen Crane  MA Trinity Univ of San Antonio 1965
844 ROY Mother Michel  The Function of Crane and Dreiser in American Literary Naturalism  MA Boston Coll 1965
845 RUSHING Leah St J  Stephen Crane and the Quality of Moral Concern  MA Lamar Technological Univ 1968  126 p
846 SANDERSON Sandra D  Themes in the Poetry of Stephen Crane  MA Baylor Univ 1965  106 p
847 SCHMITTLEIN Albert E  Colors and Shadows: Stephen Crane as a War Correspondent and the Stories He Wrote from His Associations and Experiences  MA Columbia Univ 1953  109 p
848 SCHWEPPE Erna G  Stephen Crane: An Interpretative and Critical Study  MA St Mary's Univ of San Antonio 1941  75 p
849 SCOTT Winifred P  Prose Texture and Narrative Structure in *The Red*

*Badge of Courage* MA Southern Illinois Univ at Carbondale 1965 103 p
850 SHAH Dorothie C An Approach to Understanding Literature: Meaning in "The Monster" MA Cornell Univ 1966
851 SHAIR Susan N Stephen Crane: A Tragic Vision MA Columbia Univ 1960 171 p
852 SIMONEAUX Katherine G Color Imagery in Selected Prose Works of Stephen Crane MA Univ of Southwestern Louisiana 1966 110 p
853 STONE Albert E Jr Stephen Crane's Children: A Literary Analysis MA Columbia Univ 1955 125 p
854 SWADLEY D R Impressionism in the Prose Fiction of Stephen Crane MA North Texas St Univ 1955
855 TANGUAY Norman J The War Theme in the Works of Stephen Crane MA Univ of Maine 1969 98 p
856 TEMPLIN Ann B The Use of Color in Stephen Crane's Poetry MA Ohio St Univ 1965 99 p
857 THOMAS Margery A Stephen Crane and War MA Univ of Kentucky 1944 107 p
858 THOMPSON Dorothy M The Literary Art of Stephen Crane MA Univ of Texas at El Paso 1959 82 p
859 THOMS Glen E Color Images in the Poetry of Stephen Crane MA Fairleigh Dickinson Univ 1964 37 p
860 TOLAN Stephanie S The Concept of Love in the Poetry of Stephen Crane MA Purdue Univ 1967 110 p
861 WALKER Herbert J Stephen Crane's *Whilomville Stories*: A Study of Humor and Determinism MA Bowling Green St Univ 1966
862 WARD Mildred The Naturalistic Vein of Stephen Crane's Writings M Ed Henderson St Coll nd
863 WESTBROOK Max Irony in the Fiction of Stephen Crane MA Univ of Oklahoma 1953
864 WILSON Fred E Stephen Crane's Presentation of War MA North Texas St Univ 1964
865 YOUNG Nancy B The Literary Reputation of Stephen Crane in America MA Univ of North Carolina at Chapel Hill 1952 133 p
See also 2450, 2634, 3067, 3894, 4401, 6255

## FRANCIS MARION CRAWFORD

866 ASHBURNE Jim G Francis Marion Crawford, Prince of Story Tellers: A Critical Biography MA Southern Methodist Univ 1932
867 BONGIORNO Carmela Roman Scenes and Characters in the Work of the American Novelist F Marion Crawford MA Ca Foscari (Italy) 1935
868 FEENEY Sr Mary H Frances Marion Crawford, 1854-1909: A Biography and Critical Study MA Univ of Maine 1954 174 p
869 NORTON Sr Elizabeth Marion Crawford: A Great American Romantic Novelist MA Boston Coll 1941
870 POWERS Daniel Francis Marion Crawford and the Vogue of the Historical Novel MA Columbia Univ 1941
871 RALEY Sr Agnes L Study of the Novels of Francis M Crawford MA Boston Coll 1940
872 ROSSI Anna Francis Marion Crawford and His Italian Novels MA Ca Foscari (Italy) 1938
873 ZUCK Constance F Francis Marion Crawford: An Analysis of His Novels MA Univ of Kansas 1967

## DAVY CROCKETT

874 APRAD Joseph J David Crockett: An Original MA Univ of Iowa 1965
875 BAILY Edith David Crockett and Augustus Baldwin Longstreet as Pioneers in the Democratic Literature of America MA Louisiana St Univ 1936
876 CROCKETT Frank Q A Study of the Politics of "The Honourable David Crockett, M C" MA Univ of Mississippi 1930

877 DOWELL Ruth B  The Congressional Career of David Crockett  MA Columbia Univ 1925
878 FISH Sandra L  Davy Crockett: The Speaker and the Image  MA Univ of Oklahoma 1965
879 GATES Margaret H  Fact and Fiction in the Early Biographies of David Crockett  MA Univ of Illinois at Urbana 1929
880 KELLOGG Oliver L  David Crockett and the Dark Ages in American Literature  MA Columbia Univ 1955  105 p
881 TOSO Paola  David Crockett: The Man and the Legend  MA Ca Foscari (Italy) 1958

## E E CUMMINGS

882 AGTE Lloyd M  E E Cummings' Use of Parentheses as Poetic Technique in *Collected Poems, 1923-1954*  MA Sul Ross St Coll 1966
883 BIRD Rita M  The Poetry and Prose of E E Cummings  MA Ohio St Univ 1948
884 BLACKMAN Marcia  Guillaume Apollinaire and E E Cummings  MA Columbia Univ 1953  73 p
885 BONTEMPO Carol L  Curving Nevers of Wherewhen: Functional Shift in the Poetry of E E Cummings  MA Ohio St Univ 1969  238 p
886 BRADEN Wilbur S  E E Cummings' Sonnets  MA Washington St Univ at Pullman 1964
887 BRYANT S R  The World View of E E Cummings  MA North Texas St Univ 1967
888 COHEN Allan R  E E Cummings  BA Amherst Coll 1959
889 CORSON Edward W Jr  "Beyond Life and Death": An Analysis of the Merits and the Limitations of Ironic Structuring in the Poetry of E E Cummings  BA Amherst Coll 1954
890 DASGUPTA Pranabendu  Nature of "Obscurity" and "Difficulty" in E E Cummings' Poems  MA Univ of North Carolina at Chapel Hill 1962
891 GREEN Judith A  E E Cummings and American Transcendentalism  MA Hunter Coll 1964
892 HARRIS Karl D  Motifs of Time and Nature in the Poetry of E E Cummings  MA Univ of Tennessee 1969  110 p
893 HOLBROOK Thomas A  Love as a Basis for the Poetry of E E Cummings  MA Syracuse Univ 1966  130 p
894 JACKSON Sandra L  Bacchanalian Innocence: A Study of E E Cummings' Philosophy as It Is Expressed in His Prose  MA Connecticut Coll 1968
895 KRAMER Lisbeth J  E E Cummings: A New Search for Grace  MA Columbia Univ 1961  115 p
896 LASSER Michael L  Technique in the Poetry of E E Cummings: A Justification of Innovation  MA Brooklyn Coll of City Univ of New York 1958  122 p
897 LINDQUIST Carol A  E E Cummings on the Nature of Man  MA Bowling Green St Univ 1963
898 MATHESON Terence J  An Analysis of the Influence of the Unworld on the Individual as Expressed in the Prose and Poetry of E E Cummings  MA Univ of Manitoba (Canada) 1967
899 MULLEN Patrick B  Humor in the Poetry of E E Cummings  MA North Texas St Univ 1965
900 MUNOZ Mary E  The Meaning of Death and Its Symbols in the Poetry of E E Cummings  MA Univ of Iowa 1965
901 MURPHY Barbara  An Examination of the Concept of Love in the Poetry of E E Cummings  MA Univ of Iowa 1965
902 MURRAY Pat  Cummings: An Experiment in Language, Consciousness and Time  BA Univ of British Columbia (Canada) 1968
903 NETCEL Theresa  The Philosophy of E E Cummings  MA Columbia Univ 1962  113 p
904 O'NEILL Michael T  Cubist Elements in the Poetry of E E Cummings  MA Long Island Univ 1967  114 p

905 ORBISON Douglas  Sensibility and the Art of E E Cummings  MA Columbia Univ 1954  148 p
906 ORDEMAN John T  "An Author of Pictures, a Draughtsman of Words": E E Cummings as Poet and Painter  MA Columbia Univ 1960  182 p
907 PAYNE Diane M  The Roles of Imagined Speaker and Listener in Selected Poems of E E Cummings  MA Univ of Minnesota 1965
908 PERRY Edith B  E E Cummings: A Study  MA Univ of New Mexico 1949
909 REESE Sr Diane  Movement in Relation to Diction and Imagery in E E Cummings' Elegy "My Father Moved Through Dooms of Love"  MA Catholic Univ of America at San Rafael 1969
910 SHVEIGER Raya  Tradition and Innovation: A Study of Form in the Sonnets of E E Cummings  MA Northeast Missouri St Coll 1960
911 SIMON Gabriele J  E E Cummings: Of Love and Death a Marriage  MA Columbia Univ 1959  53 p
912 STRONGIN Lynn  "Actually Flowers": Romanticism in E E Cummings' Poetry  MA Stanford Univ 1965
913 TAL-MASON Patricia  "Mortally Immortal": A Study of E E Cummings' Concept of the Individual, Based on *i: Six Non-Lectures*  MA Univ of Miami 1966
914 VINCENT Jeffrey S  E E Cummings: The Development of an Artist  BA Rutgers St Univ 1969  78 p
915 ZIPSE Erwin C  Aspects of Thought, Style and Mechanical Form in E E Cummings' Poetry  MA Univ of Rhode Island 1956
916 ZULANDT George K  The Poetic Techniques of E E Cummings  MA Ohio St Univ 1957

## GEORGE WILLIAM CURTIS

917 LINEHAN Marion W  George William Curtis and the Near East in the Travel Book Tradition of the Nineteenth Century  MA Texas Christian Univ 1968  78 p
918 SMART F A  George William Curtis as Literary Critic  MA Boston Univ 1948

## THE DANAS

919 GRIFFIN Lloyd W  Selected Letters of Richard Henry Dana, 1815-1882  MA Univ of Maine 1947  396 p
920 WALLACE Florence M  A Study of R H Dana's Critical Attitude Toward the Political Situation of His Time  MA Univ of Iowa 1931
See also 390

## DONALD DAVIDSON

921 CROSBY Richard W  Three Poets as Social Critics: Donald Davidson, John Crowe Ransom, Allen Tate  BA Amherst Coll 1963
922 FREEZE Leslie H  The Poetry of Donald Davidson  MA Univ of Kansas 1964

## REBECCA HARDING DAVIS

923 GALE M S  Short Stories of Rebecca Harding Davis  MA Ohio St Univ 1933
924 LAMBERT Maude E  Rebecca Harding Davis as a Social Critic  MA Univ of North Carolina at Chapel Hill 1959  70 p

## JOHN WILLIAM DeFOREST

925 ANDERSON Edith C  John William DeForest: Pioneer American Realist  MA Fresno St Coll 1958  156 p
926 BRIGHT Elizabeth M  An Analysis of the Methods Used by John William DeForest in Translating His Personal War Experiences

into Realistic Fiction as Shown in *Miss Ravenal's Conversion* MA Univ of Louisville 1949
927 CARVER Rosetta P John William DeForest: Portrayer of the Civil War MA Florida St Univ 1951
928 FAGGIANI Lester A Aspects of the Fiction of John William DeForest MA Columbia Univ 1953 87 p
929 HALL Doris B The Southern Poor-White in the Writings of William DeForest and Other Northern Writers, 1860-1880 MA Univ of North Carolina at Chapel Hill 1963
930 HILL Jerry H The Novels of John William DeForest MA Univ of Vermont 1969 115 p
931 KINNARD Karolyn K An Historical and Critical Study of John William DeForest's *Miss Ravenal's Conversion from Secession to Loyalty* MA Univ of Texas at Austin 1966
932 PRIDDY Ruth M A Proposed Anthology of Selections from John William DeForest MA Univ of Pittsburgh 1959
933 SHEMWELL Arthur L Jr John William DeForest: In Critical Perspective MA Columbia Univ 1961 83 p

## MARGARET DELAND

934 BEARD Catherine Margaret Deland's Use of the Deus Ex Machina in the Old Chester Stories MA Univ of Kentucky 1948 72 p
935 BELL Hattie M Margaret Deland's Old Chester and Its People MA George Peabody Coll for Teachers 1931
936 DEBENNING Evelyn M The Literary Career of Margaret Deland MA Oklahoma St Univ 1948 53 p
937 HARVEY William M Didacticism in the Fiction of Mrs Margaret Deland MA Univ of Pittsburgh 1930
938 NOLAN Earleene D Margaret Wade Deland MA Louisiana St Univ 1939
See also 5636

## JOSEPH DENNIE

939 FITZHERBERT Eleanor M An Edition of the "Farrago" Essays of Joseph Dennie, 1768-1812 MA Univ of Maine 1942 199 p
940 McLEISTER Walter E Joseph Dennie and the Port Folio MA Univ of Pittsburgh 1939
941 RAMSEY Vernelle The Place of Joseph Dennie in American Literature M Ed Henderson St Coll nd

## BERNARD DeVOTO

942 BEAL Barbara M The Significance of Bernard DeVoto on the Interpretation of Mark Twain MA Univ of Arizona 1960 120 p
943 SAWEY Sara C Bernard DeVoto and the Metaphysical Critics: The Book That Isn't There MA Univ of Texas at Austin 1966 114 p

## EMILY DICKINSON

944 BAKER Mary G Emily Dickinson's Knowledge of the Classical and European Philosophers and Their Influence on Her Prose and Poetry MS Univ of Massachusetts 1933
945 BARNETT Joan W The Soul's Distinct Connection with Immortality: Emily Dickinson's Experience of Poetic Inspiration MA Auburn Univ 1964 82 p
946 BARNHILL M E The Poetry of Emily Dickinson MA Ohio St Univ 1929
947 BLACKWELL Bonnie Self-revelation in the Works of Emily Dickinson MA Univ of Texas at Austin 1937 152 p
948 BLEVINS Winfred E Jr Emily Dickinson: The Critics and Approximate

Rhyme   MA Columbia Univ 1962   57 p
949 BOLIN Donald W   Emily Dickinson and the Nature Tradition   MA Ohio St Univ 1956
950 BROOKER Jewel S   Rhetorical Patterns in Emily Dickinson's Poetry   MA Univ of Florida 1964
951 BUSSOLA Carla   Emily Dickinson   MA Ca Foscari (Italy) 1942
952 CADWELL Floralyn   The Sources of the Poetic Mind in Emily Dickinson   MA Univ of Hawaii 1926   94 p
953 CANAN Jessie E   The Religion of Emily Dickinson   MA Univ of Pittsburgh 1933
954 CLAY Winfred E   Some Influences of Emily Dickinson's Father Which Support Later Life of Seclusion   MA Univ of Texas at El Paso 1966   68 p
955 CLINE Ruth A   A Bibliography of Emily Dickinson's Writings and Analysis from January 1, 1931 to January 1, 1950   MA Univ of Kentucky 1950   98 p
956 CONLON Mary R   The Mystical Quality in the Poetry of Emily Dickinson   MA St Bonaventure Univ 1966
957 CONWAY Marion L   A Study of Certain Elements of Emily Dickinson's Poetic Style   MA George Peabody Coll for Teachers 1936
958 CORFIELD Bertha M   The Problem of Originality in the Techniques of Emily Dickinson and Edna St Vincent Millay   MA Boston Univ 1934
959 COUSINEAU Jeanine   Emily Dickinson's Concept of Freedom and the Power of Will   MA Univ of New Hampshire 1962   52 p
960 CROWDER Anna M   Some Aspects of Emily Dickinson's Prosody   MA East Tennessee St Univ 1964
961 CULLEN Sr Helen M   Color Imagery in the Poems of Emily Dickinson   MA Boston Coll 1960
962 DICKIE Jane A   Emily Dickinson:  Ironist   MA Columbia Univ 1943
963 DICKINSON George T   A Study of the Poetry of Emily Dickinson   MA North Texas St Univ 1938
964 DORGAN Gerard L   Biblical Imagery in the Poetry of Emily Dickinson: The Revelation of St John the Divine   MA Boston Coll 1966
965 DOROUGH Ivy A   Emily Dickinson: A Critical Analysis of Her Ideas About Nature   MA Univ of Texas at Austin 1940   139 p
966 DUQUE Manuel R   Emily Dickinson's "Aptitude for Bird": A Study of Selected Poems   MA Bucknell Univ 1969
967 EARWOOD Orpha   Nature in the Poems of Emily Dickinson   MA Univ of Texas at Austin 1938   113 p
968 ELLIOTT G D   The Solitary Dissenter: A Study of Emily Dickinson's Concept of God   MA North Texas St Univ 1968
969 ENNIS Carol A   Heretical Implications in the Poetry and Letters of Emily Dickinson: A Study   MA C W Post Coll 1964   56 p
970 ESPY George   Dualism in the Poetry of Emily Dickinson   MA Atlanta Univ 1965
971 FALEN Doris J   The Spiritual Journal of a Poet: Emily Dickinson's Inability to Honor or Dismiss the "Faith of the Fathers"   MS Kansas St Coll at Pittsburg 1959
972 FARMER Mary J   Color in the Poems of Emily Dickinson   MA Univ of Denver 1964
973 FAUST Ruby J   Scope and Intensity in Emily Dickinson's Love Poetry   MA Auburn Univ 1964   228 p
974 FILLMORE Lily M   The Life and Poetry of Emily Dickinson   MA Boston Univ 1934
975 FLANIGAN Robert C   The Nature Poetry of Emily Dickinson   MA Univ of Pittsburgh 1957
976 FLETCHER Eleanor R   The Poetic Genius of Emily Dickinson: An Interpretation   MA Univ of Texas at Austin 1940   115 p
977 FLY Richard D   The Thematic Use of Astronomical Imagery in the Poetry of Emily Dickinson   MA Univ of Hawaii 1963   109 p

978  FORSYTH Sr Celine M  Tension as a Principle of Design in the Poems of Emily Dickinson  MA San Diego Coll for Women 1967  89 p
979  FORTENBERRY Imogene  Imagery in the Poetry of Emily Dickinson  MA Texas Technological Univ 1950  80 p
980  FOWLER M J  Emily Dickinson's Originality as a Poet  MA Boston Coll 1934
981  FRANCIS Clifton N Jr  The Household Imagery of Emily Dickinson  MA Lamar Technological Univ 1962  137 p
982  FUJITA Nozomi  Emily Dickinson's Poetic Theory  MA Univ of Massachusetts 1970  56 p
983  GARNES David F  A Dim Capacity for Wings: Concepts of the Self in Emily Dickinson's Poetry  MA Columbia Univ 1965  76 p
984  GONSOR Robert L  Nature, Science and Emily Dickinson  MA Univ of Massachusetts 1961
985  GOODE Lehoma B  A Comparison of the Early and Late Poetry of Emily Dickinson  MA Wake Forest Univ 1966
986  GREEN Lola B  Emily Dickinson in Facts and Fiction  MA Texas Technological Univ 1942  53 p
987  HALL Sr M Jeremias  A Comparative Study of Death-consciousness in John Donne and Emily Dickinson  MA Siena Hts Coll 1959  217 p
988  HALPIN Mary C  The Metaphysical in Emily Dickinson's Poetry  MA Boston Univ 1947
989  HARRIS Jack E  A Study of the Insect Images of the Poetry of Emily Dickinson  MA West Virginia Univ 1969  73 p
990  HARRIS Ruth  Emily Dickinson: A Forerunner of Imagism  MA Boston Univ 1944
991  HAYASHI Kyoko  Concept of Friendship in the Poems of Emily Dickinson  MA Northeast Missouri St Coll 1960
992  HENNING Catherine A  The Riddle as Literary Form in the Poetry of Emily Dickinson  MA Univ of Western Ontario (Canada) 1967
993  HERTZ Renee L  Emily Dickinson: Orthodoxy and Heterodoxy  MA Columbia Univ 1950
994  HOGAN Sr Rosaria  An Evaluation of Emily Dickinson's Newly Discovered Poems  MA Boston Coll 1948
995  HOLT Beverly  The Major Themes of Imagery in the Poetry of Emily Dickinson  M Ed Henderson St Coll nd
996  HOWARD Wilma W  The Insufficient Solution: Emily Dickinson's Religious Beliefs  MA San Diego St Coll 1958  101 p
997  HUBERT Thomas H  Emily Dickinson's Father as a Shaping Influence in Her Poetry  MA Auburn Univ 1969
998  JOHNSTON Frank D Jr  Evolution of a Mystic as Revealed in the Love Poems of Emily Dickinson  MA Univ of Pittsburgh 1948
999  JOSEPH E E  Poetry of Emily Dickinson  MA Ohio St Univ 1933
1000  KASELL Walter B  Emily Dickinson: Poetry in a Neutral Universe  BA Amherst Coll 1966
1001  KELEHER Julia  Emily Dickinson: A Study of Her Life and Poetry  MA Univ of New Mexico 1931
1002  KIDD Katherine H  The Magnetism of Emily Dickinson  MA Midwestern Univ 1953  56 p
1003  KIRBY Constance  Religious Imagery in Emily Dickinson's Love Poems  MA Butler Univ 1964
1004  KRAUSE Stephen A  The Symbolic Expression of the Concrete Universal and Its Effect in Selected Lyrics of Emily Dickinson  MA Niagara Univ 1966
1005  KWOK Eunice G  The Structure of Emily Dickinson's Poetry  MA Louisiana St Univ 1942
1006  LANDIS Sarah E  The Religion of Emily Dickinson as Revealed in Her Letters and in Her Poems  MA Univ of Mississippi 1941  130 p
1007  LANG Ruth S  The Relationship Between New England Transcendentalism and Emily Dickinson  MA Brooklyn Coll of City Univ of New York 1953  116 p

1008 LEDWELL Alice R  A Study of the Critical Reputation of Emily Dickinson, 1913-1933  MA Univ of Hawaii 1961  65 p
1009 LEWIS Elizabeth C  The Drift of Eastern Gray: Death as Frontier in the Poetry of Emily Dickinson  MA Univ of Delaware 1969  129 p
1010 LOVERING Joseph P  The Religious Character of Emily Dickinson's Verse  MA Boston Univ 1948
1011 LOWREY Robert E  "Which Ruby's Mine?": Emily Dickinson's Search for a Meaningful Existence  MA Texas Agricultural and Mechanical Univ 1964  80 p
1012 LYNCH Judith M  True Poems: The Poetic Tradition of Emily Dickinson  MA Univ of Notre Dame 1966
1013 MacBAIN Judith A  At Last to be Identified: A Study of the Self as Expressed in the Poetry of Emily Dickinson  MA Northeast Missouri St Coll 1964
1014 McCARTY Rachel E  Images and Ideas in Emily Dickinson's Poetry  MA Ohio St Univ 1936
1015 McCLASKEY Martha J  Concepts of the Divine in the Poetry of Emily Dickinson  MA Northeast Missouri St Coll 1959
1016 McDONALD H S  The Poetry of Emily Dickinson and Edna St Vincent Millay  MA North Texas St Univ 1968
1017 McGARY Sr Mary L  Emily Dickinson, "The New England Nun": A Justification of Her Title from Her Writings  MA Univ of Texas at Austin 1943
1018 McGOWAN Clare  The Question of Mysticism in the Poetry of Emily Dickinson  MA Boston Coll 1950
1019 McGRATH Sara A  The Language of a Poet: A Study of Verbal Techniques in Emily Dickinson's Poetry  MA Columbia Univ 1962  63 p
1020 McINTIRE Virginia S  Emily Dickinson's Self-image  MA Univ of New Hampshire 1965  56 p
1021 MAIER Justine L  The Existential Self in the Life and Work of Emily Dickinson  MA St Louis Univ 1961  84 p
1022 MARTIN Mary K  Emotional Balance in the Poetry of Emily Dickinson  MA West Texas St Univ 1944  99 p
1023 MASIUK Carol A  Emily Dickinson and Mysticism  MA Tufts Univ 1963
1024 MAYER Nancy D  Emily Dickinson's Struggle with the Orthodox Protestant Tradition: An Analysis of the Poems  MA Univ of Maryland at College Park 1968  69 p
1025 MILLER Jon  A Study of the Confusion of Lover and God in Emily Dickinson's *Bolts of Melody*  MA Univ of Houston 1953  92 p
1026 MILLS Ruth B  Wing Imagery in Emily Dickinson's Poetry  MA Lamar Technological Univ 1968  101 p
1027 MIYATAKE Teiko R  Emily Dickinson: Tradition and the Individual Talent  MA Ohio St Univ 1951
1028 MOORE Murial M  The Idea of God in the Poetry of Emily Dickinson  MA Boston Univ 1930
1029 MOREY Frederick L  The Tragic Implication of Emily Dickinson's Poetry  MA Univ of Maryland at College Park 1966  68 p
1030 MORRIS Claire M  The Influence of Emily Dickinson on Four Recent Poets: Lizette Woodworth Reese, Sara Teasdale, Elinor Wylie, and Edna St Vincent Millay  MA Univ of Southern California 1942
1031 MURPHY Janys A  Theme of Death in the Poetry of Emily Dickinson  MA Northeast Missouri St Coll 1958
1032 MYERS Marian H  The Mail of Anguish: The Humor of Emily Dickinson  MA Univ of Richmond 1969  81 p
1033 NYLAND Gertrude C  The Personalistic Idealism of Emily Dickinson  MA Boston Univ 1930
1034 ORSINI David M  Emily Dickinson: Puritan and Transcendental Influences  MA Brown Univ 1966
1035 PATTERSON Ollie M  Emily Dickinson: A Critic of Life  MA George Peabody Coll for Teachers 1930

1036 PAYZANT Marion  A Study of the Puritan Element in Emily Dickinson
     MA Univ of Montana 1931  81 p
1037 PELZ Karen L  Gem-tactics: Jewel Imagery in Emily Dickinson's Poetry
     MA Univ of Delaware 1967  50 p
1038 PETREE Ruth L  Introduction to Dickinson's Arisbas  MA Univ of
     Tennessee 1929
1039 PHIPPS Mona C  Syntax, Metaphor and Meaning in Emily Dickinson's
     Poetry  MA Univ of Oklahoma 1957
1040 PORTER Jenny L  The Divina Commedia of Emily Dickinson  MA Texas
     Christian Univ 1949  120 p
1041 POSTEN Beulah  A Study of the Versions of the Romantic Episode in
     the Life of Emily Dickinson  MA St Mary's Univ of San Antonio
     1939  95 p
1042 PRICE Opal R  The Reputation of Emily Dickinson Between 1910 and
     1930  MA Univ of Mississippi 1950  71 p
1043 QUINN Frances M  Mysticism in the Poems of Emily Dickinson
     MA St Mary's Univ of San Antonio 1941  73 p
1044 REDDY Kamala C  The World of Emily Dickinson  MA Univ of Delaware
     1966  109 p
1045 REID John L  The Love Element in the Life and Poetry of Emily Dickinson
     MA Columbia Univ 1961  75 p
1046 REINKE Elizabeth L  Puritan and Transcendental Influences on
     Emily Dickinson's Philosophy  MA Columbia Univ 1935
1047 RENEY Sr M Michelle  Transcendentalism in Emily Dickinson's Poetry
     MA Boston Coll 1962
1048 RICKER Hazel  Emily Dickinson as a Woman and a Poet  M Ed Henderson
     St Coll nd
1049 ROBERTS James L  Emily Dickinson: The Reflection of Her Life in
     Her Art  MA Univ of Mississippi 1954  128 p
1050 ROBEY Annie L  Emily Dickinson: A Forerunner of Modern American
     Poetry  MA Univ of Oklahoma 1928
1051 ROBINSON Ellen H  Emily Dickinson's Religious Thought  MA Arkansas
     St Coll 1964
1052 ROBYN D J  Emily Dickinson and Nature  MA North Texas St Univ 1945
1053 RUNKEL Peter R  Revolt and Tradition in the Thought of Emily Dickinson
     MA Univ of the Pacific 1958  48 p
1054 SCANLAN Grace S  Emily Dickinson: Theatrical Aspects of Her Poetry
     MA Rivier Coll 1966
1055 SHAY Sr Mary I  Emily Dickinson's Prose  MA Boston Coll 1935
1056 SHEEHAN Sr Helen T  Emily Dickinson: The Non-conventionalist as
     Revealed by Her Legal Images  MA Boston Coll 1964
1057 SHUTTS Julia F  The Spirit of Childhood in the Poetry of Emily Dickinson
     MA Univ of Pittsburgh 1933
1058 SITZ Herbert A  Student and Teacher Preferences Among Certain Poems
     of Emily Dickinson  MA Mankato St Coll 1958  39 p
1059 SKEY Miriam A  A Comparison of Emily Dickinson's Poetry and Haiku
     Poetry  MA Univ of Toronto (Canada) 1966
1060 SMEYAK Marcia A  The Metaphysical Conceit in the Poetry of
     Emily Dickinson  MA Univ of Pittsburgh 1961
1061 SOMSEN Julia A  A Formal Feeling: Emily Dickinson and the Art of
     Meditation  MA Univ of Wyoming 1965
1062 STEELE Mildred M  Emily Dickinson as Portrayed in Novels, Plays and
     Short Stories  MA Univ of Kentucky 1952  77 p
1063 TANNER Audra B  The Effects of Disquietude upon Emily Dickinson's
     Life and Poetry  MA Midwestern Univ 1953  117 p
1064 TAYLOR Sue  The Art of Emily Dickinson  MA Univ of Texas at Austin 1925
1065 TERRIS Virginia R  Ambiguity in Emily Dickinson's Poetry  MA Adelphi
     Univ 1965
1066 THRIFT William B  Nature Imagery in the Poetry of Emily Dickinson
     MA St Mary's Univ of San Antonio 1966  65 p

1067 TODD S Richard Jr  The Secret Dancer: An Essay on Some Poems of Emily Dickinson  BA Amherst 1962
1068 VEACH Jessie A  The Central Flint: A Consideration of Edward Dickinson as the Crucial Influence in the Development of the Poet Emily Dickinson  MA Southern Illinois Univ at Carbondale 1961  92 p
1069 VIETS Marjorie R  Emily Dickinson's Character as Revealed by Her Poetry  MA Boston Univ 1931
1070 WAJIMA Shiro  Emily Dickinson and Her Search for Self-identity  MA Univ of Hawaii 1963  58 p
1071 WHITAKER Rosemary  Emily Dickinson: Her Attitudes Toward Death, Immortality and God  MA Univ of Tulsa 1959  92 p
1072 WHITE Janice L  Sound in Emily Dickinson's Poetry  MA Univ of Mississippi 1965  108 p
1073 WHITE Mary J  Emily Dickinson and the Civil War  MA Univ of North Carolina at Chapel Hill 1960
1074 WILLIAMS A E  The Personality of Emily Dickinson as Revealed in Her Poetry  MA Boston Univ 1938
1075 WILLIAMS Patricia A  Emily Dickinson: Religious Unorthodoxy  MA Columbia Univ 1965  68 p
1076 WILSON Gwendean F  Predominant Influences in the Life of Emily Dickinson  M Ed Henderson St Coll nd
1077 WILSON James R  Emily Dickinson: Her Reading  MA Univ of Tulsa 1948
1078 WILSON Ruth D  Emily Dickinson and the Traditional Church  MA Univ of Oklahoma 1946
1079 WOOD Frances L  People in the Poetry of Emily Dickinson  MA Ohio St Univ 1950
1080 WOOD Thomas E  The Charms of Emily Dickinson  BA Amherst Coll 1961
1081 WORST Kathleen  The Literary Reputation of Emily Dickinson  MA Columbia Univ 1935
1082 WORTH Douglas G  Syntax as Strategy: An Approach to the Poetry of Emily Dickinson  MA Columbia Univ 1964  61 p
See also 1510, 4976, 6600

## THOMAS DIXON

1083 LUTZ Sr M Angelita  Thomas Dixon's Contribution to American Literature with Special Reference to the Original Manuscript of *The Root of Evil*  MA St Bonaventure Univ 1948
1084 MINTON Lucile  A Study of Thomas Dixon, Southerner  MA Univ of Georgia 1938
See also 6999

## J FRANK DOBIE

1085 CAMBRON Roga  Five Texas Novelists (James Frank Dobie, Donald Joseph, Norma Patterson, Dorothy Scarborough, and John William Thomason)  MA East Texas St Univ 1941
1086 KEYSER Mildred B  J Frank Dobie: Artist in Depth  MA Univ of Texas at El Paso 1961  94 p
1087 PINKHAM Sibyl V  Life and Work of J Frank Dobie  MA George Peabody Coll for Teachers 1933

## HILDA DOOLITTLE

1088 FRANK Kathryn G  The Art of Hilda Doolittle Aldington  MA Univ of Pittsburgh 1957
1089 GALLOWAY Ruth D  Theme and Imagery in the Poetry of Hilda Doolittle  MA West Texas St Univ 1965  209 p
1090 MILICIA Joseph Jr  A Study of *Palimpsest*: A Novel of H D  MA Columbia Univ 1964  101 p
1091 SALMON J C  Hilda Doolittle  MA Boston Univ 1938

## JOHN DOS PASSOS

1092 ALLEN A J  World War I in the Novels of John Dos Passos  MA Rice Univ 1966
1093 BARIL James R  John Dos Passos and His Libertarianism  MA Washington St Univ at Pullman 1961
1094 BEIN Morris  The Ideological Development of John Dos Passos  MA Univ of Louisville 1940
1095 BERNARDIN Charles W  A Perilous Passage: John Dos Passos  MA Boston Coll 1942
1096 BREEDLOVE N E  An Analysis of John Dos Passos' *Streets of Night* and Its Seminal Effect on *Manhattan Transfer* and *U S A*  MA Rice Univ 1968
1097 CARR James O  The Critical Reputation of John Dos Passos from *U S A* to *Midcentury*  MA Hunter Coll 1965
1098 DAWSON V  Contrasting Attitudes Towards War and American Society Between 1920 and 1961 in the Works of John Dos Passos and Norman Mailer  MA Univ of London (England) 1965
1099 DUFOUR Richard E  Jeremiah in the Wilderness: Style and Structure in the Novels of John Dos Passos  MA Univ of Vermont 1962  182 p
1100 EVANS William A  John Dos Passos: The Collectivist Technique  MA Univ of Southern Mississippi 1959
1101 GIUSTI Lola  John Dos Passos  MA Ca Foscari (Italy) 1949
1102 GRANT Herbert L  Edwin Lawrence Godkin: An Analysis of His Political and Economic Thought and John Dos Passos: *An Exile's Return*  BA Amherst Coll 1955
1103 GREEN Janet E  The City: Central Element in Cela's *La Colmena* and Dos Passos' *Manhattan Transfer*  MA Emory Univ 1965
1104 GULISH George  The Novels of John Dos Passos  BA Rutgers St Univ 1959  52 p
1105 HUFNELL William J  John Dos Passos: A Critical Study of Seven Novels  MA Temple Univ 1965  65 p
1106 KING Merton P  John Dos Passos' *U S A*  MA Univ of Texas at Austin 1953  132 p
1107 McGREGOR Maxine D  John Dos Passos as a Literary Pioneer in *U S A* and *District of Columbia*  MA Howard Payne Coll 1970  118 p
1108 MONT Sylvia  John Dos Passos  MA St Univ of New York at Albany 1936
1109 NORDIN David G  The Dissolution of the Dos Passos Hero and the Structure of *One Man's Initiation* and *Three Soldiers*  MA Bowling Green St Univ 1960
1110 OUELLETTE Allen J  Three Character Types and "The System" in Five Representative Novels of John Dos Passos  MA Univ of Maine 1969  90 p
1111 PARELLO Stephen M  Three Writers Between Wars: Case Studies of John Dos Passos, Robert Sherwood and Archibald MacLeish  BA Rutgers St Univ 1951  92 p
1112 PIETENS Bradley G  Impressionism in John Dos Passos' *U S A*  MA Univ of South Dakota 1966
1113 ROSSELOT Gerald S  Radical Characters in the Novels of John Dos Passos as Reflectors of His Shift in Political Point of View  MA DePauw Univ 1959  125 p
1114 SPEER Michael D  The Contribution of Journalism to the Creative Writing of John Dos Passos and Erskine Caldwell  MA Univ of Tulsa 1967  74 p
1115 STAGGS Kenneth W  John Dos Passos' *District of Columbia*: An Analysis  MA Univ of Texas at Austin 1956  140 p
1116 WALKER Earl H  John Dos Passos: A Witness to Unpopular Truths  MA Long Island Univ 1965  134 p
1117 WEADOCK Virginia L  John Dos Passos' Artistic Use of the Sacco-Vanzetti Case in *U S A*  MA Bowling Green St Univ 1960
1118 WILLIG Charles L  John Dos Passos: Art and Ideology  MA Oklahoma St

Univ 1964   100 p
1119   WILSON James R   A Study of the Interrelations Between Dos Passos' Personal Philosophy, Objectives and Techniques and the Influence of the Zeit-geist on Them   MA Univ of the Pacific 1940   94 p
1120   WINNER Anthony   The Progress of an Indignant Pilgrim: An Analysis of the Basic Themes in John Dos Passos' Work   MA Columbia Univ 1954   210 p
1121   WORKMAN Robert F   Two Novelists and Their Views of War (Dos Passos and Mailer)   MA Ohio St Univ 1961   52 p
See also 213, 214, 1159, 1551, 2826, 3082, 3760

## THEODORE DREISER

1122   AL-KHATIB Issam M   The Philosophical Development of Theodore Dreiser   MA Indiana Univ 1964
1123   ARNOLD Ann J   Naturalism in Dreiser's Female Characters   MA Univ of Mississippi 1969
1124   BARNES Marion S   Theodore Dreiser's Changing Concept of Morality   MA Univ of Southern Mississippi 1957
1125   BERNECHE Lawrence   The Evolution of "Creative Divinity": Spirituality in the Novels of Theodore Dreiser   MA Chico St Coll 1965   97 p
1126   BISHOP Bert O   A Study of the Correlation of Theodore Dreiser's Journalistic Experience to His Work as a Creative Artist   MA Southern Illinois Univ at Carbondale 1960   64 p
1127   BRITTON Joe S   Dreiser's Views of Woman   MA Southern Illinois Univ at Carbondale 1957   66 p
1128   BURG David F   From Naturalism to Socialism: The Politics of Theodore Dreiser   MA Washington St Univ at Pullman 1960
1129   CARLITZ Barbara B   The Unnatural Woman: A Study of Dreiser's Major Women Characters   MA Rice Univ 1964
1130   CERRUTI James   Theodore Dreiser: The Man and His Attitude   MA Syracuse Univ 1941   164 p
1131   CHEEVES Dorothy   The Presuppositions of Theodore Dreiser   MA La Verne Coll 1969   66 p
1132   COLEMAN Glenna   The Cynicism and Skepticism of Theodore Dreiser   M Ed Henderson St Coll nd
1133   CORKRUM Ralph E Jr   Theodore Dreiser: A Study of His Short Stories   MA Washington St Univ at Pullman 1953
1134   DICKINSON W E   A Critical Study of Theodore Dreiser's "Trilogy of Desire"   MA Wesleyan Univ 1951
1135   DIEM Vu T   The Significance of the Women in Dreiser's Trilogy   MA Univ of Hawaii 1964   53 p
1136   FISCHMAN Bernard S   Theodore Dreiser's "Autobiography"   MA Univ of Pittsburgh 1950
1137   FRANKLIN Pauline M   American and English Criticism of Theodore Dreiser   MA Univ of Iowa 1926
1138   FRAZIER Alexander S   The Influence of Darwinism on Theodore Dreiser's Concept of the American Businessman in Selected Novels   MA Bowling Green St Univ 1966
1139   HAILEY Virginia L   Religion in the Novels of Theodore Dreiser   MA Southern Illinois Univ at Carbondale 1951   64 p
1140   HANDY William J   Dreiser's Naturalistic Philosophy   MA Univ of Oklahoma 1949
1141   HARMAN William C   The Women in Theodore Dreiser's Novels *The Financier*, *The Titan* and *The Stoic*   MA Bowling Green St Univ 1966
1142   HOROVITZ Sydney   Theodore Dreiser and Some Aspects of American Society   MA Univ of Pittsburgh 1947
1143   JOHNSON Gwen   The Satirical Elements in *Jennie Gerhardt*   MA Brigham Young Univ 1965   68 p
1144   KORES Maryjo A   The Search for Personal Identity and Meaning in

*Sister Carrie, Winesburg, Ohio* and the Novels of Herbert Gold
MA Ohio St Univ 1960   75 p
1145   LEMON Alma R   The Moral Intensity in the Major Works of Theodore Dreiser
M Ed Henderson St Coll nd
1146   LEWIS Robert E   Unified Reality: A Study of the Novels of
Theodore Dreiser   MA Univ of Idaho 1951
1147   McCONNELL Julian C   The Problem of the Christian Ethic in Three
Modern Novels   MA Columbia Univ nd
1148   McNAMARA Owen   Aspiration as Spirit and Theme in Theodore Dreiser's
Novels   MA Univ of Rhode Island 1963   86 p
1149   McTAGUE Sylvia H   Dreiser the Iconoclast: His Attack on Marriage
MA Univ of Mississippi 1968
1150   McWHIRTER George E   Economic Determinism as a Factor in the Verisimilitude of Dreiser's Novels   MA Texas Technological Univ 1936
1151   MAYHALL Fan   Religion and Morality in the Works of Theodore Dreiser
MA Mississippi St Univ 1963   106 p
1152   MILLER Jerry L   Journey into the Twentieth Century: A Study of
Theodore Dreiser's Development as a Poet   MA Indiana Univ 1964
1153   MILLER Judith L   A Character Analysis of Carrie Meeber and Jennie Gerhardt   MA Brigham Young Univ 1963   93 p
1154   MITCHELL Richard   The Creative Force and the Inner Light: A Study
of Theodore Dreiser's *The Bulwark*   MA Syracuse Univ 1960   86 p
1155   MOLDENHAUER J J   Theodore Dreiser and the High Financier: A Study
in Naturalism and the Business Age   BA Amherst Coll 1956
1156   MOYLES Robert G   Theodore Dreiser: The Reluctant Naturalist
MA Memorial Univ (Canada) 1967
1157   NEEL Stephen E   Theodore Dreiser and H L Mencken: Prototypes for
America's Identity Crisis, 1900-1925   BA Amherst Coll 1969
1158   O'BANNON Robert H   Theodore Dreiser and the Question of Moral
Responsibility   MA Univ of Mississippi 1947   113 p
1159   OLIVELLA Torrents   The Theme of Success in American Fiction from
1900-1941 with Special Reference to Dreiser, Lewis, Fitzgerald
and Dos Passos   M Phil Univ of London (England) 1967
1160   ORA John P Jr   Theodore Dreiser: The Lobster and the Squid
MA Univ of North Carolina at Chapel Hill 1962
1161   RUFFIN Mary S   The Exemplification of Certain Ideas of Theodore Dreiser
Through the Protagonists in *Sister Carrie, Jennie Gerhardt* and
*An American Tragedy*   MA Virginia St Coll 1953   57 p
1162   SALATORE Nicholas T   The Development of Dreiser's Frank Cowperwood
as Based upon the Life of Charles Tyson Yerkes   MA Temple Univ
1963   48 p
1163   SANDSBERRY J C   Naturalism in the Novels of Theodore Dreiser
MA North Texas St Univ 1950
1164   SAWICKI Robert M   Theodore Dreiser and *An American Tragedy*: From
the American Dream to the American Nightmare   MA Columbia Univ
1965   156 p
1165   SHAPIRO Charles K   Dreiser and the American Dream   MA Indiana Univ 1955
1166   SLEEPER Mary E   The Treatment of Women in the Novels and Short
Stories of Theodore Dreiser   MA Univ of Maine 1964   71 p
1167   STOKES Peter B   Technique and Temperament in Dreiser's *Sister Carrie*
MA Univ of Toronto (Canada) 1964
1168   STORY Suzanne   Human Action and Responsibility in Theodore Dreiser's
*An American Tragedy* and Richard Wright's *Native Son*   MA Univ of
Texas at Austin 1965   68 p
1169   STOUT Rebecca A   The City as Setting in Theodore Dreiser's *Jennie Gerhardt*: The Role of the City in the Naturalistic Tradition
MA Univ of North Carolina at Chapel Hill 1966
1170   THOMAS Leroy   Dreiser's Utilization of Autobiographical Material in
His Novels   MA Oklahoma St Univ 1959   110 p
1171   VENTO Irma D   Dreiser's Concept of Man   MA Univ of Texas at Austin

1964   87 p
1172   WHITAKER Eleanor M   A Descriptive Analysis of Theodore Dreiser's Non-fiction Work   MA Univ of Maryland at College Park 1966   94 p
1173   WHITFIELD Jozelle   Some Representative Women in the Novels of Theodore Dreiser: A Study by Comparison   MA Texas Christian Univ 1969   100 p
1174   WILKERSON James C   The Altruistic Thought of Theodore Dreiser in Seven Representative Novels   MA Univ of Florida 1952
1175   ZEHENTMAYR Aurelia   Treatment of the American Businessman in the Novels of Theodore Dreiser   MA North Texas St Univ 1965
See also 844, 3123, 3426, 3688, 4401, 6204

## PAUL LAURENCE DUNBAR

1176   LAWSON Victor   The Poetry and Prose of P L Dunbar   MA Howard Univ 1939   128 p
1177   SCHILLER Josephine L   Paul Laurence Dunbar   MA Univ of Texas at Austin 1943   152 p

## FINLEY PETER DUNNE

1178   GEIERMAN Alvin J   Finley Peter Dunne: Humorist, Satirist, Vital Historian   MA Univ of Toledo 1952
1179   WILLIAMS Joseph P Jr   Finley Peter Dunne and the Irish-American Dialect   MA Columbia Univ 1963   88 p
See also 3804

## BOB DYLAN

1180   BALL Carolyn D   Bob Dylan: Contemporary Minstrel   MA Univ of Maryland at College Park 1967   182 p
1181   HYDE Sally J   Dylan: A Production Thesis   MA Chico St Coll 1969   219 p
1182   McDONOUGH John W   Bob Dylan: The Romantic Sensibility in the Modern Cauldron   MA Univ of North Carolina at Chapel Hill 1968

## JONATHAN EDWARDS

1183   BARKAN Chester M   Jonathan Edwards: His Theory of Divine Sovereignty   MA Brooklyn Coll of City Univ of New York 1959   65 p
1184   CHENNAULT Henry L   An Examination of the Sermon Style of Jonathan Edwards   MA Univ of Oklahoma 1963
1185   COLLINS Frances   Jonathan Edwards: A Puritan Man of Letters   MA Univ of Kansas 1941
1186   CONSTANTINIDES Janet C   A Study of the Sermon Style of Jonathan Edwards   MA Univ of Oklahoma 1966
1187   D'AMATO Camilla N   The Practical Element in Jonathan Edwards   MA Columbia Univ 1940
1188   IRVING Donald C   Style in the Personal Narrative of Jonathan Edwards   MA Southern Illinois Univ at Carbondale 1962   87 p
1189   KNIGHT John A   James Dana's Criticism of Jonathan Edwards' Concept of Freedom of the Will   MA Univ of Oklahoma 1953
1190   READER Maxwell   Two Views of Man in American Literature: A Comparison of Jonathan Edwards and Ralph Waldo Emerson   MA Univ of Vermont 1961   234 p
1191   REEVES Troy   Imagery in the Sermons of Jonathan Edwards   MA Univ of Kansas 1962
1192   SCHLICK Carol A   A Comparative Rhetorical Analysis of Sermons by Jonathan Edwards and William Franklin Graham   MA Miami Univ at Oxford 1966
1193   THORBURN James A   Some Aspects of Edwards' Prose Style   MA Ohio St Univ 1951

1194 TREADWELL Pauline N  Jonathan Edwards' Philosophy of the Will  M Ed Henderson St Coll nd
1195 WORSTER Donald E  Jonathan Edwards: The Nature of Religious Conversion and Its Rhetorical Impetus  MA Univ of Kansas 1965
See also 5714

### EDWARD EGGLESTON

1196 ALLEN Crawford W  The Contributions of Edward Eggleston to the Development of the Realistic Novel in America  MA Univ of Oklahoma 1932
1197 BROWN J Richard  An Investigation of the Technique of Edward Eggleston  MA San Diego St Coll 1961  121 p
1198 COYNE Leah  Edward Eggleston: Recorder of Pioneer Life in the Ohio Valley  MA Univ of Kansas 1937
1199 GLOSSUP Loretta C  A Study of Ideas in the Writings of Edward Eggleston  MS Illinois St Univ at Normal 1950
1200 GREER Wynis  Edward Eggleston (1837-1902): A Critical and Biographical Study  MA Southern Methodist Univ 1934
1201 LEMMON Margaret A  Edward Eggleston's *The Hoosier Schoolmaster*  MA Univ of Texas at Austin 1948  134 p
1202 LOGAN Harlan D  An Unpublished Journal of Edward Eggleston with Supplementary Notes and Letters  MA Indiana Univ 1935
1203 McIVER Jane M  Edward Eggleston as a Realist  MA Univ of Toledo 1944
1204 RIST Ray C  The Nature and Importance of Religion in America's Frontier Society as Presented in the Novels of Edward Eggleston  MA Southern Illinois Univ at Carbondale 1955  74 p
1205 ROWLAND Lionel L  The Idea of Progress in the Writings of Edward Eggleston  MA Lamar Technological Univ 1969  118 p

### T S ELIOT

1206 ABOLIN Nancy  T S Eliot: The Difference Twenty Years Made  MA Columbia Univ 1961  55 p
1207 ADELMAN Irving  A Gestalt Study of T S Eliot's *Four Quartets*  MA Columbia Univ 1951
1208 ALLEN Mabel W  The Concept of Love in the Plays of T S Eliot  MA Columbia Univ 1960  59 p
1209 ANGER Helen M  A Study of *The Cocktail Party* by T S Eliot  MA Columbia Univ 1953  25 p
1210 AULT Donald D  Time and T S Eliot  MA Kent St Univ 1965
1211 BALTAY Virginia R  T S Eliot in Education  MA Univ of Massachusetts 1967
1212 BELL Joan R  T S Eliot's Martyr-saints in *Murder in the Cathedral*, *The Family Reunion* and *The Cocktail Party*  MA Ball St Univ 1966  88 p
1213 BELLAVIA Rita M  Eliot and Critics at Midcentury  MA Indiana Univ of Pennsylvania 1962  54 p
1214 BILZ Doris  The Two Ways to Salvation in the Plays of T S Eliot  MA Columbia Univ 1962  51 p
1215 BONANDER Alice  The Image of *Murder in the Cathedral*  MA Brooklyn Coll of City Univ of New York 1962  70 p
1216 BOYD Jacquelyn M  The Presentation of Ritual Sacrifice in T S Eliot's *The Waste Land* and Garcia Lorca's *Poeta en Nueva York*  MA Purdue Univ 1968  73 p
1217 BREWER Charles W  An Integrated Account of the Poetry and Prose of T S Eliot  MA Univ of Texas at Austin 1967  57 p
1218 BREWER Winnoa D  T S Eliot: Sneered, Jeered and Cheered by His Critics  M Ed Henderson St Coll nd
1219 BROOKS Jerry  Eliot's Critical Method: Its Intent and Achievement  MA George Washington Univ 1957
1220 BROWN John L  T S Eliot's Anti-Miltonic Prejudice  MA Univ of Vermont 1962  105 p

1221 BUCK Mrs Charles C  The Religious Development of T S Eliot  MA Texas Arts and Industries Univ 1951
1222 BURNS Richard J  The Biblical Reference in T S Eliot's Poems  MA Boston Coll 1951
1223 BUTTURUFF Douglas R  The Influence of F H Bradley's Appearance and Reality on T S Eliot's Concept of Impersonal Poetry  MA Georgetown Univ 1965  54 p
1224 BYERS Marion H  Eliot the Metaphysical  MA Columbia Univ 1940
1225 CAMMACK Sr Mary A  *Murder in the Cathedral*: A Study of the Particular Problem of Martyrdom and Eliot's Dramatic Intention  MA Univ of Hawaii 1960  33 p
1226 CAREY Susan  A Study of the Major Animal Images in the Poetry of T S Eliot  MA West Virginia Univ 1969  106 p
1227 CARRUTH Gorton V  A Comparative Study of the Major Critical Concepts of Jacques Riviere and T S Eliot  MA Columbia Univ 1954  169 p
1228 CICCHESE Sr Louise M  The Significance of Christian Influence in T S Eliot's *Four Quartets*  MA Boston Coll 1962
1229 COLLINS Jean K  An Introduction to the Poetry of T S Eliot: A Selective Handbook  MA Univ of Richmond 1951  109 p
1230 COX Paul  Murder and Mr Eliot: A Study in Attitude  MA Columbia Univ 1960  183 p
1231 CROOKSHANKS Linda  The Man-woman Relationship as Symbolic of the Isolation Theme in Selected Works of Thomas Sterns Eliot  MA East Tennessee St Univ 1965
1232 DANIEL Elizabeth A  From Horror to Glory: T S Eliot's Vision of the World, 1909-1943  MA Univ of Mississippi 1953  82 p
1233 DARDAC Jack  If There Were Only Water Amongst the Rock: A Biblical Interpretation of *The Wasteland*  MA Brooklyn Coll of City Univ of New York 1960  50 p
1234 D'EASUM Lille  T S Eliot's Use of the Philosophy of Time in His Poetry  MA Univ of British Columbia (Canada) 1969
1235 DE BLASIO Maria A  T S Eliot: Poet, Critic, Dramatist  MA Smith Coll 1939
1236 DELISLE Fanny  The Metaphysical Influence on T S Eliot  MA Univ of New Hampshire 1967  80 p
1237 DEMPSEY William J  T S Eliot and Tradition  MA Columbia Univ 1951
1238 DENHAM Alice  T S Eliot: His Theory and Practice of Poetic Drama  MA Univ of Rochester 1950  121 p
1239 DE QUESNAY Maurice  The Influence of William Temple's Theology upon T S Eliot's "Burnt Norton"  MA Louisiana St Univ 1966
1240 DOOLAN J  T S Eliot's *The Waste Land*: A Textual Commentary and Full Introduction Including a Critical Appreciation of the Poem and Discussion of Its Relation to His Earlier and Later Works; with a Bibliography and Two Appendices  MA Univ of London (England) 1961
1241 DORAN James P  T S Eliot: A Poetic Journey to the Absolute  MA Columbia Univ 1962  76 p
1242 DOUGLAS Kathryn F  The Dramatic Theory and Practice of Thomas Stearns Eliot  MA Auburn Univ 1952  107 p
1243 DOYLE James P  The Modern Dilemma and the *Four Quartets*  MA Boston Coll 1968
1244 DUECK Jake E  Existentialism and T S Eliot's *The Waste Land*  MA Western Washington St Coll 1966  70 p
1245 EGAN Sr M Antonine  The Will in T S Eliot's Early Poetry  MA Boston Coll 1952
1246 EKBERG Linnea W  The Swedish Translation and Understanding of the Poetry of T S Eliot  MA Univ of Massachusetts 1968  78 p
1247 ELLIOTT Ruth  Echoes of Eliot's *The Waste Land* in Three Modern American Novels  MA Univ of the Pacific 1967  63 p
1248 EMERSON Robert L Jr  T S Eliot: "The Third Voice of Poetry"  MA Texas Christian Univ 1961  127 p

1249 EZCH Marjory  A Study of the Critical Problems Involved in the Elucidation of T S Eliot's *The Waste Land*  MA Univ of Pittsburgh 1951
1250 FITCHEN Allen N  Poetry Redefined: A Study of Some of the Major Works of T S Eliot  BA Amherst Coll 1958
1251 FITZPATRICK Eve  To Redeem the Time: A Study of Time in T S Eliot's Drama and Poetry  MA Coll of the Holy Names at Oakland 1970
1252 FLEISCHER Constance L  The Communicator and the Communicants in the Major Poetry of T S Eliot  MA Univ of Miami 1966
1253 FORESTER William S  T S Eliot's Dramatic Method: A Correlation of Critical Opinion  MA Univ of Louisville 1964
1254 FOSTER Elizabeth T  T S Eliot: Circle of Infinity  MA East Texas St Univ 1965
1255 FREEMAN John  Allusion by Quotation in *The Waste Land*  MA Columbia Univ 1954  105 p
1256 GREEN Christene L  T S Eliot: A Study of His Drama in Relation to His Earlier Poetry and Essays  MA Texas Arts and Industries Univ 1954
1257 GROVER Shannon  T S Eliot: His Concept of Language  MA Univ of Toronto (Canada) 1964
1258 HANLIN Hilda M  T S Eliot's Water Motif: A Unifying Symbol  MA Kent St Univ 1966
1259 HARRIS W E  A Study of Thomas Stearns Eliot's *The Cocktail Party*  M Ed Henderson St Coll nd
1260 HARTE Marcia  Resolution in Dostoevsky and Eliot: *The Brothers Karamazov* and *Four Quartets*  MA Columbia Univ 1960  137 p
1261 HAYDEN Polly W  A Study of Christian Principles in *Murder in the Cathedral, The Family Reunion* and *The Cocktail Party*  MA West Chester St Coll 1966
1262 HAYNES Michael A  Themes of Purgation and Rebirth in Three T S Eliot Poems  MA Ball St Univ 1968  53 p
1263 HENDERSON Nellie G  Spiritual Quests of T S Eliot's Dramatic Heroes  MA Univ of Southern Mississippi 1968
1264 HILL Carol L  The Music in T S Eliot's *Four Quartets*  MA Wichita St Univ 1965
1265 HILL Dorothy M  An Interpretative Analysis of T S Eliot's *Four Quartets*  MA Univ of Pittsburgh 1948
1266 HILTON Charles  The Revolt of T S Eliot Against Wordsworthian Tendencies in Nineteenth Century Poetry  MA Univ of Montana 1933  70 p
1267 HOLDER Kenneth  A Transformational Analysis of Selected Works of T S Eliot  M Ed Henderson St Coll nd
1268 HOLLIDAY Howard J  Seriocomic Juxtapositions in the Poetry of T S Eliot  MA Univ of Texas at Austin 1967
1269 JARMOL Helene A  A Syntactic and Figurative Analysis of the Language of T S Eliot in *The Love Song of J Alfred Prufrock*  MA C W Post Coll nd  84 p
1270 JENSEN H  An Analysis and Appraisal of T S Eliot's *Four Quartets*  BA Univ of British Columbia (Canada) 1959
1271 JOHNSON Joyce M  A Study of Eliot's Use of Greek Tragedies in His Three Modern Plays  MA Univ of Kentucky 1958  131 p
1272 JONES Lloyd A  An Examination of T S Eliot's Cultural Criticism in the Light of His Debt to Matthew Arnold  MA Oklahoma St Univ 1950
1273 JONES Louise B  T S Eliot: A Study  MA Baylor Univ 1950  105 p
1274 KELLY Sr Joanne  Religious Universality in the Works of T S Eliot  MA Xavier Univ of New Orleans 1965
1275 KIDDER Rushworth M  T S Eliot: The Development of a Dramatic Language  MA Columbia Univ 1966  127 p
1276 KREMER Lillian  A Study of T S Eliot's Use of Urban and Industrial Imagery  MA Brooklyn Coll of City Univ of New York 1964  43 p
1277 KRONE Gerald S  Studies for a Production of T S Eliot's *Murder in the*

*Cathedral* MA Washington Univ at St Louis 1958
1278 LAING H W  The Development of the Religious Thought of T S Eliot MA North Texas St Univ 1967
1279 LANE Barbara J  Samuel Johnson and T S Eliot Concerning John Dryden MS Illinois St Univ at Normal 1968
1280 LANE Marilyn J  Major Images in the Poetry of T S Eliot  MA Univ of Southern Mississippi 1959
1281 LASKEY Howard G  Esotericism in Certain Poems of T S Eliot  MA Univ of Rhode Island 1960
1282 LEE Helen  The Religion of T S Eliot  M Ed Temple Univ 1946  201 p
1283 LEIRIS Helene  Loneliness and Faith in the Twentieth Century (Focusing on T S Eliot)  MA Univ of Maine 1968  122 p
1284 LESTER W P  The Literary Criticism of T S Eliot  MA Boston Univ 1942
1285 LEVRET Sr Marie C  *The Waste Land*; "What the Thunder Said": A Reading MA Georgetown Univ 1964  65 p
1286 LIVINGSTON James T  The Effect of Christian Belief upon the Literary and Social Criticism of T S Eliot  MA Texas Christian Univ 1953  120 p
1287 LOYOLA Sr Mary  T S Eliot's Verse Drama  MA Univ of Saskatchewan (Canada) 1966
1288 McDOWELL James V  Time in the Works of T S Eliot  MA Baylor Univ 1950  109 p
1289 McLAUGHLIN Franklin B Jr  The Outsider Viewed Through Modern Poetry: A Study of the Alienated Individual as Reflected in the Poetry of T S Eliot, W H Auden, Conrad Aiken, Robinson Jeffers and Archibald MacLeish  MA Villanova Univ 1964
1290 MAGNER James E Jr  A Consideration of T S Eliot's Theory of Ultimates MA Univ of Pittsburgh 1960
1291 MARTIN J  Water Imagery in the Poetry of T S Eliot  MA Pennsylvania St Univ 1965
1292 MAYESKI Sr M Immaculata  A Comparative Study of the Functions of Imagery, Lyric and Dramatic, as Exemplified in T S Eliot's *Ash Wednesday* and *The Family Reunion*  MA Coll of the Holy Names at Oakland 1963
1293 MEEK Peter H  T S Eliot: The Early Years  BA Amherst Coll 1965
1294 MILLER David L  Ritual Patterns in *The Cocktail Party*  MA Bowling Green St Univ 1963
1295 MIRSKY Murray  The Critical Theory of T S Eliot  MA Brooklyn Coll of City Univ of New York 1941  100 p
1296 MITIGUY Mary E  The Comic Spirit in T S Eliot  MA Univ of Vermont 1954  104 p
1297 MIYAKE Akiko  Some Aspects of Romantic Irony in T S Eliot's Poetry (1909-1922)  MA Duke Univ 1966
1298 MONTGOMERY Peter C  *The Waste Land* as City  MA Univ of Alberta (Canada) 1966
1299 MOORE Sr M Reginald  T S Eliot's *Paradiso*  MA Dominican Coll of San Rafael 1955
1300 MORIARTY Patricia A  T S Eliot and the Problem of Communication for the Poet in the Modern World  MA Hunter Coll 1964
1301 MURPHY Sr Mariedel  The Theme of Purgation in T S Eliot  MA Boston Coll 1949
1302 NATTERSTAD Jerry H  T S Eliot: A Study of Religion in His Early Poetry  MA Southern Illinois Univ at Carbondale 1961  68 p
1303 NELSON Elizabeth J  T S Eliot and the Anglo-Catholic Tradition MA Univ of Maryland at College Park 1957
1304 NELSON Gary  Thematic and Technical Influences of Tristan Corbiere and Arthur Rimbaud on the Poetry of T S Eliot  MA Coll of the Holy Names at Oakland 1969
1305 NEWELL Frances W  The Critical Theories of T S Eliot  MA Univ of Arkansas 1933

1306 NORDMAN Ted H  The Problems of Poetic Drama in Relation to a Production of *The Cocktail Party*  MA Ohio St Univ 1955
1307 NORTHCUT Mary N  T S Eliot: Loves Sacred and Profane  MA Southern Methodist Univ 1965
1308 NOVIK Geraldine M  Time in T S Eliot's "Burnt Norton"  BA Univ of British Columbia (Canada) 1966
1309 OGDEN Thomas H  Failure of Language in the Poetry of T S Eliot  BA Amherst Coll 1968
1310 OTNESS Lillian G  A Reconciliation of Opposites: Coleridge and T S Eliot  MA Univ of Idaho 1961
1311 PAK Tae-yong  Metaphysical Parallels Between *The Cocktail Party* and the Book of Job  MA Bowling Green St Univ 1966
1312 PAPPAS Dionysia M  The Worlds of T S Eliot and C P Kavaphes  MA Hunter Coll 1961
1313 PARKER D G  Frustration and Quest in the Poems and Plays of T S Eliot  MA North Texas St Univ 1969
1314 PETRELLA Mary C  T S Eliot: The Sweeney Poems  MA Univ of New Hampshire 1957  73 p
1315 PHILLIPS Judith B  The Efficacy of the Word in T S Eliot's *Four Quartets*  MA Syracuse Univ 1963  64 p
1316 PHILLIPSEN Edwin  T S Eliot and the Nature of God  MA Univ of Denver 1964
1317 PIERCE Flora M  Time in the Poetry of T S Eliot  MA Southern Illinois Univ at Carbondale 1956  124 p
1318 PINSKY Robert  The Religious Drama of T S Eliot  BA Rutgers St Univ 1962  62 p
1319 PONGRACE Marie B  T S Eliot's Romantic Repertoire  MA Univ of Texas at Austin 1963  348 p
1320 POPE W J  The Early Works of T S Eliot  MA Univ of London (England) 1950
1321 PORTER Mary M  Language, Imagery and Syntax in *Four Quartets*  MA Auburn Univ 1968
1322 PRESTON John F  The Development and Function of the Image in the Poetry of T S Eliot, 1909-1922  MA Univ of British Columbia (Canada) 1967
1323 PRICE Margaret M  Primitive Mythology in the Poetry of T S Eliot  MA Univ of Texas at Austin 1964  116 p
1324 RABKIN Gerald E  T S Eliot's Dramatic Dialectic  MA Ohio St Univ 1952
1325 RAFFEL Burton  The Role of Things in T S Eliot's Poetry: A Study in Sensibility  MA Ohio St Univ 1949
1326 RAKOWSKI Leonard F  Myth and Magic in T S Eliot's Poetry  MA Columbia Univ 1954  128 p
1327 RAY Robert J  The Poetic Techniques of T S Eliot and Ezra Pound: A Comparative Study  MA Univ of Texas at Austin 1959  143 p
1328 REAGAN Roberta R  The Evolution of Poetic Techniques in Selected Dramas of Thomas Stearns Eliot  MA Bowling Green St Univ 1960
1329 REED Paul R  The American and British Criticism of T S Eliot as a Dramatist  MA Univ of Maine 1961  145 p
1330 RICHMAN Daniel J  The Autonomy of Meaning in T S Eliot's Poetry  MA Long Island Univ 1967  57 p
1331 RITTER Sue A  The Evolution of T S Eliot's Time Images  MA Butler Univ 1969
1332 RIVERA-RODRIQUEZ Judith  T S Eliot's Search for Spiritual Value  MA Univ of Texas at El Paso 1963  80 p
1333 RODGERS Ruth A  T S Eliot: A Lifetime's Effort  MA Syracuse Univ 1951  115 p
1334 ROSSO Bernice M  Patterns of Imagery in T S Eliot's Early Poems, 1917-1930  MA Coll of the Holy Names at Oakland 1967
1335 SCHUCHARD Walter R  The Development of T S Eliot's Theory of Tradition  MA Univ of Texas at Austin 1967  86 p
1336 SCHUESSLER Lorna J  T S Eliot: Poetic Drama Theory and Practice

MA Temple Univ 1965  43 p
1337 SCOTT Virgil J  The Relation of Theory and Practice in the Poetry of T S Eliot  MA Ohio St Univ 1937
1338 SEARS Sr M Placide  Structure of Biblical Allusion in *The Waste Land* of T S Eliot  MA Univ of Notre Dame 1964
1339 SHAHEEN Abdel-Rahman A  Form and Content in *The Waste Land*  MA Mississippi St Univ 1963  98 p
1340 SHANDS Michael F  Human Love in T S Eliot: From Futility to Fulfillment  MA Univ of Texas at Austin 1967  111 p
1341 SHARMA Jitendra K  The Problem of Time and Human Consciousness in T S Eliot  MA Univ of Toronto (Canada) 1963
1342 SHEA Mary T  The Classicism of T S Eliot  MA Columbia Univ 1943
1343 SHORT R L  Christian Doctrine in the Plays of T S Eliot  MA North Texas St Univ 1962
1344 SIEVERT William  Toward T S Eliot's "Preludes": A Study of the Esthetic Backgrounds of "Abstract" Poetry  MA Columbia Univ 1961  102 p
1345 SMITH Harold J  T S Eliot and the Baudelairean Tradition  BA Amherst Coll 1962
1346 SMITH Julia A  T S Eliot and St John of the Cross: The Mystical Element in *Ash Wednesday* and *Four Quartets*  MA Univ of Texas at Austin 1958  72 p
1347 SMITH Mahlon H  Catholic Orthodoxy in the Plays of T S Eliot  BA Rutgers St Univ 1961  74 p
1348 SNELL Sr Marie V  An Interpretative Study of the Symbolism in Part IV "Death by Water" of *The Waste Land*  MA Siena Hts Coll 1947  86 p
1349 SOUCY Armand  T S Eliot and the Classic: Its Role and Definition  M Ph Univ of Montreal (Canada) 1963
1350 STEINGOLD Faye S  Two Attitudes Toward Spring: "General Prologue" and *The Waste Land*  MA Univ of Wyoming 1965
1351 SUTTON George W  The Criticism of T S Eliot Applied to His Own Poetry  MA Univ of Mississippi 1960  191 p
1352 SUTTON W E  The Critical Thought of T S Eliot  MA Ohio St Univ 1938
1353 SWANSON Gretchen N  The Objective Correlative in T S Eliot's Verse Drama  MA St Cloud St Coll 1968  90 p
1354 SWANSON Margaret S  An Analysis of the Fusion of Music-hall Elements with Ritual and Dramatic Myth in T S Eliot's Verse Plays  MA Municipal Univ of Omaha 1967
1355 TANASSO Elda M  T S Eliot and Some Poetry of the Seventeenth Century  MA Columbia Univ 1943
1356 TATE John U  A Reading of T S Eliot's *The Family Reunion*  MA Univ of North Carolina at Chapel Hill 1956  113 p
1357 TAYCHMAN Milena  John Davidson and T S Eliot  MA Univ of Maryland at College Park 1967  98 p
1358 TERRELL Carroll F  T S Eliot: "Gerontion"  MA Univ of Maine 1950  152 p
1359 THOMPSON Larry G  Form and Theme in Three Plays of T S Eliot  MA Brigham Young Univ 1967  118 p
1360 TORRENTS John E  A Comparison of the Historical, Dramatic and Production Aspects of T S Eliot's *Murder in the Cathedral* and Jean Anouilh's *Becket*  MA Hunter Coll 1965
1361 UNGER Leonard H  A Study of T S Eliot's *Ash Wednesday*  MA Louisiana St Univ 1938
1362 VILLANUEVA Agnes  T S Eliot: The Growth of His Religious Sensibility  MA Univ of Denver 1965
1363 VonAUW A  The Critical Theory and Practice of T S Eliot  MA Wesleyan Univ 1937
1364 VON DOEMMING Jeanne M  Continuity in the *Four Quartets*: Culmination of Eliot's Concept of Tradition  MA Georgetown Univ nd
1365 WASSERSTEIN Alan G  *The Waste Land* and Eliot's Pure Aesthetic  BA Amherst Coll 1968

1366  WEINBERG Kerry C  T S Eliot and Charles Baudelaire  MA Temple Univ 1957
1367  WEISKEL Thomas F  The Integrity of T S Eliot  BA Amherst Coll 1967
1368  WERNER Reginald L  T S Eliot and the Greek Drama: A Study of His Dramaturgy  MA Columbia Univ 1955  94 p
1369  WEST John O  The Poetic Development of T S Eliot  MA Texas Technological Univ 1951
1370  WILHELMI Nancy O  T S Eliot's Critical Evaluation of the Six Major Romantic Poets  MA Univ of Texas at Austin 1966
1371  WILKIE Brian F  Matthew Arnold and T S Eliot as Literary Critics  MA Univ of Rochester 1952  166 p
1372  WILLIAMS T J  T S Eliot: Theorist of the Elite  MA Univ of Texas at El Paso 1950  120 p
1373  WILLIAMSON Mervyn W  A Critical Study of the Imagery in *The Waste Land*  MA Univ of Texas at Austin 1953  218 p
1374  WRIGHT Ronald K  Eliot's Use of Words: A Categorical Enquiry into the Language of T S Eliot's Early Verse  MA Univ of Kentucky 1961  207 p
1375  WULFF Gisela E  Das Problem der Realitat bei Gottfried Benn und T S Eliot  MA Univ of Alberta (Canada) 1965
1376  ZACHARY Robert Y  The Character of the Symbol in the Poetry of T S Eliot  MA George Washington Univ 1949  64 p
1377  ZAULI-NALDI Camilla  *Murder in the Cathedral*  MA Ca Foscari (Italy) 1949
1378  ZERKINE Aziza  T S Eliot and Charles Baudelaire: Two Modern Christian Poets  MA Columbia Univ 1964  41 p
See also 150, 1644, 2745, 2890, 3266, 4314, 4754, 5234, 5236, 6554, 6801

## RALPH ELLISON

1379  BELL Bernard W  Anger in the Novels of Ralph Ellison, John O Killens and James Baldwin  MA Howard Univ 1966  167 p
1380  COWSKY David L  Blindness and Distorted Vision Symbolism in *Invisible Man* by Ralph Ellison  MA Bowling Green St Univ 1966
1381  HASKINS Alma F  The Nightmare of Invisibility: A Study of the Relationship of Theme and Structure in Ralph Ellison's *Invisible Man*  MA Ohio St Univ 1968  94 p
1382  HEIBERG Anne  The Impetus Toward Integration: An Investigation of the Fiction of Ellison, Wright and Baldwin  MA Stanford Univ 1964
1383  McNELIS Sr Marie A  Ralph Ellison: Negro Novelist  MA Boston Coll 1964
1384  POLSGROVE Carol C  Aspects of the Grotesque: Ralph Ellison's *Invisible Man*  MA Univ of Louisville 1969  75 p
1385  STICK Ethel  Picaresque Elements in *Invisible Man*  MA Mankato St Coll 1968  57 p
1386  TURNGREEN John A  Ralph Ellison's *Invisible Man*  MA Claremont Graduate School 1966
See also 4104, 5511, 6952

## RALPH WALDO EMERSON

1387  ABEL Arthur R  The Imagery in Emerson's Essay "Nature"  MA Univ of Rochester 1956  95 p
1388  ANDERSON Edna S  Emerson's Concept of Genius  MA Univ of North Dakota 1965
1389  ANDERSON Larry W  A Paradox in Ralph Waldo Emerson's Transcendentalism  MA Miami Univ at Oxford 1966
1390  ANDREWS William D  Emerson and Thoreau: An Intellectual and Stylistic Analysis  MA Ohio St Univ 1967  74 p
1391  BANKSTON Dorothy H  A Study of the Imagery in Selected Prose Works of Ralph Waldo Emerson  MA Univ of Southwestern Louisiana 1966  102 p
1392  BAY Anthony F  Emerson and Confucius  MA Univ of Tennessee 1956

1393 BEARD Gladys M  An Analysis of Ralph Waldo Emerson's Concepts of the Over-soul and Immortality  MA Shippensburg St Coll 1965
1394 BELL George E  Emerson and Baltimore: A Biographical Study  MA Univ of Maryland at College Park 1968  69 p
1395 BELTZ Lynda A  "Intrepid Pedlar of Ideals": Ralph Waldo Emerson, Lecturer  MA Indiana Univ 1963
1396 BENNETT Winifred E  Emerson: Optimist  MA Univ of Oklahoma 1904
1397 BLACKWELDER James R  Ralph Waldo Emerson's Contributions to *The Dial*  MA Wake Forest Univ 1964
1398 BLAYLOCK Johnnie B  Ralph Waldo Emerson and Charles Chauncy Emerson: A Study of Similarities in Their Thought  MA Northeast Louisiana Univ 1970  70 p
1399 BODGE Richard A  Six Principal Years (1836-1841) in the Life and Philosophy of Ralph Waldo Emerson  MA Boston Univ 1948
1400 BOUIT Mildrid O  Emerson's Attitude Toward Orthodox Christianity: The Religious Sources of His Esthetic  MA Fresno St Coll 1969  64 p
1401 BOULTER Jessie L  The Intellectual and Spiritual Development of Ralph Waldo Emerson  MA Univ of New Mexico 1944
1402 BRENNAN Mary E  The Influence of Emerson upon Walt Whitman  MA Univ of North Dakota 1935  96 p
1403 BRODIE Jeweldean  The Personal and Literary Relationship of Ralph Waldo Emerson and Walt Whitman  MA Univ of Oklahoma 1927
1404 BURRUM High H  Emerson's Conception of Christ  MA George Peabody Coll for Teachers 1929
1405 BUSS Janet L  Concord as Seen Through the Writings of Emerson, Thoreau, Bronson Alcott and Hawthorne  MA Boston Univ 1950
1406 CAULKINS Cora M  Emerson as a Nature Poet  MS Purdue Univ 1902
1407 CHAPMAN Margaret E  Emerson's Use of the Symbol  MA Univ of Texas at Austin 1930
1408 CHASTEEN Nina  Nineteenth Century Critics and the Poetry of Ralph Waldo Emerson  MA East Texas St Univ 1964
1409 CLAYTON Donald R  The Immanence of Sentiment: A Preface to Ralph Waldo Emerson's "Nature"  MA Florida St Univ 1962
1410 COBB Sharon S  The Love Poetry of Ralph Waldo Emerson  MA Columbia Univ 1965  68 p
1411 COLE Mary L  Ralph Waldo Emerson as an Observer of Mid-nineteenth Century England  MA Columbia Univ 1942
1412 CONKLIN Lillian M  Mystical Elements in Emerson's Thought  MA North Texas St Univ 1966
1413 COSBY Amine  An Analysis of Emerson's Reading  MA Ohio St Univ 1936
1414 COWAN Louise S  Some Aspects of Emerson's Poetic Diction  MA Texas Christian Univ 1947  74 p
1415 CREWS Helen  The American Author in Europe, 1830-1860 (Emerson, Lowell, Longfellow, Hawthorne)  MA Southern Methodist Univ 1934
1416 DECARY Yves  The Idea of the Divine in the Writings of R W Emerson  MA Univ of Montreal (Canada) 1964
1417 DEMENT Wanda P  The American Dream: Three Distortions of Emersonian Concepts  MA West Texas St Univ 1966  124 p
1418 D'HAENE Sr Henry F  Unity in Variety: Emerson's Prose  MA Florida St Univ 1963  119 p
1419 DILDY Urban D  Ralph Waldo Emerson: Transcendentalist  M Ed Henderson St Coll nd
1420 EATON Clement  Spiritual Kinship of Plato and Emerson  MA Univ of North Carolina at Chapel Hill 1920
1421 ELLIOTT F S  Emerson as a Lecturer  MA Univ of North Carolina at Chapel Hill 1931
1422 ELLIS Hilda J  The Personality of Ralph Waldo Emerson as Revealed in His Letters  MA Ohio St Univ 1942
1423 FELDER Annie G  Emerson's Reading from 1820 to 1860  MA Univ of Texas at Austin 1928

1424  FELTS Sara S  Emerson's Theory of Diction in Relation to His Poetry  MA Univ of Tennessee 1952  58 p
1425  FITZGERALD Margaret  Emerson's Theory of Education  MA Baylor Univ 1957  101 p
1426  FRIEDLANDER Jack  A Comparison of the Aspects of Romanticism in the Poetry of Johann Wolfgang Von Goethe and Ralph Waldo Emerson  BA Univ of Delaware 1950  83 p
1427  GARTNER Dennis D  Emerson's Theory of Greek and Roman Myths and Their Uses in His Poems and *Essays, First and Second Series*  MA Univ of North Dakota 1965
1428  GAUSE M J  Emerson's Theory of Learning  MA North Texas St Univ 1962
1429  GIRAULT Emily S  The Political Ideas of Ralph Waldo Emerson  MA Univ of Rochester 1949  105 p
1430  GLASRUD Bruce A  The Impact of the Frontier on Ralph Waldo Emerson's Transcendentalism  MA Eastern New Mexico Univ 1963
1431  GOREN Leyla  Elements of Brahmanism in the Transcendentalism of Emerson  MA Columbia Univ 1962  70 p
1432  GRAHAM Katherine T  Survival and Revival of Emersonianism  MA St Univ of New York at Albany 1932
1433  GRIFFIN Bonnie C  Evidences of Coleridge's Influence upon the Development of Emerson's Religious Ideas and upon His Main Theories of Nature, Soul, Mind and Criticism  MA Auburn Univ 1939
1434  HABOSIAN Mary  Puritan's Progress: A Study of Emerson's Understanding of Goethe  MA Tufts Univ 1961
1435  HAHN Lewis E  Emerson as a Lecturer  MA Univ of Texas at Austin 1929
1436  HALVORSON Nelius O  Growth of Emerson's Reputation up to the Time of His Death in 1882  MA Univ of Iowa 1925
1437  HANCOCK Arthur S  Emerson, Lowell, Poe and Whitman on the Functions of Poetry  MA Columbia Univ 1923
1438  HARBBELL G S  Some Foci of Emerson's Philosophical Teachings  MA Wesleyan Univ 1916
1439  HARRISON J P  Emerson's Representative Men  MA North Texas St Univ 1948
1440  HAZARD Alice M  The Reciprocal Relations of Emerson and Thoreau and the Impact of Thoreau's Ideas on Our Times  MA Boston Univ 1935
1441  HEMKE Marie D  Emerson and German Literature  MA Northwestern Univ 1917
1442  HERRERA Virginia  Emerson's Conception of the Poet  MA Univ of Mississippi 1953  109 p
1443  HILDEBRAND V O  Emerson's Ideal of Education  MA North Texas St Univ 1941
1444  HIRSCH Tim  The Dialectical Unity of Emerson's Later Essays  MA Bowling Green St Univ 1967
1445  HOCK Cassie H  A Contrast of Two American Essayists: Ralph Waldo Emerson and Jose Enrique Rodo  MA Oklahoma St Univ 1927
1446  HOELTJE Hubert H  Emerson and Alcott in Iowa, with Notes on the History of Iowa, 1855-1885  MA Univ of Iowa 1926
1447  HOLMES Doris  The Individualism of Emerson and Thoreau  MA Boston Univ 1929
1448  HUGHES William H  The Influence of Emerson on Whitman Before 1855  MA Univ of Arkansas 1930
1449  HUMMEL Wilhelmine E  Is Emerson Entirely Platonic?  M Ed Temple Univ 1932  84 p
1450  HUTCHINS M Viletta  Emerson: His Educational Ideas and Their Modern Application  MA St Univ of New York at Albany 1931
1451  HUTCHINSON Alfred R  Emerson's Contemporary Reputation: An Interpretation of Literary Opinion in England and America, 1836-1882  MA Oklahoma St Univ 1958
1452  IREY Eugene F  Emerson's Opinions of Daniel Webster  MA Univ of Colorado 1946
1453  JACKSON Dan S  Emerson and Nietzsche: Their Ideas on History  MA Univ of Texas at Austin 1952  111 p

1454  JACOBS Louise B  Emerson's Conception of Childhood  MA George Peabody Coll for Teachers 1931
1455  JOHNSON James K  Ralph Waldo Emerson's Relationship with Five Magazines, 1835-1850  MA Univ of Iowa 1966
1456  JONES Helen F  The Anti-intellectualism in the Essays of Ralph Waldo Emerson  MA Univ of Kentucky 1937
1457  JONES Nancy E  Emerson's Reputation as a Poet, 1838-1888  MA Univ of Texas at Austin 1943  179 p
1458  JONES Nancy J  Three American Nature Poets:  Emerson, Lanier, Whittier  MA Columbia Univ 1945
1459  KHIRALLA George  Aspects of Democracy in Emerson's Essays  MA Boston Univ 1947
1460  KURRE Dorothy L  The Soaring Orbit of the Muse:  Emerson's "Merlin" and "Bacchus"  MA Washington Univ at St Louis 1968  53 p
1461  LADU A I  Conception of the Ego in the Writings of Ralph Waldo Emerson and Walt Whitman  MA Univ of North Carolina at Chapel Hill 1927
1462  LAYTON J S  Emerson's Theory of Tragedy  MA Univ of North Carolina at Chapel Hill 1941
1463  LEE Roland F  A Study of Emerson's Essay "Compensation"  MA Ohio St Univ 1947
1464  LINDENBERG John G  Ralph Waldo Emerson's Natural Symbols in Action  MA Tufts Univ 1965
1465  LINDQUIST Vernon R  Emerson and Bangor:  An Analysis and History of Their Reciprocal Influence  MA Univ of Maine 1968  198 p
1466  LOVE Lanelle E  Emerson's Use of the Term Moral Sentiment  MA Univ of Texas at Austin 1938  96 p
1467  LOWE Ruth H  The Influence of Emanuel Swedenborg on Ralph Waldo Emerson as Shown in "Nature"  MS Auburn Univ 1947  82 p
1468  McCANN Ruth V  Emerson's Religious Development  MA Univ of California at Berkeley 1916
1469  McGINLEY William J  The Spiritual-cosmic Doctrine of Ralph Waldo Emerson  MA Univ of Texas at El Paso 1964  92 p
1470  McGOLDRICK Stephanie E  Swedenborg, Emerson and the Soul  MA Univ of New Hampshire 1966  66 p
1471  McQUISTON Raymer  The Relation of Ralph Waldo Emerson to Public Affairs  MA Univ of Kansas 1921
1472  MARING Anne S  Emerson's Indebtedness to Swedenborg  MA Texas Arts and Industries Univ 1960
1473  MAROTTE Beatrice E  The Influence of Emerson on Hawthorne  MA Rutgers St Univ 1934
1474  MATTHEWS Richard D  Emerson's Hopes and Fears for America  MA Ohio St Univ 1952
1475  MATTHIS L C  The Influence of Negro Slavery on Emerson's Concept of Freedom  MA North Texas St Univ 1946
1476  MEECH Lydia J  Parallels of Thought in Emerson and Coleridge  MA Rutgers St Univ 1934
1477  MENTIN E H  Emerson's Conception of Personality  MA Wesleyan Univ 1917
1478  MIDDLEBROOK Leah H  Emerson's Conception of Self-reliance and Compensation  MA Baylor Univ 1937  100 p
1479  MITCHELL Amy N  Plato, Rousseau, Emerson and the Knowledge of Self  MA Florida St Univ 1964
1480  MONGAN Adele  The Influence of Ralph Waldo Emerson on Edwin Arlington Robinson  MA Columbia Univ 1954  110 p
1481  MOODY Blaine D  Emerson's "Frigid Fear":  The Nature of "Coldness" in His Early Life and Thought  MA Bowling Green St Univ 1958
1482  MORAN Virginia A  Circle and Dialectic:  A Consideration of Emerson's Interest in Hegel  MA Columbia Univ 1962  102 p
1483  MOSES Mary R  The Reflections of Ralph Waldo Emerson's Life and Thoughts in Selected Works  M Ed Henderson St Coll nd
1484  MUMFORD Dorothy  The Idea of Progress in Ralph Waldo Emerson  MA Univ

of North Carolina at Chapel Hill 1930
1485 O'DONNELL Barbara N  The Calvinistic Element in Emerson's *Journals*  MA Ohio St Univ 1941
1486 O'GARA Edward J  The Influence of Coleridge on Emerson's Theory of Poetry  MA Univ of Vermont 1941  80 p
1487 OTEY Rheba W  Progress and Providence:  The Myth of Time in Emerson and Hawthorne  MA Ohio St Univ 1969  78 p
1488 PARKER Lois  Man and God-reality According to Emerson, Whitman and MacLeish:  A Continuum in American Literature  MA Sul Ross St Coll 1965
1489 PARKMAN Mary R  Emerson and Walt Whitman:  A Study in Contrasts  MA Univ of Vermont 1930  81 p
1490 PAULITS Br F Joseph  Emerson's Philosophy of Nature, Spirit, Man and the Poet, Drawn from the Essays, the Poems and Nature  MA Univ of Pittsburgh 1950
1491 PINER Ouilda  A Study of Emerson's Poetic Art  MA Univ of Texas at Austin 1931
1492 PORTER Nora W  Emerson and Thoreau  MA Ohio St Univ 1943
1493 POWELL Aileen  Classical Mythology in Emerson's Writings  MA Univ of Texas at Austin 1929
1494 PRICE Mary McK  A Comparison of Ralph Waldo Emerson's Concepts of Ideal Character and Nineteenth Century English Character  MA Texas Christian Univ 1962  82 p
1495 PROUD Geoffrey F  Religion, God and Jesus Christ in the Manuscript Sermons of Ralph Waldo Emerson  MA Boston Coll 1966
1496 PUCKETT Cecil E  Emerson and Swedenborg or, "The Mystic"  MA Washington Univ at St Louis 1953
1497 READING Elinor L  The Critical Reception of Ralph Waldo Emerson, 1836-1841  MA Columbia Univ 1965  85 p
1498 REWAK William J  The Transcendental Philosophy of Ralph Waldo Emerson  MA Gonzaga Univ at Spokane 1958
1499 RIGGS Lisette  Emerson's Catholic Friends  MA Univ of Maryland at College Park 1940  67 p
1500 ROBERTSON Dora E  Ralph Waldo Emerson as a Critic of Literature  MA Univ of Kansas 1929
1501 ROBINSON Michael L  The Aesthetic Amalgam:  A Study of Emerson  MA Brigham Young Univ 1970  104 p
1502 ROLLINS Henry B  Ralph Waldo Emerson as an Editor  MA Univ of North Carolina at Chapel Hill 1948  83 p
1503 RUBIO Marya P  Ralph Waldo Emerson and Hinduism:  A Study of the Over-soul and Self-reliance  MA Univ of Houston 1960  85 p
1504 RUFF Patricia A  Ralph Waldo Emerson on Tour to the West, 1850-1870  MA Lamar Technological Univ 1969  209 p
1505 SADLER George M  Emerson and the South  MA Duke Univ 1934
1506 SAVAGE Dorothy H  Emerson's Idealism and the Problem of Evil  MA Western Washington St Coll 1967  165 p
1507 SCHMIDT Joseph E  Emerson and Arnold as Critics of Six Writers  MA Univ of Iowa 1949
1508 SCOTT Anna M  A Rhetorical Analysis of Ralph Waldo Emerson's Anti-slavery Speeches  MA Texas Christian Univ 1964
1509 SCOTT William D  The Harmony of Ralph Waldo Emerson and Nature  M Ed Henderson St Coll nd
1510 SHANE Margaret B  A Study in Similarity:  Ralph Waldo Emerson and Emily Dickinson  MA George Washington Univ 1954  78 p
1511 SHERWOOD Rachel  Transcendentalism in the Private Journals of Ralph Waldo Emerson  MA Univ of Richmond 1964  102 p
1512 SILVA Joseph D  Emerson's Concept of Immortality  MA Univ of New Hampshire 1965  39 p
1513 SLACK Robert C  Emerson and Schopenhauer:  A Comparison  MA Univ of Pittsburgh 1941

1514 SMITH Ben L  Emerson Epiphanies in Whitman  MA Fresno St Coll 1968  40 p
1515 SMITH Ena B  The Delicate Mercuries:  Emerson's Attitude Toward Women  MA Univ of Colorado 1946
1516 SMITHLINE Arnold  The Reasons for Emerson's Break with Unitarianism  MA Brooklyn Coll of City Univ of New York 1952  70 p
1517 SNIPES David M  Emerson's "Nature":  Analysis and Synthesis  MA Univ of North Carolina at Chapel Hill 1968
1518 SROKA Suzanne G  Influence of Montaigne Upon Emerson  MA St Univ of New York at Albany 1932
1519 STEVENSON Florence C  The Romantic Philosophers:  Ralph Waldo Emerson and Johann Gottlieb Fichte  MA Columbia Univ 1950
1520 SULLIVAN Hazel  The Reflection of Life Influences in Ralph Waldo Emerson's Works  M Ed Henderson St Coll nd
1521 SULLIVAN Virginia  The Educational Ideas and Opinions of Ralph Waldo Emerson and Henry David Thoreau  MA Univ of Puget Sound 1966
1522 SUMIDA Alice  Emerson and Oriental Philosophy  MA Columbia Univ 1966  113 p
1523 TANZY Conrad E  Browning and Emerson:  A Study in Parallel Ideas  MA Ohio St Univ 1952
1524 THOMAS Ruth E  Motivations for Artistic Expression in Ralph Waldo Emerson  MA Ohio St Univ 1936
1525 TU Hsin Y  Emerson Through Chinese Eyes  MA Florida St Univ 1949
1526 VALENTINE Charles B  Emerson and Slavery After 1850  MA Virginia St Coll 1956  73 p
1527 VOGEL Dan  Decade of Rebellion:  A Study of Contemporary Reputation of Ralph Waldo Emerson During the Period 1832-1840  MA Rutgers St Univ 1949
1528 WALLACE Harry J  The Influence of Ellen Louisa Tucker on the Life and Thought of Ralph Waldo Emerson  MA Univ of Maryland at College Park 1969  58 p
1529 WEBB Ralph W  Personal Influences of Emerson  MA East Texas St Univ 1938
1530 WHALEY Betty P  Style in Emerson's Prose  MA Univ of Maryland at College Park 1961  126 p
1531 WILLIAMS Paul A  Emerson's Ideas on Democracy  MA Boston Univ 1938
1532 WILSON Thomas H  Emerson's Doctrine of Illusions  MA Univ of Oklahoma 1940
1533 WIMBERLY Jessie N  The Relationship of Emerson and Montaigne in Life and Thought  MA Univ of Texas at Austin 1937  120 p
1534 WOLFE Don M  Emerson and the Democratic Ideal  MA Univ of Pittsburgh 1927
1535 WOOD Barry A  Emerson as a Process Philosopher  MA Univ of British Columbia (Canada) 1968  104 p
1536 WOODS Hazel M  Critical Opinion of Emerson Since 1920  MA Univ of Texas at Austin 1940  172 p
1537 WORSHAM Myra Z  Greek and Roman Mythology in the Poetry of Emerson  MA George Peabody Coll for Teachers 1937
1538 WORTHAM Thomas E  Ralph Waldo Emerson's Critical Estimates of His Literary Contemporaries  MA George Peabody Coll for Teachers 1929
See also 90, 1190, 1598, 2479, 2673, 4128, 4987, 5749, 5796, 6502, 6568, 6660, 6666

## JOHN ERSKINE

1539 SISSA Irene  John Erskine  MA Ca Foscari (Italy) 1946
1540 STEVENS H F  John Erskine's Literary Critical Theory and Practice  MA Boston Univ 1940

## W C FALKNER

1541 OWEN Virginia R  W C Falkner: A Critical and Biographical Study  MA Univ of Mississippi 1930
1542 PURYEAR Mary J  Life and Legend of Colonel W C Falkner as Source for Colonel John Sartoris  MA Florida St Univ 1969  98 p
1543 WATTS Mary E  Two William Falkners: A Study in Contrast  MA Univ of Texas at Austin 1941  65 p

## JAMES T FARRELL

1544 BOWKER Alvin W  The Human Static: An Evaluation of the Writing of James T Farrell Based on His Literary Criticism  MA Univ of Maine 1960  137 p
1545 BYRNES Raymond A  Roman Catholicism in James T Farrell's *Studs Lonigan*  MA Mankato St Coll 1966  55 p
1546 COX John F  An Analysis of the Religious Conflicts in the Danny O'Neill Pentalogy of James T Farrell  MA Arizona St Coll at Flagstaff 1965
1547 HOLMAN Hortense G  James T Farrell and Richard Wright: A Study in Comparative American Naturalism  MA North Carolina Central Univ 1957  133 p
1548 HOPKINS Derrell C  Naturalism in the Novels of James T Farrell  MA Howard Univ 1959  145 p
1549 JOANNIDES John M  The Decline of Social Inter-relationships in the Family, the Church and Traditions in American Life as Seen in James T Farrell's Trilogy *Studs Lonigan*  MA Morehead St Univ 1968  50 p
1550 KLAR Lloyd A  An Analysis of the Short Story Technique of James T Farrell  MA Texas Christian Univ 1953  123 p
1551 PARMANTIE Peter A  The Great Depression as Seen by James T Farrell, John Dos Passos and John Steinbeck  MS Illinois St Univ at Normal 1960
1552 ROSENTHAL Maurice M  The Novels of James T Farrell: A Study in Social Forces and the Individual  MA Univ of New Mexico 1952
1553 SCOBLE William F  James T Farrell: The Themes of Naturalism  MA Chico St Coll 1969
1554 SOLENSTEN John M  A Study of Naturalism in James T Farrell's *Studs Lonigan*  MA Mankato St Coll 1961  61 p

See also 6835

## WILLIAM FAULKNER

1555 ABBOTT Horace P  The Mind and "The Old Meat": Vision and the Verities in Faulkner's Ethic  MA Univ of Toronto (Canada) 1964
1556 ABBOTT Priscilla A  Family Relationships in Faulkner's Novels: Microcosm of the South's Degeneration  MA Texas Christian Univ 1966  132 p
1557 ALBRITTON Sue P  Faulkner's Lost Women of the Aristocracy  MA Univ of Mississippi 1968
1558 ALDRIDGE Henry B  The Function of Imagery in the Narratives of William Faulkner's *Absalom, Absalom!*  MA Univ of North Carolina at Chapel Hill 1968
1559 ALEXANDER Esther McC  A Critical Analysis of the Roles of Lucas Beauchamp in William Faulkner's *Go Down, Moses* and *Intruder in the Dust*  MA Univ of North Carolina at Chapel Hill 1963
1560 ALLEN Billups S  Faulkner's Soldiers  MA Univ of Mississippi 1968
1561 ALLEN George R  The Hatch and Brood of Time: Temporal Structure in the Major Novels of William Faulkner  MA Univ of Alaska 1964  101 p
1562 ALLEN James D  William Faulkner: The Regeneration of a Myth, A Study of the "Yoknapatawpha Saga"  BA Amherst Coll 1962

1563 ANDERSON Eleanor S  Decadence in the Old South as Seen in William Faulkner's *The Sound and the Fury*  M Ed Henderson St Coll nd

1564 ANDERSON Jean M  William Faulkner as Moralist: *A Fable*  MA Univ of the Pacific 1959  72 p

1565 ARANT Fairlie  The South of William Faulkner as Seen in *Absalom, Absalom!*  MA Columbia Univ 1961  98 p

1566 ARMSTRONG Richard A  Yoknapatawpha and the Natchez Trace: A Study of Regional Influences on William Faulkner and Eudora Welty  MA Columbia Univ 1955  65 p

1567 BALKMAN B A  The Role of Women in the Work of William Faulkner  MA North Texas St Univ 1968

1568 BARFOOT Anne  Social Opportunism in Balzac and Faulkner  MA Univ of Southern Mississippi 1967

1569 BARGER Stanley F  Cash Bundren and the Funeral Journey in Faulkner's *As I Lay Dying*  MA Univ of New Hampshire 1969  80 p

1570 BARNETT Bill M  Relationship of Point of View and Theme in Three Novels of William Faulkner  MA Auburn Univ 1960

1571 BEAUCHAMP Gorman L  Archetypes in William Faulkner's *The Bear*  MA Univ of Houston 1966  123 p

1572 BELL H H Jr  Lucius Priest and Ike McCaslin: A Comparative Study of Their Initiation Into Manhood  MA Univ of Maryland at College Park 1965  77 p

1573 BELLOMY Joyce  Christ Figures in the Novels of William Faulkner  MA Univ of Texas at Austin 1958  92 p

1574 BENNETT Myrtalee A  The Endurance Theme in William Faulkner's Major Novels  MA Hardin-Simmons Univ 1968

1575 BENTON Robert R Jr  The Unity of *Go Down, Moses*: A Study of Faulkner's Revisions  MA Univ of North Carolina at Chapel Hill 1963

1576 BLANCHARD Jo A  Five Major Themes in the Fiction of William Faulkner  MA East Tennessee St Univ 1966

1577 BLAY Francis B  Faulkner's Debt to the 1890's  MA Washington St Univ at Pullman 1961

1578 BLISSARD Thomasina  The Role of the Negro in William Faulkner's Yoknapatawpha Series  MA Vanderbilt Univ 1948

1579 BONHAM Ronald A  Unreality as Inhumanity: Faulkner's "Ike" McCaslin and the Failure of Humanism  MA Univ of Manitoba (Canada) 1967

1580 BONIN Jane F  The Place of *The Reivers* in William Faulkner's Yoknapatawpha Chronicle  MA Univ of Southwestern Louisiana 1966  101 p

1581 BONTEMPO Edward F  The Role of the Narrator in *Go Down, Moses*  MA Ohio St Univ 1967  63 p

1582 BORDEN David M  William Faulkner: A Study of the Family  BA Amherst Coll 1959

1583 BOSTIAN Frieda F  A Study of William Faulkner's *As I Lay Dying*  MA Univ of North Carolina at Chapel Hill 1966

1584 BOWER Richard  William Faulkner's Reputation in France, 1931-1950  MA Hunter Coll 1966

1585 BOYD Mary J  Faulkner's Primitives and the Timeless Values  MA Hunter Coll 1967

1586 BRADLEY Wanda H  Idealism Versus Realism in William Faulkner  M Ed Henderson St Coll nd

1587 BRANAM Harold F  Faulkner's Icons: The Earth-mother Figures  MA Temple Univ 1967  91 p

1588 BRIGHT Michael M  Alienation in William Faulkner's *Light in August*  MA Boston Coll 1968

1589 BROACH Kathleen  An Ethical Vision of Life: A Review of William Faulkner's *The Sound and the Fury*  M Ed Henderson St Coll nd

1590 BRODSKY Louis D  Man and Nature: A Study of Animal Imagery in *As I Lay Dying*, *Old Man* and *The Bear*  MA Washington Univ at St Louis 1967  68 p

1591 BROWN Jewell L  Faulkner's Preachers  MA Univ of Texas at Austin 1966 111 p
1592 BUICE Joe C  An Evaluation of William Faulkner's *Requiem for a Nun* MA Univ of Texas at Austin 1963  72 p
1593 BURGHDURF Cheryl J  The Women in Faulkner's Novels  MA Univ of Maine 1969  119 p
1594 BURLESON Shirley D  The Snopes Trilogy  M Ed Henderson St Coll  nd
1595 BYRNE Sr Mary E  From Tradition to Technique: Development of Character in Joyce and Faulkner  MA Univ of Southern Mississippi 1969
1596 CAIN R E  The Social Hierarchy of the South in the Works of William Faulkner  MA North Texas St Univ 1954
1597 CARTER Bernice B  Justice and Retribution in the Novels of William Faulkner  MA Univ of Houston 1967  99 p
1598 CARTER Stephen L  A Study of Similarities in Faulkner and Emerson  MA West Texas St Univ 1968  70 p
1599 CASWELL Robert W  The Fire and the Hearth: Conflict and Affirmation in William Faulkner  MA Univ of Vermont 1954  137 p
1600 CHAMPION Eugenia L  The Characteristics of William Faulkner's Yoknapatawpha County  MA Texas Arts and Industries Univ 1955
1601 CHAPPELL Charles M  The Defeat of the Indian in Faulkner's Wilderness  MA Emory Univ 1965
1602 CHICANO Phyllis A  Faulkner on *The Sound and the Fury*: A Reader's Interpretation  BA Univ of Delaware 1969  37 p
1603 CHRISTEN Elizabeth L  The Presentation of Consciousness in *As I Lay Dying* by William Faulkner and *L'emploi du Temps* by Michel Butor  MA Purdue Univ 1967  94 p
1604 CLUNE Sr Maria P  William Faulkner and the Theme of Isolation  MA Villanova Univ 1964
1605 COK Georgette W  The Faulknerian Woman: A Study  MA Dalhousie Univ (Canada) 1966
1606 COLEMAN Clara R  Faulkner's Snopeses, 1929-1939  MA Univ of North Carolina at Chapel Hill 1964
1607 COLEMAN Irwin W  The Negro Problem in William Faulkner's Yoknapatawpha Series  MA Univ of Texas at Austin 1956
1608 CONNORS Greta M  William Faulkner and His Critics, 1926-1950  MA Univ of Maine 1957  79 p
1609 COOLEY John R  Three Initiations in Faulkner's Fiction  MA Syracuse Univ 1960  135 p
1610 COOPER Richard A  An Interpretation of Faulkner's *Pylon*  MA Univ of North Carolina at Chapel Hill 1968
1611 CORDER Jimmie W  The Enduring Was: William Faulkner's Treatment of Time  MA Texas Christian Univ 1954  81 p
1612 COSSABOOM Bruce  The Pattern of Ironic Inversion in William Faulkner's *Light in August*  MA Univ of Wyoming 1965
1613 CRISWELL Helen P  William Faulkner: His Complexity and Ambiguity  MA Butler Univ 1950
1614 DANCE Daryl C  An Analysis of William Faulkner's *Light in August*  MA Virginia St Coll 1963
1615 DEAHOFE Winfield A  The Realism, Romanticism and Irony of William Faulkner  MA Univ of Minnesota 1936
1616 DEAN Harry N  A Study of the Horse and the Mule in William Faulkner's Fiction  MA Univ of Tennessee 1969  64 p
1617 DEAUQUIER Sybil  William Faulkner's Concept of Knowledge Beyond Reason  MA North Texas St Univ 1964
1618 DEETER Gary D  The Ambivalent Affirmation: A Study of Faulkner's Christian Symbolism  MA Kansas St Teachers Coll 1966
1619 DE MARIS Ronald E  Faulkner's Folk Heroes: The Poor White Hero from Regional Stereotype to Mythic Protagonist  MA Trinity Coll at Hartford 1965
1620 DEW Marian N  A Study of William Faulkner's *Requiem for a Nun*  MA Univ of North Carolina at Chapel Hill 1962

1621  DEW Ozella E  Structure and Theme in Faulkner's *Go Down, Moses* Stories  MA Univ of Texas at Austin 1965  160 p
1622  DISTELZWEIG Howard L  Faulkner's Determinism: A Study of Selected Novels  MA Ohio St Univ 1966  63 p
1623  DONELAN Shirley B  Language as Related to Style in William Faulkner's "The Old Man"  MA Ball St Univ 1964  65 p
1624  DRAPER Lowell A  William Faulkner's Tense Shifts: A Study of the Relation Between William Faulkner's Tense Shifts and His Time Themes  MA Fresno St Coll 1964  68 p
1625  DUDLEY Michael D  *Light in August*: A Study of Loneliness and Rigidity of Spirit  MA Univ of Mississippi 1969
1626  EBDON Priscilla A  Faulkner's Colonels: Reality and Fiction  MA Univ of Maryland at College Park 1969  99 p
1627  EDWARDS M J  Time in the Structure of the Novels of William Faulkner  M Phil Univ of London (England) 1968
1628  ELLIS Janet B  An Analysis of Parallel Narrative Structure in the Novels of William Faulkner  MA Northern Illinois Univ 1966
1629  ENGLISH Dorothy  The Poet's Voice: A Study of Christianity in William Faulkner's Novels  MA Univ of Texas at El Paso 1966  101 p
1630  EVERETT Maxine S  Folklore in William Faulkner's Yoknapatawpha Fiction  MA Texas Technological Univ 1961  110 p
1631  FARRAR Winifred H  Moral Intention in the Work of William Faulkner: A Call for Positive Action  MA Univ of Southern Mississippi 1962
1632  FAUGHT P K  Metamorphosis of Faulkner's Short Stories  MA North Texas St Univ 1961
1633  FAULKNER Francys K  A Character Analysis of William Faulkner's Trinity of Consciousness MA Arkansas St Coll 1965
1634  FERNSTERMAKER John J  Moral Responsibility in Faulkner's Yoknapatawpha: The Aristocratic Women and Their Female Descendants  MA Ohio St Univ 1967  125 p
1635  FIREMAN Judith K  The Rhetoric of *Absalom, Absalom!*  MA Columbia Univ 1966  68 p
1636  FISHER Arnold  The Shape of Morality in the Novels of William Faulkner  MA Columbia Univ 1954  98 p
1637  FITCH Betty A  William Faulkner's Use of the Negro as a Fictional Pivot  MA North Carolina Central Univ 1965
1638  FITZGERALD Pauline M  The Purple Within Faulkner's Grotesqueries  MA Univ of Mississippi 1969
1639  FIVEASH Martha S  "Go Slow, Now": An Evaluation of Faulkner's Attitudes Toward Equality  MA Univ of Houston 1968  151 p
1640  FLEMING David W  The Theme of Alienation in Selected Works from William Faulkner's Early Fiction  MA Oklahoma St Univ 1969  29 p
1641  FOLSOM Gordon R  Folk Narrators of Yoknapatawpha County: Suggestions for a Reinterpretation of William Faulkner  MA Univ of New Hampshire 1951  99 p
1642  FORBUS Jere K  The Function of Game Imagery in Faulkner's Sartoris Myth  MA Univ of Massachusetts 1969  79 p
1643  FORGEY Susan M  William Faulkner's Use of Commentator-narrator Characters: V K Ratliff and Gavin Stevens  MA Univ of Colorado 1966
1644  FOURIER Ruth G  The "Prufrock" Theme in the Novels of William Faulkner  MA Univ of South Carolina 1948
1645  FOWLKES Bessie I  A Study of William Faulkner's Literary Reputation in the United States, 1926-1952  MA North Carolina Central Univ 1955  61 p
1646  FRAME Gary A  William Faulkner and Sherwood Anderson: A Study of a Literary Relationship  MA Univ of British Columbia (Canada) 1968  109 p
1647  FREY Edith T  The Young White Male Protagonist in Selected Works of Faulkner  MA Ohio St Univ 1967  69 p
1648  FRIEDLAND Ronald L  The Tragic Hero in William Faulkner  MA Columbia

Univ 1960  166 p
1649 FRIEND Robert III  Humor in Jason's Section of William Faulkner's *The Sound and the Fury*  MA Univ of North Carolina at Chapel Hill 1963
1650 FULKERSON Sarah J  The Evolution of *The Bear* from "Lion": William Faulkner's Revisions  MA Georgetown Univ 1968  160 p
1651 FUNK Margaret A  A Guide to the Fiction of William Faulkner  MA Washington Univ at St Louis 1949
1652 GALBRAITH Margaret E  Faulkner's Trilogy: Technique as Approach to Theme  MA Univ of British Columbia (Canada) 1962  108 p
1653 GANIM John M  House of Smoke: The Theme of Abstraction in the Major Works of William Faulkner  BA Rutgers St Univ 1967  59 p
1654 GATE Judy E  Down the Long Corridor: A Study of Child Characters in Faulkner's Fiction  MA Univ of Tennessee 1966
1655 GEORGER Audrey J  Faulkner's Innocents  MA St Louis Univ 1966  76 p
1656 GILLILAND Joe D  Sin and Redemption in Faulkner  MA Univ of Texas at Austin 1955
1657 GLENN Barbara M  Humor in the Works of William Faulkner  MA Virginia St Coll 1965
1658 GOODMAN Gerald T  The War Fiction of William Faulkner  MA Miami Univ at Oxford 1966
1659 GOURLEY Dan M  The Unity of *Go Down, Moses*  MA Univ of Texas at Austin 1966  129 p
1660 GRANT Robert E  The Poor White in Yoknapatawpha County, Mississippi: William Faulkner, Sole Owner and Proprietor  BA Amherst Coll 1955
1661 GRAVES John A  Techniques in the Fiction of William Faulkner  MA Columbia Univ 1948
1662 GRAY Betty J  The Role of Women in Four Faulkner Novels  MA St Coll of Iowa 1966
1663 GREET Thomas Y  The Southern Legend in Yoknapatawpha Fiction of William Faulkner  MA Univ of North Carolina at Chapel Hill 1950  150 p
1664 GREGG Alvin L  A Critical Analysis of William Faulkner's *The Bear*  MA Texas Technological Univ 1957  94 p
1665 GRIFFIN Ernest G  William Faulkner and the Tragic Ritual  MA Columbia Univ 1951
1666 GROMAN George L  William Faulkner and the Changing Social Structure of the South  MA Columbia Univ 1951
1667 GROPPE John D  The Predatory Females of William Faulkner: A Study of *Mosquitoes, Sanctuary* and *The Wild Palms*  MA Columbia Univ 1969  84 p
1668 GROSSI Joseph L  The Function of William Faulkner's Sartorises  MA Univ of Rhode Island 1967  111 p
1669 GROVER Elizabeth B  Puritanism in Faulkner's *Light in August*  MA Temple Univ 1966  58 p
1670 GULLATTEE Latinee  Social Realism in the Writings of William Faulkner  MA Howard Univ 1953  270 p
1671 HALL Patsy A  Faulkner's *The Sound and the Fury*  MA Univ of Texas at Austin 1958  145 p
1672 HALSELL Roberta J  The Thematic Value of Faulkner's Yoknapatawpha County Heroines  MA Northeast Louisiana Univ 1968  142 p
1673 HAMBLIN Bobby W  Faulkner's Suspense: A Study in Literary Technique  MA Univ of Mississippi 1965  96 p
1674 HAMMOND Alexander L  The Tragic Conflict in William Faulkner's Major Works  MA Univ of Redlands 1966
1675 HARDY Thomas W  Two Unifying Devices in Faulkner's *The Hamlet*  MA Univ of North Carolina at Chapel Hill 1968
1676 HARTSELL Anne D  The Snopes Clan in William Faulkner's Fiction  MA East Tennessee St Univ 1963
1677 HASKEL Peggy I  William Faulkner and Ivan Bunin: Their Worlds  MA Univ of Texas at Austin 1952  77 p
1678 HEBAISHA Hoda A  Faulkner's Revisions in *The Bear*  MA Columbia Univ

1960   138 p
1679 HEFNER Lonnie D   The Concept of Love in Novels of William Faulkner
     MA Univ of Texas at Austin 1955   159 p
1680 HEIMER Jackson W   William Faulkner and the Contemporary Social Scene
     (1920-1950)   MA Univ of Kentucky 1952   88 p
1681 HEINEMANN Fredrik J   Quentin Compson and Southern Guilt   MA Univ of
     Delaware 1966   36 p
1682 HENDERSON Charles G   Faulkner's Snopeses: The Genesis and Growth
     of a Symbol   MA Univ of Delaware 1967   86 p
1683 HIATT David F   William Faulkner and the Yoknapatawpha Negro   MA Univ
     of New Mexico 1956
1684 HILFER Anthony C   William Faulkner and Jacobean Drama: A Comparison
     MA Columbia Univ 1960   88 p
1685 HILL James A   The Narrative Technique of William Faulkner   MA Univ of
     Texas at Austin 1947   103 p
1686 HILLIARD Lewis J   A View of Faulkner's Women   MA Southern Illinois
     Univ at Carbondale 1959   93 p
1687 HOAR Victor M   William Faulkner's John Sartoris: A Study in Derivation
     MA Univ of Connecticut 1958
1688 HOFFMAN Roberta M   Tragedy: From Athens to Yoknapatawpha   MA Columbia
     Univ 1961   167 p
1689 HOPKINS Gertrude M   The Secret Cause: A Study of Pursuit and Flight
     in William Faulkner's Early Work   MA Univ of Maryland at College
     Park 1969   80 p
1690 HUBBARD Minnie G   Parallels to Calvinism in the Works of William Faulkner   MA Ft Hays Kansas St Coll 1961   153 p
1691 HULL Donald L   *Sartoris:* A Study of the Hero   MA Columbia Univ 1960
     95 p
1692 HUPP Ellen K   William Faulkner: The Primitive Initiation Rite
     MA Univ of Texas at Austin 1966   87 p
1693 INGRAM Betty P   Reappraisal of Faulkner's *Light in August*   MA North
     Carolina Central Univ at Durham 1964   45 p
1694 JACOBOWSKY Nadia A   William Faulkner's *The Bear*   MA Ohio St Univ 1957
1695 JAMES Sharon   The Theme of *Go Down, Moses*   MA Arkansas St Coll 1966
1696 JEMISON Richard K   A Study of the Naturalism in Faulkner's *The Hamlet*
     MA Ohio St Univ 1963   109 p
1697 JOBES Lavon M   William Faulkner: The Sins and the Curse   MA Municipal
     Univ of Omaha 1961
1698 JOHNSON Barbara A   Snopesism: A Study of the Snopeses in the Writings
     of William Faulkner   MA West Texas St Univ 1969   95 p
1699 JOHNSON James L   Among Her Cloudy Trophies: A Study of Feminine
     Archetypes in Faulkner's *The Hamlet*   MA Fresno St Coll 1969   42 p
1700 JOHNSON Marguerite   *As I Lay Dying*: Some Observations on Ambiguity,
     Reality and Form   MA Columbia Univ 1963   88 p
1701 JONES Elizabeth K   Faulkner's Construction of Four Snopes Characters
     MA Univ of Houston 1966   152 p
1702 JONES Mary J   Four Themes in Faulkner: The Land, the Design, the
     Past and the Negro   MA Univ of Houston 1964   132 p
1703 JUNKIN Lorraine S   William Faulkner's Use of Stream of Consciousness
     MA Shippensburg St Coll 1966
1704 KAIMOWITZ Benita R   The Crack in the Urn: A Study of Women in the
     Writings of William Faulkner   MA Sarah Lawrence Coll 1966
1705 KEYES Claire J   The Concept of Optimism and Its Development in the
     Novels of William Faulkner   MA Boston Coll 1964
1706 KNOX Nancy D   A Study of William Faulkner's Poor White Characters
     MA Oklahoma St Univ 1969
1707 KOMINARS Sheppard B   Encounter with Satan: A Study of Dostoyevski,
     Mann and Faulkner   MA Columbia 1959   124 p
1708 KOZLOSKI Danielle P   Camus' *L'Etranger* and Faulkner's *Light in August*:
     Parallels and Contrasts   MA Purdue Univ 1968   93 p

1709 KRUSE Harriet M  Some Aspects of Wit and Humor in William Faulkner's Fiction  MA Washington St Univ at Pullman 1958
1710 KURTZ Ralph F  William Faulkner and Ernest Hemingway Depict the "Lost Generation"  MA Indiana Univ of Pennsylvania 1966  75 p
1711 MISKIN Ruth  The Absurdity of Justice in Yoknapatawpha County, Mississippi  MA Wayne St Univ 1965
1712 MOFFETT Judith L  Blood and Doom in Faulkner  MA Colorado St Univ 1966
1713 MOORE Jeanette F  An Interpretation of the Theme of Snopesism in the Works of William Faulkner  MA North Texas St Univ 1964
1714 MORRIS H B  The Anticonventionalism of William Faulkner  MA Boston Univ 1941
1715 MORRISON Sr Mary K  Faulkner's Joe Christmas: Character Through Voice Structure  MA St Louis Univ 1960  87 p
1716 MOSELEY Francis S  The Statement of Time in William Faulkner  MA Long Island Univ 1968  88 p
1717 MULLADY Eileen T  The Problem of Unity in William Faulkner's *Go Down, Moses*: A Critical History  MA Univ of North Carolina at Chapel Hill 1968
1718 MURDOCK Marilan  The Individual and the Family: A Study of Conflict and Union in Selected Novels of William Faulkner  MA Columbia Univ 1965  115 p
1719 NAGY Carolyn E  The World of Nature in Some Typical Stories of William Faulkner  MA Columbia Univ 1955  93 p
1720 NELB Bob F  Obsessed Heroes in the Novels of William Faulkner  MA Texas Technological Univ 1967  73 p
1721 NESSELHOF John M  Negro in the Prose of William Faulkner  MA Univ of Kansas 1950
1722 NEWMAN Jules  The Religion of William Faulkner: An Inquiry into the Calvinist Mind  MA Columbia Univ 1953  130 p
1723 NICHOLAS Roberta J  Love and a Power Struggle in William Faulkner's *Wild Palms*  MA Univ of Maryland at College Park 1967  74 p
1724 NIGLIAZZO Marc A  The Indians in the Works of William Faulkner  MA Texas Arts and Industries Univ 1967  71 p
1725 O'BRIEN Matthew C  William Faulkner and the Civil War  MA Univ of Maryland at College Park 1968  103 p
1726 OLSEN Frederick B  Faulkner's Dramatic Psychology  MA Indiana Univ 1955
1727 ORAVETS Andrew J  The Misfortune of Time: Alienation in William Faulkner  MA Ohio St Univ 1966  80 p
1728 ORR Ellen E  Faulkner's Manipulation of Time as It Affects Selected Characters from Two Novels  MA Illinois St Univ at Normal 1969
1729 OVERTON Dave  The Role of V K Ratliff  BA Univ of British Columbia (Canada) 1964
1730 PAGE Ralph S  William Faulkner and the Grotesque  MA Univ of Houston 1963  138 p
1731 PARK William J  Harmony in Discord: A Study of Faulkner's *Light in August*  MA Columbia Univ 1954  114 p
1732 PARKER Margaret M  William Faulkner: Symbolic Prophet  MA Texas Christian Univ 1961  77 p
1733 PEARCE Jon R  The Double Vision of William Faulkner  MA Univ of Toronto (Canada) 1963
1734 LAMAR Lewis W  Faulkner's Use of Nature  MA Auburn Univ 1968
1735 LAN Rev Augustine P  William Faulkner: Criticism in Catholic Periodicals  MA John Carroll Univ 1964
1736 LANCEBY Jane K  Faulkner's Use of Myth in Three Novels: A Critique of the Criticism  MA Texas Technological Univ 1969  133 p
1737 LANSFORD Henry H  The Clash of Emotions: Irony in the Writings of William Faulkner  MA Univ of Southern Mississippi 1959
1738 LARKIN Brenda M  Negro Characters in Selected Novels of William Faulkner  MA Washington St Univ at Pullman 1965
1739 LARSEN Wendell W  The Christ Figure in *A Fable*  MA Washington St Univ

1740 LASSETER Victor K  Love and Money in William Faulkner's Snopes Trilogy at Pullman 1960  MA Florida St Univ 1963
1741 LAUTERMILCH Steven J  The Reality and the Dream: A Study in the Manner of William Faulkner  MA Ohio St Univ 1966  76 p
1742 LAWSON Deanna H  Faulkner's Women: 1929-1940  MA Middle Tennessee St Univ nd
1743 LEACH Frances H  A Statistical Analysis of Selected Factors of William Faulkner's Language Style in *The Sound and the Fury*  MA Indiana Univ of Pennsylvania 1964  80 p
1744 LEE B Y  The South in Faulkner's Novels: Myth and History  MA North Texas St Univ 1969
1745 LePARTE Patricia L  Definition of the Situation: Its Importance in Theme Development and Character Portrayal in Faulkner's *The Sound and the Fury* and *As I Lay Dying*  MA Univ of Rhode Island nd
1746 LEVINS Lynn G  The Four Narrative Perspectives in *Absalom, Absalom!*  MA Univ of North Carolina at Chapel Hill 1966
1747 LEWIS Margaret D  Racial Attitudes in Three Works by William Faulkner: *Go Down, Moses*, *Light in August* and *Absalom, Absalom!*  MA Temple Univ 1968  45 p
1748 LIGON Linda C  From Poetry to Prose: The Metamorphosis of Faulkner's Art  MA Oklahoma St Univ 1966
1749 LONG Pierre  Imagery in the Prologue of Faulkner's *Mosquitoes*  MA Univ of Illinois at Chicago Circle 1970
1750 LONGLEY John L  The Problem of Evil in Three Novels of William Faulkner  MA Univ of Tennessee 1949
1751 LORD Maryanne F  An Experiment in Linguistic Analysis of the Prose Style of William Faulkner  MA Univ of Houston 1965  107 p
1752 LOWDERBAUGH Thomas E  Thematic Unity in the Novels of the Snopes Trilogy  MA Univ of Maryland at College Park 1967  76 p
1753 LYON Ruth M  William Faulkner's Experiments with Point of View  MS Kansas St Coll at Pittsburg 1961
1754 McCORMICK Beverly H  The Comic Hero in the Fiction of William Faulkner  MA Univ of Maine 1969  105 p
1755 McFADDEN Nancy  Faulkner's Women in the Structure of His Yoknapatawpha World, 1929-1936  MA Univ of North Carolina at Raleigh 1959  74 p
1756 McHANEY Thomas L  The Image of the Railroad in the Novels of William Faulkner, 1926-1942  MA Univ of North Carolina at Chapel Hill 1963
1757 McNAMES Donna G  Functions of Gothicism in William Faulkner's Trilogy  MA Chico St Coll 1969  31 p
1758 MAGRUDER William T  Character Identities in William Faulkner's *A Fable*  MA Univ of Mississippi 1963  93 p
1759 MALUSKI Anne-Marie  *Requiem pour une Nonne* Adapte par Camus de *Requiem for a Nun* de W Faulkner  MA Columbia Univ 1963  60 p
1760 MAMOLI Rosella  William Faulkner as a Story Writer  MA Ca Foscari (Italy) 1964
1761 MANGANO Kathryn F  A Comparative Thematic Study in the Major Novels of Faulkner and Dostoevsky  MA Arizona St Univ 1966
1762 MARSHALL Jean S  Thematic Imagery in William Faulkner's *Absalom, Absalom!*  MA Brigham Young Univ 1969  50 p
1763 MATTHEWS Rex O  William Faulkner: A Study in Technique  MA Univ of Washington at Seattle 1948
1764 MAURER Barbara S  Thematic Development in the Works of William Faulkner  MA Univ of Louisville 1962
1765 MELROSE Mona M  An Encyclopedia of Characters in the Novels of William Faulkner  MA Univ of Hawaii 1955  100 p
1766 MELTABARGER Beverly A  Rules and Circumstances: The Young Protagonist and the Social Codes in Faulkner's Fiction  MA Univ of British Columbia (Canada) 1967

1767  MEYER Ruth A   Ethical Concepts in Faulkner's Negro Characters
      MA Mankato St Coll 1966   66 p
1768  MILLER Ruth Z   A Study of Genealogy in the Works of William Faulkner
      to Discover What Happened to the American Dream   MA George Washington
      Univ 1961   222 p
1769  MILLGATE Eunice J   Short Stories into Novels:  A Textual and Critical
      Study of Some Aspects of Faulkner's Literary Method   MA Leeds Univ
      (England) 1963
1770  PEDERSEN Penny   Thomas Sutpen in *Absalom, Absalom!*:  A Study of the
      Multiple Points of View   BA Univ of British Columbia (Canada) 1970
1771  PHILLIPS Ruth V   Humor in William Faulkner's Novels Based on the
      Yoknapatawpha Tradition   MA Univ of Wyoming 1965
1772  PILKINGTON James P   The Place of *Sanctuary* in Faulkner's Scheme of
      Novels   MA Vanderbilt Univ 1946
1773  POE Mary C   The Price of Cain:  A Study in the Use of Violence by
      William Faulkner   MA Brooklyn Coll of City Univ of New York 1967
      44 p
1774  POKE Jack O   A Comparative Examination of the Humor of William Faulkner
      and Mark Twain   MA Texas Arts and Industries Univ 1963
1775  POLLARD Rebecca A   The Negro as Victim in William Faulkner's Fiction
      MA Univ of Texas at Austin 1967   175 p
1776  PORTERFIELD Christopher   Faulkner's Snopes Trilogy:  A Study of
      *The Hamlet, The Town* and *The Mansion*   MA Columbia Univ 1965
1777  POSTON Thomas H   Structural Techniques and Patterns in William Faulkner's
      *The Sound and the Fury*   MA Univ of Maryland at College Park 1969
      146 p
1778  POXSON David M   The Critical Reception of William Faulkner in America
      MA Michigan St Univ 1948
1779  PYLAND J L   The Decay of the Yoknapatawpha Aristocracy in the Works
      of William Faulkner   MA North Texas St Univ 1962
1780  RAMSEY William C   A Critical Interpretation of William Faulkner's
      *The Unvanquished*   MA Univ of North Carolina at Chapel Hill 1967
1781  RANDALL Emma   Themes and Concepts in Selected Works of William Faulkner
      M Ed Henderson St Coll nd
1782  RASCO Kay F   The Yoknapatawpha Woman   MA Univ of Mississippi 1953   107 p
1783  RAU Suzanne G   "Snopesism" in Faulkner's Trilogy   MA Univ of Rhode
      Island 1966   88 p
1784  REIRDON Suzanne R   Caddy, the Tragic Figure in *The Sound and the Fury*
      MA Texas Christian Univ 1969   88 p
1785  RICHARDSON Mary S   Temporal Conflict and Spiritual Dilemma in Three
      Novels by William Faulkner   MA Univ of Houston 1959   81 p
1786  RICHEY Dauthor J   A Study of Sibling Relationships in Selected Writings
      of William Faulkner   MA Bowling Green St Univ 1965
1787  RIDLEY Norma   The Revisions of William Faulkner's *Go Down, Moses*
      MA Univ of Arkansas 1955
1788  ROBB Mary C   William Faulkner:  An Estimate of His Contribution to
      the Modern American Novel   MA Univ of Pittsburgh 1952
1789  ROBBIANO Hugo   A Comparison and Contrast of *The Sound and the Fury* and
      *Light in August*   MA Fairleigh Dickinson Univ 1969   108 p
1790  ROCCHIO Anthony M   Faulkner's Outrage   MA Univ of Rhode Island 1967   82 p
1791  RODNON Stewart   William Faulkner and the Negro   MA Brooklyn Coll of
      City Univ of New York 1952   72 p
1792  ROERECKE Howard H   William Faulkner's Jason Compson:  A Major Portrayal
      of Malice Without Motive   MA Columbia Univ 1958   62 p
1793  ROGERS Rebecca N   An Index and Concordance to the Characters of
      William Faulkner   MA Univ of Mississippi 1964   317 p
1794  ROTH Russell F   William Faulkner:  An Experiment in Existential Reading
      MA Univ of Minnesota 1948
1795  ROTHER Carole A   Motifs of Alienation in William Faulkner's *As I Lay
      Dying*   MA McGill Univ (Canada) 1965

1796 RUDNICK Lois P  The Grail and the Urn:  A Study of William Faulkner's Women Characters  MA Tufts Univ 1968
1797 RUFFIN Paul D  Faulkner's Dark Hero, Flem Snopes  MA Mississippi St Univ 1968  88 p
1798 SABEY F Peter  Faulkner and the Guilt of the South: A Study of the Individual Southern Conscience as It Is Seen in William Faulkner's Novels, 1929-1932  BA Amherst Coll 1956
1799 SAMPLE Dorothy J  The Wilderness Theme in *Go Down, Moses*  MA Louisiana St Univ 1966
1800 SAMPSELL Paul H  The Ambiguous Christ: The Development, Use and Meaning of the Christian Materials in the Fiction of Faulkner  MA Univ of Pittsburgh 1962
1801 SATHER Margareeta J  A Study of the Theme of Negro Endurance in the Writings of William Faulkner  MA Univ of Louisville 1966
1802 SCHMIDT Gerald L  William Faulkner's *The Hamlet*: A Study and Interpretation  MA Ohio St Univ 1967  67 p
1803 SCHWARTZ Elizabeth B  *Light in August*: The Individual in the Community  MA Carnegie-Mellon Univ 1966
1804 SEALE William A  The Journey as Technical Device in the Novels of William Faulkner  MA Texas Arts and Industries Univ 1965
1805 SEYMOUR Betty J  The Individual and the Problem of Self-definition on Faulkner: Isolation and Gesture in *Light in August, Absalom, Absalom!* and *As I Lay Dying*  MA Univ of Richmond 1967  109 p
1806 SHARP Etta R  Symbolism in Five Novels by William Faulkner  MA East Tennessee St Univ 1957
1807 SHELL Janet C  Classical Allusions in the Works of William Faulkner  MA Univ of Maryland at College Park 1968  74 p
1808 SHELTON Frank  Three Aspects of Blackness: Faulkner's *Sanctuary, Light in August, Absalom, Absalom!*  MA Columbia Univ 1963  96 p
1809 SHERMAN Edward F  The Southern Jurisprudence of William Faulkner  MA Univ of Texas at El Paso 1966  118 p
1810 SHUMAKER Harvey W  The Changing Appraisal of Faulkner's *The Sound and the Fury*  MA Kent St Univ 1964
1811 SILVERMAN Yvonne  The Hour Before the Dawn: A Study of William Faulkner's Treatment of the Negro  MA Columbia Univ 1954  121 p
1812 SIMMEN Edward R  *The Sound and the Fury* and *As I Lay Dying*: A Comparison  MA Univ of Texas at Austin 1959  71 p
1813 SIMONS Madeleine A  An Introduction to William Faulkner's Art  MA Miami Univ at Oxford 1947
1814 SIMPSON Hassell A  William Faulkner's Negroes: A Study in Changing Attitudes  MA Florida St Univ 1957
1815 SINCLAIR Geraldine  Faulkner's *Light in August*  BA Univ of British Columbia (Canada) 1968
1816 SLAUGHTER Catherine R  Some Aspects of Transcendentalism in William Faulkner's Story *The Bear*; *Death Comes for the Archbishop*, a Study in Style; a Comparison of "Lycidas" and "Thyrsis" in Terms of Dr Johnson's Criticism of "Lycidas"  MA Brigham Young Univ 1960  84 p
1817 SMITH Ann M  The Development of the Temple Drake Type of Heroine in the Fiction of Selected Southern Novelists of the Twentieth Century  MA Trinity Univ at San Antonio 1965
1818 SMITH Grace H  Faulkner's Flem Snopes in *The Hamlet*  MA Univ of Texas at Austin 1964  70 p
1819 SMITH James H  William Faulkner's *Sartoris* and Snopes: A Study in Tradition and Anti-tradition  MA Univ of Mississippi 1957  89 p
1820 SMITH Kearney I  The Function of Food and Shoe Imagery in Unifying *Light in August*  MA Univ of North Carolina at Chapel Hill 1968
1821 SMITH Mary E  Faulkner's Myth  MA Univ of Rhode Island 1957
1822 SMITH Paul  William Faulkner's *The Sound and the Fury*: An Explication

1823 and Evaluation  MA Univ of Rochester 1931  102 p
1823 SMITHERS Betty J  The Christ Figure in William Faulkner's Novels
      MA Univ of Idaho 1955
1824 SOLOMON Linda N  William Faulkner as an American Humorist  MA Columbia
      Univ 1965  70 p
1825 SPRINGER Cecil L  The Problem of Humanity in Faulkner's Yoknapatawpha
      Stories  MA Texas Technological Univ 1961  77 p
1826 STACK Mildred R  The Frontier Tradition in *The Hamlet* and Selected
      Stories by William Faulkner  MA Univ of Texas at Austin 1962  124 p
1827 STAHR Alden  Flem Snopes: The Epitome of Evil in Faulkner's Trilogy
      MA Lehigh Univ 1965
1828 STANLEY Don  Character and Value in William Faulkner's *Absalom, Absalom!*
      BA Univ of British Columbia (Canada) 1969
1829 STANTON Brian E  Theme, Characterization and Imagery in William Faulkner's *Light in August*  MA Brigham Young Univ 1966  81 p
1830 STEEGE Martin T  Battling the "Reducto Absurdum": Quentin Compson
      as a Hamlet Figure  MA Bowling Green St Univ 1967
1831 STEINBERG Ronnie A  Archetypal Symbols in William Faulkner's *Light in August*: The Adventure of the Hero  MA Univ of Miami 1966
1832 STEVENS Patsy A  The Tragic Lives of the Yoknapatawpha Women
      MA West Texas St Univ 1969  102 p
1833 STEVENS Sandra K  Structural and Thematic Aspects of Humor in
      Faulkner's Trilogy  MA Univ of Tennessee 1964
1834 STILLEY Hugh M  William Faulkner and George Washington Harris:
      Frontier Humor in the Snopes Trilogy  MA Univ of British Columbia
      (Canada) 1965  152 p
1835 STONEBACK Harry R  Faulkner's Use of Dialect  MA Univ of Hawaii 1966  40 p
1836 STUART Barbara F  Multiple Narration in William Faulkner's *The Sound and the Fury*  MS Illinois St Univ at Normal 1968
1837 STUTMAN Suzanne T  Faulkner's Woman: Promise and Peril  MA Temple
      Univ 1965  42 p
1838 TANNER Jimmie E  The Twentieth Century Impressionistic Novel: Conrad
      and Faulkner  MA Univ of Oklahoma 1964  216 p
1839 TERRY Eleanor F  Representative Children in William Faulkner's Fiction
      MA Mississippi Coll 1965
1840 THEEMLER Lyman W  Primitivism and Masculinity in the Works of
      William Faulkner  MA Univ of Pittsburgh 1960
1841 THETFORD James W Jr  William Faulkner: A Critical Estimate  MA Vanderbilt Univ 1935
1842 THOMAS Nell H  The Negroes in William Faulkner  MA Univ of Mississippi
      1952  118 p
1843 THOMPSON Evelyn J  Buffs, Clowns and Wits: Three Comic Types in
      Faulkner  MA Texas Technological Univ 1967  72 p
1844 TILLSON Minto L  The Unity of *Go Down, Moses*  MA Temple Univ 1965  80 p
1845 TODD June F  William Faulkner: The Yoknapatawpha Novels and the Nobel
      Prize Speech  MA Southern Illinois Univ at Carbondale 1954  119 p
1846 TOMARKEN Carol J  Tradition and the Process of Personal Identity in
      *The Bear*, *Light in August* and *Absalom, Absalom!*  MA Univ of
      Toronto (Canada) 1966
1847 TOMMY-MARTIN Yves  Searching for a Tradition: A Study of William Faulkner's *The Sound and the Fury* and *Absalom, Absalom!*  BA Amherst Coll
      1958
1848 TRAVIS Mildred K  Woman as Nature: Major Women in Faulkner's Novels
      MA Mississippi St Univ 1962  56 p
1849 TREMBLAY William A  William Faulkner's Myth of the South in the Snopes
      Trilogy  MA Clark Univ at Worcester 1969
1850 UZZELL Minter  William Faulkner: His Message and His Methods  MA Univ
      of Tulsa 1951
1851 VAUGHN Sue C  William Faulkner's Use of Judaic-Christian Tradition in
      Six Major Works  MA Eastern New Mexico Univ 1969

1852  VOGT Kathleen M  Toward a Definition of the Hero: A Study of Two Major Characters in the Work of William Faulkner  MA Bowling Green St Univ 1958
1853  VOTH Ruth A  William Faulkner and the Gothic Tradition  MA Univ of Maryland at College Park 1958  91 p
1854  VOYLES James R  Quest for Identity: A Study of the Adolescent Character in the Novels of William Faulkner  MA Univ of Louisville 1964
1855  WAGSTAFF Lyle  An Interpretation of William Faulkner  MA Univ of Utah 1940
1856  WALKER Martha W  An Annotated Bibliography of the William Faulkner Section of the Shaw Collection of Contemporary Authors in the University of Tulsa's McFarlin Library  MA Univ of Tulsa 1965  34 p
1857  WARDERS Donald F  Character Consciousness of God in Faulkner's Novels  MA Univ of Kansas 1964
1858  WATSON Arlene E  Yoknapatawpha Redmen: Faulkner's Indians  MA Purdue Univ 1965  96 p
1859  WATSON Betty L  A Study of Women Character Types in Novels of William Faulkner  MA Univ of Houston 1968  93 p
1860  WEBER Kenneth L  Aviation in the Fiction of William Faulkner  MA Ohio St Univ 1964  118 p
1861  WEBER Robert E  The Search for Identity in the Early Novels of William Faulkner  MA Syracuse Univ 1951  206 p
1862  WEBNER William T  An Analysis of Some Techniques of Characterization in the Novels of William Faulkner  MA Howard Univ 1964  108 p
1863  WELCH Josephine C  William Faulkner: His Relation to His Material  M Ed Henderson St Coll nd
1864  WHISENHUNT Della B  Negro-White Relations in the Fiction of William Faulkner  MA Univ of Oklahoma 1960
1865  WHITESIDE George A  A Study of William Faulkner's *A Fable*  MA Columbia Univ 1959  189 p
1866  WHITMORE Stephen C  Faulkner: Style and a Definition of Nature  BA Amherst Coll 1954
1867  WILCHER Olivia B  A Classification of William Faulkner's Negro Characters  MA Howard Univ 1963  96 p
1868  WILEY William J  William Faulkner's Yoknapatawpha Characters  MA Univ of Texas at Austin 1952  187 p
1869  WILLIAMS Kay  A Study of the Calvinist and New Humanist Philosophies as the Basis of Faulkner's *Light in August*  MA Univ of Mississippi 1967
1870  WILLIAMS Mary C  Faulkner's "Dead Humor"  MA Univ of Florida 1965
1871  WILLIAMS Mary M  The Critical Reputation of Faulkner's Novel *Sanctuary*  MA North Carolina Central Univ 1966  60 p
1872  WILLIS Virginia S  Man and the Machine in Four Faulkner Novels  MA East Tennessee St Univ 1968
1873  WILSON Charmayne  Theme and Technique in Faulkner's *The Sound and the Fury* and *Light in August*  MA Texas Technological Univ 1963  100 p
1874  WINKEL Carol A  The I-Thou Theme in Faulkner's Yoknapatawpha Chronicle  MA Texas Christian Univ 1965  123 p
1875  WITHERINGTON Paul  William Faulkner's *Light in August*: A Critical Analysis  MA Univ of Texas at Austin 1960
1876  WOLINSKI Mabel J  The Relationship of White and Negro Characters in the Works of William Faulkner and Ellen Glasgow  MA Florida St Univ 1960
1877  WOOD Dorothy F  A Study of William Faulkner's Use of the Negro as a Symbol  MA Chico St Coll 1955  49 p
1878  WOODWARD Charles L  The Spirit and the Letter of the Law in William Faulkner's Yoknapatawpha County  MA Municipal Univ of Omaha 1966
1879  WRIGHT Jerry T  Negro Dialect in Selected Novels of William Faulkner

```
         MA East Tennessee St Univ 1969
1880  WRIGHT Ray G  Humility and Pride:  Pharisaism in the Writings of
         William Faulkner  MA Univ of Houston 1967  80 p
1881  WYNN Leila D  The Decline of Faulkner's Art  MA Univ of Texas at
         Austin 1955  175 p
1882  YEARGIN Margaretta K  Violence in the Modern Novel as Shown in the
         Works of Faulkner, Caldwell, Steinbeck and Hemingway  M Ed Henderson
         St Coll nd
1883  YOUNG Ann M  William Faulkner's Sense of the Poetic  MA Clemson Univ 1968
1884  YOUNG Sau H  Cultural Tensions in William Faulkner and Hawaiian Myth
         MA Ohio St Univ 1953
1885  YOUNGBLOOD Sarah H  Decadence in the "Mythic" Novels of William Faulkner
         MA Univ of Oklahoma 1951
See also 198, 1541, 1542, 1543, 2646, 2745, 3003, 3426, 3562, 4029,
         4081, 5412, 5649, 6144, 6876, 6992
```

### EUGENE FIELD

```
1886  COLBERT Sr Mary T  A Critical Study of Eugene Field  MA St Louis Univ
         1935  72 p
1887  KIRKPATRICK Loucillah F  The Humor of Eugene Field  MA Univ of Tulsa
         1952  102 p
1888  NUSSBAUM Jean C  American Types and Themes in Eugene Field's Verse
         MA Univ of Texas at Austin 1939  67 p
1889  TAYLOR Pearl L  An Analytical Study of Eugene Field's Poetry Written
         About Children  MA George Peabody Coll for Teachers 1928
```

### DOROTHY CANFIELD FISHER

```
1890  ATWATER Inez Marion  The Realism of Dorothy Canfield Fisher  MA Boston
         Univ 1935
1891  CRAIG Marjory  Domestic Problems in the Novels of Dorothy Canfield
         MA George Peabody Coll for Teachers 1931
1892  MITCHELL Jacques A III  Dorothy Canfield Fisher: A Critical Analysis
         MA Florida St Univ 1963
1893  SCHLEY Jewell B  In Marble and Mud: A Biographical and Critical
         Study of Dorothy Canfield Fisher  MA Texas Arts and Industries Univ
         1943
1894  WILLIAMS Gladys V  Mrs Dorothy Canfield Fisher's Views on Society,
         Education and the Problems of Sane Living as Revealed in Her
         Writings  MA Univ of Kansas 1930
1895  WILSON D B  Parallelism Between the Philosophy of John Dewey and
         the Art of Dorothy Canfield  MA Boston Univ 1942
```

### VARDIS FISHER

```
1896  ALLEY Kenneth D  Vardis Fisher: The Vridar Hunter Tetralogy
         MA Southern Illinois Univ at Carbondale 1956  70 p
1897  HANKS Ida M  Antelope, Idaho, in the Novels of Vardis Fisher
         MA Univ of Idaho 1942
1898  HANSON Donna N  Vardis Fisher's Search for Truth  MA Mankato St Coll
         1969  87 p
1899  PARKINSON Linda F  Wider than Mormonism: Vardis Fisher's Prophets and
         His Vision of Man  MA Univ of Idaho 1965
```

### CLYDE FITCH

```
1900  BERNET A M  Clyde Fitch's Interpretation of Women Characters  MA Univ
         of South Dakota 1920
1901  FASH W G  The Life and Work of Clyde Fitch  MA Wesleyan Univ 1940
```

1902 JOHNSON Dean C  Realism in the Drama of Clyde Fitch  MA Univ of Kansas 1956
1903 NORSWORTHY Frances  Clyde Fitch's Treatment of Melodrama  MA Louisiana St Univ 1937
1904 PAYNE Ruth D  A Study of Clyde Fitch  MA Univ of Kansas 1917

## F SCOTT FITZGERALD

1905 ADAMS Theodore S  Structural Problems in Four Novels of F Scott Fitzgerald  MA Ohio St Univ 1948
1906 ADKINS Carl A  Toward a Dramatic Structure: The Evolution of F Scott Fitzgerald's Artistry in His Short Story Characterizations  MA Univ of Idaho 1964
1907 ALLMAN Margaret H  A Study of Technique in Five Short Stories by F Scott Fitzgerald: "May Day", "The Diamond as Big as the Ritz", "Absolution", "The Rich Boy" and "Babylon Revisited"  MA Univ of North Carolina at Chapel Hill 1959  87 p
1908 ARBO Evelyn A  A Study of the Treatment of Wealth in the Fiction of F Scott Fitzgerald and Edith Wharton  MA Univ of Maine 1955  95 p
1909 ARUTUNOFF Anatoly A  Trends in Character Description in the Short Stories of F Scott Fitzgerald  MA Univ of Tulsa 1961  83 p
1910 BAILEY Nancy I  Moral Values in the Novels of F Scott Fitzgerald  M Phil Univ of Toronto (Canada) 1966
1911 BALLMAN Patricia G  Zelda Sayre and the Heroines in the Major Novels of F Scott Fitzgerald  MA St Cloud St Coll 1969  88 p
1912 BARBOUR Brian H  The Critical Reputation of F Scott Fitzgerald, 1930-1951  MA Kent St Univ 1966
1913 BARTON J F  F Scott Fitzgerald: Interpreter of the Jazz Age  MA Univ of Texas at El Paso 1950  95 p
1914 BATTON Catherine  Symbolism and Imagery in *Tender is the Night*  BA Univ of British Columbia (Canada) 1961
1915 BENNETT Ellen E  Three Uncollected Works of F Scott Fitzgerald  MA Fresno St Coll 1965  66 p
1916 BERGQUIST Harold E  The Use of Narrator and the Point of View in the First Three Volumes of F Scott Fitzgerald's Short Stories  MA Columbia Univ 1953  115 p
1917 BODIN Miriam I  F Scott Fitzgerald and the American Dream of Success  MA St Univ of New York at Buffalo 1966
1918 BREMMER John F  The Function of the Women Characters in the Novels of F Scott Fitzgerald  MA Oklahoma St Univ 1967  96 p
1919 BROWN Paul A  A Study of the Women in the Novels of F Scott Fitzgerald  MA Arizona St Univ 1966
1920 BRYER Jackson R  The Critical Reputation of F Scott Fitzgerald, 1920-1960: An Annotated Bibliography  MA Columbia Univ 1960  313 p
1921 BURKS S L  Structural and Thematic Development in the Novels of F Scott Fitzgerald  MA North Texas St Univ 1948
1922 CALABIA Florentine  The Heroines of F Scott Fitzgerald and the Literature on Women and on Love  MA Columbia Univ 1963  118 p
1923 CARTER Julia L  An Analysis of the Influences on the Writings of F Scott Fitzgerald  MA Arkansas St Coll 1966
1924 COOK Jerome E  Attitudes Toward Wealth in the Works of F Scott Fitzgerald  MA Univ of Texas at Austin 1965
1925 COOPER Donald M  Geographical Themes in F Scott Fitzgerald  BA Amherst Coll 1968
1926 COX Sr Eva M  Overtones of Existentialism in the Novels of F Scott Fitzgerald  MA Gonzaga Univ at Spokane 1966
1927 DAMBRAUSKAS Cynthia K  F Scott Fitzgerald's Creation of Character: A Study of the Artistic Transformation of Biographical Experience into Fiction  MA Ball St Univ 1970
1928 DUMMITT Colleen M  Thought Structures in the Novelistic Art of

1929  F Scott Fitzgerald and Sinclair Lewis  MA Morehead St Univ 1969  203 p
1929  ELLINGER Ramona J  F Scott Fitzgerald's Dark Night: A Study of Fitzgerald's Short Fiction  MA Univ of Oklahoma 1966
1930  ELLIOTT Lorris T  The American Nightmare: A Study of F Scott Fitzgerald and James Baldwin  MA Univ of British Columbia (Canada) 1965
1931  ELSON Judith L  The Romantic Hero in F Scott Fitzgerald's *All the Sad Young Men*  MA Univ of North Carolina at Chapel Hill 1968
1932  EVANS Robert A  The Destructive Element and the Quest for Values in the Novels of F Scott Fitzgerald  MA Central Connecticut St Coll nd
1933  FACHILLA Louise A  The Development of the Narrator Device in Fitzgerald's Novels  MA Vanderbilt Univ 1904
1934  GRAY Richard S  Fitzgerald the Novelist: A Critical Study  BA Amherst Coll 1953
1935  GROSS Dalton  Recurrent Patterns in the Novels of F Scott Fitzgerald  MA Southern Illinois Univ at Carbondale 1961  50 p
1936  HABERSTROH Charles J Jr  The Failure of Love in the Major Novels of F Scott Fitzgerald  MA Villanova Univ 1965
1937  HAUENSTEIN Joyce A  F Scott Fitzgerald's Heroines: A Study of the "New" Woman and Her Destructive Influence  MA Bowling Green St Univ 1966
1938  HILDEBRAND Carol J  A Study of the Heroines in the Novels of F Scott Fitzgerald  MA Baylor Univ 1968  168 p
1939  HILL Hamlin L  The Social Testament of F Scott Fitzgerald  MA Univ of Texas 1954  158 p
1940  HOLLAND James E  The Idea of Honor in the Novels of Scott Fitzgerald  MA Univ of Texas at Austin 1966  97 p
1941  HOUGHTON Russell E  F Scott Fitzgerald as a Spokesman for the "Lost Generation"  MA Boston Univ 1946
1942  ISON David L  Chiaroscuro and Color Symbolism in the Novels and Selected Short Stories of F Scott Fitzgerald  MA Oklahoma St Univ 1966
1943  JENSEN Vernon H  The Romantic Eden: A Study of Felt Alienation in the Short Fiction of Scott Fitzgerald  MA Brigham Young Univ 1967  32 p
1944  JOHANNSEN Pauline R  Estrangement in the Twenties: An Application of Socio-psychological Categories of Alienation to F Scott Fitzgerald's *The Great Gatsby*  MA Northern Arizona Univ 1970
1945  JUSTICE Mary H  F Scott Fitzgerald's Characterization of Women  MA Univ of Southern Mississippi 1965
1946  KEETCH Brent  F Scott Fitzgerald's *The Great Gatsby* and the Great American Dream  MA Utah St Univ at Logan 1967
1947  KINNEY John C  The Variable Popularity of the Works of F Scott Fitzgerald  MA Univ of Arizona 1957  95 p
1948  KLUG Jack B  F Scott Fitzgerald's "Top Girl": A Study of His Women Characters in Three Major Novels  MA Texas Agricultural and Mechanical Univ 1965
1949  KRUSE Margaret A  F Scott Fitzgerald: Actor and Spectator  MA Hunter Coll 1959
1950  LACKEY June E  Historical Reality and Illusion in F Scott Fitzgerald's Fiction  MA Texas Technological Univ 1966  80 p
1951  LANDRUM Roger L  Imagery in F Scott Fitzgerald's *The Great Gatsby*  MA Bowling Green St Univ 1960
1952  LaPOTA Margherite E  The Use of Archetypes in the Short Stories of F Scott Fitzgerald  MA Univ of Tulsa 1965  74 p
1953  LERCH John H  Moral Significance in the Novels of F Scott Fitzgerald  MA Ohio St Univ 1950
1954  LORD Mary J  The First-rate Intelligence in F Scott Fitzgerald  MA Washington St Univ at Pullman 1967
1955  LOVE Alan C  Late Victorian Social Expression in the Novels of F Scott Fitzgerald  MA Texas Agricultural and Mechanical Univ 1966

83 p
1956 LUCHTEL Patricia M  F Scott Fitzgerald's *Tender is the Night*: A Discussion of the Development of the Novel and Its Alleged Credibility Gap  MA Univ of Louisville 1969  111 p
1957 McINERNEY Thomas J  Autobiographical Elements in the Works of F Scott Fitzgerald  MA Boston Coll 1948
1958 MIAZGA Ronald C  Views of Upper Class Americans by Fitzgerald, Santanyana and Marquand  MS Illinois St Univ at Normal 1967
1959 MILFORD Nancy  Zelda Fitzgerald: An Informal Study in Biography  MA Columbia Univ 1964  154 p
1960 MILLER Lawrence E  The Concept of Man in F Scott Fitzgerald's Novels  MA McMaster Univ (Canada) 1967
1961 MOONEY Henry F  Comments on Some Symbols in F Scott Fitzgerald's *The Great Gatsby*  MA Boston Coll 1964
1962 MOORE Joan S  F Scott Fitzgerald: Ironist  MA Univ of Houston 1962  81 p
1963 MORGAN Rita A  F Scott Fitzgerald's Novels: Their Catholic Elements  MA Univ of Maryland at College Park 1968  101 p
1964 NORTON Sarah B  The Jazz Age as Reflected in the Writing of F Scott Fitzgerald  MA Baylor Univ 1966  182 p
1965 PARNELL Helen A  F Scott Fitzgerald and Self-consistency  MA Univ of Oklahoma 1953
1966 PEROSA Sergio  The Art of F Scott Fitzgerald (Now Published by the Univ of Michigan Press in 1965, in the Italian Edition in 1961)  MA Ca Foscari (Italy) nd
1967 PERRY John D  The Sinister Side of Paradise: A Study of the Influence of Compton MacKenzie on F Scott Fitzgerald  MA Temple Univ 1963  66 p
1968 PFEIFFER John F  Fitzgerald and Glamor: An Interrelation of His Fact and Fiction  MA Duke Univ 1965
1969 PUZIO Elaine M  F Scott Fitzgerald: The Fated Prophet of "The Lost Generation"  MA Fairleigh Dickinson Univ 1969  137 p
1970 REIF Anthony  The Style of Scott Fitzgerald  BA Univ of British Columbia (Canada) 1965
1971 RIGGS Jerry A  Insanity in the Novels of F Scott Fitzgerald  MA Univ of Mississippi 1967
1972 ROBINSON Clayton R  The Development of Social Criticism in the Stories of F Scott Fitzgerald  MA Univ of Southern Mississippi 1960
1973 ROESSNER William P  Fitzgerald's Treatment of the Romantic Personality  MA Univ of Rochester 1951
1974 SCHROEDER Richard  Personalities and Personages: A Study of the Protagonists in F Scott Fitzgerald's Novels  MA Univ of New Mexico 1965
1975 SEYMOUR Elizabeth  An Analysis of Tragedy in F Scott Fitzgerald's Novels  MA Univ of Tulsa 1949
1976 SKEELS Ralph A  F Scott Fitzgerald: The Futility of Success  MA Univ of Idaho 1950
1977 SOLAND Carol  Fitzgerald's Women Characters  MA Tufts Univ 1965
1978 STALEY Thomas F  Fitzgerald's Five Heroes: A Study in Projection  MA Univ of Tulsa 1958  101 p
1979 STANTON Judith M  F Scott Fitzgerald: The Function of the Money Motif  MA Univ of Maine 1967  90 p
1980 STEEN James T  The Art of Scott Fitzgerald  MA Univ of Pittsburgh 1950
1981 STORM Donna O  The Feminine Mystique in F Scott Fitzgerald's Jazz Age  MA Univ of Wyoming 1966
1982 TAYLOR Frances F  The Fitzgerald Myth: A Study of Zelda Sayre Fitzgerald  MA Vanderbilt Univ 1964
1983 THOMPSON Kathleen A  The Comic Aspects of *The Great Gatsby*  MA Univ of Florida 1964
1984 UNTHANK Luisa T  F Scott Fitzgerald's Concept of the Rich  MA East

Carolina Univ 1965
1985 VIVERETTE Jacob A Jr  F Scott Fitzgerald's *Tender is the Night*: A Reexamination of the Novel with Emphasis Upon Its Viewpoint and Theme  MA Univ of North Carolina at Chapel Hill 1949  142 p
1986 WALFORD Thorp L  The Ambivalence of F Scott Fitzgerald  MA Univ of Louisville 1955
1987 WARREN Clifton L  F Scott Fitzgerald: His Materials and His Methods  MA Univ of Richmond 1954  97 p
1988 WHITTINGTON Joseph R  Fictional Form in Two Novels by F Scott Fitzgerald  MA Univ of Oklahoma nd
1989 WILLIAMS Thomas W Jr  The Last Extremity: F Scott Fitzgerald in Hollywood  MA Univ of Mississippi 1967
See also 168, 1159, 2820, 2928, 2967

## GEORGE FITZHUGH

1990 BALDWIN Mary F  The Social Theories of George Fitzhugh  MA Univ of Texas at Austin 1933
1991 BROOKS F J  George Fitzhugh: A Study in Antebellum Southern Thought  MA Univ of Chicago 1937

## JOHN GOULD FLETCHER

1992 FLETCHER Amine W  John Gould Fletcher: Imagist Poet  MA Columbia Univ 1920
1993 HAUN Frederic E  The Allusive Method of John Gould Fletcher: An Analysis  MA Vanderbilt Univ 1946
1994 McMARTIN Christina M  A Study of the Poetry of John Gould Fletcher  MA Occidental Coll 1945
1995 PIERCEY Mary A  John Gould Fletcher  MA Univ of Texas at Austin 1941
1996 YEN Barbara Y  The Oriental Background of John Gould Fletcher  MA Columbia Univ 1939

## STEPHEN C FOSTER

1997 CHISOLM Mary L  Stephen Collins Foster and His Songs  MA Univ of Kentucky 1936
1998 ETHERIDGE Jane  Stephen Foster and the American Folk Ballad  MA Southern Methodist Univ 1934
1999 WRIGHT Denton J  A Literary Study of the Content of Stephen C Foster's Songs  MA George Peabody Coll for Teachers 1927

## JOHN FOX Jr

2000 BRAME Walter H  The Life and Longer Stories of John Fox Jr  MA George Peabody Coll for Teachers 1933
2001 PAGE Ruth E  John Fox Jr and His Mountain Folk  MA Univ of Texas at Austin 1938
2002 SHEERAN Joseph A  John Fox Jr: A Critical Appreciation  MA Catholic Univ of America at Washington, D C 1939
2003 STOUT Glen W  A Critical Evaluation of the Fictional Works of John Fox Jr  MA Columbia Univ 1961  82 p

## WALDO FRANK

2004 COX Mary H  Waldo Frank's Treatment of Women  MA Univ of Louisville 1942
2005 SHARPE Mitchell R  The Novels of Waldo Frank: A Search for American Form  MA Auburn Univ 1954

## BENJAMIN FRANKLIN

2006 CARROLL R W  Benjamin Franklin: Colonial Agent to Great Britain, 1757-1762  MA Univ of North Carolina at Chapel Hill 1937
2007 FLAIG Neno N  A View of the Religious Beliefs of Benjamin Franklin  M Ed Henderson St Coll nd
2008 HEATER E Kathryn  The Thought Development of Benjamin Franklin Viewed Through His Biography and Works  MA Boston Univ 1931
2009 HOOVER Louise  The Composition and Interpretation of Selected Bagatelles by Benjamin Franklin  M Ed Henderson St Coll nd
2010 KENNEDY Robert V  A Brief Study of the Sayings of Poor Richard  MA George Peabody Coll for Teachers 1923
2011 OBER Ronald W  The Contribution of Benjamin Franklin to Religious Thought in America  MA Boston Univ 1948
2012 PAUL Clara G  Benjamin Franklin as an Essayist  MA Univ of Pittsburgh 1932
2013 RUFFING Anita L  The Backgrounds of Benjamin Franklin's Educational Theories  MA Ohio St Univ 1945

## HAROLD FREDERIC

2014 AMEND Alan E  Harold Frederic's *The Damnation of Theron Ware*: A Stylistic Analysis  MA Fresno St Coll 1963  67 p
2015 BUTCHER Lory A  Women as Types in Three Novels by Harold Frederic  MA Chico St Coll 1968  65 p
2016 COPELAND Marion W  The Treatment of Religious Denominations in the Novels of Harold Frederic  MA Syracuse Univ 1961  135 p
2017 DARNELL Donald G  The American Fiction of Harold Frederic: A Study of Its Development  MA Univ of Oklahoma 1961
2018 GEORGE Sharon K  Harold Frederic and the Question of Ethical Responsibility  MA Univ of Texas at Austin 1965
2019 GRAGG Perry E  Harold Frederic and the New Woman  MA Univ of Texas at Austin 1955  112 p
2020 PRICE Richard P  Harold Frederic and the Transition Between the Victorian and Modern Novel  MA Syracuse Univ 1956  72 p
2021 REDDERSON Theresa T  Harold Frederic's Short Fiction  MA Colorado St Univ 1969
2022 SMALL George A  The Novels of Harold Frederic  MA Univ of New Mexico 1952
2023 TEITZ Barbara A  Three Neglected Novels in American Literature by Joseph Kirkland, Harold Frederic and E W Howe  MA Columbia Univ 1954  67 p
2024 THOMAS Peggy  Harold Frederic: Writer and Viveur  MA Columbia Univ 1937
2025 VAN DER BEETS Richard  Harold Frederic's Contemporary Mohawk Valley Novels: A Social Indictment  MA Univ of Idaho 1963

## MARY E WILKINS FREEMAN

2026 BENNETT George N  A Critical Study of Mary Wilkins Freeman  MA Univ of Oklahoma 1948
2027 BILLINGS Constance  The New England Backgrounds in the Short Stories of Mary E Wilkins  MA Boston Univ 1930
2028 BOTTOMS Mollie R  Mrs Freeman's Characterizations of Women in One Hundred and Fifty Stories  MA George Peabody Coll for Teachers 1929
2029 CARLSON Mary J  Mary E Wilkins Freeman: Artist or Lady?  MA Univ of Vermont 1965  126 p
2030 FOYS Richard M  A Study of Image and Symbol in Selected Works of Mary E Wilkins Freeman  MA Bowling Green St Univ 1967
2031 GEARY Sr Mary  A Study of the Diction in Certain Stories by Mary Wilkins Freeman: A Contribution to the Historical Dictionary

of American English  MA Univ of Kansas 1932
2032 GLENN Clara M  Mary E Wilkins Freeman as an Interpreter of New England  MA Univ of Texas at Austin 1941  177 p
2033 GRAHAM Elta F  The Short Stories of Mary Wilkins Freeman  MA Louisiana St Univ 1944
2034 HALEY F R  Mary E Wilkins Freeman's Typical Heroines  MA Boston Univ 1939
2035 HANDLEY Ruth E  A Critical Evaluation of the Short Stories Written by Mary E Wilkins Freeman Before 1900  MA Auburn Univ 1957
2036 LAVI Gay E  The Changing American Scene: As Depicted by Mary E Wilkins Freeman, George Washington Cable and Bret Harte  MA Univ of Pittsburgh 1962
2037 LOGVIN Rayna  The Characterization of Women in the Short Stories of Mary Wilkins Freeman  MA Columbia Univ 1963  88 p
2038 LUNDQUIST Richard A  The Image of Declining New England in the Fiction of Mary Wilkins Freeman  MA Stanford Univ 1965
2039 ROSS Leah H  Mary E Wilkins Freeman's Short Stories of New England Villagers  MA Univ of Kansas 1957
See also 2592

## ALICE FRENCH

2040 MARTIN Theodore K  The Social Philosophy of Alice French  MA Louisiana St Univ 1941
2041 SCHMALENBECK Hildegard  A Study of the Literary Reputation of Alice French (1850-1934)  MA Univ of Texas at Austin 1946  208 p
2042 SEWELL Rebecca  Alice French: The "Octave Thanet" of Literature  MA Southern Methodist Univ 1934

## PHILIP FRENEAU

2043 BAKER Donald C  The Literary Theories of Philip Freneau  MA Univ of Mississippi 1950  157 p
2044 BRITTAIN Linda C  Philip Freneau's Speculations About Life and Death  MA Utah St Univ at Logan 1967  57 p
2045 COWIE Jane E  The Political and Social Satire of Philip Freneau from 1772-1815 with Special Reference to the Influence of the English Satirists of the Eighteenth Century upon His Writings  MA Univ of Rochester 1948  177 p
2046 GOOLD E H Jr  Philip Freneau's Humanitarian Interests  MA Univ of North Carolina at Chapel Hill 1941
2047 GOUCH Ruth L  Philip Freneau: Poetic Interpreter of the American Spirit of His Time  M Ed Henderson St Coll nd
2048 MARSH Philip M  The Familiar Essays of Philip Freneau  MA Univ of Maine 1931  158 p
2049 MOORE Penelope  A Comparison of Characteristic Elements in the Poetry and Prose of Philip Freneau  MA Univ of Mississippi 1960  120 p
2050 PARIS Matthew  Philip Freneau: The Search for Form  MA Brooklyn Coll of City Univ of New York 1967  46 p
2051 STRAIN Joseph H  Philip Freneau's Uncollected Robert Slender Letters  MA Boston Coll 1949
2052 WOOD Marion T  An Edition of the *Satires Against the Tories* by Hugh Henry Brackenridge, Philip Freneau and James Madison  MA Columbia 1961  72 p

## ROBERT FROST

2053 ABRONS Mary G  Through a Glass Darkly: Some Poetry of Robert Frost  MA Sarah Lawrence Coll 1966
2054 ADAMS Jane G  A Study of Treatments of the Book of Job by Robert Frost and Archibald MacLeish  MA Texas Christian Univ 1964  130 p

2055 ADAMS John F  The Estrangement of Man and Woman and Its Resolution in the Poetry of Robert Frost  MA Auburn Univ 1967
2056 ALDEN Edith C  An Estimation of Robert Frost  MA Boston Univ 1930
2057 ASHBY Anna L  Frost and Thoreau: Poets of One Persuasion  MA Univ of Texas at Austin 1965  64 p
2058 BACON Kenneth H  Sound is the Gold in the Ore: The Early Poetry of Robert Frost  BA Amherst Coll 1966
2059 BAILEY Light  A Study of Robert Frost: The Wise Countryman Commenting on Civilization  MA Univ of Houston 1964  105 p
2060 BEEDE M F  The Dramatic Elements in the New England Characterizations of Frost, Robinson and Amy Lowell  MA Ohio St Univ 1929
2061 BERTSCH Esther R  The Creative Process in Robert Frost: An Aid to Creative Expression  MA Ball St Univ 1951  85 p
2062 BISHOP Beth S  The Ideas in Robert Frost's Poetry: A Revaluation  MA Univ of Rochester 1950  80 p
2063 BLUM Alan M  "The Way of Understanding is Partly Mirth": A Critical Study of the Work of Robert Frost  BA Amherst Coll 1969
2064 BOSE Roberta H  The Pessimistic Side of Robert Frost  MA Oklahoma St Univ 1965  124 p
2065 BOTHWELL Etta K  The Range of Loneliness in the Poems of Robert Frost  MA Auburn Univ 1967
2066 BOURN Colin E  Robert Frost and Edward Thomas: Influence by Way of Encouragement  MA Univ of Massachusetts 1966
2067 BROOKS A F  Examples of Process in the Lyric Structure of Robert Frost  MA Wesleyan Univ 1967
2068 CANZONERI Robert W  Man's Relationship to Man, Nature and God in the Poetry of Robert Frost  MA Univ of Mississippi 1951  139 p
2069 CARVER Myrna G  Robert Frost: A Poet Both Provincial and Universal  MA Ft Hays Kansas St Coll 1942  176 p
2070 CAVANAGH Evelyn G  A Study of Robert Frost's Poetry  MA Univ of Tulsa 1947
2071 CLARK Jackie  Major Themes in Selected Works of Robert Frost  M Ed Henderson St Coll  nd
2072 COOK Larry W  Indirection and Meaning in the Poetry of Robert Frost  MA Texas Technological Univ 1958  74 p
2073 DANIEL McAfee  New England Reflected in the Poetry of Robert Frost  MA Baylor Univ 1960  140 p
2074 DEVAL Anne M  The Adjectives in Robert Frost's Poetry  MA Univ of Vermont 1959  68 p
2075 DJOS Matts G Jr  The Union of Opposites in the Poetry of Robert Frost  MA Univ of Idaho 1968
2076 DORN David A  Existential Attitudes in the Poetry of Robert Frost  MA Mankato St Coll 1966  54 p
2077 DREW Sandra H  The Dialectical Pattern in Robert Frost's Dramatic Narrative Poetry  MA Oklahoma St Univ 1963  124 p
2078 DUNKELBERG Dorothy S  A Paradox of Breadth: A Parallel Study of Robert Frost and Ernest Hemingway  MA Clemson Univ 1965
2079 DUNNING Sarah E  Robert Frost: A Portrait  MA Ohio St Univ 1939
2080 DYSINGER Helen H  Robert Frost: Parable of Love and Marriage  MA Univ of New Hampshire 1969  56 p
2081 EMBRY Cecelia W  The Ominous in Robert Frost  MA Univ of Texas at Austin 1965  84 p
2082 FAN Hao-ying  Lyrical and Dramatic Elements in the Early Poetry of Robert Frost  MA Mount Holyoke Coll 1965
2083 FELEY Ruth A  Robert Frost: The Man and His Works  MA Boston Univ 1935
2084 FINLEY John H  Robert Frost's Theory of Speech Tones  MA Washington St Univ at Pullman 1941
2085 FITZPATRICK Donald C  Robert Frost's Theory of Poetry  MA Temple Univ 1964  54 p
2086 FORD Mary A  The Metamorphosis of Robert Frost's Masks  MA Memphis

St Univ 1969
2087 FLYNN William J  Robert Frost: A Critical Study  MA Univ of New Mexico 1930
2088 GAGE Eleanor M  Significance of Nature and of Man to Robert Frost  MA St Univ of New York at Albany 1939
2089 GAHARAN Charles A  The Theme of Choice in the Poetry of Robert Frost  MA Louisiana Technological Univ 1969  46 p
2090 GARNER Cecilia T  Drama in Robert Frost's Poetry  MA North Carolina St Univ at Raleigh 1969  73 p
2091 GERBER Jack  Robert Frost's Uses of the Dramatic Monologue  MA Auburn Univ 1964  113 p
2092 GREEN Freida E  What the Critics Think About Robert Frost  M Ed Henderson St Coll nd
2093 HARVILL Laura O  Robert Frost and Existentialism  MA Lamar Technological Univ 1962  114 p
2094 HAYFORD James H  The Direction of Robert Frost: A Study in Cultural Orientation  MA Columbia Univ 1942
2095 HENN Shirley E  A Comparative Evaluation of the Robert Frost Materials in the Rare Book Room of the University of North Carolina Library  MA Univ of North Carolina at Chapel Hill 1965
2096 HERSCHAFT Patricia A  New England's Problem and Robert Frost's Solution  MA Boston Univ 1948
2097 HICKS Ruth S  A Way of Teaching Robert Frost's Poetry  MA Ohio St Univ 1961  122 p
2098 HOFFMAN Ruth O  Antitheses in Robert Frost's Poetry  MA Florida St Univ 1952
2099 HOLDEN Donald  The Dramatic Narratives of Robert Frost  MA Ohio St Univ 1952
2100 HORNBACK William B  The Bucolic Influence on the Poetry of Robert Frost  MA Univ of Kentucky 1950  87 p
2101 HOYT Irene S  The Evidence of the Dramatic in Robert Frost's Poetry  MA Brigham Young Univ 1963  113 p
2102 HUNT Harriett B  Robert Frost as Poet and Teacher  MS Illinois St Univ at Normal 1957
2103 HUNTINGTON S H  A Study of the Literary Relations of Robert Frost and Edward Thomas  MA Ohio St Univ 1938
2104 JACOBSON Harold A  A Study of Some Negative Criticisms of Robert Frost  MA Bowling Green St Univ 1954
2105 JENKINS Annibel  Symbols for Further Thought: A Study of the Figurative Language of Robert Frost  MA Baylor Univ 1943  203 p
2106 JOLLY Robert P  Robert Frost as a Dramatic Poet  MA Univ of North Carolina at Chapel Hill 1951  100 p
2107 JONES Ida D  Robert Frost: Poet of the Soil  M Ed Temple Univ 1933  237 p
2108 JUDD Dorothy W  A Study of Robert Frost as a Lyric Poet  MS Purdue Univ 1959  71 p
2109 KANE Sr Benigna  A Comparative Study of New England Character as Developed in the Poems of Robert Frost and E A Robinson  MA Boston Coll 1966
2110 KELFER Gail  The Sardonic in the Poetry of Robert Frost  M Ed Slippery Rock St Coll 1967  98 p
2111 KENNEDY Mary M  Barriers in the Poetry of Robert Frost  MA Emory Univ 1966
2112 KIDD Walter E  Robert Frost: Yankee Classicist  MA Univ of Oregon 1935
2113 KIMMELL E L  The Idea of God in Robert Frost's Poetry  MA Boston Univ 1938
2114 KIMMINS Pollyanna P  Restraint in the Works of Robert Frost  MA West Texas St Univ 1948  78 p
2115 KING Lenore F  Robert Frost and the New Humanism  MA Texas Arts and Industries Univ 1953

2116  KREISMAN Arthur  The Recent New England Pulitzer Prize Winners: Frost, Coffin, Hillyer  MA Boston Univ 1943
2117  KROPP Maura C  The Tragic Element in the Poetry of Robert Frost: A Critical Viewpoint  MA Univ of North Carolina at Chapel Hill 1965
2118  LABOON M  A Study of the Element of Terror in the Poetry of Robert Frost  MA Duquesne Univ 1965
2119  LAYTON Patricia  Performer and Poet: Robert Frost's Poetical Technique  MA Brigham Young Univ 1968  81 p
2120  LEONARD John M  Robert Frost: The Poetic Process  MA Univ of Wyoming 1965
2121  LIEBHAFSKY Hertha  Robert Frost and New England  MA Univ of Texas at Austin 1940  85 p
2122  LUKE Edith J  The Man-Nature Dialogue in the Poetry of Robert Frost  MA North Texas St Univ 1965
2123  LUNDEEN David F  The Critics, the Poetry and Robert Frost  BA Amherst Coll 1954
2124  LYON Anna M  Recurrent Themes in the Poetry of Robert Frost  MA Auburn Univ 1948  153 p
2125  McCAIN Carolyn  Robert Frost: Man on Quest  MA Univ of Texas at El Paso 1967  94 p
2126  McCALL Gloria M  Robert Frost as a Public Personality  MA Texas Christian Univ 1965  118 p
2127  MacVICAR Margaret B  The Human Element in Robert Frost  MA Boston Univ 1944
2128  MAHAR Anthony S  The Play-element in the Poems of Robert Frost  MA Univ of Massachusetts 1966
2129  MAHER Virginia M  Robert Frost: Poet Laureate of New England  MA St Louis Univ 1936  84 p
2130  MAHLA Dorothy K  Robert Frost's Contribution to the Dramatic Monologue Tradition  MA St Mary's Univ of San Antonio 1964  106 p
2131  MAUCH Russell C  A Study of Limitations of Robert Frost  MA Univ of Massachusetts 1968  86 p
2132  MOORE Stanley G  Robert Frost: The Negative Critical Response  MA Univ of North Carolina at Chapel Hill 1965
2133  MYERS N B  Human Relationships in the Poetry of Robert Frost  MA North Texas St Univ 1969
2134  NARDUCCI Patricia C  The House Metaphor in the Poetry of Robert Frost  MA Pennsylvania St Univ 1965
2135  NICHOLSON Lillian L  The Art of Robert Frost  MA Univ of Texas at Austin 1929
2136  NOACK R B  Robert Frost's Ethics: A Study of His Personal Beliefs as Revealed by His Poetry  MA Texas Technological Univ 1952
2137  NOBLE Lucille  The Dramatic Element in the Poetry of Robert Frost  MA St Louis Univ 1940  77 p
2138  NOLAN C E  Robert Frost: His Treatment of Nature and Humanity  MA Boston Univ 1942
2139  O'CONNOR M R  Robert Frost, New England Poet: A Study in Aesthetics  MA Boston Coll 1935
2140  OGILVIE J T  From Woods to Stars: A Study of the Poetry of Robert Frost  MA Wesleyan Univ 1953
2141  OHTA Kaoru  Textual Variations in Robert Frost's Poems  MA Univ of Massachusetts 1969  218 p
2142  PECKHAM Barbara A  "A Lantern Light from Deeper in the Barn": A Study of the Ideas, Deeds and Style of Robert Frost  MA Northeast Missouri St Coll 1964
2143  PENDERGRAF Rozzell C  A Study of the Imagery in the Poetry of Robert Frost  MA Univ of Tulsa 1956  145 p
2144  PENDERGRAFT Joyce H  The Adverse Criticism of the Poetry of Robert Frost  MA Univ of Tulsa 1965  82 p
2145  PENNINGTON Patricia G  Robert Frost: Synecdochist of Poetry

M Ed Henderson St Coll nd
2146 PICHETTE Kathryn H  Robert Frost's Theory of Poetry  MA Univ of Texas at El Paso 1959  85 p
2147 POWERS Margaret A  Quest for Meaning: A Study of Six Meditative Poems by Robert Frost  MA Univ of Massachusetts 1967
2148 RANNEY Z F  The Commonplace in Robert Frost's Poetry  MA Boston Univ 1938
2149 RAY Linda L  The White World of Robert Frost  MA Emory Univ 1966
2150 REESE Olyarie S  A Study of Techniques for Providing for Individual Differences in the Teaching of the Poetry of Robert Frost Through the Exploration of Sight, Sound and Feeling  M Ed Howard Payne Coll 1969  157 p
2151 RICHARDSON Anne  Distinctive Qualities of the Poetry of Robert Frost  MA Texas Arts and Industries Univ 1944
2152 RIEDER Judy E  Robert Frost's Theme of Isolation  MA Univ of Kansas 1964
2153 RILEY Mary E  Robert Frost: Cheerful Interpreter of New England  MA Univ of New Hampshire 1959  50 p
2154 RINDLAUB Katherine G  Robert Frost's Philosophy of Life  M Ed Temple Univ 1935  91 p
2155 SCHREIBER Ruth J  The Women in Robert Frost's Poetry  MA Univ of Mississippi 1952  97 p
2156 SCHROEDER Reinhard U  Robert Frost and Thomas Stearns Eliot: A Comparison  MA Univ of Texas at Austin 1966
2157 SHAW Myrtis  A Study of the Poems of Robert Frost  MA George Peabody Coll for Teachers 1932
2158 SHENNUM Marion  Nature's Creatures in Robert Frost's Poetry  MA West Texas St Univ 1963  109 p
2159 SHORT Gertrude M  Robert Frost's Place in Contemporary American Poetry  MA Boston Univ 1932
2160 SILBER Cornelius A  Landscape and the Poetry of Robert Frost  MA Univ of Toronto (Canada) 1965
2161 SIM Lee K  An Evaluation of the Poetry of Robert Frost  BA Acadia Univ (Canada) 1966
2162 SIMMS Kristina  Three Views of Man's Relation to Nature in Robert Frost's Poetry  MA Stephen F Austin St Univ 1966
2163 SIPPLES Harold J  Man and Nature in Robert Frost's Poetry  MA Univ of Rhode Island 1965  43 p
2164 STERNBERG Joseph  "Ten-step": Anti-beauty in the Poetry of Robert Frost  MA Univ of Massachusetts 1966
2165 STORMS Clifford B  The Tribute of the Current to the Source: A Critical Study of the Poetry of Robert Frost  BA Amherst Coll 1954
2166 TEMPLE Helen F  The Country Characters of Robert Frost  MA Boston Univ 1946
2167 THIBODEAU Mother Marie-Helena  Symbolism and Universality in Robert Frost's Dramatic Narrative Poetry  MA Boston Coll 1963
2168 THOMAS Paul J  Robert Frost and Personalism  MA Univ of Kansas 1962
2169 THOMPSON Margaret H  The Local and Universal Elements in the Poetry of Robert Frost  MA Boston Univ 1934
2170 THWEATT James K Jr  Robert Frost's Epistemology  MA Univ of Kansas 1963
2171 TSCHUMY Ruth D  The Astronomy Poems of Robert Frost  MA Univ of North Carolina at Chapel Hill 1968
2172 TUA Lynda M  The Hills of View: A Study of Robert Frost's View of Man's Relationship to Nature and Other Men  MA Fairleigh Dickinson Univ 1969  84 p
2173 VOGEL Nancy S  Robert Frost and Andrew Wyeth: Closeness to the Swaying Line  MA Univ of Kansas 1965
2174 WALL Linda F  The Snow Poetry of Robert Frost  MA Univ of Tennessee 1969  47 p
2175 WALSH John F  The Possibility of Ultimate Despair: A Study of the

Pessimism in the Poetry of Robert Frost  MA Univ of Massachusetts 1968  61 p
2176 WALZ Sr Vincent  The Doubleness of Nature in Robert Frost's Poetry and Paradox  MA St Louis Univ 1968  222 p
2177 WARNER Gertrude  The Metrics, Imagery and Philosophy of Robert Frost  MA Univ of New Mexico 1936
2178 WEINSAFT Malcolm H  Robert Frost and the World of Nature: An Ordering of the Poems  BA Amherst Coll 1959
2179 WELLS J I  Robert Frost: Poet of New England  MA North Texas St Univ 1941
2180 WEYNAND Isbella  Selected Phases of the Critical Interpretation of the Poetry of Robert Frost  MA St Mary's Univ of San Antonio 1939  72 p
2181 WHITE P F  Ambivalence in the Poetry of Robert Frost  MA North Texas St Univ 1967
2182 WYSS Hal H  Robert Frost: A Bleak, Darkly Realistic Poet  MA Ohio St Univ 1964  54 p
2183 ZAGRANSKI Richard A  Robert Frost's Imagery  MA Univ of Massachusetts 1969  86 p
See also 4314, 4325, 5236, 6650

## HENRY BLAKE FULLER

2184 HADAS David  Henry Blake Fuller: A Study of the Bachelor Dilettante in His Novels  MA Columbia Univ 1954  62 p
2185 HOMAN Nancy L  The Voracious Woman Theme in Selected Novels of Henry Blake Fuller  MA Bowling Green St Univ 1963
2186 LINDER Robert A  The Literary Career of Henry Blake Fuller  MA Univ of Mississippi 1962  151 p
2187 McGUIRE Linda S  A Thematic Study of the Novels of Henry Blake Fuller  MA Univ of Mississippi 1965  101 p
2188 MOYER Ray W  Fuller, Well Forgotten: A Study of the Chicago Novelist, Henry Blake Fuller  MA Fresno St Coll 1955  66 p

## MARGARET FULLER

2189 ACORD Joan P  Margaret Fuller's Views on Socialism  MA San Diego St Coll 1966  217 p
2190 ADAMS Mary S  Two Women Transcendentalists: Margaret Fuller and Elizabeth Palmer Peabody  MA Univ of Houston 1968  135 p
2191 COHEN Lauren W  Margaret Fuller: Nineteenth Century Romantic Heroine  MA Colorado St Univ 1968  121 p
2192 DWYER Sr M Timothee  Margaret Fuller: A Literary Critic  MA Boston Coll 1956
2193 FILLER Lorelle  Sarah Margaret Fuller Ossoli: An Interpretation in the Light of Contemporary and Subsequent Criticism  MA Univ of Tennessee 1943
2194 GROSBERG Charlotte R  Margaret Fuller: From Rebel to Revolutionary  MA Washington Univ at St Louis 1949
2195 HALL Clare J  Margaret Fuller's Connection with the Feminist Movement  MA Univ of Texas at Austin 1955  173 p
2196 HINKLE William C  Margaret Fuller as Exponent of Transcendental Thinking: A Study of Margaret Fuller's Religious and Philosophic Ideas  MS Auburn Univ 1951  78 p
2197 McKAY Mae B  Margaret Fuller (Ossoli): The Gnomon of *The Dial*  MA Ohio St Univ 1942
2198 MILLER Mary R  Margaret Fuller's Part in the Language Interests of American Transcendentalism  MA Univ of North Carolina at Raleigh 1946  84 p
2199 PALMER Sarah G  Margaret Fuller: Friend of Emerson  MA Auburn Univ 1943

2200 PAULIN Ruth N  Margaret Fuller: Literary Critic  MA Univ of Pittsburgh 1925
2201 PENTA Constance  Fuller's Folly: The Eccentric World of Margaret Fuller and the Greeleys  MA Columbia Univ 1960  196 p
2202 SCHOFIELD Joan B  Margaret Fuller: Studies in Her Life, Thought and Criticism  MA Boston Coll 1966
2203 SPROUSE Veda B  The Relationship Between Margaret Fuller and Nathaniel Hawthorne  MA Duke Univ 1965
2204 SUMMERS Hazel  Margaret Fuller: A Study of the Nature and Extent of Her Literary Contacts  MA Texas Christian Univ 1929  113 p
2205 TAYLOR Ruth M  A Chronological Outline of American Literature from 1607 to 1820  MA Univ of Maine 1934  96 p
2206 THURMAN Kelly  Margaret Fuller in Two American Novels: *The Blithedale Romance* and *Elsie Venner*  MA Univ of Kentucky 1945  63 p
2207 TULL Martha A  Contemporary Portraiture of Margaret Fuller  MA George Peabody Coll for Teachers 1929
2208 WEBB Marie A  Margaret Fuller: Feminist of the Nineteenth Century  MA Columbia Univ 1936
2209 WILSON Janice E  An Inquiry Into Selected Writings of Margaret Fuller as They Appeared in *The Dial* Magazine, 1840-1844  MA San Jose St Coll 1966
See also 2455, 2522

## LUCY FURMAN

2210 BROWNING Robert L  A Study of the Humor in the Early Works of Lucy Furman  MA Univ of Louisville 1961
2211 LANDRUM Louise M  A Study of Kentucky Mountain Dialect Based on Lucy Furman's *Quare Women*  MA Univ of Kentucky 1930
See also 6996

## HAMLIN GARLAND

2212 ARRIETA Mauro  Early Life and Art of Hamlin Garland, "First Farmer in American Fiction"  MA Univ of Texas at El Paso 1960  114 p
2213 BASKETT Donald L  Protest in the Middle-Border Short Stories of Hamlin Garland  MA Northeast Missouri St Teachers Coll 1965
2214 BLAIR John W  Garland's and Lewis' Treatment of the Prairie Town as a Phase of American Realism  MA Univ of South Dakota 1951
2215 BRACK P L  Realism in Hamlin Garland's Prose Fiction  MA North Texas St Univ 1950
2216 BULL C E  Hamlin Garland: A Son of the Middle Border  MA Boston Univ 1939
2217 BYNUM Lucy S  Hamlin Garland and the Arena  MA Univ of Texas at Austin 1940  77 p
2218 CRYMES Judith A  Farm Life in the Short Stories of Hamlin Garland  MA George Peabody Coll for Teachers 1931
2219 DOWDY Shirley  Hamlin Garland: The Wavering Realist  M Ed Henderson St Coll nd
2220 DUBARD Louise L  Hamlin Garland: Forerunner of American Literary Naturalism  MA Univ of Mississippi 1962  150 p
2221 DUFFY J B  Western Realism of Hamlin Garland  MA Boston Coll 1937
2222 EDWARDS Geraldine T  Hamlin Garland: Social Historian  M Ed Henderson St Coll nd
2223 FLINT Joyce M  What "Is" and "What Is to Be": A Study of Pioneer and Farm Women in Hamlin Garland's Books of the Middle Border  MA Washington St Univ at Pullman 1966
2224 FRANK William L  Hamlin Garland and the Theory of Veritism: A Study of the Literary and Social Ideas in His Short Stories, Novels and Social Essays  MA Univ of Southern Mississippi 1957

2225 HARVEY Josephine S  Hamlin Garland as a Reformer  MA Texas Arts and Industries Univ 1948
2226 HOLTKAMP Louise E  Hamlin Garland: A Critical Biography  MA Southern Methodist Univ 1929
2227 IRWIN Norma  Hamlin Garland: Perennial Pioneer  MA Univ of Florida nd
2228 KNUDSON Keith D  A Study of the Poetry of Hamlin Garland  MA Washington St Univ at Pullman 1957
2229 KOEHLER Thomas H Jr  Hamlin Garland: His Fiction and Criticism  MA Univ of Mississippi 1965  87 p
2230 LEE Jane E  Hamlin Garland and His Works on the Middle Border  MA Howard Univ 1951  141 p
2231 LIGHT Grace  Social Interest in the Prose Works of Hamlin Garland  MA Univ of Kansas 1919
2232 McCASLAND Louvenia J  A Study of Music as Used by Hamlin Garland  MA Texas Technological Univ 1969  90 p
2233 MILES Nellie  Treatment of Nature in the Fiction of Hamlin Garland  MA Univ of Iowa 1932
2234 PICKARD Fannie P  The Development of Hamlin Garland's Literary Purpose and Its Effect on His Technique  MA Univ of Iowa 1922
2235 PRESTON Donald E  The Development of Hamlin Garland's Theory of Realism  MA Univ of Iowa 1964
2236 ROSSI Dorothy D  A Critical Examination of the Short Stories of Hamlin Garland  MA Colorado St Univ 1968  77 p
2237 SANT Thomas A  Hamlin Garland: A Veritist of the Nineties  MA Univ of Idaho 1938
2238 SETTLE Elizabeth A  The Paradox of Garland's Escape from Reality: A Biographical and Critical Study of His Stories  MA Univ of Oklahoma 1944
2239 STAGGS Barbar M  The Women of Hamlin Garland's Collected Early Short Stories  MA Univ of Tulsa 1967  66 p
2240 STIENECKER Wertha  The Literary Theory and Practice of Hamlin Garland  MA Univ of Pittsburgh 1938
2241 SWANK Dorothy L  Literary Techniques of Hamlin Garland  MS Kansas St Coll at Pittsburg 1940
2242 TODD Daniel O  The Treatment of Nature in the American Novel  MA Univ of Iowa 1931
2243 TOMLINSON Bernice E  An Interpretation of the Personality of Hamlin Garland as Revealed by a Study of His Series of Chronicles: Some New Light on Hamlin Garland  MA Univ of Oklahoma 1945
2244 WEISS Miriam  Hamlin Garland's Lecture Tours: A Study of Their Context, Extent and Purpose  MA Memphis St Univ 1964
2245 WHIPPLE A A  Hamlin Garland's Ideas of Middle Age as Seen in the Characters of His Books  MA Univ of North Carolina at Chapel Hill 1945
2246 WIRTH Bernard  Nature in the Works of Hamlin Garland  MA Univ of Kansas 1925
See also 603, 3069, 3159, 6478

## ELLEN GLASGOW

2247 ASHLEY S B  An Evaluation of *The Sheltered Life* by Ellen Glasgow  MA Univ of Connecticut 1951
2248 ASPRAY Ruth M  Ellen Glasgow and the New South  MA Univ of Washington at Seattle 1927
2249 ATKINS Dorothy W  Ellen Glasgow: Novelist of Change  MA Ohio St Univ 1942
2250 BAXTER Clara M  The Southern Community in Ellen Glasgow's *In This Our Life*  M Ed Henderson St Coll nd
2251 BENHAM Oliver J  The Continuance of Romance in American Fiction  MA Central Washington St Coll 1969  76 p

2252 BLANCO Sr Margaret C  Ellen Glasgow: Her Contribution to the Novel of Manners  MA St John's Univ 1948
2253 BUNCOME Marie H  The Life and Works of Ellen Glasgow  MA Howard Univ 1952  128 p
2254 BURKETT Eva M  Virginia Life as Portrayed by Ellen Glasgow  MA George Peabody Coll for Teachers 1930
2255 BURNS James T Jr  Three Main Themes in the Works of Ellen Glasgow  MA Columbia Univ 1951
2256 BUSHMAN Claudia L  Old Values and New: The Heroines of Ellen Glasgow, Edith Wharton and Willa Cather  MA Brigham Young Univ 1963  62 p
2257 BUTTS Barbara  Ellen Glasgow and the New South  MA Univ of Mississippi 1941  236 p
2258 CANTRELL Francesca W  The Part That the Negro Played in the Novels of Ellen Glasgow  MA Univ of Florida 1951
2259 CARTER Alice B  The Repetitions in Ellen Glasgow's Novels  MA Univ of South Carolina 1933
2260 CHALK Nancy E  The Early Naturalism of Ellen Glasgow  MA Univ of Texas at Austin 1967  126 p
2261 CLEMENTS Margie P  Ellen Glasgow and the Victorian Morality in the South  MA William and Mary Coll 1930
2262 COLLIER Fay  Ellen Glasgow's Methods of Visualization in *Vein of Gold*  MA Sam Houston St Coll 1941
2263 COPELIN Pauline S  Symbolism in the Later Novels of Ellen Glasgow  MA Midwestern Univ 1953  135 p
2264 DANN Lois M  The Novels of Ellen Glasgow  MA Columbia Univ 1946
2265 DAVIS Mary L  Patterns and Changes in Family Life in Ellen Glasgow's Novels  MA Mississippi St Univ 1967  65 p
2266 DYKES Freydis T  The Moral Framework of the American Novel  MA Louisiana St Univ 1966
2267 EDWARDS Ava L  Women and Girls in Nine Recent Novels by Ellen Glasgow  MA George Peabody Coll for Teachers 1933
2268 FERGUSON Vivian L  Ellen Glasgow: Portrayer of the Changing Status of Women  MA Texas Arts and Industries Univ 1953
2269 FINNELL Flora  The Social Philosophy of Ellen Glasgow  BA Hunter Coll 1941
2270 FLOMERFELT Oriene  The Negro in the Novels of Ellen Glasgow  MA Univ of Missouri 1945
2271 GALLOWAY Nancy G  Ellen Glasgow and the New South  MA Univ of Oklahoma 1964
2272 GARRETT Catherine C  Ellen Glasgow's Virginia Dream  MA Longwood Coll 1968
2273 GARSON Helen  Local Color in the Work of Ellen Glasgow  MA Univ of Georgia 1947
2274 GILBORN Alice C  Ellen Glasgow: Between Two Worlds  MA Univ of Delaware 1968  93 p
2275 GLENDON Patricia E  An Analysis of the Three Important Themes in Seven of Ellen Glasgow's Novels  MA Univ of Rhode Island nd
2276 GOOD Ruth  The Southern Woman in Ellen Glasgow's Novels  MA Univ of North Carolina at Chapel Hill 1950  112 p
2277 GREGORY Laura B  Miss Glasgow and Social Readjustment  MA Univ of South Carolina 1932
2278 GUILMARTIN Alice J  Clarification of Ellen Glasgow's Perspectives  MA Boston Univ 1947
2279 HALL Henry M  The Novels of Ellen Glasgow: A History of Manners  MA Univ of Idaho 1950
2280 HARTMAN John L  Age and Change in Four Glasgow Novels  MA Mississippi St Univ 1959  72 p
2281 HARVEY Helen A  The Validity of the Depiction of the Depression in Ellen Glasgow's Novels  MA Indiana Univ of Pennsylvania 1965  112 p
2282 HARWOOD Mary L  A Study of Ellen Glasgow's Prose Style in Five

Selected Novels  MA Washington St Univ at Pullman 1958
2283 HAUSS Mary A  Virginia Life in the Novels of Ellen Glasgow  MA Duke Univ 1931
2284 HAVEL Lillian K  Political, Economic and Social Transition in Virginia Following the Civil War as Shown in Ellen Glasgow's Novels  MA Univ of Nebraska 1947
2285 HOLMES Agatha  An Analysis and Interpretation of Ellen Glasgow's *Barren Ground*  M Ed Henderson St Coll nd
2286 HOUGHTON Everett A  Ellen Glasgow as a Critical Historian of the South  MA Miami Univ at Oxford 1944
2287 JACOBS Pansy E  The Economic, Social and Religious Life of the People of Virginia as Seen in the Country Novels of Ellen Glasgow  MA Virginia St Coll 1953  71 p
2288 JOINER Sarah B  The Women Characters in Ellen Glasgow's Novels  MA Duke Univ 1941
2289 JOST Nancy R  Ellen Glasgow's Social Panorama of Virginia  MA Univ of Southern Mississippi 1953
2290 JULIAN Elizabeth A  The Tragedy of Everywoman, as It Was Lately Enacted in the Commonwealth of Virginia: A Study of the Feminine Characters in the Novels of Ellen Glasgow, Along with Biographical Considerations of the Richmond Lady  MA Univ of Mississippi 1962  318 p
2291 LEVY Amelia R  Ellen Glasgow's Lost Generations  MA Univ of Texas at El Paso 1956  141 p
2292 McCOLLUM Nancy M  Ellen Glasgow: Virginia Satirist  MA Univ of Georgia 1964
2293 McLENNAN Marie C  Ellen Glasgow's Theories of Fiction  MA Univ of Pittsburgh 1947
2294 MANTOR Ruth  Fortitude in Ellen Glasgow  MA Univ of Texas at Austin 1948  78 p
2295 MARIMON Rosa B  Some Distinguishing Characteristics of Ellen Glasgow's Novels  MA Univ of Utah 1937
2296 MITCHELL Mary E  Idealism and Realism in the Novels of Ellen Glasgow  MA Univ of Texas at El Paso 1964  82 p
2297 MOORE Clara W  Ellen Glasgow's Method of Characterization in *Barren Ground*  MA Sam Houston St Coll 1939
2298 MYER Elizabeth G  The Social Situation of Women in the Novels of Ellen Glasgow  MA Brown Univ 1947
2299 NORRED Barbara A  A Study of the Middle Class Character in the Novels of Ellen Glasgow  MA Univ of Mississippi 1958  118 p
2300 OAKS Mildred R  The Virginian Gentlewoman: A Study of Ellen Glasgow's Development in the Realistic Treatment of a Social Type  M Ed Temple Univ 1939  87 p
2301 OPPENHEIM Abe  Some Studies in Ellen Glasgow's Concept of Fortitude  MA Columbia Univ 1961  190 p
2302 PATTERSON Mary K  Ellen Glasgow: Social Historian  MA Wofford Coll 1939
2303 PHELPS Sylvia E  The Novels of Ellen Glasgow  BA Univ of Delaware 1940  66 p
2304 PORTER Dorothy  Description in Ellen Glasgow's Novels  MA Univ of Nebraska 1925
2305 PORTER Maud D  Lack of Dramatic Art in Ellen Glasgow's Novels  MA Univ of Nebraska 1927
2306 RAITT Mildred D  Ellen Glasgow and Her Virginia Tradition  MA Columbia Univ 1955  46 p
2307 RAMPEY Wesley L  Ellen Glasgow and the Virginia Tradition  MA Univ of Oklahoma 1962
2308 RAMSEY Edna J  Social Concepts of Ellen Glasgow as Shown in the Treatment of Characters  MA Univ of Oklahoma 1942
2309 RAYBURN Harriet S  The Cultural Relations of the South as Discussed in the Novels of Ellen Glasgow  MA Whittier Coll nd

2310 REEVES Ruth "Father, I Have Written a Book": A Study of Characterization in Ellen Glasgow's Novels  MA Univ of Houston 1948  88 p
2311 REIMERS Frances D  Character as Grace in the Novels of Ellen Glasgow: A Legacy  MA Univ of Rhode Island 1968  175 p
2312 RIKER Joyce R  The Major Women Characters in Ellen Glasgow's Novels: The Southern Belle and the "New Woman"  MA Univ of Houston 1968  127 p
2313 RINGHEIM Barbara J  Ellen Glasgow's Interpretation of Human Action and Ethics as Reflected in Her Novels and Essays  MA Stanford Univ 1948
2314 ROGERS Margaret A  Negroes in the Novels of Ellen Glasgow  MA George Washington Univ 1955  201 p
2315 ROSENTHAL Yvette C  Ellen Glasgow as a Realist  MA Univ of Texas at Austin 1936
2316 SCHOPPE Jean L  Ellen Glasgow the Novelist  MA Univ of Vermont 1939  134 p
2317 SIMPSON Rosa G  Feminism in the Novels of Ellen Glasgow  MA Univ of Maine 1957  174 p
2318 SMART Catherine  Ellen Glasgow's Interpretation of the South  MA Univ of North Carolina at Chapel Hill 1948
2319 STALNAKER Susan L  Major Male Characters in the Novels of Ellen Glasgow  MA West Virginia Univ 1969  68 p
2320 STEVENS Lucile  Miss Glasgow's Treatment of Virginia Scenes and People  MA Univ of Kansas 1933
2321 WAGNER Charlotte A  Two Frontiers: A Study in the Major Novels of Ellen Glasgow and Willa Cather  MA Columbia Univ 1953  90 p
2322 WALDEN Mary  Ellen Glasgow and Social Democracy  MA Texas Arts and Industries Univ 1943
2323 WETMORE A B  The "Vein of Iron" in Ellen Glasgow  MA Boston Univ 1940
2324 WHITE I R  Ellen Glasgow: Virginia Rebel  MA North Texas St Univ 1956
2325 WILKINS Ruth J  Ellen Glasgow's Virginia: The Background of Her Novels  MA Univ of Richmond 1951  90 p
2326 WOODHAM Louise K  Ellen Glasgow: A Portrayer of the Southern People  MA Birmingham-Southern Coll 1936
2327 WORLEY Harriet C  Ellen Glasgow: Author or Character? The Autobiographical Element in Miss Glasgow's Later Novels  MA Univ of Tennessee 1965
2328 WORLEY Veronica  Parallels in Ellen Glasgow's Portrayals of Women  MA Northeast Louisiana Univ 1966  77 p
See also 435, 514, 531, 552, 1876, 4340, 4709, 4710, 6415, 6986, 6988, 6996, 6999

## CAROLINE GORDON

2329 GRIFFIS Marcia W  The Sense of Order in Caroline Gordon's Early Novels  MA Mississippi St Univ 1967  79 p
2330 RAWLINGS Margaret G  Caroline Gordon's Theory and Use of Point of View  MA Univ of North Carolina at Chapel Hill 1964
2331 WISE Kenneth K  The Art of Caroline Gordon and the Religious Theme in Her Novels  MA Columbia Univ 1960  161 p

## HORACE GREELEY

2332 BONNER Thomas N  Horace Greeley and Secession, 1860-1861  MA Univ of Rochester 1948  112 p
2333 MICHAEL Cecelia K  Horace Greeley and Fourierism in the United States  MA Univ of Rochester 1949  150 p
See also 2205

## JULIAN GREEN

2334 COLLINS Margaret J  The American Heritage of Julian Green  MA Ohio St

       Univ 1958
2335   DISMUKES Jaqueline H   La Psychologie de Julian Green a Travers Sa Vie
       Et Son Oeuvre   MA Univ of Mississippi 1950   101 p
2336   GRANT R L   The Gothic Element in Julian Green   MA Boston Coll 1959
2337   SHERIFF Donald L   Darkness and Night in the Novels of Julian Green
       MA Kansas St Teachers Coll 1966
See also 2679

## PAUL GREEN

2338   ANDERSON Ruth W   Paul Green: A Study of His Life, His Writings
       and His Portrayal of the Negro   MA Birmingham-Southern Coll 1937
2339   ASHLEY Oscar R   The Negro Characters in the Plays of Paul Green
       MA George Peabody Coll for Teachers 1942
2340   COE Berenice   Paul Green: The American Dramatist   MA Southern
       Methodist Univ 1944
2341   COX Louise H   Paul Green's Negro Folk Plays: A Criticism   MA Univ
       of Texas at Austin 1949   123 p
2342   CREIGHTON Ruth   Paul Green and His Drama   MA Univ of South Carolina
       1929
2343   DEVIN Philip L   Form and Structure in Paul Green's Tragedies
       MA Indiana Univ 1967
2344   DIXON Bessie L   The Negro Character in American Drama (Paul Green,
       Joel Chandler Harris, DuBose Heyward, Irwin Russell)   MA Howard
       Univ 1936
2345   JUST Ethel H   Negro American Folk-plays of Paul Green with Special
       Reference to Their Sociological Value   MA Boston Univ 1936
2346   KAVANAUGH John M   A Study of Paul Green's Negro Plays   MA Louisiana
       St Univ 1937
2347   KEATON Eloise R   Religious Themes in Modern Drama (1890-1940)
       MA Univ of Tennessee 1946
2348   LINNEY Daniel A   Social Problems in the Plays of Paul Green   MA Univ
       of North Carolina at Chapel Hill 1964
2349   LOCKHART Malcolm W   The Negro in American Drama (Paul Green,
       DuBose Heyward, Georgia Douglas Johnson, Willis Richardson)
       MA Louisiana St Univ 1932
2350   MEREDITH Claire   The Decline of the Southern Aristocratic Tradition
       in American Drama: Paul Green, Lillian Hellman, Tennessee Williams,
       and Joshua Logan   MA Columbia Univ 1962   117 p
2351   MIDDLETON F S   Paul Green's South: A Land of Contrasts   MA North
       Texas St Univ 1955
2352   PAINE John R   The Plays of Paul Green   MA Occidental Coll 1938
2353   POWER Helen L   The Development of the Folk Drama in North Carolina
       with Special Reference to the Plays of Paul Green   MA Univ of
       Southern California 1945
2354   PRITCHARD Arthur S   Paul Green's Early Plays on Negro Life   MA Texas
       Christian Univ 1966   112 p
2355   REDD LaVerne M   The Plays of Paul Green: A Study of Technique
       MA Fisk Univ 1936
2356   ROURKE Margaret E   Paul Green: Folkwriter   MA Univ of Illinois at
       Urbana 1934
See also 6986, 6996

## LOUISE IMOGEN GUINEY

2357   KEATING Sr Mary A   Militancy of L I Guiney   MA Boston Coll 1939
2358   QUIGLEY Mary E   Louise I Guiney: The Craft of Poetry   MA Boston Coll
       1943
2359   RUHL Urvan E   Louise Imogen Guiney   MA Columbia Univ 1942

2360  WALSH Sr M James   The Lyric Affinities of Louise Imogen Guiney
        MA Boston Coll 1946
2361  WENNERBERG Sr Tia A   Louise Imogen Guiney   MA Boston Coll 1935
See also 4239

## CORRA HARRIS

2362  BLACKSTOCK Walter Jr   Corra Harris: An Analytical Study of Her Novels
        MA Vanderbilt Univ 1944
2363  JOHNSON A W   A Critical Biography of Corra Harris   MA Univ of North
        Carolina at Chapel Hill 1940
2364  REEVES Ruby C   Corra Harris: Her Life and Works   MA Univ of Georgia
        1937
See also 6996

## GEORGE WASHINGTON HARRIS

2365  BLACK William P   Sut Lovingood as Seen by George Washington Harris
        MA Duke Univ 1966
2366  BOYKIN Carol   A Study of the Phonology, Morphology and Vocabulary
        of George Washington Harris' Sut Lovingood Yarns   MA Univ of
        Tennessee 1966
2367  GENTRY Robert B   The Animal Motif in the Sut Lovingood Yarns
        MA Univ of Tennessee 1966
2368  HEFLIN John J Jr   George Washington Harris' Sut Lovingood: A Bio-
        graphical and Critical Study   MA Vanderbilt Univ 1934
2369  LATTA Charles M   Reason in Fooldom: George Washington Harris'
        Sut Lovingood   MA Univ of Louisville 1967   182 p
2370  STEWART James E   George Washington Harris: A Critical Study
        MS Kansas St Coll at Pittsburg 1963
See also 1834, 6016

## JOEL CHANDLER HARRIS

2371  BARNES Madeleine T   Joel Chandler Harris' *Nights with Uncle Remus*:
        The Question of Origin   MA Univ of Kansas 1965
2372  DANCE Willis L   Georgia Life in the Stories of Joel Chandler Harris
        MA Duke Univ 1933
2373  ELLISON Rhoda C   Joel Chandler Harris   MA Columbia Univ 1929
2374  FISHER Alice M   Studies in Uncle Remus   MA Colorado Coll 1933
2375  GREEN Sue B   A Bibliography of Joel Chandler Harris   MA Emory Univ
        1939   43 p
2376  HENDERSON Mary M   Folklore in the Uncle Remus Stories   MA Univ of
        South Carolina 1932
2377  HODGE Llewellyn B   A Descriptive and Critical Analysis of *Uncle Remus'
        Magazine*   MA Univ of Georgia 1948
2378  JOHNSON Charles W   An Annotated Check List of Joel Chandler Harris
        Manuscripts in the Memorial Collection of the Emory University
        Library   MA Emory Univ 1934   156 p
2379  KELLY Kathleen E   The Uncle Remus Stories: A Portrayal of the
        Plantation Negro   M Ed Duke Univ 1946
2380  LAVIN Elizabeth I   A Survey of Early and Later Critical Opinion of
        the Work of Joel Chandler Harris   MA St John's Univ 1940
2381  McKNEELY Lewis M   An Analysis of the Local Color Elements in the
        Novels of Joel Chandler Harris   MA Emory Univ 1943   134 p
2382  McLEOD Agnes A   Joel Chandler Harris   MA Columbia Univ 1914
2383  NOLL Irene   The Types of Poor Whites in the Stories of Joel Chandler
        Harris   MA Univ of Kansas 1934
2384  NORWOOD Lila R   A Literary History of Joel Chandler Harris' "Uncle
        Remus"   MA Univ of Texas at Austin 1944   133 p
2385  ROBERTS Evangeline   Joel Chandler Harris and the Georgia Group of

Writers  BA Univ of Oklahoma 1919
2386 STEVENS Annie W  An Inquiry into the Sources of the Beast Tales of Joel Chandler Harris  MA Columbia Univ 1921
2387 STROTHER Louise M  Joel Chandler Harris  MA Univ of Georgia 1936
2388 TAYLOR Celia B  Cherokee and Creek Folklore Elements in the Uncle Remus Stories: A Comparison of the Tales by Joel Chandler Harris and Legends of the Southeast  MA Auburn Univ 1959
2389 TAYLOR Sr Marie C  The Development of the Literary Personality and the Inspiration of the Work of Joel Chandler Harris  MA Villanova Univ 1945
2390 TUBB Hilda  Characteristics of Negroes and Animals in the Uncle Remus Stories  MA George Peabody Coll for Teachers 1925
2391 UNDERWOOD Josephine K  Joel Chandler Harris' Portrayal of Negro Life After the War  MA George Peabody Coll for Teachers 1931
2392 WALTON David A  A Study of Compensation in *Uncle Remus: His Songs and Sayings*  MA Bowling Green St Univ 1966
2393 WASHBURN B E  The Uncle Remus Stories  MA Univ of North Carolina at Chapel Hill 1909
2394 WHITTEN Nannie M  A Study of the Fiction of Joel Chandler Harris  MA Univ of Mississippi 1959  138 p
2395 WILLIAMSON May  Joel Chandler Harris  MA Oglethorpe Univ 1937
See also 2344, 3562, 4704

## BRET HARTE

2396 AX Gladys  The Later Bret Harte  MS Univ of Toledo 1958
2397 BEEDE Lillian E  The Relation of Bret Harte to the Short Story  MA Univ of California at Berkeley 1917
2398 BEKUS Albert J  Bret Harte and the Southwest Humorists  MA Auburn Univ 1966
2399 BRANLETTE Gloria  Bret Harte's Literary Reputation in American and British Periodicals, 1868-1902  MA Univ of Texas at Austin 1946  112 p
2400 CARLTON Golda  Bret Harte: Portrayer of the Forty-niner  MA Florida St Univ 1951
2401 CRANE C L Jr  The Decline in the Literary Reputation of Bret Harte  MA Univ of North Carolina at Chapel Hill 1939
2402 DILDY Ora  The Relationship of Character and Setting in Bret Harte's "Local Color"  M Ed Henderson St Coll nd
2403 DOTTS Grace B  Bret Harte's Indebtedness to Charles Dickens  MA Univ of California at Berkeley 1917
2404 DUCKETT Margaret  A Study of Racial Intolerance as a Phase of Social Criticism in the Writings of Bret Harte  MA Univ of North Carolina at Chapel Hill 1941
2405 EYRING Rose  A Study of the Criticism and Literary Reputation of Bret Harte  MA Columbia Univ 1937
2406 FOLEY Sr Gilmary  Bret Harte: A Study of His Literary Career  MA Siena Hts Coll 1955  55 p
2407 FRANCIS Nola B  A Critical Analysis of Selected Works of Bret Harte  M Ed Henderson St Coll nd
2408 GEEHERN Richard J  Bret Harte's "Other California": A Study of His Knowledge and Use of Spanish-Californian Material  MA Univ of North Carolina at Chapel Hill 1949  123 p
2409 GOOLD Martha L  The Literary and Personal Relationships of Bret Harte and Mark Twain  MA Univ of North Carolina at Raleigh 1948  85 p
2410 HARPER Bena H  The Humor of Bret Harte  MS Kansas St Coll at Pittsburg 1964
2411 HOLMES Dolores E  The Relation of Five of Bret Harte's Better Known Short Stories to the Actual Facts of California Life  MA Univ of Idaho 1935
2412 JACKSON Joyce W  Bret Harte and the Short Story  MA George Peabody

Coll for Teachers 1928
2413 LEAHY Anna C  The Spanish-Californian in the Short Stories of Bret Harte  MA George Peabody Coll for Teachers 1931
2414 LEHAM Anthony  The Technique of Contrast in "The Luck of Roaring Camp"  MA Claremont Graduate School 1965
2415 MACK Garnett L  Bret Harte as Literary Artist  MA George Washington Univ 1966  123 p
2416 MacPHERSON Dorothy B  The Technique in the Stories of Bret Harte  M of Letters Univ of California at Berkeley 1911
2417 MOORE Joseph A  Realism in Bret Harte  MA Boston Univ 1934
2418 PODOLYN Joseph C  Local Color in the Short Story with Special Reference to Francis Bret Harte  M Ed Temple Univ 1926  88 p
2419 RESNICK Robert B  Life on the Frontier as Seen in the Early Sketches and Tales of Bret Harte  MA Boston Univ 1948
2420 SHOOK Bessie L  The Mind of Bret Harte  MA Univ of Texas at Austin 1919
2421 SPANGLER Lazelle  The Short Story in the Far West from the Time of Bret Harte to the Present  MA Univ of Oklahoma 1931
2422 THROCKMORTON Jean L  A Study of Bret Harte's Condensed Novels  MA Univ of Kansas 1942
2423 WEBB Mary H  Western Humor in Bret Harte  MA Baylor Univ 1950  130 p
2424 WILKINS Lily W  Local Color and Spanish Loan Words in the Works of Bret Harte  MA Texas Technological Univ 1934
2425 WOODS Hernando J Jr  A Bret Harte Lexicon  MA Univ of Florida 1953
See also 2036, 2721, 6074

## NATHANIEL HAWTHORNE

2426 ADAMS Linda  Half-told Tales About Nathaniel Hawthorne  MA Univ of Oklahoma 1964
2427 ALFF Joyce M  Hawthorne's Use of the Legend of the Wandering Jew  MA Univ of Houston 1968  114 p
2428 ALLEN Charles W  Hawthorne: Skeptic  MA Univ of Louisville 1962
2429 ALLEN Frederick C  Hawthorne's Puritanism and Transcendentalism Modified by His Central Human Interest  MA Boston Univ 1934
2430 ANDERSON Judith A  Hawthorne's Use of Experience in *The Blithedale Romance*  MA Texas Agricultural and Mechanical Univ 1967  132 p
2431 ASSAD Thomas J  Hawthorne's *Marble Faun* and Catholicism  MA Boston Coll 1953
2432 ASTOR Saul D  Hawthorne's Treatment of Children  MA Columbia Univ 1950
2433 AUSTIN Allan D  Echoes and Parallels in Reviews of Hawthorne, 1837-1850: A Testing of Melville's Claim to Originality in "Hawthorne and His Mosses"  MA Univ of Massachusetts 1967  125 p
2434 AUSTIN Lettie J  Puritanism in the Works of Nathaniel Hawthorne  MS Kansas St Coll at Pittsburg 1947
2435 AUVENSHINE Anna B  A Critical Analysis of Hawthorne's *The Marble Faun*  MA Baylor Univ 1968  112 p
2436 BATTISTEL M L  Puritanism and Romanticism in Nathaniel Hawthorne's Work  MA Ca Foscari (Italy) 1941
2437 BEAMER George C  Hawthorne's Use of Contrast; Charles Kingsley's Christian Democracy  MA Univ of Texas at Austin 1968  53 p
2438 BEANE Margaret A  The Sin of Pride and the Tragedy of the Human Soul: Dominant Forces in Hawthorne's Conception of Evil  MA Univ of Colorado 1966
2439 BECKER John E  The Moral Meaning of *The Scarlet Letter*  MA St Louis Univ 1958  129 p
2440 BEGGS J K  The Problem of the Artist in Society: Hawthorne, James and Hemingway  MA North Texas St Univ 1960
2441 BEHLER Violet E  Pride and Penalty in Hawthorne's Tales  MA Butler Univ 1960
2442 BIGNELL Dorothea  The Gothic Element in Hawthorne  MA Univ of Iowa 1934

2443 BIRDSONG Theda P  Witchcraft and Supernaturalism in the Works of Nathaniel Hawthorne  MA Northeast Louisiana Univ 1965  99 p
2444 BIRNEY Gaylord A  The Conflict Between Moral and Aesthetic Commitment in *The Marble Faun* and in the *Notebooks* of Nathaniel Hawthorne  MA Ohio St Univ 1962  44 p
2445 BLOOD Diana B  The Use of Allegory by John Bunyan and Nathaniel Hawthorne  MA Tufts Univ 1960
2446 BOARDMAN Edward J  Isolation in Some of Hawthorne's Tales and Stories  MA Columbia Univ 1967  71 p
2447 BOOTH Ida L  *The Scarlet Letter*: A Study of Sin and Its Atonement  MA Univ of Kansas 1914
2448 BORSOTTI Catherine  Hawthorne's Ambivalent Reaction to Catholicism  MA Hunter Coll 1966
2449 BORZA Anne M  Three Studies in English: Henryson's *Fables*; Swift and Pope; and Hawthorne's Roger Malvin  MA Pennsylvania St Univ 1966
2450 BOYD Joann  A Comparison of the Symbolism in Hawthorne's *The Scarlet Letter* and Crane's *Red Badge of Courage*  MA East Tennessee St Univ 1959
2451 BRAMLETTE William H  Hawthorne's Religious Ideals  MA Indiana Univ 1950
2452 BRANDLY Thelma O  The Influence of Hawthorne's Ancestry, Family Relationships, Friends and Environment on His Writings  MA Oklahoma St Univ 1955  66 p
2453 BRANNEN Ann C  Hawthorne's Use of Contemporary Life in His Shorter Narratives  MA Univ of Texas at Austin 1942  145 p
2454 BREITENBERG Katherine  The Moral Conservation of Nathaniel Hawthorne  M Ed Henderson St Coll nd
2455 BREWINGTON Patsy D  Hawthorne and Margaret Fuller: A Study in Literary and Personal Relationships  MA North Carolina Central Univ 1955  75 p
2456 BRYAN Louis H  Hawthorne's *Man of Science*  MA Texas Technological Univ 1970  58 p
2457 BURGIN Cornelia A  The Critical Reputation of Nathaniel Hawthorne's *The Scarlet Letter*  MA Texas Christian Univ 1966  147 p
2458 BURNS Elinor M  Did Transcendentalism Influence the Fiction of Nathaniel Hawthorne?  MA Boston Univ 1929
2459 CARDEN Geraldine J  Bibliography of the Criticism of *The Scarlet Letter*, 1946-1966  MA Univ of Tennessee 1970  99 p
2460 CAREY N B  A Study of the Problem of Evil in Hawthorne's Major Novels  MA Wesleyan Univ 1950
2461 CARIOU Paul L  That Democrat: Hawthorne  MA Univ of Maine 1969  121 p
2462 CARR Jerry G  Hawthorne's Uses of Colonial History  MA Mississippi St Univ 1963  62 p
2463 CAVANAUGH Dorothea E  The "Spotless Maiden": A Type Character in the Fiction of Nathaniel Hawthorne  MA Univ of Rhode Island 1967
2464 CHILDERS Dwight M  The Humanization Theme in the Published Fiction of Nathaniel Hawthorne  MA Univ of North Carolina at Chapel Hill 1967
2465 CHURCHILL Dorothy O  Hawthorne's Dark Women  MA Purdue Univ 1966  55 p
2466 CHURCHILL Jerry H  The Thematic Significance of Falsehood in *The Scarlet Letter*  MA Univ of Iowa 1965
2467 CLAYTON L R  Hawthorne's Romantic Transmutation of Colonial and Revolutionary War History  MA North Texas St Univ 1969
2468 COBB Elinor N  The Sources and Originals of Some of Hawthorne's Female Characters  MA Columbia Univ 1935
2469 COHEN Benjamin B  "Eternal Truth": A Study of Nathaniel Hawthorne's Philosophy  MA Indiana Univ 1950
2470 COHEN Herbert J  The Man of Religion in the Fiction of Nathaniel Hawthorne  MA Hunter Coll 1967
2471 COLVILLE Derek K  Hawthorne's Use of Historical and Legendary Sources as Shown by Certain Tales and Novels Based on Such Sources

MA Washington Univ at St Louis 1952
2472 COOK Frances K  Hawthorne's Women  MA Mississippi St Univ 1967  58 p
2473 COOKE Alice L  A Study of the Sources of Hawthorne's Shorter Narratives  MA Univ of Texas at Austin 1923
2474 COSBY Mabel A  Hawthorne's Comments on His Contemporaries  MA George Peabody Coll for Teachers 1937
2475 COX David K  Romance Techniques of Characterization in *The House of the Seven Gables*  MA Univ of North Carolina at Chapel Hill 1967
2476 CRAIG Vetres K  Symbolism in the Fiction of Nathaniel Hawthorne  MA Texas Arts and Industries Univ 1945
2477 CRAIN Cordelia D  A Study of Motive and Character in the Romances of Nathaniel Hawthorne  MA Univ of California at Berkeley 1919
2478 CRAWFORD Roselle W  A Study of Aspects of the American Character as Revealed by Nathaniel Hawthorne and Mark Twain  MA East Texas St Univ 1954
2479 CRONMILLER Lance G  Architecture in Nineteenth Century American Prose, the Concord Group: Hawthorne, Emerson and Thoreau  MS Temple Univ 1966  110 p
2480 CROSS Alice F  Hawthorne's Conception of Sin in Relation to Characterization in His Novels  MA Univ of Oklahoma 1941
2481 CROWLEY Suzanne M  The Question of the Hawthorne Influence in the Early Tales of Henry James, 1864-1875  MA Ohio St Univ 1968  132 p
2482 DAVIES Harold L  Hawthorne: The Artist in the Novel  MA Colgate Univ 1965
2483 DAVIS Marilyn D  Side-scenes Into Hawthorne's Artistry: His Use of Children in Tales and Sketches  MA Lehigh Univ 1966
2484 DAVLIN Jean L  The Role of Women in Hawthorne's Life and Writings  MA Texas Christian Univ 1965  99 p
2485 DECKER Joseph P  Outcasts in the Universe: A Study of the Scientists in Hawthorne's Short Stories  MA Texas Agricultural and Mechanical Univ 1963  57 p
2486 DELVENTAL Linda M  The Interpolated Tales in Hawthorne's Novels  MA Columbia Univ 1961  91 p
2487 DICKERSON Maurine  Hawthorne and the Emancipation of Women  MA Oklahoma St Univ 1951  123 p
2488 DIXON Betty L  Love and Isolation in Hawthorne's Fiction  MA Butler Univ 1962
2489 DOUGLAS Harold J  Hawthorne and Maturin: A Study in Parallels  MA Univ of Tennessee 1951  66 p
2490 DUKE Pauline R  Gothic Elements in Four Novels of Nathaniel Hawthorne  MA Univ of Tulsa 1967  68 p
2491 DULOCK Jerre A  Hawthorne's Symbolism in Seven Stories in *Mosses from an Old Manse*  MA Texas Woman's Univ 1966
2492 DUNCAN Effie L  An Historical and Critical Study of Hawthorne's *The House of the Seven Gables*  MA Univ of Texas at Austin 1950  183 p
2493 DUNCAN June A  Ritual and Archetype in the Work of Nathaniel Hawthorne  MA Univ of Oklahoma 1962
2494 DUNSON D C  Hawthorne's Philosophy of Art  MA North Texas St Univ 1967
2495 EASTMAN June  Comic Stereotypes in the Tales of Nathaniel Hawthorne  MA Ball St Univ 1960  87 p
2496 ELAM Julia C  Symbolism in the Works of Nathaniel Hawthorne  MA Virginia St Coll 1964
2497 ELENBURG Mary J  A Critical Analysis of the Background and Content of *The Blithedale Romance*  MA Univ of Texas at Austin 1965  82 p
2498 ELKINS Lucy E  Three of Hawthorne's Heroines Discussed as Tragic Figures  MA Columbia Univ 1952  63 p
2499 ELLSWORTH Mary E  Studies in Simplicity: The Blonde Maiden in the Works of Nathaniel Hawthorne  MA Columbia Univ 1963  147 p
2500 EMMANUEL Carol  Attitudes Toward Guilt in Selected Works of Hawthorne

and Dostoevsky  MA Bowling Green St Univ 1963
2501 ENGEL Frances H  A Basis in Fact in Hawthorne's *The Blithedale Romance*  MA Auburn Univ 1944
2502 ESTES E D Jr  Characterization of Women in the Fiction of Nathaniel Hawthorne  MA North Texas St Univ 1956
2503 EVANS Margaret  Hawthorne: A Study of the American Notebooks as a Source of His Romances and Tales  MA Univ of Kansas 1929
2504 EVRARD Isabel  Nathaniel Hawthorne's Use of Folklore  MA St Louis Univ 1936  63 p
2505 FERGUSON Joyce B  An Examination of Nathaniel Hawthorne's Treatment of Nineteenth Century Intellectual Ideas in Three Romances: *The Scarlet Letter, The House of the Seven Gables, The Blithedale Romance*  MA Wittenburg Univ 1969  130 p
2506 FERRELL Margaret J  Dissolving the Gross Actuality of the Fact: Hawthorne's Attack on Matter  MA Univ of Oklahoma 1967  194 p
2507 FERRELL Margaret J  Hawthorne's Use of Four Myths  Ba Univ of Oklahoma 1963
2508 FOSTER Emily E  The Puritan Spirit and the American Revolution: Hawthorne Versus Bancroft  MA Ohio St Univ 1969  50 p
2509 FRANZ Doris C  Relationship of the Social Life of Hawthorne's Novels to That of His Times  MA Baylor Univ 1955  178 p
2510 GEORGE Edythe  The Characterization of Women in Hawthorne's Fiction  MA Howard Univ 1963  125 p
2511 GEYER Charles W  Hawthorne, Allegorist and Artist: The Use of Idea as Technique in *The Scarlet Letter*  MA Auburn Univ 1960
2512 GOLDSMITH O K  Hawthorne's Use of Symbolism in Four Romances  MA North Texas St Univ 1943
2513 GOODRICH Ruth  A Comparative Study of the Narrative Art of Nathaniel Hawthorne and Robert Louis Stevenson  MA Univ of California at Berkeley 1921
2514 GOODRICH Vera L  A Critical Analysis of Puritanism in the Works of Nathaniel Hawthorne  M Ed Temple Univ 1936  94 p
2515 GOULD Arthur J  Hawthorne and the Problem of Evil  MA Columbia Univ 1937
2516 GOULD Warren  Nathaniel Hawthorne, Franklin Pierce and the Presidential Election of 1852  MA George Washington Univ 1955  68 p
2517 GRAVES Martha M  The Characters in the Stories of Nathaniel Hawthorne  MA George Peabody Coll for Teachers 1933
2518 GRAY Alma A  Recent Criticism of Hawthorne's American Novels  MA St Mary's Univ of San Antonio 1949  80 p
2519 GREEK Betty L  A Study of Hawthorne's Sentence Structure  MA Ohio St Univ 1945
2520 GRUENERT Charles F  Hawthorne's Views on the Fine Arts  MA Indiana Univ 1940
2521 GURIAN Jay P  The Language Pattern of *The Blithedale Romance*  MA Univ of Hawaii 1958  66 p
2522 GUSHEE Anne E  Nathaniel Hawthorne and Margaret Fuller  MA Columbia Univ 1955  72 p
2523 GUSTAFSON Sandra  The Dark and Fair Ladies in the Novels of Nathaniel Hawthorne  MA Univ of Kansas 1965
2524 HACKETT Barbara B  Hawthorne's Treatment of Nature  MA Mississippi St Univ 1964  73 p
2525 HAIGHT Helen R  Hawthorne's Multiple Choice in Symbolism  MA Univ of New Mexico 1947
2526 HALL Blaine H  Hawthorne's Comic Vision: The Smile Behind a Black Veil  MA Brigham Young Univ 1965  106 p
2527 HALLACY Anita R  The Concept of Sin in the Works of Nathaniel Hawthorne  MA Brooklyn Coll of City Univ of New York 1950  59 p
2528 HAMMILL Mildred A  Nathaniel Hawthorne's Attitudes Toward Organized Christianity  MA Baylor Univ 1969  104 p

2529  HANBY Mary L  Hawthorne and His Friends  MA Univ of Pittsburgh 1934
2530  HANLEY Joseph L  Light Out of Darkness: The Felix Culpa in the Works of Nathaniel Hawthorne  MA Temple Univ 1963  86 p
2531  HARDIN James B  The Power and Illusion of Place: Setting and Point of View in Hawthorne's Novels  MA Syracuse Univ 1968  106 p
2532  HARKEY Alice P  Supernaturalism in the Works of Nathaniel Hawthorne  MA Univ of Arizona 1940
2533  HARKINS Mary E  Hawthorne's Use of American Backgrounds in His Novels  MA Univ of Texas at Austin 1941  107 p
2534  HARMON A O  Hawthorne's Reading  MA Univ of North Carolina at Chapel Hill 1925
2535  HARPER Sandra M  A Study of "The Old Manse" as a Framework for a Collection of Short Stories  MA Ohio St Univ 1965  66 p
2536  HARRELL R C  Medieval Echoes in Hawthorne  MA Univ of North Carolina at Chapel Hill 1924
2537  HARRINGTON Richard B  Hawthorne's Heroines  MA Univ of Texas at Austin 1954  97 p
2538  HARRIS Frederick C  The Development of the Artist in the Tales of Nathaniel Hawthorne  MA Pennsylvania St Univ 1966
2539  HARRIS John B  Elements of Puritanism in Nathaniel Hawthorne  MA Brigham Young Univ 1956  94 p
2540  HARRISON William D  Nathaniel Hawthorne as a Critic of Literature  MA Univ of Iowa 1921
2541  HART Beryl G  The Short Story as Written by Hawthorne  MA Univ of Iowa 1913
2542  HAWKINS Jane  An Analysis of the Social Assumptions Underlying Hawthorne's Fiction  MA Ohio St Univ 1936
2543  HAWTHORNE Manning  The Youth of Hawthorne  MA Univ of North Carolina at Chapel Hill 1937
2544  HEFFERNAN Gerald D  Sin and Retribution in Nathaniel Hawthorne's *The Scarlet Letter*  MA Niagara Univ 1965
2545  HEITZMAN Mary B  Hawthorne's Use of Sin in *The Scarlet Letter*  MA Moorhead St Coll 1966
2546  HELGESON Carol M  Isolation in the Life and Writings of Nathaniel Hawthorne  MA Washington St Univ at Pullman 1948
2547  HIGGINBOTHAM Lynn A  Hawthorne's Use of Folklore in Selected Novels and Tales  MA West Virginia Univ 1968  60 p
2548  HILL Douglas B Jr  A Study of the Observer in the Writings of Nathaniel Hawthorne  MA Columbia Univ 1963  111 p
2549  HOLE Lucy E  Hawthorne's Humor  MA Univ of Oklahoma 1947
2550  HOLLOWAY Glenna  Hawthorne's Treatment of the Problem of Sin  MA Univ of Texas at Austin 1936
2551  HOPKINS Annie P  A Dictionary of the Characters Found in the Romances and Tales of Nathaniel Hawthorne  MA Univ of Kansas 1916
2552  HOPTIAK Elaine  A Study of Nathaniel Hawthorne's "Young Goodman Brown"  MA Univ of North Carolina at Chapel Hill 1967
2553  HOWARD Anne B  Hawthorne's Magnetic Chain: The Achievement of Humanity  MA Univ of New Mexico 1966
2554  HOWARD Lucinda L  A Study of the Criticism of *The House of Seven Gables*  MA Univ of Tulsa 1969  52 p
2555  HOWZE Louie J  Hawthorne's Use of His English Notebooks  MA North Texas St Univ 1965
2556  IRBY Laurens H  Hawthorne's Use of Calvinism as a Literary Device  MA Clemson Univ 1969
2557  JOHN Finnie E  Hawthorne and His Wife: A Bibliographical Study  MA Univ of Maryland at College Park 1969  96 p
2558  JOHNSON Bobbie S  A Study of the Motivation for Arthur Dimmesdale's Confession in *The Scarlet Letter*  MA Univ of Mississippi 1966
2559  JOHNSON Johnile  Symbolic Gesture in Nathaniel Hawthorne's Life  MA Northeast Louisiana Univ 1964  126 p

2560  JOHNSON Lyndon E  An Analysis of Four Short Stories by Hawthorne  MA Mankato St Coll 1967  72 p
2561  JOHNSON Mary G  Hawthorne:  The Welcome Intruder  MA Texas Technological Univ 1966  73 p
2562  JOHNSON Wendell S  Hawthorne and *The Pilgrim's Progress*  MA Ohio St Univ 1949
2563  JOHNSTON Wilma M  Hawthorne's Use of History  MA Louisiana St Univ 1939
2564  JONES Bayard H  Hawthorne and German Romance:  Hawthorne's Artistic Relationship to Hoffman, Tieck and Musaus; Based on a Comparison of Volksmarchen and Kunstmarchen  M of Letters Univ of California at Berkeley 1912
2565  JONES Jennie M  Recurrent Themes in Hawthorne  MA Louisiana St Univ 1939
2566  JONES M M  Symbolic Narrative of Hawthorne and Elinor Wylie  MA Boston Univ 1938
2567  JONES Phyllis J  Nathaniel Hawthorne:  An Early Psychologist  M Ed Henderson St Coll nd
2568  JONES Tandy  Nathaniel Hawthorne, Mark Twain and Carl Sandburg as Writers for Children  MA Duke Univ 1957
2569  JORDAN William D  Hawthorne and New England Transcendentalism  MA Univ of Texas at Austin 1952  276 p
2570  JULIAN Hilda  Significant Ideas in Hawthorne's Stories  MS Kansas St Coll at Pittsburg 1943
2571  KANNENBERG Bettie A  Hawthorne's Use of the Bible in Five of His Novels  MA Univ of Texas at Austin 1949  111 p
2572  KARTIGANER Donald M  The Isolation of Nathaniel Hawthorne  MA Columbia Univ 1960  100 p
2573  KAWAKUBO Keisuke  Physical Appearance in Hawthorne's Fiction  MA Duke Univ 1966
2574  KEANE John C  *Fanshawe*:  A Study of Hawthorne's First Novel  MA Butler Univ 1959
2575  KEEFE Sr Bernadette M  Nathaniel Hawthorne:  A Balanced Christian View of Man  MA Boston Coll 1965
2576  KELIHER Agathe M  Ambiguity as a Literary Device in Hawthorne's Tales  MA Columbia Univ 1964  98 p
2577  KELLET Jane W  Hawthorne's Use of Mirror Symbolism in His Writings  MA Univ of North Carolina at Greensboro 1968
2578  KELSAY Alleen  Nathaniel Hawthorne:  Artist Puritan  MA Univ of Texas at El Paso 1952  82 p
2579  KENDALL Ella F  Types of Characters in Hawthorne's Tales and Romances  MA North Texas St Univ nd
2580  KENNEDY Sally P  The Wandering Jew in Nathaniel Hawthorne's Short Fiction  MA Univ of Tennessee 1965
2581  KIKEL Rudy J  Thomas Howell's "Ruine the Rewarde of Vice"--A Microedition; Tennyson's Final Whirl--An Analysis of *The Death of Oenone, Akbar's Dream and Other Poems*; and the World of Beatrice--A Critical Survey and Analysis of Hawthorne's "Rappaccini's Daughter"  MA Pennsylvania St Univ 1965
2582  KIM Yong-chol  Hawthorne's Treatment of the "Fortunate Fall" in Fiction: A Reconsideration  MA Univ of Hawaii 1964  92 p
2583  KLIGERMAN Jack M  The Use of the Comic in Nathaniel Hawthorne's *The House of Seven Gables*  MA Syracuse Univ 1962  97 p
2584  KOLB Alfred  Color:  A Key to the Interpretation of Character, Theme and Tone in Nathaniel Hawthorne's Major Novels  MA Syracuse Univ 1960  144 p
2585  KRAMER Marilyn H  A Study of Nathaniel Hawthorne's Theories About Power  MA Brooklyn Coll of City Univ of New York 1960  63 p
2586  KRUSE Alice M  Hawthorne and Children  MA Univ of Kentucky 1943  106 p
2587  KUYENDALL Thomas R  Nathaniel Hawthorne:  The Role of Humor and Gaiety in Life and in Art  MA Lamar Technological Univ 1969

2588 LAKEHOMER Leona  Hawthorne in Transition: 1842-1845  MA Claremont Graduate School 1965
2589 LAMB M  Puritanism as Romantic Structure in Hawthorne  MA Univ of Connecticut 1951
2590 LANXNER William  The Development of Hawthorne's Attitude Toward Sin as Seen in *The Scarlet Letter* and His Earlier Writings  MA Columbia Univ 1955  65 p
2591 LAWSON Robert N  Nathaniel Hawthorne's Use of Supernatural Elements in *The Scarlet Letter*  MA Univ of Kansas 1961
2592 LEATHERS Bertha M  The Literary Kinship of Nathaniel Hawthorne and Mary Wilkins Freeman  MA Univ of New Hampshire 1951  50 p
2593 LEEPER Helen I  The Moral Purpose of Hawthorne's Fiction  MS Kansas St Coll at Pittsburg 1936
2594 LEVERONI Richard  That Which Was Lost: The Transformation Theme in Three Novels by Nathaniel Hawthorne  MA Columbia Univ 1966  74 p
2595 LEWIS Bradford  The Role of the Protagonist in the Short Stories of Nathaniel Hawthorne  MA Univ of Vermont 1966  243 p
2596 LEWIS Ruth N  Nathaniel Hawthorne's Version of the Greek Myths  MA Univ of Maryland at College Park 1963  66 p
2597 LINK Robert L  Hawthorne and Puritanism: A Study in Conflict  MA Columbia Univ 1954  45 p
2598 LIPE Louise C  Image and Symbol in Nathaniel Hawthorne's *The Scarlet Letter* and *The Marble Faun*  MA Univ of Tulsa 1966  155 p
2599 LOEFFLER Sr Paul C  *The Marble Faun*: The Focal Point of Hawthorne's Religious Convictions  MA Siena Hts Coll 1958
2600 LYERLY Ralph H  Hawthorne's Treatment of Nature in His Three Chief American Romances  MA Univ of North Carolina at Chapel Hill 1946  156 p
2601 LYON Frances L  The Idea of Communication in Hawthorne's *Blithedale Romance*  MA Univ of Oklahoma 1962
2602 McBRIDE Ruth H  Hawthorne's Use of Setting in His Novels  MA Univ of Kansas 1925
2603 McCALL Dan  "Pride" as Subject in *The Blithedale Romance*  MA Columbia Univ 1963  81 p
2604 McCOY Cecil V  Hawthorne's View of Puritanism  MA Univ of Mississippi 1959  130 p
2605 McCRAW Melrose H  A Study of the Women in Nathaniel Hawthorne's Major Novels  MA Univ of Tulsa 1961  134 p
2606 McCRORY M D  A Study of the Stylistic Technique of Nathaniel Hawthorne in the Creation of Romance  MA North Texas St Univ 1967
2607 McCULLOH Ruth S  Hawthorne's Use of "Money, a Root of Evil"  MA Ohio St Univ 1942
2608 McDONALD Sherry  Sin and Its Consequences in Selected Works of Nathaniel Hawthorne  M Ed Henderson St Coll nd
2609 McKEE Ruth E  Hawthorne: A Study of the Modifications Which Took Place in His Attitude Toward Sin  MA Univ of Hawaii 1930  59 p
2610 McKEIRNAN Agnes C  A Classification of the Short Stories of Nathaniel Hawthorne  MA Univ of Idaho 1936
2611 McKEITHAN Dell  Nathaniel Hawthorne's Satire of Transcendentalism in "The Artist of the Beautiful"  MA Univ of North Carolina at Greensboro 1965
2612 McKIBBEN Leila J  Hawthorne's Notebooks and the Uses He Made of Them  MA Univ of California at Berkeley 1914
2613 MacMILLAN M M  Nathaniel Hawthorne's Use of the Concept of Innocence  MA Ohio St Univ 1943
2614 MADDEN Emily M  Perceptible Consequences of Sin in Hawthorne and Poe  MA Virginia St Coll 1958  58 p
2615 MADDEN Sr Mary R  The Concept of Sin in Hawthorne's Fiction  MA Indiana Univ 1964
2616 MAGEE Mary K  Nathaniel Hawthorne's Concept of Christianity  MA Temple

Univ 1963   93 p
2617   MAHER Mary S   Thematic Roles of Women in Hawthorne's Fiction   MA Univ of Arizona 1960   103 p
2618   MAJOR Mildred   The Gothic Element in Hawthorne's Short Stories   MA Univ of Tennessee 1949
2619   MARSH L A   The Critical and Poetic Theories of Nathaniel Hawthorne   MA Univ of North Carolina at Chapel Hill 1943
2620   MARTIN Horace D   Tales from Hawthorne Selected and Edited for High School Use   MA George Peabody Coll for Teachers 1922
2621   MAY Judith A   The Paradox of the Fortunate Fall in Hawthorne's Major Romances   MA San Diego St Coll 1967   113 p
2622   MAYES Thomas R   Hawthorne's Attitude Toward Progress and Reform   MA Mississippi St Univ 1962   80 p
2623   MECK E C   Ghosts in Hawthorne and James   MA Ohio St Univ 1927
2624   MEHLMAN Mary M   Tradition and the Symbolism of *The Marble Faun*   MA Boston Coll 1950
2625   MEREDITH Glen   The Gothic Influences on the Novels of Nathaniel Hawthorne   MA Univ of Kansas 1955
2626   MILLER J D   Religion as a Factor in the Literary Career of Nathaniel Hawthorne   MA North Texas St Univ 1952
2627   MILLS Lorraine G   Salem as a Source of the American Gothic in the Works of Nathaniel Hawthorne   MA Univ of Maryland at College Park 1958   97 p
2628   MITCHELL Stephanie L   The Narrator's View of Hester Prynne: A Study of Narrative Commentary About Hester Prynne in Hawthorne's *The Scarlet Letter*   MA Univ of New Mexico 1966
2629   MOORE Ruth S   A Study of the Artistic Use of Native Materials in Hawthorne's Novels   MA Univ of Houston 1958   111 p
2630   MOSS Richard F   The Transcendental Vision of Hawthorne, Poe and Melville as Seen in Some of Their Short Stories   MA Univ of Massachusetts 1959
2631   MOSS Winnie H   Hawthorne's *The Marble Faun*: An Historical and Critical Study   MA Univ of Texas at Austin 1940   210 p
2632   MULLANE Sr Mary C   Silent Hawthorne Speaks from His Secret Heart   MA Boston Coll 1938
2633   NEEL Yvonne L   Hawthorne's Abortive Use of Tragedy   MA Univ of Mississippi 1964   91 p
2634   NEIDHARDT Frances E   The Influence of Nathaniel Hawthorne on Stephen Crane: A New Source Study   MA Hardin-Simmons Univ 1966
2635   NEWBOLD Mary R   The History of Hawthorne Criticism   MA Univ of Iowa 1924
2636   NEWPORT Vivian   Hawthorne's Portrayal of Sin   MA Univ of Arizona 1940
2637   NICHOLS Grace E   Hawthorne's Conscious Use of Art Principles   MA Univ of Iowa 1932
2638   NUTTER Dell   Hawthorne: Master of the Short Story   MA West Texas St Univ 1966   89 p
2639   O'CONNOR Sr Mary C   Hawthorne's Attitude Toward the Catholic Church as Revealed in *The Marble Faun* and His French and Italian Journals   MA Siena Hts Coll 1943   49 p
2640   OSTRANDER Joan   Characterization Themes and Symbolism in the Works of Nathaniel Hawthorne, with Reference to the Personality Theories of Karen Horney   MA Univ of South Dakota 1965
2641   O'SULLIVAN Robert T   Nathaniel Hawthorne: The Relationship of the Paradoxes and His Calvinism   MA Columbia Univ 1965   69 p
2642   PALMER Lewis H   A Study of the Friendship Between Nathaniel Hawthorne and Herman Melville   MA Syracuse Univ 1947   127 p
2643   PANDIT Manorma   An Analysis of the Major Fictional Works of Nathaniel Hawthorne   MA Pacific Univ 1966
2644   PASINETTI Pier   The Tragic Element in Hawthorne   MA Louisiana St Univ 1936
2645   PENDLETON James D   Sin and the Head-heart Conflict in *The Scarlet Letter*   MA Univ of North Carolina at Chapel Hill 1959

2646  PENNY Beverly J  Regional Guilt and Shame in Selected Novels of Hawthorne and Faulkner  MA Louisiana St Univ 1966
2647  PERKINS Kenneth  Symbolism in Hawthorne  MA Univ of California at Berkeley 1916
2648  PETRICK Ann  Nathaniel Hawthorne: Artistic Ideals  MA Brooklyn Coll of City Univ of New York 1957  148 p
2649  PHILLIPS Mary D  The Conflict of the Head and the Heart in the Works of Nathaniel Hawthorne and Herman Melville  MA Chico St Coll 1961  73 p
2650  PICCINI Laura  Nathaniel Hawthorne: The Story-teller and the Novelist  MA Ca Foscari (Italy) 1936
2651  PIKET Diane  Isolation in Hawthorne's Writing  BA Univ of British Columbia (Canada) 1967
2652  PORT Ruth E  Destructive Effects of the Doctrine of Election in *The Scarlet Letter* and Selected Tales by Nathaniel Hawthorne  MA Univ of Maryland at College Park 1968  106 p
2653  PREBUS Helen McI  Dantesque Concepts in Nathaniel Hawthorne's "The Birthmark" and "Rappaccini's Daughter"  MA Ohio St Univ 1969  53 p
2654  PRESSLEY Ruth  Hawthorne's Use of Symbolism  MA Univ of Texas at Austin 1921
2655  PROPER Stanton H  Hawthorne's Fictional Children  MA Univ of Massachusetts 1969  49 p
2656  PROSSER Michael H  Solitude in Context in Hawthorne's Works  MA Ball St Univ 1959  74 p
2657  PULLIN Zula  The Influence of Hawthorne's European Experiences on His Writings  MA Louisiana St Univ 1937
2658  PULVIRENTI Agatina  Hawthorne  MA Ca Foscari (Italy) 1931
2659  QUESENBERY Virginia E  The Static Quality of the Art of Nathaniel Hawthorne as Revealed Through a Study of His Recurrent Themes  MA Univ of Oklahoma 1940
2660  RAMEE Elizabeth E  Hawthorne's Use of Symbols in His Romances  MA Univ of Texas at Austin 1969  141 p
2661  REDMOND John O  The Ambiguity of Hawthorne's Puritanism  MA Ohio St Univ 1960  56 p
2662  REED Angie C  The Psychology of Hawthorne's *Twice-told Tales*  MA Boston Univ 1947
2663  REID Alfred S  Concepts of God and Satan in the Major Romances of Nathaniel Hawthorne  MA Univ of Florida pre-1952
2664  RICHARDSON John W  Sin and Symbolism in Hawthorne  MA Univ of Louisville 1965
2665  RIEDLING Gerald L  Hawthorne's Concept of the Artist  MA Univ of Louisville 1962
2666  RIGGS Roy A  Hawthorne and Contemporaneous Taste in Short Fiction, 1825-1850  MA Ohio St Univ 1947
2667  RISMILLER Anne B  Marble and Mud: A Study of Hawthorne's *The Blithedale Romance*  MA Ohio St Univ 1966  43 p
2668  RISSOVER Fredric  The Characters in Hawthorne's American Romances as an Indication of the Development of Hawthorne's Fictional Practice  MA Univ of Cincinnati 1965
2669  RITCH Betty R  The Critical Reputation of *The Scarlet Letter*  MA Oklahoma St Univ 1956  72 p
2670  RODEWALD F A  The Use of Art Objects in the Fiction of Nathaniel Hawthorne  MA North Texas St Univ 1959
2671  ROSS M  Nathaniel Hawthorne and Brook Farm  MA Univ of Pittsburgh 1932
2672  ROSSER Deba M  Hawthorne's Human Heart  MA Univ of Tulsa 1962  99 p
2673  ROULSTON Charles R  *The Scarlet Letter*, Emerson and New England Idealism  MA Indiana Univ 1960
2674  ROWE Myra O  Views on the Villains in Selected Works of Nathaniel Hawthorne  MA Northeast Louisiana Univ 1965  95 p
2675  RUKAS Nijole M  "Expression" in Hawthorne  MA Tufts Univ 1961
2676  SAKAMOTO Tatsuyoshi  A Study of Number in the Noun in *The Scarlet*

*Letter* MA Univ of Texas at Austin 1953 90 p
2677 SAKS Barbara J Historical Allegory: A Study of Three Tales by Nathaniel Hawthorne MA Columbia Univ 1965 122 p
2678 SAYERS DeEtta L Hawthorne's Use of Art in *The Marble Faun* MA Univ of Texas at Austin 1965 218 p
2679 SCARBOROUGH Charles W The Influence of Hawthorne and Poe on the Work of Julian Green MA Univ of Maryland at College Park 1969 124 p
2680 SCHANER Julia E Hawthorne: Realist, Puritan, Idealist MA Univ of California at Berkeley 1917
2681 SCHAUP Susanne M The Theme of Isolation in Selected Works of Nathaniel Hawthorne MA Auburn Univ 1963
2682 SCHLESINGER Emily K Hawthorne's "Rappacini's Daughter": A Survey of Criticism and Comment MA Univ of Maryland at College Park 1965 84 p
2683 SCHOEN Carol B The House of the Seven Deadly Sins: Theme and Structure in Hawthorne's *The House of Seven Gables* MA Columbia Univ 1963 129 p
2684 SCHUMACHER John F Hawthorne in Maine MA Univ of Maine 1967 111 p
2685 SCOTT John H Hawthorne: *Twice Told Tales* MA Northwestern Univ 1907
2686 SERENI Emma Hawthorne's Short Stories MA Ca Foscari (Italy) 1964
2687 SERPICO Lucille M Franklin Pierce and Nathaniel Hawthorne: A Lifetime Friendship MA Univ of New Hampshire 1960 59 p
2688 SHOHAN Herschel S Structure and Symbolism of Hawthorne's *The Marble Faun*: A Preliminary Essay MA Columbia Univ 1955 109 p
2689 SHUMAKER I C Attitudes of Life in the Works of Nathaniel Hawthorne and Edith Wharton MA Ohio St Univ 1933
2690 SIEK Priscilla P Nathaniel Hawthorne's Conception of Art, the Artist and the Spectator MA Roosevelt Univ at Chicago 1960
2691 SMITH Clare R Nature in Hawthorne's Art in Particular Respect to His American Fiction MA Columbia Univ 1951
2692 SMITH Clyde A Thematic Craftsmanship in the Novels of Nathaniel Hawthorne MA Oklahoma St Univ 1958 99 p
2693 SMITH Jack E Jr Archetypal Patterns in *The Scarlet Letter* MA Kent St Univ 1966
2694 SMITH Laura Hawthorne's Use of Characters MA East Texas St Univ 1966
2695 SMITH Maureen J A Study of Dramatizations of Nathaniel Hawthorne's *The Scarlet Letter* MA Florida St Univ 1963
2696 SODERGREN Mary F Horatio Bridge: Friend of Hawthorne MA Univ of Maine 1966
2697 SPARROW M S Symbolism and Allegory in the Writings of Nathaniel Hawthorne MA Univ of North Carolina at Chapel Hill 1919
2698 SPILLANE Sr James M Nathaniel Hawthorne: Fashioned by Solitude MA Boston Coll 1948
2699 STAEHLE Jane T Hawthorne's Theory of Historical Fiction MA Ohio St Univ 1962 67 p
2700 STANTON Robert B The Significance of the Women in Hawthorne's American Romances MA Indiana Univ 1955
2701 STARK Alice W The Treatment of Nature in the Works of Nathaniel Hawthorne MA Univ of Texas at Austin 1936
2702 STEELE Marie T Nathaniel Hawthorne and Transcendentalism MA Univ of New Hampshire 1956 66 p
2703 STEELE Sue C The Structure of the International Novel as Revealed in Nathaniel Hawthorne's *The Marble Faun*, Henry James' *The Portrait of a Lady* and William Dean Howells' *Indian Summer* MA Eastern Kentucky Univ 1967 163 p
2704 STEIN William B Hawthorne's *The Scarlet Letter*: A Re-evaluation MA Univ of Florida nd
2705 STOCKTON Marijim Nathaniel Hawthorne's Concept of Perfection MA Duke Univ 1965
2706 STOTT Jon C Nature Symbolism and Moral Isolation in Hawthorne

2707 STOUT Janis P  Nathaniel Hawthorne and the Idea of Human Brotherhood
MA Univ of British Columbia (Canada) 1965
2708 STRAIN William H  Hawthorne and Abolition  MA Lamar Technological Univ 1968  192 p
2709 STRAUSS Mary T  A Study of Nathaniel Hawthorne's Treatment of Sin and Conscience  MA Indiana Univ 1942
2710 STROMMER Diane W  Hawthorne's Dark Lady and the Adamic Myth  MA Univ of Pittsburgh 1961
2711 SUGG Robert E  The Impassive Male in the Fiction of Nathaniel Hawthorne  MA Ohio St Univ 1965  71 p
2712 SULLIVAN Joan R  Nathaniel Hawthorne's Conception of the Effects of Sin in *The Scarlet Letter* and *The Marble Faun*  MA Ft Hays Kansas St Coll 1966
2713 SUSTAFSON Sandra L  The Dark and Fair Ladies in the Novels of Nathaniel Hawthorne  MA Arkansas St Coll 1966
2714 SYKES James T  The Religious Intolerance of the American Puritans as Viewed by Nathaniel Hawthorne  MA Univ of Kansas 1966
2715 TALEY Seniha A  Symbols in Hawthorne's Fiction  MA Kent St Univ 1965
2716 TALMAN Thomas S  The Central Moment in Selected Short Stories of Nathaniel Hawthorne  MA Northeast Missouri St Coll 1958
2717 TEPLITSKY Alan  Hawthorne's Parody: *The House of Seven Gables*  MA Columbia Univ 1969  124 p
2718 THEL Caroline H  A Comparative Study of Two Methods of Teaching *The House of Seven Gables*  MA Columbia Univ 1963  166 p
2719 THERIAULT Albert A  Hawthorne's Use of the Philosophy of the Imperfect in His Analysis of Evil  MA Univ of Pittsburgh 1931
2720 THOMPSON Anne  A Study of the Synthesis of Ideas, Fact and Fiction in *The Blithedale Romance*  MA Univ of Rhode Island 1961  212 p
2721 TILLSON Olive  Choice and Treatment of Setting and Character in the Short Stories of Nathaniel Hawthorne and Bret Harte  MA Long Island Univ 1967  93 p
2722 TORRES John B  Structure in *The Marble Faun*  MA Univ of California at Berkeley 1918
2723 TOWLE Calvin K  A Study of Puritanism as Seen by Nathaniel Hawthorne in *The Scarlet Letter* and by Arthur Miller in *The Crucible*  MA Washington Univ at St Louis 1956  136 p
2724 TREECE Dorothy Y  The Theme of Redemption in Hawthorne's Four Major Novels  MA Columbia Univ 1961  70 p
2725 TRENT Louise K  The American Girl in Europe: Hawthorne and James  MA Southern Illinois Univ at Carbondale 1960  160 p
2726 TUCKER Callie H  Nathaniel Hawthorne's Treatment of Sin  MA Univ of Tennessee 1950
2727 TUFTS M A  The Characteristic Importance of Solitude in Hawthorne's Life and Works  MA George Peabody Coll for Teachers 1934
2728 TURNER Frederick W  Hawthorne's Functional Use of the Fine Arts in *The Marble Faun*  MA Univ of North Carolina at Chapel Hill 1932
2729 TURRELL Carolyn R  Nathaniel Hawthorne and Brook Farm  MA Ohio St Univ 1961  59 p
2730 UPTON Dorothy L  The Minor Figures in the Four Principal Novels of Hawthorne  MA Ohio St Univ 1946
2731 VEHRS Geneive S  A Study of the Office-holding Years of Nathaniel Hawthorne and Their Effect Upon His Creative Ability  MA Columbia Univ 1960  93 p
2732 VEIT Richard C  Nathaniel Hawthorne: The Complete Man  MA San Diego St Coll 1955  120 p
2733 VOLLMANN Phillip D  The Common Man in Hawthorne's Short Stories  MA Columbia Univ 1961  213 p
2734 WAGES Jack D  Hawthorne's Minister  MA Ohio St Univ 1959  56 p
   MA Univ of Texas at Austin 1963  99 p

2735 WALDRON Randall H  The Development of Hawthorne's Powers of Characterization  MA Univ of Louisville 1964
2736 WALLIS Kathyrn C  Hawthorne's Use of the Gothic Tradition  MA Univ of Oklahoma 1959
2737 WARREN Linda  Prometheus Encircled: An Interpretation of Fire Symbolism in the Works of Nathaniel Hawthorne  MA Columbia Univ 1963  111 p
2738 WASHBURN I A  Three Inconsistencies in Hawthorne's Unfinished Romance: *Septimius Felton*  MA Univ of North Carolina at Greensboro 1964
2739 WEAR Catherine R  The Influence of the Graphic Arts Upon Those Works of Nathaniel Hawthorne Written Before 1853  MA Texas Christian Univ 1954  92 p
2740 WEAVER Josephine A  The Art of Hawthorne's Shorter Narratives  MA Univ of Texas at Austin 1936
2741 WELLS Susan M  The Development of Nathaniel Hawthorne's Plots and Settings  MA Univ of Mississippi 1962  162 p
2742 WHITE Claris B  The Puritanistic Writings of Nathaniel Hawthorne  M Ed Henderson St Coll nd
2743 WHITESELL Phyllis C  A Study in Sin in the Romances of Nathaniel Hawthorne  MA Univ of Texas at Austin 1963  103 p
2744 WICKHAM Linda R  The Conception of Art and the Artist in Hawthorne's Major Fiction  MA Ohio St Univ 1967  82 p
2745 WILLIAMS Philip E  The Biblical View of History: Hawthorne, Twain, Faulkner and Eliot  MA Univ of Pennsylvania 1964
2746 WILLIS S H  Treatment of Nature in Hawthorne  MA Univ of North Carolina at Chapel Hill 1924
2747 WILSON Barbara M  Hawthorne's Use of Folklore in the First (1837) Edition of the *Twice Told Tales*  MA Univ of Kansas 1962
2748 WILSON Dorothy W  An Aristotelian Criticism of the Characters in Nathaniel Hawthorne's Four Major Novels  MA Auburn Univ 1959
2749 WILSON Leonard L  Hawthorne's Changing Religious Emphasis in *The Blithedale Romance* and *The Marble Faun*  MA Ohio St Univ 1963  97 p
2750 WINN Shirley C  From Transgression to Character Change: A Reflection of the Deviating Spirit of Man as Unfolded Through Nathaniel Hawthorne's Symbolism  MA Univ of Houston 1965  153 p
2751 WOODWARD Robert H  Hawthorne's Women: A Study of Character Types  MA Indiana Univ 1955
2752 WYATT D C  Mask-veil Imagery in Hawthorne's Fiction  MA North Texas St Univ 1969
2753 ZELDITCH Bernice A  Hawthorne's Showmen  MA Stanford Univ 1964
2754 ZELLER Margaret A  Hawthorne's Theories of Fiction  MA Univ of Kansas 1949
2755 ZOBARSKAS Nola M  *Fanshawe*, a Study: An Examination of Nathaniel Hawthorne's First Published Work  MA Columbia Univ 1962  49 p
See also 363, 674, 1405, 1415, 1473, 1487, 2203, 2206, 3868, 3982, 4043, 4063, 4091, 4192, 4771, 4839, 4968, 5416

## PAUL HAMILTON HAYNE

2756 HARDENDORFF Victor H  Paul Hamilton Hayne and the North  MA Duke Univ 1942
2757 JOHNSON Tezzie O  Paul Hamilton Hayne: A Representative Southern Poet  MA Univ of Texas at Austin 1943  112 p
2758 PARKS Lillian L  An Appraisal of Paul Hamilton Hayne's Sonnets in the American Sonnet Tradition  MA Univ of North Carolina at Chapel Hill 1946  84 p
2759 PLYLER Conrad A  Paul Hamilton Hayne: A Man of Letters  MA Wofford Coll 1935
2760 RODGERS Elena  The Life and Poetry of Paul Hamilton Hayne  MA Louisiana St Univ 1937

2761 TAYLOR Francesca B  Nature in the Poetry of the South: Paul Hamilton Hayne and Sidney Lanier  MA Univ of Texas at Austin 1918
2762 WILLIAMS Rose E  Margaret Junkin Preston, Poetess of Virginia Based Chiefly on the Correspondence with Paul Hamilton Hayne  MA Duke Univ 1940

## LAFCADIO HEARN

2763 BASS Gaston R  Lafcadio Hearn: His Life and His Literary Thought  MA Univ of Mississippi 1946  128 p
2764 CLARK Christopher T  The Bohemian as Moralist: The Paradox of Lafcadio Hearn  MA Georgetown Univ 1966  112 p
2765 COHN Meyer  Lafcadio Hearn  MA Columbia Univ 1916
2766 COLLINS Henry H  Lafcadio Hearn and Japan  MA Columbia Univ 1917
2767 CORTALE Frank  A Context for Some of Lafcadio Hearn's Views on Japanese Life and Folk-ways  MA Brooklyn Coll of City Univ of New York 1962  56 p
2768 CRAVEN Dorothy H  Lafcadio Hearn as an Interpreter and Critic of the British Poets  MA Univ of Kansas 1941
2769 DERRICKSON Howard S  Biographies of Lafcadio Hearn  MA Washington Univ at St Louis 1942
2770 DOROUGH Charles D  The Life and Mind of Lafcadio Hearn  MA Univ of Texas at Austin 1936
2771 FLANAGAN V M  Lafcadio Hearn  MA Ohio St Univ 1927
2772 GARIG Aminie R  Lafcadio Hearn: The Man and His Works  MA Louisiana St Univ 1929
2773 GAULDING Roxie G  Lafcadio Hearn in New Orleans  MA Duke Univ 1939
2774 GREEN Innes E  The Treatment of Death in the Writings of Lafcadio Hearn  MA Northeast Louisiana Univ 1966  95 p
2775 GROSS Sylvia W  Some Aspects of the Orientalism of Lafcadio Hearn  MA Brooklyn Coll of City Univ of New York 1942  90 p
2776 HAMLIN Sr Mary A  Southern Regionalism in the Writings of Lafcadio Hearn  MA George Peabody Coll for Teachers 1942
2777 JORDAN Gerald M  The Literary Criticism of Lafcadio Hearn Based on Lectures Given at the University of Tokyo During 1896-1902  MA Univ of Southern California 1948
2778 KAWAMURA Kinichi E  Lafcadio Hearn's Life and His Interpretation of Japan and the Japanese People  MA Boston Univ 1934
2779 KILEY George B  The Social Attitudes of Lafcadio Hearn  MA Univ of Pittsburgh 1947
2780 KO Hibu  Lafcadio Hearn: His Life and His Japanese Works  MA Univ of Mississippi 1963  109 p
2781 KRUGER Charles F  Lafcadio Hearn's Published Lectures on English Literature Viewed in the Light of Catholic Philosophy  MA St Louis Univ 1928  83 p
2782 LIPTZIN Solomon  Lafcadio Hearn: The Teacher  MA Columbia Univ 1922
2783 LOVELL E S  Lafcadio Hearn: His Writing as a Reflection of His Life and Personality  MA Boston Univ 1941
2784 McADOW Margaret A  A Descriptive Bibliography of the Writings of Lafcadio Hearn (1850-1904)  MA Texas Christian Univ 1966  233 p
2785 McKINNON William T  The Life and Work of Lafcadio Hearn  MA Univ of South Carolina 1926
2786 MESTAYER Myrtle  Lafcadio Hearn in New Orleans  MA Louisiana St Univ 1932
2787 NELSON Bonnie  A Study of Lafcadio Hearn's Understanding of Beauty  MA Columbia Univ 1963  52 p
2788 NORRIS Onalee W  Lafcadio Hearn: Local Colorist  MA Texas Arts and Industries Univ 1952
2789 PATTERSON Vernon K  Lafcadio Hearn: The Teacher in Japan  MA Univ of Southern California 1946

2790  PIERCE Bertha M  Lafcadio Hearn in Louisiana  MA George Peabody Coll for Teachers 1928
2791  PLEASANTS Martha G  Lafcadio Hearn: His Life and Work  MA Tulane Univ 1905
2792  RAVETCH Paul H  Lafcadio Hearn's Appraisal of Japanese Life and Culture  MA Brooklyn Coll of City Univ of New York 1948  51 p
2793  RUSSELL Carol S  Lafcadio Hearn in Japan: His Life, Critics, Lectures, Fairy Tales  MA Univ of Texas at Austin 1958  97 p
2794  SUZUKI Kazudo  A Critical Study of the Sources of Lafcadio Hearn's Japanese Folk Tales  MA Univ of Southern California 1941
2795  SWANSON Kathryn  A Study of the Development of Lafcadio Hearn's Style  MA Univ of Minnesota 1928
2796  WARD Allie M  Lafcadio Hearn: Interpreter of Japanese Life  MA Univ of Oklahoma 1939
2797  WEISS Dorothy  Lamp Unto Himself: A Study of the Influences in the Life of Lafcadio Hearn, as They Were Reflected in His Major Themes  MA Fairleigh Dickinson Univ 1962  56 p
2798  WERTHEIM Martha H  Definite and Precise Use of Color in Selected Writings of Lafcadio Hearn  MA Bowling Green St Univ 1955
2799  WILKES Anita E  Lafcadio Hearn: Orientalist  MA Columbia Univ 1937
2800  YOUNG Dorothy T  Lafcadio Hearn's Tokyo Lectures  MA Columbia Univ 1943

## JOSEPH HELLER

2801  BARLOW Michael M  *Catch 22:* Man in an Alien Society  MA Univ of British Columbia (Canada) 1969  55 p
2802  JOHNSON Maridee A  Joseph Heller: A Study in Style  MA Washington St Univ at Pullman 1970
2803  KALTER Michael J  A Critical Interpretation and Explication of *Catch 22*  MA Univ of Iowa 1965
2804  KOGAN Richard A  Joseph Heller's *Catch 22* and the American Novel of the Absurd  MA Colorado St Univ 1968
See also 2915, 4020

## LILLIAN HELLMAN

2805  BENJAMIN Madeline L  The Social and Historical Vision of Lillian Hellman  MA Ohio St Univ 1967  130 p
2806  BREAULT Sr Mary A  A Comparative Analysis of the Structure of Selected Plays by Lillian Hellman and William Inge  MA Siena Hts Coll 1963  51 p
2807  BROWN Kent R  Lillian Hellman and Her Critics  MA Univ of California at Santa Barbara 1967  165 p
2808  DESSLER Harold  Lillian Hellman: An Evaluation  MA Univ of North Carolina at Chapel Hill 1948
2809  ESTRIN Mark W  An Evil World Well-made: The Plays of Lillian Hellman  MA Columbia Univ 1961  104 p
2810  FISHER Lois H  A Critical Analysis and Evaluation of Lillian Hellman's Dramatic Works  MA Univ of Pittsburgh 1960
2811  KALAHER Lucille F  The Theme of Evasive Idealism in the Plays of Lillian Hellman  MA Univ of Wyoming 1964
2812  PARRISH James A  A Study of the Plays of Lillian Hellman  MA Florida At Univ 1949
2813  ROBERTSON Helen E  Lillian Hellman and the Psychology of Evil  MA Univ of Texas at Austin 1964  116 p
2814  SCHEMERHORN Leora H  Lillian Hellman: Craftsman, Moralist, Thinker  MA Stetson Univ 1966
2815  SHROPSHIRE Anne W  The Plays of Lillian Hellman: A Study of Contemporary Drama  MA Univ of Kentucky 1946  149 p
See also 2350, 4570

## ERNEST HEMINGWAY

2816 ADAMS Barbara E  *A Farewell to Arms*: A Modern Grail Quest  MA San Diego St Coll 1967  149 p
2817 ADLER J  The Concept and Presentation of the Hero in the Novels and Stories of Hemingway  MA Univ of London (England) 1962
2818 ALLRAN Barbara M  Autobiographical Elements in Hemingway's *In Our Time*  MA Univ of North Carolina at Chapel Hill 1963
2819 AMELL Karin  A Reception Study of Ernest Hemingway  MA Univ of Kansas 1957
2820 ANTONIN Claudine  The Legacy of Romantic Love in *The Sun Also Rises* and *The Great Gatsby*  MA Univ of North Carolina at Greensboro 1970
2821 ARCHER F B  A Study of the Interrelationship or the Philosophy and Art of Ernest Hemingway  MA Univ of Texas at El Paso 1954  111 p
2822 ARTHUR Harold M  Hemingway's Nick Adams Stories: A Psychological Interpretation  MA Univ of Rhode Island 1968  83 p
2823 ARTHUR Henry  Metaphysical Tendencies in Hemingway's Short Stories  BA Univ of British Columbia (Canada) 1968
2824 ASLAM Jamsheda  Hemingway's Attitude Toward Women as Implied in His Major Novels and Short Stories  MA Texas Agricultural and Mechanical Univ 1964  54 p
2825 AULD John H  An Analysis of the Leit-motif of Learning in Three Novels by Ernest Hemingway  MA Univ of Rhode Island 1965  92 p
2826 BAILEY Carolyn S  The "Ironic Gap" in Hemingway's *The Sun Also Rises* and in Dos Passos' *The Big Money*  MA Ohio St Univ 1967  78 p
2827 BELTZ George W  The Treatment of War in Ernest Hemingway's Novels  MA Southern Illinois Univ at Carbondale 1950  100 p
2828 BERMAN Paul I  Ernest Hemingway and the Spanish Civil War  MA Hunter Coll 1957
2829 BILLINGS Robert S  Hollywood and Hemingway: A Critical Inquiry Into the Ability of Hollywood to Adequately Present the Works of Ernest Hemingway  MA Boston Univ 1948
2830 BIRD Agnes P  The Realism of Ernest Hemingway  MA Univ of Texas at Austin 1948  120 p
2831 BLACKBURN David W  Ernest Hemingway: A Will to Live  BA Amherst Coll 1953
2832 BLOODWORTH William A Jr  Ernest Hemingway and the American Tradition  MA Lamar Technological Univ 1967  99 p
2833 BLOTT Stewart G  Romance Conventions in *For Whom the Bell Tolls*  BA Univ of British Columbia (Canada) 1966
2834 BOURKE Robert L  Cradle of the Horns: An Examination of the Hemingway Death Mystique  MA Brigham Young Univ 1966  91 p
2835 BOWEN Carey S  The Use of Understatement in the Short Stories of Ernest Hemingway  MA Univ of North Carolina at Chapel Hill 1964
2836 BRAVO Maria E  Hemingway and Castile  MA Univ of North Carolina at Chapel Hill 1964
2837 BRIDGE Josiah  The Craft of Ernest Hemingway  MA Columbia Univ 1955  71 p
2838 BROER Lawrence R  Pattern of Revolt: A Short and Long View of the Death of Ernest Hemingway  MA Florida St Univ 1963
2839 BRUMFIELD Barbara M  Loneliness in the Novels and Short Stories of Ernest Hemingway  MA Univ of Mississippi 1963  96 p
2840 BRYANT Ella L  Hunting and Fishing and Hemingway  MA North Texas St Univ 1964
2841 BURDESHAW Monica D  Religious Values in the Fiction of Ernest Hemingway  MA Univ of Texas at El Paso nd
2842 CALDWELL Julia  Ernest Hemingway and Society: From Rejection to Acceptance  MA Univ of Mississippi 1968
2843 CALLAHAN Michael A  "And Into the Trees": A Study of Death as the Central Unification of Ernest Hemingway's Thought  MA Gonzaga

Univ 1959
2844 CAMPBELL Curtis E  The Significance of Suffering and Death in Some of Ernest Hemingway's Works  MA Virginia St Coll 1962  73 p
2845 CAMPBELL John W  The Development of the Reputation of Ernest Hemingway  MA Western St Coll of Colorado 1959  190 p
2846 CANFIELD Elizabeth C  A Study of Existential Attitudes in the Fiction of Ernest Hemingway  MA Indiana Univ of Pennsylvania 1964  94 p
2847 CANO Janet M  The Burlesque of Tragedy: A Study of the Comic in Hemingway's Writings  MA Univ of Kansas 1964
2848 CASH Thomas H Jr  Ernest Hemingway and Death  MA Univ of Kentucky 1951  100 p
2849 CASSELL Marcia H  The Role of the Female Characters in Selected Works of Ernest Hemingway  MA Univ of Tennessee 1969  143 p
2850 CHAMBERS Chrysostamus  A Study and Evaluation of Representative Criticism of Ernest Hemingway's Early Novels and Short Stories  MA Temple Univ 1963  129 p
2851 CHANG Barbara S  What's in a Style? Ernest Hemingway's Art of Writing  MA Idaho St Univ 1964
2852 CHARPENTIER Kathleen A  A Study of Imagery in Selected Short Stories of Ernest Hemingway  MA Univ of North Carolina at Chapel Hill 1965
2853 CHERMSIDE Robert A  Ernest Hemingway: A Writer of Episodes  MA Univ of Richmond 1952  90 p
2854 CHILCOTE Sanford M  The Nada Theme in Four Novels by Ernest Hemingway  MA Univ of New Hampshire 1967  75 p
2855 CLARK Elvis G  A Search for Meaning in Life as Reflected in the Works of Ernest Hemingway  MA Arkansas St Coll 1964
2856 CLAYTON John D  Ernest Hemingway: The Writer as a Reporter  MA Univ of Tulsa 1956  168 p
2857 CONRAD Ralph W  Development of the Hemingway Hero  MS Kansas St Coll at Pittsburg 1958
2858 COOK M K  Representation of the Social Class Structure in the Fiction of Ernest Hemingway  MA North Texas St Univ 1957
2859 CORNELIUS Gilbert D  Alienation and Unification in the Short Fiction of Ernest Hemingway  MA Univ of North Carolina at Chapel Hill 1967
2860 COSTELLO Mary  Hemingway's Old Men  MA Boston Coll 1965
2861 COURRIEU Andree  A Comparative Study of Camus and Hemingway  MA Louisiana St Univ 1966
2862 CRAFT Harvey M  The Development of the Hemingway Protagonist  MA Univ of Southern Mississippi 1956
2863 CRIGLER Cornelia A  A Study of Certain Symbols in Ernest Hemingway's Writings  MA Arkansas St Coll 1964
2864 CVETANOVSKI Save  Naturalistic Elements in Three of Hemingway's Novels  MA Univ of Texas at Austin 1968
2865 DAVENPORT Maxine M  Hemingway's Cyclic Patterns  MA Colorado St Univ 1967
2866 DAVIS Benjamin E  The Sensibility of the Hemingway Hero  MA San Diego St Coll 1965  126 p
2867 DAVIS J B  Dominant Themes in the Novels of Ernest Hemingway  MA North Texas St Univ 1961
2868 DePASQUAL J A  The Use of Light Imagery in the Fiction of Ernest Hemingway  MA North Texas St Univ 1967
2869 DOBBS Lewis L  Ernest Hemingway: The Universal Themes  MA Univ of Kansas 1963
2870 DODGE William S  A History of the Criticism of Ernest Hemingway's Novels  MA Univ of Rhode Island 1966  85 p
2871 DOERFEL Hanspeter R  The Craft of Ernest Hemingway  MA DePauw Univ 1958  88 p
2872 DORRINGTON Paul E  Ernest Hemingway and the Rules of the Game  MA Boston Coll 1955
2873 DOWDLE Mary  The Themes, Style and Influence of Ernest Hemingway

M Ed Henderson St Coll nd
2874 DUGAN Norman M  Two Literary Interpretations of the Spanish Civil War: The Fiction of Ernest Hemingway and Ramon Sender  MA Fort Hays Kansas St Coll 1965
2875 EASTBURN Esther W  A Hemingway Sequence: From Jakes Barnes to Santiago  M Ed Henderson St Coll nd
2876 EDGAR Catherine G  Hemingway's Concept of the Heroine  MA Arkansas St Coll 1966
2877 EICHEL Seymour  A Study of Ernest Hemingway's Nick Adams Stories  MA Columbia Univ 1954  99 p
2878 EXLEY Jo E  The Bridge Motif in the Fiction of Ernest Hemingway  MA Univ of Houston 1969  85 p
2879 FAHEY John  Whom Nature's Self Upholds: Wordsworth and Hemingway and Their Code Heroes  MA Gonzaga Univ 1966
2880 FARESE J B  Patterns of Secular Redemption in the Novels and Short Stories of Ernest Hemingway  MA Wesleyan Univ 1956
2881 FARQUHAR Robin H  Ernest Hemingway: The Pattern of the Quest  MA Univ of British Columbia (Canada) 1964
2882 FAULKNER John E  Hemingway's Nick Adams Stories  MA Rutgers St Univ 1962
2883 FERBER Daniel A  Hemingway, a Modern Stoic: A Study in Literature and Philosophy  MA Indiana Univ 1956
2884 FIELD Mary J  Hemingway's Developing Art and Its Culmination in *The Old Man and the Sea*  MA Univ of Texas at Austin 1956
2885 FISHER Dale A  The Hemingway Style  MA Hunter Coll 1966
2886 FLOURNOY Morris  A Thematic Analysis of Ernest Hemingway  MA Univ of Tulsa 1960  81 p
2887 FRANDSEN Coleen W  The Women in the Writings of Ernest Hemingway  MA Univ of Idaho 1957
2888 FREEMAN Arvella  The Historical Bases for *A Farewell to Arms* and *For Whom the Bell Tolls*  MA East Tennessee St Univ 1966
2889 FULTON Robert C III  Hemingway's Heroes  BA Amherst Coll 1962
2890 GAITHER Nell W  The Dolphin as Symbol in Three Modern Works: Ernest Hemingway, *The Old Man and the Sea*; William B Yeats, "Byzantium"; T S Eliot, *The Waste Land*  MA Univ of North Carolina at Greensboro 1970
2891 GARVER Jay A  War Themes from the Fiction of Ernest Hemingway  MA Indiana Univ of Pennsylvania 1965  83 p
2892 GATBONTON Erlinda S  A Study of Structure in the Short Stories of Ernest Hemingway  MA Univ of Maryland at College Park 1965  110 p
2893 GULDE Karmen  Hemingway's Use of Nature in Fiction  MA Butler Univ 1970
2894 GUNNING Emily  Hemingway's Heroines  MA Univ of Texas at El Paso 1965  128 p
2895 HAMILTON William T  Ernest Hemingway's Contributions to *Esquire*  MA Univ of Maryland at College Park 1963  72 p
2896 HARDYMAN Joyce W  Initiative and the Heroes in Three Hemingway Novels: The Movement from Defeat to Undefeat  MA Morehead St Univ 1969  50 p
2897 HARRELL R B  Structure as a Literary Technique in the Major Novels of Ernest Hemingway  MA North Texas St Univ 1956
2898 HAYES Susanne F  Hemingway's Style  MA Ohio St Univ 1963  79 p
2899 HENCHEY Richard F  Ernest Hemingway: An Ethical Study  MA Univ of Massachusetts 1955
2900 HERRIN Lois  Ernest Hemingway's Realism  M Ed Henderson St Coll nd
2901 HINCE Thaddeus E  A Discussion of Two Types of Women in the Fiction of Ernest Hemingway  MA Indiana Univ of Pennsylvania 1965  92 p
2902 HOLLOMAN Curtis C  With No Before and No After: Ernest Hemingway on Courage and Cowardice  MA Univ of Mississippi 1968
2903 HOOD Constant  The Use of Water in the Writing of Ernest Hemingway  MA North Texas St Univ 1960
2904 HOWARD David C  *The Old Man and the Sea*: The Achievement of a Moral

Position  MA Texas Christian Univ 1968  104 p
2905 HUGHES Douglas A  Hemingway and Camus: A Comparative Study of Four Novels  MA Univ of Idaho 1965
2906 ING Shirley J  Hemingway's War Novels  MA Univ of Texas at Austin 1954  84 p
2907 INGARGIOLA Nina A  Man: His World, His Struggles, His Victories-- A Study of Ernest Hemingway  MA Hunter Coll 1958
2908 JACKSON Margaret A  Hemingway as Symbolist  MA Univ of North Carolina at Chapel Hill 1967
2909 JACOBS Joan C  A Study of Ernest Hemingway's Literary Use of the Bullfight  MA Univ of Rhode Island 1965  105 p
2910 JACOBS William H  The Short Stories of Ernest Hemingway: An Examination Into the Relationships Between His Fictional World and the Diction Used in Creating It  MA Univ of the Pacific 1962  104 p
2911 JARRARD Norman E  The Critical Reception of Ernest Hemingway, 1940-1950: *For Whom the Bell Tolls; Across the River and Into the Trees*  MA Univ of North Carolina at Chapel Hill 1954
2912 JOHNSTON Velma L  Hemingway's Experiment in Africa  MA Univ of Texas at Austin 1961  117 p
2913 JONES John A  Hemingway Among the Critics: The Critical Reception of Hemingway's Works to 1954  MA Univ of Kentucky 1957  239 p
2914 JORDAN R A  Characterization of the American Abroad in the Fiction of Ernest Hemingway  MA North Texas St Univ 1961
2915 KALUZYNSKI Thomas A  A Separate Peace: A Comparison of *A Farewell to Arms* to *Catch 22* and *The Deathmakers*  MA Ohio St Univ 1968  66 p
2916 KIM Suk-Joo  Aspects of the Heroes' View of Life and Their Ethics in Ernest Hemingway's Six Novels  MA Univ of Rhode Island 1958
2917 KLEBANOW James E  Hemingway and Existentialism  BA Amherst Coll 1964
2918 KNIGHT John F  Hemingway's Santiago as Wounded Hero  MA Chico St Coll 1966
2919 KNOX Juanita  Character Traits Common to Ernest Hemingway and Two of His Fictional Characters  M Ed Henderson St Coll nd
2920 KUEKER Ted  The Treatment of War in Hemingway's Works with Special Emphasis on *A Farewell to Arms*  MA Mankato St Coll 1965  49 p
2921 KURTZMAN Mary C  Ernest Hemingway's *Across the River and Into the Trees*: A Critical Evaluation  MA Univ of Texas at El Paso 1968  96 p
2922 LAUER Carl A  Ernest Hemingway's Use of Physical Aspects  MA Illinois St Univ at Normal 1967
2923 LEE Tong C  An Analysis of the Structure of Hemingway's *In Our Time*  MA Univ of Hawaii 1959  114 p
2924 LEWIS Margaret C  Ernest Hemingway's Spanish War: Dispatches from Spain, 1937-1938  MA Univ of Louisville 1969  190 p
2925 LIGGERA Joseph J  Hemingway in the Transcendental Tradition  MA Tufts Univ 1963
2926 LIGGERA Lanayre D  Love and Death in Hemingway's *Across the River and Into the Trees*  MA Tufts Univ 1969
2927 LUEDEMAN Gertrude  The Narrative Technique of Ernest Hemingway  MA Univ of Texas at Austin 1942  161 p
2928 LYNCH Beverly A  Search for the Twentieth Century Woman in the Works of Hemingway and Fitzgerald  MA West Texas St Univ 1966  143 p
2929 McFADDEN Mary H  Hemingway and Religion  MA Temple Univ 1968  54 p
2930 McKEE Mary H  An Annotated Bibliography of the Ernest Hemingway Section of the Shaw Collection of Modern Authors in the University of Tulsa's McFarlin Library  MA Univ of Tulsa 1964  37 p
2931 McKOIN Florence  Ernest Hemingway and His First Novel  M Ed Henderson St Coll nd
2932 MacLAY Robert F  Romantic Idealism and Other Paradoxes: Love, Death and Despair in the Literature of Ernest Hemingway  BA Rutgers St Univ 1969  61 p
2933 MacLEOD Norman  Hemingway's View of the Bullfight: Tragedy and Ritual

MA Univ of North Carolina at Chapel Hill 1951  118 p
2934 MAINORD Daisy L  A Study of the Parallels Between the Work of Ernest Hemingway and That of Pablo Picasso  MA Ball St Univ 1966  67 p
2935 MALMSHEIMER Lonna M  Ernest Hemingway: The *Esquire* Years  MA Pennsylvania St Univ 1965
2936 MALONE Francis N  A Study of the Dialogue in the Novels and Stories of Hemingway  MA Kent St Univ 1964
2937 MANCUSO Joseph C  The Cinematic Technique of Montage: Its Use in Films and in the Writings of Ernest Hemingway  MA Univ of New Hampshire 1967  33 p
2938 MARTYANOVA Olga P  The Vision of Ernest Hemingway: Character, Code and Style  MA Univ of Alberta (Canada) 1966
2939 MAZEIKA Edward J  Existential Categories in Some Works of Hemingway and Camus  MA Univ of Houston 1958  71 p
2940 MELVIN Byron W  Ernest Hemingway and the British Temper  MA Univ of Southern Mississippi 1963
2941 MILLER Glenn P  Ernest Hemingway's *The Fifth Column*: A Production and Evaluation  MA Washington St Univ at Pullman 1965
2942 MILLIS Walter III  Translating Fortune: A Study of Some Early Works by Ernest Hemingway  BA Amherst Coll 1954
2943 MINCHEW Sue  Hemingway's Women: Real-life and Fictional  MA Mississippi St Univ 1969  66 p
2944 MORGAN Leger J Jr  Escapism and Search in the Major Works of Ernest Hemingway  MA Univ of Mississippi 1968
2945 MORRISON Nona L  The Use of -ing Verbals in Hemingway's *The Sun Also Rises*  MA Univ of Texas at Austin 1951  60 p
2946 MUSSETTER Sally A  Struggle and Victory in the Works of Ernest Hemingway and Andre Malraux  MA Ohio St Univ 1962  115 p
2947 NAHAL Sudarshna  The Woman in Ernest Hemingway's Fiction  MA Long Island Univ nd  78 p
2948 NELMS Patricia M  Ernest Hemingway's Women: Their Roles and Reality  MA Eastern New Mexico Univ 1969
2949 NELSON Margaret  Hemingway and the Individual: The War Novels  BA Univ of British Columbia (Canada) 1970
2950 NEUWIRTH Louise M  Hemingway on War  MA Hunter Coll 1959
2951 ORR Diane B  Women in Hemingway's Fiction  MA Texas Christian Univ 1969  106 p
2952 PEARSON Roger L  A Study of the Religious Symbolism and Imagery in Ernest Hemingway's Five Major Novels  MA Univ of Rhode Island 1963  143 p
2953 PERRIN Margaret L  A Study of the Change in Ernest Hemingway's Philosophy and Tone Through an Analysis of His Uses of the Techniques of Humor  MA Stetson Univ 1965
2954 PITTMAN William L  Ernest Hemingway: Matador Without a Cape; the Influence of the Bullfight Upon the Writing of Ernest Hemingway  MA Butler Univ 1956
2955 PORTER John  Style and Structure in *The Sun Also Rises*  MA Columbia Univ 1963  79 p
2956 PRATT John C  Ernest Hemingway: The Impulse Toward Catholicism  MA Columbia Univ 1960  135 p
2957 PRESLEY Margie C  An Analysis of Elements of Style in Ernest Hemingway and William Faulkner  MA East Tennessee St Univ 1969
2958 PREWETT Jim  A Linguistic Analysis of Ernest Hemingway's Prose Style in *A Farewell to Arms*  MA Univ of Houston 1966  165 p
2959 PRITCHARD Walter L Jr  War in the Fiction of Ernest Hemingway  MA Columbia Univ 1965  65 p
2960 PRUITT Phyllis B  The Change That Makes the Movement That Makes the Hemingway Short Story: A Study in Technique  MA Univ of North Carolina at Greensboro 1970
2961 QUIGG Joanne M  Hemingway and the Spanish Sensibility  MA Univ of

Oklahoma 1966
2962 REAGAN Richard S  The Sporting Life of Ernest Hemingway: Sports as Matter and Metaphor in the Life and Works of Ernest Hemingway  MA Villanova Univ 1965
2963 REARDON J D  Hemingway's Secret Community: The Order of Brusadelli  MA Univ of Connecticut 1951
2964 RICHARD Blakeney J  Irony and Pity: A Study of the Women in the Fiction of Ernest Hemingway  MA Univ of Mississippi 1963  104 p
2965 ROBBINS Elizabeth L  Hemingway and Pictorial Art  MA Univ of North Carolina at Greensboro 1970
2966 ROCHFORD John J  The Focus of Narration in Three Early Novels by Ernest Hemingway  MA Boston Coll 1959
2967 ROEGNER Judith L  Hemingway and Fitzgerald: A Comparison of Their Literary Styles and Themes  MA Fairleigh Dickinson Univ 1965  66 p
2968 ROOS Daniel F  The Irony in *The Sun Also Rises*  MA Univ of Maryland at College Park 1969  80 p
2969 ROSENBLUM Harriet S  An Analysis of the Time of the Spanish Civil War in the Writings of George Orwell, Ernest Hemingway and Andre Malraux  MA Ohio St Univ 1954  84 p
2970 RUMSEY Albert E  The Protagonist in Three American Novels of the Spanish Civil War: *Adventures of a Young Man, For Whom the Bell Tolls, Wide Is the Gate*  MA Univ of North Carolina at Chapel Hill 1954  93 p
2971 RUPRIGHT Michael P  The Heroes and Themes of Ernest Hemingway's *To Have and Have Not* and *For Whom the Bell Tolls*  MA Ohio St Univ 1965  61 p
2972 RYAN Anna G  The Adamic Myth in the Works of Ernest Hemingway  MA Rice Univ 1964
2973 SANTACROCE Patrick J  The Influence of Spain and Spanish Tradition Upon Selected Writing of Ernest Hemingway  MA Niagara Univ 1965
2974 SASSO Laurence J  A Study of the Grotesque in Selected Works by Ernest Hemingway  MA Univ of Rhode Island 1967  119 p
2975 SCHMIDT Barbara  What's In a Style?  Ernest Hemingway's Art of Writing  MA Univ of North Carolina at Chapel Hill 1964  95 p
2976 SEIBERT Robert E  A Critical Edition of the First Two Parts of Spender's *Vienna;* Four Views of Lady Duff: A Study of the Original of Hemingway's Lady Brett Ashley; and Man as God in a Godless World: A Study in Renaissance Tragedy  MA Pennsylvania St Univ 1965
2977 SHAFER Mary J  Ernest Hemingway's Literary Reputation in England: 1926-1968  MA Roosevelt Univ at Chicago 1968
2978 SILIO Thomas A  Prescription for Death: A Study of Ernest Hemingway's Code of Living  MA Univ of Maine 1968  130 p
2979 SIMPSON Sue K  Ernest Hemingway's View of His Society  MA Mississippi St Univ 1964  96 p
2980 SMITH B J  War as a Factor in the Fiction of Ernest Hemingway  MA North Texas St Univ 1957
2981 SOLDERER Anna E  English Translations from German Criticism on Ernest Hemingway  MA Southern Illinois Univ at Carbondale 1961  117 p
2982 SORENSEN Eugene C  The Hemingway Ethical Code  MA Mankato St Coll 1960  108 p
2983 STAFFORD Edward P  The Use of the Idea of Death in the Writings of Ernest Hemingway  MA George Washington Univ 1956  107 p
2984 STAROSCIAK Kenneth P  Hemingway's Tragic Vision in *A Farewell to Arms*  MA Univ of Rhode Island 1965  162 p
2985 STEWART Doris A  A Study of the Dimensional Quality in the Writing of Ernest Hemingway  MA Univ of Houston 1958  91 p
2986 STOCKSTILL Michael A  Ernest Hemingway: The Quest for Autonomy  MA Mississippi St Univ 1967  101 p
2987 STRICKLER Jo H  The Love Ethic of Ernest Hemingway  MA Univ of Mississippi 1969

2988 SWEITZER Robert H  Style, Structure and Meaning in Hemingway's Metaphysic of Time  MA Ohio St Univ 1966  56 p
2989 TANNER Jimmie E  The Romanticism of Ernest Hemingway  MA Univ of Oklahoma 1957
2990 THAYER Helen D  The Significance of Animals in the Work of Ernest Hemingway  MA Brooklyn Coll of City Univ of New York 1950  142 p
2991 THOMPSON Larry C  Ernest Hemingway's Impressionistic Style  MA Univ of Richmond 1969  62 p
2992 THOMPSON Mattie B  Ernest Hemingway's Treatment of Love and Marriage  MA Howard Univ 1963  117 p
2993 THURMAN Lynda H  The Hero and the Heroic Qualities in Certain Selected Short Stories and Novels of Ernest Hemingway  MA Northeast Louisiana Univ 1967  125 p
2994 TIBBETTS Bruce H  Futility and Value in the Novels of Ernest Hemingway  MA Univ of Tulsa 1966  86 p
2995 TYSON Barbara M  Ernest Hemingway:  The Writer's Search for Values  MA Univ of Texas at Austin 1959  164 p
2996 VANDIVER Samuel E  The Education of Nicholas Adams: An Examination of a Theme Development in Hemingway's Short Stories  MA Univ of Texas at Austin 1958
2997 VAN METER Martha E  An Analysis of the Writing Style of Ernest Hemingway  MA Texas Arts and Industries Univ 1963  332 p
2998 VILLANE Maria V  Hemingway and the Universal  MA Illinois St Univ at Normal 1969
2999 VON MASZEWSKI Betty D  Hemingway and Baroja:  A Comparison  MA Univ of Texas at Austin 1963  85 p
3000 WADE Clyde G  Ernest Hemingway:  Moral Historian of the Twentieth Century  MA Univ of Mississippi 1954  145 p
3001 WAGENER James W  Hemingway's Women Characters:  A Reassessment  MA Univ of Texas at Austin 1967  104 p
3002 WAITERS Ruby C  The Unifying Theme in *To Have and Have Not*: A Novel by Ernest Hemingway  MA Univ of North Carolina at Chapel Hill 1963
3003 WALKER Don D  Hemingway, Anderson and Faulkner:  Three Studies in Mytho-symbolism in American Literature  MA Univ of Utah 1947
3004 WALSH Joan M  Symbolism in *A Farewell to Arms* and Its Relevance to Hemingway's Philosophy  MA Boston Coll 1961
3005 WALZ Lawrence  The Use of Contrasts in Hemingway's Short Stories  MA Univ of North Carolina at Chapel Hill 1965
3006 WEST John F  Death in Hemingway  MA Univ of North Carolina at Chapel Hill 1949  186 p
3007 WHITE Zella B  Hemingway's Use of the Adjective Clause  MA San Diego St Coll 1966  69 p
3008 WILKERSON Martin J  A Critical Analysis of Ernest Hemingway's *For Whom the Bell Tolls*  M Ed Henderson St Coll nd
3009 WILSON Don H  The Spanish Concept of Honor in Hemingway  MA Univ of Louisville 1964
3010 WITHEY L M  Treatment of the Rootless Man in the Short Stories of Hemingway, Salinger, Stafford and Welty  MA Wesleyan Univ 1957
3011 WYCHE Lois M  The Archetypal Dark Woman in Hemingway's Fiction:  The American Bitch versus the European Dark Lady  MA Univ of North Carolina at Greensboro 1969
3012 WYMER George  Jake Barnes and Frederic Henry:  An Examination of the Interaction of Nada and the Code in *The Sun Also Rises* and *A Farewell to Arms*  MA Chico St Coll 1968  110 p
3013 YARUP Robert L  Nick Adams and the Pragmatic Attitude in Hemingway's Short Stories  MA West Virginia Univ 1967  150 p
3014 YATES Robert L  Irony in the Novels of Ernest Hemingway  MA Washington St Univ at Pullman 1965
3015 YONG E B  Characterization of the Heroine in the Fiction of Ernest Hemingway  MA North Texas St Univ 1956

3016  YOUNT Dorothy F  Hemingway's Critical Reception in Spain from 1940 to the Present  MA Univ of North Carolina at Greensboro 1966
3017  ZONA Sr Mary F  The Philosophy of Ernest Hemingway as Revealed in His Code Heroes  MA Boston Coll 1967
See also 178, 188, 764, 783, 801, 809, 829, 1710, 1882, 2078, 2440, 3199, 3385, 3688, 4029, 5783, 6076, 6253

## CAROLINE LEE HENTZ

3018  BERDAN Alan  Caroline Lee Hentz: Northern Defender of Southern Tradition  MA St John's Univ 1948
3019  CARTER Maude  A Study of Caroline Lee Hentz: Sentimentalist of the Fifties  MA Duke Univ 1942
3020  ENLOE Harvey M  A Criticism of Mrs Caroline Lee Hentz  MA Auburn Univ 1936
3021  HARDY Evelyn  Mrs Caroline Lee Hentz: A Woman of Her Time  MA Auburn Univ 1935
3022  MORAN Neva R  Caroline Lee Hentz, an Early Southern Novelist: A Study of the Life and Works of Mrs Caroline Lee Hentz  MA Birmingham-Southern Coll 1937
3023  WHICHARD Lindsay R  Caroline Lee Hentz: Pro-slavery Propagandist  MA Univ of North Carolina at Chapel Hill 1951  80 p
See also 5630

## JAMES A HERNE

3024  McCARTHY Joseph A  The Theatre Libre (Boston, 1891) and James A Herne's *Margaret Fleming*  MA Univ of North Carolina at Chapel Hill 1962
3025  OLF Julian M  James A Herne and Early American Realism  MA Columbia Univ 1965
3026  TALLMAN Richard S  The Depths and Heights of James A Herne  MA Univ of Maine 1968  104 p
3027  WEISS Irene R  James A Herne and the Development of Realism in the Drama  MA Brooklyn Coll of City Univ of New York 1943  119 p

## ROBERT HERRICK

3028  HOLABACH Philip  The Use of Symbolism in the Fiction of Robert Herrick  MA Washington St Univ at Pullman 1966
3029  LINKER Isadore M  Robert Herrick: American Apostle of Integrity  MA Univ of Pittsburgh 1953
3030  LOMAX Katherine F  Problem Novels of Robert Herrick  MA Boston Coll 1943
3031  McMANUS Marie A  The Short Stories of Robert Herrick: With a Criticism and Evaluation  MA Univ of New Hampshire 1953  522 p

## JOHN HERSEY

3032  BROWN Jennie M  John Hersey's War Novels: *The Wall, A Bell for Adano* and *The War Lover*  M Ed Henderson St Coll nd
3033  HUDSPETH Robert N  The Growth of Nihilism: Four Novels of John Hersey  MA Syracuse Univ 1963  77 p

## DuBOSE HEYWARD

3034  BAILEY Rosalie V  DuBose Heyward: Poet, Novelist, Playwright  MA Duke Univ 1941
3035  CREIGHTON Nannie E  DuBose Heyward and His Contribution to Literature  MA Univ of South Carolina 1933
3036  MacFIE Anne E  The Representation of Aristocrats in the Novels of DuBose Heyward  MA Univ of North Carolina at Chapel Hill 1958  93 p

3037 WHITESIDES Glenn E  DuBose Heyward and the Mediums of *Porgy*  MA Florida St Univ 1960
See also 2344, 2349, 6996, 6999

## MARIETTA HOLLEY

3038 DAVIS Clifford E  Marietta Holley: Humorist and Crusader  MA Univ of Pittsburgh 1936
3039 PIERCE Jane L  Marietta Holley's (Josiah Allen's Wife) Techniques of Humor  MS Kansas St Coll at Pittsburg 1961
See also 3804

## OLIVER WENDELL HOLMES

3040 BEADLE John A  A Comparative Study of the Medical and Literary Writings of Oliver Wendell Holmes  MA Univ of Iowa 1929
3041 BOEWE Charles E  A Study of the Medical Career of Oliver Wendell Holmes  MA Syracuse Univ 1949  109 p
3042 BOONE Dorothy D  A Study of Scientific Determinism in the Novels of Oliver Wendell Holmes: *Elsie Venner, The Guardian Angel* and *A Mortal Antipathy*  MA North Carolina Central Univ 1959  75 p
3043 CARR Ella G  Religious Attitudes as Found in the Works of Oliver Wendell Holmes  MA Ohio St Univ 1941
3044 CARSTENSEN Vernon R  The Literary Background of Oliver Wendell Holmes  MA Univ of Iowa 1932
3045 CHANDLER M  Some Eighteenth Century Traits of Oliver Wendell Holmes  MA Univ of Pittsburgh 1933
3046 DEAN Paula T  Oliver Wendell Holmes as a Novelist  MA Texas Technological Univ 1967  104 p
3047 GOODMAN R E  Critical Doctrines in Oliver Wendell Holmes  MA Ohio St Univ 1927
3048 HALL Eliza P  The Religious Opinions of Oliver Wendell Holmes  MS Northwestern Univ 1900
3049 LEVY Nora  Women in the Poetry of Holmes and Lowell  MA Hardin-Simmons Univ 1935
3050 McGRAW Mary H  An Analysis of the Literary Principles in Oliver Wendell Holmes' Breakfast-table Series  MA Univ of Oklahoma 1954
3051 MOORE Mayme M  Heredity and Psychology in the Novels of Oliver Wendell Holmes  MA St Mary's Univ of San Antonio 1949  80 p
3052 REED Jeanette  A Study of Holmes, Lowell and Twain as American Humorists  BA Univ of Oklahoma 1910
3053 ROGERS Geraldine P  Science as an Influence on the Writings of Oliver Wendell Holmes  MA Univ of Kansas 1939
3054 WEAVER Alma K  Dr Holmes: The Occasional Poet  M Ed Temple Univ 1932  80 p
3055 WHITTON Willa M  A Study of the Art of Holmes' Essays  MA Univ of Texas at Austin 1938  82 p
See also 674, 2206, 3775, 4968

## SAM HOUSTON

3056 BROWN Patricia J  The Rhetorical Practice of John Minor Botts, John J Crittenden and Sam Houston as Southern Unionists in 1860  MA Ohio St Univ 1968  154 p
3057 MITCHELL Yetta G  An Evaluation of Sam Houston's Oratory  MA Univ of Southern California 1945
3058 STEPHENS Andrew J  A Calendar of the Writings of Sam Houston in the Various Collections in Austin, Texas  MA Univ of Texas at Austin 1927

## SIDNEY HOWARD

3059 ADAMS Henry H  The Late Sidney Howard  MA Columbia Univ 1940
3060 FRANCIS Nelle T  Sidney Howard: Playwright  MA Univ of Texas at Austin 1942  155 p
3061 GRESSMAN Malcolm G  *The Late Christopher Bean* by Sidney Howard  MA Ohio St Univ 1950
3062 HELSER Ethel R  Sidney Howard  MA Ohio St Univ 1943
3063 HENDRY Kathleen  The Plays of Sidney Howard  MA Columbia Univ 1952  47 p
3064 STEWART Walter A  A Project in Stage Direction for the Production of Sidney Howard's *The Silver Cord*  MA San Diego St Coll 1966  321 p
3065 SWINNEY Donald H  Principles of Characterization in Sidney Howard's Plays  MA Univ of Idaho 1947

See also 213, 214

## E W HOWE

3066 HECKERT Della J  A Critical Study of *E W Howe's Monthly*  MS Kansas St Coll at Pittsburg 1962
3067 MARKEY Mary M  The American Village: As Revealed in the Autobiographical Fiction of E W Howe, Stephen Crane and Clarence S Darrow  MA Bowling Green St Univ 1961
3068 SHANNON Robert S  A Study of the Diction and Phraseology in Ed Howe's *The Story of a Country Town*  MA Univ of Kansas 1929
3069 SOLLERS Frances W  Howe, Kirkland and Garland: Beyond Regionalism  MA Univ of Idaho 1970
3070 WOODHOUSE Willard L  The Writings and Philosophy of E W Howe  MA Univ of Kansas 1941

See also 2023

## WILLIAM DEAN HOWELLS

3071 BALL Thelma  The Plays of William Dean Howells  MA Louisiana St Univ 1944
3072 BASS Altha L  The Social Consciousness of William Dean Howells  MA Univ of Oklahoma 1921
3073 BELL Ruth B  Professional Men in the Novels of William Dean Howells  MA George Peabody Coll for Teachers 1938
3074 BOBO Sandra B  William Dean Howells' Use of Yankee Humor and the Yankee Character in *The Rise of Silas Lapham* and *A Hazard of New Fortunes*  MA Auburn Univ 1968
3075 BOYD George W  Social Criticism in the "Hazard" Trilogy of William Dean Howells  MA Univ of Kentucky 1941
3076 BROOKS Violet F  A Comparison of William Dean Howells and Sinclair Lewis' Treatment of Characters of Mixed Blood as Seen in *An Imperative Duty* and *Kingsblood Royal*  MA North Carolina Central Univ 1963  56 p
3077 BROWN Olive B  William Dean Howells and Mark Twain  MA Columbia Univ 1914
3078 BRUNTON Frances D  Social Satire in the Farces of William Dean Howells  MA Univ of Pittsburgh 1935
3079 BUXTON Teresa L  A Study of the Relationship of William Dean Howells and Samuel L Clemens  MA Bucknell Univ 1930
3080 CAPLAN Eleanor D  The Ambivalence of Howells' Critical Reception of Twain  MA Univ of Massachusetts 1966
3081 CARLSON Patricia H  William Dean Howells: The Development of His Social Criticism; the Influence of Tolstoi  MA Univ of Houston 1967  60 p
3082 CASTRO Evelyn H  The Delineation of New York City in Two Novels: *A Hazard of New Fortunes* by William Dean Howells and *Manhattan Transfer* by John Dos Passos  MA Univ of Hawaii 1948  113 p
3083 CLARK Ann F  William Dean Howells' Ideals of Journalism Applied to His

|      | Attempted Practice on the *Cosmopolitan* MA Bowling Green St Univ 1963 |
|------|---|
| 3084 | CLARK Martha M  William Dean Howells: Critic of Twentieth Century Writers  MA Southern Illinois Univ at Carbondale 1953  56 p |
| 3085 | CLEGG Marian L  Courtship as Portrayed by W D Howells  MA La Verne Coll 1968  82 p |
| 3086 | CLEGG Minerva P  William Dean Howells as a Literary Critic  MA Univ of Maine 1957  83 p |
| 3087 | CLEVELAND Gertrude C  New England in the Novels of William Dean Howells  MA Univ of Maine 1957  153 p |
| 3088 | CORNELIUS Patricia P  William Dean Howells' Critical Realism: Reviews Published in the *Atlantic Monthly*, 1866-1880  MA Texas Christian Univ 1967  60 p |
| 3089 | COX Mary E  William Dean Howells and Naturalism  MA Marquette Univ 1952 |
| 3090 | CUTHBERT Martha M  Criticism of Fiction in the Novels of W D Howells  MA Univ of Tennessee 1965 |
| 3091 | DAESCHNER Naomi  The Dramatic Works of William Dean Howells  MA Univ of Kansas 1930 |
| 3092 | DAVIS Mildred D  Family Life as a Fictional Theme in William Dean Howells  MA Bowling Green St Univ 1949 |
| 3093 | DAYTZ Phyllis  William Dean Howells and the Controversy over Realism: 1886-1892  MA Columbia Univ 1951 |
| 3094 | DOBBINS Dorothy R  William Dean Howells' Growing Interest in the Influence of Environment on Character as Reflected in His Novels from 1881 to 1890  MA Univ of North Carolina at Chapel Hill 1968 |
| 3095 | DUBE Anthony  The Failure of William Dean Howells as a Playwright  MA Univ of Texas at El Paso 1964  80 p |
| 3096 | EBERSOLE Nelle A  William Dean Howells in Ohio  MA Bowling Green St Univ 1942 |
| 3097 | ELLIOTT James K  Americans Abroad in the Writings of William Dean Howells and Henry James  MA Oklahoma St Univ 1958  64 p |
| 3098 | ERWIN Ulrike  William Dean Howells and the American Woman  MA Syracuse Univ 1967  93 p |
| 3099 | FARR Jan R  William Dean Howells: A Study of the Economic Novel and the Utopian Dream and Father Coughlin, the Radio Priest  BA Amherst Coll 1955 |
| 3100 | FLEUR Leo Y  William Dean Howells and the American Drama  MA Columbia Univ 1941 |
| 3101 | FORBIS Dorothy M  The Concept of "Realism" in the School of Howells: Critical Interpretation of the New Trend in American Fiction by Writers for the *Atlantic Monthly*, 1866-1881  MA Univ of Texas at Austin 1942  160 p |
| 3102 | GARROW Argyle S  The Short Novels of William Dean Howells  MA Univ of North Carolina at Chapel Hill 1966 |
| 3103 | GETZELS Jacob W  William Dean Howells: Victim of Transition  MA Columbia Univ 1936 |
| 3104 | GREVE Frank J  William Dean Howells: The Sentimental Realist  BA Amherst Coll 1967 |
| 3105 | GROVE James L  Toward Complicity: Six Religious Figures Created Between 1874 and 1886 by William Dean Howells  MA San Diego St Coll 1965  166 p |
| 3106 | HANNA Willard A  William Dean Howells  MA Ohio St Univ 1937 |
| 3107 | HOLDEN Jack B  Journalistic Influences in William Dean Howells  MA Hardin-Simmons Univ 1969 |
| 3108 | HUGHEY C M  An Analysis of the Characterizations of Women in the Novels of William Dean Howells  MA Ohio St Univ 1932 |
| 3109 | JANN Reid  The Literary Criticism in Howells' *Easy Chair*  MA Southern Methodist Univ 1933 |
| 3110 | JOHNSON Richard T  A Realist's View of Evil: A Study of Four of Howells' Novels  MA Univ of British Columbia (Canada) 1966 |
| 3111 | JOHNSTON Ella B  William Dean Howells as a Critic  MA Univ of Kentucky |

3112 JONES Jimmy W  Howells and Alger: The Problem of Business Ethics in American Fiction from the Civil War to 1885  MA Texas Christian Univ 1967  69 p
3113 JOYCE Alice B  The Courtship Theme in Howells' Fiction  MA Ohio St Univ 1960  68 p
3114 KELLEY Carolyn E  Realism in the 1890's and Today with Particular Emphasis Upon the Influence of William Dean Howells  MA St Univ of New York at Albany 1934
3115 KESTLER Mary  Howells' Personal and Literary Association with Clemens  MA Duke Univ 1932
3116 KOHLMEYER Helen B  Realism in Howells and Arnold Bennett  MS Illinois St Univ at Normal 1969
3117 LAUCK Ada B  The Influence of Tolstoy on William Dean Howells: A Study Particularly of Ethical Parallels  MA Univ of Iowa 1924
3118 LIGHT Pansy  William Dean Howells as a Critic and Theoretician of the Short Story  MA Auburn Univ 1954
3119 LYNCH John E  From Narration to Dramatic Characterization: The Impact of Drama on Howells' Literary Development Between 1870 and 1879  MA San Diego St Coll 1967  281 p
3120 McAULIFFE Cornelius P  Structural Contrasts of Character and Theme in William Dean Howells' Major Social Novels  MA San Diego St Coll 1967  89 p
3121 McBRIDE Sara  Setting in the Novels of William Dean Howells  MA Univ of Iowa 1919
3122 McDANIEL Allen J Jr  The Ministers in William Dean Howells' Novels  MA Hardin-Simmons Univ 1968
3123 MARTIN Alonzo L  The Character of the Businessman in the Novels of William Dean Howells, Frank Norris and Theodore Dreiser  MA Univ of Louisville 1950
3124 MAYER Charles W  Satire and Humor in William Dean Howells' Fiction  MA Ohio St Univ 1954
3125 MAYES Martha A  Religion in the Work of William Dean Howells  MA Univ of Mississippi 1957  130 p
3126 MILES E R  William Dean Howells: The Development and Demonstration of His Theory of Fiction Through 1892  MA North Texas St Univ 1947
3127 MITCHELL Mary  A Study of the Early Novels of William Dean Howells  MA Columbia Univ 1964  50 p
3128 MOLDENHAUER Mary L  An Analysis of the Biographical Basis for the Political, Economic, Social and Literary Theories of William Dean Howells  MA Univ of Omaha 1966
3129 MOORE Howard K  William Dean Howells' Editorship of the *Atlantic Monthly*  MA Boston Univ 1940
3130 MOORHEAD Ruth  The Social Philosophy of William Dean Howells  MA Univ of Pittsburgh 1937
3131 MORGAN Myrtle V  Women Characters in the Novels of William Dean Howells  MA Univ of Maine 1962  196 p
3132 NOLAN Joseph S  A Comparison of the Novel and Play Forms of *The Rise of Silas Lapham*  MA Ohio St Univ 1964  82 p
3133 O'MARRA Barbara S  William Dean Howells: Critical Theories and Criticism  MA Univ of Mississippi 1952  93 p
3134 PAC URAR George  Howells in Canada  MA La Verne Coll 1968  53 p
3135 PUGH Lotta  A Study of the Women in the Novels of William Dean Howells  MA Ohio St Univ 1924
3136 PULLIAM Robert  The Businessman as an Ethical Character in the Novels of William Dean Howells  MA Southern Illinois Univ at Carbondale 1950  92 p
3137 REIBEL Dorothy E  A Bibliographical Guide to the Study of William Dean Howells  MA Univ of North Carolina at Chapel Hill 1946  104 p
3138 RILEY Clark  The Candid Camera of William Dean Howells  M Ed Henderson

St Coll nd
3139 RUDOLPH Edwin P  A Study of the Evidences of Puritanism in the Novels of William Dean Howells  MA Ohio St Univ 1944
3140 RUTENBER Ralph D Jr  The Opinions of William Dean Howells on the Novel  MA Columbia Univ 1940
3141 RYAN James P  The Satiric Howells: An Explication of a Novel  MA Texas Christian Univ 1968  76 p
3142 SANDERS Martha A  The Evolution of the Literary Theory of William Dean Howells  MA Auburn Univ 1954
3143 SARASOHN Cecilia L  The Literary Reputation of William Dean Howells, the Novelist, from the Point of View of His Contemporaries  MA Columbia Univ 1940
3144 SHARPE D R  William Dean Howells' Theory of Realism in Prose Fiction  MA Univ of North Carolina at Chapel Hill 1944
3145 SNOOK Donald G  Humor in the Early Novels of William Dean Howells  MA Auburn Univ 1966
3146 SPENCER Anna  The Realism of William Dean Howells  MA Univ of Kansas 1914
3147 SPILHAUG Berit  William Dean Howells and Two Contemporary Norwegian Realists  MA Univ of Kansas 1961
3148 STERN Jerome H  William Dean Howells: The Later Phase  MA Univ of North Carolina at Chapel Hill 1967
3149 STROUP Betty A  A Re-evaluation of William Dean Howells' Treatment of New England Characters  MA Univ of Pittsburgh 1948
3150 SUMNER Ruth  Women as Portrayed in the Novels of William Dean Howells  MA George Peabody Coll for Teachers 1938
3151 TAYLOR Hilda  Howells' Realistic Theory of Art  MA Univ of Iowa 1909
3152 TAYLOR James W  Swedenborgianism in the Fiction of William Dean Howells  MA Univ of Kansas 1959
3153 THOMPSON Genevieve  William Dean Howells' *The Rise of Silas Lapham*: A Critical and Historical Study  MA Univ of Texas at Austin 1946  99 p
3154 TURNER Peggy  William Dean Howells: Dramatist  MA North Texas St Univ 1954
3155 WEBER Eva  The Literary Code of William Dean Howells  MA Univ of Iowa 1923
3156 WILSON Benjamin H  Quiet Realism: Women Writers in the William Dean Howells' Tradition  MA Univ of North Carolina at Chapel Hill 1965
3157 WILSON Martha B  The Feminism of William Dean Howells  MA Butler Univ 1970
3158 WILSON Rachel L  William Dean Howells' Concepts of Marriage  MA Bowling Green St Univ 1962
3159 YORK Dorothy C  A Study of the Personal and Literary Relationships of William Dean Howells and Hamlin Garland  MA North Carolina Central Univ 1962  84 p
3160 ZUBER Lucy L  William Dean Howells in Columbus, 1851-1852, 1857, 1858-1861  MA Ohio St Univ 1954
See also 12, 257, 259, 2703, 3284, 4340, 6096

## LANGSTON HUGHES

3161 ARMSTEAD T J  The Social Realism of Langston Hughes and Sterling Brown  MA Boston Univ 1946
3162 BLUE Illa J  A Study of the Poetry of Langston Hughes  MA North Carolina Central Univ 1945  150 p
3163 BURNS Loretta S  The Black Metropolis in the Poetry of Langston Hughes  MA Ohio St Univ 1967  66 p
3164 FARRELL Mary D  Protest, Pride and Langston Hughes: A Study of the Themes of His Non-musical Three-act Plays  MA Univ of Delaware 1965  45 p

3165 HALL Rubye M  Realism in the Poetry of Langston Hughes  MA Univ of Oklahoma 1959
3166 HILL Eloise H  Langston Hughes: Versatile Spokesman for His Race  MA Northeast Missouri St Coll 1957
3167 KITAMURA Takao  Langston Hughes: American Negro Poet  MA Howard Univ 1966  130 p
3168 ZEIDMAN Nathalie  The Image of the Negro Through the Eyes of Langston Hughes  MA Roosevelt Univ at Chicago 1962

See also 3537

## JAMES GIBBONS HUNEKER

3169 DYNNER Audrey J  James Gibbons Huneker: A Study of His Influences on American Literary Taste  MA Ohio St Univ 1947
3170 JONES Anne L  James Huneker: A Critical Study  MA Univ of Texas at Austin 1939  157 p

## JOSEPH HOLT INGRAHAM

3171 FRENCH Warren G  Joseph Holt Ingraham: Southern Romancer, 1809-1860  MA Univ of Texas at Austin 1948
3172 TURNIPSEED James O  Joseph Holt Ingraham: His Life and Works  MA Auburn Univ 1938

## WASHINGTON IRVING

3173 ANDERSON Martha D  Washington Irving's *Sketch Book* and the Establishment of a Nineteenth Century American Literary Tradition  MA Univ of Tennessee 1966
3174 BENNING Rita J  Character Sketches of Selected Works from Washington Irving's *Sketch Book*  M Ed Henderson St Coll nd
3175 BLACK Michael  The American Face of Washington Irving: An Examination of the Writings Attributed to Diedrich Knickerbocker  MA Columbia Univ 1963  147 p
3176 BOWLES Lester  Irving's Influence on Poe  MA Southern Methodist Univ 1936
3177 BROWN Richard  A Stylistic Comparison of Washington Irving's *Sketch Book* and Charles Dickens' *Sketches by Boz*  MA Ohio St Univ 1969  83 p
3178 CLARK Graves G  The Development of the Surprise Ending in the American Short Story from Washington Irving Through O Henry  MA Columbia Univ 1931
3179 CRAFTS Helen  Washington Irving in Modern Criticism  MA Ohio St Univ 1936
3180 CRAIG Edward J  "Legends of the Conquest of Spain": Irving's Treatment of His Sources  MA Univ of Rhode Island 1968  64 p
3181 DAVIS Gordon  A Study of Irving's Interest in Painting as Reflected in His Literary Work  MA Univ of Iowa 1931
3182 DREWRY Galen N  Satire in Washington Irving's *Knickerbocker's History of New York*  MA Univ of North Carolina at Chapel Hill 1952  97 p
3183 DUGGAR John W  Elements of Romanticism in the Works of Washington Irving  MA Univ of Southern Mississippi 1952
3184 FLYNN L J  Washington Irving: The Humorist  MA Boston Univ 1926
3185 HOFFMAN Louise M  Irving's Use of Spanish Sources in *The Conquest of Granada*  MA Univ of Arizona 1944
3186 INGRAM Pauline E  An Analysis of Characterization in *Diedrich Knickerbocker's History of New York*  MA Univ of Oklahoma 1952
3187 KISKA Pauline L  The Western Writings of Washington Irving  MA Univ of Texas at El Paso 1956  174 p
3188 LAMB John P  Washington Irving and the Tradition of American Humor  MA Univ of Kansas 1954
3189 McCOLLUM Wanda A  Irving the Humorist  MA Univ of Tulsa 1945

3190  McDANIEL C Y  Washington Irving's Interest in the Drama  MA Univ of North Carolina at Chapel Hill 1929
3191  NETHERCUTT Betty G  Washington Irving's Use of Spanish Sources in *The Life and Voyages of Christopher Columbus*, *The Conquest of Granada* and *The Alhambra*  MA Univ of North Carolina at Chapel Hill 1950  104 p
3192  OLIVER Ethel C  Washington Irving as a Biographer  MA Boston Univ 1948
3193  OWENS Lucille  Washington Irving as a Humorist  M Ed Henderson St Coll nd
3194  PARKER Jean L  The Period of Reawakened Americanism in the Life and Works of Washington Irving, 1832-1842  MA Columbia Univ 1953  89 p
3195  PARKER Patti J  The Influence of Travel on Washington Irving's Writings  M Ed Henderson St Coll nd
3196  POMIDOR Walter J  Washington Irving's *The Life and Voyages of Christopher Columbus*: The Restructuring of the Spanish Sources as a Romantic Biography  MA John Carroll Univ 1964
3197  PROWN Jules D  Washington Irving's Interest in Art and His Influence on American Painting  MA Univ of Delaware 1956
3198  RANDALL Robert B  Washington Irving and the Theatre  MA Univ of Oklahoma 1948
3199  RECORD Verna S  Syntactic Patterns in the Writing of Irving, Cooper and Hemingway  MA San Diego St Coll 1964  90 p
3200  REED Henry R  Foreign Influence on the Work of Washington Irving  MA Boston Univ 1934
3201  REID L P  Washington Irving's Interpretation of America  MA Univ of North Carolina at Chapel Hill 1921
3202  RUSHING Lethe  Washington Irving: The First Man of American Letters  M Ed Henderson St Coll nd
3203  RYAN Sr Mariola  Washington Irving: Wit and Man of Sentiment  MA Boston Coll 1954
3204  SCHMIDT M C  American Sketch Books from Irving to Longfellow  MA Univ of Minnesota 1931
3205  SEMMLER Henry C  Washington Irving's *A Tour on the Prairies*  MA Univ of North Carolina at Chapel Hill 1965
3206  SERDAREVIC Bosilka  An Analysis of Some English and German Influences on Washington Irving's *Sketch Book*  MA Columbia Univ 1963  45 p
3207  SMITH Pearl A  Irving's *Astoria*: A Critical Edition (Chapters One to Five)  MA Washington St Univ at Pullman 1934
3208  SPILLMAN Ralph R  Washington Irving's Literary Reputation Among American Authors and Critics, 1820-1860  MA Univ of North Carolina at Raleigh 1946  106 p
3209  STAHLMAN Lucille  Folk Sources and Analogues of Irving's *Alhambra*: A Study of Four Representative Tales  MA American Univ 1966
3210  TOBIASSON Loran J  The Tradition of the Sketch as Seen in Irving's *Sketch Book* and *Bracebridge Hall*, Longfellow's *Outre-mer* and Kennedy's *Swallow Barn*  MA Brigham Young Univ 1968  109 p
3211  TRACY Len G  The Origin of the Rip Van Winkle Legend and the Different Manner of Its Presentation in the Media of the Short Stories  MA Univ of Kentucky 1933
3212  VAN LOEN Helen R  The Masks of Washington Irving  MA Long Island Univ 1967  120 p
3213  WEATHERSPOON Mary A  Irving's Treatment of Politics in His Early Works  MA Univ of Texas at Austin 1965  89 p
3214  WELCH Edna S  A Study of Irving's Origins  MA Univ of Texas at Austin 1932
3215  WEST Elsie L  The Portrayal of the New York Dutch in American Fiction from Washington Irving to the Present  MA Columbia Univ 1951
3216  WHITBECK Earl C  Local Color in Washington Irving's Tales of the Hudson  MA St Univ of New York at Albany 1929
3217  WHITE Naomi J  The Interest of Washington Irving in Music, Painting and Architecture  MA Univ of Oklahoma 1935
3218  WISEMAN Earl F  Washington Irving's Use of American Literary Materials

MA George Washington Univ 1940   64 p
3219  WOODY Dana D   Washington Irving: Artist of the Picturesque   MA Univ of Richmond 1965   71 p
See also 696, 704, 4732, 4771, 4968

## SHIRLEY JACKSON

3220  FERGUSON M G   The Novels of Shirley Jackson: A Critical-analytical Study   MA North Texas St Univ 1970
3221  MARPLE Jewel   The Daemonic in Shirley Jackson   MA Washington St Univ at Pullman 1966

## HENRY JAMES

3222  ABADIE Francine L   Henry James and French Art: An Evolving Point of View   MA Univ of Massachusetts 1964
3223  ADAMS Jennifer M   Henry James and the Sentimental Novel of the Nineteenth Century   MA Univ of Maryland at College Park 1960   94 p
3224  AGLER Sharon P   English and American Societies as Seen in Four Nouvelles by Henry James   MA La Verne Coll 1969   107 p
3225  AITKEN Johan L   Henry James, the Involved Creator: A Study of Motivation in Three Major Works   MA Dalhousie Univ (Canada) 1964
3226  ALDERSON Thomas R   A Critical Analysis of the Characters of Isabel and Madame Merle and Their Conflict in Henry James' *The Portrait of a Lady*   MA Univ of the Pacific 1964   93 p
3227  ALEXANDER Doris F   Ambiguities in the Renunciations of Henry James   MA San Diego St Coll 1964   347 p
3228  ANDERSON Alexander J   Aspects of Narrative Techniques in Three Novels of Henry James   BA Rutgers St Univ 1968   59 p
3229  ANDERSON H M   Henry James' Estimate of Women Novelists   MA Univ of North Carolina at Chapel Hill 1942
3230  ANDERSON Marillene   The Compositional Key: A Study of Henry James' Prefaces in Relation to *The Ambassadors, The Wings of the Dove* and *The Golden Bowl*   MA Univ of Louisville 1964
3231  ARNETT Molane D   Development of the Minor Characters in James' Fiction: 1864-1881   MA Eastern Kentucky Univ 1969   104 p
3232  ARNOLD John W   James and the Concept of Nullity   MA Univ of Massachusetts 1964
3233  AUGHTRY Charles E   Henry James and Puritanism   MA Univ of Oklahoma 1951
3234  BAILEY Alma L   Henry James' Portrayal of the American Character   MA Colorado St Univ 1938   134 p
3235  BATTEN Catherine A   Turgenev and James: A Comparison   MA Univ of Toronto (Canada) 1964
3236  BATTILANA Maria G   Venice as Setting and Symbol in Henry James' Fiction   MA Ca Foscari (Italy) 1967
3237  BEAMS David   A Study of Henry James' *The Sense of the Past*   MA Columbia Univ 1960   119 p
3238  BERLAND Alwyn   Henry James and the Nature of Civilization   M Litt Cambridge Univ (England) 1954
3239  BERMAN Robert H   Henry James: The Plastic Arts in *The Europeans, Daisy Miller* and *An International Episode*   MA Columbia Univ 1960   87 p
3240  BERTRAM Ray M   The Critical Prefaces of Henry James   MA Univ of Kentucky 1937
3241  BLACKBURN Alexander L   Flaubert and the Realism of Henry James   MA Univ of North Carolina at Raleigh 1955   84 p
3242  BLAKELY Patricia P   A Pictorial Conception of Henry James in Selected Works   M Ed Henderson St Coll nd
3243  BLICKMAN Miriam F   Metaphor as Used in Four Short Novels of Henry James: *The Siege of London, The Aspern Papers, The Pupil* and *The Beast in the Jungle*   MA Columbia Univ 1959   82 p

3244 BOE Margaret A  Theme and Image in Henry James' *The Ambassadors*  MA Columbia Univ 1963  87 p
3245 BOUVIER Rosetta H  Types of "Innocents" in Selected Works of Henry James  MA Bowling Green St Univ 1962
3246 BRICKMAN Carol L  The Imagery of Motion in *The Portrait of a Lady*  MA Univ of Vermont 1969  80 p
3247 BRIGGS Ruth C  Henry James and William Dean Howells: A Study of Some Aspects of Their Personal and Literary Relationship  MA Univ of Maine 1956  185 p
3248 BRODY Alan  The Use of the Theatrical Form in Henry James' *The Awkward Age*  MA Columbia Univ 1964  80 p
3249 BROSIUS Mary F  Henry James and the Aristocratic Situation  MA Univ of Pittsburgh 1949
3250 BROWN Marjorie R  Women and the International Theme in Henry James' Works  MA George Peabody Coll for Teachers 1937
3251 BRYANT Paul T  A Glossary of the Critical Terms of Henry James  MA Univ of Oklahoma 1956
3252 BUCKLEY Connie  The Symbolic and Dramatic Functions of the Golden Bowl in Henry James' Novel *The Golden Bowl*  MA Brigham Young Univ 1969  78 p
3253 BUCKNER Phea R  Parental Patterns in Selected Novels of Henry James  MA Northeast Louisiana Univ 1963  65 p
3254 BUGG Virginia F  The Manuscript of Henry James' "Four Meetings": A Typescript Reproduction and Collation with the First Published Text  MA Univ of Louisville 1969  72 p
3255 BUKOWSKY Helen S  The Heroine in Henry James: A Psychological Reality  MA Brooklyn Coll of City Univ of New York 1951  69 p
3256 BURNS Aileen I  Art and Its Correlation with Life as Expressed in Certain Novels of Henry James  MA Brigham Young Univ 1969  57 p
3257 BYRD Joseph S  The Versions of Henry James' *Daisy Miller*  MA Univ of North Carolina at Chapel Hill 1960
3258 CAMP J T  Direct and Indirect Methods of Presenting Character in Selected Novels of James and Galsworthy  MA Ohio St Univ 1931
3259 CAMPBELL May E  The Use of the Supernatural in the Short Stories of Henry James and Edith Wharton  MA Univ of Texas at Austin 1938  130 p
3260 CARNEFIX Virginia E  The European Background in the Novels of Henry James  MA Butler Univ 1939
3261 CARROLL Benjamin H Jr  The Supernatural in the Writings of Henry James  MA Louisiana St Univ 1939
3262 CLARK Robert L  James' *The Turn of the Screw*: The Governess and the Ghosts  MA Columbia Univ 1959  118 p
3263 COHEN Willy  Henry James: The War Years, 1914-1916  MA Hunter Coll 1964
3264 COLEMAN Alice C  Scattered Radiance: A Critical Study of a Selected Group of Heroines Taken from the Nouvelles of Henry James Written During the Years 1888 to 1897  MA San Diego St Coll 1951  124 p
3265 CONNELL Ettabel D  A Comparison of Henry James' Use of Dramatic Irony Concerning the Theme of the American in Europe in *The American* and *The Portrait of a Lady*  MA Texas Agricultural and Mechanical Univ 1968  78 p
3266 COOPER Judith J  Two Portraits of a Lady by Henry James and T S Eliot  MA Columbia Univ 1961  110 p
3267 COSPER Vivian C  Henry James and the Well-made Play  MA Rice Univ 1962
3268 CRANE Rochelle  Henry James as a Drama Critic  MA Columbia Univ 1966  69 p
3269 CRAWFORD Quay  James' Art: "A Social Stumbling-block"  MA Mississippi St Univ 1961  67 p
3270 CROMER V W  The Development of Henry James' "Scenic" Method in the Novels and Stories After 1895: A Study of a Dramatic Genius Which Could Not Be Expressed on the Stage and Its Realization in Prose Fiction  MA Univ of London (England) 1963
3271 CZAJA Helen M  The Artist as Portrayed by Henry James  MA Coll of

the Holy Names at Oakland 1959
3272 DARDEN Frances E  The Americans in Henry James' Fiction  MA Univ of Mississippi 1949  158 p
3273 DAVIS Leona G  On a Certain Blindness in Henry James: A Study of His Jewish Characters  MA Univ of Pittsburgh 1961
3274 DAVIS Patricia A  Problems of Identity in Henry James' *The Bostonians*  MA Ohio St Univ 1966  57 p
3275 DENNY William L  An Enquiry Into the Significance of the Supernatural Novellas of Henry James  MA Univ of Houston 1951  101 p
3276 DI SALVO Leta P  A Study of the Criticism of the Works of Henry James from 1920 to 1930  MA Syracuse Univ 1948  81 p
3277 DOERSAM J B  Objects of Art in the Tales and Little Novels of Henry James  MA Ohio St Univ 1926
3278 DONADIO Stephen  Henry James: The Lost Relation  MA Columbia Univ 1965  81 p
3279 DUGAN Robert J  The Inner Harmony of Henry James' Novels  MA Boston Coll 1963
3280 DUNCAN Kirby L  Henry James: The Development of a Moral Philosophy  MA Texas Technological Univ 1964  73 p
3281 DUNCAN Susan G  A Study of Henry James' Two Versions of *The Outcry*  MA Univ of North Carolina at Chapel Hill 1966
3282 DURR Robert A  The Night Journey in *The Ambassadors*  MA Univ of Connecticut 1952
3283 DUTTON Joseph F  The Influence of Henry James in the Novels of Edith Wharton  MA Butler Univ 1953
3284 EBERWINE L A  The Women of James and Howells, 1875-1885  MA Ohio St Univ 1931
3285 ERICKSON Peter B  Unseen Uses of Society in the Later Novels of Henry James  BA Amherst Coll 1967
3286 FIGG Robert McC III  Henry James' American Man in Europe  MA Univ of North Carolina at Raleigh 1954  91 p
3287 FINKLE Jonathan  The Controlling Consciousness in James' *The Golden Bowl*  MA Hunter Coll 1967
3288 FINNEY Martha C  The Unique Instrument: A Study of Point of View in the Novels of Henry James  MA Univ of Iowa 1965
3289 FLAXMAN Erwin  *Lessons of the Master*: The Image of the Artist in Henry James  MA Temple Univ 1964  47 p
3290 FLETCHER Gwendolyn S  The Free-hanging Nudal: A Study of the Structure of *The Wings of the Dove*  MA Georgetown Univ 1969  87 p
3291 FLOWEDAY Frances E  Humour in the Serious Novel: A Study of the Sources and Function of the Humour in Henry James' *The Portrait of a Lady*, Using P G Wodehouse's *The Code of the Woosters* for Purpose of Reference  MA Univ of Manitoba (Canada) 1967
3292 FRANKLIN Rosemary F  Henry James' Prefaces to the New York Edition: An Index and an Analysis  MA Wake Forest Univ 1964
3293 FRIGERIO Eugenia  The Theatre of Henry James  MA Ca Foscari (Italy) 1961
3294 GAAL M M  Character Development of the Heroines in the Novels of Henry James  MA Ohio St Univ 1932
3295 GARBUIO Fiorella  *Roderick Hudson* by Henry James  MA Ca Foscari (Italy) 1969
3296 GARRIGAN Kristine O  The Imagination of Atrocity: A Study of Henry James' *The Sacred Fount*  MA Ohio St Univ 1964  158 p
3297 GILLINGHAM Emma L  A Study of Two Women in Henry James' Novels  MA Illinois St Univ at Normal 1965
3298 GOOCH Dixie R  Recognizable Patterns of Characterization and Plot Structure in Five Major Novels by Henry James  MA Clemson Univ 1967
3299 GORAN Sylvester L  The Fraudulent Artist in Henry James  MA Univ of Pittsburgh 1960
3300 GOTS Barbara A  Religious Imagery in the Novels of Henry James  MA Temple Univ 1966  94 p

3301 GRAY Anne K  The Death of the Heart in Three Nouvelles of Henry James  MA San Diego St Coll 1968  56 p
3302 GREENHAW Charles R  The Ghostly Tales of Henry James  MA North Texas St Univ 1965
3303 GRELLA George  The Sacred Struggles: Imagery and Meaning in the Last Three Novels of Henry James  MA Univ of Kansas 1965
3304 GRUMET Marilyn L  The Innocents of Henry James  MA Ohio St Univ 1966  43 p
3305 HAMON Mary S  The Use of the Child as a Literary Device by Henry James and Carson McCullers  MA Univ of Texas at Austin 1964  100 p
3306 HANLEY John M  The Artist in the Work of Henry James  MA McMaster Univ (Canada) 1965
3307 HAYES Thomas  The Influence of Ivan Turgenev on Henry James  MA American Univ 1966
3308 HAZARD Francine P  A Comparison of the Novel and Play Forms of Henry James' *The American*  MA Ohio St Univ 1963  80 p
3309 HEMBREE Charles W  Imagery and Architectonics in Henry James' *The Golden Bowl*  MA Univ of Oklahoma 1963
3310 HOCKS Richard  Henry James and Pragmatic Thought  MA Univ of North Carolina at Chapel Hill 1967
3311 HOGG Ruth S  From Setting to Scene in Henry James: A Study of *Roderick Hudson*, *The Tragic Muse* and *The Wings of the Dove*  MA Univ of Toronto (Canada) 1966
3312 HOLT K C  The Henry James' Finale as Developed in the Novels  MA Ohio St Univ 1929
3313 HORRELL Joyce T  Names and Their Significance in the Novels and Tales of Henry James (1870-1900)  MA Univ of Maryland at College Park 1963  99 p
3314 HORWITZ Dawn L  Henry James: The Dramatic Years and Their Influence on His Craft; a Comparison of *The Portrait of a Lady* and *The Wings of the Dove*  MA Columbia Univ 1960  83 p
3315 HOVANEC Evelyn A  Roger Lawrence and Rowland Mallet: A Study of James' Ambivalent Heroes  MA Duquesne Univ 1966
3316 HOWARD John K  Morality and the Economic Marriage  MA Univ of Vermont 1966  106 p
3317 HUMPHERYS Anne  The Broken Bowl: A Comparative Study of the Criticism of *The Golden Bowl*, a Novel by Henry James  MA Columbia Univ 1962  129 p
3318 HUNTER Glen D  The "Trapped" Spectator in Four of James' Novels  MA Auburn Univ 1967
3319 IACONO W R  *The Ambassadors*: The Dialect of Action and Repose  MA Rice Univ 1968
3320 ILLINGWORTH Elsie J  The Young Woman in the Novels of Henry James  MA Univ of Saskatchewan (Canada) 1964
3321 INGBER Marcia R  The Renunciation of Joy: A Study of Henry James' Male Characters in *The Princess Casamassima*, *The Ambassadors*, *The Wings of the Dove* and *The Bostonians*  MA Tufts Univ 1963
3322 JAMES Gordon  The Affective Level of Henry James' Novels  MA Texas Technological Univ 1932  45 p
3323 JAMES Norman  Henry James' Criticism of American Literature from 1865 to 1879  MA Univ of Maryland at College Park 1950  104 p
3324 JOHNSON Avis L  A Selective Study of Henry James' Revisions for the New York Edition  MA Kansas St Univ 1965
3325 JONES Alan K  The Concept of Choice in Certain Novels of Henry James  MA Texas Technological Univ 1962  64 p
3326 JORDAN Anna G  Scholarly and Critical Studies of Henry James' *The Portrait of a Lady*, 1943-1958: A Survey  MA Georgetown Univ 1961
3327 JULIAN James L  Henry James' Characterization of Women  MA Univ of Texas at Austin 1940  199 p
3328 KELLEY David J  A Consideration of the Theme of Good and Evil in

Selected Short Fiction of Henry James  MA Univ of Rhode Island 1967  81 p

3329 KEYES Daniel  The Writer as a Character in Modern American Fiction: Henry James to Thomas Wolfe  MA Brooklyn Coll of City Univ of New York 1961  84 p
3330 KNEEBONE Sydney A  A Critical Study of *The Wings of the Dove*  MA Univ of Pittsburgh 1948
3331 KNIGHT William N  Henry James: The Other Side of Silence--A Study of Narrative Evolution  BA Amherst Coll 1961
3332 KNIGHTON Ellen S  Americans Abroad in Novels of Henry James  MA West Texas St Univ 1950  70 p
3333 KOCH Dorothy A  Morality in the Criticism of Henry James  MA Univ of Pittsburgh 1933
3334 LANDON Emalou G  Henry James: A Critical Study of *The Ambassadors*  MS Kansas St Coll at Pittsburg 1963
3335 LAUX Margaret  A Study of the Art-property Images in Henry James' *The Golden Bowl*  MA Georgetown Univ 1958  87 p
3336 LAWSON Jack B  Henry James: Truth and Art  MA Southern Illinois Univ at Carbondale 1958  112 p
3337 LEIBEL Paulette  Technique and Form in Six Tales of Henry James  BA Univ of British Columbia (Canada) 1968
3338 LEIKEN Hope L  Henry James: Social Critic  MA Columbia Univ 1941
3339 LEVIN Elaine B  Floral Imagery and the Jamesian Woman  MA Brooklyn Coll of City Univ of New York 1956  82 p
3340 LEWIS Linda G  Through a Glass Darkly: The Literary Reputation of Henry James  MA Univ of Richmond 1962  112 p
3341 McCLARE Dale A  Henry James' *The Portrait of a Lady*: A Character Analysis of Isabel Archer  MA Gonzaga Univ 1966
3342 McDOWELL Alfred B  Henry James' Attitude Toward America, 1900-1916  MA Bowling Green St Univ 1968
3343 McGRATH Neva E  The Prefaces of Henry James: Their Additions to His Critical Theory  MA Columbia Univ 1935
3344 McLAUGHLIN Lula E  The Personality of Henry James  MA Univ of California at Berkeley 1920
3345 McMULLEN Michael  A Study of the Imagery of Character in Henry James' *The Wings of the Dove*  MS Kansas St Coll at Pittsburg 1966
3346 MAIXNER Paul R  The Structure of James' *The Ambassadors*  MA Columbia Univ 1955  78 p
3347 MANLY William M  Imagination and Reality in Henry James  BA Amherst Coll 1956
3348 MARSON Antonio  *The Portrait of a Lady* by Henry James  MA Ca Foscari (Italy) 1969
3349 MARTIN Ann H  A Critical Analysis of Henry James' *The Golden Bowl*  MA Univ of North Carolina at Raleigh 1949  184 p
3350 MASON David J  Two Masks of the Master: Some Henry James Themes as Fiction and Drama  MA Columbia Univ 1950
3351 MATHEWS Robin D  Plastic Form in Henry James' Novel *The Ambassadors*  MA Ohio St Univ 1958
3352 MAY Susan H  The Illusion of Time in the Fiction of Henry James  MA Univ of Delaware 1961  84 p
3353 MAYNARD Sr Ann R  The Renunciation Theme in Henry James  MA Coll of the Holy Names at Oakland 1966
3354 MAZZELLA Anthony J  Mrs Grose and *The Turn of the Screw*  MA Columbia Univ 1964  119 p
3355 MEYER Emily  Imagery and Vision in *The Golden Bowl* and *The Ambassadors*  MA Columbia Univ 1962  58 p
3356 MILLER Evelyn E  *The Turn of the Screw* by Henry James: A Redaction and Analysis  MA Univ of Connecticut 1958
3357 MILLER Richard H  A Critical Analysis of Henry James' *The Princess Casamassima*  MA Columbia Univ 1960  61 p

3358  MILLER Violet L  Parties as Symbol and Pattern in the Later Novels of Henry James  MA Univ of Texas at Austin 1963  105 p
3359  MISSIO Rita  Henry James and the Theatre  MA Ca Foscari (Italy) 1957
3360  MONHERRAN Marie  Henry James' Treatment of France  MA Cornell Univ 1965
3361  MOORE Rachel H  A Study of the Moral Choice in Selected Works of Henry James  MA Baylor Univ 1969  161 p
3362  MORGAN Joanne C  Henry James' Art of Narration  MA DePauw Univ 1963  48 p
3363  MORTON Doris B  Woman's Changing Role in American Civilization as Portrayed by Henry James and Edith Wharton  MA Univ of Texas at Austin 1964
3364  MOTARD Pierre P  Henry James' Ghostly Stories and the Haunted Mind of the Artist  MA Ohio St Univ 1952
3365  NANGERONI Olga M  Henry James in Italy  MA Columbia Univ nd
3366  NEFF Allen R  The Imagery in Henry James' Short Stories of the 1890's  MA Ohio St Univ 1957
3367  NELSON Susan A  Studies in the Development of Consciousness in the Fiction of Henry James  MA Univ of Oklahoma 1960
3368  NEUMAN Mary A  The Social Purpose of Henry James' Art  MA Howard Univ 1967  184 p
3369  NOYES Naomi  Complexity and Guest: Henry James and Society  MA Hunter Coll 1962
3370  NYENHUIS Mary E  The Dramatic Illusion in Browning's Dramatic Monologues and James' Later Novels  MA Ohio St Univ 1960  94 p
3371  O'CONNELL Mary C  An Introduction to Henry James  MA Boston Univ 1948
3372  O'CONNELL Susan V  The Jamesian Passion  MA Univ of Massachusetts 1965
3373  ODUM Martha K  Interruption in the Stream: Henry James' Use of Parentheses in "The Bench of Desolation"  MA Univ of North Carolina at Chapel Hill 1965
3374  OLNEY Clarke  Earlier Short Stories of Henry James  MA Univ of Pittsburgh 1926
3375  O'NEIL Sr Marie T  Henry James: The Use of Symbols to Effect an Impression of Life  MA Boston Coll 1962
3376  ONLEY Gloria E  Henry James and the Zeitgeist  MA Univ of British Columbia (Canada) 1966
3377  OTTERVIK Eric Van T  Henry James' *The Sacred Fount*: A Critical Study  MA Univ of Pittsburgh 1961
3378  OWEN E E  Wit as an Instrument of Moral Discrimination in the Later Novels of Henry James  MA Univ of London (England) 1966
3379  OYZON Crescenciana K  A Study of Symbolism in the Last Three Complete Novels of Henry James  MA Boston Coll 1960
3380  OZICK Cynthia  Parable in Henry James: The Twentieth Century Novels  MA Ohio St Univ 1950
3381  PAROISSIEN David  Henry James and His Use of the Vampire Emblem  MA New Mexico Highlands Univ 1966
3382  PEROTTI Valerie J  Three Ghostly Tales of Henry James: A Study of Irony  MA Duquesne Univ 1966
3383  PERRIN Edwin N  The Multiplication of Touches: A Study of the Late Jamesian Style  M Litt Cambridge Univ (England) 1959
3384  PINCUS Harriet  Henry James and Humane Consciousness  MA Brooklyn Coll of City Univ of New York 1955  88 p
3385  PORTERFIELD Nolan  The Storeyism of Henry James and Ernest Hemingway: Parables Between *The Ambassadors* and *The Sun Also Rises*  MA Texas Technological Univ 1964  70 p
3386  POWELL Douglas J  Henry James' Treatment of Romantic Love in the Early Tales  MA Wake Forest Univ 1966
3387  PRITCHARD Orpha B  Parallels in the Short Stories of Henry James, Edith Wharton and Willa Cather  MA Univ of Maryland at College Park 1941  68 p
3388  QUINT Muriel E  Henry James and His Aesthetic Idealism  MA Univ of

New Hampshire 1954 249 p
3389 RASCO Lavon  The Point of View from Which Henry James Tells His Novels  MA Univ of Mississippi 1949  105 p
3390 RASKIN Jonah  Henry James: The Historical Imagination  MA Columbia Univ 1964  92 p
3391 REICH Rosalie  A Study of Henry James' Use of Imagery in *The Ambassadors*  MA Brooklyn Coll of City Univ of New York 1955  52 p
3392 REID Alice  The Illusion of Personality: An Analysis of Seven Short Stories by Henry James  MA Lehigh Univ 1966
3393 RICHMOND Lee J  Henry James and the Comedy of Love: A Study of Three Late Novels  MA Syracuse Univ 1962  127 p
3394 RODGERS Claud D  *The Wings of the Dove*: An Affirmation of Impressionism  MA Univ of Louisville 1967  132 p
3395 ROESER K M  Color Description in Meredith, Hardy and James  MA Ohio St Univ 1913
3396 ROGERS Rita  The Genius of Henry James' *The Turn of the Screw* and an Analysis of the Critical Interpretations of the Novel  MA Univ of South Dakota 1962  70 p
3397 ROSE Zelda  An Inquiry Into the Significance of Certain Recurrent Themes in the Ghostly Tales of Henry James  MA Columbia Univ 1954  96 p
3398 ROSEMOND Leslie  The Golden Bowl, Image and Symbol, as It Appears in the Novel of That Name, Written by Henry James  MA Ohio St Univ 1922
3399 ROUILLARD Harriet L  Henry James and the Life of Art  MA Smith Coll 1934
3400 SAINER Stefanie  Henry James' Concept of the Painter's Intuition, Particularly as Reflected in the Novel *Roderick Hudson*  MA Columbia Univ 1959  78 p
3401 SANDERS Errol F  The Relationships Between the Sexes in the Three Great Novels of James' Major Phase  MA Univ of Georgia 1965
3402 SCHINDELMAN Lily  Types of Modern Women in Meredith and James  MA Ohio St Univ 1925
3403 SCHOLES James B  American and British Criticism of Henry James, 1916-1953  MA Univ of North Carolina at Chapel Hill 1961
3404 SCHWARTZ Joan C  Henry James' *The Sacred Fount*: A Study of Critical Interpretations  MA Columbia Univ 1964  85 p
3405 SCHWERTMAN Mary P  Henry James' Portraits of Ladies  MA Univ of North Carolina at Chapel Hill 1968
3406 SEGAL Alan F  The House of a Million Windows: Henry James and a New England Moral Tradition  BA Amherst Coll 1967
3407 SENTER Mark L  Henry James' Use of Garden Imagery and Garden Settings in *The Portrait of a Lady*, *The Spoils of Poynton* and *The Ambassadors*  MS Kansas St Coll at Pittsburg 1967
3408 SHELLY Elizabeth W  Nature Imagery in Henry James' *The Wings of the Dove* and *The Golden Bowl*  MA Temple Univ 1965  56 p
3409 SILVERMAN Dorothy H  Henry James: The Art of Life  MA Univ of Delaware 1956  56 p
3410 SILVERMAN Judith  The Collector and the Connoisseur: Henry James' Use of Art Objects with Special Attention to *The Spoils of Poynton* and *The Golden Bowl*  MA Columbia Univ 1960  90 p
3411 SIMES M E  The Little Novels of Henry James  MA Ohio St Univ 1918
3412 SMITH M H  The American Businessman in the Novels and Stories of Henry James  MA North Texas St Univ 1969
3413 SNYDER L E  Evidence of the Painter in the Early Short Stories of Henry James  MA Ohio St Univ 1927
3414 SOLOMON Rose M  A Study of the Fictional Writers in the Ten Tales of Henry James  MA Indiana Univ of Pennsylvania 1966  77 p
3415 SPANOS Bebe  Reality and Significance in the Shorter Fiction of Henry James  MA Univ of Pittsburgh 1947
3416 SPECK Paul S  A Structural Analysis of *Rowland Mallet*: Henry James'

Misnomer  MA Auburn Univ 1969
3417 SPEEGLE K S  A Study of the Characters in the Novels of Henry James  MA North Texas St Univ 1949
3418 STANDISH Evelyn Y  The Aesthetic Consciousness of Henry James  MA Florida St Univ 1949  44 p
3419 STANLEY Emily B  The Use of Setting in the Novels of Henry James  MA Univ of Florida 1956
3420 STEELE H G  Revelations of Method in Henry James' Prefaces to His Novels Compared to Analyses of His Art by Other Critics  MA Ohio St Univ 1933
3421 STEPANIUK Anna  Displacement in Henry James  MA Univ of Western Ontario (Canada) 1963
3422 STONE Francis B  The Shorter Fictions of Henry James: A Critical Study  MA Univ of Pittsburgh 1930
3423 STONE Susan L  Henry James' *Julia Bride*: An Analysis  MA Univ of North Carolina at Chapel Hill 1967
3424 STONE Vesta L  Themes in the Earliest Tales of Henry James  MA Univ of Tulsa 1968  62 p
3425 SULLENBERGER Tom E  The Abuse of Confidence as a Major Theme in the Novels of Henry James  MA North Texas St Univ 1966
3426 SULLIVAN William J  Studies on James, Dreiser and Faulkner  MA Univ of Utah 1966
3427 SWEARINGEN J E  Morality in Three of the Later Novels of Henry James  MA North Texas St Univ 1962
3428 SWEARINGEN Wilba S  Money in Four of the Early Novels of Henry James  MA North Texas St Univ 1966
3429 SWEIVEN Edrig G  Light as a Mode of Revelation in Three Novels of Henry James: *The Portrait of a Lady*, *What Maisie Knew* and *The Awkward Age*  MA Texas Technological Univ 1968  51 p
3430 SZALA Alina  Henry James' Shorter Fiction: A Study in Structural Development  MA Columbia Univ 1959  95 p
3431 TADASEO Ruth T  The Humanism of Henry James: Major Premise of His Later Phase  MA Texas Technological Univ 1959  53 p
3432 TARLETON Robert M  A Study of Henry James' Development of the Narrator as a Technical Device in Three Selected Works  MA Univ of the Pacific 1962  99 p
3433 THOMAS Audrey G  Henry James in the Palace of Art: A Survey Evaluation of James' Aesthetic Criteria as Shown in His Criticism of Nineteenth Century Painting  MA Univ of British Columbia (Canada) 1963
3434 THOMAS Carol E  Four Novels of Henry James: The Point of View  MA Auburn Univ 1968
3435 THORNHILL E E  A Study in the Fact and the Symbolism of Henry James' *The Golden Bowl*  MA Ohio St Univ 1925
3436 TURNER Dorcas A  Henry James' Tales of Tormented Children  MA Texas Technological Univ 1968  98 p
3437 WAGNER Linda W  Heredity and Character in Selected Novels of Henry James  MA Bowling Green St Univ 1959
3438 WARD Marjorie A  The Philosophical Position of Henry James  MA Univ of Kansas 1953
3439 WESTBROOK Frankie L  The Artist Stories of Henry James  MA Univ of Oklahoma 1953
3440 WILDA Adrienne R  Henry James' View of Evil in His Writings from 1888-1899  MA Univ of New Mexico 1952
3441 WILSON J M  The Nature and Function of Dialogue in the Short Stories of Henry James  MA Univ of London (England) 1965
3442 WINKS Patricia L  The Adoption Theme in the Novels of Henry James  MA Columbia Univ 1961  120 p
3443 WINSOR Philip  The Observer in Henry James  MA Columbia Univ 1955  84 p
3444 WOLFE Bertie B  Significant Patterns of Imagery in the Works of

Henry James  MA Univ of Houston 1966  132 p
3445  WOOD B N  Patterns of Imagery in Henry James' *The Ambassadors*  MA North Texas St Univ 1968
3446  ZARA Bertha R  The Figure in the Carpet: Patterns of Myths, Fairy Tales and Bible Stories in the Fiction of Henry James  MA Hunter Coll 1960
3447  ZUANELLI Elisabetta  *The Turn of the Screw* by Henry James  MA Ca Foscari (Italy) 1968
See also 2440, 2481, 2623, 2703, 2725, 3097, 3449, 6436, 6441

## WILLIAM JAMES

3448  CLIFT Blanche  William James as an Educator  M Ed Temple Univ 1932
3449  DAVIDSON Gilbert A  William James as a Critic of Henry James  MA San Diego St Coll 1958  73 p
3450  JACKSON Peggy M  The Theory of Experience in the Philosophy of William James  MA Univ of Oklahoma 1965
3451  PATCH Alice  William James, Self-actualizer: A Study of Continuing and Creative Growth  MA Univ of New Hampshire 1959  117 p
3452  SHIRAHAMA Kyukio  The Effect of William James' Pragmatism on His Religious Philosophy  MA Univ of Oklahoma 1968
See also 3982, 5192

## RANDALL JARRELL

3453  EISIMINGER Sterling K  The Poetry of Randall Jarrell: A Study of Its Critical Acceptance and the Poet's Development of His Major Themes and Motifs  MA Auburn Univ 1968
3454  GILLIKIN Dure J  Conventions in Randall Jarrell's War Poems  MA Univ of North Carolina at Chapel Hill 1958  95 p
3455  HONEYCUTT Irene B  Randall Jarrell: A Study of His World, His War, His Woods  MA East Tennessee St Univ 1969
3456  HUGHES Betty S  The Dream Motif in the Poetic Works of Randall Jarrell  MA Lamar Technological Univ 1966  148 p
3457  KILLGALLON Donald A  The Literary Criticism of Randall Jarrell  MA Univ of Maryland at College Park 1966  72 p
3458  KOBLER Jasper F  The Three Voices of Randall Jarrell  MA Univ of Houston 1959  121 p
3459  SKATES Craig B  Randall Jarrell and the Inhumanity of Obscurity  MA Univ of Southern Mississippi 1968
3460  STURTEVANT Donald F  A Study of the Criticism and Poetry of Randall Jarrell  MA Syracuse Univ 1964  99 p
3461  VARDAMIS Alex A  Randall Jarrell: Poem and "Marchen"  MA Columbia Univ 1967  77 p
See also 5109

## ROBINSON JEFFERS

3462  ALLEN Irwin M  The Symbolism of Robinson Jeffers  MA Univ of Houston 1949  56 p
3463  BAILEY Lucy  The California Background in the Poetry of Robinson Jeffers  MA Univ of Kansas 1934
3464  BENTON Johnny  An Interpretative Analysis of Robinson Jeffers' *The Women at Point Sur*  MA Univ of Oklahoma 1967  263 p
3465  BRADFORD Mary J  A Spirit for the Stone: Themes and Ideas in the Poetry of Robinson Jeffers  MA Univ of Tulsa 1953  136 p
3466  BROPHY Robert J  Structure, Symbol and Myth in Selected Narratives of Robinson Jeffers  MA Univ of North Carolina at Chapel Hill 1966
3467  BUFFUM Molly S  A Study of the Reputation of Robinson Jeffers Before 1930  MA Univ of Wyoming 1965

3468  BUTLER Dennis R  Elements of German Ideal Philosophy in the Poems of Robinson Jeffers  MA Midwestern Univ 1967  112 p
3469  CARNES Frank F  The Poetry of Robinson Jeffers  MA Univ of Mississippi 1949  115 p
3470  CAVANAUGH Jerald D  Tragedy and the Tragic Hero in the Carmel Narratives of Robinson Jeffers  MA Univ of Pittsburgh 1962
3471  CLARK Bruce B  A Study of the Longer Carmel Narrative Poems of Robinson Jeffers  MA Brigham Young Univ 1947  126 p
3472  COMBS John E  The Weltanschauung of Robinson Jeffers  MA Butler Univ 1963
3473  COX Mary M  The Role of Women in the Narrative Poetry of Robinson Jeffers  MA Univ of North Carolina at Chapel Hill 1964
3474  CROWE Charles T  Robinson Jeffers: The Ultimate Destiny of Man  MA Southern Illinois Univ at Carbondale 1958  52 p
3475  CZERMAK Herbeth  For the Strong There Are Left the Mountains: Robinson Jeffers' Solution to the Dilemma of Modern Man  MA Univ of New Hampshire 1961  83 p
3476  DODEZ M Leon  Robinson Jeffers' "Roan Stallion": An Analysis and Appraisal for the Oral Interpreter  MA Ohio St Univ 1960  269 p
3477  EARISMAN Delbert L  Robinson Jeffers as a Nature Poet  MA Columbia Univ 1955  128 p
3478  EATON David J  An Evaluation of Robinson Jeffers as a Lyric Poet  MA Univ of Maine 1967  97 p
3479  FRITZ Donald E  The Concept of Time in the Poetry of Robinson Jeffers  MA Texas Technological Univ 1969  88 p
3480  GORDON Dudley W  Robinson Jeffers Disputes Death  MA Fairleigh Dickinson Univ 1960  85 p
3481  HARING Jo M  Permanence: Robinson Jeffers' Poetic Theory  MA Southern Illinois Univ at Carbondale 1959  75 p
3482  HART William D  Robinson Jeffers: A Study of "The Tower Beyond Tragedy", with a Copy of the Unpublished Manuscript of the Drama  MA Columbia Univ 1951
3483  JOHNSON Emily C  Robinson Jeffers and the Problem of Humanity  MA Univ of Kentucky 1948  53 p
3484  KENDALL Jack L  A Correlation of the Philosophical Judgments in the Poetry of Robinson Jeffers  MA Univ of Kansas 1948
3485  LANE Margaret A  Nature in the Poetry of Robinson Jeffers  MA Southern Illinois Univ at Carbondale 1953  83 p
3486  LEE Jae N  Destructive Forces of Introversion: A Study of the Poetry of Robinson Jeffers  MA Univ of Idaho 1960
3487  LIPSON Benjamin H  Robinson Jeffers and the Paradox of Humanism  MA Columbia Univ 1951
3488  LYNN Justine  The Study of the Jeffers' Symbol for Introversion  MA Univ of Kentucky 1939
3489  McDOWELL Charlotte B  A Study of Robinson Jeffers' Adaption of Euripedes' *Medea*  MA Oklahoma St Univ 1961
3490  MARIA Francis  Robinson Jeffers and His Poetry  MA Boston Univ 1937
3491  MONJIAN Mercedes C  Robinson Jeffers: A Study in Inhumanism  MA Univ of Pittsburgh 1958
3492  ORR Thomas J  Parallels to Hinduism in the Poetry of Robinson Jeffers  MA Ohio St Univ 1969  97 p
3493  PHELPS Harry C  Shifted Emphasis: The Concept of Tragedy in the Poetry of Robinson Jeffers  MA Florida St Univ 1950
3494  POWERS Velma M  An Interpretative Analysis of Robinson Jeffers' *Medea*  MA Univ of Oklahoma 1950
3495  REMALEY Peter P  The Doctrines of Inhumanism in the Poetry of Robinson Jeffers  MA Kent St Univ 1965
3496  RIDGEWAY Ann M  A Study in Inhumanism: Action Symbols in the Shorter Poems of Robinson Jeffers  MA Bowling Green St Univ 1957
3497  ROTHMAN Abby B  The Electra Myth from Aeschylus to Robinson Jeffers

MA Columbia Univ 1954  82 p
3498 SANDERS Elisabeth A  Robinson Jeffers' Philosophy of Inhumanism
MA Texas Technological Univ 1958  80 p
3499 SCOFIELD Sandra V  Robinson Jeffers: His Myth of Man's Innate Evil
MA Univ of Maryland at College Park 1968  63 p
3500 SHIELDS Jerry A  Robinson Jeffers and His Savior-inhumanist Dilemma
MA Duke Univ 1966
3501 SMITH Muriel I  Principal Themes in Robinson Jeffers' Book *The Beginning and the End*  MA Univ of Redlands 1965
3502 SPIESE Richard D  Robinson Jeffers: Aesthetic Theory and Practice
MA Univ of New Mexico 1966
3503 STAMPER James M  A Preliminary Examination of Robinson Jeffers' Poetry as It Suggests a Geopoetics  MA Univ of Kentucky 1946  186 p
3504 WRUBEL David  Primitivism and Robinson Jeffers: A Survey and a Study
MA Columbia Univ 1940
See also 1289, 4247, 4811

## THOMAS JEFFERSON

3505 BLACKMAN Herbert N  Thomas Jefferson and the Natural Sciences
MA Columbia Univ 1936
3506 CAREY Alma P  Thomas Jefferson's Ideal University: Dream and Actuality
M Ed Univ of Texas at Austin 1937
3507 EUBANKS Seaford W  A Vocabulary Study of Thomas Jefferson's *Notes on Virginia*  MA Univ of Missouri 1940
3508 JOHNSON Axel  The Principles of Thomas Jefferson  MA Univ of Kansas 1908
3509 LEDDY A F  Thomas Jefferson  MA Boston Coll 1933
3510 LICHTENSTEIN William  The Pacifism of Thomas Jefferson: Its Underlying Philosophy and Its Practical Application  MA Columbia Univ 1935
3511 LOKENSGARD Hjalmar  The Aristocratic Element in Jefferson's Educational Plan  MA Univ of Iowa 1932
3512 STOUT Belle M  Interest in Science in Early American Writers with Special Reference to Thomas Jefferson  MA Univ of Iowa 1928
3513 YINGLING George S  The Rights of Man as Understood by Thomas Jefferson
MA Ohio St Univ 1944
See also 31, 362

## SARAH ORNE JEWETT

3514 BECK Margaret F  France and the French in the Life and Work of Sarah Orne Jewett  MA Univ of Rhode Island 1964  104 p
3515 BENSTEN June M  Sarah Orne Jewett: An Interpretation of Her Work
MA Brooklyn Coll of City Univ of New York 1967  78 p
3516 BLOMENKAMP Alfrieda  Sarah Orne Jewett: A Study in Regionalism
MA Univ of Texas at Austin 1945  173 p
3517 BRETZ Leslie S  The Pastoral Mode in Sarah Orne Jewett's *The Country of the Pointed Firs*  MA Univ of North Carolina at Chapel Hill 1968
3518 BRYAN Jessie F  Sarah Orne Jewett's Interpretation of Maine Life
MA Univ of Maine 1930  209 p
3519 BRYANT Rosemary  The Realism of Sarah Orne Jewett  MA Southern Illinois Univ at Carbondale 1962  87 p
3520 CHESLER Pearl  Sarah Orne Jewett: From *Deephaven* to *Pointed Firs*
MA Columbia Univ 1967  56 p
3521 COLLINS Michael F  Humor in the Art of Sarah Orne Jewett  MA Univ of North Carolina at Chapel Hill 1964
3522 DAVIES Carolyn S  The Relationship Between Nature and Character in the Works of Sarah Orne Jewett  MA Ohio St Univ 1965  65 p
3523 DONAHUE Marie A  Sarah Orne Jewett: New England Realist  MA Univ of New Hampshire 1955  89 p
3524 FAUST Margaret  Sarah Orne Jewett: A Study  MA Univ of Kansas 1928

3525 FRIZZELL Jane  The Pastoral in the Art of Sarah Orne Jewett  MA Univ of North Carolina at Chapel Hill 1968
3526 KISH Dorothy  Effect of the Economic Decline of New England Coastal Towns on the Writing of Sarah Orne Jewett  MA Univ of Pittsburgh 1961
3527 LAUGHLIN A T  New England Characteristics in the Stories of Sarah Orne Jewett  MA Boston Univ 1942
3528 LINKEY Alice  The Characters in the Short Stories of Sarah Orne Jewett  MA George Peabody Coll for Teachers 1929
3529 MAGOWAN Robert A Jr  Pastoral Conventions in the Art of *Country of the Pointed Firs*  MA Columbia Univ 1960  65 p
3530 MILLER Betty L  Yankee Woman as Portrayed by Sarah Orne Jewett  MA Univ of Idaho 1956
3531 MORAN Marianne W  A Critical Analysis of Sarah Orne Jewett's *Country of the Pointed Firs*  MS St Cloud St Coll 1963  87 p
3532 OEHING Martha F  New England and New England Characters in the Work of Sarah Orne Jewett  MA Univ of Pittsburgh 1930
3533 PARSONS Helen V  A Critical Study of *The Tory Lover* by Sarah Orne Jewett  MA Univ of Maine 1969  115 p
3534 SEARS Sr Catherine M  Impressionism and the Art of Sarah Orne Jewett  MA Boston Coll 1951
3535 TRAFTON Burton W  Little Kingdom Down East: A Psychological Perspective on the World of a Gifted Child, Sarah Orne Jewett, 1849-1909  MA Univ of New Hampshire 1957  199 p
3536 WILE Richard L  Voyage to Dunnet Landing: The Development of Sarah Orne Jewett's Use of Structure  MA Univ of Vermont 1969  161 p

## JAMES WELDON JOHNSON

3537 BAKER Ruth T  The Philosophy of the New Negro as Reflected in the Writings of James Weldon Johnson, Claude McKay, Langston Hughes and Countee Cullen  MA Virginia St Coll 1941  92 p
3538 BARKSDALE Howard R  James Weldon Johnson as a Man of Letters  MA Fisk Univ 1936
3539 CLARK Peter W  A Study of the Poetry of James Weldon Johnson  MA Xavier Univ at New Orleans 1942
3540 CRAWFORD Lucille H  The Musical Activities of James Weldon Johnson  MA Fisk Univ 1941
3541 GEAR Alice J  Career and Writing of James Weldon Johnson  MA Univ of Kansas 1936
See also 6953, 6961, 6964, 6965, 6967, 6996

## MARY JOHNSTON

3542 CHAPMAN Mary E  Mary Johnston: From Virginian to American  MA Longwood Coll 1966
3543 CONSON Virginia J  The Virginia History in the Historical Novels of Mary Johnston  MA George Peabody Coll for Teachers 1936
3544 PATTERSON Dorothya R  Mary Johnston as a Novelist  MA Southern Methodist Univ 1941
3545 YOUNG Claire S  Development of American Life as Shown in Mary Johnston's Novels  MA George Peabody Coll for Teachers 1932
See also 6996

## RICHARD MALCOLM JOHNSTON

3546 BRINSON Lessie B  Richard Malcolm Johnston: Georgia Author  MA Univ of Georgia 1927
3547 DYAR Pat M  Schools and Teachers of Richard M Johnston  MA Univ of Georgia 1940
3548 EYLER Clement M  Richard Malcolm Johnston and His *Dukesborough Tales*

MA Columbia Univ 1926
3549 HENDRICKS Edna  Richard Malcolm Johnston  MA Univ of Georgia 1936
3550 MARTIN Minerva  Richard Malcolm Johnston: A Local Colorist  MA Louisiana St Univ 1937
3551 PITTMAN Frances E  Middle Georgia Life in the Fiction of Richard Malcolm Johnston  MA Duke Univ 1941
3552 WOOD James W  Richard Malcolm Johnston  MA Univ of South Carolina 1931
See also 3805

## JAMES JONES

3553 HERLONG Henry K Jr  The Body and Soul of the Artist in the Works of James Jones  MA Univ of Tennessee 1965
3554 IRSFELD John H  The Military Mystique in James Jones' *From Here to Eternity*  MA Univ of Texas at Austin 1966  120 p

## LEROI JONES

3555 HASKER Ann K  Jones' Use of Dramatic Irony: *The Silver King* Through *The Liars*  MA Univ of Rochester 1951  56 p
3556 MAYS Mardess  Leroi Jones: A Study of His Writings  MA Howard Univ 1966  108 p

## SYLVESTER JUDD

3557 BROCKWAY Philip J  Sylvester Judd: Novelist of Transcendentalism  MA Univ of Maine 1940  157 p
3558 HOLMES Dorothy B  Sylvester Judd: His Philosophy of Reform  MA Univ of Vermont 1940  196 p

## JOHN PENDLETON KENNEDY

3559 ADAMS Christopher A  Study of the Life and Works of John Pendleton Kennedy  MA Trinity Coll of Hartford 1940
3560 BOYER Innes  The Note Book of John Pendleton Kennedy  MA Columbia Univ 1935
3561 CALLAHAN Br Francis P  John Pendleton Kennedy: Novelist, 1795-1870  MA Villanova Univ 1943
3562 GOFORTH Juanita  Evolution of the Negro Character in Fiction by Six Representative Southern White Writers: Kennedy, Simms, Page, Harris, Caldwell, Faulkner  MA East Tennessee St Univ 1965
3563 HARRISON Thomas D  The Novels of John Pendleton Kennedy, 1832-1840  MA Emory Univ 1948
3564 JACKSON Katie L  John Pendleton Kennedy as an Interpreter of Southern Life and History  MA Univ of Texas at Austin 1940
3565 KEAN William A  Factors That Limited the Literary Productivity of John Pendleton Kennedy  MA Columbia Univ 1952  101 p
3566 LEWIS Dimples  A Critical Study of the Literary Works of John Pendleton Kennedy  MA Univ of Georgia 1940
See also 3210

## JACK KEROUAC

3567 BINGHAM Irwin D  Jack Kerouac: The Odyssey of Existential Man  MA Univ of Oklahoma 1966
3568 CANE Suzanne  The Duluoz Legend: The Zen Influence on Jack Kerouac  MA Brooklyn Coll of City Univ of New York 1965  74 p
3569 LEMIRE Bernice M  Jack Kerouac: Early Influences  MA Boston Coll 1963
See also 3760, 6543

## GRACE ELIZABETH KING

3570 HUGHES Katherine E  Grace Elizabeth King:  A Study in Local Color  MA Univ of Texas at Austin 1951  155 p
3571 JASTREMSKI Sarah L  Grace King  MA Louisiana St Univ 1929
3572 JONES Eunice E  The Short Stories of Grace Elizabeth King  MA Univ of Kansas 1936

See also 451, 464, 465, 468

## MARTIN LUTHER KING JR

3573 McGREGOR Marjorie  Martin Luther King Jr:  An Analysis of His Washington March Speech  MA Univ of Oklahoma 1965
3574 SAUNDERS Richard L  Dr Martin Luther King's Intellectual Resources as Studied in Two Selected Speeches  MA San Diego St Coll 1967  146 p

## CAROLINE M KIRKLAND

3575 HALL Tom H  The Works of Caroline Matilda Kirkland  MA Univ of Toledo 1941
3576 SCHICK Nancy W  The Western Writings of Caroline M Kirkland  MA George Washington Univ 1963  162 p

See also 3069

## JOSEPH WOOD KRUTCH

3577 GREEN Joseph G  Joseph Wood Krutch:  Critic of the Drama  MA Indiana Univ 1965
3578 PAVICH Paul N  Joseph Wood Krutch:  Western Nature Essayist  MA Colorado St Univ 1968

See also 6996

## OLIVER LA FARGE

3579 BROKAW Zoanne S  Oliver La Farge:  His Fictional Navajo  MA Univ of Arizona 1965
3580 DYSON James W  Intimate Study of the Life and Writings of Oliver La Farge  MA George Peabody Coll for Teachers 1935
3581 FRIEDMAN Philip  Oliver La Farge:  The Scientist as Literary Artist  MA Univ of New Mexico 1959
3582 HARVEY Robert A  Oliver La Farge as a Literary Interpreter of Navajo Indian Culture  MA Oklahoma St Univ 1949

See also 694

## SIDNEY LANIER

3583 ATKINSON Eleanor M  A Study of the Poetic Art of Sidney Lanier  MA Univ of Texas at Austin 1928
3584 BARBER Evon M Jr  Sidney Lanier  BA Univ of Oklahoma 1916
3585 BELTON James E  The Reading Done by Sidney Lanier  MA Univ of Illinois at Urbana 1937
3586 BERGBAUER Sr Corda M  Elements of English Romanticism in Sidney Lanier  MA Villanova Univ 1964
3587 BLITCH Lila M  Sidney Lanier:  Artist, Critic and Human Being  MA Univ of Maryland at College Park 1935  122 p
3588 BROWN P E  A Study of Lanier's Verse Technique  MA Univ of Chicago 1921
3589 BRYAN W F  Sidney Lanier's Poems:  A Study in Style and Content  MA Univ of North Carolina at Chapel Hill 1908
3590 BURNETT Gussie  A Study of Lanier's Poetic Art  MA Hardin-Simmons Univ 1928
3591 CABANISS Jelks H  Sidney Lanier:  The Man and His Poetry  MA Univ of

Alabama 1907
3592 CAPON Reginald L  The Literary Critical Ideas of Sidney Lanier  MA Boston Univ 1936
3593 COKER Lavinia C  A Study of Sidney Lanier's Attitude Toward Human Limitations  MA Univ of South Carolina 1933
3594 CONRATH Mary C  The Poetic Technique of Sidney Lanier  MA Stetson Univ 1933
3595 COX Alice B  Sidney Lanier as a Nature Poet  MA Columbia Univ 1910
3596 CREDO Ethel  The Use of Figures of Speech in Lanier's Longer Poems  MA Univ of Texas at Austin 1938  129 p
3597 DAVIS J Ray  The Treatment of Nature in the Poetry of Sidney Lanier  MA North Texas St Univ 1938
3598 DEBERRY Margie J  The Role of the Lanier Brothers in the Dialect Movement of the United States  MA North Carolina Central Univ 1956  61 p
3599 EARNEST Elizabeth  Sidney Lanier  MA George Washington Univ 1923
3600 EGLESTON Louise A  Sidney Lanier as a Critic and Interpreter of American Life  MA Univ of North Carolina at Chapel Hill 1931
3601 ELLIOTT Winifred M  The Adam Image and the Christ Image in the Poetry of Sidney Lanier  MA Texas Christian Univ 1963  89 p
3602 FESMIRE William S  Contours of Lanier Criticism: A Study of the Critical Reputation of Sidney Lanier  MA Mississippi St Univ 1965  147 p
3603 FIFE Herzl  A Critique of the Prosody of Sidney Lanier  MA New York Univ 1933
3604 FITZPATRICK Grace M  Sidney Lanier: A Study in the Development of Literary Craftsmanship  MA St John's Univ 1940
3605 FORSYTHE Gladys M  Sidney Lanier the Man  MA Univ of Maryland at College Park 1928
3606 GALBRAITH Evelyn M  The Poetry of Sidney Lanier: A Study in Diction and Imagery  MA Univ of Missouri 1948
3607 GARNETT Anna M  Sidney Lanier's Theory of Verse  MA Colorado St Univ 1946
3608 GLOVER Erma W  The Literary Reputation of Sidney Lanier's "The Centennial Meditation of Columbia"  MA Univ of North Carolina at Chapel Hill 1964
3609 GRISWOLD Frances C  Sidney Lanier: His Theories of Verse in Relation to His Practice  MA Univ of Illinois at Urbana 1927
3610 GUMMOW Willette A  A Study of Imagery in Lanier's Poetry  MA Univ of Southern California 1948
3611 HAIRE Sr Mary E  Sidney Lanier: A Knight of Chivalry in His Life  MA Boston Coll 1937
3612 HALBROOK Mamie S  A Study of the Music of Sidney Lanier's Poetry  MA George Peabody Coll for Teachers 1931
3613 HANLEY Evelyn A  Music and Prosody: An Analysis of Lanier's Verse  MA New York Univ 1937
3614 HEMRICH Jeanne M  A Comparative Study of *Charles Auchester* by Elizabeth Sara Sheppard and *Tiger-Lillies* by Sidney Lanier with Particular Emphasis Upon Their Musical Content  MA Univ of Southern California 1942
3615 HENDERSON Irene S  Sidney Lanier's Imagery  MA Southwestern Univ 1938
3616 HOFFMAN Mary E  Sidney Lanier  MA Ohio St Univ 1931
3617 HOLLISTER Cora  Sidney Lanier as a Critic of Literature  MA New York Univ 1932
3618 HOUSMAN Anna B  Sidney Lanier as a Citizen of the World  MA Columbia Univ 1925
3619 HOWARD Chester J  A Study of the Religion of Sidney Lanier  MA Texas Christian Univ 1962  101 p
3620 KERR Carl A  Sidney Lanier as Poet: A Study of the "Intermittent Mist of Defect"  MA Ohio St Univ 1954

3621  KING Emily B  The Elements of Rousseauism in the Work of Sidney Lanier  MA Duke Univ 1935
3622  KING Mildred B  Sidney Lanier's Social Philosophy as Revealed in His Works  MA Univ of Arizona 1941
3623  KNOLL Margaret F  The Poetry of Sidney Lanier  MA Pennsylvania St Univ 1933
3624  KRAMER Rosella C  Sidney Lanier's Theory and Practice of Poetry  MA Columbia Univ 1926
3625  LIPSCHITZ Louis  Sidney Lanier: His Place in American Literature  MA New York Univ 1931
3626  McCASKILL Agnes S  Sidney Lanier  MA Oglethorpe Univ 1936
3627  McCORVEY Eleanor P  The Poetry of Sidney Lanier  MA Univ of Alabama 1906
3628  McGRATH Sr Catharine M  An Appreciation of the Poetry of Sidney Lanier  MA Villanova Univ 1948
3629  MARSH Alice M  Love in Search of a Word: A Romantic Biography of Sidney Lanier  MA Southwestern Univ 1929
3630  MOORE Lelia Z  Religious Element in Sidney Lanier's Works  MA Univ of Kansas 1924
3631  OLSON Ruth H  The Poetry of Sidney Lanier  MA Univ of Nebraska 1935
3632  OWINGS Ralph S  Sidney Lanier: A Man of His Times  M Ed Wofford Coll 1935
3633  PEARCE Eva F  The Influence of Music on the Literary Career of Sidney Lanier  MA Columbia Univ 1913
3634  PERRY Margaret E  Sidney Lanier: A Transitional Figure in American Literature  MA Univ of Alabama 1939
3635  PRIDDY Jewell C  The Southern Scene as Reflected in the Works of Sidney Lanier  MA Univ of Southern California 1945
3636  PULLEN Sr M Consuela  Imagery of Sidney Lanier  MA Catholic Univ of America at Washington, D C 1940
3637  RITCHEY Liane M  Sidney Lanier's Two Springs: Music and Poetry  MA Indiana Univ of Pennsylvania 1965  47 p
3638  SALLEE Jesse D  Sidney Lanier as a Literary Critic  MA Boston Univ 1910
3639  SCHILLER Rose L  A Study of Sidney Lanier as Critic  MA Ohio St Univ 1950
3640  SEALS Thomas D  Lanier as a Metrist  MA Columbia Univ 1918
3641  SHAW Edwin P  An Application of Sidney Lanier's Theories of Poetic Composition to His Poem "The Symphony"  MA East Carolina Univ 1964
3642  SHIELDS Margaret V  A Concordance of Sidney Lanier's Poems Excluding the Dialect and Unrevised Early Poems  MA Duke Univ 1938
3643  SIMONTON Carol H  Sidney Lanier: Critic of Society  MA Northeast Louisiana Univ 1968  94 p
3644  SMITH Jessie D  Illustrative Material for a Study of Lanier's Poems  MA George Peabody Coll for Teachers 1927
3645  SMITH Leland C  The Literary Reputation of Sidney Lanier  MA Univ of North Carolina at Chapel Hill 1946  64 p
3646  SMITH Melanie M  Sidney Lanier: The Poet as Prophet for a Culture  MA Howard Payne Coll 1969  138 p
3647  SPIVEY Herman E  A Critical Bibliography for the Years 1917-1922 of Representative American Authors  MA Univ of North Carolina at Chapel Hill 1929
3648  STEELE Joy H  The South in the Works of Lanier  MA Clemson Univ 1968
3649  STRAIN Jennie  Sidney Lanier and His Poetry  MA Univ of Washington at Seattle 1930
3650  STRICKLAND Anna B  The Bible and Mystical Elements in Works of Sidney Lanier  MA George Peabody Coll for Teachers 1935
3651  TILLMAN Ruth J  A Study of Sidney Lanier's Criticism of George Eliot's Works  MA North Carolina Central Univ 1953  57 p
3652  UPPMAN Ingegerd M  Old-world Influences on the Poems of Sidney Lanier  MA Stanford Univ 1921
3653  WATKINS Hortense  A Study of the Religious Concepts of Sidney Lanier

MA Southern Methodist Univ 1947
3654 WEAVER Lester  Sidney Lanier:  The New Southerner  MA George Peabody Coll for Teachers 1917
3655 WEED Marguerite  The Ethical and Religious Beliefs of Sidney Lanier  MA Columbia Univ 1932
3656 WHEELER Harold P  Lanier's Conception of the Poet  MA Duke Univ 1929
3657 WHITAKER George W Jr  Sidney Lanier as a Critic of His Times  MA Univ of South Carolina 1947
3658 WILLCOCKSON Ruth  The Rhythmical Principles and Practices of Sidney Lanier  MA Univ of Chicago 1928
3659 WILSEY Collin M  Certain Influences of Contemporary Science Upon the Critical Theory and Practice of Sidney Lanier  MA Univ of South Carolina 1942
See also 1458, 2761, 4830, 4897, 6577

## RING LARDNER

3660 BELCH George E  Ring Lardner: Satirist and Humorist  MA Univ of Texas at Austin 1953  104 p
3661 CARUTHERS Clifford M  The Fictional World of Ring Lardner: His Positive and Negative Values  MA Univ of Kansas 1961
3662 TRIBBLE Joan F  The Busher Returns: A Selection of Ring Lardner Stories  MA Univ of Louisville 1968  310 p
3663 WECKERLE Cyrus W  Ring Lardner: Post-war Humorist  MA Univ of Pittsburgh 1937
See also 168

## HUGH SWINTON LEGARE

3664 COATES K D  Hugh Swinton Legare: Literary Critic  MA Univ of North Carolina at Chapel Hill 1932
3665 WILLIS Larry J  The Character and Literary Style of Hugh Swinton Legare  MA Univ of South Carolina 1928

## ALFRED HENRY LEWIS

3666 MANZO Flourney  Alfred Henry Lewis: Western Story Teller  MA Univ of Texas at El Paso 1966
3667 TURNER Tressa  Life and Works of Alfred Henry Lewis  MA Univ of Texas at Austin 1936

## SINCLAIR LEWIS

3668 ALBERT Wilma W  The Methodology of Sinclair Lewis  MA Syracuse Univ 1948  80 p
3669 ALLEN Elda M  An Analysis of Three Characters of Sinclair Lewis: Carol in *Main Street*, Leora in *Arrowsmith* and Fran in *Dodsworth*  MA Texas Agricultural and Mechanical Univ 1968  110 p
3670 AUSMUS Martin R  The Evolving Social Attitudes of Sinclair Lewis as Revealed Through His Type-characters  MA Univ of Oklahoma 1959
3671 BALDUCCI Assunta  Men and Women Characters in the Works of Sinclair Lewis  MA Ca Foscari (Italy) nd
3672 BASS Mary  A Portrait of Sinclair Lewis as Revealed in Selected Works  M Ed Henderson St Coll nd
3673 BLAKELY Mary L  Sinclair Lewis and His Critics  MA Ft Hays Kansas St Coll 1956  80 p
3674 BOULANGER Fernand  The Idea of Culture in the Major Novels of Sinclair Lewis  MA Univ of Montreal (Canada) 1964
3675 BREWER Callie F  Sinclair Lewis: The Man Who Revitalized American Literature  M Ed Henderson St Coll nd

3676 CALLENDER Nevada M  The Seven Ages of Sinclair Lewis:  A Study in the Relation of Sinclair Lewis to His Age  MA Univ of Houston 1949  55 p
3677 CARSLEY Anne N  A Re-evaluation of the Novels of Sinclair Lewis  MA Univ of Mississippi 1959  187 p
3678 CLARK L T  The America of Sinclair Lewis  MA Boston Univ 1938
3679 CONNALLY Marie B  Sinclair Lewis:  Social Critic  MA Univ of Texas at El Paso 1956  156 p
3680 COWSER R G  Characterization of the Nonconformist in the Novels of Sinclair Lewis  MA North Texas St Univ 1954
3681 DABALA Clara  Sinclair Lewis' *Babbitt*:  A Study in Social Criticism  MA Ca Foscari (Italy) 1957
3682 DAVENPORT Albert E  Sinclair Lewis:  Leader of the Conflict with Conformity in Three Novels:  *Main Street*, *Babbitt* and *Arrowsmith*, 1920-1925  MA Univ of the Pacific 1962  99 p
3683 DAVEY Francis F  Critical Reception of Sinclair Lewis  MA Columbia Univ 1951
3684 DAVIS Jack L  The Satire of Sinclair Lewis  MA Washington St Univ at Pullman 1959
3685 DESMOND F J  Satirical Aspects of Sinclair Lewis  MA Boston Coll 1935
3686 ELLENER Leslie  Shifting Values in Sinclair Lewis  MA Univ of British Columbia (Canada) 1969
3687 FERGUSON Judith A  Sinclair Lewis and the Critics:  A Bibliography of Criticism with an Essay on His Critical Reputation  MA Univ of Maryland at College Park 1970  132 p
3688 FLIPPEN Charlie C Jr  The Influence of Journalistic Experience on Three American Novelists:  Sinclair Lewis, Ernest Hemingway and Theodore Dreiser  MA Univ of North Carolina at Chapel Hill 1966
3689 GRANT Gary L  A Study of the Religious Satire in Four Novels by Sinclair Lewis:  *Main Street*, *Babbitt*, *Elmer Gantry* and *The God Seeker*  MA West Texas St Univ 1964  100 p
3690 HARPER Esther B  A Social Study of Sinclair Lewis' Major Novels  MA Univ of Texas at Austin 1946  147 p
3691 HARRIS Mark  Sinclair Lewis:  An Apostle of the Full Life  MA Williams Coll 1931
3692 HEARN Charles R  Sinclair Lewis' Treatment of Marriage in His Novels  MA Southern Illinois Univ at Carbondale 1960  88 p
3693 HEY Ernest W  Social Criticism in the Novels of Sinclair Lewis  MA Boston Univ 1937
3694 HOFHEINZ Wilburn  A Critical Study of Sinclair Lewis' *Dodsworth*  MA Univ of Texas at Austin 1952  91 p
3695 HUBBARD Elijah  Satire in the Novels of Sinclair Lewis and Nathaniel West  MA Columbia Univ 1966  51 p
3696 KLEMAS Regina M  The Satiric Depiction of Organized Religion in the Novels of Sinclair Lewis  MA Univ of Maryland at College Park 1966  76 p
3697 KNIGHT Karl F  A Comparison of the Methods of Social Criticism Employed by Sinclair Lewis and John P Marquand  MA Univ of North Carolina at Chapel Hill 1957  108 p
3698 LAGNEAU John D  The Satire of Sinclair Lewis  MS Kansas St Coll at Pittsburg 1941
3699 LITTLE Claude F Jr  Marriage in the Novels of Sinclair Lewis  MA Texas Christian Univ 1959  144 p
3700 MAGERS Anita J  The Small Town in Satire:  A Comparison of Sinclair Lewis' *Main Street* and Stephen Leacock's *Sunshine Sketches of a Little Town*  MA Univ of Texas at Austin 1966
3701 NELSON Arnette  Sinclair Lewis:  The Influence of His Sauk Center Boyhood on His Major Novels  MA Univ of South Dakota 1965
3702 NELSON Faye McC  The American Town as Portrayed by Sinclair Lewis  MA George Peabody Coll for Teachers 1931
3703 NORMAN H M  Satire on American Life as Portrayed in the Novels of

             Sinclair Lewis  MA North Texas St Univ 1940
3704  OWEN David S  The Romance of Sinclair Lewis  MA Ohio St Univ 1952
3705  PARSONS Mildred L  Sinclair Lewis: Social Satirist  MA Ft Hays Kansas
      St Coll 1951  61 p
3706  PECK Richard W  Sinclair Lewis and Europe  MA Southern Illinois Univ
      at Carbondale 1959  78 p
3707  PETTY W Everett  A Critical Analysis of the Novels of Sinclair Lewis
      BA Rutgers St Univ 1958  151 p
3708  RAMSEY Lillian A  Much-traveled Main Street: A Study of Sinclair Lewis'
      Midwestern Towns  MA San Diego St Coll 1958  101 p
3709  RAY Martha E  Types of Women: A Study of Women Characters in the
      Novels of Sinclair Lewis  MA Univ of Southern Mississippi 1957
3710  RUGG Hazel E  Relationships Observed in the Novels of Sinclair Lewis
      and James Branch Cabell  MA Ohio St Univ 1932
3711  SADLER Elizabeth L  Sinclair Lewis' Idealists  MA Univ of Mississippi
      1948  101 p
3712  SCALES Gail M  Sinclair Lewis' Attitude Toward the Midwest  MA Fair-
      leigh Dickinson Univ 1969  102 p
3713  STEPHENSON Carrie C  The Transposition of Business and Religion in the
      Novels of Sinclair Lewis  MA Brigham Young Univ 1964  90 p
3714  STEWART A E  The Satire of Sinclair Lewis  MA Boston Univ 1940
3715  THOMPSON Tina M  The Village in Sinclair Lewis' Novels  MA Univ of
      Texas at Austin 1940  108 p
3716  VENABLE Sue N  A Study of Religion in the Novels of Sinclair Lewis
      MA Univ of Tulsa 1965  91 p
3717  VERSINGER Nicole M  Sinclair Lewis as a Social Critic  MA Southern
      Illinois Univ at Carbondale 1951  55 p
3718  WALTON Moselle  The Repressed Individual in the Novels of Sinclair
      Lewis  MA Mississippi St Univ 1963  73 p
3719  WERMERS Bernard F  The Development of Sinclair Lewis as a Novelist
      MA Boston Univ 1948
3720  WIGGINS Jean K  Sinclair Lewis' Treatment of Parents in His Novels
      MA Univ of Georgia 1965
3721  WOOD David C  Juxtaposition as a Satiric Technique in Sinclair Lewis'
      *Main Street*, *Babbitt* and *Elmer Gantry*  MA Bowling Green St Univ 1959
See also 166, 1159, 1928, 2214, 3076, 4161, 5268, 6962,

ABRAHAM LINCOLN

3722  BLACK Joanna  Abraham Lincoln as He Appears in Poetry  MA Univ of
      New Mexico 1942
3723  DEVIN Philip L  Historical Fact and Dramatic Form: Three Plays About
      Abraham Lincoln  MA Indiana Univ 1961
3724  McCANN Richard A  The British Publicists and Abraham Lincoln, 1860-1916
      BA Amherst Coll 1959
3725  McFADDEN Louis B  Lincoln and Education  MA Univ of Iowa 1935
3726  NEFF Elizabeth  Abraham Lincoln as a Character in American and English
      Drama  MA Univ of Oklahoma 1942
3727  REDMOND Mary M  A Critical Study of the Historical Interpretation of
      Lincoln in Three Modern Plays  MA Univ of Iowa 1942
3728  RYAN George B  Abraham Lincoln: The Law and His Writings  MA Univ
      of Louisville 1960
3729  SCHUG C H  Lincoln's Use of Imagery as a Persuasive Device  MA Ohio
      St Univ 1931
3730  SPRINGMAN Lelia R  A Bibliography of Lincoln Poetry Chronologically
      Arranged and Classified According to Subject Matter  MA Washington
      Univ at St Louis 1943  159 p
3731  WILLIAMS Christine M  Abraham Lincoln in Poetry and Drama  MA Univ
      of Oklahoma 1925
See also 5329

## VACHEL LINDSAY

3732 BRADBURY David L  Vachel Lindsay and His Heroes  MS Illinois St Univ at Normal 1969
3733 CLEVELAND William H  American History and Folklore in Vachel Lindsay's Poetry  MA Univ of Texas at Austin 1939  210 p
3734 DEW Jerene V  Vachel Lindsay as an Interpreter of American Life  MA Univ of Kansas 1937
3735 EVANS M E  Vachel Lindsay as Seen Through His Literature and Art  MA Ohio St Univ 1932
3736 GODBOLD Mavis  An Analytical Study of Vachel Lindsay's Poems  MA George Peabody Coll for Teachers 1930
3737 HARBECK Carl C  Vachel Lindsay: American Poet  MA St Univ of New York at Albany 1933
3738 JEWETT Elizabeth  The Social Philosophy of Vachel Lindsay, Carl Sandburg and Edgar Lee Masters  MA Boston Univ 1942
3739 KIMBALL Roland C  Vachel Lindsay and the Gospel of Beauty  MA Univ of New Hampshire 1956  47 p
3740 KRAMER Roy E  Vachel Lindsay: The Poet as Painter  MA Univ of Houston 1959  70 p
3741 LEE Ruth E  The Teaching of Lindsay's Poetry with an Annotated Bibliography  MS Illinois St Univ at Normal 1949
3742 LERNER Carl  Bible in Vachel Lindsay  M Ed Temple Univ 1934  132 p
3743 McLAIN Idie M  A Study of Vachel Lindsay  MA Univ of Texas at Austin 1935
3744 OBERLIN Benjamin G  A Study of the Work of Vachel Lindsay  MA Univ of Texas at El Paso 1959  126 p
3745 RAY I E  Some Aspects of Vachel Lindsay's Americanism as Reflected in His Writings  MA North Texas St Univ 1944
See also 5147

## WALTER LIPPMANN

3746 FORD David W  Walter Lippmann: His Place in American Political Thought  BA Amherst Coll 1958
3747 KUKLIS Robert D  The Democratic Faith of a Young Intellectual: An Interpretation of Walter Lippmann's Early Writings  BA Amherst Coll 1961
3748 SALTER Alice B  Contributions of Walter Lippmann to an Understanding of Public Opinion  MA Univ of Iowa 1932
3749 SULLIVAN John J  Walter Lippmann: The Search for Mastery, 1889-1920  MA Boston Coll 1968

## ROSS LOCKRIDGE

3750 HOOPLE Robin P  Ross Lockridge's Attitude Toward History in His Novel *Raintree County*  MA Syracuse Univ 1954  162 p
3751 ROTH Toni  The Golden Bough in *Raintree County*  MA Brooklyn Coll of City Univ of New York 1965  89 p
3752 SHELDON Robert H  The Riddle of Ross Lockridge's *Raintree County*  MA Colorado St Univ 1966
3753 THORNE Charles D  An Interpretation of *Raintree County*  MA Univ of Tulsa 1955  102 p

## JACK LONDON

3754 ANDREW Loyd D  Jack London: Pioneer Naturalist  MA Univ of Texas at El Paso 1956  127 p
3755 BOUCHER James J  The Political and Economic Opinions of Jack London  MA Univ of Kentucky 1936

3756  CARROLL Joseph P  Jack London: Socialist Writer  MA Univ of Kansas 1967
3757  COLLEY Nellie M  The Romanticism and Realism in Jack London's Works  MA Louisiana St Univ 1939
3758  DISHINGER Mary L  Jack London's Indictment of Capitalism  MS Illinois St Univ at Normal 1966
3759  DOZIER M D  The Conflict Between Individualism and Socialism in the Life and Novels of Jack London  MA North Texas St Univ 1948
3760  FEIED Frederick J  The Hobo in the Works of Jack London, John Dos Passos and Jack Kerouac  MA Columbia Univ 1961  74 p
3761  FINDLEY Emma S  The Dichotomy of Jack London  MA Baylor Univ 1967  179 p
3762  FREEMAN Harold A  Jack London and the Problem of Poverty  MA Univ of Iowa 1932
3763  FULKERTH Robert C  Naturalism in the Works of Jack London  MA Chico St Coll 1969  70 p
3764  FULLER Frank A  Jack London and Critical Realism  MA Roosevelt Univ at Chicago 1965
3765  GRANT Norman  Social Consciousness in Selected Works of Jack London  MA Univ of Maine 1965
3766  HEWICK Walter E  An Analysis of Jack London's Naturalism  MA Howard Univ 1967  117 p
3767  HORTON Arthur L Sr  Jack London's Reputation as a Novelist  MS Auburn Univ 1951  105 p
3768  KAYS Marjorie  Jack London's *The Valley of the Moon*: A Textual and Critical Study  MA Ohio St Univ 1948
3769  LEVITT Morton P  The Social and Economic Writings of Jack London  MA Columbia Univ 1960  66 p
3770  NICHOL John W  Local Color in the Alaskan Stories of Jack London  MA Ohio St Univ 1948
3771  SCHMEDAKE Dorothy M  Dichotomy in the Works of Jack London  MA Washington Univ at St Louis 1944
3772  SHAW Edward A  Jack London: Social Critic  MA Univ of Oklahoma 1956
3773  SPARKS Eva C  The Quiet Ones: A Study of Jack London's Lesser Heroes  MA Mississippi St Univ 1967  109 p
3774  YOUNG Thomas D  The Political and Social Thought of Jack London  MA Univ of Mississippi 1948  210 p
See also 4362

## HENRY WADSWORTH LONGFELLOW

3775  ADAMS Pearl  A Background Study of the Poetry of Longfellow, Lowell and Holmes  MA Univ of Iowa 1924
3776  ALEXANDER Dorothy O  The Bible in the Poetry of Longfellow  M Ed Temple Univ 1935  62 p
3777  BASS M L  The Epic Element in *Hiawatha*  MA North Texas St Univ 1953
3778  BOND William D  Longfellow's Use of the Bible  MA Univ of Texas at Austin 1925
3779  CARROW Elizabeth L  Longfellow's Treatment of Nature and Use of Imagery in *Evangeline*  BA Univ of Delaware 1954  52 p
3780  CHOVANETZ Martha B  A Study of Longfellow's *Tales of a Wayside Inn* in Relation to Their Sources  MA Univ of Texas at Austin 1938  139 p
3781  COPPEDGE Dora  American Materials Used in Longfellow's Poetry  MA George Peabody Coll for Teachers 1938
3782  DOTY F M  American Background in Longfellow's *The Song of Hiawatha*  MA North Texas St Univ 1940
3783  ENLOW Ruth E  Compare and Contrast the Oklahoma Indian with the Indian Portrayed in Longfellow, Cooper and Neilhardt  MA Oklahoma St Univ 1926  151 p
3784  FERUGLIO Silvia  Longfellow Considered as a Link Between America and Europe  MA Ca Foscari (Italy) 1933
3785  HEILMAN E W  The Sources of *Hiawatha*  MA Boston Univ 1913

3786 KAUFMAN Abraham  Some Aspects of Longfellow's Prose in Relation to His Artistic Development  MA Roosevelt Univ at Chicago 1958
3787 KSHEMSANT Suprapada  Longfellow's Use of Indian Sources in *The Song of Hiawatha*  MA Univ of North Carolina at Chapel Hill 1952  99 p
3788 McCABE E J  Catholicity of Longfellow's Works  MA Boston Coll 1930
3789 MATHERNE Br Adrian  A Study of the Prose Works of Henry Wadsworth Longfellow  MA St Mary's Univ of San Antonio 1950  65 p
3790 METFESSEL Carol S  Romanticism and the Genesis of Longfellow's Art  MA Univ of Iowa 1924
3791 NERONE Beato N  Italy in Longfellow's Works  MA Ca Foscari (Italy) 1940
3792 RADLEY Virginia L  Longfellow and the Protestant Hymns  MA Univ of Rochester 1952  87 p
3793 RILEY Margaret  Additional Helps in the Teaching of *Evangeline*  MA St Coll at Fitchburg 1940
3794 ROSS Bernard M  Longfellow's Place in American Literature  MA St Bonaventure Univ 1966
3795 SCHNEIDER Stewart P  A Study of the Maine Background in the Works of Henry Wadsworth Longfellow  MA Columbia Univ 1950
3796 STODDART Helen G  Longfellow in England  MA Indiana Univ 1942
3797 SULLIVAN Sr Mary C  A Comparison of the Religious Spirit to be Found in Some of the Poems of Lamarline and of Longfellow  MA Boston Coll 1944
3798 TAYLOR Joyce  Henry W Longfellow's Theory of Poetry  MA Univ of Mississippi 1948  87 p
3799 TURNER E H  The Use of the Bible in Longfellow's Poetry  MA North Texas St Univ 1948
3800 VOLTOLINA Ada  A Poet of Goodness:  Henry Wadsworth Longfellow  MA Ca Foscari (Italy) 1924
3801 WEEKS Florence H  A Study of Longfellow's *Hiawatha* in Connection with Finnish Epic *Kale Vala*  MA Smith Coll 1914
3802 WORMELL Marian A  A Study of Longfellow's Use of Biblical Allusions and Its Implication for Bible Study by Teachers of Elementary and Junior High School Literature  MA Univ of Idaho 1934
See also 1415, 3204, 3210, 4968

## AUGUSTUS BALDWIN LONGSTREET

3803 ALTSCHUL Debra  Augustus Baldwin Longstreet:  Manners and Morals in Southwestern Folk Humor  MA Columbia Univ 1960  79 p
3804 BURTON Luthera H  Seven American Humorists:  Selections Edited with an Introduction (Augustus B Longstreet, G H Dirby, Henry W Shaw, M Holley, E W Nye, F P Dunne, G Ade)  MA Univ of Maine nd
3805 HOWARD William  Three Nineteenth Century Georgia Humorists:  A Comparative Study of the Writings of Augustus Baldwin Longstreet, William Tappan Thompson and Richard Malcolm Johnston  MA Auburn Univ 1950
3806 SITTON Lucy B  Nature in the Works of Augustus Baldwin Longstreet  MA Univ of Oklahoma 1949
3807 ZULA Marian I  Augustus Baldwin Longstreet:  Humorist  MA Univ of South Carolina 1940
See also 875

## ROBERT LOVEMAN

3808 FRIEDMAN Helen A  Robert Loveman:  Belated Romanticist  MA Univ of Alabama 1932
3809 SORRELLS Daniel J  Robert Loveman:  Man and Poet  MA Univ of Georgia 1937
See also 6996

## THE LOWELLS

3810 AKEY John  Liturgical Imagery in the Poetry of Gerard Manley Hopkins, Thomas Merton and Robert Lowell  MA Univ of Vermont 1950  97 p
3811 ALBERTA Robert C  History of the Literary Reputation of James Russell Lowell with Special Attention to Biographical and Critical Studies  MA Univ of Pittsburgh 1931
3812 APPLEGATE Bessie B  Lowell's Estimate of Contemporary Men of Letters  M of Letters Univ of California at Berkeley 1911
3813 BARRETT Thomas R  A Poet in Babylon: An Essay on the Poetic Worlds of Robert Lowell  MA Univ of New Hampshire 1960  89 p
3814 BARRY David A  The World and Beyond: A Study of Robert Lowell's *Lord Weary's Castle*  MA Columbia Univ 1965  71 p
3815 BOWMAN Mary E  The Biblical Allusions in the Poetry of James Russell Lowell  MA Univ of Kansas 1930
3816 BRAMLETTE Josephine M  The Art of Amy Lowell  MA Univ of Texas at Austin 1929
3817 BRUMLEVE Sr Eric M  Robert Lowell: His World-view  MA St Louis Univ 1966  105 p
3818 BYGRAVE Lurline  Robert Lowell: Archetypal Patterns in His Poetry  MA Bowling Green St Univ 1963
3819 CAMFIELD Gretta T  The Grotesque in the Poetry of Robert Lowell  MA Univ of Texas at Austin 1967  80 p
3820 CARLIN Jayne C  James Russell Lowell on National Language and Literature  MA Univ of Florida 1952
3821 CASEY Mary E  Color Symbolism in Literature with Particular Reference to the Poetry of Amy Lowell  MA Boston Coll 1951
3822 CLAYTON Janice U  James Russell Lowell and the *Biglow Papers*: A Yankee Champions the "Amerikin Idee"  MA Univ of Texas at El Paso 1967  116 p
3823 COFFEY Jeanette E  Religious Perplexity in the Poetry of Lowell  MA Univ of Iowa 1933
3824 CRAIGIE A L  Amy Lowell's Development as Poet and Critic  MA Ohio St Univ 1935
3825 DE CURTIS Sr Edvige  L'Italia Nil Pensiero di James Russell Lowell  MA Columbia Univ 1942
3826 DONOHUE Roberta J  Robert Lowell's Vision of Life as Presented in *Lord Weary's Castle*  MA Boston Coll 1966
3827 EVERETT Grace  James Russell Lowell's Ideas Concerning Death and Immortality  MA George Peabody Coll for Teachers 1939
3828 FAUDI Susan M  Amy Lowell: A Study in Imagism  MA Washington Univ at St Louis 1932
3829 FOGARTY Janice C  Robert Lowell: Puritan Pragmatist  MA Villanova Univ 1965
3830 FOLEY Rita M  The Lowell Offering  MA Univ of New Hampshire 1944  114 p
3831 FORD Mary J  The Themes and Forms of Amy Lowell's Poetry  MA Columbia Univ 1942
3832 FOREMAN Cora G  Nature in the Poetry of James Russell Lowell  MA Hardin-Simmons Univ 1933
3833 GADDY C F  James Russell Lowell's Knowledge and Use of Classical Mythology  MA Univ of North Carolina at Chapel Hill 1925
3834 GRUNEWALD William  Lowell and German Culture  MA Univ of Iowa 1932
3835 HALFDON Leif  Lowell as an Exponent of New England Thought on the Annexation of Texas and the Mexican War with an Historical Survey of the Early Anti-slavery Struggle in the United States  MA Univ of North Dakota 1911  70 p
3836 HATLEY Inez  Amy Lowell and the Far East  MA Univ of Texas at Austin 1936
3837 HAWKINS Ruth  The Use of Mythology in Lowell's Poetry  MA Univ of Idaho 1928
3838 HEARTZ G W  Democracy in the Poetry of Lowell and Whitman  MA Boston

Univ 1919
3839 HEIMSATH Charles H  A Study of Lowell's Poetic Art  MA Univ of Texas at Austin 1922
3840 HOLFORD Carolyn  Mythic Themes and Literary Analogues in Lowell's *Prometheus Bound*  MA North Texas St Univ 1970
3841 HORNE M M  A Study of the Development of Americanism in James Russell Lowell  MA Univ of North Carolina at Chapel Hill 1934
3842 HOWE Herbert B  The Religion of James Russell Lowell: An Investigation of the Writings of Lowell  MA Williams Coll 1921
3843 KRAMER Larry L  The Sharp Knife of God: A Study of Robert Lowell's Religious Poetry  MA Ohio St Univ 1963  52 p
3844 LACY Lois E  James Russell Lowell and the Antislavery Movement  MA Univ of Maryland at College Park 1934  137 p
3845 LEWIS Robert P  The Poet's Cornerstone: A Study of Robert Lowell's *Lord Weary's Castle*  MA Columbia Univ 1964  73 p
3846 MAHER Alberta M  The Literary Reputation of James Russell Lowell as a Poet from 1841 to 1933  MA Columbia Univ 1935
3847 NASH A G  Amy Lowell: Her Contribution to Literature  MA Boston Univ 1926  109 p
3848 NEWCOMB Mary E  Classical Mythology in the Poetry of James Russell Lowell  MA Univ of Kansas 1928
3849 PHELPS Frances M  James Russell Lowell's Philosophy of Life  MA Louisiana St Univ 1941
3850 PICKARD Charlotte V  Amy Lowell: Critic  MA Univ of Texas at Austin 1939  111 p
3851 PLOCEINNIK E J  James Russell Lowell: Good Satirist or Better Critic?  MA Boston Coll 1929
3852 PRESTURICH L Ann  Charles Jacobs Peterson: Editor and Friend of Lowell and Poe  MA Columbia Univ 1939
3853 RILEY Susan B  A Critical Study of Amy Lowell's Experiments in Verse Forms  MA George Peabody Coll for Teachers 1927
3854 ROPETER Marie  The Force of James Russell Lowell in American Literature  MA Ohio St Univ 1931
3855 ROYALL S L  James Russell Lowell and *The Boston Miscellany*  MA Univ of North Carolina at Chapel Hill 1934
3856 SEQUEIRA Amy  The Theme of Loneliness in the Poetry of Amy Lowell  MA Univ of Kansas 1962
3857 SHAPIRO Joseph  Amy Lowell and Her Critics  MA Brooklyn Coll of City Univ of New York 1940
3858 SMITH Stewart H  Robert Lowell's *Colloquy in Black Rock*  MA Columbia Univ 1966  72 p
3859 SOLOMON Lewis R  "O to Break Loose": The Virtuosity of Robert Lowell  BA Amherst Coll 1968
3860 TAPER Phyllis A  Robert Lowell's *Old Glory*: The Effect of Lowell's Attitude Toward Violence on His Use of the Sources  MA Columbia Univ 1966  79 p
3861 TERRELL B S  Lowell's Opinion of His Contemporaries  MA North Texas St Univ 1942
3862 TRUJILLIO Br Augustine B  A Critical Analysis of Amy Lowell's Polyphonic Prose  MA St Mary's Univ of San Antonio 1940  73 p
3863 TYREE Mabel I  The Arthurian Legend as Treated by Four American Poets: James Russell Lowell, Richard Hovey, Madison Cawein, Edwin Arlington Robinson  MA Univ of Kentucky 1938
3864 WARD John C  Robert Lowell: The Poetry of Feeling  BA Amherst Coll 1966
3865 WELLS Carolyn  James Russell Lowell as an Editor  MA Southern Methodist Univ 1933
3866 WHITE Charles C Jr  An Analytical Study of Amy Lowell's Experiments in Poetry  MA Southern Illinois Univ at Carbondale 1956  76 p
3867 WHITTON Helen F  The Validity of Lowell's Opinions of His Contemporaries as Revealed in *A Fable for Critics*  MA Univ of Texas at Austin 1938

118 p
3868 WOLD Janet  Robert Lowell's *Old Glory*: A Comparison with Its Sources in Hawthorne and Melville  MA Univ of Wyoming 1965
3869 WOLF Howard R  Robert Lowell: An Historic Vision  MA Columbia Univ 1960  66 p
See also 1415, 1437, 2060, 3049, 3052, 3775, 4156, 4314, 4987, 5109, 6666

## CHARLES FLETCHER LUMMIS

3870 GARDNER Esther  A Study of the Life and Works of Charles Fletcher Lummis  MA Univ of New Mexico 1941
3871 OGDEN Florence R  Charles Fletcher Lummis: His Life and Works  MA Univ of Texas at Austin 1940  55 p

## MARY McCARTHY

3872 COLLINS Verna A  Mary McCarthy: Critic with a "Cold Eye"  MA Columbia Univ 1965  81 p
3873 ROCK Mary H  Mary McCarthy as a Social Critic in Her Fiction  MA East Tennessee St Univ 1965

## CARSON McCULLERS

3874 BARKOWSKY Edward R  The Theme of Spiritual Isolation in the Major Works of Carson McCullers Prior to 1962  MA Texas Technological Univ 1968  57 p
3875 BARNETT Gene A  The Tragic Theme of Carson McCullers  MA Univ of Oklahoma 1953
3876 BERVIN Arthur E  The Haunted Search: Allegory in the Works of Carson McCullers  MA Univ of Redlands 1965
3877 BROWN Peggy  Characters as Symbols in the Fiction of Carson McCullers  MA Eastern New Mexico Univ 1965
3878 BURNSIDE Patricia  Carson McCullers: A Study of Disillusionment  MA Univ of Texas at El Paso 1967  76 p
3879 CARY Elizabeth E  A Production Book for *The Member of the Wedding*  MA Kansas St Univ 1966
3880 CONTEY Catherine B  Recurring Motifs in the Works of Carson McCullers  MA Fairleigh Dickinson Univ 1968  120 p
3881 COVER Josephine E  Carson McCullers: A Song of Loneliness and Love  MA Lamar Technological Univ 1969
3882 DAVIS David H  The Tragic Idealists of Carson McCullers  MA Claremont Graduate School 1965
3883 DAVIS Karla J  An Analysis of the Grotesque in the Novels of Carson McCullers  MA Ohio St Univ 1967  137 p
3884 FRAZIER Adelaide H  A Consideration of Imagery in Carson McCuller's *The Ballad of the Sad Cafe*  MA Northeast Louisiana Univ 1969  105 p
3885 GIPSON Patricia R  The Limitations of Loneliness: A Critical Study of Carson McCullers  MS Univ of Oklahoma 1966
3886 GOOLD Linda  Belonging: A Study of Love in Novels of Carson McCullers  MA Brigham Young Univ 1970  102 p
3887 GRENTHOT Joan S  The Loving and the Lonely: An Analysis of the Themes and Characters of Carson McCullers  MA Columbia Univ 1952  68 p
3888 HARTMANN Ruth A  Carson McCullers: The Relation of Isolation to Love  MA Univ of Texas at Austin 1965  86 p
3889 HILTON Ruth  Compensatory Factors in Carson McCullers' Lonely and/or Depraved Characters  M Ed Henderson St Coll nd
3890 HULL Anne T  Carson McCullers and the Hazard of Human Existence  MA Univ of Massachusetts 1961
3891 JASKOL Helen S  Characterization in the Novels of Carson McCullers as Seen Through the Dialogue  MA Ohio St Univ 1955

3892 KENDALL Donald  Carson McCullers: The Sense of Dread  MA Columbia Univ 1961  53 p
3893 LEMLEY Raymond E  A Study of Alienation in the Novels of Carson McCullers  MA Southern Connecticut St Coll 1965
3894 LOWE Margaret A  Isolation in the Works of Carson McCullers and Stephen Crane  MA Brigham Young Univ 1968  90 p
3895 LYONS Helene G  The Grotesque World of Carson McCullers and Tennessee Williams  MA Univ of Maine 1967  69 p
3896 McCARTHY Lawrence J  Carson McCullers: Her Fiction, 1936-1960  MA Florida St Univ 1961
3897 McGUIGGAN Sr Kathryn L  The Adolescent as Symbolic Figure in Carson McCullers  MA Boston Coll 1965
3898 MARTIN Virginia A  A Discussion of the Works of Carson McCullers  MA Columbia Univ 1954  136 p
3899 MERRICK Addison H  Dark in the Golden Glare: A Study of Carson McCullers  MA Univ of Vermont 1956  142 p
3900 MILES Betty L  A General Critical Study of the Works of Carson McCullers  MA Univ of Louisville 1964
3901 OLSON Charles  The Use of the Grotesque in the Novels of Carson McCullers  MA Midwestern Univ 1969  91 p
3902 PHILLIPS Robert S  The Gothic Vision of Carson McCullers  MA Syracuse Univ 1963  103 p
3903 REESE Regina  The Quest for Identity in the Novels of Carson McCullers  MA Univ of Mississippi 1969
3904 RODENBERGER Molcil L  A Study of Techniques of Characterization in the Works of Carson McCullers  MA Texas Agricultural and Mechanical Univ 1967  98 p
3905 SANTORO William D  Carson McCullers: Classics from the South  MA Columbia Univ 1955  77 p
3906 SMITH Kyle A  The Isolated Individual in the Novels of Carson McCullers  MA North Texas St Univ 1965
3907 SULLIVAN Margaret S  Carson McCullers: An Analysis of Four Major Works  MA Auburn Univ 1961
3908 WALKER John D  Thematic Unity in the Novels and Stories of Carson McCullers  MA Univ of Texas at Austin 1956  134 p
3909 WEBSTER Virginia G  The Style of Carson McCullers: Realism and Symbolism  MA Oklahoma St Univ 1964  104 p
See also 6144, 6356

## JAMES STEELE MacKAYE

3910 BURCHINAL Kenneth H  Realism in the Plays of James Steele MacKaye  MS Kansas St Coll at Pittsburg 1961
3911 DuBURON E V  Steele MacKaye's Place in the American Theatre  MA Univ of New Hampshire 1938  107 p

## ARCHIBALD MacLEISH

3912 BLUM Harriet  Archibald MacLeish: Development of a Poetic Language for Verse Drama  MA Columbia Univ 1961  158 p
3913 BROWN William J  The Influence of Bernal Diaz' *True History of the Conquest of New Spain* on Archibald MacLeish's *Conquistador*  MA Univ of North Carolina at Chapel Hill 1958  137 p
3914 BUNGE Margritt  The Poet as Mentor of His Nation and Age: Erlich Kastner and Archibald MacLeish, a Comparison  MA Southern Illinois Univ at Carbondale 1960  109 p
3915 FOSTER Margaret  Development of the Poetic Technique of Archibald MacLeish  MA Ohio St Univ 1934
3916 FRANKS Barbara L  The Philosophic Implications Inherent in Archibald MacLeish's Pulitzer Prize Winning Play  MA Ball St Univ 1963  128 p

3917 JACKSON Mabel E  The Verse Plays of Archibald MacLeish  MA Univ of Pittsburgh 1960
3918 JORDAN Cedric R  The Direction, Production and Historical Background of Archibald MacLeish's *J B*  MA San Diego St Coll 1964  315 p
3919 KEEFE Sr M St David  Man as the Hero in the Poetry and Drama of Archibald MacLeish  MA Boston Coll 1963
3920 POTTER J L  The Poetic Development of Archibald MacLeish  MA Wesleyan Univ 1944
3921 ROBBINS Dorothy  A Critical Analysis of the Play *J B*  M Ed Henderson St Coll nd
3922 SCHNEIDER Ethel D  *Conquistador*: Archibald MacLeish's Debt to the Diary of Bernal Diaz  MA Univ of Idaho 1941
3923 SHELTON Richard W  Certain Aspects of Prosody in the Verse Drama of Archibald MacLeish  MA Univ of Arizona 1961
3924 SIMMONS Billie  Archibald MacLeish's Use of Source Material in *Conquistador*  MA Univ of Texas at Austin 1941  68 p
3925 STASIO Marilyn L  The Theme of Alienation in the Poetry of Archibald MacLeish  MA Columbia Univ 1961  100 p
3926 VRESWYK Paul W  A Critical Study of Archibald MacLeish's *J B*  MA Washington St Univ at Pullman 1960
3927 WAPLINGTON Frances  *J B*  BA Univ of British Columbia (Canada) 1966
See also 1111, 1289, 1488, 2054, 4539

## NORMAN MAILER

3928 ALLEN Richard A  The Evolution of the Social and Political Thought of Norman Mailer  MA Mankato St Coll 1968  100 p
3929 BERG Odean E  Naturalism in the Novels of Norman Mailer  MA Mankato St Coll 1966  67 p
3930 BINGHAM Robert D  Norman Mailer and the New Left  BA Amherst Coll 1969
3931 COHN Steven M  Radicalism in Search of Reality: A Reading of Norman Mailer  BA Amherst Coll 1969
3932 EPSTEIN Arthur D  The Theme of Integrity in Norman Mailer  MA Indiana Univ 1961
3933 SCHAIBLE Harry  Norman Mailer: The Quest for an American Heroism  MA Columbia Univ 1963  204 p
See also 1098, 1121

## BERNARD MALAMUD

3934 CAMPBELL Sharon  Theme and Character in Bernard Malamud's Fiction  MA Washington St Univ at Pullman 1966
3935 CARTER Allan B  The Role of Woman in Malamud's Novels  MA Univ of Rhode Island 1967  108 p
3936 DOLLARD Peter A  The Prose Fiction Metaphor and the Works of Bernard Malamud  MA Univ of Wyoming 1965
3937 KOFOSKY Rita N  Bernard Malamud: A Bibliography of His Work and Its Critical Reception  MA Univ of Maryland at College Park 1968  75 p
3938 LAVENDER Tresea G  The Suffering Hero in the Early Fiction of Bernard Malamud  MA Texas Technological Univ 1968  99 p
3939 McDONALD Cynthia A  A Study of Recurring Themes in the Fiction of Bernard Malamud  MA North Carolina Central Univ 1967  52 p
3940 McNILLE Rose C  Myth and Fantasy in the Early Works of Bernard Malamud  MA Ohio St Univ 1969  73 p
3941 RICHTEL Anne  The Schlemihl Motif in the Short Stories of Bernard Malamud  MA Fresno St Coll 1966  137 p
3942 RUTHERFORD Bruce  The Ironic World of Bernard Malamud  MA Univ of Connecticut 1965
3943 SHERMAN William D  The Hero as Athlete in Contemporary American Fiction: The Baseball Novels of Bernard Malamud and Mark Harris

MA St Univ of New York at Buffalo 1964
See also 5511

## WALTER MALONE

3944 CORBAN Emma R  The Life and Works of Walter Malone  MA Univ of Mississippi 1930  256 p
3945 STITH Mary E  Walter Malone: Jurist, Poet, Man  MA George Peabody Coll for Teachers 1927
See also 6996

## EDWIN MARKHAM

3946 GOFORTH Lydia G  Edwin Markham: A Critical Study  MA Univ of Texas at Austin 1952  89 p
3947 HARDING Agatha L  Edwin Markham's Poetry Considered in the Light of His Social Theories  MA Univ of Idaho 1931
3948 HENDRICKSON Andrew  The Life and Works of Edwin Markham  MA Columbia Univ 1935
3949 QUAID Lena D  An Analytical Study of Edwin Markham's Poems  MA George Peabody Coll for Teachers 1928

## JOHN P MARQUAND

3950 CHERRY William G  The Past Versus the Present in the Novels of John P Marquand  MA East Carolina Univ 1966
3951 RIPPER Goldie C  The Treatment of the Businessman in the Novels of John P Marquand  MA Texas Christian Univ 1964  72 p
3952 WESTBROOK James S Jr  John P Marquand: Social Historian  MA Columbia Univ 1950
See also 1958, 3697

## EDGAR LEE MASTERS

3953 BOWLES John C  Edgar Lee Masters' Attitude Toward Women as It Is Reflected in *Across Spoon River* and *Spoon River Anthology*  MA DePauw Univ 1965  33 p
3954 EATON Orville L  Edgar Lee Masters' Philosophy of Life in the Small Town as It Is Reflected in His Poetry  MS Kansas St Coll at Pittsburg 1940
3955 FLYNN Cornelius J  Midwest America (1880-1925) as Seen Through a Study of *Spoon River Anthology* and *The New Spoon River* by Edgar Lee Masters  MA Univ of New Hampshire 1953  29 p
3956 LADD H G  A Critical Biography and Bibliography of Edgar Lee Masters  MA Univ of New Hampshire 1941  201 p
3957 MASTERS Gertrude B  The Fatalism of Edgar Lee Masters  MA Bowling Green St Univ 1938
3958 SLOBBE Vanda  Edgar Lee Masters Ed il Valore Della *Spoon River* Intesa Come Documento del Realismo Americano  MA Ca Foscari (Italy) 1950
3959 WOLF Sidney R  A Study of Naturalism in Edgar Lee Masters' *Spoon River Anthology*  MA Oklahoma St Univ 1940  43 p
See also 3738, 5147

## COTTON MATHER

3960 ESTEY Rebecca J  Cotton Mather and the Superstitions of the Early Period of American Literature  MA Boston Univ 1928
3961 SMITH Mary E  Cotton Mather: Puritan and Progressive  MA Smith Coll 1929
3962 YOUNG Dora J  Cotton Mather, Leader in the American Enlightment, Gide and His Counterfeiters and Shakespeare and Fletcher, Elizabethan Collaborators  MA Brigham Young Univ 1958  118 p

## HERMAN MELVILLE

3963 ADLER Carl H   The Symbolic Role of Costume in Herman Melville's Prose   MA Roosevelt Univ at Chicago 1961
3964 ALEXANDER Sydney   The Evolution of Melville's Protagonist from *Typee* Through *Moby Dick*   MA Univ of Southern Mississippi 1954
3965 ALFORD William P   The Dubious Light: A Study of the Problems of Race and Perception in Mid-nineteenth Century America as Expressed Particularly in the Writings of Herman Melville   BA Amherst Coll 1970
3966 ALLEN Alvin   *Moby Dick*: A Centenary of Criticism   MA Brooklyn Coll of City Univ of New York 1953   41 p
3967 ALLEN James S   A Critical Study of *The Confidence Man* by Herman Melville   MA Univ of Texas at Austin 1946   66 p
3968 ALRIDGE Robert E   Melville's *Pierre* and *Billy Budd*: A Study of the Ideals Versus Actualities Theme   MA Mississippi St Univ 1964   65 p
3969 AMBROSETTI Ronald J   Melville's Cloister and Hearth   MA Bowling Green St Univ 1968
3970 ANDERSON Betty C   Subtleties of Communication in Melville   MA Univ of North Carolina at Chapel Hill 1969   161 p
3971 ANDREWS Patricia B   A Critical Study of *The Confidence Man*   MA Univ of Oklahoma 1961
3972 ATKINSON Jeanne M   Drummond of Light: Herman Melville's "The Encantadas"   MA Univ of Massachusetts 1963
3973 AVINGER James   Moral Solipsism in Melville   MA Texas Technological Univ 1964   70 p
3974 BABIN James L   Herman Melville and the Idea of Moral Tradition   MA Duke Univ 1965
3975 BAGLEY Carol L   Melville's *Pierre*: A Freudian Interpretation   MA Washington St Univ at Pullman 1963
3976 BAIRD Louise   *Mardi*: The Narrative Voice   MA Univ of Hawaii 1968   113 p
3977 BALL Cecil R   Herman Melville and His Significance in Modern Letters   MS Univ of Maryland at College Park 1934   99 p
3978 BALL Kenneth R   A Study of Critical Problems in *Benito Cereno*   MA Univ of Texas at Austin 1962   93 p
3979 BANET Robert A   The Uses of Irony in *Moby Dick*   MA Univ of Louisville 1956
3980 BARNET Judith M   The Vastness of the Joke: Further Dimensions of Parody in *Moby Dick*   MA Brown Univ 1966
3981 BARTINI Arnold G   Melville in the Berkshires: A New Outlook   MA Boston Coll 1959
3982 BEHAR Judith   The Idea of the Absurd in Melville, Hawthorne and William James   MA Univ of Connecticut 1958
3983 BENNETT Georgia M   Melville's Humor   MA Univ of Mississippi 1953   166 p
3984 BERGSTROM Robert F   Man and His Religion in the Novels of Herman Melville: *Typee* Through *Moby Dick*   MA Duke Univ 1966
3985 BICKLEY Robert B   Master and Servant in Melville   MA Duke Univ 1965
3986 BIGGERSTAFF Donald R   Thematic Sexuality in Melville's *Moby Dick*   MA Trinity Univ of San Antonio 1965
3987 BLANSETT Barbara N   Melville's *Pierre*: An Indictment of Transcendentalism   MA Univ of Houston 1958   111 p
3988 BLAU Rachel M   An Explication of Melville's *Timoleon*   MA Columbia Univ 1964   165 p
3989 BORTON John C Jr   Herman Melville: The Philosophical Implications of the Literary Techniques in *Moby Dick*   BA Amherst Coll 1960
3990 BOWERS James A   A Study in Design, Scenery and Lighting for a Production of *Billy Budd*   MA Ohio St Univ 1952
3991 BOYD Nancy C   A Comparative Study of Melville's *Pierre* and Dostoevsky's *The Idiot*   MA Ohio St Univ 1963   42 p
3992 BRANOM Ethel C   A Study of the Origins of Herman Melville's Fiction   MA Univ of Texas at Austin 1934

3993 BRENNAN Sr M Thomas  The Idea of Fate in Herman Melville's *Moby Dick*  MA Siena Hts Coll 1948
3994 BROWN Charles T  Medical Men and Medical Matters in Melville's Works  MA Univ of Arizona 1966
3995 BURKE Merle M  Herman Melville's Attitude Toward the South Sea Islands  MA Univ of Pittsburgh 1937
3996 BURNS Robert A  Melville's Early Novels:  A Study of Artistic Development  MA Kansas St Teachers Coll 1965
3997 BURTNER William T Jr  A Study of Alienation and Acceptance in Selected Works of Herman Melville  MA Miami Univ at Oxford 1965
3998 CANADAY Nicholas Jr  The Ambiguity of Melville's *Billy Budd*  MA Univ of Florida 1955
3999 CARMICHAEL K J  Herman Melville's Literary Reputation  MA Univ of North Carolina at Chapel Hill 1929
4000 CARPENTER Joyce M  The Structure of Melville's *Clarel*  MA Boston Coll 1964
4001 CARPENTER Marie C  The People of Herman Melville's Novels  MA Univ of Texas at Austin 1935
4002 CATES David G  Melville's Rejection of Christianity  MA Univ of Maine 1969  115 p
4003 CHASE Oliver S  Owen Chase's Narrative of the Shipwreck of the Whaleship *Essex* and Its Influence on Herman Melville's *Moby Dick*  MA Columbia Univ 1962  112 p
4004 CHIRICO Elizabeth M  Melville's Use of Imagery in *The Piazza Tales*  MA Brooklyn Coll of City Univ of New York 1952  89 p
4005 CHISHOLM Sr Joseph J  Herman Melville's Use of Biblical Symbolism in *Pierre, Clarel, Billy Budd*  MA Boston Coll 1959
4006 CHUN Woo Y  Appearance and Reality in the Later Works of Melville  MA Ohio St Univ 1964  82 p
4007 CLARK Janet T  Images of Identity in *Moby Dick, The Red and the Black* and *Steppenwolf*  MA Univ of Massachusetts 1967  57 p
4008 CLARK Marden J  Elements of Aristotelian Tragedy in Melville's *Moby Dick*  MA Brigham Young Univ 1949  133 p
4009 CLEMENS Richard A  Herman Melville:  Concerning the Disproportionate Ratio of Boojums to Snarks  MA Fairleigh Dickinson Univ 1969  45 p
4010 COCKMAN Nelda R  The Influence of Camoes' *The Lusiads* on Melville's *Moby Dick*  MA Univ of North Carolina at Greensboro 1969
4011 COFFMAN Stanley K Jr  The Pessimism of Herman Melville:  An Analysis of *Mardi* and *Moby Dick*  MA Ohio St Univ 1940
4012 COGGINS Paul E  A Critical Study of Herman Melville's Short Fiction from 1853 to 1856  MA Univ of Oklahoma nd
4013 COOPER Barbara  Herman Melville's *Billy Budd*  MA Hunter Coll 1961
4014 COVINGTON Sterling C  A Critical Study of Herman Melville's *Clarel*, a Poem and Pilgrimage in the Holy Land  MA Univ of Texas at Austin 1944  151 p
4015 CRAIG Claude A  Missionaries and Ministers in the Novels of Herman Melville  MA Univ of Tennessee 1964
4016 CRAIG Phyllis  Herman Melville  MA Univ of Pittsburgh 1929
4017 DANIEL Mary B  A Critical and Historical Analysis of Melville's "The Encantadas"  MA Univ of Houston 1969  147 p
4018 DAVIS N C  A Study of Herman Melville's *Mardi*  MA Ohio St Univ 1938
4019 DeKANTER Carolyn L  Herman Melville:  Immortal Icarus  MA Univ of Texas at El Paso 1966  92 p
4020 DENNISTON Constance  The Romance-parody:  A Study in Melville, Twain, Purdy and Heller  MA Kansas St Teachers Coll 1965
4021 DENTON Lynnard W  Melville's Investigation and Rejection of Major Victorian Philosophies as Illustrated in *Clarel*  MA Eastern New Mexico Univ 1966
4022 DEVEAU Joyce H  Resignation and Despair:  The Philosophical Journeys of Melville and O'Neill  MA Univ of Delaware 1963  69 p

4023 DIBBELL Adam  Sir Thomas Browne, Stylistics and Style of *Moby Dick*  MA Claremont Graduate School 1966
4024 DODGE Gerald H  Melville and *Moby Dick*: The Royalty Motif  MS St Cloud St Coll 1963  46 p
4025 DOERING Ann H  Melville's "Bartleby the Scrivener": A Review of Scholarship and Interpretation  MA Bowling Green St Univ 1966
4026 DRYDEN Edgar A  The Relationship Between Narration and Theme in Herman Melville's *Moby Dick* and *Pierre*: A Study in Point of View  MA Univ of Rhode Island nd
4027 DUGGAN Jesse E  The Progeny of Ahab: A Study of the Monomaniacs in Herman Melville's *Clarel*  MA Univ of Texas at El Paso 1969  124 p
4028 EARLY Joseph D  The Influence of the Young America Movement on Melville's *Israel Potter*  MA Texas Christian Univ 1966  98 p
4029 EGNER R A  The Relationship Between the Hunter and the Hunted: *Moby Dick*, *The Old Man and the Sea* and *The Bear*  MA North Texas St Univ 1963
4030 ELLEN Terence H  The Voyaging Mind: A Study of the Narrator in Melville's Early Books  BA Amherst Coll 1967
4031 EUTSLER Nellvena D  An Interpretative Analysis of Herman Melville's "The Encantadas"  MA East Carolina Univ 1968
4032 FAITH John C  Herman Melville's Civil War Poetry  MA Columbia Univ 1961  86 p
4033 FENNER June M  The Loom of Fate in *Moby Dick*  MA Univ of Texas at Austin 1965  100 p
4034 FIELD Jane T  The Quality of Melville's Comic Characters  MA San Diego St Coll 1963  157 p
4035 FITCH Mary J  The Prose Style of Herman Melville  MA Oklahoma St Univ 1940  109 p
4036 FLEISHMAN I P  Melville's Use of Language in *Moby Dick*  MA Wesleyan Univ 1967
4037 FORMAN Delta K  Herman Melville: Rebel  MA Univ of Texas at Austin 1939  129 p
4038 FORREY R J  The Divided Empire: A Study of the Divided World in Melville's Work  MA Wesleyan Univ 1958
4039 FOWLKES Glenn C  The Idea of Natural Goodness in the Writings of Herman Melville  MA Ohio St Univ 1946
4040 FRAZIER Mary E  The Function of Narrative Point of View in Melville's Short Stories  MA Columbia Univ 1961  86 p
4041 FREY Gary E  Ahab: Negative Romantic and Neurotic  MA Gonzaga Univ 1965
4042 FRIEDERICH Reinhard H  Calms in Melville's Prose Works  MA Univ of Houston 1966  105 p
4043 FULTON Mary F  The Relation Between Melville and Hawthorne, 1850-1851  MA Univ of Oklahoma 1963
4044 GLOVER J Denis  The Mesmerized, Heartless Adam in *Moby Dick*  MA Columbia Univ 1962  85 p
4045 GLUECK Michael W  The Witcheries of Weather: A Seasonal Approach to *Moby Dick*  MA Columbia Univ 1961  117 p
4046 GOODINE Lenwood O  Herman Melville's Attitude Toward Man  MA Univ of Manitoba (Canada) 1966
4047 GOREN Yildiz N  The Sultan of the *Pequod*: The Sources of Authority in *Moby Dick*  MA Univ of Florida 1955
4048 GRAFF Frances B  *White Jacket* and *Billy Budd*: Herman Melville's Changing View of Man in a Militaristic Society  MA Univ of Tennessee 1966
4049 GRAY Rockwell Jr  Unamuno and Melville: A Comparative Study  MA Columbia Univ 1963  166 p
4050 GREENE Nancy B  Melville and the Pallid Jesus: A Study of the Christ-figure in *Billy Budd*  MA Butler Univ 1968
4051 GREENWOOD Keith M  The Sea in *Moby Dick* and the Plays of Eugene O'Neill

MA Columbia Univ 1954  70 p
4052 GRENBERG Bruce L  An Analysis of the Structure of *Moby Dick*  MA Univ of North Carolina at Raleigh 1958  115 p
4053 GRIFFITH Eve G  A Study of Eight Short Stories by Herman Melville  MA Ohio St Univ 1962  66 p
4054 GRINNAGE Willadine M  A Critical Analysis and Evaluation of *Benito Cereno*  MA Howard Univ 1949  130 p
4055 GUILMETTE Rev Emile  The Solidarity of Humanity and Creation in *Moby Dick*  MA Boston Coll 1964
4056 GUNTER Larry B  Youth and the Incomprehensible World: A Study of Character and Theme in Herman Melville's *Redburn, White Jacket* and *Billy Budd, Foretopman*  MA Coll of the Holy Names at Oakland 1963
4057 GUPTA Raj K  A Critical Study of Form and Style in Herman Melville's *Pierre*: Or, the Ambiguities  MA Univ of Rhode Island 1962  83 p
4058 HACKWORTH Robert A  The Alienation of Herman Melville  MA Univ of North Carolina at Chapel Hill 1969  79 p
4059 HAMILTON Mae H  The Influence of Religious Thought on Melville's Literary Career  M Ed Henderson St Coll nd
4060 HAWKINSON Bruce R  Emotive Prose in *Moby Dick*: A Stylistic Study  MA Univ of Kansas 1962
4061 HAWTHORNE Ruth J  Melville's *Confidence Man*: A Critical Study  MA Syracuse Univ 1951  98 p
4062 HENCH Michael M  Melville's Final Romantic Object  MA Univ of Massachusetts 1967
4063 HERMANN Lila  The Literary and Personal Relations of Herman Melville and Nathaniel Hawthorne  MA Univ of North Carolina at Chapel Hill 1945
4064 HEWITT Elizabeth C  "This Two-fold Enormousness": A Study of Melville's Use of Christian Myth in *Moby Dick*  MA Tufts Univ 1968
4065 HILL Robert W  The Poet and the Poetry in Melville's *Mardi*  MA Univ of North Carolina at Chapel Hill 1964
4066 HILL Starline  Primitive Innocence: The Strand of Continuity in Herman Melville's Works  MA Northeast Louisiana Univ 1965  85 p
4067 HILTY Mae F  An Interpretation of Melville's *Mardi*  MA Univ of Texas at Austin 1942  104 p
4068 HODGE William H  The Plinlimmon Pamphlet as a Guide to the Interpretation of *Billy Budd*  MA Univ of New Hampshire 1967  76 p
4069 HOGAN Patricia  Herman Melville's Use of Nature in "The Encantadas" and Selected Poems  MA Univ of New Mexico 1966
4070 HOLT Eunice S  Symbolism in *Moby Dick*  MA West Texas St Univ 1952  171 p
4071 HOLT Winfield A  Herman Melville's *Benito Cereno*: The New England Sceptic on Abolition  MA Columbia Univ 1961  60 p
4072 HOOVER Walter B  The Existential Melville  MA Univ of Alberta (Canada) 1966
4073 HOUSTON Neal B  The Clergy in the Novels of Herman Melville  MA Univ of Texas at Austin 1961  100 p
4074 HOWARD I B  Elements of the Byronic Hero in Captain Ahab  MA North Texas St Univ 1969
4075 HOWELL Mary E  Melville's Narrenschiff: Theme Implementation Through Character Types in *The Confidence Man*  MA Univ of Southern Mississippi 1969
4076 HUCKABAY Evert K  Melville's Spiritual Isolation: The Loss of the Elizabethan World-picture  MA Oklahoma St Univ 1969  47 p
4077 HULL Myra E  Histories of American Literature  MA Univ of Kansas 1920
4078 IRELAND Donald B  An Analysis of the Social Assumptions Underlying Four of the Novels of Herman Melville: *Typee, Omoo, Mardi* and *Moby Dick*  MA Ohio St Univ 1939
4079 ISHAQ Saada  Herman Melville as an Existentialist: An Analysis of

His Philosophical Novels  MA Kansas St Teachers Coll 1966
4080  JACKSON Grace  Symbolism in Herman Melville's *Mardi*  M Ed Henderson St Coll nd
4081  JEWELL Patricia A  The Adolescent Idealist: A Study of *Pierre, The Sound and the Fury* and *The Catcher in the Rye*  MA Columbia Univ 1966  67 p
4082  JONES Walter D  Herman Melville: The Middle Years--a Reappraisal  MA Auburn Univ 1954
4083  JOSEPH Vasanth D  A Study of the Relationship Levels of Language to Action and Symbol in Herman Melville's *Moby Dick*  MA Northeast Missouri St Coll 1961
4084  JUNKIN Sr Mary W  Color Symbolism and Providence in Melville  MA St Louis Univ 1958  75 p
4085  KAPLAN Sidney  Herman Melville on the Negro and the Slave  MA Boston Univ 1948
4086  KENNEDY Patricia B  God, Woman and Herman Melville  MA Univ of Houston 1964  90 p
4087  KENWORTH Genevieve E  Herman Melville's Use of Symbol and Allegory in a Selected Group of Four Novels with Attention Given to Patterns of Symbols and Equivalents Among the Symbols  MA Univ of Rhode Island 1955
4088  KENYON George R  Basic Conflicts of Attitude in Herman Melville  MA Univ of Pittsburgh 1949
4089  KETTERER David A  Melville's Allegoric Interpretations of the White Whale: A Study of the Empirical "a priori" Relationship Between Method and Meaning in *Mardi, Moby Dick, The Confidence Man* and *Billy Budd*  MA Carleton Univ (Canada) 1965
4090  KEVORKIAN David M  The Conflict Between Primitive and Civilized Modes of Existence in Herman Melville's *Billy Budd*  MA Univ of Rhode Island 1963  90 p
4091  KINNEY Frances W  The Personal and Literary Relations of Melville and Hawthorne  MA Univ of Kentucky 1932
4092  KISS Katie G  Rediscovery of Herman Melville  MA Northeast Missouri St Coll 1958
4093  KNOX William A  Melville's Use of the Naturally Good Man  MA Oklahoma St Univ 1960
4094  KOCH Christopher  *The Confidence Man*: Melville's Satire of Human Nature  MA Columbia Univ 1960  87 p
4095  KOENIG Barbara  The Concept of the Mask in Three Novels by Herman Melville  MA Univ of Rochester 1958  141 p
4096  KOHPAY Bernice  Satire in the Fiction of Herman Melville  MA Univ of Kansas 1935
4097  KRAMER Eleanor B  The Condor's Quill: An Analytical and Historical Study of the Style of Herman Melville's *Moby Dick*  MA Univ of the Pacific 1962  152 p
4098  KREGOR Karl  The Function of Emblematic Conventions in Melville's *Moby Dick*  MA Syracuse Univ 1965  90 p
4099  LACERVA Patricia A  Development of Satire in the Novels of Herman Melville  MA Auburn Univ 1962
4100  LACEY William R  Melville's Expression of Personal Dubiety in *Moby Dick* Through the Use of Ambivalent Time-eternity Symbolism  MA Mississippi St Univ 1959  86 p
4101  LANGFORD Thomas  Biblical Illusions in *Billy Budd*  MA Univ of California at Riverside 1956
4102  LEBOWITZ Shirley  Melville's Conception of Fate  MA Univ of Houston 1966  96 p
4103  LEE A R  The Development of the Meaning of "Sociality" in Selected Writings of Herman Melville  MA Univ of London (England) 1965
4104  LOURIE Richard M  Shadows of Invisibility: A Comparative Study of Herman Melville's *Benito Cereno* and Ralph Ellison's *Invisible Man*

MA Columbia Univ 1960   110 p

4105  LOWREY Lucille Y  The Character-type of Innocence in Herman Melville's *Billy Budd*  MA Ball St Univ 1965   54 p

4106  McCARTHY Kevin M  Melville's Use of His *Journal* for *Clarel*  MA Univ of North Carolina at Chapel Hill 1966

4107  McCLINTOCK Patricia R  The Glance of Melancholy: Herman Melville's Perception of Man and His World  MA Univ of Massachusetts 1967   71 p

4108  McCLUNG Judy  Melville's *Mardi*: Structure, Imagery and Theme  MA Univ of Oklahoma 1965

4109  McDONALD Eleanor M  The Many Faces of Faith in Herman Melville's *Clarel*  MA Bowling Green St Univ 1965

4110  MacDONALD Robert D  *Moby Dick* as a Reaction Against Emersonian Transcendentalism  MA McMaster Univ (Canada) 1963

4111  McDOWELL Oneita C  The Epic Writer's Use of Technique as Demonstrated by Melville in *Moby Dick*  MA West Texas St Univ 1960   68 p

4112  McGOUGHRAN J H  Changes in Critical Views of *Moby Dick*  MA Univ of Kansas 1950

4113  McINTYRE James M  A Study of Herman Melville's Theory of Freedom of the Will  MA Univ of Pittsburgh 1952

4114  McKEE Jessie  Elements of Transcendentalism in the Writings of Herman Melville  MA Univ of North Carolina at Chapel Hill 1925

4115  McLEAN Kathleen R  Melville's Narrative Poems  MA Univ of Idaho 1965

4116  MacMASTER June  Melville and Mother: Myth and Symbol in the Early Novels  MA Univ of Alberta (Canada) 1963

4117  MacMILLAN Kenneth D  The Alternate Perception: The Theme of Companionship in Some of Melville's Novels  MA Univ of Toronto (Canada) 1966

4118  McQUILKIN Robert R  The Religious Problem in Melville's *Clarel*  MA Columbia Univ 1962   100 p

4119  MANNING William E  Symbolism and Myth in Melville's *Pierre*  MA Louisiana Technological Univ 1966   126 p

4120  MARINO Pilar E  Herman Melville on Primitivism: A Study of Four Novels  MA Columbia Univ 1966   75 p

4121  MARTIN Bettejane  Herman Melville: A Study of the Conflict Between the Self and Society in His Novels  MA Ohio St Univ 1961   75 p

4122  MARTINEZ Inez  Melville's Transcendentalism  MA St Louis Univ 1965   118 p

4123  MITCHELL Donna P  *Mardi*, *Moby Dick* and *Pierre*: A Survey of Allegorical Interpretations  MA Texas Technological Univ 1970   89 p

4124  MOMBERGER Philip  Ishmael's Odyssey: Melville and the American Voyage  MA Columbia Univ 1963   199 p

4125  MULLINS Patricia A  The Development of Themes and Method in Herman Melville's Novels Through *Moby Dick*  MA Univ of Texas at Austin 1963

4126  NICHOLS James  The Face of Innocence: A Study of the Development of the Young Protagonist in *Redburn* and *White Jacket*  MA Univ of North Carolina at Chapel Hill 1966

4127  NNOLIM Charles E  Melville's *Benito Cereno*: A Study in Meaning of Name Symbolism  MA Bemidji St Coll 1968

4128  O'COURT Mary E  The Insular Tahiti of W O Mitchell and R W Emerson Versus the Appalling Ocean of S Ross and H Melville  MA Univ of Toronto (Canada) 1966

4129  OLSON C J  The Growth of Herman Melville, Prose Writer and Poetic Thinker  MA Wesleyan Univ 1933

4130  OWEN Charles F  The Development of Symbol in Melville's *White Jacket*  MA Univ of Nevada 1966

4131  PARKER Thomas V  A Study of the Autobiographical References and Themes in the Shorter Prose Works of Herman Melville  MA East Carolina Univ 1966

4132  PERREY Robert T  *Billy Budd*: Interpretations and Non-interpretations  MA Roosevelt Univ at Chicago 1964

4133  PETERSON Jean  The Mississippi as Interpreted by Herman Melville and

Mark Twain  MA Western New Mexico Univ 1964
4134  PHARR Milton E  The Short Stories of Herman Melville: With Emphasis on *Benito Cereno*, "The Belltower" and "Bartleby"  MA Columbia Univ 1959  65 p
4135  PILKINGTON William T Jr  A Study of Melville's *Benito Cereno*  MA Texas Christian Univ 1963  99 p
4136  PITMAN John  Herman Melville's Civil War Poetry  MA Univ of Florida nd
4137  PIZARRO Jorge  The Theme of Quest in Melville's *Typee, Mardi, Redburn* and *White Jacket*  MA Univ of Denver 1965
4138  POPE Katherine V  Reward and Punishment and Herman Melville  MA Univ of Houston 1966  133 p
4139  POTTER David  American Magazine Opinion of Herman Melville from 1846 Through 1852  MA Rutgers St Univ 1939
4140  PRANG Edna L  *Moby Dick* and Oil Parallels and Fusions in the Whaling Industry Compared to the Petroleum Industry  MA Texas Woman's Univ 1964
4141  PRINCE Flora N  Ahab's Ivory House: Form and Technique in *Moby Dick*  MA Auburn Univ 1956
4142  RACICOT Ann M  Melville's Ishmael: A Study of Critical Opinion  MA Barry Coll 1966
4143  RAMPERSAD Arnold  *Israel Potter*: Melville's Three Armageddons  MA Bowling Green St Univ 1968
4144  RATHBUN Roger C  The Conflicts of "Civilization, Philosophy and Ideal Virtue in "Bartleby the Scrivener" and Other Works of Herman Melville  MA Ohio St Univ 1966  84 p
4145  RAY Richard E  Melville's Sea Imagery: A Search for Patterns of Sea Images in Seven Selected Novels by Herman Melville, 1846-1890  MA Indiana Univ of Pennsylvania 1965  291 p
4146  REDEKOP Ernest H  Appearance and Reality: The Confidence Man in Melville and Mann  MA Univ of Toronto (Canada) 1963
4147  RIEDELL Frances  The Existential Attitudes of Free Will and Alienation in Herman Melville's Novel *Moby Dick*  MA Mankato St Coll 1968  71 p
4148  RIESEN Charles F  From Farce to Irony: An Interpretation of the Comic Spirit in Herman Melville  MA Univ of Houston 1957  196 p
4149  RILEY Clark  Herman Melville: Characterization in *Moby Dick*  M Ed Henderson St Coll nd
4150  ROBERTSON Thomas L Jr  Narrative Technique in the Prose Work of Herman Melville  MA Univ of Mississippi 1950  174 p
4151  ROCCO Maria L  Herman Melville in His Narrative Work  MA Ca Foscari (Italy) 1942
4152  ROCKEFELLER Larry  A Study of the Starbuck Archetype in Melville's *Moby Dick* and *Billy Budd*  MA Bowling Green St Univ 1963
4153  ROSENHEIM Judith  Melville's Portrayal of Heroism in *Moby Dick*  MA Hunter Coll 1960
4154  ROSKOS Nancy L  Symbolism in the Short Novels of Herman Melville  MA Northeast Missouri St Coll 1959
4155  ROSS Martin W  Melville: A Confrontation with Primitivism  BA Rutgers St Univ 1968  86 p
4156  ROSS Ruth B  Herman Melville and Robert Lowell: *Benito Cereno*  MA Columbia Univ 1965  105 p
4157  RUSSELL J J  Epic Qualities in *Moby Dick*  MA North Texas St Univ 1952
4158  SCHAEFLE James W  Melville's *Moby Dick*: A Collection of Criticism  MA Univ of Maryland at College Park 1950  107 p
4159  SCHEUER Alice  A Reading of Melville's *Mardi*  MA Univ of Hawaii 1952  184 p
4160  SCHMIDT Roderic W  An Explication of Herman Melville's *Billy Budd*  MA Whittier Coll nd
4161  SCHMIDT Sanford M  *Moby Dick, Elmer Gantry* and *Lolita*: From Novel to Film  MA Washington Univ at St Louis 1963  56 p
4162  SCHROEDER Linda  Satan and Ahab: The Sin of Pride Contrasted

|   |   |
|---|---|
| 4163 | MA San Diego St Coll 1968 139 p<br>SCOTT Kay K  Herman Melville's Interest in the Problem of Evil in the World  MA Univ of Tulsa 1962  89 p |
| 4164 | SEXTON Estelle  Melville's Religion  MA Univ of Mississippi 1943  269 p |
| 4165 | SHAPIRO Bernard H  A Study of Certain Literary and Biographical Influences on Melville's Creative Method as Reflected by Some of His Novels and Short Stories  MA Univ of Massachusetts 1956 |
| 4166 | SHIN Kyun K  A Study of the First Person Narrators in Melville's Short Stories  MA Univ of Hawaii 1964  122 p |
| 4167 | SILBERMAN Donald J  Form and Point of View in Melville's Fiction  MA St Univ of New York at Buffalo 1965 |
| 4168 | SILTZBACH Marguerite K  Melville's "The Encantadas": A Mariner's Tale of the Act of Seeing  MA Columbia Univ 1963  129 p |
| 4169 | SIMSON George K  The Characters of Herman Melville's *Clarel*  MA Washington St Univ at Pullman 1957 |
| 4170 | SLADE Leonard A  A Review of Some Theories of the Symbolism of the White Whale in *Moby Dick*  MA Virginia St Coll 1965 |
| 4171 | SMITH Rex A  A Critical Study of Herman Melville's *Pierre*  MA Univ of Texas at Austin 1959  76 p |
| 4172 | SNOW John H  Melville and Aeschylus: A Similarity of Tragic Vision  MA Columbia Univ 1950 |
| 4173 | STARK Sidney Jr  Melville's Spiritual Biography as Seen in Four Characteristic Sea Novels  MA Columbia Univ 1951 |
| 4174 | STEINHAGEN Margaret J  The Term "Epic" as Applied to *Moby Dick*  MA Georgetown Univ 1958  91 p |
| 4175 | STUMP Reva J  Herman Melville's Battle-pieces and Aspects of the War Analyzed in Relation to His Prose  MA Ohio St Univ 1949 |
| 4176 | SUITOR John H  Social Criticism in the Novels of Herman Melville  MA Univ of Vermont 1948  120 p |
| 4177 | SUTHERLAND Helen L  The Early Novels of Herman Melville  MA Rice Univ 1956 |
| 4178 | SUTTON William A  The Reading of Herman Melville Through the Year 1857  MA Ohio St Univ 1937 |
| 4179 | TART James D  Herman Melville: The Hot Heart's Shell; an Inquiry Into the Origins and Development of Melville's Religious and Philosophical Ideas as Revealed Through His Novels  MA Washington Univ at St Louis 1949  130 p |
| 4180 | TAYER Delma W  Point of View as Key to the Narrative Structure, Symbolism and Theme of *Moby Dick*  M Ed Central Washington St Coll 1964  66 p |
| 4181 | TIPPETTS Robert H  Comparison and Contrast as Techniques of Character Development in *Moby Dick*  MA Brigham Young Univ 1969  161 p |
| 4182 | TURNER Harold  Melville's Seagoing Uncle: Norwest John  MA Columbia Univ 1964  124 p |
| 4183 | VALENTE Joseph B  An Analysis of Gothicism in Herman Melville's *Redburn*, *Moby Dick* and *Pierre*  MA Univ of Vermont 1969  75 p |
| 4184 | VATHING Gale S  The Imagery in Herman Melville's Shorter Poetry  MA Washington St Univ at Pullman 1963 |
| 4185 | VINECOUR Ada  Herman Melville and the Problem of Evil  MA Boston Univ 1944 |
| 4186 | WAGEMAN James C  Fire Imagery in Melville's Novels  MA Univ of Hawaii 1964  69 p |
| 4187 | WAHLQUIST Jeniveve J  The Character Evolution of Melville's Evil Agent, John Claggart  MA Brigham Young Univ 1970  74 p |
| 4188 | WALKER Robert H  An Evaluation of Herman Melville's *Billy Budd*  MA Univ of Texas at Austin 1958  90 p |
| 4189 | WALTERS E L  Some Social Criticism Expressed in Herman Melville's Shorter Narrative Works  MA Univ of North Carolina at Chapel Hill 1940 |
| 4190 | WARD Dean A  Characterization in the Novels of Herman Melville |

Previous to, and Including, *Moby Dick*  MA Univ of North Carolina at Chapel Hill 1932
4191 WARING Philip B  Many a Brave Unbodied Scheme: A Study of Herman Melville's Writings During the Four Years That Followed *Moby Dick*  MA Columbia Univ 1959  121 p
4192 WASHBURN M B  Melville and Hawthorne Compared and Contrasted  MA Boston Univ 1941
4193 WEBBER Joan M  "Thomas Browne Our Ensample": A Study of Thomas Browne's Influence on the Style of Melville's *Mardi*  MA Univ of Rochester 1952  88 p
4194 WHEELER Otis B  Humor in Herman Melville  MA Univ of Texas at Austin 1947  156 p
4195 WHEELOCK Alan S  Out of the Swing of the Sea: Melville and the Mountains  MA Hunter Coll 1965
4196 WHITEHEAD C  Melville's "Bartleby": A Selective Review of Scholarship and Criticism and an Interpretation  MA Univ of Toledo 1970
4197 WILLIAMS Joann F  Melville the Minister: An Analysis of Melville and His Men of God  MA Northeast Louisiana Univ 1966  91 p
4198 WILLIAMS Shirley J  Fatalism in Melville's Prose and Poetry  MA Univ of Mississippi 1954  170 p
4199 WILLIAMSON Don T  The Development of Herman Melville's Character-types Through the Early Works to Their Culmination in *Clarel*  MA Midwestern Univ 1967  91 p
4200 WILSON Jack H  Adumbrations of *Moby Dick* in *Redburn* and *White Jacket*  MA Univ of North Carolina at Raleigh 1957  73 p
4201 WITTEVELD Peter J  Camus' Doctrines of the Absurd in Melville's *Moby Dick*  MA DePauw Univ 1969  42 p
4202 WOMACK John P  The Friendship Theme in the Novels of Herman Melville  MA Univ of Texas at Austin 1956  87 p
4203 WOOD S E  Herman Melville as Novelist  MA Boston Univ 1940
4204 WOODEN Warren W Jr  An Analytical Study of the Style of *Typee*  MA Univ of Mississippi 1967
4205 WOODFIELD Ernest E  The Absurd Reality in the Works of Herman Melville  MA Chico St Coll 1968  108 p
4206 WOODWORTH Don W  Two Views of the Nature of Man: Calvinism and Melville's *Pierre*  MA Indiana Univ 1956
4207 WYLIE Rolfe A  Symbolism and Mysticism as Used by Herman Melville  M Ed Henderson St Coll nd
4208 YEAGER O S  Herman Melville  MA Univ of Texas at El Paso 1951  109 p
4209 YEN Margaret S  Image, Symbol and Theme in Melville's *Mardi*, *Moby Dick* and *Pierre*  MA McMaster Univ (Canada) 1965
4210 YOAKAM William E  A Study of Herman Melville's Poetical Techniques  MA Bowling Green St Univ 1950
4211 YOUNG Charles L  In the Shadow of the Leviathan: A Study of Melville's Use of Animal Symbolism  MA Univ of Tennessee 1969  62 p
4212 YOUNG Charles R  Herman Melville's Females (as Studied in the Novels and His Family Circle)  MA Columbia Univ 1951
4213 YOUNG Lorna D  Christian Ethics and *Billy Budd*  MA Univ of Rochester 1952  138 p
4214 YOUNG Miriam  The Decline of the Tragic Figure in American Literature as Seen in Historical Perspective: A Study of Captain Ahab and Willy Loman as Opposite Figures in the Decline  MA Columbia Univ 1964  66 p
4215 ZAGGER Jacquelynn A  An Analysis of the Criticism of Herman Melville's *Billy Budd*  M Ed Slippery Rock St Coll 1969  84 p
4216 ZIPES Jack D  A Second Voyage with *Redburn*  MA Columbia Univ 1960  72 p
See also 672, 674, 704, 709, 2433, 2630, 2642, 2649, 3868, 4810, 4839, 6600

## H L MENCKEN

4217  ATWELL Br James S  Two Studies in Twentieth Century American Literature, Eclipse and Emergence: H L Mencken's "Dark Years" and the Advent of His Second Career and J F Powers' *Morte D'Urban* and Religious Satire and Prophetic Theme  MA Univ of Maryland at College Park 1968  84 p
4218  BERNHARDT William F  H L Mencken: Critic of American Life  MA Columbia Univ 1951
4219  BERRY Warren P  The Political Thought of H L Mencken  MA Univ of California at Santa Barbara 1960  120 p
4220  BROWN Barbara I  The Political Thought of H L Mencken, Inception--1923  MA John Hopkins Univ 1966
4221  COOPER Guy L  The Influence of H L Mencken in the Critical Revolt of the 1920's  MS Kansas St Coll at Pittsburg 1956
4222  COOPER Sharon T  H L Mencken's Social Critism in *The American Mercury*  MA Univ of Texas at Austin 1967  125 p
4223  GILLIS Adolph  H L Mencken as Critic  MA Columbia Univ 1928
4224  HASSLER David B  Satirical Technique in the Social Criticism of H L Mencken  MA Univ of Texas at El Paso 1963  155 p
4225  KRAMORIS Ivan J  The Principles of Literary Criticism of H L Mencken  MA Marquette Univ 1938
4226  LOUNSBURY Marion B  H L Mencken: A Study of His Style  MA Texas Technological Univ 1953
4227  SAMUELS Barry  H L Mencken and the Quest for Kultur in the 1920's  BA Rutgers St Univ 1965  179 p
4228  SHUFORD Cecil E  An Evaluation of the Influence of H L Mencken and *The American Mercury* Upon American Thought  MA Northwestern Univ 1929
4229  STONE Edward  Henry Louis Mencken's Debt to Friedrich Wilhelm Nietzsche  MA Univ of Texas at Austin 1937  123 p
4230  STRAWN Robertson I  The Critical Theories of H L Mencken and the Purpose Underlying His Criticism  MA Univ of Kansas 1934
4231  SULLIVAN Esther  Critical Theory of H L Mencken  MA Ohio St Univ 1928
4232  TERRY Taylor B  H L Mencken's Religious Skepticism: An Attitude Contradicted by His Life and Actions  MA Univ of Texas at El Paso 1956  91 p

See also 336, 1157

## ADAH ISAACS MENKEN

4233  DAVIS Kate W  Adah Isaacs Menken: Her Life and Poetry in America  MA Southern Methodist Univ 1944
4234  LEACH Catherine  Adah Isaacs Menken: The Biography of an American Actress  MA Louisiana St Univ 1937
4235  RIBACK William H  The Life and Works of Adah Isaacs Menken  MA Northwestern Univ 1933

## JAMES MICHENER

4236  BRYLAWSKI Linda B  Heroes of Epic Figures in James A Michener's *Hawaii*  MA Univ of Maryland at College Park 1970  69 p
4237  LUDWIG Albert W  The Making of a Literary Career: Michener's Use of His War Experiences in the Pacific  MA Southwest Texas St Univ 1966

## EDNA ST VINCENT MILLAY

4238  BLODGETT Malcolm H  Edna St Vincent Millay: The Person, the Prescence, the Poet  MA Columbia Univ 1960  130 p
4239  CALLAHAN Sr M Edward  Edna St Vincent Millay and Louise Imogen Guiney: A Study in Contrast  MA Boston Coll 1942

4240 CARTLEDGE Mary C  Studies in the Work and Critical Reception of Edna St Vincent Millay  MA Columbia Univ 1942
4241 COLLETTE Jean  The Lyric Poetry of Edna St Vincent Millay  MA Univ of Idaho 1932
4242 DAUDET Margaret E  Elements of Distrust in the Poetry of Edna St Vincent Millay  MA Univ of Pittsburgh 1953
4243 DENNIS Martha J  The Imagery of Edna St Vincent Millay  MA Univ of Mississippi 1962  130 p
4244 DOYLE Mary M  The Satiric Trend of Thought in the Poetry of Edna St Vincent Millay  MA Boston Coll 1940
4245 EANES Ellagene J  The Types of Edna St Vincent Millay's Poetry  MA Univ of Texas at Austin 1940
4246 EDWARDS Larry D  The Sonnets of Edna St Vincent Millay  MA Univ of Louisville 1966  80 p
4247 HUGHES R N  Poetic Technique in the Verse of Edna St Vincent Millay, Robinson Jeffers and Edwin Arlington Robinson  MA Ohio St Univ 1932
4248 JACKSON Sarah W  Literary Allusions to the English Bible in the Lyric Poetry of Edna St Vincent Millay  MA Univ of Maine 1964  87 p
4249 JENSON M P  Edna St Vincent Millay  MA Univ of Texas at El Paso nd
4250 LAMBERT B  The Poetry of Edna St Vincent Millay  MA Wesleyan Univ 1956
4251 LAWS Herbert L  *Fatal Interview*: A Study and a Review of Its Critical Reception  MA Univ of Tennessee 1957  94 p
4252 McEACHERN Mary J  Edna St Vincent Millay and the Love Lyric  MA Univ of Texas at Austin 1966  116 p
4253 MACHIN Janet M  Gesture of Defiance: An Analysis of Edna St Vincent Millay's *A Few Figs from Thistles*  MA Texas Agricultural and Mechanical Univ 1967  83 p
4254 O'CONNOR J T  Poetry of Edna St Vincent Millay  MA Boston Coll 1932
4255 OSCAR Rebecca E  Edna St Vincent Millay and the Great Tradition  MA Univ of Texas at Austin 1940  93 p
4256 PITRELLA Mary A  Edna St Vincent Millay: Life, Poetry and Criticism  MA Univ of Rochester 1951  156 p
4257 SMITH Jane D  The Masonry of Art: A Study of the Sonnets of Edna St Vincent Millay  MA Temple Univ 1967  36 p
4258 STEWART Lola M  Edna St Vincent Millay's Philosophy of Life as Reflected in Her Poetry  MS Kansas St Coll at Pittsburg 1938
4259 TOMEI Sr M Corita  Edna St Vincent Millay: A Study in Contrast Between Her Earlier and Later Works  MA Boston Coll 1949
See also 503, 958, 1016, 1030

## ARTHUR MILLER

4260 AARON Chloe W  Arthur Miller: Evolution of an American Playwright  MA George Washington Univ 1966  122 p
4261 BARDEN Mary L  A Critical Analysis of Moral Concepts in Three Plays by Arthur Miller  MA Univ of Houston 1962  51 p
4262 BARRETT Elizabeth T  The Role of Law in Arthur Miller's Drama  MA Univ of Alberta (Canada) 1966
4263 BRADLEY Carol A  Arthur Miller's Use of Ibsen's Retrospective Exposition  MA Ohio St Univ 1969  76 p
4264 BURGE Barbara J  Arthur Miller: Social Critic  MA Univ of Pittsburgh 1961
4265 CALDWELL Michael S  Arthur Miller: A Critical Analysis of *Candida*  M Ed Henderson St Coll nd
4266 CAMPBELL Dorothy  Arthur Miller: A Critical Analysis of the Play *All My Sons*  M Ed Henderson St Coll nd
4267 CHAPMAN George  *The Death of a Salesman*: A Psychological Study  MA Texas Arts and Industries Univ 1950
4268 CLARK J W  Arthur Miller's *The Death of a Salesman*: An Instance of Modern Tragedy  MA Wesleyan Univ 1958

4269  CONSTABLE C R  *All My Sons* by Arthur Miller  MA Ohio St Univ 1949
4270  DeWAIDE Sandia L  The Female Characters in the Plays of Arthur Miller  MA San Diego St Coll 1967  121 p
4271  ERWIN Martin N  The Use of Blocks of Past Time in Arthur Miller's *Death of a Salesman*  MA Univ of North Carolina at Chapel Hill 1965
4272  FISHER William C  *Death of a Salesman*: A Drama for the High School Performer  MA Texas Christian Univ 1969  236 p
4273  FLANNERY Cathleen B  The Theme of Responsibility in the Plays of Arthur Miller  MA Univ of Maryland at College Park 1966  44 p
4274  FOREMAN Howard E  Arthur Miller and Modern Tragedy  MA Colorado St Univ 1967
4275  FRELING Roger N  A Study of the Principal Characters in Arthur Miller's Plays  MA Oklahoma St Univ 1961  53 p
4276  FUNK Elaine M  *The Crucible* as Drama and Polemic  MA Univ of Maryland at College Park 1968  81 p
4277  GENTRY Glenda E  Spatial Form in Arthur Miller's *Death of a Salesman* and *After the Fall*  MA Univ of Redlands 1965
4278  GILLIARD Frederick W  Dignity in Arthur Miller's Drama  MA Univ of Montana 1965
4279  HANNETT Beverly A  A Twentieth Century Morality Play: Arthur Miller's *Death of a Salesman*  MA St Univ of New York at Buffalo 1966
4280  HEEMANN Paul W  Arthur Miller's *The Crucible*: A Study of the Playwright's Dramatic Theory and Method  MA Univ of North Carolina at Chapel Hill 1959  77 p
4281  HEISS Rolland L  The Search for Identity and Love in Arthur Miller's Plays  MA Ball St Univ 1969  92 p
4282  HITCHENS Gordon  Attention Must Be Paid: A Study of Social Values in Four Plays by Arthur Miller  MA Columbia Univ 1962  193 p
4283  HOY J C  Contemporary American Society as Reflected in the Plays of Arthur Miller  MA Wesleyan Univ 1960
4284  McANANY Emile G  The Tragic Commitment: A Study of Arthur Miller's Heroes in His Plays and His Critical Writings  MA St Louis Univ 1960  131 p
4285  McBRIDE Jane M  An Existential Examination of Arthur Miller  MA Univ of Houston 1963  80 p
4286  MITTELSTET Sharron R  Social Conscience in Arthur Miller  MA West Texas St Univ 1968  100 p
4287  MOOR Gulliume  Form and Meaning in Arthur Miller's *After the Fall*  MA Roosevelt Univ at Chicago 1966
4288  POLHEMUS Ann S  Arthur Miller and Greek Tragedy  MA Univ of North Carolina at Chapel Hill 1960
4289  PRIDDY Barbara H  The Fall of the Fortress: Thematic Progression in Arthur Miller's Major Plays  MA Univ of Louisville 1969  77 p
4290  REYER Paul  Arthur Miller's Concept of Tragedy: Its Application to His Works  MA Univ of Arkansas 1952
4291  RINGER Linda K  Human Relationships in the Major Works of Arthur Miller  MA Baylor Univ 1965  100 p
4292  SCHWALB Sanford  Thematic Developments in Arthur Miller's Plays  MA Univ of Tennessee 1965
4293  SMITH Phyllis S  Arthur Miller: A Writer of Tragedy  MA East Carolina Univ 1967
4294  SPILLER Ellen B  The Influence of Henrik Ibsen on Arthur Miller  MA Univ of Houston 1965  86 p
4295  STANLEY Linda C  Guilt in Arthur Miller  MA Univ of Rhode Island 1966  67 p
4296  STARK Howard J  Arthur Miller's Concept of Tragedy  MA Univ of the Pacific 1962  151 p
4297  WOOD Carolann  Arthur Miller: Is It Possible for the Individual to Shape His Own Destiny?  MA Univ of Massachusetts 1967

See also 83, 2723, 4214, 4539, 4652, 6672, 6734

## HENRY MILLER

4298 CROSS Robert L  The Henry Miller Circle in Paris, 1930-1939  MA Univ of Kansas 1961
4299 DeWOSKIN Ronald M  The Wisdom of the Heart: An Introduction to the Works of Henry Miller  MA Roosevelt Univ at Chicago 1962
4300 FOULON Marie H  Henry Miller: A Humanist  MA Univ of Louisville 1961
4301 GALVIN John R  *Tropic of Cancer* and *Leaves of Grass*  MA Columbia Univ 1962  84 p
4302 GRIFFIN David W  The Possibility of Joy: Henry Miller's Place in the American Tradition  MA Columbia Univ 1951
4303 HEFLING Ronald J  The Ego-protagonist in *The Rosy Crucifixion*  MA Wichita St Univ 1966
4304 KIMBLE Stephen B  Henry Miller: The Conditions and Achievement of Freedom  MA Univ of Idaho 1966
4305 LINDWALL Wilbert J  Henry Miller as Surrealist  MA San Diego St Coll 1967  179 p
4306 PEACOCK Valerie S  Imagery, Style and Aesthetic Theory in the Novels of Henry Miller  MA Fresno St Coll 1968  86 p
4307 WYNDHAM Harald P  Portrait of the Artist as Surrealistic Hero: An Analysis of *Tropic of Capricorn*  MA Bowling Green St Univ 1969
See also 6512

## JOAQUIN MILLER

4308 BUCHANAN Betty  Non-American Elements in Joaquin Miller  MA Washington St Univ at Pullman 1943
4309 LUDBERG Everetta B  Joaquin Miller: A Study of His Life and Work  MA Univ of Idaho 1927

## SILAS WEIR MITCHELL

4310 BURRELL Norma P  A Study of the Novels of Silas Weir Mitchell  MA Univ of Mississippi 1961  115 p
4311 HEFLEY Aruella B  Silas Weir Mitchell: Pioneer in Psychotic Characterization  MA Texas Technological Univ 1959  125 p

## HARRIET MONROE

4312 FABIAN Edith  Harriet Monroe and Her Place in the American Poetic Renaissance  MA Brooklyn Coll of City Univ of New York 1947  70 p
4313 McKNIGHT Velda W  Harriet Monroe's Contribution to Contemporary Poetry  MA Univ of Texas at Austin 1941  123 p
4314 SMITH Elizabeth M  Poets as Critics: A Study of Four Moderns (Harriet Monroe, Amy Lowell, Robert Frost and T S Eliot)  MA Baylor Univ 1950  218 p

## WILLIAM VAUGHN MOODY

4315 BAUGH Rosa M  William Vaughn Moody: An Interpretation  MA Univ of Texas at Austin 1926
4316 BOYD Carrie B  William Vaughn Moody as Poet  MA George Peabody Coll for Teachers 1937
4317 GOODWYN Frank  Eastern and Western Traditions as Reflected in the Writings of William Vaughn Moody  MA Texas Arts and Industries Univ 1941
4318 KING Ellen M  Religion in William Vaughn Moody's Works  MA Southern Illinois Univ at Carbondale 1956  81 p
4319 LICKTEIG Sr Mary A  William Vaughn Moody: A Study  MA Univ of Kansas 1924

4320  REAVER J R  A Study of the Poetic Dramas of William Vaughn Moody
      MA Ohio St Univ 1938
4321  STEPHENS Mary M  Symbolism in the Poetic Dramas of William Vaughn Moody
      MA Butler Univ 1944
4322  WOLFRUM Annie L  Non-dramatic Poetry of William Vaughn Moody
      MA Texas Arts and Industries Univ 1952
See also 5683

## MARIANNE MOORE

4323  HUMPHREY Jewel S  Marianne Moore and the Art of Poetry:  A Study of
      Her Theory and Practice  MA Oklahoma St Univ 1964  143 p
4324  LESLEY Bonnie A  Values in Use:  Theme and Imagery in the Poetry of
      Marianne Moore  MA West Texas St Univ 1968  184 p
4325  ROSS Jane M  Images of Nature in the Poetry of Marianne Moore and
      Robert Frost  MA Columbia Univ 1959  153 p
4326  SHELBOURN Judith A  Poetic Synthesis:  A Study of Form and Subject
      in the Poetry of Marianne Moore  MA Univ of British Columbia
      (Canada) 1967

## PAUL ELMER MORE

4327  CERVANTES Rachel S  Paul Elmer More and the New England Heritage
      MA Columbia Univ 1958  109 p
4328  SUGARBAKER Everett  Paul Elmer More:  Editor of *The Nation*  MA Univ
      of Kansas 1944
See also 206, 5362

## GOUVERNEUR MORRIS

4329  BUTLER Martin J  The Practical Patriot:  Gouverneur Morris  MA Boston
      Coll 1958
4330  HAUSER Richard P  A Critical Examination of the Diary and Letters of
      Gouverneur Morris to Determine Their Adequacy as a Source for
      Historical Writing  BA Amherst Coll 1956

## JOHN MUIR

4331  HARMON Philip M  John Muir:  Wilderness Evangelist  MA Brigham Young
      Univ 1968  84 p
4332  ONTHANK Charlotte  John Muir's Contribution to Literature  MA Boston
      Univ 1921
See also 5802

## MARY NOAILLES MURFREE

4333  BRAUM Maryalice  Mary Noailles Murfree:  A Study of Her Short Stories
      Dealing with the Mountain Folk  MA Univ of Kansas 1943
4334  BYRD Eva M  The Life and Writings of Mary Noailles Murfree  MA Univ
      of Tennessee 1937
4335  COUSINS Paul M  Charles Egbert Craddock  MA Columbia Univ 1920
4336  CURTIS J L  The Dialect Writing of Charles Egbert Craddock in the
      Light of the Author's Background  MA Univ of North Carolina at
      Chapel Hill 1942
4337  HARRIS Isabella D  Charles Egbert Craddock as an Interpreter of
      Mountain Life  MA Duke Univ 1933
4338  JOHNSON Euner G  Mary Noailles Murfree as a Writer of Local Color
      Fiction  MA Univ of Mississippi 1961  119 p
4339  MAGEE Mary V  Charles Egbert Craddock and Her Background  MA Louisiana
      St Univ 1935

4340 MILLS Fanny H  Nature Coloring in the American Novel with Emphasis Upon Its Use in the Works of Craddock, Allen, Howells, Glasgow, Cather and Ostenso  MA Univ of Virginia 1928
4341 MOONEY Mary S  An Intimate Study of Mary Noailles Murfree, Charles Egbert Craddock  MA George Peabody Coll for Teachers 1928
4342 OGLE Gladys L  Mary Noailles Murfree (Pseudonym: Chalres Egbert Craddock)  MA Columbia Univ 1924
4343 OTJEN Mary E  A Descriptive Analysis of the Short Stories of Mary Murfree (Charles Egbert Craddock)  MA Oklahoma St Univ 1938  56 p
4344 SHERMAN Marian C  The Local Color Motif in the Writings of Mary Noailles Murfree (Charles Egbert Craddock)  MA Ohio St Univ 1944
4345 SPENCE Eleanor B  Collected Reminiscences of Mary N Murfree  MA George Peabody Coll for Teachers 1928
4346 SWINK Lottie H  The Literary Reputation of Charles Egbert Craddock with an Annotated Selected Bibliography of Craddock for 1884 to June, 1968  MA Univ of North Carolina at Chapel Hill 1968
4347 TROUY Fr Lucien  Charles Egbert Craddock and the Southern Mountains and Mountaineers  MA Catholic Univ of America at Washington, D C 1932
4348 WELSH Clara I  An Evaluation of the Writings of Mary Noailles Murfree  MA Univ of Pittsburgh 1930

## GEORGE JEAN NATHAN

4349 COHN Sanford L  George Jean Nathan: The Yearbooks  MA Columbia Univ 1954  93 p
4350 FOGELMAN Frances  George Jean Nathan as a Critic  MA Boston Univ 1937
4351 FRICK Constance  The Dramatic Criticism of George Jean Nathan  MA Indiana Univ 1945
4352 WEAVER Bruce J  A Comparative Study of the Critical Theories of George Jean Nathan and Stark Young  MA Kansas St Coll at Pittsburg 1966

## ROBERT NATHAN

4353 GREEN Marianne D  Spiritual Aspects of Robert Nathan as Reflected in His Works  MA Univ of Texas at Austin 1960
4354 HODGKINSON Patricia  The Substance and Form of Robert Nathan's Fantasy  MA Univ of Pittsburgh 1948
4355 KOLLOR Diane M  Robert Nathan's Use of Fantasy  MA Texas Christian Univ 1966  93 p

## JOHN G NEIHARDT

4356 BOWDEN Lois  Mike Fink: The Last of the Keel-boatmen (John Neihardt, T B Thorpe, J M Field, Emerson Bennet)  MA Columbia Univ 1928
4357 DONNELLY Jean M  John G Neihardt: Epic Poet  MA Univ of Arizona 1934
4358 HOMAN John  Mike Fink: The Spoiler as Culture Hero (John Neihardt, T B Thorpe, J M Field, Emerson Bennet)  MA Southern Illinois Univ at Carbondale 1964  72 p
See also 694, 3783, 5147

## FRANK NORRIS

4359 ALTENBERND August L  The Intellectual Currents in *The Octopus*: A Study of the Naturalism of Frank Norris  MA Ohio St Univ 1949
4360 ANDERSON Grace  A Dictionary of Characters in the Novels of Frank Norris  MA Univ of Kansas 1933
4361 ANDERSON Robert G  Frank Norris and the Realism War  MS Illinois St Univ at Normal 1966
4362 BARNEY Danford  "La Bete Humaine": A Study of the Bestial Imagery in Frank Norris and Jack London and the Conflicts Which Are Illiminated by Such a Study  MA Univ of Colorado 1966
4363 BEDNO Howard M  The Short Works of Frank Norris  MA Roosevelt Univ at

Chicago 1961
4364 BLISS Bonnie M  The Emergence of the Non-hero in American Fiction 1850-1915 and His Significance to the Novels of Frank Norris  MA Syracuse Univ 1967  115 p
4365 BOWDRE Paul H  Naturalism and the Novels of Frank Norris  MA Univ of Mississippi 1960  124 p
4366 BRAUN Margaret M  Male-female Relationships in the Novels of Frank Norris  MA Univ of Texas at Austin 1967  78 p
4367 BRINKLEY Thomas E  Frank Norris' Naturalistic Psychology  MA Univ of North Carolina at Chapel Hill 1964
4368 CIFELLI Edward M  The Other Side of Naturalism: Frank Norris and the Theme of Love  MA Texas Technological Univ 1967  104 p
4369 COHEN Paul E  "The Boy Zola" at Harvard: A Study in Frank Norris' Development  MA Univ of Maine 1968  104 p
4370 COLEMAN Thomas C III  Norris' Debt to Zola: A Study in Literary Influence  MA Univ of Louisville 1950
4371 CRIDER A B  Romantic Elements in Five Novels of Frank Norris  MA North Texas St Univ 1967
4372 DIAMOND Naomi J  Primordial Imagery in the Novels of Frank Norris  MA Ohio St Univ 1949
4373 DUNBAR John R  Naturalism in the Novels of Frank Norris with Particular Reference to *McTeague*, *The Octopus*, *The Pit* and *Vandover and the Brute*  MA Univ of Oregon 1937
4374 FREDIN Robert W  Polarity and Conflict: A Study of Ethical Theory in Selected Novels of Frank Norris  MA Utah St Univ at Logan 1967
4375 HATFIELD Francis H  A Study of the Life and Works of Frank Norris, American Author, 1870-1902  MA Univ of Texas at El Paso 1957  99 p
4376 HAUSMANN Reid D  Sex and the Novels of Frank Norris  MA Ohio St Univ 1965  100 p
4377 HAZLERRIG J O  Naturalism in the Novels of Frank Norris  MA North Texas St Univ 1961
4378 HELLMAN David  Frank Norris' Theory of the Novel  MA Rutgers St Univ 1939
4379 HENSGEN Morgan D  Frank Norris' Use of Historical Materials in *The Octopus*  MA Texas Christian Univ 1968  79 p
4380 HILL Marion V  A Study of the Thematic Forces in the Novels of Frank Norris  MA Bowling Green St Univ 1954
4381 JACKSON Frank L  The Nature of Tragedy in the Fiction of Frank Norris  MA Univ of Idaho 1950
4382 JONES Jeanette H  A Critical Study of the Short Stories of Frank Norris  MA Auburn Univ 1965
4383 LATHROP Paul G  The Animal Imagery of Frank Norris  MA Chico St Coll 1966  106 p
4384 LEE U S Jr  Frank Norris: A Definition  MA Howard Univ 1936  131 p
4385 LEITZ Robert C  Muckraking Elements in Frank Norris' *The Octopus*  MA Texas Agricultural and Mechanical Univ 1969  101 p
4386 LETIZIA Louise M  Frank Norris: A Study in Contrasts and Contradictions  MA Univ of Pittsburgh 1950
4387 LOUGHLIN James L  An Analysis of the Naturalism of Frank Norris  MA Univ of New Mexico 1937
4388 McGINN Richard J  The Characterization of Women in the Novels of Frank Norris  MA Columbia Univ 1954  100 p
4389 MERIDETH Robert D  Intellectual Consistency and Artistic Value in *The Octopus*  MA Oklahoma St Univ 1958  68 p
4390 MORRIS Ethiel V  Frank Norris' Trilogy on American Life  MA Univ of Kansas 1928
4391 MORRIS Homer H  A Critical Study of Frank Norris' *McTeague*  MS Kansas St Coll at Pittsburg 1963
4392 MORTON Warren W  The Importance of Frank Norris as a Novelist  MA Tufts Univ 1932

4393 OEHLK Roger W  Frank Norris  MA Univ of Iowa 1966
4394 PADDEN Sr Mary J  Frank Norris' Conception of Romanticism as Realized in His Fiction  MA Univ of Oregon 1932
4395 PALMER Oronona M  Frank Norris: A Triumph of Victorian Conscience  MA Brigham Young Univ 1969  116 p
4396 PARSHALL Rodney L  A Critical Study of the Structural Quality of Three Naturalistic Novels by Frank Norris  MA Bowling Green St Univ 1958
4397 PIERSON Robert C  The Use of Symbols in the Novels of Frank Norris  MA Midwestern Univ 1956  118 p
4398 PULLIAM Jim F  Frank Norris and the Brute Concept  MA Univ of Tulsa 1968  78 p
4399 REISS John H  Characterization in the Four Major Novels of Frank Norris  MA Univ of Louisville 1966
4400 SEIGEL Robert K  Frank Norris as a Sociological Novelist  MA Butler Univ 1962
4401 SNYDER Joseph M  The Development of the Naturalistic Hero: As Seen in the Works of Norris, Dreiser and Stephen Crane  MA George Washington Univ 1969  80 p
4402 SPAW George  The Influence of Emile Zola on the Novels of Frank Norris  MA Hunter Coll 1963
4403 STARR Carma J  Frank Norris' Mixed Allegiance to Romanticism and Naturalism  MA Auburn Univ 1964  91 p
4404 TRAGER Thomas N  The Influence of Professor Joseph Le Conte in the Major Novels of Frank Norris  MA Ohio St Univ 1965  49 p
4405 WAGNER William D  Frank Norris' Theory of Fiction as Applied in Selected Short Stories  MA Bowling Green St Univ 1960
4406 WALES Anita M  The Development of Frank Norris as a Writer of Fiction  MA Univ of California at Berkeley 1918
4407 WALSH Thomas P  The Naturalistic Influence of Emile Zola on Frank Norris  MA Univ of Oklahoma 1963
See also 3123

## FLANNERY O'CONNOR

4408 ADERHOLT Martha  Flannery O'Connor's Thematic Use of Family Relationships  MA Univ of Tennessee 1969  143 p
4409 BALCER Joan  Flannery O'Connor's Christian Insight Revealed by Style and Content  MA Aquinas Coll 1966
4410 BRUCE Duane F  The Regional and Religious Dimensions of Flannery O'Connor's Fiction  MA Univ of North Carolina at Chapel Hill 1967
4411 BUSH George D  An Author Looks at Her Work: An Approach to Flannery O'Connor  MA Univ of Tennessee 1965
4412 CASEY Margaret E  Teilhardianism in the Fiction of Flannery O'Connor  MA Boston Coll 1968
4413 CHERRY Charles L  Theme, Structure and Symbol in Flannery O'Connor's *The Violent Bear It Away*  MA Univ of North Carolina at Chapel Hill 1966
4414 COULBOURN Mildred E  Flannery O'Connor's Displaced Persons  MA Duke Univ 1966
4415 DELAFIELD Carter  Flannery O'Connor: Prophet and Evangelist  MA Univ of North Carolina at Greensboro 1966
4416 DeMOUY Jane K  Damascus Road: Epiphany and Theme in the Works of Flannery O'Connor  MA Univ of Maryland at College Park 1967  99 p
4417 DREYER Ladonna J  The Truth Shall Make You Free: Flannery O'Connor's Ideology as Reflected in Her Prose  MA West Texas St Univ 1969  96 p
4418 DULA Martha A  The State of Man as It Is Portrayed in Flannery O'Connor's *Wise Blood*  MA Univ of North Carolina at Chapel Hill 1967
4419 EVANS Florence T  Flannery O'Connor and Modern Man  MA St Mary's Univ of San Antonio 1964  63 p
4420 FLOERCHINGER Sharon M  The Rat-gray and the Wooden Leg: The Meaning

of the Grotesque in Flannery O'Connor  MA Wichita St Univ 1966
4421 FREEMAN Warren E  The Social and Theological Implications in Flannery
 O'Connor's *A Good Man Is Hard to Find and Other Stories*  MA Univ
 of North Carolina at Chapel Hill 1962
4422 GALVIN Elizabeth H  Point of View in the Works of Flannery O'Connor
 MA Texas Arts and Industries Univ 1968  139 p
4423 GILBERT Mary R  Solar and Lunar Imagery in Flannery O'Connor's Short
 Stories  MA Boston Coll 1968
4424 GILLIKIN Sandra A  The Face of Evil: A Study of Irony in Flannery
 O'Connor's *The Violent Bear It Away*  MA East Carolina Univ 1968
4425 GUILKA Mother Therese E  Flannery O'Connor's Violent World  MA Boston
 Coll 1966
4426 HARDWICK Patricia A  The Longer Fiction of Flannery O'Connor  MA Ohio
 St Univ 1965  48 p
4427 HART Gary V  The Eucharistic Symbol and the Concept of Grace in the
 Works of Flannery O'Connor  MA Pepperdine Coll 1969
4428 HOLLOWAY Phyllis S  The Power of Shock: A Study of the Central
 Figures in Flannery O'Connor's Fiction  MA East Tennessee St Univ
 1969
4429 HUFF Carol A  Flannery O'Connor and the Technique of Characterization
 MA Texas Christian Univ 1968  63 p
4430 MARONEY Janet M  The Grotesque in Flannery O'Connor  MA Columbia Univ
 1962  77 p
4431 MATCHETTE William A  Southern Protestantism in the Fiction of
 Flannery O'Connor  MA North Texas St Univ 1970
4432 MILLS Elizabeth M  Mannerist Art and the Fiction of Flannery O'Connor:
 A Combination of Parallels  MA Univ of Texas at El Paso 1967  105 p
4433 MOORE Lofton S  Flannery O'Connor: A Description Analysis of Her
 Fiction  MA Univ of Idaho 1965
4434 MORLEY Irene  The Unknown Self in Flannery O'Connor's Novels
 MA Columbia Univ 1966  59 p
4435 NEWMAN William S  Flannery O'Connor's Distinctive Use of Place in Her
 Novels and Short Stories  MA Univ of Tennessee 1965
4436 OUZTS Cuyler E  Flannery O'Connor's Use of the Grotesque  MA Texas
 Christian Univ 1968  91 p
4437 PERRIN Elaine  The Unique Achievement of Flannery O'Connor  MA Texas
 Technological Univ 1969  86 p
4438 PRITCHARD Alice S  Violence in Flannery O'Connor's Fiction  MA Univ
 of Maryland at College Park 1967  99 p
4439 SCALIA Linda F  The Theological Vision of Flannery O'Connor in
 *Everything That Rises Must Converge*  MA Northeast Louisiana Univ
 1968  72 p
4440 SCAMBRAY Terry A  Flannery O'Connor's Christian Vision  MA Fresno St
 Coll 1969  69 p
4441 STUMBO Carol  The Technique of the Grotesque in the Writings of
 Flannery O'Connor  MA Morehead St Univ 1968  61 p
4442 TIERNEY Sr Marie R  The Displaced Person Motif in Flannery O'Connor's
 Works  MA Boston Coll 1967
4443 WARD Sr Mary B  Children in the Fiction of Flannery O'Connor
 MA Georgetown Univ 1967  93 p
4444 WISEMAN William J  Idiots Clapping in Church: The Fiction of
 Flannery O'Connor  MA Univ of Tulsa 1968  102 p
4445 WOOD Ralph C  The Scandal of Redemption: Religious Meaning in the
 Novels of Flannery O'Connor  MA East Texas St Univ 1965
4446 YORK Beth M  An Ax for the Frozen Sea Within Us: Flannery O'Connor's
 Prose  MA West Texas St Univ 1965  164 p
See also 490, 6356

## CLIFFORD ODETS

4447 BURT David J  A Prose Larger Than Life: A Study of the Diction and Dialogue in Two Plays of Clifford Odets  MA North Texas St Univ 1966
4448 CONNORS James F  Analysis of Plays of Clifford Odets  MA Boston Coll 1948
4449 CRAWFORD Margaret A  The Artistry and Significance of Clifford Odets  MA Univ of Texas at El Paso 1956  116 p
4450 DRAKE James A  Clifford Odets: Dramatist of Frustration  MA Ohio St Univ 1942
4451 FAIGEN Anne G  The Dramas of Clifford Odets: Variations on a Constant Theme  MA Univ of Pittsburgh 1957
4452 FARISH Annie L  A Legend of Sorrow: Odets and Wexley in the Thirties  MA Mississippi St Univ 1968  80 p
4453 GILLESPIE Harold R  The Plays of Clifford Odets: A Critical Study  MA Univ of Texas at Austin 1956  180 p
4454 HOPPER Arthur B Jr  Man's Search for Values in the Early Plays of Clifford Odets  MA Univ of North Carolina at Chapel Hill 1961
4455 LAUGHNER Carl L  Clifford Odets: A Critical Evaluation of Ten Dramas  MA Univ of Pittsburgh 1955
4456 MILLER Jeanne-Marie A  Clifford Odets and the Dramatic Ferments of the 1930's  MA Howard Univ 1963  281 p
4457 NIELSEN Karl  Clifford Odets: Critic of the American Dream  MA St Univ of New York at Albany 1969
4458 RICHEY Robert D  *Awake and Sing* by Clifford Odets  MA Ohio St Univ 1948
4459 STIGDON Clement F Jr  A Critical Evaluation of the Contribution of Clifford Odets to the American Theatre  MA Indiana Univ 1950

## JOHN O'HARA

4460 BABBS John E  John O'Hara's *Assembly*: Descendant of *Winesburg, Ohio*  MA Ohio St Univ 1962  65 p
4461 CHAMBERS Jean M  John O'Hara's Lantenego Novels: Society as Seducer and Destroyer  MA Southwest Texas St Univ 1966
4462 GRIPPO Helen G  The Tragedy of the Commonplace: John O'Hara's Vision of Reality in His Short Fiction  MA Univ of North Carolina at Raleigh 1970  64 p
4463 KRAUSE D P  The Naturalistic Technique of John O'Hara  MA North Texas St Univ 1963
4464 NAGEL James E  Characterization and Morality in the Novels of John O'Hara  MA Univ of Tennessee 1964
4465 PAYNE Mary B  The Tragic Visionary: An Analysis of John O'Hara's Major Protagonists  MA Univ of Mississippi 1963  132 p
4466 RICKMAN Sidney M  John O'Hara: Psychological Patterns in His Major Works  MA Univ of Mississippi 1965  112 p
4467 ROGERS Henry P  The Applied Axioms of Social Psychology as Carried by the Language of Alfred Eaton's Attitudes in John O'Hara's *From the Terrace*  MA Morehead St Univ 1969  73 p

## O HENRY

4468 BEARDSHEAR William M  The Style and Plot Structure of O Henry's Short Stories  MA Columbia Univ 1913
4469 CARTER Elizabeth H  O Henry: The Sultan of the Short Story  MA Univ of Hawaii 1931  42 p
4470 CONNALLY Lucy B  A Study of the Social Background of the Characters in O Henry's New York Short Stories  MA North Texas St Univ 1940
4471 CRICHLOW Isabel L  O Henry's Social Attitudes  MA Ohio St Univ 1951
4472 ECHOLS Myrtle M  O Henry: Perfectionist of the Short Story  M Ed Henderson St Coll nd
4473 FAGGETT Harry L  Characterization in O Henry  MA Boston Univ 1945

4474  FELKER Violet  A Study of O Henry's Southeastern Types  MA Stetson Univ 1935
4475  HARRELL Mary S  O Henry's Texas Contacts  MA Univ of Texas at Austin 1935
4476  HIXON Carolyn  The Literary Reputation of O Henry  MS Auburn Univ 1951  80 p
4477  HOWELL Dana M  Settings and Characters of O Henry's Texas Stories  MA George Peabody Coll for Teachers 1937
4478  HUNTLEY Stephen M  O Henry: An American Story Teller  MA Univ of South Carolina 1920
4479  LONG Eugene H  O Henry as Seen by the Critics  MA Baylor Univ 1931  72 p
4480  MacANDREW James F  A Critical Analysis of the Literary Reputation of O Henry  MA Columbia Univ 1938
4481  MARTIN J F  Method of O Henry  MA Boston Coll 1934
4482  MEADORS Olive G  Types of Character Portrayed in O Henry's New York Stories  MA George Peabody Coll for Teachers 1930
4483  MITCHELL Eleen R  The Dramatizations of O Henry's Short Stories  MA Auburn Univ 1965
4484  NEUMANN Ray  The Origin of the Pen Name O Henry  MA St Mary's Univ of San Antonio 1945  141 p
4485  PIKE Cathleen M  O Henry in North Carolina  MA George Peabody Coll for Teachers 1938
4486  REED Dorris I  O Henry and Henry Lawson: A Comparative Study  MA Univ of Texas at Austin 1959  101 p
4487  RODDEY Cammie  O Henry: The Picaroon  MA Winthrop Coll 1945
4488  ROSANS Rita  O Henry: Sentimental Fatalist  MA Univ of Delaware 1968  74 p
4489  SEAMAN Gertrude A  Tendencies Shown in the O Henry Prize Memorial Stories from 1920-1930  MA Hunter Coll 1936
4490  SCOLES David L  A Study of O Henry's Southwestern Types  MA Stetson Univ 1934
4491  SMITH Joyce A  O Henry: Pioneer in the Development of the American Short Story  M Ed Henderson St Coll nd
4492  SPENCER Maud  The Influence of O Henry's Life and Character on His Short Story  MA Boston Univ 1932
4493  TAPP George H  The Attitude of O Henry Toward His Work  MA George Peabody Coll for Teachers 1929
4494  TAYLOR Virginia W  The Narrative Art of O Henry  MA Univ of Texas at Austin 1936
4495  TOWNLEY Janice F  O Henry and the Southern Literary Tradition  MA Auburn Univ 1963
4496  WATSON Grace M  O Henry on *The Houston Post*  MA Univ of Texas at Austin 1934
4497  WOODWARD Vinola S  O Henry's Use of the Malapropos and Related Devices  MA Stetson Univ 1935
4498  YANG Helen  A Study of O Henry's Social Attitudes as Reflected in His New York Short Stories  MA Atlanta Univ 1966
4499  YATES Arminda T  O Henry's Use of Dialect in Portraying American Character  MA Hardin-Simmons Univ 1948
See also 3178, 6996

## EUGENE O'NEILL

4500  AMLIE Elizabeth  Development of Eugene O'Neill as a Dramatist  MA Univ of Iowa 1934
4501  AMMAN Marguerite  Eugene O'Neill as a Playwright  MA Boston Univ 1936
4502  AMORATI Anna  Eugene O'Neill and the Classical Myths  MA Ca Foscari (Italy) 1958
4503  BACON Eugene  The Force Theme in the Plays of Eugene O'Neill  MA Univ of Toledo 1956

4504 BALDWIN M E  Eugene Gladstone O'Neill: Studies in Dramaturgy  MA St Univ of New York at Albany 1940
4505 BALL Dayton  Eugene O'Neill: Dramatist of Illusion Versus Reality  MA Columbia Univ 1951
4506 BASS Joan W  A Study: The Influence of Sigmund Freud on the Plays of Eugene O'Neill  MA Univ of North Carolina at Chapel Hill 1967
4507 BELL Cyrene  Dramatic Experiment in the Plays of Eugene O'Neill  MA North Texas St Univ 1941
4508 BELL George H  O'Neill's Use of Irony, Masks and Impersonation in *The Great God Brown*  MA Univ of North Carolina at Chapel Hill 1964
4509 BOCCHIERI Salvatore  The Spirit of the Sea in the Early Plays of Eugene O'Neill  MA Ca Foscari (Italy) 1945
4510 BRADY Marion B  Orin and Orestes: A Study of Eugene O'Neill's Modern Transcription of the *Oresteia*  MA Brigham Young Univ 1950  76 p
4511 BREWER Sr Marie C  Eugene O'Neill: His Search for a Mother  MA Boston Coll 1963
4512 BRICK Seymour  Eugene O'Neill: The Deterioration of a Dramatist  MA Univ of Arizona 1936
4513 BRYER Jackson R  The Disintegration of Character Development in the Plays of Eugene O'Neill  BA Amherst Coll 1959
4514 BUDD Dirk R  The Power of Love in the Plays of Eugene O'Neill  MA Columbia Univ 1959  111 p
4515 BUKER Barbara V  The Influence of the Greek Technique in the Works of Eugene O'Neill  MA Boston Univ 1945
4516 BYRNS Ethel I  Symbolism in Eugene Gladstone O'Neill's Dramas  MA Oklahoma St Univ 1931  57 p
4517 CALLAHAN Harry R  A Proposed Production of Eugene O'Neill's *The Great God Brown*  MA Univ of North Carolina at Chapel Hill 1964
4518 CAMPBELL Dorothy  Eugene O'Neill's Tragic Sense  M Ed Henderson St Coll nd
4519 CHABROWE Leonard E  The Classical Idea of Eugene O'Neill  MA Columbia Univ 1960  293 p
4520 CHASE Elizabeth  The Trend of Modern Drama as Shown in the Works of Eugene O'Neill  MA Boston Univ 1930
4521 CLARK Kathleen  The Problem of Incest in Three Selected Modern Dramas: Henrick Ibsen's *Ghosts*, Eugene O'Neill's *Desire Under the Elms* and Tennessee Williams' *A Streetcar Named Desire*  MA North Carolina Central Univ 1963  64 p
4522 CLEM Marguerite D  Dual Personality and the Plays of Eugene O'Neill  MS Kansas St Coll at Pittsburg 1938
4523 CLEMENT Mildred D  Eugene O'Neill: The Comic Mask  MA Texas Christian Univ 1950  124 p
4524 COEN Marie H  Eugene O'Neill: Achieving Universal Themes Through Autobiographical Material  MA Fairleigh Dickinson Univ 1968  125 p
4525 COLES Violet C  A Chronological Analysis and Interpretation of the Plays of Eugene Gladstone O'Neill  MA Ft Hays Kansas St Coll 1930  118 p
4526 COOPER Kitty  The Evolution of Eugene O'Neill  MA Ohio St Univ 1929
4527 COOPER Melvin  Patterns of Development in the Plays of Eugene O'Neill  MA Univ of Toronto (Canada) 1966
4528 COSGROVE James D  The Fathers in the Plays of Eugene O'Neill  MA Ohio St Univ 1961  56 p
4529 COUCH Caroline E  Nemesis in Eugene O'Neill  MA Hardin-Simmons Univ 1932
4530 CROUCH Pearl V  The Religious Theme in Eugene O'Neill's Plays  MA Univ of Texas at El Paso 1956  114 p
4531 CUSHING Anita L  The Father Figure in the Plays of Eugene O'Neill  MA Univ of Maryland at College Park 1967  92 p
4532 DAVIDSON Ivan H  An Analysis of Selected Plays of Eugene O'Neill from 1913-1934  MA Indiana Univ 1966
4533 DEEMAN Andrew J  The Folk Element in Eugene O'Neill's Negro Dramas

MA St Louis Univ 1936  58 p
4534 DERANEY Beverly R  O'Neill on the Broadway Stage, 1946-1965  MA Boston Coll 1966
4535 DEVINE Sr Mary E  Eugene O'Neill: A New Approach  MA Temple Univ 1965  51 p
4536 DRAKE Jessee  Eugene O'Neill as an Impressionist and Expressionist  MA Hardin-Simmons Univ 1951
4537 DRUCKER Trudy  Eugene O'Neill's "Greek Dream in Tragedy"  MA Fairleigh Dickinson Univ 1965  90 p
4538 EHRENKRANZ Louis  Reality and Illusion in the Expressionistic Plays of Eugene O'Neill  MA Hunter Coll 1959
4539 ELLISON Jerome  God on Broadway: Deity as Reflected in the Work of Seven Playwrights Prominent in the Twentieth Century American Commerical Theater; O'Neill, Wilder, MacLeish, Williams, Miller, Albee, Chayofski  MA South Connecticut St Coll 1966
4540 EMMONS Janet L  Eugene O'Neill's Treatment of the Negro in the Drama of the 1920's  MA Univ of North Carolina at Chapel Hill 1961
4541 EWING L J  The Influence of Strindberg on Eugene O'Neill  MA Ohio St Univ 1930
4542 EYLER Marion  August Strindberg and Eugene O'Neill  MA Univ of Maryland at College Park 1942  103 p
4543 FALK Signi L  Twisted Personalities from the Plays of Eugene O'Neill  MA Univ of Hawaii 1933
4544 FELDMAN David E  Mythic Hero in Modern Garb: The Hero Pattern in Several of Eugene O'Neill's Plays  MA Syracuse Univ 1967  111 p
4545 FELDMANN Hans E  Eugene O'Neill's Last Four Plays: An Interpretation  MA Univ of Maryland at College Park 1965  101 p
4546 FENNELL E J  Eugene O'Neill's Theory and Practice of Tragedy  MA North Texas St Univ 1951
4547 FISH Margaret  A Comparative Study of Eugene O'Neill and the Decadent Elizabethan Dramatists  MA Brigham Young Univ 1934
4548 FIX Ressie J  Henrik Ibsen and His Influence on Modern Dramatists, Particularly Eugene O'Neill  MA DePauw Univ 1929  154 p
4549 FOUKS Toby R  The Poet-artist: A Study of a Theme in the Plays of Eugene O'Neill  BA Univ of British Columbia (Canada) 1962
4550 FOWLER Anne N  Symbolism in the Plays of Eugene O'Neill  MA Texas Arts and Industries Univ 1955
4551 FREEMAN Max  Eugene O'Neill  MA Univ of Kentucky 1926
4552 GEARHART Evelyn S  The Philosophy of Eugene O'Neill as Reflected in the Inner Consistency of His Dramas  MA Univ of Oregon 1935
4553 GORMAN Sr Monica  Eugene O'Neill's *Mourning Becomes Electra*: Interpretative Analysis  MA Boston Coll 1961
4554 GREENWALT Sr Mary A  Character Relationships as Dramatic Device in *The Iceman Cometh*  MA Boston Coll 1965
4555 HACHADOURIAN Sadie B  Eugene O'Neill's "Island" Symbolism  MA Univ of Massachusetts 1969  62 p
4556 HAGEN Doris M  The Theme of Illusion in the Plays of Eugene O'Neill  MA Columbia Univ 1960  59 p
4557 HALLAUER John W  Exposition in Terms of Climax in O'Neill's Tragedies  MA Ohio St Univ 1942
4558 HAUSSMAN Courtney L  The Theme of the Mask in Eugene O'Neill's Plays  MA Univ of Wyoming 1964
4559 HENDRICKS Richard  Eugene O'Neill and the Psychological Drama  MA Ohio St Univ 1939
4560 HENSLEY Donald M  Eugene O'Neill's Use of Greek Dramatic Themes  MA Univ of North Carolina at Raleigh 1954  70 p
4561 HERZOG John L  The Influence of Guilt in the Plays of Eugene O'Neill  MA Mankato St Coll 1967  57 p
4562 HICKS Annie A  The Emergence of Eugene O'Neill as a Playwright  MA Howard Univ 1966  137 p

4563 HIGHSMITH James M  Eugene O'Neill: Apprenticeship with Dramatic Presentationalism  MA Univ of North Carolina at Chapel Hill 1967
4564 HILL Bette  The Illusion Theme in Nine Plays by Eugene O'Neill  MA Baylor Univ 1964  101 p
4565 HILLES Olive R  The Anatomy of Eugene O'Neill's Expressionism  MA Oklahoma St Univ 1937
4566 HINDMAN Pamela K  Eugene O'Neill's Treatment of Religion, Love and Illusion  MA Southern Illinois Univ at Carbondale 1962  99 p
4567 HOUSTON Ralph H  Dramatic Expressionism in the Works of Eugene O'Neill  MA Univ of Texas at Austin 1934
4568 HUMPHREY Margaret R  Dramatic Utilization and Development of the Women Characters in O'Neill's Plays  MA Ohio St Univ 1935
4569 HUNT Doris A  American Criticism of the Plays of Eugene O'Neill  MA Univ of North Carolina at Raleigh 1952  90 p
4570 HYNES Carolyn  An Analysis of Nine Tragedies by American Playwrights: Eugene O'Neill, Maxwell Anderson and Lillian Hellman  MA Univ of Houston 1954  214 p
4571 JETTON J K  Aristotelian Elements in Tragic Drama from Sophocles to O'Neill  MA North Texas St Univ 1960
4572 JOHNSON Barbara F  The Impact of the Year 1912 on the Plays of Eugene O'Neill  MA Clemson Univ 1964
4573 JOHNSON Marjorie K  An Analysis of the Artistic Process in Creating the Character of Mary Tyrone in *Long Day's Journey Into Night*  MA Ohio St Univ 1966  92 p
4574 JONES Carol L  An Examination of Four O'Neill Plays as Tragedies  MA Univ of Arizona 1961  103 p
4575 JONES Myrl G  Eugene O'Neill and the Poet  MA West Texas St Univ 1963  78 p
4576 JOSEPHS Lois S  Eugene O'Neill: The Variable Philosophy of His Plays  MA Univ of Pittsburgh 1956
4577 KAUFFMANN LeRoy  An Analysis of the Influence of Friedrich Nietzsche on Eugene O'Neill  MA Univ of Houston 1961  128 p
4578 KIMBALL Janet G  The Women in the Plays of Eugene O'Neill  MA Univ of Pittsburgh 1951
4579 KOINM Albert J  Elements of Greek Tragedy in Three Eugene O'Neill Plays  MA Texas Agricultural and Mechanical Univ nd  66 p
4580 KRUPP Kathleen M  Some Structural Problems in the Plays of Eugene O'Neill  MA Univ of Pittsburgh 1960
4581 LAMUN Jo A  A Study of the Greek Concept of Fate as Utilized in Three Plays by Eugene O'Neill  MA Univ of Colorado 1965
4582 LANG Marie E  A Study of the Influence of the Greek Tragedians on the Dramatic Work of Eugene O'Neill  MA Univ of Hawaii 1948  116 p
4583 LaRUE Carolyn  The Irish Nationalistic Traits in Eugene O'Neill  MA Univ of Pittsburgh 1948
4584 LAWRENCE Harry W  Studies in Eugene O'Neill  MA Univ of Delaware 1942  79 p
4585 LAWSON Wayne P  A Comparative Study of Three Pairs of Plays by Federico Garcia Lorca and Eugene O'Neill  MA Ohio St Univ 1966  93 p
4586 LEARY Cecil A  The Theme of Illusion in Three Late Plays by Eugene O'Neill  MA Univ of Kansas 1965
4587 LEMAY Loraine  The Influence of August Strindberg on Eugene O'Neill  MA Univ of New Hampshire 1965  50 p
4588 LEMBO Louis J  Eugene O'Neill and Expressionism  MA Villanova Univ 1966
4589 LINDLEY Arthur  Eugene O'Neill: The Late Plays  MA Columbia Univ 1964  76 p
4590 McCOPPIN Alice  Eugene O'Neill: A Critical Analysis of *Mourning Becomes Electra*  M Ed Henderson St Coll nd
4591 McDANIEL Camille  Eugene O'Neill in Contemporary Drama  MA Univ of Idaho 1923

4592 McGHEE Esther J  The Secret Lives of the Women in Eugene O'Neill's Plays: A Study in Dramatic Technique  MA Howard Univ 1954  127 p
4593 MacKENZIE Eleanor H  Eugene O'Neill: A Social Critic  MA Columbia Univ 1940
4594 McLANE Elva R  Death and Immortality in Eugene O'Neill  MA Howard Univ 1940  66 p
4595 McMULLAN Barbara L  The Theme of Illusion in Plays by Eugene O'Neill  MA Texas Agricultural and Mechanical Univ 1965  90 p
4596 MAHAN Lorena W  Frustration in the Plays of Eugene O'Neill  MA Hardin-Simmons Univ 1947
4597 MARSHALL Sue S  Eugene O'Neill: A Study of Human Value in the Early Plays  MA Univ of North Carolina at Chapel Hill 1966
4598 MARTIN June M  Eugene O'Neill in Search of a Faith  MA Univ of North Carolina at Raleigh 1958  78 p
4599 MASON Martha N  An Analysis of the Characters in Eugene O'Neill's *The Iceman Cometh*  MA Indiana Univ 1967
4600 MASON Walter S Jr  The O'Neill Plays  MA George Peabody Coll for Teachers 1933
4601 MASTERS Robert W  Fate as It Appears in the Works of Eugene O'Neill  MA Indiana Univ 1935
4602 MASTROW William  "Fate" in Eugene O'Neill  MA Brooklyn Coll of City Univ of New York 1955  117 p
4603 MAZAHER K H  Eve, the Apple and Eugene O'Neill  MA North Texas St Univ 1963
4604 MEIER Doris E  Eugene O'Neill: A Critical Analysis of *The Great God Brown*  M Ed Henderson St Coll nd
4605 MICHELSEN Cleo  The Spiritual Dilemma of Modern Man in the Tragic Formula of Eugene O'Neill  MA George Washington Univ 1952  235 p
4606 MILKEY Lucy M  Eugene O'Neill: A Critical Analysis of the Play *Strange Interlude*  M Ed Henderson St Coll nd
4607 MILLIGAN Janet P  Eugene O'Neill: Tragic Dramatist  MA Southern Illinois Univ at Carbondale 1954  88 p
4608 MINOTT Ada C  Eugene O'Neill and the Critics: A Study of Critical Opinions Concerning the Works of America's Foremost Dramatist  MA Univ of Maine 1947  160 p
4609 MOFFETT Alexander S  The Sickness of Today: A Study of Five Plays by Eugene O'Neill  MA Univ of North Carolina at Chapel Hill 1963
4610 MONTAGNA Anna  The Expressionism of Eugene O'Neill in *The Emperor Jones* and *The Hairy Ape*  MA Ca Foscari (Italy) 1967
4611 MOORE Nancy  The Influence of the Greek Drama Upon Eugene O'Neill's *Mourning Becomes Electra*  MA Butler Univ 1934
4612 MORELLI Angelo  Studies on Eugene O'Neill  MA Ca Foscari (Italy) 1930
4613 MOSKOWITZ Marcia M  Eugene O'Neill's Vision of Woman: A Study of Four O'Neill Heroines  MA Fairleigh Dickinson Univ 1968  83 p
4614 MULHALL Sr M Sabina  Conscious Role-playing in *Long Day's Journey Into Night* and *A Touch of the Poet*  MA Boston Coll 1968
4615 MULLALY Gerard E  Self-dispossession as Tragedy in the Last Plays of Eugene O'Neill  MA Univ of New Brunswick (Canada) 1966
4616 NEWMAN Charles E  Eugene O'Neill: Social Critic  MA Washington Univ at St Louis 1947  140 p
4617 NORWOOD Kittie R  A Study of Escapism in the Works of Eugene O'Neill  MA Midwestern Univ 1964  131 p
4618 OSEROFF Joel R  A Nietzschean Approach to Eugene O'Neill's *A Tale of Possessors Self-dispossessed*  MA Univ of North Carolina at Chapel Hill 1968
4619 O'TOOLE Austin J  The Impossibility of Happiness for the Protagonists of Six Plays by Eugene O'Neill  MA Univ of Rhode Island 1966  158 p
4620 PACE Antoinette L  Man's Search for Identity and the Failure of Love in the Family Plays of Eugene O'Neill  MA Univ of Massachusetts 1968  47 p

4621  PALMER Charlotte  The Theme of Illusion in the Plays of Eugene O'Neill  MA C W Post Coll 1964  133 p
4622  PARILLARD Dan  Eugene O'Neill and *The Great God Brown*  MA West Texas St Univ 1960  103 p
4623  PARKER Karen F  Eugene O'Neill: The Struggle for Communication  MA Brigham Young Univ 1962  97 p
4624  PARKER Thomas W  *Long Day's Journey Into Night*: An Insight Into the Plays of Eugene O'Neill  MA Univ of Arizona 1957  71 p
4625  PAUL Br Amian  Eugene O'Neill's Use of Tone in Stage Directions of Three Plays  MA Univ of Rhode Island 1965  129 p
4626  PAYNE Dana E  Motives Underlying the Obsessions Exhibited by Characters in the Plays of Eugene O'Neill  MA Virginia St Coll 1966
4627  PAYTON Marjorie C  The Pipe Dream as a Dramatic Device in Eugene O'Neill's Plays  MA Howard Univ 1960  127 p
4628  PERRY James  The Diminishing Hero in the Works of O'Neill  MA Xavier Univ of New Orleans 1965
4629  PETERS Betty L  The Tragic Stature of the Characters of Eugene O'Neill  MA Univ of Idaho 1953
4630  PETTIE Ralph P  A Bibliography of Books and Articles Concerning Eugene O'Neill and His Work  MA Univ of Maine 1956  141 p
4631  PHILLIPS Robert L Jr  Jung's *Psychology of the Unconscious* in Three Plays of Eugene O'Neill  MA Univ of North Carolina at Chapel Hill 1963
4632  PICKERING Christine  The Influence of Friedrich Nietzsche's Philosophy on the Tragic Drama of Eugene O'Neill  MA East Texas St Univ 1964
4633  PILCHER Marie H  O'Neill's Universality  MA Florida St Univ 1952
4634  PINES Sergio  Eugene O'Neill, Part I: The Early Works  MA Ca Foscari (Italy) 1962
4635  POOL Martin V Jr  Eugene O'Neill's Life and Its Twin-like Qualities in *Long Day's Journey Into Night*  M Ed Henderson St Coll nd
4636  POSTON Charles D  The Emancipated Woman in the Plays of Eugene O'Neill  MA Univ of Texas at Austin 1965  92 p
4637  QUICK Edna N  Eugene O'Neill and His World  MA Boston Univ 1930
4638  RANSOM Mae F  The Dramatic Reputation of Eugene O'Neill  MA Howard Univ 1966  96 p
4639  RASCO R C  The Use of the Mask in the Plays of Eugene O'Neill  MA North Texas St Univ 1961
4640  RAY Helen H  Eugene O'Neill's Expressionism  MA Univ of Texas at El Paso 1958  147 p
4641  REUMERT Patricia  The Strindberg Influence on O'Neill's Expressionistic Plays  MA Univ of Houston 1964  153 p
4642  REYNOLDS Paula  Puritanism in *Mourning Becomes Electra* by Eugene O'Neill  MA Baylor Univ 1969  89 p
4643  RHODES Raymond H  The Influence of Greek Tragedy on Eugene O'Neill  MA Stanford Univ 1939
4644  RICE Evelyn A  Eugene O'Neill: A Search for Permanence  MA Boston Coll 1966
4645  RINDFLEISCH Greg  A Director's Prompt Book for a Staged Production of Eugene O'Neill's *The Great God Brown* with a Critical Analysis of the Use of Masks  MA Mankato St Coll 1966  121 p
4646  ROAHEN Richard L  Eugene O'Neill: The Playwright and His Plays  MA Univ of Kansas 1928
4647  ROBERTS William H  The Development of Eugene O'Neill: An Analysis and Partial Integration of the Criticisms of O'Neill's Work  MA Univ of Kansas 1948
4648  RUEDI Norma P  Eugene O'Neill: American Exponent of Expressionism  MA Southern Methodist Univ 1932
4649  SAMS Oscar E Jr  The Cultural Background of Eugene O'Neill as Reflected in His Plays  MA Univ of Tennessee 1938
4650  SAMUELSON Jane E  Eugene O'Neill's Expressionism  MA Univ of Maine 1962  100 p

4651 SANTRY Agnes T  The Development of Eugene O'Neill  MA Boston Univ 1929
4652 SCHAPIRO Joanne B  Towards Tragic Realism: O'Neill and Miller  MA Columbia Univ 1962  118 p
4653 SCHMIDT Peter  Man's Existence in a Materialistic World: Eugene O'Neill's Search for the Meaning of Life in Four of His Early Plays  MA Syracuse Univ 1965  86 p
4654 SCHOENDALLER Katherine P  A Study of the Women Characters in the Long Plays of Eugene Gladstone O'Neill  MA Ft Hays Kansas St Coll 1941  197 p
4655 SCHOLES James B  Comparative Studies in the Plays of Eugene O'Neill  MA Univ of Kansas 1949
4656 SCHWAN Fred O  A Study of Eugene O'Neill's Dramatic Technique  MA Columbia Univ 1965  92 p
4657 SEIDEL Reginald F  Tragedy and Eugene O'Neill  MA Fairleigh Dickinson Univ 1969  164 p
4658 SEWELL Harold R  The Concept of God in the Plays of Eugene O'Neill  MA Baylor Univ 1956  179 p
4659 SHARP Donald B  Themes of Illusion and Their Tragic Significance in O'Neill's One-act Plays  MA Univ of Alaska 1963  97 p
4660 SIMMONS Linda W  The Influence of Family Environment on Eugene O'Neill's Plays  MA Baylor Univ 1969  102 p
4661 SIMMONS V B  The Mystical Trend in Naturalistic Drama with Special Reference to Eugene O'Neill  MA Ohio St Univ 1928
4662 SPARROW Martha C  The Influence of Psychoanalytical Material on the Plays of Eugene O'Neill  MA Northwestern Univ 1931
4663 SPELMAN John W  Direction of Eugene O'Neill's *Desire Under the Elms*  MA Purdue Univ 1965
4664 SPENCER Madeline  Eugene O'Neill's Adaptation of the Lazarus Story in *Lazarus Laughed*  MA Stanford Univ 1964
4665 SPONAGLE Alice P  Expressionism in Eugene O'Neill  MA Univ of Arizona 1934
4666 STENSON Melbourne J  Dominant Influences of the Dramas of Eugene O'Neill  MA North Carolina Central Univ 1964  66 p
4667 STEWART Juanita W  Eugene O'Neill and American Materialism  MA Howard Univ 1952  102 p
4668 STEWART Sara G  Folklore in the Plays of Eugene O'Neill  MA Univ of North Carolina at Raleigh 1951  108 p
4669 STONER Madge P  O'Neill's Women Characters: A Literary and Psychological Analysis  MA Univ of Louisville 1937
4670 STONER Peter A  Expressionism in the Drama of Eugene O'Neill  MA Univ of Vermont 1937  52 p
4671 STOUT Naomi G  A Study of Pipe Dreams in the Last Plays of Eugene O'Neill  MA Univ of North Carolina at Greensboro 1968
4672 STRAUGHN Laurlene  The Stage of Eugene O'Neill  MA Univ of Pittsburgh 1943
4673 STREATER Gloria L  Justifications for Violations of Social, Moral and Religious Laws and Codes by Women Characters in the Plays of Eugene O'Neill  MA Howard Univ 1967  141 p
4674 STUDER William P  A Study of Selected Theatrical Devices Used in the Published Plays of Eugene O'Neill  MS St Cloud St Coll 1965  113 p
4675 SWANSON Ralph N  *Anna Christie*: A Study of the Revisions of Chris Christopherson by Eugene O'Neill  MA Univ of North Carolina at Chapel Hill 1963
4676 TANNER H A  Eugene O'Neill: The Man and His Work  MA Boston Univ 1923
4677 TARANTINO Floriana  Symbolism in the Plays of Eugene O'Neill  MA Boston Univ 1941
4678 TAYLOR L John  William Blake--Christian Critic of Christianity, Prophecy and Poesy: An Imaginary Conversation Between William Wordsworth and Joseph Smith and Eugene O'Neill, a Man of Thought and Feeling in an Era of Unbelief  MA Brigham Young Univ 1960  27 p

4679 THOMAS Ruth B  The Use of Obsessions and Delusions as a Tragic Device in the Major Plays of Eugene O'Neill  MA Univ of the Pacific 1942  88 p
4680 THOMSON Carol L  The Earth Mother in O'Neill: The Archetype in the Plays from 1922-1931  MA Chico St Coll 1967  67 p
4681 TIDWELL Dewitt  Eugene O'Neill: A Critical Analysis of *The Emperor Jones*  M Ed Henderson St Coll nd
4682 TROWBRIDGE Clinton W  The Quest for Union in the Plays of Eugene O'Neill  MA Univ of Florida 1952
4683 TRUAX Elizabeth  Eugene O'Neill's Dramatic Debt to August Strindberg  MA Rutgers St Univ 1958
4684 TUOHEY Joseph P  The Autobiographic in the Plays of Eugene O'Neill  MS Purdue Univ 1961  72 p
4685 TUXBURY Francis K  The Visual and Auditory Devices in Representative Plays of Eugene O'Neill  MA Univ of New Hampshire 1949  56 p
4686 TYSON John P  Eugene O'Neill and the Roman Catholic Doctrine of Grace  MA Texas Christian Univ 1961  108 p
4687 UKA Kalu  Themes and Characterization in Some Plays of Eugene O'Neill and Tennessee Williams  MA Univ of Toronto (Canada) 1965
4688 UNDERWOOD Maurine P  Plot-structure in Certain Plays of Eugene O'Neill  MA Univ of Texas at Austin 1938
4689 VERBIEREN Dianne R  Three Tragic Visions in the Plays of Eugene O'Neill  BA Acadia Univ (Canada) 1965
4690 VIRSIS Rasma A  Eugene O'Neill: Isolation as a Result of Family Tragedy  MA Univ of Massachusetts 1963
4691 WARREN Nancy M  Basic Philosophic Themes in the Drama of Eugene O'Neill  MA Univ of Louisville 1939
4692 WASHINGTON Jack A  The Influence of Certain Places Upon the Plays of Eugene O'Neill  MA Howard Univ 1949  91 p
4693 WHITAKER D  Themes and Technique in the Plays of Eugene O'Neill During the Period 1921-1931  M Phil Univ of London (England) 1967
4694 WILBERT Charles L  Dramatic Repetition in Three Plays of Eugene O'Neill: *The Emperor Jones*, *Mourning Becomes Electra* and *The Iceman Cometh*  MA Ohio St Univ 1966
4695 WILLIAMS Earl M  The Influence of Freud on the Plays of Eugene O'Neill  MA Univ of Mississippi 1954  57 p
4696 WOOD Nancy R  An Analysis of the Settings of the O'Neill Dramas  MA George Peabody Coll for Teachers 1933
4697 WRIGHT David J  Flight from Reality in O'Neill's Later Plays  MA Bowling Green St Univ 1960
See also 203, 213, 214, 252, 580, 4022, 4051, 6672

## JAMES OPPENHEIM

4698 FREEMAN William W  The Poetry of James Oppenheim  MA Ohio St Univ 1967  102 p
4699 SACKS Harold H  James Oppenheim and *The Seven Arts*  MA Columbia Univ 1955  77 p

## THOMAS NELSON PAGE

4700 ABERNATHY Robert  The Southern Planter Portrayed in Fiction of Thomas Nelson Page  MA George Peabody Coll for Teachers 1933
4701 ALLBRITTEN Geraldine  The Conception of the Southern Aristocracy in the Fiction of Thomas Nelson Page  MA Univ of Kansas 1933
4702 BITTINGER Mary S  The Historical Validity of Representative Short Stories of Thomas Nelson Page  MA Vanderbilt Univ 1945
4703 BRIDGERS Frank E Jr  Thomas Nelson Page's Treatment of Southern Plantation Life  MA Duke Univ 1933
4704 BROWN Dorothy W  The Negro Problem in the Fiction of Thomas Nelson Page,

Joel Chandler Harris and George Washington Cable; 1880-1900 MA Texas Christian Univ 1950 217 p

4705 CRAVER Sadie B  Thomas Nelson Page  MA Southern Methodist Univ 1944
4706 DAVIS Mary M  Children in Thomas Nelson Page's Stories of Children  MA George Peabody Coll for Teachers 1931
4707 HOWARD Helen E  The Negro in the Fiction of Thomas Nelson Page  MA George Peabody Coll for Teachers 1932
4708 McFADIN Maude A  Thomas Nelson Page as a Short Story Writer  MA Univ of Kansas 1935
4709 MOORE Eva L  Two Virginia Regionalists: A Comparison of the Materials and Methods of Thomas Nelson Page and Ellen Glasgow  MA Univ of Missouri 1931
4710 RANDALL Helen L  Thomas Nelson Page and Ellen Glasgow as Interpreters of Southern Women  MA Univ of Iowa 1933
4711 SMITH Mary P  Thomas Nelson Page: The Literary Interpreter of Ole Virginia (1850-1880)  MA Auburn Univ 1936
See also 6988, 6999

## WALTER HINES PAGE

4712 BENNETT Caroline  Walter Hines Page: Political Thinking, 1900 to 1913  MA Columbia Univ 1934
4713 HOLT Mildred E  Walter Hines Page: A Study of His Influence on Our Entry Into World War I  MA Vanderbilt Univ 1946
4714 MINOR Olive  Walter Hines Page's Reconstruction Policy with the *Atlantic Monthly*  MA Columbia Univ 1934

## THOMAS PAINE

4715 ANGRIST Eugene P  Principle and Practice: An Interpretation of Paine's "Rights of Man"  BA Amherst Coll 1959
4716 CASEY William T  Thomas Paine: Patriot and Propagandist; an Evaluation of His *The American Crisis*  MA Boston Coll 1952
4717 DUPUIS Elroy  A Comparison of Certain Aspects of Revolutionary Thought as Found in the Writings of Thomas Paine and Jean-Jacques Rousseau  MA Univ of North Carolina at Chapel Hill 1937
4718 ETHERIDGE Billie W  Thomas Paine, Revolutionary Rhetorician: His Abilities and Rewards  MA Univ of Texas at El Paso 1966  73 p
4719 GAINES Betty L  Religious Philosophy of Thomas Paine  MA Univ of Texas at Austin 1951  83 p
4720 HAHN Bill E  Thomas Paine: Literary Patriot  M Ed Henderson St Coll nd
4721 KING Montgomery W  Thomas Paine: His Relationship to English and French Radicalism, 1791-1794  MA Howard Univ 1937  47 p
4722 LORENZI Robert  Thomas Paine: A Study of His Unpopularity  MA Fairleigh Dickinson Univ 1966  70 p
4723 MERRIMAN Lockwood  Thomas Paine's Attitude Toward Revealed Christianity  MA Columbia Univ 1940
4724 METZGAR Joseph V  Thomas Paine: A Study in Social and Intellectual History  MA Univ of New Mexico 1965
4725 MILLER Mary S  The Influence of the Bible on the Writings of Thomas Paine  MA George Washington Univ 1932  120 p
4726 SAUNDERS J M  The Political Theories of Thomas Paine  MA Univ of North Carolina at Chapel Hill 1926

## THEODORE PARKER

4727 CARTER Lewis L  Transcendentalism in the Philosophy of Theodore Parker: An Approach to the Movement Through the Individual  MA Syracuse Univ 1949  119 p
4728 CATHEY Bill R  The Transcendentalism of Theodore Parker  MA North Texas

St Univ 1965

## FRANCIS PARKMAN

4729 DIETER Joseph M  Francis Parkman:  The Historian as Literary Man  MA Howard Univ 1966  73 p
4730 ELLIS David C  A Discussion of Francis Parkman, Historian  M Ed Slippery Rock St Coll 1967  44 p
4731 FORD Arthur L  A Study of How Francis Parkman Used His Notes for *The Oregon Trail*  MA Bowling Green St Univ 1960

## JAMES KIRKE PAULDING

4732 BURNEY Mary A  The Development of the Literary Style of James K Paulding Through Association with Washington Irving  MA Univ of Southwest Louisiana 1968  68 p
4733 GEORGE J Mishell  James Kirke Paulding:  A Literary Nationalist  MA George Washington Univ 1941  122 p
4734 GOERLICH Dorothy S  James Kirke Paulding as Satiric Humorist  MA Univ of Toledo 1943
4735 TERRELL Barbara L  An Analysis of the Fiction of James Kirke Paulding  MA Univ of Texas at Austin 1956  120 p
4736 WALKER Virginia A  James Kirke Paulding:  Precursor of Realism  MA Auburn Univ 1958
4737 WATKINS Floyd C  James Kirke Paulding:  Nationalist and Man of Letters  MA Emory Univ 1947  166 p

## WILLIAM ALEXANDER PERCY

4738 DICKEY Benjamin W  William Alexander Percy:  An Alien Spirit in the Twentieth Century  MS Auburn Univ 1951  212 p
4739 TALLEY May R  A Study of the Poems of William Alexander Percy  MA East Texas St Univ 1939
See also 6996

## JULIA PETERKIN

4740 JORDAN Mary R  The Prose Fiction of Julia Peterkin:  A Study of Technique  MA Fisk Univ 1936
4741 MOORE Laura L  The Life and Fiction Writings of Julia Peterkin  MA George Peabody Coll for Teachers 1930
See also 6996

## DAVID GRAHAM PHILLIPS

4742 BOYVEY Mary R  David Graham Phillips:  Social Novelist  MA Univ of Texas at Austin 1945  89 p
4743 FELDMAN Abraham  A Survey of the Life and Novels of David Graham Phillips  MA Univ of New Mexico 1945
4744 JAEHNIG Robert D  Forgotten American Odyssey:  A Critical Re-evaluation of David Graham Phillips' *Susan Lenox*  MA Syracuse Univ 1965  136 p

## EDGAR ALLAN POE

4745 ADAIR Margaret C  Literary Techniques and Death Symbolism in Selected Short Stories of Edgar Allan Poe  MA Northeast Louisiana Univ 1968  161 p
4746 ADAMS Eugenia I  Poe's Relation to the French Symbolists  MA Univ of Texas at Austin 1939  108 p
4747 ALBRIGHT Thelma  Poe's Interest in Contemporary Affairs  MA Duke Univ 1937

4748 ALEXANDER A S  The Changing Character of the Increasing Interest in Edgar Allan Poe  MA Univ of Oregon 1928
4749 ALEXANDER Jean  Poe and Baudelaire: A Study of Comparative Literature  MA Univ of Chicago 1918
4750 ALLAN Carlisle V  The Military Services of Edgar Allan Poe  MA Columbia Univ 1925
4751 ALLEN John N  The Possibility of a New World: A Study of the Settings in Selected Tales of Edgar Allan Poe  MA Univ of Idaho 1969
4752 ALLEN Ruth C  Edgar Allan Poe's Doctrine of the Single Effect  MA Duke Univ 1936
4753 ANDERSON Lorine  A Century of Dandyism: From Poe and Baudelaire to Wallace Stevens  MA Columbia Univ 1954  131 p
4754 ANDRA Carl E  Those Ravens and Cats of Mr Poe: Myth, Eliot and *The Elder Statesman*; and "Pas de Deux", an Original Story  MA Brigham Young Univ 1964  21 p
4755 ATKINSON James B  Moral Implications in the Poetry of Edgar Allan Poe and Arthur Rimbaud  MA Columbia Univ 1961  149 p
4756 AYALA Esperanza  Edgar Allan Poe's Place in Literature  MA Texas Arts and Industries Univ 1943
4757 BAILEY Patricia R  Poe and Griswold  MA Columbia Univ 1948
4758 BAIRD Ruth C  The Modernity of Edgar Allan Poe's Criticism  MA Vanderbilt Univ 1943
4759 BALLARD Ruby T  Poe as a Critic  MA Baylor Univ 1948  125 p
4760 BANCROFT Anne D  Poe's Theory of Poetry and the Doctrine of Art for Art's Sake  MA Stanford Univ 1927
4761 BAREFOOT Spencer W  Sources of Poe's Tales  MA Univ of Oklahoma 1931
4762 BEARZATTO Giovanni  The Strange Life and the Weird Stories of Edgar Allan Poe  MA Ca Foscari (Italy) 1941
4763 BEASLEY Annie R  A Study of the Gothic Elements in *The Narrative of Arthur Gordon Pym* and Some of Poe's Selected Tales  MA North Carolina Central Univ 1959  56 p
4764 BERCES Francis A  Poe, Opium and Imagination  MA Wake Forest Univ 1966
4765 BLACK Henry M  The Gothic Element in Poe  MA Univ of Iowa 1934
4766 BOCKES Douglas T  Edgar Allan Poe and the Gothic Tradition  MA Syracuse Univ 1948  66 p
4767 BODY Lois M  The Influence of the Gothic Novel on the Works of Edgar Allan Poe  MA Univ of Illinois at Urbana 1941
4768 BOJE Louise M  Notes on Poe's Criticisms in Burton's *Gentleman's Magazine*  MA Columbia Univ 1924
4769 BONDURANT Agnes M  Poe's Richmond  MA Duke Univ 1941
4770 BOST W R  First-person Narration in Edgar Allan Poe's Tales  MA North Texas St Univ 1968
4771 BOYD William P  The Beginnings of the Short Story in America (Poe, Hawthorne and Irving)  MA Univ of Texas at Austin 1926
4772 BRADFIELD Elizabeth  A Study of Poe's Narrative Art  MA Univ of Texas at Austin 1933
4773 BRASWELL John W  Poe as a Critic  MA Duke Univ 1931
4774 BRODIE Bernard  Poe as an Artist  MS Temple Univ 1926  26 p
4775 BRODY Paul  Poe's *Eureka*: Madness, Prophecy or Simply the Product of the Intellectual Climate of the 1840's  MA Brooklyn Coll of City Univ of New York 1954  119 p
4776 BROWN Christine H  Edgar Allan Poe: Gothicism and Its Background in Selected Short Stories  M Ed Henderson St Coll nd
4777 BROWN Marion F  Poe in France  MA Columbia Univ 1914
4778 BROWN Ruth  Unpublished Correspondence of Poe  MA Hunter Coll 1936
4779 BROWNE Robert E  Art and Artifice in the Poetry of Poe  MA Columbia Univ 1964  344 p
4780 BROWNLEE May  Edgar Allan Poe and Charles Baudelaire  MA Columbia Univ 1912
4781 BRYANT Anne  Poe and *Godey's Lady's Book*  MA Duke Univ 1940

4782  BUDDE Nelda  The Reading of Edgar Allan Poe  MA Univ of Kansas 1946
4783  BURBANK Blanche  Edgar Allan Poe's Literary Criticisms of Women Writers  MA Univ of Texas at Austin 1937  130 p
4784  BURNETTE Bernard J  Poe's *Narrative of A Gordon Pym*: A Work Divided  MA Florida St Univ 1969
4785  BUTLER Susan P  Elements of Mysticism in the Work of Poe  MA Southwestern Univ 1927
4786  CALDWELL Henry H  The Other Poe  MA Columbia Univ 1921
4787  CARPENTER Florence M  Poe and Balzac in the Detective Story and the Tale of the Grotesque and Arabesque  MA Univ of California at Berkeley 1919
4788  CARPENTER William H  Some Mental Aspects of Edgar Allan Poe  MA Univ of Maryland at College Park 1935  88 p
4789  CASTELLANI Quintilia  Supernatural and Macabre Elements in Edgar Allan Poe  MA Ca Foscari (Italy) 1954
4790  CASTILLON Pauline S  The French Language and Literature in the Prose Works of Edgar Allan Poe  MA Texas Christian Univ 1965  129 p
4791  CATE Julian O  Edgar Allan Poe and the Romance Languages  MA Univ of Texas at Austin 1937  205 p
4792  CAUTHEN Irby B Jr  A Descriptive Bibliography of Criticism of Edgar Allan Poe, 1827-1941  MA Univ of Virginia 1942
4793  CHERRY Kenneth H  Poe's Sound Effects: Alliteration, Assonance and Consonance  MA Univ of Tennessee 1965
4794  CHIABRANDI Ada P  The Influence of Edgar Allan Poe on Charles Baudelaire  MA Boston Univ 1930
4795  CLANTON Doris D  Edgar Allan Poe's Reputation in the Twentieth Century as a Short Story Writer  MA Auburn Univ 1959
4796  COFFEY Thomas P  An Evaluation of Edgar Allan Poe as a Critic of His Contemporaries  MA St Mary's Univ of San Antonio 1947  76 p
4797  CONWAY John D  Evil and Poe: A Study of "The Fall of the House of Usher"  MA Illinois St Univ at Normal 1965
4798  COX Fay  *Graham's Magazine* and Edgar Allan Poe  MA Duke Univ 1931
4799  COX John L  Classical Tendencies in Poe's Criticism  MA Univ of North Dakota 1932  43 p
4800  CROWDER Ashby B  Poe as a Critic of Women Writers  MA Univ of Tennessee 1966
4801  CURRIE Elizabeth L  A Study of the Influence of Women Upon Edgar Allan Poe  MA Cornell Univ 1940
4802  DAVIS Georgia M  Investigations Since 1909 Concerning the Biography of Edgar Allan Poe  MA Univ of Colorado 1929
4803  DAY Marjery F  Literary Kinship of Edgar Allan Poe and August Strindberg  MA Univ of Kansas 1926
4804  DEATON Frances W  Poe's Tendencies as a Writer of Fiction as Shown in His Early Tales  MA Northwestern Univ 1928
4805  DeFATO Grace R  The Critical Reception of Edgar Allan Poe's *Narrative of Arthur Gordon Pym*  MA Columbia Univ 1960  85 p
4806  DIEHL P H  Imagination of Poe  MA Boston Coll 1933
4807  DIX William S Jr  The Gothic Element in the Short Stories of Edgar Allan Poe  MA Univ of Virginia 1932
4808  DOLBEE Cora E  Poe's Place in Southern Criticism  MA Univ of Kansas 1911
4809  DOWDEN Wilfred S  Some Influences of E T A Hoffman Upon Edgar Allan Poe  MA Vanderbilt Univ 1940
4810  DOWER John W  Poe and Melville: The Vision of Evil and the Annihilation of the Self  BA Amherst 1959
4811  DUBOISE Novella E  A Study of Some Parallel Ideas Found in the Literary Works of Edgar Allan Poe and Robinson Jeffers in the Light of Scientific Progress  MA Univ of Kentucky 1942
4812  EARLE Ethel J  Poe's Philosophy of Literary Composition as Exemplified in His Poems  MA Boston Univ 1932
4813  EIKLEBERRY Doris L  Poe's Criticism in the Light of Recent Studies

MA Univ of Illinois at Urbana 1947
4814 EISENMAN Mayette B   Edgar Allan Poe and the South   MA New York Univ 1940
4815 El KHALDI Hasson B   Casual and Instinctive Resemblances Between Poe and the Oriental   MA Boston Univ 1931
4816 ENGLEKIRK John E   Notes on the Influence of Poe in Spanish-American Literature   MA Northwestern Univ 1928
4817 ENGLISH Carroll N   Mythological Allusions in Poe's Tales and Poems   MA Univ of Texas at Austin 1936
4818 ESPY Robert B   The Poe-Osgood Affair: A Study of the Relations of Edgar Allan Poe and Frances Sargent Osgood   MA Washington and Lee Univ 1941
4819 ESTEY Helen S   The Objectivity of Poe   MA Univ of Kansas 1913
4820 EVANS Elizabeth   The Narrator in Three Tales by Edgar Allan Poe   MA Univ of North Carolina at Chapel Hill 1960
4821 FARIS Paul P   The Poetry of Edgar Allan Poe: A Study in Diction   MA Univ of Missouri 1928
4822 FEAZEL Delmar D   Poe's Literary Borrowings   MA Southern Illinois Univ at Carbondale 1950   90 p
4823 FEINSTEIN George W   *The Raven*: A Drama in Prologue and Five Acts   MA Univ of North Dakota 1937
4824 FLANNERY Peggy A   Edgar Allan Poe in Anthologies of American Literature, 1849-1899   MA Duke Univ 1945
4825 FLIBBERT Joseph T   The Uncanny in Poe: A Study in Narrative Technique   MA Boston Coll 1963
4826 FLOWERS Frank C   Poe and the Problem of God   MA Louisiana St Univ 1939
4827 FORT J Carter Jr   Satire in the Works of Edgar Allan Poe   MA Vanderbilt Univ 1939
4828 FRED Raymond M   Mural Representing Edgar Allan Poe and His Work   MA Univ of North Dakota 1947
4829 FREEMAN Jennie Y   A Study of the Criticism of Edgar Allan Poe   MA Columbia Univ 1907
4830 FREUND Sr M Aloysia   Metrical Theories of Poe and Lanier: A Comparative Study   MA Loyola Univ at Chicago 1937
4831 FULLER Louise F   Poe and Puckler-Muskau: "The Domain of Arnheim" and *The Tour of a German Prince*   MA Univ of Tennessee 1966
4832 GALE Marjorie H   The Thwarted Poe   MA Boston Univ 1945
4833 GAY Pauline M   The Tell-tale Cane: Death of Edgar Allan Poe   MA Univ of Texas at El Paso 1967   59 p
4834 GILL Lucile A   Poe's Influence in American Literature   MA Univ of Texas at Austin 1925
4835 GILLEN Madeline M   Personal Incidents and Theories in the Poetry of Edgar Allan Poe   MA Boston Univ 1940
4836 GLASHEEN Minnie A   The Relationship of Poetry to Music in the Poems of Edgar Allan Poe   MA Boston Univ 1934
4837 GLIMP Isie T   The Women in the Life of Edgar Allan Poe   MA St Mary's Univ of San Antonio 1944   90 p
4838 GOLDZUNG Valerie J   The Theory and Practice of Annihilation Themes and Images in the Works of Edgar Allan Poe   MA Univ of Massachusetts 1966
4839 GOODFRIEND Robert E   Transformation of the Gothic: A Study of the Veil in the Works of Poe, Hawthorne and Melville   MA Stanford Univ 1965
4840 GORDON Vera   Nathaniel Parker Willis: Friend of Poe   MA Columbia Univ 1961   234 p
4841 GRAVELY William H Jr   The Lunar Voyage in Literature from Lucian to Poe   MA Univ of Virginia 1934
4842 GRIGGS Earl L   Notes on Edgar Allan Poe's Pinakidia   MA Columbia Univ 1923
4843 HALL Thomas   Science and Pseudo-science in Poe's Works   MA North Texas St Univ 1938
4844 HALLORAN Sr M Thomas   The Superiority of the Technique of Edgar Allan Poe

Over That of James Sheridan LeFanu in the Treatment of the Weird MA Catholic Univ of America at Washington, D C 1934
4845 HANKS Lacola L  The Narrative Art of Edgar Allan Poe  MA North Texas St Univ 1939
4846 HANSARD J Douglas  Poe and Chekhov  MA Oglethorpe Univ 1934
4847 HART Charles W  Poe's Humor in the *Tales of the Folio Club*  MA Catholic Univ of America at Washington, D C 1935
4848 HARWOOD Sprigg  Sources of Poe's Tales  MA Southern Methodist Univ 1940
4849 HAVERSTICK Iola S  The Two Voyages of Arthur Gordon Pym  MA Columbia Univ 1965
4850 HAWKES Helen S  Poe's Use of Gothic Romance in His Prose Tales  MA Univ of Idaho 1928
4851 HECKMAN Franklin J  Edgar Allan Poe:  The Critic  MA Pennsylvania St Univ 1926
4852 HENSLEY Virgil W  Edgar Allan Poe as Critic:  In Theory and Practice  MA Univ of Tulsa 1965  97 p
4853 HERRING Louise L  Poe's Habits of Composition  MA Univ of Texas at Austin 1937  147 p
4854 HIGHUM Clayton D  Poe's Consistency of Practice in the Short Story  MS St Cloud St Coll 1960  92 p
4855 HILL Johnsie C  American Criticism of Poe, 1909-1937  MA Duke Univ 1938
4856 HILL Nellie M  Edgar Allan Poe as a Critic  MA Univ of Arkansas 1933
4857 HILTY James R  Why the French Like Edgar Allan Poe  MA Univ of Pittsburgh 1929
4858 HITCHCOCK Lila  The Favorite Books of Roderick Usher  MA Pacific Univ 1964
4859 HOLDEN R E  Poe as a Novelist  MA Univ of Ohio 1933
4860 HOLT Jerry G  Poe's Existential Predicament  MA Univ of Oklahoma 1967
4861 HOLUB Peter F  Poe's Rhythmical Creation of Beauty  MA Univ of Pittsburgh 1948
4862 HONEYCUTT Julian B  Edgar Allan Poe's Attitude Toward the Immortality of the Soul  MA Louisiana St Univ 1920
4863 HOOLE William S  Edgar Poe and His Times  MA Wofford Coll 1931
4864 HUBBELL Harold B  Edgar Allan Poe's Use of Source Material in Three Sea Tales  MA Columbia Univ 1948
4865 HUTTER Revecca T  The Devices of Edgar Allan Poe as Seen in *Narrative of Arthur Gordon Pym* and Other Tales  MA Memphis St Univ 1963
4866 HYNEMAN Esther  A Bibliography of Poe Criticism  MA Columbia Univ 1962  263 p
4867 JACKSON David K Jr  Poe and the *Southern Literary Messenger*  MA Duke Univ 1930
4868 JAEGER Robert O  The Influence of Edgar Allan Poe on the Leading "Modernista" Writers of Latin America  MA Washington Univ at St Louis 1947
4869 JENKIN Leonard  States of Consciousness in the Writings of Edgar Allan Poe  MA Columbia Univ 1964  125 p
4870 JOHNSON Falk S  Edgar Allan Poe as a Critic of Poetry  MA Wake Forest Univ 1936
4871 JONES Dan P  The Language of Poe's Vision:  The Significance of *Eureka* in Relation to the Fictional and Poetic Works of Edgar Allan Poe  MA Univ of Texas at Austin 1964  75 p
4872 KAFKA Karl A  Edgar Allan Poe as Judge of America in the *Southern Literary Messenger*  MA Brooklyn Coll of City Univ of New York 1937  56 p
4873 KEATHLEY Lona  A Study of the Religious and Ethical Implications in the Works of Edgar Allan Poe  MA Sul Ross St Coll 1965
4874 KELLEY Rhoda A  The Reputation of Edgar Allan Poe in America, 1875-1909  MA Duke Univ 1937
4875 KELLY Herbert L  Four of Poe's Women and the Contemporary Magazine Heroine  MA San Diego St Coll 1965  97 p

4876 KELLY Sr M Olive  The Mechanics of the Grotesque and Arabesque in the Works of Edgar Allan Poe  MA Duquesne Univ 1946
4877 KELLY Ruth  The Influence of Thomas de Quincey on Edgar Allan Poe  MA Univ of Southern California 1938
4878 KENDRICK Muriel S  The Mentality of Poe Viewed Through His Life and Works  MA Boston Univ 1930
4879 KENNEDY B A  The Romanticism of Edgar Allan Poe  MA Boston Univ 1942
4880 KIRBY Robert R  A Study of Repetition and Self-plagiarism in Poe's Reviews  MA Univ of North Carolina at Chapel Hill 1958  63 p
4881 KOCH Mary L  The Marginalia as a Reflection of Poe's Interests in History, Science, the Arts, Philosophy and Literature  MA Univ of Texas at Austin 1962
4882 LaNEVE George L  Poe and Science Fiction  MA Univ of Pittsburgh 1960
4883 LAZAR Beverly B  Edgar Allan Poe's Theories of Prose Fiction  MA Univ of Tennessee 1965
4884 LEVY David  The Counterfeit Revelation: A Study of the Junction of Life, Death and Eternity in the Works of Edgar Allan Poe  MA Univ of Montreal (Canada) 1966
4885 LEWIS Ruby P  A Study of Imagery in the Poems of Edgar Allan Poe  MA Univ of Southern California 1947
4886 LINDLEY John M  Aspects of Individualism in Edgar Allan Poe  BA Amherst Coll 1966
4887 LINVILLE Jane J  A Study of Some of the Literary and Legendary Sources of Poe's *Gold Bug*  MA Columbia Univ 1947
4888 LITTLE Sally V  An Analysis of the Angle of Narration in the Tales of Edgar Allan Poe  MA Univ of Houston 1957  111 p
4889 LOCHER Edward W  A Study of the Elements of Mystery and Terror in the Tales of E T W Hoffmann and E A Poe  MA Univ of California at Berkeley 1908
4890 LODEWICK Mary S  The Use of the Supernatural in Edgar Allan Poe  MA Univ of Louisville 1965
4891 LUBKA Bernice  A Comparative Study in the Aesthetics of Paul Valery and Edgar Allan Poe  MA Columbia Univ 1948
4892 LYON Joette E  Edgar Allan Poe: Frontiersman of the Short Story  MA Duquesne Univ 1936
4893 MABBOTT Thomas O  New Light on Poe  MA Columbia Univ 1921
4894 McANDREW William W  The Fugitive Vision of Edgar Allan Poe  MA Tufts Univ 1966
4895 McAULEY Patricia H  The French Reception of Poe's *Arthur Gordon Pym*  MA Memphis St Univ 1966
4896 McCALL Inez S  Place-setting in the Short Story with Special Study of Poe and Maupassant  MA Univ of California at Berkeley 1909
4897 McCALMAN Marjorie B  An Inquiry Into the Musical Aspects of the Literature of Poe, Lanier, Whitman  MA Univ of Tulsa 1956  71 p
4898 McELROY Maurine D  Auditory Imagery in Poe's Poetry  MA Hardin-Simmons Univ 1941
4899 McMANUS Mary H  Unusual Words and Phrases in the Writing of Edgar Allan Poe  MA Virginia St Coll 1967
4900 McNAIR Hallie  The Reputation of Edgar Allan Poe in America, 1849-1875  MA Duke Univ 1932
4901 McPHERSON Maud E  The Genius of Edgar Allan Poe as Manifested in His Tales  MA George Washington Univ 1905
4902 McWHINNEY Norman N  The Sense of Humor of Edgar Allan Poe  MA Univ of Pittsburgh 1959
4903 MARQUARDT Helen L  Edgar Allan Poe and Friedrich Gerstaecker: A Comparison  MA Pennsylvania St Univ 1933
4904 MARSHALL Carol E  Edgar Allan Poe's Philosophy of Man and the Universe  MA Univ of Virginia 1943
4905 MARTIN Princess  Poe's Use of Landscape  MA North Texas St Univ 1942
4906 MASSELLO William  Edgar Allan Poe and Modern Science  MA Univ of Texas

at El Paso 1965  82 p
4907 MATHEWS Gary S  Horror Imagery in the *Narrative of Arthur Gordon Pym*  MA Texas Technological Univ 1969  111 p
4908 MAZOW Julia  The Fugitive Character in Selected Works of Edgar Allan Poe  MA Univ of Houston 1969  137 p
4909 MEXXANOTTE John J  Significance of Myth Making in Poe's Poetry  MA Southern Connecticut St Coll 1965
4910 MIDDLEBROOK Mary E  An Analysis of the Influence of Edgar Allan Poe Upon Charles Baudelaire  MA Baylor Univ 1941
4911 MILLER Arthur M  The Influence of Edgar Allan Poe on Ambrose Bierce  MA Stanford Univ 1932
4912 MILLER Newton E  A Study of Poe's Use of Imaginary and Extraordinary Voyages  MA Univ of Texas at Austin 1940  102 p
4913 MORAN Catharine R  Edgar Allan Poe  MA George Washington Univ 1920
4914 MORRIS Elizabeth G  Science Fiction in the Tales of Edgar Allan Poe  MA Univ of South Carolina 1948
4915 MATCHENBACH Frank  Edgar Allan Poe's "Prisoner" Theme  MA Univ of Texas at El Paso 1969  123 p
4916 MURPHY Winnie A  The Literary Relations of Poe with Bryant, Hawthorne and Lowell  MA Univ of North Carolina at Chapel Hill 1937
4917 NAKAMURA Junichi  Edgar Allan Poe's Relations with New England Writers  MA Duke Univ 1938
4918 NEAL Sharon B  Edgar Allan Poe and the Shadow That Haunted Him  MA Univ of Texas at El Paso 1969  85 p
4919 NELSON Sydney L  The Sources of Poe's Later Tales (1841-1849)  MA New York Univ 1942
4920 NEWBERRY Elizabeth  A Comparison of the Short Stories of Poe and Maupassant  MA Univ of Tennessee 1934
4921 NOVACK Aaron  The Imagery of Edgar Allan Poe  MA Brooklyn Coll of City Univ of New York 1941  76 p
4922 NULL Stephanie  Literary Allusion in Poe's Tales  MA Univ of Massachusetts 1969  43 p
4923 ORR Sr M St Mary  Mental Mechanisms in Edgar Allan Poe  MA Catholic Univ of America at Washington, D C 1934
4924 OTT Catherine R  A Study of Edgar Allan Poe's Use of the Dominant Will to Live in His Prose Fiction  MA Univ of Rhode Island 1965  85 p
4925 PACKENHAM Howard E  Poe's Literary Theories and Their Application in His Creative Works  MA Univ of Idaho 1933
4926 PAGE Trudie M  Edgar Allan Poe: Enigmato Critics  M Ed Henderson St Coll nd
4927 PAPPAS Gus M  A Dream Within a Dream: A Study of the Women in the Tales of Edgar Allan Poe  MA Kent St Univ 1964
4928 PARTRIDGE Claire E  Religious Tendencies of Edgar Allan Poe  MA Boston Univ 1931
4929 PATTEN Lawrence  Poe's Treatment of Terror in Fiction  MA Univ of North Carolina at Chapel Hill 1940
4930 PAYNE Velma  Poe's Influence in English Literature  MA Univ of Texas at Austin 1929
4931 PEACH Susie  The Influence of the Gothic on Poe's Prose Tales  MA Univ of Alabama 1935
4932 PENNER John T  Edgar Allan Poe and the *Broadway Journal*  MA Columbia Univ 1965  109 p
4933 PERCIVAL Mary M  Poe's Editorship of the *Southern Literary Messenger*  MA Columbia Univ 1926
4934 PERLMAN Helen D  Edgar Allan Poe: His Use of Source Material in the Stories of 1840  MA New York Univ 1942
4935 PERRY Ethel M  The Influence of Gothic Romance on the Fantastic Tales of Edgar Allan Poe  MA Boston Univ 1930
4936 PLANT John F  Charles Baudelaire Et la Pensee Litteraire d'Edgar Allan Poe  MA Univ of British Columbia (Canada) 1967

4937 POHLER Lola E  Poe's Sense of His Own Worth: A Study of Pride and Humiliation  MA Univ of Texas at Austin 1940  119 p
4938 POINDEXTER John  The Gothic Tradition in Poe  MA Vanderbilt Univ 1948
4939 PRESTON Fannie R  A Comparative Study of the Works of Edgar Allan Poe and Gustavo Adolfo Becquer  MA Univ of Texas at Austin 1920
4940 PUGH Anna E  The Ways in Which Edgar Allan Poe Has Used Connotative Material and Expressions  MA Univ of Florida 1931
4941 PURCELL I M  Actual Place in Poe's Prose  MA Duquesne Univ 1942
4942 QUINN Mary W  The Women of Poe's Poems and Tales  MA Boston Coll 1951
4943 RANDLE Flo A  A Study of Destructive Forces in the Tales of Edgar Allan Poe  MA Univ of Texas at Austin 1962  147 p
4944 RASCO Edna E  The Technique of Effect: A Study of Poe's Narrative Method  MA North Texas St Univ 1941
4945 RAY Ruth M  Sources of the French Quotations in Poe's Works  MA Columbia Univ 1924
4946 RESNICK Seymour  The Influence of Edgar Allan Poe on Jose Asuncion Silva  MA New York Univ 1943
4947 RICHEY Evlyn B  An Interpretation of Edgar Allan Poe's "The Fall of the House of Usher"  MA Northwestern Univ 1937
4948 RIDDLE Mary J  Three Chapters on *Eureka* as Metaphysic, Science and Theme  MA Colorado St Univ 1968  76 p
4949 RIESS Lynda P  The Philosophy of Edgar Allan Poe in *Eureka*  MA Baylor Univ 1967  183 p
4950 RODGERS Joseph  The Verse-melody of Edgar Allan Poe  MA St Louis Univ 1939  51 p
4951 ROLAND Albert  Edgar Allan Poe: A Study in Poetic Technique  MA Univ of Kansas 1951
4952 ROSENBLATT William F Jr  The Aesthetic Theory and Practice of Edgar Allan Poe  M Phil Vanderbilt Univ 1932
4953 RUSKA Margaret K  Edgar Allan Poe: Frustrated Dramatist  MA Univ of Texas at Austin 1965  180 p
4954 SADOCK Geoffrey J  The Haunted Palace: The Figure of the Dying Heroine in Edgar Allan Poe  MA Tufts Univ 1966
4955 SCHNEIDER Josephine M  French Criticism of Poe, Especially Since 1900  MA Univ of South Carolina 1929
4956 SEARS Vera M  The Philosophy of Edgar Allan Poe  MA Univ of Oklahoma 1936
4957 SEAWELL Elizabeth  Poe's Interest in Contemporary Affairs  MA Columbia 1928
4958 SEIGLER Milledge B  Gothicism in Poe's Short Stories  MA Duke Univ 1936
4959 SEXTON Richard J  The Minor Criticism of Edgar Allan Poe  MA Fordham Univ 1935
4960 SHAW Dorothy B  The World of Edgar Allan Poe's Short Stories  MA Howard Univ 1960  136 p
4961 SHEERIN William V  The Nature of the Influence of Edgar Allan Poe on French Poetry  MA Fordham Univ 1933
4962 SHUCK Emerson C  Poe and Science  MA Ohio St Univ 1939
4963 SIEDLECKI Peter A  Fool's Gold in the Mainstream of American Literature: The Popular Position of Poe and Twain  MA Niagara Univ 1966
4964 SILVIA Barbara J  Poe: Short Story Author and Critic  MA Univ of Rhode Island 1964  74 p
4965 SIMPSON Helen  Edgar Allan Poe's Doctrine of Effect  MA Southern Methodist Univ 1936
4966 SLOANE David E  Early Nineteenth Century Medicine in Poe's Short Stories  MA Duke Univ 1966
4967 SMITH Carl Y  The Vocabulary of Edgar Allan Poe  MA George Peabody Coll for Teachers 1939
4968 SMITH Mamie  Literary Fads and Fashions in America of the 1830's (Poe, Hawthorne, Irving, Lowell, Holmes, Longfellow, Whittier)  MA Univ of Texas at Austin 1926

4969  SMITH Mary E   Imagery in the Poetry of Edgar Allan Poe   MA Univ of Oklahoma 1937
4970  SMITH Sarah F   Poe and Anderson: A Study in the Tradition of the Short Story   MS Auburn Univ 1949   89 p
4971  SNOEK Nico   Death in Poe's Fiction   BA Univ of British Columbia (Canada) 1963
4972  SNYDER Lulu N   A Study of Edgar Allan Poe's "Fall of the House of Usher"   MA Columbia Univ 1926
4973  SPEAKE Margery M   The Development of the Poe Biography Before Woodberry   MA Columbia Univ 1928
4974  SPEAR Dorothy A   Edgar Allan Poe in Germany   MA Columbia Univ 1913
4975  STEEN Gladys E   Poe's Indebtedness to the Periodicals of His Time   MA Univ of Texas at Austin 1931
4976  STEWART Katherine K   French Criticism of Four American Poets: Poe, Whitman, Dickinson, Robinson   MA Univ of Kansas 1938
4977  STITH Mary E   Imagery in the Poetry of Edgar Allan Poe   MA Univ of Oklahoma 1937
4978  STOVALL Jennie   Fantastic Effects in Poe's Stories: A Study of the Use of the Supernatural   MA Univ of Texas at Austin 1937   108 p
4979  STRANGE Arthur F   The World of Edgar Allan Poe   MA Columbia Univ 1959   93 p
4980  STRINGER Alan W   States of Suspended Decay in the Works of Edgar Allan Poe   MA Univ of New Mexico 1964
4981  STRUGGLES Eva   Edgar Allan Poe as a Critic   MA Columbia Univ 1918
4982  STUTZMAN Dorles C   The Development of Edgar Allan Poe as a Short Story Writer   MA Univ of Illinois at Urbana 1933
4983  TEWELL Dan J   A Dissertation of Poe's Literary Principles as Illustrated by His Prose Narratives   MS Kansas St Coll at Pittsburg 1935
4984  THARP James B   Poe and Maupassant   MA Univ of Illinois at Urbana 1924
4985  THEURER Lydia A   A Study of the Literary Criticism of Edgar Allan Poe   MA Stetson Univ 1942
4986  THORNTON Edythe C   Poe as Theoretical and Practicing Critic   MA Vanderbilt Univ 1940
4987  TIPTON Lois   Symbolism in American Literature (Poe, Emerson, Whitman and Lowell)   MA Univ of Texas at Austin 1936
4988  TREAT Ariss   A Study of the Influence of Edgar Allan Poe on the Critical Thinking of Charles Baudelaire   MA San Diego St Coll 1959   123 p
4989  TRIMBLE Louise M   A Study of the Works of Edgar Allan Poe for the Secondary Schools   M Ed Columbia Univ 1903
4990  VANN Jerry D   The Obsessed Man in the Tales of Edgar Allan Poe   MA Texas Christian Univ 1960   97 p
4991  VARNER John G   Poe and Mrs Whitman: A Study of the Documents of Sarah Helen Whitman   MA Univ of Virginia 1932
4992  VETERS Anna J   Some Notes on the Sources of Poe   MA Tulane Univ 1915
4993  VOORHEES Virginia D   The History of Opinion in America Regarding the Life of Edgar Allan Poe   MA Univ of Kansas 1943
4994  WALLACE J Hobart   A Comparison of the Short Stories of Edgar Allan Poe and Guy de Maupassant   MA Univ of Oklahoma 1919
4995  WALTON Gerald W   Edgar Allan Poe as a Literary Critic   MA Univ of Mississippi 1959   224 p
4996  WATERS Charles M   The Influence of Poe's Journalism on His Art and Criticism   MA Univ of Tennessee 1952   91 p
4997  WEED Marietta K   The Literary Fame of Edgar Allan Poe in France, 1846 to 1904   MA Univ of Illinois at Urbana 1936
4998  WEISSTEIN Ulrich W   Types of Projection in Romantic Literature: E T A Hoffmann and Edgar Allan Poe   MA Indiana Univ 1955
4999  WHITE Miriam E   Influence of Coleridge on Poe   MA St Univ of New York at Albany 1940
5000  WHITMAN Max   A Study of Poe's *Marie Roget*   MA Columbia Univ 1932

5001  WIDGER Howard D  The Reading of Edgar Allan Poe with Special Reference to Its Effect Upon His Writing  MA Univ of Illinois at Urbana 1930
5002  WILEY Virginia  The Interior Settings of Edgar Allan Poe's Short Stories  MA Duke Univ 1946
5003  WILKAS John J  Poe's Application of His Critical Standards  MA Boston Univ 1945
5004  WILKINSON Wayne B  Personal Symbolism in the Study of Selected Tales of Edgar Allan Poe  MA Univ of North Carolina at Greensboro 1964
5005  WILLIAMS Hazel S  Baudelaire, Translator of Poe, as Seen in the "Histoires Extraordinaires" and the "Nouvelles Histoires Extraordinaires"  MA Southern Methodist Univ 1934
5006  WILLIAMS John R  Poe's Treatment of the Macabre  MA Southern Methodist Univ 1947
5007  WILSON Katherine E  Satire in Poe's Works  MA Univ of North Carolina at Chapel Hill 1924
5008  WILTSHIRE Evelyn  Influence of Nineteenth Century English Poetry on Edgar Allan Poe  MA Yale Univ 1939
5009  WINKELMAN Janie  Does Edgar Allan Poe Conform to His "Principles of Composition"?  M Ed Henderson St Coll nd
5010  WOOD Marie L  An Autobiographical Interpretation of the Poems of Edgar Allan Poe  MA Univ of Texas at Austin 1951  168 p
5011  WOODS Carrie S  The Narrator in Poe's Tales of Horror  MA Texas Woman's Univ 1965
5012  WRANEK William H Jr  The Psychology of Poe  MA Univ of Virginia 1926
5013  YOUNG Sallie S  Edgar Allan Poe in Relation to His Times  MA North Texas St Univ 1940
5014  ZIMMERMAN Michael P  A Study of *Eureka*: Poe's Last Testament  MA Columbia Univ 1960  128 p
See also 365, 1437, 2614, 2630, 2679, 3176, 3852, 5673

## KATHERINE ANNE PORTER

5015  ASHMORE Doris B  Katherine Anne Porter: Theme and Image in Her Short Stories  MA Florida St Univ 1958
5016  BAUER Shirley A  An Annotated Bibliography: Criticism of the Works of Katherine Anne Porter  MA Univ of Maryland at College Park 1969  109 p
5017  BAYLOR Robert A  Katherine Anne Porter: An Examination of Her Method, Style and Use of the Short Novel  MA Columbia Univ 1952  93 p
5018  BUCKEYE Robert W  That Complete Statement Which Is Literature: A Study of the Fiction of Katherine Anne Porter  MA Purdue Univ 1963  167 p
5019  CECH Eugene J  Exiles in Time: Katherine Anne Porter's Sense of the Past  MA Univ of California at Riverside 1957
5020  CLAMPITT Thelma F  An Examination of Characters in the Fiction of Katherine Anne Porter  MA Oklahoma St Univ 1959  68 p
5021  COUNCIL Mary J  The Collected Fiction of Katherine Anne Porter: A Doubter's World in Miniature  MA Univ of Texas at El Paso 1957  167 p
5022  CUNNIFF Anne T  The Allegory in Katherine Anne Porter's *Ship of Fools*  MA Boston Coll 1966
5023  CURRAN Henry G  Structure and Theme in the Short Novels of Katherine Anne Porter  MA Columbia Univ 1960  114 p
5024  ENGLE Marjorie S  A Comparative Study of Familial Structure in Katherine Anne Porter's *Ship of Fools* and "Miranda" Stories  MA Bowling Green St Univ 1966
5025  EWING Mary D  Regionalism in the Short Works of Katherine Anne Porter  MA Texas Christian Univ 1965  86 p
5026  FERGUSON S M  Katherine Anne Porter's Fiction: Man in a Falling World  MA North Texas St Univ 1968
5027  FINKLESTEIN Adele D  Katherine Anne Porter  MA Columbia Univ 1947
5028  FOX Jean A  Characterization in the Work of Katherine Anne Porter

            MA Columbia Univ 1954   120 p
5029  FRANCKE Richard H  Recurring Themes in the Short Stories of Katherine Anne Porter  MA Fairleigh Dickinson Univ 1969  82 p
5030  GESSEL Michael A  "The Downward Path to Wisdom": A Study of the Fiction of Katherine Anne Porter  MA Roosevelt Univ at Chicago 1966
5031  GRAN Carlyn  Major Themes in the Fiction of Katherine Anne Porter  MA Texas Technological Univ 1963  70 p
5032  HAHAMOVITCH Lillian  Katherine Anne Porter: Point of View and Irony  MA Univ of Montreal (Canada) 1965
5033  HALL Audrie W  Aspects of the Feminine Mind in the Collected Short Stories of Katherine Anne Porter  MA Virginia St Coll 1966
5034  HANDY Deidre C  The Family Legend in the Stories of Katherine Anne Porter  MA Univ of Oklahoma 1953
5035  HENNIS Rucker S Jr  The Critical Reception of the Work of Katherine Anne Porter  MA Univ of North Carolina at Chapel Hill 1956  77 p
5036  IRBY Hazel M  Katherine Anne Porter: Her Contribution to the American Short Story  MA Univ of Texas at Austin 1951  131 p
5037  KINSER Elizabeth A  Katherine Anne Porter's Disenchanted Women  MA Univ of Tennessee 1966
5038  LACKEY Horace G  Katherine Anne Porter's Theory of Art as Revealed in Her Life and Work  MA Texas Technological Univ 1966  70 p
5039  LOEWER Edythe A  Characterization, *Old Mortality* and the Oral Interpreter  MA Univ of Oklahoma nd
5040  LOWRY Evelyn J  Katherine Anne Porter: Ironic Betrayal in "Maria Concepcion", "He" and "Flowering Judas"  MA Fresno St Coll 1965  45 p
5041  MOONEY Harry J Jr  The Fiction and Criticism of Katherine Anne Porter  MA Univ of Pittsburgh 1954
5042  MULDOON Mary M  Theme and Symbol in Selected Stories by Katherine Anne Porter  MA Boston Coll 1965
5043  NELSON Paula S  Katherine Anne Porter and the Existentialist Tradition  MA Columbia Univ 1962  116 p
5044  O'BRYAN Paul A  Katherine Anne Porter and the Satiric Tradition  MA Columbia Univ 1964  104 p
5045  O'NEILL Marie M  Name Symbolism in the Fiction of Katherine Anne Porter  MA Georgetown Univ 1968  127 p
5046  PAGE Willie E  Katherine Anne Porter: A Study in Creative Concepts  MA Florida St Univ 1959
5047  PIIPPO Laurel R  An Examination of Setting in Six Selected Short Novels of Katherine Anne Porter  M Ed Central Washington St Coll 1967  120 p
5048  RATLIFF Sandra  Illusion and Reality: A Study in *Pale Horse, Pale Rider* by Katherine Anne Porter  MA Wayne St Univ 1965
5049  ROBBINS Orville M  "True Testimony": The Short Stories of Katherine Anne Porter  MA Texas Christian Univ 1958  119 p
5050  SEWELL Joan D  The Theme of Isolation in Stories by Katherine Anne Porter  MA Univ of Houston 1965  128 p
5051  SPEER Mary T  Four Women Writers of the Southwest (Katherine Anne Porter, Mary Austin, Dorothy Scarborough and L Grace Erdman)  MA Univ of Texas at El Paso 1959  151 p
5052  STALLING Donald L  Katherine Anne Porter: Life and the Literary Mirror  MA Texas Christian Univ 1951  127 p
5053  TREITEL Renata M  Miranda's Quest in *Pale Horse, Pale Rider*  MA Univ of Tulsa 1965
5054  VOGELSANG Frederic M  The Short Stories of Katherine Anne Porter  MA Columbia Univ 1954  110 p
5055  WELCH Evie A  Some Aspects of Unity in Selected Works of Katherine Anne Porter  MA Virginia St Coll 1968
5056  WELNA Richard D  The Problems of Evil in the Stories of Katherine Anne Porter  MA Univ of Oklahoma 1961
5057  WILSON Florence J  The Narrative Technique of Katherine Anne Porter  MA Baylor Univ 1961  109 p

See also 5515

## EZRA POUND

5058 BENNETT Edward H  Ezra Pound's Critical Theory  MA Ohio St Univ 1951
5059 CASTILLO Y MENDOZA Estrella  A B C to Ezra Pound: Critic-at-large of America  MA Columbia Univ 1941
5060 CHEUNG Dominic C  Ezra Pound's Chinese Translations: Three Chinese Communist Writers; "Elegance and Ivory"  MA Brigham Young Univ 1969  127 p
5061 CHIESURA Irene  The Poetry of Ezra Pound  MA Ca Foscari (Italy) 1942
5062 CLARK Robert L  Pound's Translations of the *Ta Hio* and *Chung Yung*  MA Univ of Texas at Austin 1964  53 p
5063 CREEKMORE Hubert  The Relation of Ezra Pound to Contemporary Poets and Literary Movements  MA Columbia Univ 1940
5064 GABBARD Gregory N  Logopoeia in Ezra Pound's *Homage to Sextus Propertius*  MA Univ of Texas at Austin 1964  157 p
5065 GIFFIN David A  Myth and Reality: Classical Allusions in *The Cantos* of Ezra Pound  MA Dalhousie Univ (Canada) 1965
5066 GREEN Patricia D  The Classical Influences in Twentieth Century Poetry: Ezra Pound  MA North Texas St Univ 1966
5067 HARMON William R  Functions of the Ellipse in *The Cantos* of Ezra Pound  MA Univ of North Carolina at Chapel Hill 1968
5068 KUCZKOWSKI Richard J  Some Themes in Ezra Pound's *Pisan Cantos*  MA Columbia Univ 1966  118 p
5069 LIANG Lucille S  Ezra Pound and His Translation of the Chinese Classics  MA Brooklyn Coll of City Univ of New York 1966  101 p
5070 McDONALD Keiko I  The Japanese Tradition of Ezra Pound's Poetry: The Effects of *Haiku* and *Noh* Plays of the Formation of His Theory of Poetic Imagery  MA Sacramento St Coll 1966
5071 MACHIN Samuel J  An Analysis of Ezra Pound's Attitudes in the *Pisan Cantos*  MA Texas Agricultural and Mechanical Univ nd  124 p
5072 NEUBAUER Richard J  Ezra Pound: Theory of the Image  MA Duke Univ 1966
5073 OHLIN Peter H  Le Grand Translateur: The Theory and Practice of Ezra Pound in Selected Translations  MA Univ of New Mexico 1962
5074 PAK Ki-Dawk  The Chinese Element in Ezra Pound's Poetry  MA Bowling Green St Univ 1965
5075 PARKER Robert W  The Ezra Pound Period: A Brief Study of the Editorial Activities of Ezra Pound from 1912 to 1922  MA Columbia Univ 1959  133 p
5076 PORTER Roger J  Ezra Pound and the Search for a New Poetic  BA Amherst Coll 1958
5077 ROSE Evelyn  *Astrophel and Stella* and Ezra Pound  MA St Univ of New York at Buffalo 1966
5078 ROSENFELD Norman  The Ezra Pound Bollingen Prize Controversy  MA Univ of Pittsburgh 1957
5079 SCRIMGEOUR Gary J  A Poet's Matrix: Ezra Pound's Translations  MA Washington Univ at St Louis 1959
5080 STEVENS Lewel R  Martin Van Buren in *The Cantos* of Ezra Pound  MA Univ of Oklahoma 1959
5081 TANDY Keith A  Woven in Points of Gold: A Study of Seven of *The Cantos* of Ezra Pound  MA Columbia Univ 1962  204 p
5082 TITCHENER Louise F  Browning and Pound: A Study in Influences  MA Ohio St Univ 1964  76 p
5083 WESTBROOK Ralph R  Love as an Ordering Principle in Cavalanti, Pound and Robert Duncan  MA Univ of British Columbia (Canada) 1969  119 p
5084 WILLARD James D  Ezra Pound and Music  MA Univ of Texas at Austin 1965  77 p

See also 1327

## JAMES FARL POWERS

5085 RENEAU Patricia S  The Fiction of James Farl Powers  MA Univ of San Diego 1961
5086 ZEADY Mary A  James Farl Powers: The Problem of Evil in Selected Short Stories and *Morte D'Urban*  MA Boston Coll 1966
See also 4217, 5511

## AYN RAND

5087 CARPENTER T W  The Literary Theory of Ayn Rand  MA North Texas St Univ 1969
5088 McILNAY Philip K  Ayn Rand: Objectivism  MA Univ of California at Santa Barbara 1968  96 p

## JOHN CROWE RANSOM

5089 ALLEN Hazel M  Irony in the Poetry of John Crowe Ransom from 1917-1963  MA Univ of North Carolina at Chapel Hill 1966
5090 AYRES James B  John Crowe Ransom and the Structure of the Concrete Universal  MA Florida St Univ 1960
5091 BONDS Georgia A  Basic Themes in the Poetry of Ransom, Warren and Tate  MA Louisiana St Univ 1940
5092 BRAACK Gerhard  Myth and Metaphysics in the Critical Prose of John Crowe Ransom and Allen Tate  MA Vanderbilt Univ 1965
5093 CARLETON Emma L  The Use of Irony in the Poetry of John Crowe Ransom  MA Univ of Oklahoma 1944
5094 CLAGGETT Frank M  Tradition and Regionalism in the Works of John Crowe Ransom and Allen Tate  MA Univ of Maryland at College Park 1956  107 p
5095 CLARKE Donald L  John Crowe Ransom: A Critical Bibliography  MA Texas Christian Univ 1966  87 p
5096 COIL Karen L  The Poetry and Prose of John Crowe Ransom: A Progression from Myth to Metaphor  MA Univ of North Carolina at Chapel Hill 1968  57 p
5097 COLLINS Elizabeth A  The Criticism of John Crowe Ransom  MA Auburn Univ 1954
5098 DAVIS Jack M  John Crowe Ransom's Aesthetic of Poetry  MA Columbia Univ 1954  150 p
5099 DUFFY Donald D  The Inferential Narrator in the Poetry of John Crowe Ransom  MA Oklahoma St Univ 1969  134 p
5100 FERGUSON Charles E  John Crowe Ransom as Southern Poet  MA Texas Christian Univ 1957  115 p
5101 GORECKI John E  John Crowe Ransom's Characters: Portrayals of the Dissociated Sensibility  MA Oklahoma St Univ 1968  71 p
5102 LINGER Sarah E  Yvor Winters and John Crowe Ransom: A Study of a Critical Controversy  MA Ohio St Univ 1947
5103 MARTIN John Pierce  John Crowe Ransom's Critical Thought and Its Relation to the New Criticism  MA Boston Coll 1951
5104 ROBESON Helen  John Crowe Ransom: Dualist  MA Vanderbilt Univ 1944
5105 ROGERS David M  The Critical Theory of John Crowe Ransom  MA Syracuse Univ 1956  90 p
5106 RYAN Martin E  Analysis of the Critical Theory of John Crowe Ransom  MA Boston Coll 1952
5107 SANDIFER Harley L  Poetic and Religious Theories of John Crowe Ransom Applied to His Poetry  MA Univ of Mississippi 1956  205 p
5108 SMOTHERS Marilyn C  Dualism in John Crowe Ransom's Poems About Lovers  MA East Tennessee St Univ 1966
5109 STIFF Anna L  An Analysis of Similarity in Tone in the Poetry of Ransom, Jarrell and Lowell  MA Midwestern Univ 1965  98 p
5110 SWAINBANK Daniel R  John Crowe Ransom: The Ironist Looks at Life

BA Amherst Coll 1970
5111 WALKER Biron H  John Crowe Ransom: An Interpretation of His Poetry  MA Univ of Florida 1941
5112 WHALEN Sharon I  Tradition in Works of John Crowe Ransom and Allen Tate  MA Miami Univ at Oxford 1965
5113 WOOD Larhylia  The Use of Sound Devices in the Poetry of John Crowe Ransom  MA East Tennessee St Univ 1961
See also 921, 6996

## MARJORIE KINNAN RAWLINGS

5114 GOERING Melva R  American Folk Materials in the Fiction of Marjorie Kinnan Rawlings, Elizabeth Madox Roberts and Ruth Suckow  MA Univ of Pittsburgh 1950
5115 JENKINS Kathleen B  A Study of a Case in Florida Courts About Majorie Kinnan Rawlings' *Cross Creek*  MA Florida St Univ 1965
5116 McCUTCHEON Mary L  A Lexicographical Study of North Florida Vocabulary Set Forth in Marjorie Rawlings' *The Yearling*  MA Univ of Virginia 1940
5117 McGUIRE William J Jr  A Study of Florida Cracker Dialect Based Chiefly on the Prose Works of Marjorie Kinnan Rawlings  MA Univ of Florida 1939
5118 PECK Joseph R II  The Fiction-writing Art of Marjorie Kinnan Rawlings  MA Univ of Florida 1954
5119 SLAGLE Mary L  The Artistic Use of Nature in the Fiction of Marjorie Kinnan Rawlings  MA Univ of Florida 1953
5120 SMITH Patrick D  A Study of Marjorie Kinnan Rawlings  MA Univ of Mississippi 1959  103 p

## OPIE READ

5121 BLACKMON William F Jr  The Life of Opie Read and an Evaluation of His Works  MA Auburn Univ 1940
5122 RANSOM William S  Opie Read  MA Vanderbilt Univ 1933

## LIZETTE WOODWORTH REESE

5123 CATO Harriet E  Lizette Woodworth Reese: A Conventional Poet in an Unconventional Age  MA Winthrop Coll 1937
5124 FISHEL Virginia R  The Poetry of Lizette Woodworth Reese  MA Univ of Pittsburgh 1950
5125 McGINLEY Sr Mary W  Lizette Woodworth Reese  MA Villanova Univ 1942
5126 SIMMONS Thelma  A Study of the Poetry of Lizette Woodworth Reese  MA George Peabody Coll for Teachers 1935
See also 1030, 6996

## AGNES REPPLIER

5127 BROWN Almarine  Agnes Repplier as a Critic of Her Times  MA George Peabody Coll for Teachers 1928
5128 FARRAGHER Mother Elizabeth  Cecilia Agnes Repplier as a Catholic Novelist  MA Boston Coll 1951
5129 JAKS Sr Mary C  The Essays of Agnes Repplier  MA Univ of Texas at Austin 1936

## CALE YOUNG RICE

5130 BERE Jenny R  Cale Young Rice: A Study of His Life and Works  MA Univ of Louisville 1939
5131 SPEARS Woodridge  Examination and Analysis of the Poetic Dramas of Cale Young Rice  MA Univ of Kentucky 1946  117 p

5132  WELLS Kathryn H  Themes in the Non-dramatic Poetry of Cale Young Rice
        MA George Peabody Coll for Teachers 1929
See also 6995, 6996

## ELMER RICE

5133  FOSTER Emma J  The Unheroic Heroes of Elmer Rice  MA Univ of Idaho 1952
5134  HAMPTON Levis H  The Plays of Elmer Rice  MA Univ of Tennessee 1954
        118 p
5135  LEWIS Wilma L  The Social Concepts of Elmer Rice  MA Baylor Univ 1966
        105 p
5136  MARTIN Charles B  The Art of Elmer Rice  MA Univ of Florida 1954

## CONRAD RICHTER

5137  HATHCOCK Judith J  Pioneer Life in Trilogies by Conrad Richter and
        Ole Rolvaag  MA Texas Technological Univ 1969  76 p
5138  SKOV Mildred J  A Comparison of the Two Frontiers of Conrad Richter as
        Revelated in His Published Novels  MA Univ of Texas at El Paso 1968
        87 p
5139  THURBER Mary S  Conrad Richter's Changing America  MA Univ of Texas
        at El Paso 1954  125 p
See also 598

## LYNN RIGGS

5140  COOGAN John W  Lynn Riggs: American Innocent  MA Columbia Univ 1962
        101 p
5141  MOSKOWITZ Abraham L  An Analysis of the Use of Regional Material in
        the Plays of Lynn Riggs  MA Univ of Iowa 1939
5142  NESBITT Ilse L  A Study of Dialect in Oklahoma in the Plays of
        Lynn Riggs  MA Univ of Tulsa 1948

## JAMES WHITCOMB RILEY

5143  CLARK Icie H  A Study of the Children's Poetry of James Whitcomb Riley
        MA George Peabody Coll for Teachers 1928
5144  COOMBS Steve J  The History of the Reputation of James Whitcomb Riley
        MA Columbia Univ 1937
5145  FAGAN William  James Whitcomb Riley as a Poet of Childhood  MA Univ
        of Kansas 1915
5146  REVELL Peter  James Whitcomb Riley: A Study of His Work as Poet and
        Humorist  MA Univ of Western Ontario (Canada) 1964
5147  WADDILL George W  Local Color Elements in the Poetry of Nine Representa-
        tive Midwestern Writers (James Whitcomb Riley, Will Carleton,
        Edwin Ford Piper, Lew Sarett, John G Neihardt, Vachel Lindsay,
        Edgar Lee Masters and Carl Sandburg)  MA Northeast Missouri St Coll
        1952
See also 5453

## ELIZABETH MADOX ROBERTS

5148  BEELER Andrew J  Elizabeth Madox Roberts: Her Interpretation of Life
        MA Univ of Louisville 1940
5149  CHAMBERLIN Lorraine E  Regional Culture in the Novels of Elizabeth Madox
        Roberts  MA Univ of Idaho 1948
5150  DAVIDSON Louise B  An Analysis of the Novels of Elizabeth Madox Roberts
        MA Univ of Tulsa 1948
5151  DONLAN A C  Epic Qualities in the Writings of Elizabeth Madox Roberts
        MA Boston Univ 1938

5152 FOSTER Edward F  Elizabeth Madox Roberts:  A Critical Study  MA Ohio St Univ 1950
5153 GUEST Jessie W  Elizabeth Madox Roberts  MA East Texas St Univ 1944
5154 HAWKINS Maude M  Religious Aspects of Modern American Fiction (Elizabeth Madox Roberts)  MA Univ of South Carolina 1932
5155 KING Sr Maria D  Elizabeth Madox Roberts and the American Regional Novel  MA Villanova Univ 1943
5156 KINNARD Wade T  The Major Novels of Elizabeth Madox Roberts  MA Univ of Massachusetts 1969  107 p
5157 WEST Estella N  Kentucky as Pictured in the Writings of Elizabeth Madox Roberts  MA George Peabody Coll for Teachers 1934
5158 WOODSIDE Harriette C  Berkeleian Idealism in the Works of Elizabeth Madox Roberts  MA East Carolina Univ 1965
See also 338, 5114, 6986, 6996

## EDWIN ARLINGTON ROBINSON

5159 ANDERSON Rosemary  Edwin Arlington Robinson's Philosophy of Success and Failure  MA Univ of Texas at Austin 1936
5160 ARTHUR Ruth L  Edwin Arlington Robinson's Conception of the Successful Man  M Ed Temple Univ 1941  56 p
5161 BAKER Margaret I  Robinson's Poetical Characters  MA Baylor Univ 1945  310 p
5162 BASSOFF Bruce  *The Children of the Night* and *Captain Craig*  MA Columbia Univ 1963  134 p
5163 BEATTY Gay G  Biblical Influence on Edwin Arlington Robinson's Light Symbolism  MA Lamar Technological Univ 1966  93 p
5164 BISHOP Myra M  Structural Elements in E A Robinson's Modern Narratives  MA Univ of Texas at Austin 1939  170 p
5165 BRADDY Varnelle  The Arthurian Poems of Edwin Arlington Robinson  MA Emory Univ 1933  77 p
5166 BUDAHL Leon A  Edwin Arlington Robinson: A Modern Concept of the Arthurian Legend  MA Mankato St Coll 1962  60 p
5167 BURKS J M  The Use of Character Portrayal in the Short Poems of Edwin Arlington Robinson  MA North Texas St Univ 1951
5168 CARR Helen  The Revelation of Robinson's Poetic Personality Through a Study of the Tristram Tradition  MA Boston Univ 1950
5169 CAWLEY A W  *Tilbury Town*: A Selection of the Shorter Poems of Edwin Arlington Robinson  MA Wesleyan Univ 1959
5170 CAYLOR Margaret  Yankee Humor and Satire in E A Robinson's New England Poems  MS Kansas St Coll at Pittsburg 1962
5171 CHANT Elsie R  The Metrics and Imagery of Edwin Arlington Robinson as Exhibited in Five of His Blank Verse Poems  MA Univ of New Mexico 1930
5172 CHEN Gracia  Irony in the Poetry of E A Robinson  MA Univ of Iowa 1966
5173 CLARK B B  Edwin Arlington Robinson: A Biography and a Critical Story  MA Ohio St Univ 1925
5174 CLARKE Matthew K  Tragedy and the Poetry of Edwin Arlington Robinson  MA Columbia Univ 1954  48 p
5175 COLSON Theodore L  Edwin Arlington Robinson's Incompatible Muses  MA Syracuse Univ 1962  118 p
5176 DAUNER Margaret L  The Tragic Light in Edwin Arlington Robinson: The Use of Symbolism in Robinson's Treatment of Failure  MA Butler Univ 1940
5177 DENNIS Jeanne N  Edwin Arlington Robinson: A Survey of the Man and His Poetry  MA Univ of Vermont 1940  114 p
5178 DOBBINS Charles  Edwin Arlington Robinson's Attitudes Toward Life as Expressed in His Tilbury Town Poems  MS Kansas St Coll at Pittsburg 1958
5179 DRAKE Mary S  Character Portrayal in the Arthurian Poetry of Hovey

and Robinson  MA East Texas St Univ 1938
5180 DUFFY Mary M  The Poetry of Edwin Arlington Robinson  MA Univ of Iowa 1932
5181 EVANS M K  An Appraisal of the Poetry of Edwin Arlington Robinson  MA Ohio St Univ 1936
5182 FABIAN Robert C  The Idea of Time in the Poetry of Edwin Arlington Robinson  MA Syracuse Univ 1947  66 p
5183 FAULKNER Claude W  A Factual Basis for Critical Study of the Poetry of E A Robinson  MA Univ of Kentucky 1938
5184 FONDACARO Vincent J  The Sunlight and the Shade: A Study of the Light and Word Symbol in the Work of Edwin Arlington Robinson  MA Columbia Univ 1955  82 p
5185 FOSTER Vivian W  Aspects of Faith and Scepticism as Seen in Edwin Arlington Robinson  MA St Mary's Univ of San Antonio 1940  108 p
5186 GARVIN Sarah J  Men Characters in the Poetry of Edwin Arlington Robinson  MA George Peabody Coll for Teachers 1931
5187 GIULIANO Grace R  The Bible in the Poetry of Edwin Arlington Robinson  M Ed Temple Univ 1932  138 p
5188 GOETHALS Thomas R  Edwin Arlington Robinson's "The Man Against the Sky": A Return to Poetry  MA Columbia Univ 1954  100 p
5189 GRAHAM Don B  Friendship in the Life and Poetry of Edwin Arlington Robinson  MA North Texas St Univ 1964
5190 HAMILTON John B  The Development and Use of the Dramatic Technique in the Poetry of Edwin Arlington Robinson  MA Univ of North Carolina at Chapel Hill 1947  175 p
5191 HAROLD Jessica  Study of Women Characters in the Poetry of Edwin Robinson  MA Univ of Kansas 1933
5192 HARRIS Leila G  A Study of Edwin Arlington Robinson's Use of New Testament Ideology Implemented by the Psychology of William James as Found in His *The Varieties of Religious Experience*  MA Univ of Kentucky 1945  146 p
5193 HEFFERMAN T C  E A Robinson  MA Boston Coll 1929
5194 HOLLAND Robert B  E A Robinson: Thought and Theory  MA Univ of Mississippi 1942  119 p
5195 HOLLMAN Raymond G  Solitude in Robinson's Early Poetry  MA Southern Illinois Univ at Carbondale 1959  72 p
5196 HOLMAN Catherine E  Edwin Arlington Robinson's Struggle Against Puritanism  MA Univ of Oklahoma 1925
5197 HOOTEN Mary M  Biblical Echoes in the Poetry of Edwin Arlington Robinson  MA Univ of Florida nd
5198 HORD Mary C  Edwin Arlington Robinson  MA Univ of Texas at El Paso 1960  78 p
5199 HUNTRESS K G  Edwin Arlington Robinson: The Man and His Poetry  MA Wesleyan Univ 1935
5200 IMBLER Irene I  Studies in Failure in the Poetry of Edwin Arlington Robinson  MA Univ of Oklahoma 1960
5201 JACOBS Robert D  A Study of Edwin Arlington Robinson's Psychological Methods and Ethical Ideas and of Their Application to the Arthurian Legend  MA Univ of Mississippi 1938  141 p
5202 JOHNSON Betty M  Self-knowledge, the Key to Existence: E A Robinson's Roman Bartholow  MA Lamar Technological Univ 1966  56 p
5203 JONES Evelyn  Derelicts in the Poems of Edwin Arlington Robinson  MA Univ of Texas at Austin 1938  92 p
5204 JONES Linnie L  Images of Light and Darkness in Edwin Arlington Robinson's Poetry  MA Eastern New Mexico Univ 1962
5205 JONES Marian D  E A Robinson's Use of the Sonnet Form  MA Univ of North Carolina at Chapel Hill 1964
5206 JONES Rebecca H  Man-woman Relationships in the Poetry of Edwin Arlington Robinson  MA Mississippi St Univ 1970  92 p
5207 JOYNER Nancy C  Edwin Arlington Robinson's View of Poetry: A Study of

His Theory and His Techniques in the Late Narratives  MA Univ of
North Carolina at Chapel Hill 1966
5208 KAYE Howard J  The Arthurian Poems of Edwin Arlington Robinson
MA Columbia Univ 1965
5209 KIDD Harry L  Vestiges of Calvinism in the Works of Edwin Arlington
Robinson  MA Univ of Texas at Austin 1938  131 p
5210 KING John C  E A Robinson's Treatment of Characters  MA Boston Univ 1943
5211 LANGHAM Mackie  Characterization in the Poetry of Edwin Arlington
Robinson  MA Univ of Texas at Austin 1935
5212 LATCHEM Dorothy  Character Portrayal in the Poetry of Edwin Arlington
Robinson  MA Univ of Iowa 1934
5213 LEHRENBAUM Burton  The Dramatic Hero in the Poetry of Edwin Arlington
Robinson  MA Ohio St Univ 1950
5214 LIGGETT Walter S  The "Tristram" of E A Robinson and Its Predecessors
M Ed Temple Univ 1933  162 p
5215 LIPSEY Ann C  The Characterization in the Long Narrative Poems of
Edwin Arlington Robinson  MA Univ of Mississippi 1953  171 p
5216 LOFTON Frank S Jr  The Psychopathology of Tilbury Town  MA Southern
Illinois Univ at Carbondale 1956  68 p
5217 LOHMANN Idella D  A Study of Certain Assumptions in the Poetry of
Edwin Arlington Robinson  MA Oklahoma St Univ 1937
5218 MAGGINIS Mary A  The Growth of the Literary Reputation of Edwin Arlington Robinson  MA Columbia Univ 1936
5219 MILLER Vassar  A Study of Mysticism in the Poetry of Edwin Arlington
Robinson  MA Univ of Houston 1950  182 p
5220 MOHRHAUSER Judith R  Categories of Failure in Short Poems of Edwin
Arlington Robinson  MA Univ of Texas at El Paso 1969  81 p
5221 NEWMAN Maud B  Studies in the Versification of Edwin Arlington Robinson
with Emphasis Upon the Phrase  M Ed Temple Univ 1934  121 p
5222 NOONAN Mary A  Edwin Arlington Robinson and His Treatment of the
Arthurian Legends  MA St Louis Univ 1935  77 p
5223 OHARA David M  An Analysis of Edwin Arlington Robinson's *Merlin*
MA Univ of Hawaii 1951  117 p
5224 OLSON Olof J  Twelve Historical Figures in the Poetry of Edwin Arlington Robinson  MA Ohio St Univ 1943
5225 OROZCO G H  The Views of Edwin Arlington Robinson on Love and Marriage
MA North Texas St Univ 1967
5226 PECKLER Christina  Form and Structure in Some of Edwin Arlington Robinson's Tilbury Town Poems  MA Univ of the Pacific 1964  122 p
5227 PETERSON Nell A  The Philosophy of Edwin Arlington Robinson as It Is
Reflected in His Poetry  MS Kansas St Coll at Pittsburg 1939
5228 PETTIGREW M M  A Study of Edwin Arlington Robinson's Arthurian Poems
MA Univ of North Carolina at Chapel Hill 1938
5229 PUGH George F  Edwin Arlington Robinson: An Existential Approach
MA Baylor Univ 1967  69 p
5230 RENFREW Marion  Edwin Arlington Robinson's Philosophy as Expressed in
His Poems  MA Boston Univ 1934
5231 RHOADES Nell S  The Metrics, Imagery and Philosophy of Edwin Arlington
Robinson as Shown in His Non-blank Verse Poetry  MA Univ of New
Mexico 1932
5232 ROBERTSON Barbara K  Edwin Arlington Robinson's Conception of Art and
the Artist  MA Louisiana St Univ 1966
5233 ROCHELLE William R  Treatment of Nature in the Poetry of Edwin Arlington Robinson  MA George Peabody Coll for Teachers 1934
5234 ROLLER William D  Edwin Arlington Robinson and T S Eliot: A Comparison of Their Versification  MA East Tennessee St Univ 1964
5235 SEYMOUR C J  Development of Character Presentation in the Tristram
Story from Malory to Robinson  MA Ohio St Univ 1929
5236 SHEFFIELD Helen M  An Analysis of the Occurrences of Alliteration
Assonance and Consonance in the Poetry of E A Robinson, T S Eliot

and Robert Frost  MA East Tennessee St Univ 1964
5237 SHIVE Frances A  A Study of Ironic Humor in the Poetry of Edwin Arlington Robinson  MA Univ of Texas at Austin 1939  94 p
5238 SMITH Marguerite  The Versification and Poetic Style of Edwin Arlington Robinson's Arthurian Poems  MA Texas Christian Univ 1936
5239 STEWART Ruth A  Irony in the Poetry of Edwin Arlington Robinson  MA Western Carolina Univ 1968
5240 STRANEY Rosarii M  A Study of Character-motivation in the Arthurian Trilogy of E A Robinson  MA Univ of Pittsburgh 1950
5241 SULLIVAN Nancy A  The Women in the Longer Poems of Edwin Arlington Robinson  MA Univ of Rhode Island 1953
5242 SWEET Arthur C  The Relationship of Mechanical Form to Content in Poems from E A Robinson's "The Man Against the Sky"  MA Oklahoma St Univ 1937  22 p
5243 THOMPSON Lola R  Edwin Arlington Robinson's Treatment of the Arthurian Legends  MA Univ of Texas at Austin 1931
5244 WALKER Ralph S  Edwin Arlington Robinson and the Arthurian Tradition  MA Univ of Tennessee 1936
5245 WEEKS David S  Variations of Edwin Arlington Robinson's "Men Against the Sky" Theme as Found in Eight Poems  MA Pacific Univ 1960
5246 WEHRFRITZ Catherine M  Edwin Arlington Robinson and the Tristram Legend  MA Rutgers St Univ 1937
5247 WELLS Louise R  The Metrics and Imagery of Edwin Arlington Robinson as Exhibited in Sixteen of His Blank Verse Poems  MA Univ of New Mexico 1933
5248 WILLOWBY Lucile  A Study of Edwin Arlington Robinson with Special Attention to His Shorter Poems  MA Butler Univ 1950
5249 WILSON Fred  The Blank Verse of E A Robinson  MA Austin Coll 1932
5250 WOOD Chloe  A Study of Edwin Arlington Robinson with Especial Emphasis on New England Influence in the Life and Poetry of Robinson  MA Univ of Kansas 1938
5251 YOUNG J J  Philosophy of E A Robinson  MA Boston Coll 1936
See also 1480, 2060, 2109, 3863, 4247, 4976

## THEODORE ROETHKE

5252 ALBIN Jaquita A  Imagery in the Poetry of Theodore Roethke  MA Hardin-Simmons Univ 1966
5253 CHRISTENSEN Philip H  Soteriology and the Poetry of Theodore Roethke  MA Hunter Coll 1968
5254 ERICKSON Geneva L  Wind and Water Imagery in the Poetry of Theodore Roethke  MA Washington St Univ at Pullman 1968
5255 EVERETT Terry E  A Surfeit of Reality: Theodore Roethke's Journey Into and Out of the Abyss  MA Univ of Mississippi 1969
5256 HOWELL John R  Poetic Sequences in Theodore Roethke's *The Far Field*  MA Texas Technological Univ 1968  74 p
5257 KEVILLE Peter R  A Reading of the Poetry of Theodore Roethke  MA Columbia Univ 1966  199 p
5258 RICHARDSON Elizabeth A  "The Terrible Hunger for Objects": The Poetic Career of Theodore Roethke  MA Colorado St Univ 1969
5259 RUDOLPH Janet G  The Psychic Adventure in the Poems of Theodore Roethke  MA Univ of Nebraska 1964

## WILL ROGERS

5260 MURRAY Mary F  A Study of the Humor of Will Rogers  MA Univ of Texas at Austin 1953  76 p
5261 WALKER Lois H  Traditional American Humor and Will Rogers  MA Stephen F Austin St Univ 1942
See also 6025

## OLE E ROLVAAG

5262 ALLARD Gwendalyn E  O E Rolvaag: Interpreter of the Middle West  MA Univ of Texas at Austin 1941  113 p
5263 BROOKS Alice F  The Life and English Writings of Ole Edvart Rolvaag  MA George Peabody Coll for Teachers 1933
5264 GEYER Carolyn K  Beret in the Prairie Trilogy of Ole E Rolvaag: A Study of Character-symbol Relationships  MA Auburn Univ 1965  129 p
5265 JONES Judd  O E Rolvaag's Trilogy: A Study of the Immigrant Experience  MA Claremont Graduate School 1965
5266 JONS Cecil W  The Dominant Themes of Rolvaag's Novels: An Analytical Approach  MA Univ of Arizona 1961  149 p
5267 LEWISON Nora V  Rolvaag's Place in American Literature  MA Univ of Iowa 1935
5268 MILLER Guy G  Attitudes for Success or Failure Drawn from Three Novels of Prairie Life (Rolvaag, Cather and Sinclair Lewis)  MA Ohio St Univ 1963  36 p
5269 STOUFER Roger  Religion in the Novels of Ole Edvart Rolvaag  MA Mankato St Coll 1969  48 p
5270 WALL Margaret G  The Norwegian-American Immigrant as Depicted in the Novels of O E Rolvaag  MA Mankato St Coll 1966  70 p
5271 YARBROUGH Sadie V  The Novels of O E Rolvaag: A Critical Estimate  MA Louisiana St Univ 1941
See also 5137

## PHILIP ROTH

5272 COULBOURN Gail C  A Critical Examination of the Fiction of Philip Roth  MA Univ of Texas at Austin 1964  173 p
5273 LUBOW Diane K  The Concept of the Self in the Work of Philip Roth  MA Tufts Univ 1966
5274 TATSUGUCHI Emmeline  *Letting Go*  MA Univ of Hawaii 1969  44 p
5275 THOMAS Edwina F  An Analysis of Philip Roth's *Letting Go*  MA Univ of Texas at Austin 1968

## IRWIN RUSSELL

5276 BASKERVILLE Katherine T  The Study of the Life and Writings of Irwin Russell  MA George Peabody Coll for Teachers 1929
5277 DANIELS Will C  The Life and Works of Irwin Russell  MA Louisiana St Univ 1936
5278 NYHOLM Jens P  Irwin Russell: A Biographical and Critical Study  MA George Washington Univ 1934  116 p
5279 RICE Frank M  Irwin Russell: Biography, Criticism, Unpublished Works  MA Columbia Univ 1934
5280 SMITH Agnes E  The Life and Literary Reputation of Irwin Russell  MA Tulane Univ 1944
5281 TABB Linda E  The Significance of the Russell Circle in the Literary Development in the South  MA Columbia Univ 1930
5282 WEBB James W  New Biographical Material, Criticism and Uncollected Writings of Irwin Russell  MA Univ of North Carolina at Chapel Hill 1946  199 p
See also 2344

## FATHER RYAN

5283 DOMBROWSKI Anthony S  Father Ryan: Poet-priest of the South  MA Columbia Univ 1936
5284 FREIDEL Robert E  An Intimate Study of the Poet-priest, Abram Joseph Ryan  MA George Peabody Coll for Teachers 1930

## J D SALINGER

5285 BRYANT Doris H  Communication and Loneliness in J D Salinger  MA San Diego St Coll 1966  258 p
5286 BURNS Roland A  An Approach to J D Salinger  MA Univ of Maine 1966  99 p
5287 BURROWS David J  A Structural Analysis of *The Catcher in the Rye*  MA Univ of North Carolina at Chapel Hill 1957  64 p
5288 CALUORI Mario L  The Theme of Withdrawal and Participation in Selected Works of J D Salinger  MA Univ of Rhode Island 1966  98 p
5289 DEGENFELDER Ethel P  The Isolate in the Fiction of J D Salinger  MA Univ of Houston 1966  105 p
5290 DOWELL Delle F  Freedom of Action in Salinger's Adult Characters  MA Baylor Univ 1965  87 p
5291 FARIS Christiane B  The Pattern of Withdrawal and Return in J D Salinger and R M Rilke  MA Bucknell Univ 1969
5292 FIENE Donald M  A Bibliographical Study of J D Salinger: Life, Work and Reputation  MA Univ of Louisville 1962
5293 FRENCH Sandra S  A Study of the Sensitive Genius in the Fiction of J D Salinger  MA Northern Arizona Univ 1967
5294 GILMER Helen C  A Study of Salinger's Major Theme: Love and Squalor  MA East Tennessee St Univ 1970
5295 GRABOIS Anthony D  The World View of J D Salinger  MA Florida St Univ 1961
5296 HANES Janice E  J D Salinger's Concept of the Family  MA Ball St Univ 1970
5297 HARLOW Agda G  The Significance of the Sibling Relationship in the Writings of J D Salinger  MA Brigham Young Univ 1970  125 p
5298 HARP J T  The Awareness of Evil in the Works of J D Salinger  MA North Texas St Univ 1964
5299 HATCHER Margaret A  An Evaluation of the Uncollected Short Stories of J D Salinger  MA Texas Christian Univ 1965  144 p
5300 HATFIELD Janice F  J D Salinger: Development of the Theatrical Motif in His Works  MA Bowling Green St Univ 1965
5301 HEMPEL P A  "For Esme - With Love and Compassion": J D Salinger's "Positive" Art  MA Rice Univ 1967
5302 JOHNSON Normalee  The Problem of Communication in the Novels of J D Salinger  MA East Tennessee St Univ 1965
5303 LALLY Sr M Lalement  Compassion and Communication as Thematic Ideas in the Short Stories of J D Salinger  MA Boston Coll 1962
5304 LILLY Paul R Jr  J D Salinger: Probing New Areas of Communication  MA Boston Coll 1964
5305 LITTLE Michael V  The Value of the Family in J D Salinger  MA Univ of Delaware 1969  60 p
5306 MacGREGOR Rob R  An Annotated Bibliography for the Teacher Including a Summary of the Criticisms of Salinger's Work and Commentary on Three Aspects of the Salinger Controversy: Theme, Literary Value and the Use of His Works in High School  MA Plymouth St Coll 1965
5307 McNIFF Aquinas M  The Theme of Communication in Salinger's "For Esme - With Love and Squalor"  MA Manhattan Coll 1966
5308 MATTHEWS Jerry B  The Religious Commitments of J D Salinger  MA Baylor Univ 1966
5309 MILLER Susan  J D Salinger's "Glass" Fiction: Reconciliation of Form and Substance  MA Bucknell Univ 1970
5310 MYATT Jean E  Innocence and Mysticism in the Works of J D Salinger  MA Univ of Southern Mississippi 1962
5311 OLIVER John C  Seymour Glass: The Essential Unifying Force of Salinger's Latest Five Stories  MA Texas Christian Univ 1967  204 p
5312 PIEROTTI Sandra  J D Salinger's Seymour Glass and His Suicide  MA Univ of Santa Clara 1970
5313 PORTER M G  Love and Death in the Fiction of J D Salinger  MA North

Texas St Univ 1962
5314 SEARSON Marilyn  Young People's Identification with the Adolescent Characters in *A Catcher in the Rye* and *Look Homeward, Angel*  MA Univ of North Carolina at Chapel Hill 1965
5315 SIMS Lou A  J D Salinger: His Conception of Innocence in Modern America  MA Univ of Texas at El Paso 1961
5316 SOLOMON Robert H  Freud, Nuns and Fat Ladies: Motivation in the Work of J D Salinger  MA Temple Univ 1964  94 p
5317 STAHL George  J D Salinger: From Christianity to Zen Mysticism  MA Brooklyn Coll of City Univ of New York 1964  74 p
5318 STEPHENSON Edward R  Response to the Urban Environment as a Theme in J D Salinger  MA Boston Coll 1966
5319 TAIZ Nard N  The Genesis of Theme in Salinger: A Study of the Early Stories  MA Univ of Arizona 1966
5320 THOMPSON Robert B  Incommunicability in J D Salinger's Glass Stories  MA Stephen F Austin St Univ 1965
5321 TICKELL Judith A  Seymour Glass: A Study in the Development of a Characterization  MA Sacramento St Coll 1965
5322 WELLS Gene  A Comparison of J D Salinger's *The Catcher in the Rye* and James Joyce's *A Portrait of the Artist as a Young Man*  MA East Tennessee St Univ 1969
5323 WILLIAMS Polly F  A Study of J D Salinger's *Nine Stories*  MA Univ of Mississippi 1968

See also 2915, 3010, 4081, 5687, 5943, 5956, 5957, 5980, 6050, 6257

## CARL SANDBURG

5324 AGLESBEE Rhea S  Some Imagistic Patterns in the Poetry of Carl Sandburg  MA Lamar Technological Univ 1965
5325 ALLMOND Nola  The Social Philosophy of Carl Sandburg  MA George Peabody Coll for Teachers 1935
5326 BAIRRINGTON Ruth E  Carl Sandburg's Study of American Democracy  MA Baylor Univ 1963  162 p
5327 GILMORE Jane  Imagery in the Poetry of Carl Sandburg  MA Texas Technological Univ 1945
5328 GOZA Elsie B  Underlying Themes in the Works of Carl Sandburg  M Ed Henderson St Coll nd
5329 HARDING Billie F  Carl Sandburg's *Abraham Lincoln*  MA Texas Technological Univ 1966  93 p
5330 HEADY Ray A  Literary Techniques of Carl Sandburg  MS Kansas St Coll at Pittsburg 1938
5331 HEATH Jan H  Carl Sandburg's Evolution as an Artist  MA West Texas St Univ 1960  75 p
5332 HOFF Clayton H  Carl Sandburg's Chicago Poems  MA Washington Univ at St Louis 1951
5333 HOUTCHENS Wade W  Examination of "a Great Nail": Sandburg's Prescription for an American Morality  MA Northeast Missouri St Coll 1959
5334 HUNT Ada L  The Evolution of Sandburg's Humanism  MA Ohio St Univ 1937
5335 KIMZEY Verd D  Carl Sandburg: The Optimist  M Ed Henderson St Coll nd
5336 MENTZER Ella S  Carl Sandburg: Humanitarian and Poet Propagandist  MS Illinois St Univ at Normal 1964
5337 PALMER Edith A  Carl Sandburg: Voice of the Plain Working Man  MA Univ of Houston 1960  75 p
5338 POLOCEK Jacquiline H  Presenting Carl Sandburg, the Poet  MA Sul Ross St Coll 1964
5339 SMITH Grace  Carl Sandburg: The Voice of the People  MA Univ of Texas at El Paso 1942  114 p
5340 SPURLOCK John H  Carl Sandburg and Sociological Poetry  MA Univ of Louisville 1965
5341 STERN Catherine S  The History of Free Verse in America from the Beginning of Carl Sandburg  MA Univ of Maine 1952  196 p

5342 TENNY Marion F  Carl Sandburg: Distinctive American Traits  MA Univ of Idaho 1957
5343 WALKER D Y  Carl Sandburg and His Poetry  MA Boston Univ 1938
5344 WALKER Louise M  Carl Sandburg's Conception of the Common Man  M Ed Henderson St Coll nd
5345 WELCH Laura L  Carl Sandburg's Use of American History and Folklore  MA Univ of Texas at Austin 1940  100 p
5346 WESTALL Pauline  The Wit and Widsom of Carl Sandburg  M Ed Henderson St Coll nd
5347 WOLFSEHR Clifford  Sandburg's Use of Folk and Native Materials  MA Washington St Univ at Pullman 1947
See also 2568, 3738, 5147, 6605

## GEORGE SANTAYANA

5348 ADAMS William C  Foundations of Literary Theory in George Santayana  MA Columbia Univ 1951
5349 BOONE Sue Z  Santayana's First Sonnet Sequence, 1883-1893: The Genesis of His Mature Philosophy  MA Univ of Houston 1969  112 p
5350 BROOKS Wilma N  George Santayana: Man of Letters  MA Univ of Kansas 1948
5351 CABELL Laura W  The Literary Theories of George Santayana  MA Univ of Tennessee 1955  54 p
5352 ERICKSON Carol A  George Santayana: Critical Anomaly  MA Univ of Omaha 1966
5353 FILL Ruth M  The Philosophical Backgrounds of George Santanyana's Poetry  MA Boston Univ 1943
5354 HARDESTY Helen C  George Santayana: An Aesthetic Literary Critic  MA George Peabody Coll for Teachers 1939
5355 JOHNSON Jean E  A Study of George Santayana's *The Last Puritan*  MA Univ of Hawaii 1951  124 p
5356 JONES John B  An Interpretation of George Santayana's *The Last Puritan* in the Context of His Moral Philosophy  MA Univ of North Carolina at Chapel Hill 1951  116 p
5357 LEEPER Nora F  Religion and Morality in Santayana's Literary Works  MA Texas Technological Univ 1965  74 p
5358 MILLER Hortense  George Santayana's Philosophical Tenets in the Art Form *The Last Puritan*  MA Howard Payne Coll 1969  87 p
5359 MUNITZ Milton K  Naturalism in the Philosophy of Santayana  MA Columbia Univ 1935
5360 REEDER Dolly C  The Withdrawal of George Santayana's Early Poetry  MA Univ of Pittsburgh 1956
5361 ROWLEY Virginia L  The Relationship of Form and Content in George Santayana's *The Last Puritan*  MA Oklahoma St Univ 1969  141 p
5362 SANDERS Paul R  A Study of Humanism as a Literary Apparatus in Determining the Critical Attitude of George Santayana and Paul Elmer More to Literature  MA Univ of Kentucky 1938
5363 STORY Anne W  The Aesthetic of George Santayana  MA Boston Univ 1935
5364 SURETTE John E  Toward Santayana's Notion of Essence  MA Boston Coll 1961
5365 SWEARINGEN Jack H  *The Last Puritan*: A Study in Fictionalized Autobiography  MA Univ of Texas at Austin 1954
5366 VALENTE Frances J  An Exposition and Evaluation of George Santayana's Categorical Framework  MA Univ of Maryland at College Park 1952  82 p
See also 1958, 5579

## WILLIAM SAROYAN

5367 BRIGGS Wallace N  A Study of the Professionally Produced Plays by William Saroyan  MA Univ of Kentucky 1944  115 p
5368 DOGGETT Mary B  William Saroyan: A Critical Analysis of *The Time of*

*Your Life* M Ed Henderson St Coll nd
5369 LINDEN Patricia J  Sentimentality in William Saroyan  MA Washington St Univ at Pullman 1944
5370 MARRIN D B  William Saroyan: An American Interpreter of Our Times as Seen in His Short Stories and Dramas  MA Boston Univ 1941
5371 TOSNEY Eileen M  An Analysis of William Saroyan's Experimental Development of the American Short Story  MA Boston Coll 1946
5372 VAN RAES Robert M  The Idea of Love in the Short Stories of William Saroyan  MA Kent St Univ 1964
See also 5528

## DOROTHY SCARBOROUGH

5373 BEARD Joyce J  Dorothy Scarborough: Texas Regionalist  MA Texas Christian Univ 1965  105 p
5374 DIXON Arline H  The Development of the Novel Lectures of Dorothy Scarborough  MA Baylor Univ 1943  581 p
5375 JOHNSON Ellen L  The Unpublished Mountain Folk-songs Collected by Dorothy Scarborough  MA Baylor Univ 1941
5376 KONE Laura R  The Life and the Prose Works of Dorothy Scarborough  MA George Peabody Coll for Teachers 1930
5377 MAXWELL Mary R  Short Story Lectures of Dorothy Scarborough  MA Baylor Univ 1942  475 p
5378 MIDDLEBROOK Marjorie A  Dorothy Scarborough's Lectures on the Technique of Writing the Novel  MA Baylor Univ 1943  157 p
5379 MUNCY Elizabeth R  Dorothy Scarborough: A Literary Pioneer  MA Baylor Univ 1940  113 p
5380 TRANTHAM Carrie P  An Investigation of the Unpublished Negro Folk-songs of Dorothy Scarborough  MA Baylor Univ 1941
5381 TRUETT Luther J  The Negro Element in the Life and Works of Dorothy Scarborough  MA Baylor Univ 1967  123 p
5382 WHITCOMB Virginia R  Dorothy Scarborough: Biography and Criticism  MA Baylor Univ 1945  162 p
See also 1085, 5051, 6986

## KARL SHAPIRO

5383 BROCK Dorcas F  Karl Jay Shapiro: Prosody and Music  MA Midwestern Univ 1957  78 p
5384 GENOVESE Peter J  The Evolution of Karl Shapiro's Poetic Theories  MA Bowling Green St Univ 1965
5385 KAMINS Shirley R  A Study of Experiments in Technique in the Poetry of Karl Jay Shapiro  MA Univ of Hawaii 1965  49 p
5386 KETCHAM Julia S  Karl Shapiro: In Defense of Poetry  MA Syracuse Univ 1966  148 p
5387 MARSHALL Ina J  Four Roles of Karl Shapiro  MA Butler Univ 1954
5388 O'BRIEN William P  Search for Belief: The Poetics of Karl Shapiro  MA Pennsylvania St Univ 1965
5389 ROUSCULP Charles G  Karl Shapiro: The Theory and Practice of Poetry  MA Ohio St Univ 1952
See also 5569

## CHARLES M SHELDON

5390 JOHNSON David G  A Study of the Ideas of Charles M Sheldon  MA Univ of Kansas 1966
5391 WENSON Carl J Jr  Charles M Sheldon: A Critical Analysis  MA Kansas St Coll at Pittsburg 1966

## STUART PRATT SHERMAN

5392 BREWER Sr Mary P  The Critical Theory of Stuart Pratt Sherman  MA St Louis Univ 1929  47 p
5393 CARTER B W  A Modern Critic: Stuart Pratt Sherman  MA Boston Univ 1939
5394 CLARKE Sarah M  Stuart Sherman: His Consistency and Some of His Battles  MA Univ of Arizona 1940
5395 DAVIS Joe L  Stuart Pratt Sherman as a Literary Critic  MA Univ of Kentucky 1927
5396 FARNHAM A Z  The Writings of Stuart Pratt Sherman  MA Boston Univ 1942
5397 PRESSON Hazel  Stuart Pratt Sherman as a Literary Critic  MA Univ of Arkansas 1934

## WILLIAM GILMORE SIMMS

5398 BARRE Elizabeth F  A Study of the Indian in William Gilmore Simms' Novels and Short Stories  MA Univ of South Carolina 1941
5399 BARTON Roger A  Simms' Literary Coterie  MA Columbia Univ 1932
5400 BEKER William G Jr  William Gilmore Simms: Maecenas of the Old South  MA Univ of South Carolina 1933
5401 BRACKETT Della L  A Critical Study of the Novels of William Gilmore Simms  MA Univ of Georgia 1941
5402 BRADING Elinor  Life and Fiction of William Gilmore Simms  MA Ohio St Univ 1934
5403 BROWN R C  William Gilmore Simms as a Chronicler of the Southwest Border  MA Univ of Chicago 1925
5404 BRYAN William A  The Revolutionary Romances of William Gilmore Simms  MA Duke Univ 1933
5405 BRYANT Byron R  The Viewpoint of the Southern Aristocracy as Reflected in the Fiction of William Gilmore Simms  MA Stanford Univ 1947
5406 BUTCHER Lorene E  Use of Phrenological Ideas in the Prose Fiction of William Gilmore Simms and Harriet Beecher Stowe  MA Univ of Texas at Austin 1942  100 p
5407 CEBULL Edward A  The Authenticity and Treatment of the Historical Background in the Revolutionary Romances of William Gilmore Simms  MA Univ of Montana 1947
5408 CHAPPELL Mary  Simms and the Sectional Controversy  MA Vanderbilt Univ 1938
5409 EARLY Sr M Nazaretta  A Critical Survey of the Poetry of William Gilmore Simms  MA Villanova Univ 1942
5410 FARRIOR J E  The Use of Historical Characters by William Gilmore Simms in His Romances of the Revolution  MA Univ of North Carolina at Chapel Hill 1944
5411 FLEMING Elizabeth M  William Gilmore Simms' Portrayal of the Negro  MA Duke Univ 1965
5412 GATLIN Jesse C Jr  A Comparison of the Returned Veteran Theme in William Gilmore Simms' *Woodcraft* and William Faulkner's *Soldiers' Pay*  MA Univ of North Carolina at Raleigh 1957  81 p
5413 GIBBS John E Jr  William Gilmore Simms and *The Magnolia*  MA Duke Univ 1931
5414 GILL Elizabeth L  An Examination of Literary Nationalism in the Letters and Selected Criticism of William Gilmore Simms  MA Univ of Houston 1968  95 p
5415 GODDARD Mack A  A Study of the Backwoods Characters in the Novels of William Gilmore Simms  MA Univ of Tennessee 1964
5416 HARTLEY Dan M  The Short Stories of William Gilmore Simms: A Study of the Objective Type of Tale in Contrast to the Subjective Type as Written by Nathaniel Hawthorne  MA Univ of Virginia 1929
5417 HEEKIN Robert E  William Gilmore Simms: Novelist of Colonial and Revolutionary America  MA Univ of Cincinnati 1940

5418 HOPKINS Konrad H  Carolina Epic: A Critical Study of William Gilmore Simms' Romances of the Revolution  MA Florida St Univ 1955
5419 JONES Martin B  William Gilmore Simms  MA Univ of South Carolina 1924
5420 JUSTUS James H  The Kentucky Tragedy in Simms and Warren: A Study in Changing Milieux  MA Univ of Tennessee 1952  111 p
5421 LINDSEY Laura B  Historical Verifications of William Gilmore Simms' Revolutionary War Romances  MA George Peabody Coll for Teachers 1936
5422 LINTON E L  A Study of the Revolutionary War Novels of William Gilmore Simms  MA North Texas St Univ 1948
5423 LUKENS Nancy  The Revolutionary Novels of William Gilmore Simms  MA Columbia Univ 1924
5424 McNEIL Evelyn S  A Study of the Elements of Realism in Some Representative Novels of William Gilmore Simms  MA Univ of Houston 1965  97 p
5425 MIZER Raymond E  The Short Stories of William Gilmore Simms  MA Ohio St Univ 1946
5426 MORRIS J Allen  The Stories of William Gilmore Simms  MA Univ of North Carolina at Chapel Hill 1938
5427 MULLEN John C  William Gilmore Simms: The Relation of His Theory to His Fiction  MS Auburn Univ 1948  173 p
5428 NICHOLS Phyllis A  William Gilmore Simms: Literary and Political Nationalist  MA George Washington Univ 1947  107 p
5429 NIXON Nell M  William Gilmore Simms as a Writer of Gullah Dialect  MA Texas Technological Univ 1964  95 p
5430 ORTS Diedrich H  A Study of the Poetry of William Gilmore Simms  MA Univ of Texas at Austin 1940  93 p
5431 OTT Eleanor  Certain Aspects of the Southern Frontier as Presented in the Romances of William Gilmore Simms  MA Auburn Univ 1931
5432 POPP Klaus-Juerger  The Revolutionary Romances of William Gilmore Simms  MA Univ of Arkansas 1961
5433 SEEGERS J Conrad  The Novels of William Gilmore Simms  MA Columbia Univ 1916
5434 SILVER James W  The Back-country People in the Historical Novels of W G Simms  MA George Peabody Coll for Teachers 1929
5435 SIMPSON Francis W  William Gilmore Simms and the *Southern Quarterly Review*  MA Furman Univ 1946
5436 STANSELL Patricia A  Realistic Characterization in Simms' Border Romances  MA Texas Technological Univ 1959  61 p
5437 TEDFORD Kathryn S  Knights in Homespun and Border Buccaneers in the Novels of William Gilmore Simms  MA Univ of Missouri 1945
5438 THORNE M E  Class and Caste in the Novels of William Gilmore Simms  MA Smith Coll 1944
5439 THORPE Berenice D  Romance and Realism in the Novels of William Gilmore Simms  MA Univ of Washington at Seattle 1925
5440 WELSH John R  Southern Life and Character in the Novels of William Gilmore Simms  MA Syracuse Univ 1941  102 p
5441 WILLIAMS Patricia A  Revolutionary South Carolina in the Fiction of William Gilmore Simms  MA Univ of Maine 1964  56 p
See also 671, 682, 701, 716, 3562

## UPTON SINCLAIR

5442 ADAMS Myra J  A Study of Upton Sinclair's *The Jungle*  MA Univ of Texas at Austin 1956  97 p
5443 BUTLER Jean S  Upton Sinclair: "The Cry for Justice"  MA Univ of New Hampshire 1958  80 p
5444 CLAYTON Mary M  Upton Sinclair as a Reformer  MA Louisiana St Univ 1937
5445 DE ANGELIS Vincenzo  Upton Sinclair  MA Ca Foscari (Italy) 1933
5446 GATES George H  Upton Sinclair: Muckraker and Novelist  BA Amherst Coll 1953
5447 HENDERSON M G  The Influence of Big Business on the Writings of

Upton Sinclair  MA Boston Univ 1937
5448  LARSEN David C  The Cry for Social Justice: A Study of the Devotion of Upton Sinclair to the Cause of Socialism and Human Rights  MA Univ of Maine 1969  103 p
See also 256

## SOL SMITH

5449  ARNOLD Wayne W  Sol Smith: Chapters for a Biography  MA Washington Univ at St Louis 1939
5450  POWELL Florence A  A Biographical and Critical Study of Solomon Smith, Early American Actor and Theatrical Manager, 1801-1869  MA Ohio St Univ 1956

## FRANK L STANTON

5451  HANSON Wyoline  The Georgia Cracker in the Poetry of Frank L Stanton  MA George Peabody Coll for Teachers 1930
5452  McKELVAIN Isla  The Spirit of the New South as Reflected in the Poetry of Frank L Stanton  MA George Peabody Coll for Teachers 1922
5453  PULLEN Mabel G  A Comparative Study of the Dialect Used in the Poems of Frank L Stanton and James Whitcomb Riley  MA George Peabody Coll for Teachers 1925

## WILBUR DANIEL STEELE

5454  GOLDSTEIN S Joan  The Short Stories of Wilbur Daniel Steele  MA Columbia Univ 1950
5455  HNATOV Fred W  Wilbur Daniel Steele: The Influence of Environment on Character  MA Univ of Idaho 1951
5456  PALMQUIST Ethel  The Treatment of New England in the Short Stories of Wilbur Steele  MA Univ of Kansas 1933
5457  ROGERS Grace M  The Short Story Technique of Wilbur Daniel Steele  MA Ft Hays St Teachers Coll 1931  68 p
See also 6996

## WALLACE STEGNER

5458  HAIRSTON Joe B  Wallace Stegner  MA Univ of Texas at Austin 1966  87 p
5459  SALA Joseph P  An Analysis of the Alien and Social Man in the Fiction of Wallace Stegner  MA Univ of Maine 1969  85 p

## GERTRUDE STEIN

5460  BACZYNSKYJ Maria  Gertrude Stein's Motto "Pigeons on the Grass Alas" Als Stilistiches Mottos Im Wolfgang Koeppen's Roman *Tauben Im Gras*  MA Tufts Univ 1969
5461  BARD Elaine  Gertrude Stein: The Theory and Practice of Literature  MA Ohio St Univ 1950
5462  FINKEL Donald  For Myself and Strangers: The Esthetics of Gertrude Stein  MA Columbia Univ 1953  79 p
5463  JONES Franklin A  An Interpretation and Critique of Certain Aesthetic Motives of Gertrude Stein  MA Stanford Univ 1966
5464  LIVELY Lorraine R  A Study of the Structure of the Stories in Gertrude Stein's *Three Lives*  MA Univ of North Carolina at Chapel Hill 1959
5465  NASH Ellen B  Gertrude Stein: Opera Librettist  MA Columbia Univ 1965  90 p
5466  OELKE Karl E  Rhythm in Gertrude Stein's *Three Lives*  MA Columbia Univ 1967  62 p

5467 REID Benjamin L  Art by Subtraction: A Study of Gertrude Stein's Theory and Practice and Her Critics  MA Columbia Univ 1950
5468 RITZO Beatrice M  Gertrude Stein's Study of Art by Abstraction  MA Univ of Pittsburgh 1961
See also 6696

## JOHN STEINBECK

5469 ASTRO Richard  John Steinbeck and the Eighteenth Century: A Study in Philosophical, Religious and Emotional Analogues  MA Un v of Colorado 1965
5470 BAILEY Frances J  Religious Elements in the Works of John Steinbeck  MA Univ of Arizona 1960  137 p
5471 BAKER Mary W  Steinbeck's Ethics: A Study of Attitudes and Techniques  MA Atlanta Univ 1966
5472 BARCK Miriam L  The Role of Women Characters in John Steinbeck's Novels  MA Eastern New Mexico Univ 1958  177 p
5473 BARKLEY Judith C  John Steinbeck's Concern with Morality in His Recent Writings  MA Texas Christian Univ 1965  95 p
5474 BEARD Ann W  Configurations of Mysticism in Selected Works of John Steinbeck  MA Bowling Green St Univ 1960
5475 BOOKER Margaret M  A Study of Personal Isolation in Three Post-war Novels of John Steinbeck  MA Univ of San Diego 1967
5476 BRUCE Carles  John Steinbeck  MA Texas Technological Univ 1947
5477 BURKHOLDER Clyde J  Mysticism in John Steinbeck's Fiction  MA Univ of South Dakota 1965
5478 BURNETT Avis P  An Analysis and Allegorical Reading of John Steinbeck's The Pearl  MA Ft Hays Kansas St Coll 1965
5479 CUNNINGHAM Joy T  An Analysis of the Ideas and Themes in the Non-fiction Prose of John Steinbeck  MA Texas Agricultural and Mechanical Univ 1969  90 p
5480 DAY Robert A  Steinbeck and Social Deviance: A Study in the Sociology of Literature  MA Ohio St Univ 1969  168 p
5481 DeWHITT Bennie L  Oklahomans' Attitudes Toward John Steinbeck: 1939-1966  MA Oklahoma St Univ 1967  75 p
5482 DIGNAM Frank P  A Non-teleological Approach to Life as It Is Observed in Major Steinbeck Characters  MA Texas Arts and Industries Univ 1966
5483 DOBBINS Mary H  Character Concept in the Works of John Steinbeck  M Ed Henderson St Coll nd
5484 DODGE T R  Anti-intellectualism in the Works of John Steinbeck  MA North Texas St Univ 1968
5485 DOGGETT Iva B  The Significance of the Symbolism in John Steinbeck's To a God Unknown  MA Texas Christian Univ 1951  105 p
5486 DRAKE Sharon  Recurrent Themes in the Works of John Steinbeck  M Ed Henderson St Coll nd
5487 DUNN Royce E  A Study of Biological Influence on John Steinbeck's Proletarian Novels and Analysis of the Group-man Theory  MA Auburn Univ 1966
5488 ELLIOTT Ruth A  John Steinbeck: Man and the Tide Pool  MA Colorado St Univ 1965
5489 EMNETT Ruth B  A Study of the Symbolism in Three Novels of John Steinbeck: To a God Unknown, The Pearl and The Winter of Our Discontent  MA Morehead St Univ 1968  50 p
5490 FOWLER Varinna L  A Study of the Philosophy of John Steinbeck as Expressed in The Sea of Cortez  MA Pacific Univ 1963
5491 GABEL Sandra L  The Shift in Focus from the Group to the Individual in the Later Novels of John Steinbeck  MA St Coll of Iowa 1966
5492 GENOVESE Cheryl A  To a God Unknown: A Study of the Concept of God in Selected Works of John Steinbeck  MA Ball St Univ 1969  49 p
5493 GERSHGOL Beverly  Development of the Concept of Man's Responsibilities in the Novels of John Steinbeck  MA Columbia Univ 1953  64 p

5494  GILES James R  The Role of Religion in the Fiction of John Steinbeck  MA Texas Christian Univ 1961  117 p
5495  GOWER Ronald A  Zoology in John Steinbeck's Fiction  MA Mankato St Coll 1963  54 p
5496  GRINNELL James  A Thematic Approach to John Steinbeck's *In Dubious Battle*  MA South Dakota St Univ 1966
5497  HERNANDO Priscila M  Social World in Selected Works of John Steinbeck  MA Northeast Missouri St Coll 1958
5498  HOAG Lucile D  The Biological and Mystical Elements in John Steinbeck's Writing  MA Univ of Idaho 1943
5499  HOGAN Michael  A Study of John Steinbeck's Treatments of Property  MA Oklahoma St Univ 1966
5500  HOSEMAN Avis  John Steinbeck and Ciro Alegria: Some Comparisons Between Two Novels of Social Protest, *Grapes of Wrath* and *Broad and Alien Is the World*  M Ed Henderson St Coll nd
5501  HUGHES Jean S  Moral Values of Steinbeck's Characters  MA Mankato St Coll 1968  138 p
5502  HUNTSBERRY William E Jr  John Steinbeck and the Naturalist Tradition  MA Univ of Hawaii 1949  74 p
5503  IMBRIANO Rita A  An Interpretation and Evaluation of the Symbolism in John Steinbeck's *The Winter of Our Discontent*  MA Boston Coll 1966
5504  JESSUP Winston M  John Steinbeck as a Social Reformer  MA Univ of Ottawa (Canada) 1963
5505  JOHNSEN Edith A  John Steinbeck: A Study of Influences  MA East Tennessee St Univ 1970
5506  JONES Kyra K  Myth and Reality in John Steinbeck's *The Winter of Our Discontent*  MA Univ of Texas at Austin 1969  80 p
5507  KEETER George B  Mock-heroic Elements in the Fiction of John Steinbeck  MA West Texas St Univ 1960  103 p
5508  KHOURIE James N  Doc and His Deity: John Steinbeck's Changing Religion  MA Univ of Tulsa 1964  74 p
5509  KINNEAR Vera E  The Animal Motif in John Steinbeck  MA Univ of Texas at Austin 1955  98 p
5510  LACHTMAN Howard L  The Short Stories of John Steinbeck  MA Univ of the Pacific 1968  145 p
5511  LeCLAIR Thomas E  The Grail Myth in Five Contemporary Novels: *The Winter of Our Discontent, Invisible Man, Morte d'Urban, Other Voices, Other Rooms, The Natural*  MA Univ of Vermont 1967  208 p
5512  LEUSCHNER Grace V  A Study of the Characters in the Novels of John Steinbeck  MA Texas Technological Univ 1941  65 p
5513  LIEDLOFF Helmut  Steinbeck in German Translation: A Study of Translational Practices  MA Southern Illinois Univ at Carbondale 1962  116 p
5514  LIU Hsien-Tung  A Study of the Nature of Man in the Novels of John Steinbeck  MA Chico St Coll 1962  98 p
5515  MAASS Henry E  Mexico and Mexicans in the Fiction of Steinbeck, Morris, Traven and Porter  MA North Texas St Univ 1966
5516  McCLEARY John M  John Steinbeck: A Voice of the Proletariat  MA Univ of Texas at Austin 1940  107 p
5517  McDANIEL B A  Alienation and Reconciliation in the Novels of John Steinbeck  MA North Texas St Univ 1964
5518  MacKENDRICK Louis K  The Sentimental Formula of John Steinbeck  MA Univ of Western Ontario (Canada) 1965
5519  McLAIN Marjorie W  Symbolism and Theme in Selected Works of John Steinbeck  MA Chico St Coll 1965  103 p
5520  MAHONEY Carol A  Steinbeck's Animal Imagery: Dimension of Growth  MA Univ of Louisville 1969  130 p
5521  MARTIN Carol J  A Study of the Psychotic and Feeble-minded Characters in the Fiction of John Steinbeck  MA Univ of Texas at El Paso 1967
5522  MATHEWS Athalie G  A Study of the Social Criticism in the Works of

|      |                                                                                 |
|------|---------------------------------------------------------------------------------|
|      | John Steinbeck  MA Arizona St Coll at Flagstaff 1965                            |
| 5523 | MATHEWS Herschel R  John Steinbeck's Paisanos: A Critical Study  MA Lamar Technological Univ 1966 |
| 5524 | MAWER Randall R  The Conflict of Individual and Society in John Steinbeck's Fiction  MA Miami Univ of Oxford 1965 |
| 5525 | MEISEL Patsy A  A Critical Analysis of the Dramatic Structure of Three of John Steinbeck's Play-novels: *Of Mice and Men*, *The Moon Is Down* and *Burning Bright*  MA Mankato St Coll 1967  85 p |
| 5526 | MERREN John J  John Steinbeck: A Naturalist and Novelist  MA Lamar Technological Univ 1963 |
| 5527 | METT Margaret A  John Steinbeck's *East of Eden*: Its Myth and Philosophy  MA Mankato St Coll 1966  60 p |
| 5528 | MILLS Ronald E  Research for Technical Production and Direction of the Following Plays: *Of Mice and Men* by Steinbeck, *High Tor* by Anderson and *Beautiful People* by Saroyan  MA Eastern New Mexico Univ 1963 |
| 5529 | MYKLEBUST Geraldine  The Effects of Steinbeck's Christ Figures  MA Univ of Texas at El Paso 1965  110 p |
| 5530 | NASH Dorothy J  Steinbeck's Use of the Natural-element Symbols  MA Univ of Texas at Austin 1958  91 p |
| 5531 | NORDAN Lewis A  Variability of Theme: A Study of *The Grapes of Wrath* and *The Winter of Our Discontent*  MA Mississippi St Univ 1966  86 p |
| 5532 | OLIVER Claudette  John Steinbeck's Method of Characterization  MA Eastern Illinois Univ 1969 |
| 5533 | OLMSTEAD P R  Naturalism and the Novels of John Steinbeck  MA Wesleyan Univ 1949 |
| 5534 | OYLER M J  Character Studies in John Steinbeck's Fiction  MA North Texas St Univ 1951 |
| 5535 | PAYERLE Cornelle S  Techniques of Humour in the Works of John Steinbeck  MA Univ of British Columbia (Canada) 1966 |
| 5536 | PAYNE Jean P  The Importance of Involvement in Steinbeck's Characters  MA San Diego St Coll 1965  99 p |
| 5537 | PENNER A R  Social Criticism in the Works of John Steinbeck  MA North Texas St Univ 1961 |
| 5538 | PROCTOR I E  John Steinbeck's Characterization of Women: A Re-evaluation  MA North Texas St Univ 1969 |
| 5539 | RAISANEN Ellen A  A Study of Women in Several of John Steinbeck's Novels  MA Bowling Green St Univ 1960 |
| 5540 | REGAN John V  Steinbeck's Changing Concept of the Individual  MA Washington St Univ at Pullman 1965 |
| 5541 | RICHARDS R Neal  John Steinbeck's Use of Natural Environment  MA Brigham Young Univ 1955  146 p |
| 5542 | ROUGE Jean R  Innocence and Evil in Steinbeck  MA Univ of Massachusetts 1956 |
| 5543 | RUDZINSKI Joan K  Patterns of Animal Imagery in the Salinas Valley Fiction of John Steinbeck  MA Indiana Univ of Pennsylvania 1965  130 p |
| 5544 | SADLER Margaret R  John Steinbeck's Mythological Orientation  MA Univ of Texas at Austin 1965  94 p |
| 5545 | SANTUCHO Oscar J  Steinbeck's Treatment of the Underprivileged  MA Baylor Univ 1959  102 p |
| 5546 | SCHRADER Ellen  Continuity of Theme in Five Representative Novels by John Steinbeck  MS Illinois St Univ at Normal 1969 |
| 5547 | SCOTT Wayne H  Violence in the Fiction of John Steinbeck, 1930-1940  MA Univ of Pittsburgh 1961 |
| 5548 | SMITH Lucian R  The Ethos of John Steinbeck's Monterey Trilogy  MA Mankato St Coll 1968  55 p |
| 5549 | SMITH Wayne C  Steinbeck's Use of the Integrated Short Story-novel Form in *The Red Pony*  MA Texas Technological Univ 1967  54 p |
| 5550 | SPROULE Willard J  A Study of Mythic Patterns in John Steinbeck's Short Stories Collected in *The Long Valley*  MA Bowling Green St Univ 1965 |
| 5551 | STEPHENSON Gail D  Certain Allegorical Implications in John Steinbeck's |

Major Novels  MA Univ of Houston 1966  106 p
5552 STOREY Michael L  Naturalism and Religion: Conflicting or Synthesizing Philosophies in *The Grapes of Wrath?*  MA Niagara Univ 1965
5553 STRAUSS Lois R  John Steinbeck's Pessimistic Conception of Man's Pattern of Life  M Ed Henderson St Coll nd
5554 SWALLOW Marvin R  John Steinbeck's Use of Primitives  MA Texas Christian Univ 1952  125 p
5555 SWARTZ George  Relative Compatibility of Individualism with a Known Social Ideal in the Novels of John Steinbeck  MA Kent St Univ 1966
5556 TEPLEY Margo A  The Theme of Frustration in Selected John Steinbeck Short Stories  MS St Cloud St Coll 1969  76 p
5557 VIERY Sr Elinor J  The Development of John Steinbeck's Style: *To a God Unknown* (1933) and *East of Eden* (1952)  MA Coll of the Holy Names at Oakland 1967
5558 WARDEN R W  John Steinbeck  MA Univ of Texas at El Paso nd
5559 WELLS Ann M  A Study of John Steinbeck's Microcosms  MA Oklahoma St Univ 1965  108 p
5560 WILLIS Lonnie L  Steinbeck's Proof of the Spiritual in Man  MA Univ of Texas at Austin 1960  106 p
5561 YOSHIDA Mishiko  A Fruitless Journey: An Examination of John Steinbeck's Early Novels  MA Stetson Univ 1965
See also 40, 1551, 1882, 6540

## WALLACE STEVENS

5562 ACKERMAN Harold C Jr  A Study of Wallace Stevens' Feminine Figures  MA Univ of Kansas 1967
5563 ARTHUR Richard  The Universal Intercourse: Poetry of Wallace Stevens  MA Univ of California at Riverside 1963
5564 BARAC Vladimir  An Exegesis of Wallace Stevens' Poem "The Comedian as the Letter C"  MA Univ of Texas at Austin 1966  76 p
5565 BEASLEY Bernadine  The Formal Principal in Wallace Stevens' "Thirteen Ways of Looking at a Blackbird"  M Ed Henderson St Coll nd
5566 BENEDIKT Michael J  Baudelaire and Stevens  MA Columbia Univ 1961  79 p
5567 BRODERICK Maureen  Wallace Stevens and His Critics  MA Hunter Coll 1961
5568 BROGUNIER Joseph E  Reality and the Imagination in the Poetry of Wallace Stevens  MA Purdue Univ 1964  112 p
5569 CAMERON Dee B  The Bourgeois Artist in the Works of Thomas Mann, Wallace Stevens and Karl Shapiro  MA George Washington Univ 1968  122 p
5570 CAMPBELL John G  The Symbol of the Bird in the Poetry of Wallace Stevens  MA Columbia Univ 1958  147 p
5571 DeGRUSON Eugene H  The Gods That Boucher Killed: A Study of the Use of Classical Mythology in the Poetry of Wallace Stevens  MS Kansas St Coll at Pittsburg 1958
5572 FARFSWORTH Robert M  A Study of the Criticism of the Poetry of Wallace Stevens  MA Univ of Connecticut 1952
5573 FRISK Philip  Wallace Stevens' "The Comedian as the Letter C": An Approach  MA Mankato St Coll 1968  90 p
5574 GITTINGS Roberta L  Rilke and Stevens: A Three-stage Analysis of Poetic Meaning  MA Emory Univ 1965
5575 GREEN Marc E  Wallace Stevens and the Mortal Paradise  BA Amherst Coll 1965
5576 GUERESCHI Edward F  The Comic Persuasion in Wallace Stevens' *Harmonium*  MA Syracuse Univ 1962  126 p
5577 HARRIS Joanne P  The Use of Colour as Symbol in Wallace Stevens' *Collected Poems*  MA Univ of Toronto (Canada) 1965
5578 HARRIS Mary J  Stevens' Gods  MA Columbia Univ 1963  73 p
5579 HERMANSON Judith A  "... in a Skeptical Music" -- Harmonious Expressions of Belief: Wallace Stevens and George Santayana  MA Colorado

St Univ 1968  81 p
5580 HETHERINGTON Shirley D  Wallace Stevens' View of Poetry and the Poet  MA Univ of North Carolina at Chapel Hill 1962
5581 HILL Fred  Wallace Stevens and the Persistent Theme of the Imagination  MA Auburn Univ 1965
5582 HURLEY Ann H  Wallace Stevens: "The Gaiety of Language" (A Study of the Effect of *The Necessary Angel* on *The Rock*)  MA Brown Univ 1966
5583 JOHNSON Ludge C  Wallace Stevens: A Study of Poetic Vocabulary  MA Texas Technological Univ 1950
5584 JONES Barbara  The Theme of the Poet as Public Speaker in Mallarme and Stevens  MA Columbia Univ 1961  118 p
5585 JOSS Gerald A  Wallace Stevens: Some Relations Between Music and Poetry  MA Temple Univ 1963  72 p
5586 KABELAC Sharon L  Wallace Stevens: Reality and the Imagination  MA Ohio St Univ 1963  124 p
5587 KOSTELANETZ Anne T  Wallace Stevens and the Romantic Tradition  MA Columbia Univ 1964  137 p
5588 KREISBERG Michael M  Spiritual Fiddlings: A Study in the Poetics of Wallace Stevens  MA Univ of Montana 1966
5589 LaCASSE Sr M of St Liliane  Wallace Stevens: Some Perspectives on His Painterly Vision  MA Boston Coll 1966
5590 LAGOUDIS Jane A  The Down-falling Gold: A Study of Wallace Stevens  MA Columbia Univ 1965  93 p
5591 LEATON Anne  Wallace Stevens and the Blue Guitar: A Study of Poetic Imagination  MA Texas Technological Univ 1959  59 p
5592 LITZ Marian A  Wallace Stevens and the French Tradition  MA Columbia Univ 1958  92 p
5593 McMEEN Marilyn F  The Poet with a Captial "P": Wallace Stevens  MA Brigham Young Univ 1964  135 p
5594 MALIK Barbara A  World Images in the Poetry of Wallace Stevens  MA Univ of Saskatchewan (Canada) 1966
5595 MARESCA Dianne G  Wallace Stevens' "The Man with the Blue Guitar": A Study in Conflict  MA Ohio St Univ 1965  115 p
5596 MOSS Margaret C  Reality as Base: An Approach to the Poetry and Aesthetic Theory of Wallace Stevens  MA Univ of Texas at Austin 1965  95 p
5597 NEILL Ronald E  Wallace Stevens' "The Comedian as the Letter C": A Critical Study and Development  MA Univ of New Brunswick (Canada) 1967
5598 OLSON Charles R  Motive and Method in the Poetry of Wallace Stevens  MA Ohio St Univ 1962  62 p
5599 PACK Robert M  The Abstracting Imagination and the Comic Spirit: A Study in the Poetry and Theory of Wallace Stevens  MA Columbia Univ 1953  149 p
5600 PARKS Kae I  The Imagined Pine, the Imagined Jay: A Study of Wallace Stevens' Green and Blue Color Signs  MA Columbia Univ 1964  118 p
5601 PARSTECK Bennett J  Wallace Stevens: The Unity of Person and Place  MA Columbia Univ 1951
5602 REIMAN Alice E  The Poetry of Wallace Stevens: A Spiritual Autobiography  MA Southern Illinois Univ at Carbondale 1963  76 p
5603 RHYNE Mary R  Wallace Stevens' View of Man's Relation to His World: A Study in Metaphor  MA Univ of Tennessee 1969  108 p
5604 RICKELS Mary S  The Relationship Between Poetry and Painting in the Works of Wallace Stevens  MA Univ of Mississippi 1969
5605 RIEMER Shirley J  The War Between the Mind and Sky: A Search for Reality Through an Examination of the Sapir-whorf Hypothesis and the Poetry of Wallace Stevens  MA Carnegie-Mellon Univ 1967
5606 RIVERA-PIZARRO Walter  Some Selected Poems of Wallace Stevens Translated Into Spanish  MA Univ of Massachusetts 1965
5607 ROTHER James  Fluent Crystal: A Study of Two Central Poems by Wallace Stevens  MA McGill Univ (Canada) 1965

5608 SALISBURY Frederick E  "Poems of the Earth" in *Parts of a World*: Stevens' Non-meditative Poems  BA Amherst Coll 1970
5609 SCANLAN John F Jr  The Poetry of Wallace Stevens  MA Tufts Univ 1966
5610 SCHEPERS Jean  "A Violent Order is Disorder": An Essay on Wallace Stevens  MA Univ of Texas at Austin 1963  72 p
5611 SCHMIDT Gretchen  Wallace Stevens: A Study in Water and Light  MA Columbia Univ 1963  84 p
5612 SEDER Judy M  Wallace Stevens' *Notes Toward a Supreme Fiction*  MA Columbia Univ 1964  91 p
5613 SPANGLER Judith D  Metaphor in the Poetry of Wallace Stevens  MA Oklahoma St Univ 1967  83 p
5614 STINEFORD Raymond E  Wallace Stevens: A Study in Existential Poetry  MA Univ of New Hampshire 1964  48 p
5615 SWARTZ G Alan  The Poems of Rhetoric and Reflection: Wallace Stevens  BA Amherst Coll 1963
5616 VOGT William J  Recurrent Themes and Image Clusters in the Poetry of Wallace Stevens  MA Southern Illinois Univ at Carbondale 1953  83 p
5617 VORSTEG Robert H  The Theme of Courage in Wallace Stevens' *Harmonium*  MA Ohio St Univ 1962  74 p
5618 WESTERBECK Colin L  Color Imagery in the Poems of Wallace Stevens  MA Columbia Univ 1965  119 p
5619 WHITE Bette A  Wallace Stevens: A Series of Explications  MA Univ of New Mexico 1956
5620 WHITE Elena D  The Development of Wallace Stevens' Imagery  MA St Cloud St Coll 1968  229 p
5621 WOOD Patricia A  Wallace Stevens: An Approach to the Language of *Harmonium*  MA McMaster Univ (Canada) 1966
See also 4753

## TRUMBULL STICKNEY

5622 GRIFFING Augustus H  The Neglect of Trumbull Stickney  MA Univ of Hawaii 1959  81 p
5623 WHITTLE Amberys R  The Dust of Seasons: Time in the Poetry of Trumbull Stickney  MA Univ of North Carolina at Chapel Hill 1965

## FRANK STOCKTON

5624 CAUDILL Alma  The Juvenile Literature of Frank R Stockton  MA George Peabody Coll for Teachers 1930
5625 ELIASON Norman E  Frank R Stockton: A Critical Study  MA Univ of Iowa 1931
5626 GILL Anna L  Stockton's Stories: His Whimsical Art  MA Univ of Kansas 1927
5627 KRETSCH C  A Study of the Vocabulary in Four Works by Frank Stockton  MA Univ of Kansas 1931

## HARRIET BEECHER STOWE

5628 ADCOCK Myrna M  The Critical Reputation of *Uncle Tom's Cabin*  MA Oklahoma St Univ nd  114 p
5629 BENEDETTI Robert A  Women Characters in Harriet Beecher Stowe's Regional Writings  MA Duke Univ 1965
5630 BROWNE Margaret A  Southern Reactions to *Uncle Tom's Cabin*  MA Duke Univ 1946
5631 COXE Ruth W  Another Look at *Uncle Tom*  MA Univ of Louisville 1965
5632 ENGLISH Nedra  The Lesser Works of Harriet Beecher Stowe  MA Louisiana St Univ 1942
5633 FELL Ruth D  The Novels of Harriet Beecher Stowe: Their Relation in Purpose and Structure  MA Univ of Oklahoma 1940

5634 GRISSOM Barbara S  A Study of the Literary Reputation of *Uncle Tom's Cabin* in America, 1940-1960  MA North Carolina Central Univ 1962  31 p
5635 HEHL Loretta M  The Authenticity of *Uncle Tom's Cabin*  MA Ohio St Univ 1943
5636 HESSER Dale C  Preacher Characterization in Harriet Beecher Stowe and Margaret Deland  MA Oklahoma St Univ 1950
5637 KIRKHAM E Bruce  Harriet Beecher Stowe and the Genesis, Composition and Revision of *Uncle Tom's Cabin*  MA Univ of North Carolina at Chapel Hill 1968
5638 McCONN Nila B  The Portrayal of New England Life by Harriet Beecher Stowe  MA Univ of Kansas 1940
5639 PADGETT Thomas E  Harriet Beecher Stowe: Local Colorist  MA Univ of Texas at Austin 1962
5640 SCANDRETT Hazel V  Diction in Volume II of Harriet Beecher Stowe's Novel *Dred*  MA Univ of Kansas 1928
5641 SEIGLE Natalie R  Puritanism in the Fiction of Harriet Beecher Stowe  MA Univ of Rhode Island 1968  123 p
5642 STEWART A B  A Critique of *Uncle Tom's Cabin*  MA Univ of North Carolina at Chapel Hill 1937
See also 674, 5406

## JAMES STREET

5643 BLEVINS Cleatis E  The Literary Career of James Street, 1936-1952  MA Univ of Southern Mississippi 1952
5644 JONES William M  A Century of Mississippi History with James Street  MA Univ of Mississippi 1969

## T S STRIBLING

5645 FULLER Robert C  Thomas Sigismund Stribling  MA Auburn Univ 1939
5646 GARNER Desda  Intimate Study of Life and Writings of Thomas Sigismund Stribling  MA George Peabody Coll for Teachers 1933
5647 JARRETT Thomas D  Novels of T S Stribling  MA Fisk Univ 1937
5648 LEAMON Irma G  Satire in T S Stribling's Novels of the South  MA Univ of Southern California 1937
5649 LOVELACE Robert E  The Deep South as Seen in Stribling and Faulkner  MA Washington Univ at St Louis 1939
5650 MOORE R G  A Study of the Background and the Mechanics of the Stribling Novels  MA Univ of Ohio 1938
5651 OVERPECK Evelyn  Thomas Stribling as a Regionalist  MA Univ of Arizona 1944
See also 6986, 6996, 6999

## JESSE STUART

5652 AUSTIN Mary F  Agrarianism in the Works of Jesse Stuart  MA Texas Christian Univ 1953  97 p
5653 DICKINSON Meriwether B  A Lexicographical Study of the Vocabulary of Greenup County, Kentucky, Set Forth in Jesse Stuart's *Beyond Dark*  MA Univ of Virginia 1941
5654 JETER Virginia L  Elements of Local Color in the Prose Fiction of Jesse Stuart  MA East Tennessee St Univ 1956
5655 KNIVAL Betty J  The Autogiographies of Jesse Stuart: American Regional Writing in a Changing Society  MA Univ of Wyoming 1964
5656 McKETHAN Flora B  Folklore in the Short Stories of Jesse Stuart  MA Baylor Univ 1965
5657 McKINNEY Edith L  Jesse Stuart's Kentucky  MA Midwestern Univ 1959  94 p
5658 PENNINGTON Royce L  Jesse Stuart: His Symbolism and Vision  MA Univ

of Iowa 1965
5659 RAMEY L O  An Inquiry Into the Life of Jesse Stuart as Related to His Literary Development and a Critical Study of His Works  MA Ohio Univ at Athens 1941
5660 ROSE Mary G  Jesse Stuart: Pioneer Writer of the Kentucky Hills  MA George Peabody Coll for Teachers 1938

### RUTH McENERY STUART

5661 HOWELL I R  A Critical Biography of Ruth McEnery Stuart  MA Univ of North Carolina at Chapel Hill 1945
5662 LONGMIRE Kathryn E  A Biographical and Dialectical Study of Ruth McEnery Stuart  MA Louisiana St Univ 1935
5663 STONE Ophelia  Ruth McEnery Stuart in Dialect and Folk-lore  MA Columbia Univ 1922

### WILLIAM STYRON

5664 HERRIN William L  The Existential Evolution of Character and Theme in the Novels of William Styron  MA Univ of Tennessee 1964
5665 MERRILL C S  An Appraisal of Structure and Point of View in the Novels of William Styron  MA North Texas St Univ 1962
5666 MEYERLE Marjorie H  William Styron and *The Confessions of Nat Turner*: A Question of Literary Merit  MA Washington St Univ at Pullman 1970
5667 OLIVER Jane S  Two Progressions in William Styron's Treatment of Minority Group Characters  MA Univ of Tennessee 1969  140 p
5668 PETERSON Marilyn L  The Achievement of William Styron  MA Trinity Univ of San Antonio 1966
5669 POLLITT Dianne M  The Use of Dreams in William Styron's Works: *The Long March, Set This House on Fire, Lie Down in Darkness* and *The Confessions of Nat Turner*  MA Ohio St Univ 1969  66 p
5670 SMITH Ronald A  The Absurd Hero in the Novels of William Styron  MA Texas Agricultural and Mechanical Univ 1969  102 p
5671 STALKER James  William Styron: An Analysis of Three Works  MA Univ of Louisville 1965
5672 THOMPSON Cynthia  The Interrelation of Technique and Meaning in Styron's *Lie Down in Darkness*  MA Univ of North Carolina at Chapel Hill 1960

### FATHER TABB

5673 BROWNING Sr M Carmel  A Concordance to the Poetry of Father Tabb and a Comparative Study of the Vocabulary of Poe and Tabb  MA Catholic Univ of America at Washington, D C 1946
5674 FIDELIS Sr  An Intimate Study of the Poet-priest John Bannister Tabb  MA George Peabody Coll for Teachers 1928
5675 GLENN Sr Mary C  Father Tabb: An American Lyrist  MA Univ of Pittsburgh 1926
5676 HALE Sr M Flavia  Tone-quality in the Poetry of Father Tabb  MA Catholic Univ of America at Washington, D C 1944
5677 KELLEY Sr Miriam L  Father Tabb's Contribution to American Literature  MA Villanova Univ 1935
5678 LALLY Sr M Aquin  The Imagery of Father Tabb  MA Catholic Univ of America at Washington, D C 1948
5679 SHEEHAN Sr Mary  The Characteristic Imagery in Father Tabb's Poetry  MA Boston Coll 1952
5680 SIMAR Anselm D  Wit and Humor of Father Tabb  MA St Mary's Univ of San Antonio 1942
5681 ZALEWSKI Br Celestine  The Mysticism of John Bannister Tabb  MA Univ of Pittsburgh 1950

## BOOTH TARKINGTON

5682 BENNETT Carl D  The Literary Development of Booth Tarkington  MA Emory Univ 1944  285 p
5683 BRISTOW Eugene K  A Comparative Study of Two Indiana Playwrights: Booth Tarkington and William Vaughn Moody  MA Indiana Univ 1955
5684 BUZBY Katherine H  Newton Booth Tarkington: A Man of Letters  MS Temple Univ 1928  194 p
5685 LEE Frances B  Two Types of the American Girl in the Works of Booth Tarkington  MA St Mary's Univ at San Antonio 1943  46 p
5686 LEMON Goldie  Booth Tarkington: A Study  MA Univ of Kansas 1927
5687 MAYBERRY Susanah J  Boyhood in *Penrod, Tom Sawyer, Huckleberry Finn* and *The Catcher in the Rye*  MA Butler Univ 1962
5688 PEARSON Lewis M  Booth Tarkington's Reputation as a Social Critic  MA Univ of Maine 1965  103 p
5689 SPHAR Elizabeth A  Booth Tarkington as a Portraitist of the Middle Western Middle Class in Certain of His Works: *The Gentleman from Indiana, In the Arena, The Conquest of Canaan, The Turmoil, The Magnificent Ambersons, Ramsey Milholland, Alice Adams* and *The Midlander*  MA Univ of Kentucky 1952  138 p
5690 WARDEN Sr Loyola  Some Aspects of the American Boy in the Works of Booth Tarkington  MA St Mary's Univ of San Antonio 1939  86 p

## ALLEN TATE

5691 DARRING Walter L Jr  Allen Tate and the Scientific Spirit  MA Florida St Univ 1964
5692 GEORGE Melvin R  Tension in Poetry: A Review of the Critical Position of Allen Tate  MS St Cloud St Coll 1960  120 p
5693 HARRINGTON Ann P  Allen Tate: The Failure of the Historical Myth  MA Boston Coll 1966
5694 HUNTER Anne C  Attitudes Toward Tradition in Allen Tate's *The Fathers*  MA Univ of North Carolina at Chapel Hill 1964
5695 LEA Mary L  Allen Tate's Attitude Toward the South  MA Vanderbilt Univ 1946
5696 NORWOOD Vera L  The Critical Career of Allen Tate, 1922-1952  MA Univ of New Mexico 1968
5697 SULLIVAN Naomi C  Allen Tate: Biographer, Critic and Poet  MA Villanova Univ 1943
See also 921, 5091, 5092, 5094, 5112

## BAYARD TAYLOR

5698 FRAZIER Dorthea W  Bayard Taylor: The Romanticism of His Poetical Works  MA Ohio St Univ 1941
5699 DUBSON Mary  Local Color in the Novels and Some Important Poems of Bayard Taylor  M Ed Temple Univ 1936  88 p
5700 HEALY Kathleen  Poetic Theory and Practice of Bayard Taylor  MA Univ of Pittsburgh 1938
5701 HOFFERTY John S  Bayard Taylor: His Life, Contemporaries and Later Literary Fame  MA Boston Univ 1930
5702 HOGUE Dennis R  Bayard Taylor's Short Stories  MA Ohio St Univ 1953

## EDWARD TAYLOR

5703 ARNOLD James W  Edward Taylor: The Man, the Milieu, the Metaphor  MA Univ of Redlands 1965
5704 BERKOWITZ Morton S  Edward Taylor and the Seventeenth Century  MA Univ of Massachusetts 1968  66 p
5705 DUNN Hough-Lewis  Edward Taylor's Poetic Sequences  MA Univ of Texas

at Austin 1966  81 p
5706 FORDERHASE Earl D  The Axiological Theism of Edward Taylor  MA Univ of Oklahoma 1962
5707 GILL Sr Anne B  Edward Taylor's Metaphysical Alliance  MA Boston Coll 1949
5708 GROSE Christopher W  To the American Strand: A Study of the Poetry of George Herbert and Edward Taylor  BA Amherst Coll 1961
5709 HOWARD John D  An Analysis of the Poetic Technique of Edward Taylor's *Prepatory Meditations*  MA Univ of Maryland at College Park 1961  181 p
5710 HUENEFELD Julia  Subject and Form in Edward Taylor's *Meditations*  MA Columbia Univ 1962  72 p
5711 JANKOWSKI Theodora A  Puritan and Metaphysical Elements in the Poetry of Edward Taylor  MA Hunter Coll 1967
5712 KLEIN Paul  Edward Taylor: Renaissance Anachronism  MA Columbia Univ 1951
5713 MISCH Thomas  Edward Taylor: Colonial Metaphysician  MA Butler Univ 1950
5714 NOLL Dolores L  The Mysticism of Edward Taylor and Jonathan Edwards  MA Univ of Kentucky 1954  115 p
5715 SPEAR Guy E  Edward Taylor's Response to the Waning of Piety in Colonial Massachusetts  MA Univ of Wyoming 1964
5716 TAYLOR Jane R  Religious Emblem Books as a Source of Imagery in Edward Taylor's *Preparatory Meditations*  MA Univ of North Carolina at Chapel Hill 1963
5717 TONG Barbara L  Characteristics of the Baroque Style in Edward Taylor's Poetry  MA Roosevelt Univ at Chicago 1967
5718 WHITE James G  Edward Taylor: A Study in Puritan Poetry and Puritan Sensibility  MA Ohio St Univ 1950

## SARA TEASDALE

5719 AMINI Hannah R  Sara Teasdale: A Biographical Sketch and Critical Analysis  MA Univ of Kansas 1948
5720 DeFRANCE Helen S  Sara Teasdale  MA Univ of Pittsburgh 1939
5721 DIVER Shirley M  Sara Teasdale: An Interpretative and Critical Study  MA St Mary's Univ of San Antonio 1939  134 p
5722 LANIGAN A M  The Lyricism of Sara Teasdale  MA Boston Univ 1941
5723 LOWE Lois M  Imagery in the Poetry of Sara Teasdale  MA West Texas St Univ 1949  59 p
5724 McKNIGHT Virginia  Sara Teasdale: Her Life and Work  MA Univ of New Mexico 1937
5725 PEARCE Virginia R  A Critical Analysis of the Poetry of Sara Teasdale  MA Univ of Mississippi 1963  204 p
5726 PFEIFFER Charles G  The Development of Central Themes in Sara Teasdale's Poetry  MA George Peabody Coll for Teachers 1952
See also 1030

## HENRY DAVID THOREAU

5727 ADAMS Marla J  Henry David Thoreau's Attitude Toward the Frontier  MA Univ of North Carolina at Chapel Hill 1958  121 p
5728 ALONSO Jean A  The Ground of Walden: Thoreau's Changing Thought and the Successive Versions of *Walden*  MA Tufts Univ 1968
5729 ANASTAS Peter N Jr  A Concept of Place in Henry David Thoreau's *A Week on the Concord and Merrimack Rivers* and *Walden*  MA Tufts Univ 1967
5730 BARNIER John F  Thoreau's Mirror Image  MA San Diego St Coll 1965  89 p
5731 BATES Lorna D  The Noble Savage in the Works of Thoreau  MA Univ of Iowa 1934
5732 BECK James P  Analogical and Symbolic Approaches to Thoreau's *Walden*  MA Columbia Univ 1962  177 p

5733 BELCHER Francis T  Thoreau as a Critic of Literature  MA George Peabody Coll for Teachers 1937
5734 BERLIN Hermes R  Aspects of Henry David Thoreau's Social Thought  MA Univ of Iowa 1965
5735 BOSTON Jason  Mysticism in *Walden*  MA West Texas St Univ 1965  59 p
5736 BREEN Nancy E  A Literary Comparison of Henry David Thoreau (1817-1862) and Gerard Manly Hopkins (1844-1889)  MA Ohio St Univ 1967  89 p
5737 BRIDGEFORTH Roberta E  Thoreau and the Nature Movement in American Literature  MA Univ of Maryland at College Park 1933  117 p
5738 BURNS Henry J  The Social Philosophy of Henry David Thoreau  MA Boston Univ 1966
5739 CASE George M  *Walden:* Testing Ground for a Transcendental Assumption  MA Univ of Massachusetts 1965
5740 CHAMBERS Annie M  Family Influences on Henry David Thoreau's Writings: A Discussion and a Bibliography  MA Univ of Southern California 1965
5741 CHANDLER W J  Thoreau's Walden Experiment as an Example of American Transcendental Economic Protest  MA Univ of North Carolina at Chapel Hill 1932
5742 CHANEY Evelyn B  Meaning of a Singular Man: Henry David Thoreau  M Ed Henderson St Coll nd
5743 CHRISTIE M E  Henry David Thoreau: The Nature Mystic  M Ed Henderson St Coll nd
5744 CLAUS Jo A  Thoreau's *Journal* as a Work of Art  MA Univ of New Brunswick (Canada) 1966
5745 COLE Robert C  Thoreau's Philosophy of Observation  MA Wake Forest Univ 1964
5746 COOK Richard C  Henry Thoreau's Poetic Imagination: An Analysis of the Imagery in *Walden*  MA Univ of Maine 1959  108 p
5747 CURLEY James M  "One of These Bibles": The Orient in the Writings of Henry David Thoreau  MA Fairleigh Dickinson Univ nd  92 p
5748 DEMPSEY Don P  Thoreau's Ideas Concerning the Impact of Civilization on the American Primitive Man  MA San Diego St Coll 1964  144 p
5749 DITTMER Bernice  Thoreau, Emerson's American Scholar  MA Univ of Texas at El Paso 1965  184 p
5750 DOSS Vernon L  Thoreau's Journey to Minnesota  MA Mankato St Coll 1961  103 p
5751 DOUGLAS M C  An Examination of the Structure of *A Week on the Concord and Merrimack Rivers* by Henry David Thoreau  MA Univ of North Carolina at Chapel Hill 1940
5752 DOWELL Carol R  The Organic Role of Imagery in *Walden*  MA Columbia Univ 1961  59 p
5753 EPPERSON William R  The Style and Structure of *Walden*  MA Univ of Kansas 1963
5754 ERLICH Michael G  Henry David Thoreau's "Plea for Captain John Brown": A Rhetorical Analysis  MA Ohio St Univ 1967  130 p
5755 FAWCETT Vera E  Ancient Literature in Thoreau  MA Univ of Kansas 1926
5756 FOSTER M J  The Mysticism of Thoreau as Evidenced by His Nature Study  MA Ohio St Univ 1933
5757 FRIESEN Victor C  Sensuousness in Thoreau's Approach to Nature  MA Univ of Saskatchewan (Canada) 1965
5758 FUSSELL M B  Henry David Thoreau as a Social Critic  MA Boston Coll 1945
5759 GANNON James A  Thoreau's...Immaturity...  MA Gonzaga Univ nd
5760 GASTON Georg M  The Source and Influence of Thoreau's *Civil Disobedience*  MA Auburn Univ 1963
5761 GIMLIN Joan M  Thoreau's Concept of the Hero  MA George Washington Univ 1967  66 p
5762 GODAY Jean M  The First Half-century of Thoreau Criticism: 1850-1900  MA Tufts Univ 1952
5763 GORDON Ruth M  Thoreau the Revolutionist: A Naturalist on State and Church  MA Auburn Univ 1943

5764 GRIFFIN Margaret E  Henry David Thoreau's Theories of Genius  MA Univ of North Carolina at Chapel Hill 1967
5765 HALL Loren W  The Concepts of Time in Henry David Thoreau's *Walden*  MA Univ of Alabama 1964
5766 HARDING Walter R  The Lectures of Henry David Thoreau  MA Univ of North Carolina at Chapel Hill 1947  64 p
5767 HAUBER Margaret F  Thoreau, the Humanitarian: A Reply to Robert Louis Stevenson's Essay "Henry David Thoreau"  MA Rutgers St Univ 1939
5768 HENDRICK George  Thoreau and the *Gita*  MA Texas Christian Univ 1950  82 p
5769 HILDENBRAND Christopher A  A Bibliography of Scholarship About Henry David Thoreau: 1940-1965  MA Ft Hays Kansas St Coll 1965
5770 HILL Mary A  The Women Acquaintances of Henry David Thoreau  MA Auburn Univ 1943
5771 HOLLINGSHEAD Mary B  The Hero of Thoreau's *A Week on the Concord and Merrimack Rivers*  MA George Washington Univ 1969  79 p
5772 HUNTER Howard E  The Religious Sentiment in Henry David Thoreau's Writings  MA Ohio St Univ 1952
5773 IGA Mamoru  Similarities Between Thoreau's Religious Philosophy and Zen Buddhism  MA Brigham Young Univ 1951  120 p
5774 JOHNSTON Robert C  Aspects of Technique in Thoreau's Poetry  MA Univ of Hawaii 1967  89 p
5775 JONES Walter O  An Analysis of Henry David Thoreau's Attitude Toward Love and Friendship as Recorded in His Journal and Correspondence  MA Mankato St Coll 1960  68 p
5776 KAPLAN Robert A  Thoreau and Gandhi: A Comparison of Their Philosophies  MA Brooklyn Coll of City Univ of New York 1965  45 p
5777 KELLEY Robert J  Thoreau's Use of Structural Metaphors in *A Week on the Concord and Merrimack Rivers* and *Walden*  MA Univ of Tennessee 1969  76 p
5778 KEPLER Laurence I  The Influence of Montaigne on Thoreau  MA Univ of Iowa 1933
5779 KORTE Alan H  The Course of the Poetry of Henry David Thoreau  MA Columbia Univ 1962  85 p
5780 KROGH Lee V  Thoreau: An Inquiry Into the Question of His Status as a Poet  MA Mankato St Coll 1961  35 p
5781 LAWTON Cynthia  Henry David Thoreau as Lecturer  MA Hunter Coll 1966
5782 LEWIS Mattie L  A Comparative Study of the Spiritual and Intellectual Revelations of the *Prelude* and *Walden*  MA North Carolina Central Univ 1961  73 p
5783 LOFTON Hoseau J  Thoreau and Hemingway: A Stylistic Analysis of Their Language in Describing Nature  MA North Carolina Central Univ 1961  93 p
5784 LOLIVA Elisa  An Essay on Henry David Thoreau  MA Ca Foscari (Italy) 1928
5785 LONGER Robert M  A Study of Thoreau's Later *Journal* (1850-1861)  MA Ohio St Univ 1966  83 p
5786 LONGSHORE Robert H  Henry David Thoreau: Craftsman in Prose  MA Auburn Univ 1953  106 p
5787 McCARTY Robert S  A Symbolic Walk: Henry David Thoreau  MA Univ of Texas at El Paso 1966  75 p
5788 McKAY Alexander G  The Traveler and the Setting Sun: A Study of Thoreau's Travel Essays  MA Long Island Univ 1966  107 p
5789 MAHANAY Vera F  An Analysis of Joy in the Writings of Henry David Thoreau  MA San Diego St Coll 1964  109 p
5790 MARK Ronald N  The Quest of Purity: A Study of the Puritanism of Henry David Thoreau  MA Roosevelt Univ at Chicago 1970
5791 MARSHALL Daniel W  Henry Thoreau's Theory and Practice of Prose Composition  MA Univ of Vermont 1941  125 p
5792 MARTIN Lee J  The Poetry of Henry David Thoreau  MA Univ of Texas at

Austin 1948  109 p
5793  MEATHENIA Jack  A Study of Humor in the Writings of Henry David Thoreau  MA West Texas St Univ 1959  65 p
5794  MORGAN Emma D  An Interpretation of Thoreau's Philosophy  MA Boston Univ 1940
5795  MURRAY Margaret  The Philosophical Rebel: Henry David Thoreau  M Ed Henderson St Coll nd
5796  NICOLOFF Philip  Thoreau and Nature: The Relation of Thoreau's Non-Emersonian Attitude Towards Nature to His Experience in Nature  MA Columbia Univ 1951
5797  O'DONNELL Norbert F  Henry David Thoreau: Man of Action  MA Ohio St Univ 1941
5798  OZAWA Clara K  The Yankee Yogi at Walden Pond: A Re-evaluation  MA Univ of Hawaii 1964  95 p
5799  PARKER Martha E  Thoreau's Quest for Identity  MA Univ of Oklahoma 1964
5800  PARKYN Stanley F  Thoreau, the Identity-seeker: A Stylistic Study of *Walden*  MA Trinity Coll of Hartford 1965
5801  PARSON Sabra  Henry David Thoreau: A Study of Character  MA North Texas St Univ 1940
5802  PEARSON Lu E  American Literary Naturalists: A Study of the Nature Movement in the Works of Henry David Thoreau, John Burroughs and John Muir  MA Univ of California at Berkeley 1922
5803  PHILLIPS Emmett L  A Study of Aesthetic Distance in Thoreau's *Walden*  MA Univ of Oklahoma 1970
5804  PHILLIPS Raymond C Jr  The Dark Isthmus: A Critical Study of Henry Thoreau's *The Maine Woods*  MA Columbia Univ 1959  75 p
5805  PILLAI A K  Walden and Indian Thought  MA East Carolina Univ 1968
5806  POGER Sidney B  Sound in Thoreau  MA Columbia Univ 1959  55 p
5807  POTTER Nancy A  A Critical Study of the Journal of Henry David Thoreau  MA Tufts Univ 1947
5808  RACKLEY Betty J  Thoreau: The Anti-social Man  MA Mississippi St Univ 1965  67 p
5809  RADETSKY Peter H  Thoreau and Taoism  MA Univ of Colorado 1966
5810  REED John Q  Thoreau's Literary Reputation in the Twentieth Century  MA Univ of Pittsburgh 1948
5811  REED Robert C  Thoreau's Influence on Frank Lloyd Wright's Domestic Organic Architecture  MA Bowling Green St Univ 1960
5812  ROBINSON Anthony C  The Prometheus of Concord: An Examination of Henry David Thoreau's Translation of Aeschylus' *Prometheus Bound* and Its Influence Upon His Life and Work  MA Columbia Univ 1960  115 p
5813  ROHMAN D Gordon  *The Executive Deity*: A Rhetorical Analysis of "Economy" in *Walden*  MA Syracuse Univ 1955  82 p
5814  SANTUICO Natividad V  A Study of Thoreau's *Walden*  MA Univ of Texas at Austin 1953  52 p
5815  SIMMONS Evelyn  A Critical Study of the *Walden* Manuscript  MA Bowling Green St Univ 1942
5816  SMITH Rosamund B  The Tonic of Wildness: A Study of Thoreau's Wilderness Theme  MA Queen's Univ (Canada) 1967
5817  SMITHAM Sylvia T  Henry David Thoreau Considered in the Light of His New England Environment  MA Univ of Idaho 1935
5818  SPIKE Walter S  Henry David Thoreau's Opinion of the Pioneer  MA Univ of North Carolina at Chapel Hill 1948  62 p
5819  STEPHAN Elizabeth  Thoreau's Treatment of the Seasons  MA Boston Univ 1935
5820  STOCKTON Edwin L Jr  The Figurative and Descriptive Use of the Sea in the Creative Writing of Henry David Thoreau  MA Univ of North Carolina at Chapel Hill 1957  89 p
5821  SWANSON Margaret L  A Study of Structure in *Walden*  MA Washington St Univ at Pullman 1948

5822 SWIGART Ford H Jr  The Relationship of Man and Nature:  A Study of Thoreau's *Journal*  MA Univ of Pittsburgh 1959
5823 TERESA E Regina  Thoreau's Ideas of Nature and Art and Their Illustration in *A Week on the Concord and Merrimack Rivers*  MA Mount Holyoke Coll 1966
5824 THOMAS David A  Thoreau:  The Advocate of Freedom  MS Kansas St Coll at Pittsburg 1940
5825 TILLINGHAST Charles A  The West of Thoreau's Imagination  MA Syracuse Univ 1965  81 p
5826 WAFER James W  Realism and Romanticism in Henry David Thoreau's Works  MA Louisiana St Univ 1942
5827 WALDRUM Evelyn  Thoreau's Philosophy of Education  MA Sul Ross St Coll 1938
5828 WHITE Donald W  A Study of Thoreau's Poetry in *A Week on the Concord and Merrimack Rivers*  MA Univ of Idaho 1941
5829 WILLIAMS Frances M  Thoreau's Views on Violence  MA San Diego St Coll 1963  92 p
5830 WOOD Priscilla A  Patterns of Imagery in Thoreau's *Journal of 1854*  MA Columbia Univ 1962  109 p
5831 WYLIE Ola G  Simplicity of Life and Elevation of Thoughts in the Works of Henry David Thoreau  M Ed Henderson St Coll nd
5832 YEHLE Carol F  The Thoreauvian Dialectic:  A Study of the Nature Symbolism in *Walden*  MA Syracuse Univ 1958  86 p
See also 1390, 1405, 1440, 1447, 1492, 1521, 2057, 2479

## JAMES THURBER

5833 BROWN Trixie T  The New York Wits: James Thurber, E B White and R C Benchley  MA West Texas St Univ 1953  82 p
5834 CHISNELL Elnora J  Thurber's Runaways:  A Study of the Misfits in James Thurber's Fiction  MA Indiana Univ of Pennsylvania 1966  73 p
5835 CULVER Nova M  Satiric Elements in James Thurber  MA Univ of Texas at Austin 1953  84 p
5836 DILLE Ralph G  A Study of the Writings of James Thurber  MA Bowling Green St Univ 1952
5837 FRIESEN Paul  James Thurber:  Satirist and Humorist  MA Univ of Denver 1964
5838 GEBEL Gertrude  James Thurber:  A Humanist with Existentialist Overtones  MA Univ of Maryland at College Park 1965  69 p
5839 HEATON Cherrill P  James Grover Thurber and the Theory of the Unpleasant  MA Florida St Univ 1961  80 p
5840 KOMPASS Arthur M  The Social Individual:  Social Criticism in the Writings of James Thurber  MA Univ of New Mexico 1959
5841 RYBERG Charles L  Humor and Pathos in James Thurber's Short Stories  MA Southern Illinois Univ at Carbondale 1959  98 p
5842 SHIELDS Patricia M  The Humor of James Thurber  MA Ohio Univ 1966
5843 STONE Patricia M  The Drawings of James Thurber  MA Univ of Florida 1953

## FRANCIS O TICKNOR

5844 CHENEY Sarah A  Francis Orray Ticknor  MA Duke Univ 1934
5845 HESS Eugene D  A Study of the Life and Writings of Dr Francis Orray Ticknor  MA Auburn Univ 1933
5846 ROGERS Annie B  Francis Orray Ticknor:  Georgia Poet  MA Univ of Georgia 1928

## HENRY TIMROD

5847 BRIGHAM Lillian M  Charleston, the Background for Timrod  MA Univ of Texas at Austin 1935
5848 BROCKMAN Allan A  The Early Sonnet Form of Henry Timrod  MA Vanderbilt Univ 1946
5849 CLEMENT Norma  A Study of Speech in Selected Poems of Henry Timrod  MA East Tennessee St Univ 1968
5850 FELDER Herman M  Notes on Timrod  MA Vanderbilt Univ 1937
5851 GLASGOW Elizabeth A  Henry Timrod: A Study in Artistic Development  MA Columbia Univ 1925
5852 HARRIS James H  A Concordance to the Poems of Henry Timrod  MA Louisiana St Univ 1939
5853 JORDAN Martha R  Henry Timrod's Early Poems  MA Duke Univ 1935
5854 KELLER Mark A  The Making of a Poet: A Survey of the Critical Reaction to the Poetry of Henry Timrod, 1860-1966  MA Mississippi St Univ nd  74 p
5855 McCLIMON Grace L  Henry Timrod as Man and Poet  MA Wofford Coll 1935
5856 PATY Sadie  Henry Timrod: A Critical Study  MA Vanderbilt Univ 1943
5857 THOMAS Evelyn J  Henry Timrod: Romantic and Rebel  MA Brigham Young Univ 1955  201 p
5858 WILBURN William B  Henry Timrod: Literary Influences and Theories of Poetry  MA Univ of Mississippi 1938  98 p

## RIDGELY TORRENCE

5859 DIXON Ruth  Ridgely Torrence and the Poetic Drama  MA Ohio St Univ 1938
5860 FAIS Marilyn  The Literary Career of Frederick Ridgely Torrence: A General Survey  MA Columbia Univ 1951
5861 TOBIAS Richard C  Ridgely Torrence, Poet (1874-1950): A Biographical and Critical Study  MA Ohio St Univ 1951

## LIONEL TRILLING

5862 CRESAP Paul M  Lionel Trilling's Theories of the Novel  MA Univ of Florida 1953
5863 WINDELL Violet B  A Man Without a Myth: A Study of Lionel Trilling  MA Univ of Louisville 1958

## MARK TWAIN

5864 ABERNETHY Francis E  Mark Twain's Literary Judgements  MA Louisiana St Univ 1951
5865 ABU-TALIB Mohammed A  Peculiarities of English in Mark Twain's *Huckleberry Finn*  MA Howard Univ 1964  143 p
5866 ACKLEY Raymond P  Mark Twain and Social Darwinism  MA San Diego St Coll 1968  83 p
5867 ADAMS Erma M  The Foreign Travel Books of Mark Twain  MA Duke Univ 1935
5868 ADAMS Eva B  Joseph T Goodman: The Man Who Made Mark Twain  MA Columbia Univ 1936
5869 ADAMS Gloria J  Mark Twain's *Pudd'nhead Wilson*: An Historical and Critical Study  MA Univ of Texas at Austin 1964
5870 ADAMSON Jeanne  Mark Twain's Nemesis: His Beloved Brother, Henry  MA Univ of Texas at El Paso 1963  183 p
5871 ADELSBERG Lester S  Huckleberry Finn as Twainian Significate  MA Univ of Iowa 1965
5872 ADKINS Denise  The Growth of the Literary Reputation of Mark Twain, 1867-1935  MA Southern Methodist Univ 1935
5873 AKINS Thomas W  The Mississippi River in Literature; Chapter 2: Mark Twain and the Mississippi  MA Southern Methodist Univ 1934

5874 ALDER Phyllis  The Effect of the Concept of Slavery on Plot Pattern and Characterization in Mark Twain's *Pudd'head Wilson*  BA Univ of British Columbia (Canada) 1966
5875 ALLEN Dorothy M  Mark Twain as a Social Historian  MA Wayne St Univ 1936
5876 ALLEN Hayward F  Some Representative Political Attitudes of Mark Twain  MA Univ of Colorado 1962
5877 ALLISON Vincent M  Sam Clemens: Genesis of a Social Critic  MA Univ of Iowa 1954
5878 ANDERSON Emory E  The Americanism of Mark Twain  MA Univ of Texas at Austin 1933
5879 ANDERSON Stewart  Mark Twain and New England  MA Boston Univ 1945
5880 ANDREWS Joseph L Jr  The Stranger's Progress: A Study of Humor and Tragedy in Mark Twain's Writings  BA Amherst Coll 1959
5881 ANNOTTI Elaine M  A Re-evaluation of the Secondary School Literature Program with Particular Emphasis on *Huckleberry Finn*  MA Brown Univ 1959
5882 ARTHUR Charles S  Mark Twain's *Joan of Arc*: A Literary Analysis  MA Univ of Maryland at College Park 1966  67 p
5883 ASMUNDSSON Doris R  Mark Twain's Treatment of Joan of Arc  MA Columbia Univ 1958
5884 ATTWOOD Ruth M  Western Elements in the Works of Mark Twain  MA Univ of Denver 1935
5885 AUGUR Margaret E  Mark Twain's Reading and Its Effect Upon His Writing  MA Univ of Illinois at Urbana 1939
5886 BAER Robert G  Mark Twain and Robert Louis Stevenson in Hawaii  MA Univ of Colorado 1964
5887 BAKER E  Mark Twain in Modern Criticism  MA Ohio St Univ 1935
5888 BARKER John F  Mark Twain and Monarchy  MA Univ of Colorado 1951
5889 BASS J N  Mark Twain's Representation of the American West  MA North Texas St Univ 1953
5890 BATEMAN Jack A  Mark Twain's *A Connecticut Yankee*: A Critical Analysis  MS Kansas St Coll at Pittsburg 1964
5891 BECHTOLD Ignatius P  Mark Twain's Attitude Toward Religion  MA Univ of Notre Dame 1943
5892 BELGRADE Harry L  Critical Interpretations of Mark Twain Since 1910  MA Univ of Iowa 1940
5893 BELL Hazel L  Mark Twain's Pessimism  MA Univ of Washington at Seattle 1929
5894 BELL Marvin C  Mark Twain and His American Critics  MA Texas Christian Univ 1951  124 p
5895 BELLAMY Gladys C  Mark Twain and Slavery  MA Univ of Oklahoma 1938
5896 BELLER Hilliard I  The Style of *Huckleberry Finn*: A Statistical Study  MA Brooklyn Coll of City Univ of New York 1959  72 p
5897 BENNETT Jo W  Mark Twain: Lecturer and Entertainer  MA Southwest Texas St Univ 1948
5898 BERRY Marcia E  Metamorphosis in Mark Twain: A Study of Three Archetypes  MA Univ of Tulsa 1966  70 p
5899 BETTS Rome A  Mark Twain and Religion  MA Columbia Univ 1929
5900 BIDEWELL George I  Mark Twain's Florida Years  MA Univ of Iowa 1945
5901 BILL Joan  Science and the Philosophy of Mark Twain  MA Seton Hall Univ 1960
5902 BLACKLEY Charles E  Inversion of Role and Patterns of Reversal in the Works of Mark Twain  MA Texas Arts and Industries Univ 1968
5903 BODDEN Louise  Mark Twain on European Civilization  MA Syracuse Univ 1929
5904 BONHAM Virginia L  The Ambiguity of Innocence in Mark Twain's Novels  MA Univ of Kansas 1966
5905 BONHAM William D  *The Mysterious Stranger*: Adaptation and Presentation of Narrative Prose in Group Oral Forms  MA Southern Illinois Univ at Carbondale 1962

5906 BRASHEAR Augusta F  Chivalry as Reflected in the Works of Ariosto, Rabelais and Mark Twain  MA Louisiana St Univ 1932
5907 BRIGGS Warren M  Gulliver's Travels on the Mississippi River:  A Question of Mark Twain's Satire (and Jonathan Swift's Humour)  MA Columbia Univ 1954  156 p
5908 BROWN Anthony E  Rhetorical Device Effecting Humor in the Works of Mark Twain  MA Univ of South Carolina 1961
5909 BRUNETT Ruth A  Mark Twain in the Northwest, August 9-23, 1895  MA Univ of Washington at Seattle 1950
5910 BUNN James W  Mark Twain and Religion:  The Foundation of His Faith  MA Columbia Univ 1966  52 p
5911 BURGESS Edna L  Evidences of a Calvinistic Background in Selected Works of Mark Twain  MA Univ of Iowa 1948
5912 BURKS William M  Mark Twain:  England and the English  MA Duke Univ 1937
5913 BURNAM Thomas B  Mark Twain and the *Gilded Age*  MA Univ of Idaho 1937
5914 BURNS Rebecca S  Mark Twain and Biblical Fundamentalism After 1880  MA Duke Univ 1963
5915 BUXBAUM Melvin H  The Bad Boy in American Fiction Through *Huckleberry Finn*  MA Roosevelt Univ at Chicago 1960
5916 BUXHAUS Katherine L  An Analysis of the Vernacular in Mark Twain's Mississippi Valley Stories  MA Univ of Chicago 1924
5917 BYRD Gary D  Freedom and Determinism in Selected Writings of Mark Twain  BA Rutgers St Univ 1967  84 p
5918 CAMERON Thomas D  Mark Twain's Views on Formal Education  MA North Texas St Univ 1966
5919 CAMP Maryella  The Adolescent as Treated by Mark Twain  MA Duke Univ 1940
5920 CAMPENNI Frank J  Recurring Elements in Mark Twain's Prose  MA Univ of Iowa 1953
5921 CAPPS Mikie L  The Conscience and the Dream:  An Analysis of the Influence of Mark Twain's Determinism on Characterization and Thematic Unity in *Huckleberry Finn*  MA Texas Agricultural and Mechanical Univ 1965  114 p
5922 CARROLL Richard T  Conscience and Mark Twain  MA Colgate Univ 1964
5923 CARSON David L  Mark Twain's Pessimism:  A Study of Skeptical Elements in the Early Writings  MA Oklahoma St Univ 1964  117 p
5924 CARTER Paul J  Mark Twain:  Satirist and Representative of the Gilded Age  MA Univ of Kentucky 1935  126 p
5925 CHAMBERS N J  Repetitions in the Most Popular Works of Mark Twain  MA North Texas St Univ 1949
5926 CHRISTENSEN Elsie  Contributions of Mark Twain to Modern Religious Thought  MA Univ of Arizona 1939
5927 CHURCHMAN Charles J  Mark Twain's Treatment of Southern Life  MA Univ of Virginia 1957
5928 CLARK William G  Superstition in the Works of Mark Twain  MA Univ of Iowa 1949
5929 CLOUD Gisela M  Mark Twain's Translation of *Der Struwwelpeter* and *Die Schrecken der Deutschen Spreche*  MA Univ of Georgia 1966
5930 COCHRAN Maryanne C  Mark Twain's *Life on the Mississippi*:  An Historical and Critical Study  MA Univ of Texas at Austin 1961  165 p
5931 COFFEE Jessie  Mark Twain's Gospel as Expressed in *Pudd'nhead Wilson*  MA Sacramento St Coll 1961
5932 COGELL Elizabeth A  The Influence of Mark Twain's Reading in Science on the Ideas in *What Is Man?*  MA Univ of South Dakota 1962
5933 COLAGROSSI Maria  The Use of Dialect in Mark Twain  MA Seton Hall Univ 1964
5934 CONNOR Marie  Aunt Polly:  The Failure of Mark Twain's Women  MA Long Island Univ 1966  87 p
5935 CONNORS Mary T  Point of View in the Writings of Mark Twain  MA New

York Univ 1958
5936 COPLIN M K  Representations of Father-son Relations in the Major Novels of Samuel Clemens  MA North Texas St Univ nd
5937 CORSA Teresa K  The Image of the Guild in Juvenile Literature from the Civil War to the Publication of *The Adventures of Tom Sawyer* MA Westminster Coll of New Wilmington 1962
5938 COURTNEY Lee F  The Boggs-Sherburn Episode: A Digression in *Huckleberry Finn*  MA Texas Agricultural and Mechanical Univ 1964  53 p
5939 CRANFORD Sr M Elaine  European Influence Upon a Typical American: Mark Twain  MA Creighton Univ 1947
5940 CRIMES M M  Joan of Arc as Personal Ideal and Literary Symbol in the Life and Writing of Samuel L Clemens  MA North Texas St Univ 1958
5941 CROMWELL Judith  Mark Twain's Travel Books: A Study of His Developing Pessimism  MA Univ of Oklahoma 1964
5942 CURRAN Ronald T  Mark Twain's *Joan of Arc*: A Critical Study  MA Univ of Pittsburgh 1962
5943 DAGG Malvin H  Huck, Holden and Their Narrative Voices: A Study in Differences  BA Univ of British Columbia (Canada) 1967
5944 DANIELSON Jeannette C  Mark Twain's Attitude Toward Women as Reflected in Selected Works  MA Bowling Green St Univ 1962
5945 DAVIDSON William E  Mark Twain and Conscience  MA Univ of Missouri 1940
5946 DAVIS Billy A  Mark Twain and Medievalism: Twain's Views of the Middle Ages and of Medieval Influence in Recent Times  MA Stanford Univ 1949
5947 DE FALCO Joseph M  Ritual Journey in *Huckleberry Finn*  MA Univ of Florida 1958
5948 DeGREGORY James R  The Development of the Critical Estimates of *Huckleberry Finn*  MA John Carroll Univ 1966
5949 DeNYSE Diane R  Ross Browne and Mark Twain: The Question of Literary Influence  MA Univ of Wyoming 1965
5950 DERRICK Leland E  A Study in Mark Twain's Sources  MA Univ of Texas at Austin 1930
5951 DIRKS Richard A  Life and How to Cure It: A Study of Lies, Truths and Social Structure in Selected Works of Mark Twain  BA Amherst Coll 1955
5952 DONLEY Beatrice L  Mississippi, the Matrix of Creative Writers: An Investigation of Causes  MA Mississippi Coll 1964
5953 DOUGLAS Doris M  A Study of His Wife's Influence on Mark Twain's Life and Works  MA East Texas St Univ 1950
5954 DRABIK Stephen F  The Christian Mark Twain  MA Seton Hall Univ 1966
5955 DRY Bernice S  Expressed Opinions of Mark Twain on Government and Politics  MA Northeast Missouri St Coll 1959
5956 DUBIN Harold N  *The Adventures of Huckleberry Finn* by Mark Twain and *The Catcher in the Rye* by J D Salinger: Two Studies in Fiction of the Adolescent in Society  MA Columbia Univ 1958
5957 DUFFY Donald D  The Moral Codes of the Adolescents of Clemens, Anderson and Salinger  MA Oklahoma St Univ 1963  91 p
5958 DUSKIS Henry  Mark Twain's Journalistic Endeavors, 1868-1890  MA Univ of Southern California 1952
5959 EBERHART John R  A Study of the Pessimism of Mark Twain  MA Univ of Colorado 1949
5960 EDWARDS Corliss H  Pessimism and Determinism in the Later Writings of Mark Twain  MA Univ of Georgia 1960
5961 EDWARDS Mary P  Racial Minorities in Mark Twain  MA Michigan St Univ 1949
5962 ELLINGER Ruth N  Mark Twain's Hannibal, 1839-1853  MA Washington Univ at St Louis 1953
5963 EMBERSON Frances G  The Vocabulary of Samuel L Clemens from 1852 to 1884  MA Univ of Missouri 1932
5964 ENGLAND Erma K  Mark Twain's Attitude Toward the Negro  MA Univ of Washington at Seattle 1947

5965 ERHARD Thomas A  Aspects of Mark Twain as a Social Critic  MA Univ of New Mexico 1949
5966 ERICKSON Mary D  Huckleberry Finn: Realist Versus Romanticist  MA Univ of Montana 1960
5967 ERTMAN Irene P  Mark Twain's Use of Sources in *Pudd'nhead Wilson* and *Those Extraordinary Twins*  MS Kansas St Coll at Pittsburg 1961
5968 EVANS Charles J  Mark Twain's Treatment of Negro Characters  MA New York Univ 1951
5969 EWING Lora M  A Justification of the Ending of *Adventures of Huckleberry Finn*  MA Univ of Massachusetts 1965
5970 FAWLEY John S  Neither, Nor: A Story of the Role of the "Innocent" and the "Hero" in the Writings of Mark Twain  MA DePaul Univ 1967
5971 FERGUSON John P  Tom and Huck: Two Aspects of Conflict Within Sam Clemens  MA Columbia Univ 1958
5972 FINCK Jane A  The Evolution of Mark Twain's *Pudd'nhead Wilson* and *Those Extraordinary Twins*  MA Queens Coll of New York 1955
5973 FISCHER Douglas  Mark Twain as a Southerner  MA Univ of Arizona 1965
5974 FITZHUGH Nannie M  Mark Twain as a Satirist  MA Southern Methodist Univ 1934
5975 FLACK Frank M  Mark Twain and Music  MA Univ of Iowa 1942
5976 FLOOD Merle D  The Sociological Basis of Mark Twain's Pessimism, 1863-1889  MA Univ of Iowa 1950
5977 FORD J M  The Treatment of Human Cruelty in the Novels of Mark Twain  MA North Texas St Univ 1956
5978 FORD Marian M  Mark Twain's Determinism in His Later Works  MA Univ of Iowa 1950
5979 FORD Thomas W  An Historical and Critical Examination of Mark Twain's *Pudd'nhead Wilson*  MA Univ of Texas at Austin 1951  141 p
5980 FOSTER Charles W  A Structural and Thematic Comparison of *Huckleberry Finn* and *The Catcher in the Rye*  MA East Tennessee St Univ 1963
5981 FOSTER Vivienne N  Mark Twain the Politician  MA Columbia Univ 1927
5982 FOX John P  Mark Twain and Colonel Sellers  MA Univ of Iowa 1962
5983 FREEMAN Miriam  Mark Twain's Pessimism  MA Vanderbilt Univ 1941
5984 FREEMAN S M  The Influence of the Frontier on Mark Twain  MA North Texas St Univ 1942
5985 FRISCH Raymond L  An Investigation of the Elements of Self-reliance and Individualism in the Works of Mark Twain  MS St Cloud St Coll 1958  51 p
5986 FUJII Paul T  Mark Twain and the Tyranny of Conformity  MA Univ of Hawaii 1965  178 p
5987 FULLER Lawrence B  The Influence of Melodrama in Several Novels of Mark Twain  MA Columbia Univ 1963  68 p
5988 GAETANO Theodora A  "The Exquisite Misery of Uncertainty": A Reappraisal of Mark Twain's *Life on the Mississippi*  MA Columbia Univ 1964  77 p
5989 GAINER Ruby J  Realism in the Novels of Mark Twain  MA Atlanta Univ 1953
5990 GARDNER G C  Mark Twain as a Political Satirist  MA North Texas St Univ 1953
5991 GARNER Marguerite F  A Critical Analysis of Mark Twain's *Tom Sawyer Abroad* and *Tom Sawyer Detective*  MA Univ of Iowa 1953
5992 GARRY Sr Mary J  *Huckleberry Finn* and *A Connecticut Yankee*: Mark Twain's Satire on Romanticism in the Nineteenth Century  MA Boston Coll 1966
5993 GAVAGHAN Paul F  Mark Twain's *The Mysterious Stranger*: A Study of the Symbolism and Its Meaning  MA Catholic Univ of America at Washington, D C 1950
5994 GERCIN Berit  America as Described in Mark Twain's Writings  MA Brown Univ 1948
5995 GERGELY Emro J  Mark Twain as a Reformer  MA Univ of Pittsburgh 1929
5996 GILLESPIE Virginia  The Moral Philosophy of Mark Twain  MA Univ of Mississippi 1952  114 p

5997  GLASSER Harry A  The Question of Mark Twain's Pessimism  MA Columbia Univ 1946
5998  GNEWUCH Leon  Mark Twain: Realistic Interpreter of the Frontier and of His Age  MA Univ of Notre Dame 1938
5999  GOFF Ida E  Mark Twain and the Dreyfus Case  MA Washington Univ at St Louis 1950
6000  GOOLSBY Opal P  Certain Aspects of Mark Twain's Pessimism  MA East Texas St Univ 1958
6001  GOURLEY Mary B  Background and Sources of Mark Twain's Humor  MA Baylor Univ 1937  112 p
6002  GUNDERSON Doris V  Mark Twain's Treatment of Children in His Fiction  MA Univ of Oregon 1954
6003  HAIG Sara L  Mark Twain's American Idealism  MA Univ of Virginia 1960
6004  HALL Raymond A  Mark Twain's Relation to Robert G Ingersoll's Program of Frontier Free Thought  MA Univ of Washington at Seattle 1951
6005  HALLER John M  A Study of Mark Twain's *Personal Recollections of Joan of Arc*  MA Univ of Texas at Austin 1946  144 p
6006  HAMADA Masajiro  Mark Twain's Conception of Social Justice  MA Southern Methodist Univ 1936
6007  HAMMOCK Herman M Jr  Mark Twain: *The Mysterious Stranger*  MA East Tennessee St Univ 1965
6008  HAMSHER Carl M  Mark Twain's Use of Dialect  MA Duke Univ 1939
6009  HANKINSON Marilyn C  The Influence of the Mississippi River on Mark Twain and How It Pervaded His Writing  MA Drake Univ 1965
6010  HANSEN Mary L  Mark Twain's Burlesque of Nineteenth Century Children's Literature  MA Stanford Univ 1959
6011  HARDIN Jewell B  Feminine Types in Mark Twain's Fiction  MA Univ of Mississippi 1947  92 p
6012  HARNEY Ralph  Mark Twain: Newspaper Man  MA Univ of Wisconsin 1945
6013  HARPER Preston F  Mark Twain's *Pudd'nhead Wilson*: An Historical and Critical Study  MA Univ of Texas at Austin 1962  94 p
6014  HARRIS Ava N  Mark Twain: Literary Artist or Mere Humorist?  M Ed Henderson St Coll nd
6015  HARRISON E L  Mark Twain as a Social Critic  MA North Texas St Univ 1944
6016  HARRISON Louis H  The Influence of George Washington Harris in the Writings of Mark Twain  MA Univ of Texas at Austin 1963  84 p
6017  HARTLEY Peter E  Myth and Meaning in *Huckleberry Finn*: A Heuristic Analysis  MA Univ of Colorado 1965
6018  HAUSMAN S Jeanne  A Study of Mark Twain's Attitude Toward Women as Reflected in His Writing  MA Univ of Tulsa 1953  102 p
6019  HEATH Lucile L  The Serious Messages in Mark Twain's Humorous Writings  MA George Peabody Coll for Teachers 1927
6020  HERRICK George H  Mark Twain as Literary Critic  MA Univ of South Carolina 1948
6021  HILBERG Christine K  *Huckleberry Finn* as Hell Allegory  MA Univ of Vermont 1965  59 p
6022  HOBBS Dora M  The Spoken Art of Mark Twain  MA Univ of Oklahoma 1945
6023  HOEGEL Rolf K  Literary Use of the River in Mark Twain  MA Southern Illinois Univ at Carbondale 1956  98 p
6024  HOFFMAN Dorothy  Mark Twain and the Double  MA Tufts Univ 1966
6025  HOLLINS Mary P  A Comparative Study of the Humor of Mark Twain and Will Rogers  MA East Texas St Univ 1950
6026  HOLT James L  Mark Twain and the Negro  MA Texas Technological Univ 1967  118 p
6027  HORD Larry D  Mark Twain's Despair: A Comparison of the Deterministic Ideas of the Old Man in "What is Man?" and Satan in *The Mysterious Stranger*  MA Texas Agricultural and Mechanical Univ nd  69 p
6028  HORNE Linda S  Mark Twain's Treatment of Slavery in *Huckleberry Finn*, *A Connecticut Yankee in King Arthur's Court* and *Pudd'nhead Wilson*

MA Univ of Texas at Austin 1964   126 p
6029 HOYT Charles L   *Pudd'nhead Wilson* and a Double-barreled Detective Story: Mark Twain's Vision of the Detective Story   MA Univ of Massachusetts 1969   59 p
6030 HUMPHREY Stella O   The Development of Mark Twain's Religious Views   MA Baylor Univ 1951   170 p
6031 HUTCHESON Louise   Mark Twain's Impressions of Europe   MA Columbia Univ 1925
6032 HUTTON Lucille   Mark Twain's Methods as a Short Story Writer   MA Univ of Southern California 1933
6033 JACOBS Teresa   A Review of Some Critical Opinions About *Huckleberry Finn*   MA Pennsylvania St Univ 1964
6034 JACOBY Bertha P   Social Influence Which Affected the Life and Writings of Samuel L Clemens   MS Kansas St Coll at Pittsburg 1953
6035 JAMES Glen J   Religion and Morality as Themes in *Tom Sawyer*, *Huckleberry Finn* and *Puddn'head Wilson*   MA Univ of Georgia 1965
6036 JOHANSSON Jurt L   Voice in *Huckleberry Finn*   MA Cornell Univ 1965
6037 JOHNS Harriet   A Comparative Study of the Treatment of Joan of Arc in Selected Works   MA Univ of New Mexico 1950
6038 JOHNSON Natalie A   Mark Twain as a Social Critic   MA Columbia Univ 1940
6039 JOINER Jeannette H   Aspects of Mark Twain's Pessimism in the 1880's: An Examination of Five Books, Stressing *The Prince and the Pauper* and *A Tramp Abroad*   MA Northern Illinois Univ 1961
6040 JOLLEY Hazel B   Mathematical and Geographic Checks on Mark Twain's Accuracy in *The Adventures of Huckleberry Finn*   MA Creighton Univ 1938
6041 JONES Alfred H   Mark Twain's Criticism of American Civilization   MA Univ of Colorado 1942
6042 JONES L C   Mark Twain as a Literary Critic   MA North Texas St Univ 1953
6043 JONES Lee C   Antebellum Humor in the Old Southwest (1830-1867) as the Beginning of American Literary Realism and the Humorous Era Which Produced Mark Twain   MA Brigham Young Univ 1963   123 p
6044 JONES Patricia M   Mark Twain and the Angel of Death   MA Univ of Hawaii 1963   107 p
6045 JULIER Ann L   Mark Twain's Religious Odyssey   MA Central Connecticut St Coll 1965
6046 KANE Br Alfred   A Study of Irreverence and Pessimism in Mark Twain   MA St Mary's Univ of San Antonio 1950   76 p
6047 KEEFE Joseph C   Mark Twain's Use of Burlesque in His Treatment of Mississippi Valley Materials   MA Univ of Iowa 1960
6048 KEELING Floy   Mark Twain as a Literary Critic   MA Univ of Texas at Austin 1941   134 p
6049 KELLEY Karen M   Mark Twain's British Literary Legacy   MA Baylor Univ 1970   147 p
6050 KELLY H F   Literary Continuity from *Huckleberry Finn* to *The Catcher in the Rye*   MA Duquesne Univ 1962
6051 KENDRICK John   The Deterministic Philosophy of Mark Twain   MA Univ of Washington at Seattle 1951
6052 KEPHART Eva H   The Paradox of Mark Twain   MA Northeast Missouri St Coll 1959
6053 KERR Dell   The Humor of Mark Twain as Tested by Freud and Bergson   MA New York Univ 1956
6054 KING Frankie J   A Study of Mark Twain and Superstitions   MA East Texas St Univ 1957
6055 KINNEBREW Mary A   Mistaken Identity in Mark Twain's Major Fiction   MA Rice Univ 1964
6056 KNIES Earl A   The Lecturing of Mark Twain   MA Lehigh Univ 1960
6057 KOCH Stephen   "The Last Dream of Freedom": A Study of Mark Twain's

*The Great Dark*  MA Columbia Univ 1964  122 p
6058 KORN Thomas H  The Rebellion of Mark Twain  MA Wesleyan Univ 1948
6059 KOS Susan  *Pudd'nhead Wilson*, Not Fiction  MA Wayne St Univ 1965
6060 LAING Juanita  Mark Twain's Philosophy of Determinism  MS Kansas St Coll at Pittsburg 1962
6061 LANG Phyllis M  The Evolution of Mark Twain's Philosophy  MA Univ of Iowa 1942
6062 LEAVELL Frank H  Mark Twain's Thought as Revealed in His Travel Books  MA Baylor Univ 1953  157 p
6063 LEE Roberta B  Some Elements of Satire in the Writings of Mark Twain  MA East Texas St Univ 1952
6064 LEVINE Jack J  Mark Twain and Samuel Clemens: Freedom and the Comic Mask, 1863-1877  BA Amherst Coll 1964
6065 LIEBERMAN Herbert E  *Huckleberry Finn*: A Biblical Interpretation  MA Columbia Univ 1957
6066 LIEVENS Sr Louise  Mark Twain as Social Critic  MA De Paul Univ 1955
6067 LINGLE Gladys H  Mark Twain: His Religious Background and Its Influence on His Pessimism  MA Southern Illinois Univ at Carbondale 1962  63 p
6068 LLOYD Sarah L  Mark Twain the Speaker  MA Columbia Univ 1925
6069 LONG Alice G  Mark Twain's Humor  MA Stephen F Austin St Univ 1947
6070 LORCH Fred W  Mark Twain in Iowa  MA Univ of Iowa 1928
6071 LOVERING Virginia E  Mark Twain: Pessimist  MA Northern Illinois Univ 1953
6072 LOW David H  Offspring of the Frontier: Mark Twain and *Roughing It*  MA Columbia Univ 1953
6073 LUBER John F  Mark Twain's Western Years  MA Univ of Washington at Seattle 1950
6074 LUCAS William E  Friendship of Mark Twain and Bret Harte  MA Northern Illinois Univ 1957
6075 LUCK Susan G  Patterns of Diminutive Imagery in Selected Works of Jonathan Swift and Mark Twain  MA Bowling Green St Univ 1968
6076 LYNCH Barbara V  The Plight of Man: Twain and Hemingway  MA George Washington Univ 1969  99 p
6077 LYNETT Mary J  Rhetorical Study of Mark Twain's Speaking  MA Northern Illinois Univ 1958
6078 LYON James C  A Study of Mark Twain's Developing Use of Irony and His Growth as a Satirist as Evidenced in His Short Stories  MA Northern Illinois Univ 1966
6079 LYONS Laura C  Satire in the Short Stories of Mark Twain  MA Butler Univ 1964
6080 McCARTHY Aloysia  The Humanitarianism of Mark Twain  MA Univ of Notre Dame 1940
6081 McCLUNG Daniel H  Mark Twain's Use of the Bible in "The Man That Corrupted Hadleyburg", "Extracts from Captain Stormfield's Visit to Heaven", *Personal Recollections of Joan of Arc* and *The Mysterious Stranger*  MA Univ of Redlands 1965
6082 McGLOCKTON Yvonne E  Humor in the Early Works of Mark Twain  MA Atlanta Univ 1963
6083 McGRATH Ann M  *Huckleberry Finn*: A Novel of Ideas  MA Boston Coll 1954
6084 McGUIRE Edna E  Mark Twain as an Historical Novelist  MA Univ of Missouri 1944
6085 McGUIRE John F  Autobiography in Mark Twain's Fiction  MA Univ of Notre Dame 1948
6086 McHARG Cynthia W  An Investigation of Mark Twain's Views on War as Found in His Writings  MA Univ of Missouri 1942
6087 McHENRY Stella M  The Influence of Women Upon the Life and Literature of Mark Twain  MA Wesleyan Univ 1961
6088 McMAHAN Elizabeth E  Mark Twain and *The Damned Human Race*: A Study of Samuel L Clemens' Indictment of Humanity  MA Univ of Houston 1962  97 p

6089 McNAMARA Joseph W  Mark Twain and the Tradition of the Good Little Boy  MA New York Univ 1951
6090 McQUITTY Robert A  Mark Twain and Literary Naturalism  MA Texas Christian Univ 1963  145 p
6091 MALONEY Francis J  Mark Twain: The Heir to Southwest Humor  MA Univ of Portland 1955
6092 MANNING James F  Antiromanticism: Key to Thematic Unity of *Huckleberry Finn*  MA Boston Coll 1960
6093 MANUEL Gerald E  Mark Twain's Attitude Toward Catholicism  MA Butler Univ 1966
6094 MARCON Alberta  *Pudd'nhead Wilson* by Mark Twain  MA Ca Foscari (Italy) 1969
6095 MARTIN Alma B  The Vocabulary of Mark Twain's *Gilded Age*  MA Univ of Missouri 1929
6096 MARX Ralph R  The Literary Associations of Mark Twain and William Dean Howells  MA De Paul Univ 1940
6097 MASON Laurene D  Characters and Incidents in Mark Twain's Fiction  MA Univ of Iowa 1926
6098 MASSE Marilyn  Mark Twain: Critic of Society  M Ed Henderson St Coll nd
6099 MATHIAS Esther L  Mark Twain: Financier  MA Southwest Texas St Univ 1950
6100 MAYO Edith P  Literary and Cultural Convention in Mark Twain's Characterization of Women  MA George Washington Univ 1970  108 p
6101 MEEHAN Frances  Publication and Reception of Mark Twain's *Joan of Arc*  MA St Mary's Univ of San Antonio 1948  77 p
6102 MEHLMAN Miachael H  The Influence of the Frontier Upon Mark Twain  MA New York Univ 1962
6103 MENKE Pamela G  Mark Twain and the Forms of Escape: Childhood as Theme in Nineteenth Century American Literature  MA Univ of North Carolina at Chapel Hill 1966
6104 MEWSHAW Nell  Satire of the American Scene in the Writings of Mark Twain  MA Univ of Texas at Austin 1936
6105 MINKS Eldren W  Realistic Elements in Mark Twain's Treatment of the American Frontier  MA Mankato St Coll 1963  82 p
6106 MINNIEHAN Hallena B  Mark Twain's Portrayal of Life in the Mississippi Valley  MA Univ of Texas at Austin 1967  117 p
6107 MOLDENHAUER Joseph  Innocence and Experience: A Thematic Study in the Works of Mark Twain  MA Columbia Univ 1957
6108 MOORE George B  Mark Twain's Mississippi  MA Univ of Kansas 1937
6109 MOORE Robert H  The Use of "Nigger" in Mark Twain's *Adventures of Huckleberry Finn*  MA Univ of North Carolina at Chapel Hill 1964
6110 MORGAN Ann D  Mark Twain's "Symbolic Sad Initiation"  MA East Tennessee St Univ 1969
6111 MORGAN Elizabeth A  The Importance of Caricature in the Artistry of Mark Twain  MA Univ of North Carolina at Chapel Hill 1966
6112 MORTON Paul S  Representative Criticism of *Huckleberry Finn*, 1884 to 1932  MA Washington Univ at St Louis 1950
6113 MOSELEY Nellie L  A Vision of Humanity: Mark Twain's Use of Satiric Narrators  MA Duke Univ 1966
6114 MURPHY Alton C  Elements of Realism in the Works of Mark Twain  MA Southwest Texas St Univ 1941
6115 MURRAY James  Mark Twain's *A Connecticut Yankee in King Arthur's Court*: A Critical Study  MA Univ of Texas at Austin 1955  89 p
6116 MUSE Jeannie L  Mark Twain's Progression from Irony Into Derisive Satire  MA Mississippi Coll 1964
6117 MYERS Mitzi O  Mark Twain and Existentialism  MA East Texas St Univ 1962
6118 NEELEY William F  Mark Twain and Aristocracy  MA West Texas St Univ 1969  146 p
6119 NEFF Merlin L  The Influence of the West Upon Mark Twain  MA Univ of

Washington at Seattle 1931
6120 NEILL Annie B  Mark Twain and the Arts  MA Southern Methodist Univ 1936
6121 NELSON Agnes D  American Boyhood in Mark Twain's Fiction  MA George Peabody Coll for Teachers 1929
6122 NEUNER Maria  Mark Twain and the South  MA Kent St Univ 1964
6123 NEWMAN Maude  Mark Twain's College  MA Stephen F Austin St Univ 1941
6124 NEWMAN Patricia W  The Critical Journey of *Huckleberry Finn*  MA Mississippi St Univ 1969  81 p
6125 NILSSON Cluster M  The Serious Side of Mark Twain  MA Univ of Utah 1931
6126 NOEL Paul K  The Influence of the Mississippi on Mark Twain's Writings  MA Ohio St Univ 1926
6127 NOWELL Rose  Mark Twain in Comparison with Cervantes  MA Stetson Univ 1917
6128 NUTTER Larry W  The Changing Reputation of Mark Twain  MA West Texas St Univ 1965  112 p
6129 ODELL Jean I  Social Conditions Pictured by Mark Twain  MA Columbia Univ 1919
6130 ODLE Zelma R  Plot Structure in the Novels of Mark Twain  MA North Texas St Univ 1949
6131 OGLESBY Ethel A  An Historical and Critical Study of Mark Twain's *The Adventures of Tom Sawyer*  MA Univ of Texas at Austin 1958  151 p
6132 OSTRANDER Elizabeth H  Eve, Joan and Roxana: Reflections of Mark Twain's Life and Thought  MA Ohio St Univ 1966  50 p
6133 PACKER James E  Mark Twain's Attitude Toward the Negro Problem  MA Texas Christian Univ 1960
6134 PAINE Stephen C  An Introduction to Twain  BA Amherst Coll 1953
6135 PALMER Maude H  History of the Literary Reputation of Mark Twain in America  MA Univ of Iowa 1925
6136 PARKS Sarah R  Mark Twain's Development in the Sarcastic Repression of Moral Indignation  MA Columbia Univ 1910
6137 PASQUIER-DOUMER Marie C  Mark Twain and the Mississippi River  MA Cornell Univ 1955
6138 PATTON Frederic K  A Study of Mark Twain's Satire in *What Is Man?* and *The Mysterious Stranger*  MA New York Univ 1951
6139 PEABODY Henry W  The Degeneration of a Character: Tom Sawyer in Four Works  MA Univ of Georgia 1967
6140 PERRI Josephine M  Mark Twain: Ironic Surveyor of American Life  MA St John's Univ 1951
6141 PHLEGER R P  Mark Twain's Social and Political Ideas  MA Boston Univ 1941
6142 PICKENS Myrtle  A Critical Study of Mark Twain's *Innocents Abroad*  MS Kansas St Coll at Pittsburg 1964
6143 POCHMANN Henry A  The Mind of Mark Twain  MA Univ of Texas at Austin 1924
6144 POE John W  An Emerging Consciousness in Southern Literature in Twain, Faulkner, Warren and McCullers  MA Kansas St Teachers Coll 1964
6145 POLLOCK George W  Mark Twain's Views of Racial Minorities in America  MA Baylor Univ 1966  158 p
6146 POTTER William D  The Relation of Mark Twain's *Adventures of Tom Sawyer* and *Huckleberry Finn* to Contemporary Juvenile Literature  MA Michigan St Univ 1946
6147 POUSSON John D  Critical Attitude Towards *Huckleberry Finn*  MA Louisiana St Univ 1960
6148 POZYCHKI Mary A  *The Adventures of Huckleberry Finn*--Portrait of America: A Study of the Critical Analysis of Mark Twain from 1884 to the 1960's  MA Villanova Univ 1966
6149 PRICE Marsden  Mark Twain and the Short Story  MA Claremont Graduate School 1947
6150 PRICE Nannie L  The Pessimism of Mark Twain  MA Univ of Texas at Austin 1937  92 p

6151 PROCTOR Kenneth R  The Negro in the Works of Mark Twain  MA East Carolina Univ 1964
6152 RATCLIFFE Robert R  The Writing, Publication and Reception of *The Mysterious Stranger*  MA Univ of North Carolina at Chapel Hill 1960
6153 RAVN Holten W  Mark Twain and Nineteenth Century Scientific Thought  MA San Diego St Coll 1950  58 p
6154 REAGAN Fred C  A Comparison of the Religious Philosophies of Mark Twain and Huckleberry Finn  MA Eastern New Mexico Univ 1962
6155 RECKFORD Phillip  Some Aspects of Mark Twain's Code  MA Univ of North Carolina at Chapel Hill 1966
6156 RHODES Sr Mary T  Cervantes and Mark Twain  MA Univ of Kansas 1926
6157 RIBYN Alta V  Structure as an Element in Mark Twain's Short Story Technique  MA Univ of Iowa 1924
6158 RINGWALD Gregory M  The Anti-Catholicism of Mark Twain in Relation to Nativism  MA Boston Coll 1948
6159 ROBERSON Robert E  Mark Twain: Satirist and Critic of the Human Race  MA Emory Univ 1940  140 p
6160 ROBERTSON Margaret M  Mark Twain as a Writer of Travel  MA Columbia Univ 1926
6161 ROBINSON Duncan W  Mark Twain's Attitude Toward Aristocracy  MA Southern Methodist Univ 1933
6162 ROBINSON Vivian U  Social Criticism in the Novels of Mark Twain  MA Atlanta Univ 1963
6163 ROBISON John H  A Literature of Ideas and Mark Twain  MA Univ of Colorado 1964
6164 ROGERS J F  Representations of the Mother-son Relations in the Major Novels of Samuel Clemens  MA North Texas St Univ 1968
6165 ROGERS Rodney C  *A Tramp Abroad, A Connecticut Yankee* and Taine's *L'Ancien Regime*: An Instance of Source Adaptation in Mark Twain's Writings  MA Univ of Virginia 1965
6166 ROSA Alfred F  Mark Twain's Use of the Technique and Theme of Appearance and Reality  MA Univ of Massachusetts 1966
6167 ROSEN Nathan  The Two Worlds of Mark Twain: A Study of His Major Novels  MA Columbia Univ 1948
6168 ROWLETTE Robert O  Mark Twain's Indebtedness to Artemus Ward  MA Univ of Colorado 1957
6169 RUSSELL James G  Mark Twain: His Quest for Soul  M Ed Slippery Rock St Coll 1969  59 p
6170 RUSSELL Leslie A  Mark Twain's Prose Style as Illustrated in *Life on the Mississippi*  MA Washington St Univ at Pullman 1952
6171 ST PIERRE Jean M  The Worlds of Hannibal, Dawson's Landing and Eseldorf: A Study of Illusion and Reality in the Works of Mark Twain  MA Columbia Univ 1961  63 p
6172 SAMPLE Everett J  Mark Twain's American Reputation, 1910-1935  MA Duke Univ 1947
6173 SANDBERG James S  The Celebration of Boyhood in Mark Twain and His Middle Western Contemporaries  MA Stanford Univ 1949
6174 SAWYER Bruce D  Mark Twain's Treatment of Womanhood  MA Lamar Technological Univ 1969
6175 SAYRE I C  The Subjective or Expressionistic Element in the Short Story  MA Ohio St Univ 1925
6176 SCHAUS Hermann  A Critical Study of Mark Twain's *The Mysterious Stranger*  MA Univ of Texas at Austin 1943  167 p
6177 SCHIFFMAN Michael  Mark Twain's Humor and *The Innocents Abroad*  MA Columbia Univ 1966  75 p
6178 SCHMIDT Bernard  The Pessimism of Mark Twain  MA Syracuse Univ 1936
6179 SCHMITT Peter J  Sources and Structure in Mark Twain's *A Connecticut Yankee in King Arthur's Court*  MA Univ of Iowa 1960
6180 SCHUPBACH Deanna J  Ideality and Reality: A Study of Reactions to

*The Gilded Age* MA Univ of Texas at Austin 1963
6181 SCOTT Emmy L  Mark Twain's *Roughing It*: An Historical and Critical Analysis  MA Univ of Texas at Austin 1964  115 p
6182 SELZMAN Jack  The Alienated Character in the Works of Mark Twain  MA New York Univ 1959
6183 SHAFER Rosemary M  The Art of *Tom Sawyer*  MA Univ of Iowa 1941
6184 SHARP Marjory P  Mark Twain's Characterization of Women  MS Kansas St Coll at Pittsburg 1961
6185 SHARPE Jonnie L  The Evolution of Pessimism in the Works of Mark Twain  MA Atlanta Univ 1967
6186 SHAVELENKO Igor A  Mark Twain as a Literary Craftsman  MA Univ of Hawaii 1945  219 p
6187 SHEEN Edwin D  The Negro as Portrayed in the Works of Mark Twain  MA Univ of Illinois at Urbana 1927
6188 SHELL Peggy T  The Evolution of a Cynic: The Philosophy of Mark Twain  MA Northeast Louisiana Univ 1968  97 p
6189 SHERMAN E P  Persons and Places in Mark Twain's Fiction  MA North Texas St Univ 1947
6190 SHERMAN Jane L  "Point of View" in Mark Twain's Narrative Method: A Study of Fictional Technique in Eight Novels  MA Univ of Minnesota 1956
6191 SHIPLEY Frederick C  Mark Twain's Tragic Stories  MA Columbia Univ 1927
6192 SIEGER Marsha  Mark Twain's Use of the Child in Social Criticism  MA Hunter Coll 1967
6193 SINGLETON Marvin K  The Medievalism of Mark Twain  MA Duke Univ 1957
6194 SKAGGS Peggy D  Folklore in *Huckleberry Finn*  MA Texas Agricultural and Mechanical Univ 1965  148 p
6195 SLOAN Betty L  Biblical Allusions in Mark Twain's Long Narratives  MA Oklahoma St Univ 1963  115 p
6196 SMALL Elizabeth  Mark Twain's Attitude Toward Europe  MA Brown Univ 1950
6197 SMIGALA Barbara L  Mark Twain's Use of Groups in Analyzing Human Nature  MA Northern Illinois Univ 1960
6198 SMITH Damian  The Religion of Mark Twain  MA De Paul Univ 1947
6199 SMITH Thomas J  Mark Twain Finds the Raft: A Report of the Last Two Years as Stormfield  MA Southern Connecticut St Coll 1964
6200 SPEEKS Ida M  Humor in Selected Travel Books by Mark Twain  MA Duke Univ 1961
6201 STAMPLEMAN Jed R  Mark Twain: The Development of the Crowd as a Character  MA Univ of Massachusetts 1966
6202 STAPPENBECK Herbert L  Mark Twain and the American Indians  MA Univ of Texas at Austin 1958  59 p
6203 STARTT William  A Survey of the Early Criticism of *The Adventures of Huckleberry Finn*, 1884-1910  MA Univ of Maryland at College Park 1963  58 p
6204 STARTZMAN Patricia K  A Comparison of the Determinism of Mark Twain and Theodore Dreiser  MA Texas Agricultural and Mechanical Univ nd  107 p
6205 STEVENSON E Burleson  Mark Twain's Attitude Toward the Negro  MA Univ of Iowa 1946
6206 STOCKDALE William A  How Calvinism and Deism Influenced Mark Twain  MA Univ of Kansas 1950
6207 STORDAHL Linn M  Mark Twain and the Frontier Spirit  MA Colorado St Univ 1966
6208 STOVALL Stella S  A Critical Study of Mark Twain's *Roughing It*  MA Baylor Univ 1951  104 p
6209 STUMBO Richard R  The Literary Reputation of Mark Twain in America, 1885-1910  MA Univ of Kansas 1965
6210 SUDDATH Jennie E  Mark Twain and Henry Adams in Account with *The Gilded Age*  MA Univ of Missouri 1942

6211 SUTRINA John J  Literary Criticism Contained in the Works of Mark Twain  MA Univ of Montana 1951
6212 SUTTON Lois M  The Influence of *Don Quixote* in the Works of Mark Twain  MA Baylor Univ 1946
6213 SWAIN Louis H  Mark Twain as a Literary Critic  MA Duke Univ 1932
6214 SWANN William R  An Investigation of the Career of Mark Twain as a Journalist  MA Univ of Missouri 1941
6215 SWANSON Paul L  The Spoken Arts of Mark Twain  MA Univ of Colorado 1966
6216 SYKES Madeline M  Mark Twain's Portrayal of Women  MA Northeast Missouri St Coll 1964
6217 TANNER Jeri  A Psychological Interpretation of Mark Twain  MA East Texas St Univ 1963
6218 TAYLOR Thomas A  I Call Mark Twain to Witness  MA Columbia Univ 1950
6219 TENNEY Thomas A  Mark Twain in 1910: A Study of His Popular and Critical Standing at the End of His Career  MA Columbia Univ 1965  137 p
6220 THAYER Gail R  Native Element in the Humor of Mark Twain  MA Univ of Tulsa 1939
6221 THERRELL Katheryne D  Folklore in the River Novels of Mark Twain  MA East Texas St Univ 1966
6222 THOENI Sr M Catherine  Literary Theory and Practice in Mark Twain: A Study of Selected Techniques as Illustrated in Selected Works  MA Coll of the Holy Names at Oakland 1966
6223 THOMAS Niles B  A Study of the Determinism of Mark Twain: Selected Novels, 1885-1910, and *What Is Man?*  MA Auburn Univ 1969
6224 THOMPSON Elizabeth J  Major Trends in Mark Twain Criticism  MA Mississippi St Univ 1966  75 p
6225 THOMPSON Joseph E  A Study of the Religion of Samuel Clemens  MA New York Univ 1951
6226 THOMSON David T  Deception in *The Adventures of Huckleberry Finn*  MA Univ of Florida 1965
6227 TOCCHI Attilia  Mark Twain and the River  MA Ca Foscari (Italy) 1961
6228 TOLTON Irene  Mark Twain as a Novelist  MA Columbia Univ 1921
6229 TOMLINSON Katie L  Mark Twain's Portrait of the Negro as Compared with Selected Fiction of His Time  MA Kansas St Teachers Coll 1964
6230 TOOLE Ross W  Mark Twain's and Charles Dudley Warner's *The Gilded Age*: An Historical and Critical Study  MA Univ of Texas at Austin 1951  93 p
6231 TRAY Sr Mary P  The Sources of *Tom Sawyer*  MA Univ of Iowa 1964
6232 TRILLING Louis R  Mark Twain's Criticism  MA Columbia Univ 1925
6233 TRUITT Dona W  Conscience in the Writings of Mark Twain  MA Northeast Missouri St Coll 1967
6234 TUCKER Carolyn H  Mark Twain's Attitudes Toward the Concept of Free Will: A Study of Selected Works  MA Bowling Green St Univ 1961
6235 TUCKER Ivey W  Elements of Folk Humor in the Works of Mark Twain  MA Wesleyan Univ 1960
6236 TURNER Margery B  Mark Twain at Mid-century, 1950-1961: A Synthesis of Critical Views Fifty Years After His Death  MA Municipal Univ of Omaha 1961
6237 VAN GUNDY Helen C  The Influence of the Bible on the Major Works of Mark Twain  MA Southwest Texas St Univ 1953
6238 VAN HEUR Marion L  *Huckleberry Finn*: The Question of "Sources"  MA Reed Coll 1963
6239 VARISCO Raymond J  Narrative Point of View in Selected Short Stories of Mark Twain: The Voice of Innocence and Experience  MA Univ of Southwestern Louisiana 1969  63 p
6240 VEST Florence E  Mark Twain and His Literary Relationships  MA Univ of Minnesota 1938
6241 VETTERLI Clarence  The Evolution of Mark Twain as Political and Social Philosopher  MA Univ of Southern California 1950

6242 WARD Fadwa E  The Influence of Virginia City on Mark Twain's Writings from 1862-1872  MA Baylor Univ 1968  197 p
6243 WARD Isabelle M  Mark Twain's Interpretation of the West  MA Columbia Univ 1923
6244 WARE Mary J  A Study of Mark Twain's *Roughing It*  MA Univ of Texas at Austin 1968
6245 WARMACK Gertrude  Play and Recreational Activities Portrayed in Mark Twain's Books  MA George Peabody Coll for Teachers 1930
6246 WATKINS Elizabeth M  Mark Twain's Religion  MA Northeast Missouri St Coll 1967
6247 WATSON Romer D  Mark Twain's Mature Attitude Towards Southern Society  MA Univ of North Carolina at Chapel Hill 1967
6248 WEAVER Katherine R  The Influence of Olivia Langdon Clemens on the Work of Mark Twain  MS Auburn Univ 1946  97 p
6249 WEBB Guilford P  An Historical and Critical Analysis of Mark Twain's *The Prince and the Pauper*  MA Univ of Texas at Austin 1951  85 p
6250 WEGELIN C A  Frontier Features in Mark Twain's Attitude Toward Europe  MA Univ of North Carolina at Chapel Hill 1942
6251 WELSH John W  The Development of the American Novel  MA Northwestern Univ 1902
6252 WEXLER Janet S  The Critics on Mark Twain's Pessimism  MA Univ of Maryland at College Park 1953  152 p
6253 WHALEN Ann T  Mark Twain's and Ernest Hemingway's Treatment of the Themes of Maturing  MA Univ of South Dakota 1959
6254 WHALING Anne  The Development of Mark Twain's Style  MA Southern Methodist Univ 1934
6255 WHARTON Mary T  Mark Twain and the Naturalism of Stephen Crane  MA Northeast Missouri St Coll 1965
6256 WHITEHEAD Katherine B  Mark Twain: The Man and His Work  MA Univ of Texas at Austin 1932
6257 WILLIAMS Patricia W  The Unity of Moral Vision in *Huckleberry Finn* and *The Catcher in the Rye*  MA Texas Agricultural and Mechanical Univ 1966  96 p
6258 WILSON Benjamin H  The Evolution of Mark Twain's *The Mysterious Stranger*  MA Univ of Pittsburgh 1950
6259 WILSON Minnie M  Mark Twain: The Development of the Humorist-Novelist  MA Southern Methodist Univ 1924
6260 WINTROUB Samuel Z  An Examination of the Charges of Pessimism Against Mark Twain  MA Univ of Texas at El Paso 1967  184 p
6261 WIRTZ Richard S  Mark Twain: The Public Personality and the Genteel Tradition  BA Amherst Coll 1961
6262 WOODS June S  Mark Twain and the Rebel Angel  MA Western St Coll of Colorado 1965
6263 WORRELL Jack E  A Study of Social Satire in Representative Novels of Mark Twain  MA Univ of Houston 1960  81 p
6264 WRIGHT Edith F  The Use of Silence as a Dramatic Technique in the Writings of Mark Twain  MA De Paul Univ 1959
6265 WRIGHT Homer L  Mark Twain: An Historian of Missouri  MA Washington Univ at St Louis 1939  129 p
6266 YOUNG Mary A  The Phelps Episode in *Huckleberry Finn*  MA Emory Univ 1959
6267 ZEIGLER Mary I  The Chivalric Ideal Toward Woman in Mark Twain  MA Univ of Notre Dame 1945
6268 ZUCKERMAN Frances  Strained Laughter: A Study of Mark Twain's *Pudd'nhead Wilson*  MA Columbia Univ 1964  96 p
6269 ZWEIG Joseph R  Jonathan Swift and Mark Twain: A Study in Methods of Satire  MA Univ of Pittsburgh 1962
See also 356, 474, 674, 700, 1774, 2409, 2478, 2568, 2745, 3052, 3077, 3079, 3080, 3115, 4020, 4133, 4963, 5687, 6296

## JOHN UPDIKE

6270 ARANOVITCH Leah  John Updike: Middleness and Rewarding Moments  MA Univ of Maine 1966  77 p
6271 BOWERMAN Vicki L  The Feminine Image in the Fiction of John Updike  MA Bowling Green St Univ 1966
6272 BRANN Carol B  The Past-present Continuum in John Updike's Fiction  MA Univ of Maryland at College Park 1968  87 p
6273 BURCHARD Rachael C  John Updike's Poetry and Fiction: An Esthetic Search  MA Northern Illinois Univ 1966
6274 DAY Ronald K  Chiron's Sacrifice: A Study of John Updike's *The Centaur*  MA Fresno St Coll 1965  72 p
6275 DEEN Carol A  The Women Characters in the Novels of John Updike  MA Texas Agricultural and Mechanical Univ 1969  63 p
6276 DEFOE Glenndale M  John Updike's Use of the Absurd Hero in His Short Fiction  MA Oklahoma St Univ 1969  65 p
6277 DRISCOLL Brian G  A Consideration of Three Stories by John Updike  BA Amherst Coll 1970
6278 EPSTEIN Charlotte  Existentialism in the Fiction of John Updike  MA Fairleigh Dickinson Univ 1969  86 p
6279 FICCO Donald F  John Updike's Preoccupation with Death and His Elaboration Upon the "Death Instinct" Found in His Fiction  MA Indiana Univ of Pennsylvania 1966  96 p
6280 HOFFMAN Arnold R  The Early Achievement of John Updike: A Study of Three Novels  MA Univ of Kansas 1965
6281 KAPNER Marilyn R  The Novels of Updike: A Version of Pastoral  MA Univ of Tulsa 1968  86 p
6282 KELLEY Winifred P  A Consideration of the Portrayal of the Anti-Hero in Selected Fiction of John Updike  MA Univ of Rhode Island 1967  71 p
6283 PETERS Edmund R  Art, Music and Literature in John Updike's Fiction  MA Florida St Univ 1968
6284 QUILLEN Frank W  The Influence of Neo-orthodoxy in the Fiction of John Updike  MA East Tennessee St Univ 1969
6285 SANDERS John P  John Updike and the Tradition of Nostalgia in American Fiction  MA Ohio St Univ 1967  76 p
6286 SCHENKER Saul I  John Updike: A Theological Quest  MA Univ of Louisville 1969  118 p
6287 SHENSTONE Susan L  Karl Barth and the Novels of John Updike: Updike's Novels as Christian Testimony  MA George Washington Univ 1969  70 p
6288 VERDUIN Kathleen  The Sense of Immortality in the Fiction of John Updike  MA George Washington Univ 1969  113 p
6289 WAGNER Don H  The Use of Sexuality in the Fiction of John Updike  MA Univ of Notre Dame 1966

## JONES VERY

6290 AHEARN Marie L  Manuscript Sermons of Jones Very  MA Boston Coll 1961
6291 BUNCH David R  Jones Very: Child of God  MA Washington Univ at St Louis 1949
6292 KIME Wayne R  Jones Very: Transcendentalism's "Dreamy Mystic"  MA Univ of Delaware 1965  114 p
6293 LANG Sr Mary M  The Quietism of Jones Very  MA Boston Coll 1958
6294 NELSON Mary S  Jones Very: A Critical Study of His Sonnets  MA Trinity Coll at Hartford 1965

## ARTEMUS WARD

6295 PERKINS Velma L  A Study of Artemus Ward and His Humor  MA George Peabody Coll for Teachers 1938

6296 YOUNG S M  A Progression in American Humor:  Artemus Ward to Mark Twain  MA Wesleyan Univ 1970
See also 6168

## MERCY OTIS WARREN

6297 CONOVER Charlotte D  A Woman's View of the American Revolution:  The Writings of Mercy Otis Warren  MA Univ of New Hampshire 1946  138 p
6298 DANKERTSEN Ethel  A Study of the Life and Works of Mercy Otis Warren  MA Wagner Coll 1967

## ROBERT PENN WARREN

6299 BALLEW Margie  A Critical Analysis of Robert Penn Warren's *Band of Angels*  M Ed Henderson St Coll nd
6300 BANKOWSKY Richard J  A Natural History of Supernaturalism:  A Study of Three Poems by Robert Penn Warren  MA Columbia Univ 1954  101 p
6301 BISHOFF Robert E  Pragmatic Man in Search of Himself:  A Study of the Novels of Robert Penn Warren  MA New Mexico Highlands Univ 1966
6302 BRUBAKER DeLacy P  The Theme of the Father in the Novels of Robert Penn Warren  MA Columbia Univ 1960  211 p
6303 BYRD John C  The Troubled Southerner:  Robert Penn Warren as a Social Critic  MA Univ of Arizona 1966
6304 COLBERT William J  Robert Penn Warren:  The Enduring Search for Self-knowledge  MA Univ of Mississippi 1969
6305 COLEMAN Thomas E  Form as Function in the Novels of Robert Penn Warren  MA Univ of Louisville 1950
6306 CRAMER James M  Moral Structure in the Novels of Robert Penn Warren  BA Rutgers St Univ 1967  86 p
6307 CRICK J Brian  R P Warren and "A Poem of Pure Imagination"  MA Univ of Western Ontario (Canada) 1966
6308 DAVIS Ellen A  The Nature of Reality:  A Study of the Poetry of Robert Penn Warren  MA Univ of Southern Mississippi 1956
6309 DOOLEY Dennis M  The Awful Responsibility of Time:  A Study of Robert Penn Warren's Concept of the Hero in the Early Novels  MA Kent St Univ 1966
6310 ELKINS Dean R  A Bibliographical and Critical Essay Upon the Robert Penn Warren Collection at University of Kentucky with a Sample Catalogue  MA Univ of Louisville 1969  73 p
6311 GRIMSHAW James A  *All the King's Men*:  Tragedy or Melodrama?  MA Texas Technological Univ 1968  89 p
6312 HALVERSTADT Barbara H  The Culmination of Images in Robert Penn Warren's *Cave*  MA Univ of North Carolina at Chapel Hill 1967
6313 HILL Michael F  Primitivism in the Novels of Robert Penn Warren  MA McNeese St Univ 1966
6314 HOCHMAN Stanley  Robert Penn Warren:  Four in Pursuit of Definition  MA Columbia Univ 1952  57 p
6315 HOHL Edward D  Robert Penn Warren and Pragmatism  MA Stanford Univ 1964
6316 LANKFORD Willard P  A Consideration of the Concept of "The Speaking Voice":  How It Is Used as a Technique for Character Development in *All the King's Men*  MA Indiana Univ of Pennsylvania 1966  68 p
6317 LEWIS Ann H  The Logic of Experience:  Robert Penn Warren's Use of History in *Wilderness*  MA Emory Univ 1965
6318 McNUTT Anne S  A Critical Analysis of the Women in Robert Penn Warren's Novels  MA East Tennessee St Univ 1969
6319 McPHERSON David C  Robert Penn Warren and the South  MA Univ of Texas at Austin 1962  101 p
6320 MICHAELSON Edith L  Self-knowledge and History in Three Novels by Robert Penn Warren  MA Hunter Coll 1969
6321 NICHOLSON Paul J  Robert Penn Warren's Philosophy:  The Theme of

Knowledge in *All the King's Men*  MA Oklahoma St Univ 1962  112 p
6322 RODEN Jerry  Technique and Tragedy in the Novels of Robert Penn Warren  MA Auburn Univ 1962
6323 SAMUELS Charles T  As Brutus Killed Caesar: Tragedy in the Novels of Robert Penn Warren  MA Ohio St Univ 1958
6324 SCOTT Willye B  Robert Penn Warren: A Modern Novelist's Image of American Experience  MA North Carolina Central Univ 1964  87 p
6325 SPICEHANDLER Daniel  Self-knowledge in the Novels of Robert Penn Warren  MA Columbia Univ 1953  61 p
6326 STEADMON Jerry D  Search for Identity in the Novels of Robert Penn Warren  MA Eastern New Mexico Univ 1965
6327 WARD Frank W III  The Problem of Focus of Narration in *All the King's Men*  MA Texas Christian Univ 1959  144 p
6328 WHITE Paula S  Robert Penn Warren's Image of the South  MA Univ of Hawaii 1958  80 p
6329 WHYTE Samuel W  Agrarianism and Father Rejection in Three Robert Penn Warren Novels  MA Bowling Green St Univ 1960
6330 WILLIAMSON Jerry M  The Patterned Protagonist in Robert Penn Warren's Novels  MA Florida St Univ 1960
6331 WILSON G Ronald  Comparing and Contrasting Characters as a Device in the Development of Robert Penn Warren's Novel *Wilderness*  MA Indiana Univ of Pennsylvania 1967  33 p
See also 5091, 5420, 6144

## BOOKER T WASHINGTON

6332 BRASHIER Martha  The Background and Philosophy of an Educator: Booker T Washington  M Ed Henderson St Coll nd
6333 REED Ernest E  Educational Philosophy of Booker T Washington  M Ed Univ of Cincinnati 1928
See also 6961

## GEORGE WASHINGTON

6334 DUNDORE Isaac N  Lives of George Washington  MA Univ of Pittsburgh 1929
6335 KEENAN James F  George Washington Biography: The Reflection of History  MA Univ of Pittsburgh 1950

## HENRY WATTERSON

6336 KIRWAN Patrick S  Henry Watterson and the World War Propaganda  MA Univ of Louisville 1939
6337 KLINGBEIL Eulalia  Henry Watterson: The Personal Journalist  MA Vanderbilt Univ 1941

## NOAH WEBSTER

6338 DODGE Robert K  Noah Webster: The Liberal-conservative Shift and *The American Dictionary of the English Language*  MA Univ of Texas at Austin 1964  81 p
6339 FRY Alderson F  Noah Webster and His Blue-back Speller  MA George Peabody Coll for Teachers 1938
6340 SCOTT Henrietta T  Noah Webster: Journalist of the Federalist Party, 1793-1798  MA Boston Univ 1929

## EUDORA WELTY

6341 APPEL Alfred Jr  Endurance and Defeat: The Contrast Between the Negro and White Characters in the Short Stories of Eudora Welty  MA Columbia Univ 1960  166 p
6342 BLACKWELL Annie L  Roots Versus Yellow Guitars: Symbol and Meaning

in Selected Short Stories by Eudora Welty  MA Florida St Univ 1964
6343 BURD Mellie R  The Progression from Innocence to Experience in the Novels of Eudora Welty  MA Univ of Louisville 1967  92 p
6344 CAIRE Fred J  Through the Burning-glass: Some Themes and Techniques in the Short Stories of Eudora Welty  MA Fresno St Coll 1967  107 p
6345 CERVENKA Majorie T  Eudora Welty as a Short Story Artist  MA Univ of Texas at El Paso 1960  136 p
6346 COLE Hunter M  Eudora Welty: Literary Critic  MA Univ of Arkansas 1963
6347 DEAN Wanda J  Characterization in the Fiction of Eudora Welty  MA Oklahoma St Univ 1961  55 p
6348 DUNLAVY Marjorie F  The Three Modes of Eudora Welty's Fiction  MA Texas Christian Univ 1955  154 p
6349 ENDEL Peggy G  Strange Felicity: A Study of Eudora Welty's Use of Mythology  MA Cornell Univ 1966
6350 HAMILTON Rachel A  Eudora Welty: A Study of Her Use of Place in Fiction  MA Wagner Coll 1964
6351 HILL Neda G  Eudora Welty: Literary Aesthete  MA Mississippi St Univ 1961  112 p
6352 JOHNSON Joan D  Ratios Among Sensational, Intellectual and Attitudinal Elements in Eudora Welty's Short Stories  MA Morehead St Univ 1967  165 p
6353 LADD Alyce M  Provincialism in the Writings of Eudora Welty  M Ed Henderson St Coll nd
6354 MENEFEE Helen H  A Study of Eudora Welty's Characters: Universal Verity in Localized Situations  MA Midwestern Univ 1963  83 p
6355 REIFF Velma B  The Guiding Heart in the Fiction of Eudora Welty: A Study in Human Relationships  MA Hardin-Simmons Univ 1964
6356 RUSSELL Mary F  Loneliness, Violence and Love in the Fiction of Eudora Welty, Flannery O'Connor and Carson McCullers  MA Univ of Massachusetts 1965
6357 SCALES Sara M  Family-related Themes in the Fiction of Eudora Welty  MA Mississippi St Univ 1968  105 p
6358 SHANKMAN Sarah R  The Unity of Eudora Welty's *The Golden Apples*  MA Emory Univ 1965
6359 SIMMONS Judith G  Dominant Themes in the Writings of Eudora Welty  MA Univ of Oklahoma 1949
6360 STOUGH Phyllis  Eudora Welty: A Master Craftsman of the American Short Story  MS Auburn Univ 1951  154 p
6361 SUTTON Kathlene H  The Moment of Revelation in the Short Stories of Eudora Welty  MA Columbia Univ 1965  127 p
6362 TURILLI Edward A  The Basic Themes in the Short Fiction of Eudora Welty  MA Univ of Rhode Island 1968  80 p
6363 VAUGHN John D  Studies in the Short Stories of Eudora Welty  MA Univ of Texas at Austin 1961  110 p
6364 WILBUR Marji A  Eudora Welty and Southern Regionalism  MA Washington St Univ at Pullman 1955
See also 1566, 3010

## GLENWAY WESCOTT

6365 DILLON Martha L  Glenway Wescott: A Question of Perspective  MA Washington Univ at St Louis nd  213 p
6366 MOORE Charles A  Style and Structure: The Early Novels of Glenway Wescott  MA Univ of Texas at Austin 1965  143 p
6367 PAGNUCCO Daniel G  A Study of Theme and Technique in Three Novels of Glenway Wescott  MA Univ of Toronto (Canada) 1966
6368 PASTORE Joanna M  Glenway Wescott: Writer of the Middle West  MA Columbia Univ 1959  120 p

## NATHANAEL WEST

6369 ALEXANDER Gordon B  Images and Structure in Nathanael West's Novel Satires  MA Univ of British Columbia (Canada) 1970
6370 BALDWIN William P III  The Influence of Dada and Surrealism on the Novels of Nathanael West  MA Clemson Univ 1968
6371 BASSHAM Gail H  Nathanael West and Dostoevsky: Compatriots of the Underworld  MA Univ of Tulsa 1965  95 p
6372 BROWN Kay K  "Toe Holes for a Flight of Fancy": The Artistic World of Nathanael West  MA Ohio St Univ 1958
6373 CRAMER Carter M  The World of Nathanael West: A Critical Interpretation  MA Kansas St Teachers Coll 1966
6374 ENGLUND David L  Some Aspects of Pictorialism in the Novels of Nathanael West  MA Univ of Hawaii 1965  41 p
6375 GINKEL James  Aspects of Alienation in the Works of Nathanael West  MA Mankato St Coll 1965  100 p
6376 GOLDSTEIN Steven  The Crowd and the Protagonist in the Works of Nathanael West  MA Tufts Univ 1966
6377 GRAFTON Lola R  A Study of Nathanael West's Need for Recipience  MA Northeast Louisiana Univ 1967  174 p
6378 GRIFFIN Steve  Mythic and Archetypal Dimensions in Selected Novels of Nathanael West  MA Chico St Coll 1968  113 p
6379 HAMMER Gael W  The Fiction of Nathanael West: A Critical Study  MA Univ of Maine 1962  82 p
6380 HOWARD Anne B  Satire and Symbol in the Novels of Nathanael West  MA Univ of New Mexico 1953
6381 LIPSCOMB Mary T  Nathanael West's Peculiar Half-world: A Study of the Imagery in *Miss Lonelyhearts*  MA Univ of North Carolina at Chapel Hill 1965
6382 MALEY Donovan C  A Visual Interpretation of Nathanael West  MA San Diego St Coll 1968  31 p
6383 PIERCE Constance  Religion, Sex and Art in the Novels of Nathanael West  MA East Carolina Univ 1969
6384 PISK George M  A Fire in Dreamland: A Suggested Unifying Principle in the Works of Nathanael West  MA Univ of Texas at Austin 1959  135 p
6385 SHAFER Michael R  The Art and Influence of Nathanael West  MA Ohio St Univ 1964  75 p
6386 SOLOMON John L  Nathanael West: Twentieth Century Prophet  MA Columbia Univ 1960  78 p
6387 SPANGER John P  A Discussion of Surrealism in Selected Novels by Nathanael West  MA Chico St Coll 1967  84 p
6388 TAYLOR Corrine Y  Existential Implications in the Novels of Nathanael West  MA Washington St Univ at Pullman 1967
6389 UNGER William E  The Absurd Vision of Nathanael West  MA Ohio St Univ 1966  137 p

See also 276, 3695

## EDITH WHARTON

6390 ALDRIDGE Margaret  Traditionalism in the Novels of Edith Wharton, Ellen Glasgow and Willa Cather as Controlled by Their Personalities  MA Univ of the Pacific 1956  183 p
6391 ASKEW Melvin W  Edith Wharton's Literary Theory  MA Univ of Oklahoma 1957  187 p
6392 BALL Maryann E  Edith Wharton: The Changing Institution of Marriage  MA Univ of Idaho 1956
6393 BATTS Maxine G  Edith Wharton's Attitude Toward Divorce as Revealed in Some Major Novels  MA Texas Agricultural and Mechanical Univ 1965  86 p

6394 BEARD Hazel M  Edith Wharton's New York  MA Univ of Texas at Austin 1938  113 p
6395 BENNETT Emma S  Autobiographical Elements in Edith Wharton's Novels  MA Univ of Texas at Austin 1940  153 p
6396 BERNSTEIN Charlotte  Social Criticism of New York Urban Life, 1870-1900, as Seen in Representative Novels of Edith Wharton, William Dean Howells, Stephen Crane  MA Columbia Univ 1951
6397 BODNAR Christyna M  Edith Wharton's Ventures Into the Beyond: Her Short Stories of the Supernatural  MA Columbia Univ 1964  84 p
6398 BOWLES Elizabeth A  New York Society in Edith Wharton's Novels  MA Univ of North Carolina at Chapel Hill 1952  104 p
6399 BROAD Lyn M  Innocence and After: The Worlds of Edith Wharton  MA Fairleigh Dickinson Univ 1967  97 p
6400 BROWN Sarah L  Social Mores and Their Effects on Characters in Edith Wharton's Novels  MA Baylor Univ 1967  117 p
6401 BROWN William R  The Use of Dramatic Irony in Edith Wharton's Fiction  MA Oklahoma St Univ 1957  92 p
6402 CANADAY Dyxie D  Edith Wharton's Conception of Tragedy in Her Society Novels  MA Oklahoma St Univ 1940  58 p
6403 CARTER M E  Social Problems Found in Edith Wharton's Novels  MA North Texas St Univ 1941
6404 CORNIER G  Some Phases of American Life as Depicted in the Fiction of Edith Wharton  MA Univ of South Dakota 1920
6405 CROSS Robert L  The Idea of Family in the Novels of Edith Wharton  MA Univ of North Carolina at Chapel Hill 1966
6406 CUEN G E  Old New York Influences on Mrs Wharton's Novels  MA Univ of Texas at El Paso 1943  56 p
6407 DENNIS Eva A  Edith Wharton on the Craft of Fiction  MA Univ of Florida nd
6408 ELLIS Mary W  Edith Wharton: Reflection of Her Life in Selected Works  M Ed Henderson St Coll nd
6409 FRAAD Therese J  Aspects of Social Change in Some Novels of Edith Wharton  MA Columbia Univ 1955  70 p
6410 FRESH DuDene E  Edith Wharton's Men and Women: A Study of Techniques of Characterization  MA Univ of Hawaii 1962  89 p
6411 GIPSON Miriam R  Victimization and Moral Judgments in Edith Wharton's Novels and Novelettes  MA Univ of North Carolina at Chapel Hill 1969  127 p
6412 GRIPPA Elvira  Edith Wharton and Italy  MA Columbia Univ 1941
6413 HAYNES John B  The Trapped Individual: The Moral Dilemma in Edith Wharton's Fiction  MA Colorado St Univ 1962
6414 HESSENAUER Merrettei I  The Short Stories of Edith Wharton  MA Indiana Univ 1935
6415 HEWITT Rosalie  The Concept of the Lady in Selected Novels of Edith Wharton and Ellen Glasgow  MA Purdue Univ 1965  182 p
6416 HUGHES Arvilla J  The Women in Mrs Wharton's Novels  MA Univ of Maine 1941  98 p
6417 HUGUELET Joyce A  Morality in the Fiction of Edith Wharton  MA East Carolina Univ 1963
6418 JONES Frances  Portrait of Edith Wharton as Revealed by Her Friends and Critics  M Ed Henderson St Coll nd
6419 JONES Jean  The Voluntary Exile: Edith Wharton in France, 1914-1919  MA American Univ 1966
6420 LEEVER Richard S  Edith Wharton: Satirist  MA Univ of Texas at Austin 1949  180 p
6421 LIGHT Ellen M  Edith Wharton's European Panorama  MA Univ of Texas at El Paso 1951  110 p
6422 LOESCH Harold G  The Relationship Between Louis Bromfield and Edith Wharton  MA Kent St Univ 1964
6423 LoLORDO Mary W  The Function of Interior Decoration in Edith Wharton's

The Age of Innocence  MA Univ of North Carolina at Chapel Hill 1968
6424 McCLELLAND F Emma  Edith Wharton: A Woman of Letters  M Ed Temple Univ 1932  175 p
6425 McELROY Sr Rose M  Edith Wharton: Social Historian  MA Siena Heights Coll 1946  78 p
6426 MacLEAN Mary V  Edith Wharton: Novelist of Manners  MA Univ of Louisville 1966  96 p
6427 MOORE Jean B  Edith Wharton's Portrait of the American Scene as Revealed in Selected Works  M Ed Henderson St Coll nd
6428 MORRISON Eva V  Edith Wharton as the Critic of New York Society  MA Univ of Kansas 1936
6429 MORSE Marian J  The Human Dilemma, Divorce, in Selected Fiction of Edith Wharton  MA Univ of Houston 1967  121 p
6430 MURPHY Mary W  Edith Wharton: Her Interpretation of the American Tragedy  MA Columbia Univ 1960  118 p
6431 NASCIMENTO Daniel C  The Problem of Style in Edith Wharton's Novels with Special Emphasis Upon *The House of Mirth*  MA Univ of Maryland at College Park 1963
6432 NOWIK Nancy A  Edith Wharton's Moral Vision in Three New York Novels  MA Stanford Univ 1965
6433 PHILLIPS Edith  Edith Wharton's Women Characters  MA Univ of Texas at Austin 1939  112 p
6434 PIROZZI John P  A Study of Class in Four of the Old New York Series of Novels by Edith Wharton: *The House of Mirth* (1905), *The Custom of the Country* (1913), *The Age of Innocence* (1920) and *Old New York* (1924)  MA Fairleigh Dickinson Univ 1969  72 p
6435 POSTELL John M  The Poetry of Edith Wharton  MA Ohio St Univ 1950
6436 RALPH E R  The Extent to Which the Novels and Short Stories of Edith Wharton Show the Influence of Henry James  MA Ohio St Univ 1931
6437 RAVENEL Mary C  The Theme of Innocence in the Major Works of Edith Wharton  MA Hunter Coll 1967
6438 SENZEE Norma K  Determinism in C Major: Three Novels by Edith Wharton  MA Brigham Young Univ 1963  95 p
6439 SILVESTRI Elena  Mrs Wharton's Art of Fiction  MA Ca Foscari (Italy) 1946
6440 SIMMONS Myrtle  Character Types in Edith Wharton's Fiction  MA Univ of Mississippi 1950  255 p
6441 SIMONS Mary P  Edith Wharton and Henry James: Their Contrasting Attitudes Towards European and American Society as Shown in Their Novels  MA West Chester St Coll 1965
6442 SMITH Grace K  The Permanent Contribution: A Critical Appraisal of the Fiction of Edith Wharton  MA Univ of Vermont 1953  120 p
6443 TAGGE Ann W  Edith Wharton's Treatment of Marriage  MA Baylor Univ 1964  285 p
6444 TEICHGRAEBER S E  Art and Artifact in Selected Fiction of Edith Wharton  MA Rice Univ 1964
6445 TEN EYCK Dorothy B  Edith Wharton: A Study of Her Novels  MA St Univ of New York at Albany 1935
6446 THOMAS Brigid O  The Trapped Sensibility in Edith Wharton's Novels  MA Whittier Coll nd
6447 THOMPSON Dorothy L  Edith Wharton as a Novelist of Manners  MA Univ of Wyoming 1965
6448 TINSLEY Beverly B  Irony in the Novelettes of Edith Wharton  MA Baylor Univ 1964  218 p
6449 WARREN Ethel  A Correlation of the Life and Work of Edith Wharton  MA Ohio St Univ 1943
6450 WATSON Calvin A  An Original Television Adaptation and Production Thesis of *Ethan Frome*  MA Washington St Univ at Pullman 1957
6451 WERTHEIM Flora G  The Social Backgrounds of Edith Wharton's Novels  MA Univ of Texas at Austin 1934

6452 WHEELER Ferrel  An Analysis of Six Representative Women Characters in Edith Wharton's Novels  MA North Texas St Univ 1942
6453 WHITEHOUSE Jean H  The Primary Influences on the Characters in Edith Wharton's Novels  MA Washington Univ at St Louis 1948  107 p
6454 WHITNEL James F  The Significance of Interior Decoration for Structure and Characterization in Edith Wharton's *The House of Mirth*  MA Univ of North Carolina at Chapel Hill 1965
6455 WILLIAMS Caro-Beth S  Edith Wharton: Satirist and Social Critic  MA Texas Christian Univ 1938  168 p
6456 WOLFE Ralph H  Edith Wharton's Use of Coincidence in Some Representative Novels  MA Bowling Green St Univ 1956

See also 536, 1908, 2256, 2689, 3259, 3283, 3363, 3387

## STEWART EDWARD WHITE

6457 McCALL Alice  Stewart Edward White's Depiction of American Frontier Characters  MA Univ of Texas at Austin 1943  132 p
6458 McCALL Margery S  The Life and Works of Stewart Edward White  MA Louisiana St Univ 1939

## WALT WHITMAN

6459 ABERNATHY Peter L  Whitman and Architecture: A Study of His Influence on Sullivan and Wright  MA Univ of North Carolina at Chapel Hill 1965
6460 ARNETT Euva  Whitman: The Poet of America  MA George Peabody Coll for Teachers 1937
6461 ASHWORTH J Delmer  Walt Whitman: Editor Poet  MA Texas Arts and Industries Univ 1953
6462 AXTELL Phyllis M  Pantheistic Thought in Walt Whitman's Poetry  MA Texas Technological Univ 1968  59 p
6463 BAKER William C  The Influence of Walt Whitman on John Burroughs  MA Univ of Pittsburgh 1941
6464 BANKS Foldine W  Walt Whitman and the Vision of Democracy  MA Virginia St Coll 1967
6465 BARTHEN Helen L  Romanticism in Walt Whitman  MA Boston Univ 1931
6466 BAUMAN Elizabeth A  Whitman and the Western Movement  MA Univ of Texas at Austin 1956  144 p
6467 BECKUM Peggy C  Whitman's Use of Myth and Archetypal Patterns  MA Texas Technological Univ 1968  77 p
6468 BELL C P  Symbolism in *Leaves of Grass*  MA North Texas St Univ 1943
6469 BENTLEY Robert H  The Development of Whitman's Poetic Abilities as Reflected in "Song of the Open Road"  MA Pacific Univ 1962
6470 BETTIS Lottie L  Whitman and His Influence  MA Baylor Univ 1949  217 p
6471 BIRKY Wilbur J  Ethics in *Leaves of Grass*  MA Univ of Iowa 1964
6472 BLACK Larry D  A Critical Study of Whitman's "Calamus" Section of *Leaves of Grass*  MA Kansas St Coll of Pittsburg 1966
6473 BLOODWORTH Bertha E  Walt Whitman: Journalist  MA Univ of Florida 1955
6474 BOOZMAN A P  Walt Whitman's Influence Abroad  MA North Texas St Univ 1950
6475 BOROFF David  Walt Whitman and Science  MA Brooklyn Coll of City Univ of New York 1949
6476 BOWMAN Barclay F  Walt Whitman's Concept of War  MA Univ of Texas at Austin 1953  216 p
6477 BRADFORD Ruth A  Walt Whitman's Reaction to Politics from 1839 to 1892  MA George Washington Univ 1933  59 p
6478 BRAND Wayne E  The Literary Influence of Walt Whitman on Hamlin Garland  MA Univ of Texas at Austin 1952  126 p
6479 BREEVER Virginia M  A Tabulated Analysis of the Philosophy of Walt Whitman  MA Univ of Maryland at College Park 1926  45 p
6480 BROIDA Lucy K  Democratic Philosophy of Walt Whitman  MA Univ of

Pittsburgh 1925
6481 BROWN Miriam  The Influence of Walt Whitman on Modern American Poetry  MA Univ of Texas at Austin 1927
6482 BROWN M K  Walt Whitman and the Theatre  MA North Texas St Univ 1957
6483 BUTHOD Mary M  Walt Whitman as Poet of the American Garden Myth  MA Univ of Tulsa 1966  51 p
6484 CALDERON Pablo O  A Comparison of Walt Whitman and Jose Santos Chocano as Exponents of the Spirit of Americanism  MA Texas Technological Univ 1947
6485 CAMPBELL Carl E  The Knoxville Walt Whitman Fellowship  MA Univ of Tennessee 1956  54 p
6486 CAMPBELL Donald A  An Approach to the Internal Structure of *Leaves of Grass*  MA Univ of Alberta (Canada) 1964
6487 CARDEN Ruth  Walt Whitman and the Civil War  MA Southern Methodist Univ 1930
6488 CARLON William T  Four Masks of Walt Whitman in the 1855 Edition of *Leaves of Grass*  BA Rutgers St Univ 1966  64 p
6489 CARLSON Florence M  Pantheistic Elements in the Poetry of Walt Whitman  MA Texas Arts and Industries Univ 1950
6490 CASEY Lillian L  Walt Whitman as Judged by His Contemporaries  MA Univ of Maryland at College Park 1933  121 p
6491 CHALFANT Edna R  Walt Whitman and His Influence on the American Poets Since 1912  MA Boston Univ 1931
6492 COFFEEN Robert G  Onomastics in *Leaves of Grass*: A Study of Place Names as Materials for Poetic Use  MA Univ of North Carolina at Chapel Hill 1964
6493 COFFMAN Lucile  Whitman's Reading Before 1855  MA Univ of Texas at Austin 1929
6494 CONNOR Francis E  The Democracy of Walt Whitman as Exemplified in "Democratic Vistas"  MA Boston Univ 1948
6495 COSTA Alan M  Brazilian Editions of *Leaves of Grass*  MA Univ of North Carolina at Chapel Hill 1960
6496 COX Diana H  An Analytical and Critical Study of Walt Whitman's Civil War Poetry  MA West Texas St Univ 1962  66 p
6497 COX Hazel  Four Aspects of Walt Whitman's Philosophy  MA Univ of Houston 1940  60 p
6498 CRAWLEY Thomas E  The Structure of *Leaves of Grass*  MA Univ of North Carolina at Chapel Hill 1965
6499 CROWL John R  The Proof of a Poet: A Study of Whitman's Acceptance in the United States in the First Quarter of the Twentieth Century  MA Univ of Louisville 1967  149 p
6500 CURRIER Barbara  Walt Whitman's Literary Criticism  MA Columbia Univ 1965  137 p
6501 DAVIDSON Loren K  A Decade of Whitman Criticism and Research, 1940-1949  MA Univ of Kentucky 1955  175 p
6502 DAWSON David L  Walt Whitman's Democratic Hero: A Reconciliation of Emerson and Carlyle  MA Butler Univ 1967
6503 DE HAVEN Rhea B  Monism in the Works of Walt Whitman  MA Univ of Iowa 1932
6504 DESCLOS Br Daniel  Walt Whitman: Critique of Love  MA Boston Coll 1948
6505 DIONNE Roger C  The Birth and Death of the First Edition of *Leaves of Grass*  MA Georgetown Univ 1966  244 p
6506 DUNFORD Thomas A  Walt Whitman: An Analytic Study of the Symbolic Theme of "Manly Love" in *Leaves of Grass*  MA Bowling Green St Univ 1955
6507 DUNSTAN Marjorie G  The Structure and Meaning of Walt Whitman's "Song of Myself"  MA Univ of Hawaii 1946  106 p
6508 ECKHOFF Eugene  Whitman's Perpetual Orbit  MA St Cloud St Coll 1969  92 p
6509 EDWARDS Anne L  *Whitman, 1920*: A Play in Three Acts  MA Univ of

North Carolina at Raleigh 1953   95 p
6510  ELLIOTT Mary A   The Southern Fugitives:  Their Opposition to the Midwestern School of Whitmanesque Poetry   MA Univ of Maryland at College Park 1962   71 p
6511  FARBER Nathan   Walt Whitman and the *Brooklyn Eagle*   MA Brooklyn Coll of City Univ of New York 1937   50 p
6512  FARNUM Bruce E   Patterns of Protest:  Walt Whitman to Henry Miller   BA Amherst Coll 1962
6513  FAUER Louis C   Walt Whitman:  A Critical Analysis of the Contemporary Social Institution   MA Northeast Louisiana Univ 1970   97 p
6514  FEIN Richard J   *Leaves of Grass* and the Bible:  A Comparison of Technique, Thought and Vision   MA Brooklyn Coll of City Univ of New York 1954   114 p
6515  FLYNN Bernard F   Camps of White and Camps of Green:  The Shifting Realities of Walt Whitman's Civil War Poems   MA Chico St Coll 1969   126 p
6516  FORD Dimple L   The Importance of Whitman's Reading as Seen in His *Leaves of Grass*   MA Texas Technological Univ 1931   55 p
6517  FULGHUM Walter B   Walt Whitman and the Quakers   MA Southern Methodist Univ 1932
6518  GOLDBERG Bernard A   A Phrenological Explication of Section 15 of "Song of Myself"   MA Univ of Texas at El Paso 1967   121 p
6519  GOODSON Lester   A Critical Study of the 1856 Edition of *Leaves of Grass*   MA Univ of Tulsa 1968   168 p
6520  GOTT George E   Walt Whitman:  Poet of the Sea   MA Univ of Texas at Austin 1953   155 p
6521  GRACE C L   The Influence of Women on Walt Whitman   MA North Texas St Univ 1952
6522  GRANADE Charles J   Walt Whitman's Concept of God in "Song of Myself"   MS Auburn Univ 1950   82 p
6523  GREENOUGH Doris A   Whitman's Use of Catalogues in *Leaves of Grass*   MA Indiana Univ 1942
6524  GURLEY Nell W   Walt Whitman and the Bible   MA Baylor Univ 1935   102 p
6525  HADDAD Salwa   Walt Whitman's View of Reality   MA Univ of Kansas 1964
6526  HALL William I   The Kinds of People in Walt Whitman's Poems   MA George Peabody Coll for Teachers 1935
6527  HARGROVE Michael C   The Female Image in Whitman's Poetry   MA Texas Technological Univ 1966
6528  HARRISON Stanley R   The Flower of Her Temperament:  Walt Whitman's Material Fixation Manifested in *Leaves of Grass*   MA Brooklyn Coll of City Univ of New York 1957   66 p
6529  HARTLE A V   Whitman in Modern Criticism   MA Ohio St Univ 1935
6530  HILL Betty J   A Study in Whitman's Symbolism   MA Northeast Louisiana Univ 1962   77 p
6531  HILL Jane K   The Structure of Whitman's "Song of Myself"   MA Univ of Louisville 1949
6532  HILLIARD Sally R   Studies in the Diction of Walt Whitman's Poetry   MA Univ of Texas at Austin 1936
6533  HOMSLEY Bonnie S   Archetypal Patterns in Whitman's Poems   MA Univ of Oklahoma 1964
6534  HOSEY Adella A   A Study of Walt Whitman's Critical Opinions   MA Northwestern Univ 1931
6535  HUDSON Heather   "A Passage to More Than India":  An Exploration of Whitman's Cosmic Philsophy   BA Univ of British Columbia (Canada) 1968
6536  HUGGINS Jack R   The Influence of Walt Whitman's Social Background on His Poetry   M Ed Henderson St Coll nd
6537  IRBY Jeanine A   Elements of the Kantian Philosophy in Whitman's Poetry   MA Texas Christian Univ 1966   87 p
6538  IRELAND Harry B   The Unifying Elements in Whitman's "Song of Myself"   MA Univ of Oklahoma 1956

6539 JANSSEN Caroline F  An Annotated Bibliography of the Walt Whitman Collection in the University of Tulsa's McFarlin Library  MA Univ of Tulsa 1962  74 p
6540 JEFFERIES Roberta L  Philosophical Parallels in the Works of Walt Whitman and John Steinbeck  MA Lamar Technological Univ 1967  103 p
6541 JENSEN Millie D  Whitman and Hegel:  On the Slopes of History  MA Colorado St Univ 1960
6542 JEWELL Ross M  Whitman's Conception of the Soul as Expressed in *Leaves of Grass*  MA Indiana Univ 1950
6543 JONES Granville H  Walt Whitman, Thomas Wolfe and Jack Kerouac:  Common Origins and Common Aims  MA Columbia Univ 1961  169 p
6544 KAMEI Shunsuke  Walt Whitman's Politics:  1840-1860  MA Washington Univ at St Louis 1961  128 p
6545 KAUTZ Eloise K  An Analysis of the Critical Estimate of Whitman's *Leaves of Grass* from Its Publication in 1855 to Whitman's Death in 1892  MA Syracuse Univ 1944  140 p
6546 KAYE J  Nationalism in Whitman's Poetry, 1855-1867  M Phil Univ of London (England) 1968
6547 KELLEY A W  Walt Whitman's Knowledge and Use of the Art of Music  MA Univ of North Carolina at Chapel Hill 1924
6548 KHER Inder N  Walt Whitman and the Integral Experience  MA McMaster Univ (Canada) 1966
6549 KING Robert W  The Fruition of Beauty:  A Study of the Sources of Whitman's Style  MA Colorado St Univ 1961
6550 KOLB Harold H Jr  "Hush'd Be the Camps Today":  A Study of the Poetry of Walt Whitman  BA Amherst Coll 1955
6551 KOONCE P L  The Use of Geography in Whitman's *Leaves of Grass*  MA North Texas St Univ 1946
6552 KRUMME Edwynne F  The Religious Perspective of Walt Whitman  MA Univ of Tulsa 1962  68 p
6553 KUHN John G  The Inaudible Rhyme:  The Cyclic Artistry in Walt Whitman's Poetry  MS Purdue Univ 1960  181 p
6554 KUSPIT Judith C  Three Studies in Poetry:  Barnfield's *Cynthia*; Eliot's *The Cocktail Party* and Euripides' *Alcestis*; Whitman's 1855 *Preface*  MA Pennsylvania St Univ 1966
6555 KYTLE Juanita S  Walt Whitman and Thomas Wolfe:  Singers of America  MA Univ of Oklahoma 1946
6556 LAGG Mabel G  Walt Whitman's Friends  MA Baylor Univ 1951  106 p
6557 LANIER Mary E  The Analysis of the Whitman Travel Dialogue, 1888-1889  MA Univ of Tennessee 1969  76 p
6558 LAUTER Paul  A Secret Self as Poet:  Walt Whitman Reconsidered  MA Indiana Univ 1955
6559 LEE Lois E  A Study of the Poetic Sources of Walt Whitman  MA Univ of Hawaii 1936
6560 LEE Yun G  Versions of Death in Six Poems in Walt Whitman  MA Univ of Hawaii 1965  49 p
6561 LEIFESTE Minnie M  The Mind of Walt Whitman  MA Univ of Texas at Austin 1931
6562 LINDSAY Kathryn D  Mathematics:  A Clue to Whitman's Philosophy  MA Southern Connecticut St Coll 1965
6563 LORANCE Maurine  Oriental Ideas in *Leaves of Grass*  MA Univ of Texas at Austin 1934
6564 McCLAIN Ellamay  A Survey of the Use of Color in Walt Whitman's *Leaves of Grass*  MA Univ of Texas at Austin 1941  67 p
6565 McDONALD Janet K  Walt Whitman:  Apostle of Democracy  MA Columbia Univ 1942
6566 McGINNIS H H  Whitman's Friends and Literary Acquaintances  MA North Texas St Univ 1947
6567 MacKAY Helen H  The Romantic Concept of the Poet-Prophet and Its

Culmination in Walt Whitman  MA Univ of North Carolina at Greensboro 1970
6568 McKERAHAN Annabelle L  Whitman: An Evolution from Emerson  MA Univ of Pittsburgh 1929
6569 McMANUS Patrick F  Walt Whitman's "Knit of Identity"  MA Washington St Univ at Pullman 1962
6570 McNEIL Katherine V  Sublimity in *Leaves of Grass*  MA Texas Woman's Univ 1966
6571 MALONE Walter K  Parallels to Hindu and Taoist Thought in Walt Whitman  MA Temple Univ 1964  320 p
6572 MALONEY Violetta G  Walt Whitman and the Fine Arts, Exclusive of Music  MA Indiana Univ 1942
6573 MANNIX Edith L  Walt Whitman: Poet of Death  MA Univ of Texas at Austin 1954  175 p
6574 MARKS Alfred H  Triadic Imagery in *Leaves of Grass*  MA Syracuse Univ 1949  68 p
6575 MARTINEZ Amelia M  A Study of Critical Opinion Affecting Whitman's Art and Technique  MA Univ of Texas at Austin 1954
6576 MATHENY C A  Walt Whitman's Philosophy  MA Ohio St Univ 1928
6577 MAYNARD Amanda J  A Study of Whitman's and Lanier's Poems of the Sea  MA Univ of North Carolina at Chapel Hill 1959  87 p
6578 MEYERS Donna  Whitman and Music  MA Univ of Florida nd
6579 MILLER Wa'ne C  Walt Whitman's Next Fold of the Future  MA Columbia Univ 1961  94 p
6580 MITCHELL William H  Whitman's House of Thought: A Collective Study of the 1855 and 1856 Editions of *Leaves of Grass*  MA Columbia Univ 1936
6581 MONTGOMERY Althea E  The Ideals of Democracy Expressed in the Writings of Walt Whitman  MA Univ of Iowa 1915
6582 MORELLI Maria  Walt Whitman: An American Poet  MA Ca Foscari (Italy) 1940
6583 MOSER Rex E  Musical Effects in Walt Whitman's "Song of Myself"  MA Univ of Hawaii 1963  69 p
6584 MUKERJEE Sipra  *Leaves of Grass* and the *Bhagavad Gita*: A Comparative Study  MS Kansas St Coll of Pittsburg 1968
6585 NICKLESS Fred P Jr  Walt Whitman's Democratic Concepts  MA Tufts Univ 1949
6586 OSBURN Luke  Whitman's Main Philosophical Ideas: An Interpretation  MA Univ of Texas at Austin 1934
6587 OSIKOWSKI John  An Examination of Whitman's Ethics  MA Univ of Texas at El Paso 1953  92 p
6588 PARSONS Olive W  Whitman the Non-Hegelian  MA Indiana Univ 1942
6589 PHELPS Maxine  The Major Influences on the Life and Works of Walt Whitman  M Ed Henderson St Coll nd
6590 PICARD A M  Walt Whitman and His French Critics  MA Boston Univ 1920
6591 POWELL Delores E  The Impact of Victorianism on the Works of Walt Whitman  MA Howard Univ 1954  169 p
6592 PROPST Hattie C  Walt Whitman's Literary Reputation from the First Edition of *Leaves of Grass* in 1855 to 1919  MA Oklahoma St Univ 1942  91 p
6593 PUGH Redford  A Study of the Relative Applicability of the Term "Poet of Democracy" to Walt Whitman  MA Univ of Texas at El Paso 1966  147 p
6594 RAMOS Dorothy C  Whitman's Dialectic: The Fusion of a Philosophy and a Poetics  MA Univ of North Carolina at Chapel Hill 1967
6595 RANKIN Elizabeth R  The Problem of Identity in Whitman's "Song of Myself"  MA Univ of Oklahoma 1965
6596 RATH Sushama  Reflections of Indian Philosophy in Walt Whitman  MA Washington St Univ at Pullman 1965
6597 REGER Laura S  Walt Whitman: Basic Christian Tenets in His Work  MA Chico St Coll 1967  111 p

6598 REGISTER Willie R  Walt Whitman: An American Prophet, and the Civil War  MA Auburn Univ 1965  91 p
6599 RHO-SERVI Lidia  Walt Whitman  MA Ca Foscari (Italy) 1930
6600 RICE Nancy H  Intimations of Immortality in the Poetry of Walt Whitman, Emily Dickinson and Herman Melville  MA Univ of Massachusetts 1967  91 p
6601 RODMAN Marion R  Walt Whitman's Literary Criticism  MA Washington St Univ at Pullman 1942
6602 ROSENBLATT Paul  Whitman's Vision of the Composite American  MA Brooklyn Coll of City Univ of New York 1951  81 p
6603 ROTH George M  Walt Whitman and Socialism  MA George Washington Univ 1934  193 p
6604 RUSSELL Nancy K  Scholarly Studies of Whitman's Prosody  MA Univ of North Carolina at Chapel Hill 1961
6605 SADLER Henrietta  A Comparison of Walt Whitman and Carl Sandburg  MA Univ of Richmond 1945  86 p
6606 SALISBURY Nancy L  Whitman and Slavery  MA Univ of Texas at Austin 1952  105 p
6607 SANDER Eunice E  The Urban Element in Walt Whitman's *Leaves of Grass*  MA Ohio St Univ 1948
6608 SANDERS Mary K  *Leaves of Grass* in the Prophetic Tradition: A Study of Walt Whitman's Poetic Method  MA Univ of North Carolina at Chapel Hill 1967
6609 SCHWEGEL Douglas M  Walt Whitman's Attitude Toward the Reception of His Poetry  MA George Washington Univ 1956  89 p
6610 SEITER Richard D  The Criticism and Evaluation of Walt Whitman's "Out of the Cradle Endlessly Rocking"  MA Bowling Green St Univ 1965
6611 SIMPSON S L  Walt Whitman's Conception of Democracy  BA Univ of British Columbia (Canada) 1928
6612 SLOVER Frances  The Impact of the Bible on Walt Whitman and His Writings  MA Memphis St Univ 1960
6613 SMITH Charles A  Walt Whitman and Zen Buddhism: A Comparative Survey  MA Univ of Maine 1967  146 p
6614 SMITH Dorothy G  Walt Whitman and Democracy  MA Univ of Maryland at College Park 1938
6615 SMITH Harriet  Walt Whitman and Rabindranath Tagore: Precursors of Universal Man  MA Univ of Massachusetts 1963
6616 SMITH Patrick D  Whitman's Literary Reputation in the Twentieth Century  MS Kansas St Coll at Pittsburg 1957
6617 SOLA Renzo  Walt Whitman's Poetry  MA Ca Foscari (Italy) 1946
6618 STAGEBERG N Clifford  Whitman's Theory of Poetry  MA Univ of Iowa 1932
6619 STENBERG Marjorie N  Walt Whitman as a Literary Critic  MA Univ of Texas at Austin 1935
6620 STEPHENS Patsy L  Political and Social Topics in Walt Whitman's Poetry  MA Howard Univ 1963  183 p
6621 STEPHENS Robert O  Walt Whitman and Religion  MA Univ of Texas at Austin 1951  141 p
6622 SUHRE Margery  The "Great Chain of Being" in *Leaves of Grass*  MA Bowling Green St Univ 1940
6623 TANNER James T  The Concept of the Superman in Walt Whitman's *Leaves of Grass*  MA Texas Technological Univ 1963  76 p
6624 TANSEL Matha R  Criticism of Walt Whitman  MA Univ of Oklahoma 1936
6625 TILFORD Sallie R  Whitman's America  MA Howard Univ 1946  63 p
6626 TIMOLIN B J  Wordsworth and Whitman: A Comparative Study  MA North Texas St Univ 1944
6627 TUCKER Charles T  A Comparative Investigation of the Lives and Poetry of Walt Whitman and Hart Crane  MA Fairleigh Dickinson Univ 1967  51 p
6628 TWAY Elsa  Walt Whitman's Poetic Claims and Limitations  MA Ohio St Univ 1917
6629 ULLRICH Vera  A Study of the Critical Controversy over Walt Whitman's

Literary Defects   MA Univ of Kansas 1934
6630  UZZLE William T Jr   The Political Views of Walt Whitman   MA Univ of
      North Carolina at Chapel Hill 1958   69 p
6631  VALENTINE Lenora B   Walt Whitman's Concept of Patriotism   MA Virginia
      St Coll 1956   81 p
6632  VAN EGMOND Peter G   Walt Whitman's Study of Oratory and Uses of It
      in *Leaves of Grass*   MA Univ of North Carolina at Chapel Hill 1966
6633  WAKELAND Myrtle   Walt Whitman and Music   MA Texas Arts and Industries
      Univ 1950
6634  WALES Eula M   A Literary Expression of Whitman's Ideas of Democracy
      MA Texas Technological Univ 1932   97 p
6635  WARE Leobel   Some Functions of Whitman's Catalogues   MA Univ of Texas
      at Austin 1938   81 p
6636  WATTER Irene   The Growth of Whitman's Reputation in America   MA Southern
      Methodist Univ 1921
6637  WEIS Theodore G   Scientific Thought and Its Influence on Walt Whitman
      MA Univ of Maryland at College Park 1938   172 p
6638  WELLS Elizabeth E   The Structure of Walt Whitman's 1860 *Leaves of
      Grass*   MA Ohio St Univ 1968   60 p
6639  WHITE Lana   Walt Whitman's Treatment of Death in Prose and Poetry
      MA West Texas St Univ nd   98 p
6640  WHITENER Catherine V   Walt Whitman and the South   MA Duke Univ 1940
6641  WILLERS Alfred C   The Poetic Ideal of Photographic Realism in *Leaves
      of Grass*   MA Columbia Univ 1963   176 p
6642  WILLINGHAM John R   The Whitman Tradition in Recent American Literature
      MA Univ of Oklahoma 1953
6643  WISE LaFern   Walt Whitman's Treatment of Death   MA Southern Illinois
      Univ at Carbondale 1949   60 p
6644  WOOD Richard C   The Effect of the Civil War on the Development of
      *Leaves of Grass*   MA Columbia Univ 1950
6645  WOODELL Charles H   Poetic Theory and Practice in Whitman's *Leaves of
      Grass*   MA Wake Forest Univ 1964
6646  WOODRUM Mildred   Walt Whitman: Barnburner in Politics and Politician
      in Poetry   MA Texas Christian Univ 1966   97 p
6647  WRIGHT Verbie   The Influence of Walt Whitman's Social Background on
      "Song of Myself"   M Ed Henderson St Coll nd
6648  WROBEL Arthur   Walt Whitman and the Fowler Brothers: Phrenology Finds
      a Bard   MA Univ of North Carolina at Chapel Hill 1968
See also 704, 740, 1402, 1403, 1437, 1448, 1461, 1488, 1489, 1514, 3838, 4301,
      4897, 4976, 4987, 6859, 6925

## JOHN GREENLEAF WHITTIER

6649  BURKHARDT Mildred   The Democratic Tradition in Whittier   MA Butler
      Univ 1933
6650  CARMINE Hollie   A Comparison of John Greenleaf Whittier and Robert Frost
      as Poets of New England, Particularly Rural New England   MA Florida
      St Univ 1937
6651  CARROLL Camilla L   The Liberalism of Whittier as Reflected in His
      Life and Work   MA Ohio St Univ 1942
6652  DENNY Lois J   John Greenleaf Whittier: A Psychograph   MA Boston Univ
      1949
6653  HABEL Herbert P   The Literary Reputation of John Greenleaf Whittier
      MA Columbia Univ 1943
6654  HALLISEY H A   Whittier's Work as Influenced by His Visits to
      New Hampshire   MA Univ of New Hampshire 1940   51 p
6655  HILDEBRAND Reuben P   Whittier's Treatment of New England History and
      Legend   MA Univ of Pittsburgh 1929
6656  HOWELL Odessie   Whittier's Use of the Bible   MA Univ of Texas at Austin
      1931

6657 HUGHES James M  The Romantic Period in Whittier, 1825-1833  MA Univ of Maine 1946  174 p
6658 LUNDAY Lena M  The People of Whittier's Poetry  MA Univ of Texas at Austin 1937  147 p
6659 McDOWELL Bill D  The Influence of Women on the Literary Career of John Greenleaf Whittier  MA Texas Christian Univ 1966  106 p
6660 MILLARD Anne E  John Greenleaf Whittier's Relationship to Ralph Waldo Emerson and Transcendentalism  MA Univ of Tennessee 1965
6661 NICHOLAIDES Evangeline I  The Influence of Haverhill and Amesbury in the Life of John Greenleaf Whittier  MA Boston Univ 1944
6662 NYQUIST Millicent  John Greenleaf Whittier: Interpreter of New England  MA Univ of Kansas 1945
6663 O'BRIEN Mary L  Whittier's Poems and Their Essex County Background  MA Univ of Maine 1951  81 p
6664 OHR Mary E  Literary and Historical Allusions in Whittier's Poetry  MA Univ of Texas at Austin 1939  146 p
6665 OSBORNE R S  Whittier's Religion as It Is Expressed in His Poetry  MA Univ of North Carolina at Chapel Hill 1940
6666 PEPPER Gertrude B  The Influence of the American West on the Thought of Whittier, Emerson and Lowell  MA Univ of Mississippi 1945  196 p
6667 RABE Katie G  Whittier as a Religious Poet  MA Texas Arts and Industries Univ 1949
6668 RENZINO Giuseppina  John Greenleaf Whittier  MA Ca Foscari (Italy) 1932
6669 RICE Margaret S  John Greenleaf Whittier: The Native Spokesman of New England  MA Univ of Vermont 1933  63 p
6670 SHAW C E  The Ethical Element of Whittier  MA Boston Univ 1914
6671 SLATER Evalina  Nature in Whittier's Poetry  MA Hardin-Simmons Univ 1934
6672 SNOW Gregory  Three Views of the Puritans: Whittier, Miller and O'Neill  MA Wayne St Univ 1965
6673 SULLIVAN R M  The Religion of John Greenleaf Whittier as Revealed in His Poetry  MA Boston Univ 1941
6674 TULGAN Gertrude R  The Influence of American Transcendentalism on John Greenleaf Whittier  MA Brooklyn Coll of City Univ of New York 1951  52 p
6675 WEST Ruth  Literary Allusions in Whittier's Prose  MA Univ of Texas at Austin 1940  245 p
6676 WISE Margaret E  The Bible in the Poetry of John Greenleaf Whittier  MA George Peabody Coll for Teachers 1936
See also 1458

## RICHARD WILBUR

6677 GEIGER M Loretta  A Study of the Theme and Structure of the Poetry of Richard Wilbur  MA Villanova Univ 1966
6678 SAGE R L  Richard Wilbur's Poetry: A Celebration of Reality  MA North Texas St Univ 1968
6679 WELCH Barbara A  Richard Wilbur: Rhetorician in Modern Poetry  MA Boston Coll 1961
See also 6807

## THORNTON WILDER

6680 BUERSTETTA Esther A  Thornton Wilder: His Literary Sources and the Use He Makes of Them  MA Univ of South Dakota 1965  85 p
6681 BURDICK Winifred M  Thornton Wilder's Novels as an Expression of American Art  MA Boston Coll 1948
6682 CHAMPLIN Susan A  The Basic Conceptions of Love Presented in the Novels of Thornton Wilder  MA Eastern Illinois Univ 1968

6683 COLLIER James  Symbolism and Allegory in the Plays of Thornton Wilder  MA Univ of North Carolina at Chapel Hill 1958  111 p
6684 DE ARMENT Warren E  Thornton Wilder: Structure of the Novels  MA Univ of Pittsburgh 1961
6685 DOLAN Mary F  An Analysis of *The Skin of Our Teeth*: A Play by Thornton Wilder  MA Ohio St Univ 1955
6686 DUGAN Clare W  Brotherly Love in the Novels and Dramas of Thornton Wilder  MA Texas Arts and Industries Univ 1953
6687 HIGHSMITH James M  Thornton Wilder's Presentational Drama  MA Univ of North Carolina at Chapel Hill 1961
6688 JAMES Nancy E  Religious Meanings in the Novels of Thornton Wilder  MA Univ of Pittsburgh 1959
6689 KELLY Priscilla H  Thornton Wilder: The Dramatist  MA Univ of Massachusetts 1967
6690 KIM Sun H  Thornton Wilder and Graeco-Roman Art  MA Fairleigh Dickinson Univ 1968  78 p
6691 KIRALIS P G  A Study of Thornton Wilder's Plays: Theory in Practice  MA Boston Coll 1954
6692 LIPSON Shirley  The Esthetic and Spiritual Ideals of Thornton Wilder  MA Univ of Pittsburgh 1956
6693 McCASLAND E B  The Philosophy of Thornton Wilder as Indicated by His Plays and Novels  MA Univ of Texas at El Paso 1953  102 p
6694 McDOWELL Judith W  The Symbolic Pattern in the Plays of Thornton Wilder  MA Ohio St Univ 1966  110 p
6695 MULLINS Raymond J  The Elements of Expressionism and Epic Theatre in the Plays of Thornton Wilder  MA Ohio St Univ 1959  56 p
6696 NASMAN Diana J  Thornton Wilder and Gertrude Stein  MA Colorado St Univ 1966
6697 SCHWARZ Charlotte  Ideas in the Works of Thornton Wilder  MA Univ of Kansas 1952
6698 SCHWIENHER Esther C  A Study of Three Treatments of the "Andria" Story by Menander, Terence and Wilder  MA St Louis Univ 1933  97 p
6699 SCOTT James M  The Critical Reception of Thornton Wilder's Novels: 1926-1962  MA Univ of North Carolina at Chapel Hill 1965
6700 SMITH C J  Techniques and Content in Thornton Wilder: A Critical Re-evaluation  MA North Texas St Univ 1959
6701 THOMAS Rita M  A Study of the Dramatic Technique and Purpose of Thornton Wilder  MA Ohio St Univ 1939
6702 TOUCHEFF James R  The Optimism of Thornton Wilder  MA Ohio St Univ 1958
6703 YORK Perry L  The Distortion of Time in the Plays of Thornton Wilder  MA Florida St Univ 1965
6704 ZUCKERMAN Harvey S  Thornton Wilder: Poet of Affirmation  MA Columbia Univ 1959  119 p
See also 80, 4539

## ROGER WILLIAMS

6705 ARNER Robert D  The Poetry of Roger Williams: A Critical Edition  MA Pennsylvania St Univ 1966
6706 KING Ethel G  Roger Williams' Concepts of Freedom  MA Mankato St Coll 1964
6707 NUNNALLY Edith E  An Annotated Edition of "Mr Cotton's Letter Lately Printed, Examined and Answered by Roger Williams of Providence in New England, London, Imprinted in the Yeere 1644"  MA Brooklyn Coll of City Univ of New York 1966  49 p
6708 TOMPKINS Robert D  Aspects of Puritanism in the Thought of Roger Williams  MA Univ of Toronto (Canada) 1965
6709 WELLS Beverly R  A Comparison of the Religious Beliefs of Roger Williams and John Cotton  M Ed Henderson St Coll nd

## TENNESSEE WILLIAMS

6710 ALTSCHULER David T  The Critical Reputation of Tennessee Williams  MA Univ of Maine 1966  147 p
6711 BARTON Catherine  Some Evidence of Alienation in the Life and Plays of Tennessee Williams  MA Saint Mary's Univ (Canada) 1966
6712 BIER Charles R  Tennessee Williams: From Play to Screenplay  MA Univ of Texas at Austin 1965  95 p
6713 BOOTH Anita D  A Study of the Diction in *The Glass Menagerie*  MA North Texas St Univ 1965
6714 BOYD Jo B  Changes in Characterization in Tennessee Williams  MA Univ of Arkansas 1963
6715 BRANNON Steve F  The Fish King Myth in Tennessee Williams' *Camino Real*  MA East Tennessee St Univ 1969
6716 CALDWELL Sally S  Symbolism in the Works of Tennessee Williams  MA West Texas St Univ 1964  110 p
6717 CAMPBELL Harry T  Tragedy and Beyond in the Drama of Tennessee Williams  MA Boston Coll 1969
6718 CANNON Margaret H  The Short Stories of Tennessee Williams  MA Univ of North Carolina at Chapel Hill 1965
6719 CASKEY Jefferson D  A Study of the Heroines in Selected Plays of Tennessee Williams and Their Attempts at Personality Integration  MA Univ of Houston 1966  111 p
6720 CHAMBERLAIN Ernest E  The Human Condition in the Works of Tennessee Williams  MA Boston Coll 1963
6721 COHEN Mary D  A Study of the Characters in the Works of Tennessee Williams  MA Southern Illinois Univ at Carbondale 1959  82 p
6722 CRAIG Martha M  A Critical Analysis of Tennessee Williams' *Orpheus Descending*  M Ed Henderson St Coll nd
6723 CZIOK Vera B  Sacrifice and Atonement in the Plays of Tennessee Williams  MS St Cloud St Coll 1966  213 p
6724 DALLAMORA Eugene L  Allegorical Significance of Changes in the Revision of Two of Tennessee Williams' Plays  MA Boston Coll 1966
6725 DAVIS Betty G  The Victim and the Victimizer in the Plays of Tennessee Williams  MA East Carolina Univ 1970
6726 DeROSE Maria E  Women in the Plays of Tennessee Williams: Studies in Personal Isolation and Outraged Sensibility  MA Univ of Arizona 1966
6727 DERVIN Daniel A  The Spook in the Rainforest: An Inquiry Into the Plays of Tennessee Williams  MA Columbia Univ 1963  71 p
6728 DOERRY Karl W  Romantic Themes and Characters in the Plays of Tennessee Williams  MA Univ of Kansas 1965
6729 DRAKE Constance M  The Evolution of Love in Tennessee Williams  MA Univ of Rhode Island 1964
6730 ENGLAND Donald G  The Importance of the Past in the Plays of Tennessee Williams  MA Univ of Texas at Austin 1964  98 p
6731 ETHERIDGE Ruth J  Tennessee Williams' Women  MA Univ of Southern Mississippi 1958
6732 FEATHERS Sherrell N  Hell Hath No Fury: Feminine Characterization in Selected Plays of Euripides and Tennessee Williams  MA East Tennessee St Univ 1964
6733 FERRELL James M  A Study of the Principal Women Characters in the Published Plays of Tennessee Williams  MA East Carolina Univ 1964
6734 FLEMING Isabelle R  Chekhovian Influence and Parallels in the Works of Tennessee Williams and Arthur Miller  MA Columbia Univ 1954  78 p
6735 GARNER Nathan C  A Proposed Production of Tennessee Williams' *The Glass Menagerie*  MA Univ of North Carolina at Chapel Hill 1966
6736 GOLDBERG Mark F  Tennessee Williams: The Clue in Cronus and Zeus  BA Rutgers St Univ 1961  50 p
6737 GOMEAU Harold O  Heroines of August Strindberg and Tennessee Williams:

A Study in Anti-feminism  MA Columbia Univ 1953  134 p
6738  GUNTER J O  The Fugitive Kind in the Major Plays of Tennessee Williams  MA North Texas St Univ 1968
6739  HAGGE Helmut P  The Plastic Theatre of Tennessee Williams  MA Univ of Texas at Austin 1966  89 p
6740  HANNAH Barbara S  Tennessee Williams: Poet-Dramatist  MA Univ of North Carolina at Chapel Hill 1966
6741  HIEMEN William  "The Lonely Fugitive": A Study of the Lonely Frustrated Individuals in Selected Plays of Tennessee (Thomas Lanier) Williams  MA Mankato St Coll 1967  119 p
6742  HILTON Susan P  Old Beauty and New Truth: The Continuation of the Major Themes of Henrik Ibsen in the Plays of Tennessee Williams  MA Stetson Univ 1966
6743  HINDMAN Ira  *Night of the Iguana*: A Departure  MA Stetson Univ 1965
6744  HOWARD Joan M  Grail Quest Motif in Two Plays by Tennessee Williams  MA Boston Coll 1965
6745  KEATING Elizabeth W  Tennessee Williams and the Critical Climate to 1964: A Study of Five of the Major Plays  MA Univ of San Diego 1965
6746  KETTLER Suzette C  "A Passion for Declivity": The Retreat from Complicity in Tennessee Williams  MA Ohio St Univ 1961  106 p
6747  KVASNICKA George M Jr  The Heroic Characters of Tennessee Williams  MA Columbia Univ 1961  54 p
6748  LaPIERRE Charles M  Tennessee Williams and the Dream  MA St Louis Univ 1960  78 p
6749  LEONARD David R  The Concept of Illusion in the Plays of Tennessee Williams  MA Univ of Mississippi 1969
6750  LESTER Frank A  A Study of the Supernatural and the Symbolic in the Works of Tennessee Williams  MA Univ of Tennessee 1956  118 p
6751  LEWIS Jim G  Major Themes in Plays of Tennessee Williams  MA Baylor Univ 1964  138 p
6752  LEWIS Waverly R  The Theme of Escape in the Plays of Tennessee Williams  MA Texas Arts and Industries Univ 1967
6753  MacDONALD Edgar E  Tennessee Williams and the Tragic Tradition  MA Univ of Richmond 1953  71 p
6754  McMANUS Portia A  Tennessee Williams as a Satirist  MA Univ of Texas at Austin 1965  86 p
6755  McNEW Ulyss H  A Collection of Memorable Heroines from Tennessee Williams  MA Univ of Nevada 1966
6756  MAGUIRE Jeanne L  Sounds and Music in Tennessee Williams' Plays  MA Boston Coll 1965
6757  MARINO John A  Tennessee Williams and the Problem of Time  MA St Louis Univ 1966  97 p
6758  MASON Irene M  Man's Search for Dignity in the Plays of Tennessee Williams  MA Univ of California at Riverside 1961
6759  MORTUS Cynthia A  Southern Ladies in the Plays of Tennessee Williams  MA Boston Coll 1966  135 p
6760  OCHILTREE Fr Richard A  The Relationship of Catharsis to Aesthetic Distance in *A Streetcar Named Desire*  MA Coll of the Holy Names at Oakland 1964
6761  OUILLEN R Clark  Adapting Selected Plays of Tennessee Williams for Television Production  MA East Tennessee St Univ 1965
6762  PARR Karen H  Animal Imagery in the Plays of Tennessee Williams  MA Univ of Alaska 1966  70 p
6763  PEARSALL Elizabeth A  A Comparative Study in the Two Major Editions of Tennessee Williams' *The Glass Menagerie*  MA Univ of North Carolina at Chapel Hill 1965
6764  PERKINS Clifford C  The Legend of Laura Young: The Life and Works of Tennessee Williams  MA Columbia Univ 1951
6765  PETERSON J M  Tennessee Williams as a Social Critic  MA North Texas St Univ 1969

6766 PFLUGRAD Gerald  A Discussion of Love in the Works of Tennessee Williams  MA Chico St Coll 1965  78 p
6767 PRINCE Peter V  A Study of the Heroines in the Plays of Tennessee Williams  MA Fairleigh Dickinson Univ 1969  70 p
6768 PRUITT Virginia D  Tennessee Williams: The Relationship Between Three Selected Short Stories and Three Selected Plays  MA Univ of North Carolina at Chapel Hill 1966
6769 RADOSEVIC Nancy E  Symbolism and Other Non-realistic Techniques in the Major Plays of Tennesse Williams  MA Univ of Kentucky 1956  88 p
6770 RAGER Leora G  An Analysis of the Symbolism of the Staging Devices in the Full-length Plays of Tennessee Williams  MA Indiana Univ of Pennsylvania 1965  79 p
6771 RECK Tom S  Tennessee Williams: Social Critic of the South  MA Univ of Houston 1961  80 p
6772 REID Elizabeth T  An Interpretative Analysis of the Writing of Tennessee Williams  MA Baylor Univ 1965
6773 RHOADES John A  Problems for the Scene Designer in Tennessee Williams' Plays  MA Ball St Univ 1968  72 p
6774 RIDDICK Ruth M  The Dramatic Development of Tennessee Williams  MA Univ of Texas at Austin 1954  102 p
6775 RUTHLEDGE Jerry W  The Southern Gothic Dramas of Tennessee Williams  MA Univ of Oklahoma 1966
6776 SMALLING Doris  "Bombs of Honesty": A Study of Humor in Tennessee Williams  MA Pepperdine Coll 1970
6777 SMITH Leonidas C  Existential Categories in Eight Plays by Tennessee Williams  MA Clemson Univ 1967
6778 STEWART Judy H  The Abandoned Woman in the Dramas of Tennessee Williams  MA Morehead St Univ 1968  44 p
6779 SWANSON David R  *Cat on a Hot Tin Roof*: Directing  MFA Texas Christian Univ 1968  182 p
6780 THOMPSON Hilary  The Forms of Irony in the Plays of Tennessee Williams  MA Univ of Alberta (Canada) 1967
6781 TIPPIT Geraldine Y  A Critical Analysis of Tennessee Williams' *The Glass Menagerie*  M Ed Henderson St Coll nd
6782 TOTH Bill D  The Stories of Tennessee Williams: A Study of Their Thematic Development and Expansion Into Full-length Drama  MA Chico St Coll 1969  60 p
6783 VAN NIEUMENHUIZE Paul F  Escape Into Illusions of the South in Characters of Tennessee Williams  MA Texas Arts and Industries Univ 1963  157 p
6784 WALKER James P  Tennessee Williams' Emerging Ethic  MA Univ of Tulsa 1966  63 p
6785 WARNER Eloise W  A Study of the Use of Symbolic Structure as Employed by Tennessee Williams in Four Plays  MA Univ of Southern Mississippi 1969
6786 WATKINS Ralph F  Sex and a Southern Lady in Tennessee Williams' Plays  MA Columbia Univ 1954  189 p
6787 WHITMORE Jon S  Laughter in Tennessee Williams' Tragic Plays  MA Washington St Univ at Pullman 1968
6788 WILLIAMS Elgenia F  Feminine Frustration in the Plays of Tennessee Williams  MA Hardin-Simmons Univ 1968
6789 WILSON Rodney M  A Production Book for *A Streetcar Named Desire*  MA Kansas St Univ 1966
See also 2350, 3895, 4521, 4539, 4687

## WILLIAM CARLOS WILLIAMS

6790 ALDRICH Philip L  The Women of William Carlos Williams  MA Univ of Massachusetts 1964
6791 ALMAND Lindsay C  The Humanism of William Carlos Williams  MA Univ

of Louisville 1958
6792 BICKMAN Martin E "Beat Hell Out of It Beautiful Thing": Rhythms of William Carlos Williams BA Amherst Coll 1967
6793 BILLS Bing D The Expressionism of William Carlos Williams as Found in His Dramatic Writings MA Univ of Iowa 1966
6794 BREWER Elizabeth W "A Plan for Action to Supplant a Plan for Action": A Study of the Organization of William Carlos Williams' *Paterson* MA Univ of North Carolina at Raleigh 1970 71 p
6795 BROWN Curtis F William Carlos Williams' *Paterson*: Bridging the Span MA Columbia Univ 1953 203 p
6796 CRUM Carol D William Carlos Williams and the Plastic Arts MA Ohio St Univ 1965 124 p
6797 DUNHAM William H Short Fiction in the Poetic Career of William Carlos Williams MA Fairleigh Dickinson Univ 1969 197 p
6798 GROWE Barry S William Carlos Williams: Poetry of the Bare Hands BA Amherst Coll 1967
6799 HALPERN Martin The Early Poetry of William Carlos Williams: A Study in the Development of an "Esthetic of the Familiar" MA Univ of Rochester 1952 119 p
6800 HATLEN Burton N Method and Meaning: A Study of the Shorter Poems of William Carlos Williams MA Columbia Univ 1959 83 p
6801 HERMAN Marilynne M The Poetry and Critical Works of William Carlos Williams and Thomas Sterns Eliot MA Univ of British Columbia (Canada) 1966
6802 HILL Georgina F An Analysis of "The Desert Music" by William Carlos Williams MA Fresno St Coll 1964 59 p
6803 JOHNS Ronald J The Vocabulary of Specifications: A Study of the Language in Williams' *Paterson* MA Wichita St Univ 1966
6804 JOHNSON Ann R *Paterson*: William Carlos Williams' Poetic Manifesto MA Univ of Nebraska 1964
6805 KAHN Maxine Explorations Into the Published and Unpublished Plays of William Carlos Williams MA Fairleigh Dickinson Univ 1964 69 p
6806 KOELLE Kate L The Social Philosophy of William Carlos Williams MA Univ of New Mexico 1957
6807 LUCAS Eunice S Things in the Poetry of William Carlos Williams and Richard Wilbur MA Washington Univ at St Louis 1966
6808 NOLAND Richard W William Carlos Williams' *White Mule Trilogy* MA Columbia Univ 1961 119 p
6809 OLIVER H Allan How Deep Is the Water at the Deepest Place?: A Critical Study of *Paterson*, a Poem in Five Volumes by William Carlos Williams BA Amherst Coll 1963
6810 OTTMERS Bette J A Critical Study of the Four Major Plays of William Carlos Williams MA Texas Agricultural and Mechanical Univ 1969 106 p
6811 OWRE Brenda M America and the Self: A Study of William Carlos Williams' Quest for Poetic Themes MA Univ of Vermont 1968 142 p
6812 PASCARELLI Joseph T The Thematic Imagery of William Carlos Williams MA Fairleigh Dickinson Univ 1968 75 p
6813 PURCELL Becky An Analysis of William Carlos Williams' *Paterson* from the Point of View of His Poetic Theory MA Washington St Univ at Pullman 1965
6814 REID Mila J The Poetic Theory of William Carlos Williams MA West Texas St Univ 1968 95 p
6815 RHODES Geri M The Paterson Metaphor in William Carlos Williams' *Paterson* MA Tufts Univ 1965
6816 ROBESON John A William Carlos Williams: His Theory of Poetry MA Univ of North Carolina at Chapel Hill 1958 65 p
6817 SERPA Robert L Approaches to Poetry: William Carlos Williams and the Idiom of Poetry MA Univ of North Carolina at Chapel Hill 1967 91 p

6818 SIMMONDS Richard S  William Carlos Williams' Development of a Measure for American Poetry  MA Ohio St Univ 1964  53 p
6819 SLATE Joseph E  Form in the Poetry of William Carlos Williams  MA Univ of Oklahoma 1952
6820 STRAUB Peter F  Toward a New Edition of William Carlos Williams' *The Desert Music*  MA Columbia Univ 1966  110 p
6821 STROMMER John P  The Experience of Order in the Poetry of William Carlos Williams  MA Ohio St Univ 1965  125 p
6822 TUCKER P A  A Study in the Relationship of Form and Content in William Carlos Williams' *Paterson*  BA Univ of British Columbia (Canada) 1964

See also 748

## AUGUSTA EVANS WILSON

6823 CALLAHAN Ida B  Augusta Evans Wilson:  An Analytical Study of Her Fiction  MA Vanderbilt Univ 1943
6824 MUNK Eunice A  The Life and Writings of Augusta Jane Evans Wilson  MA Emory Univ 1948
6825 PHILLIPS Sidney C  Life and Works of Augusta Evans Wilson  MA Auburn Univ 1937

## EDMUND WILSON

6826 LENSING W E  Edmund Wilson's Development as Critic  MA Univ of Louisville 1940
6827 MARTIN Richard T  A Problem in Criticism:  Edmund Wilson's *The Wound and the Bow*  MA Univ of Louisville 1965  165 p
6828 WRIGHT Richard R  Edmund Wilson: History, Art and Man  MA Southern Illinois Univ at Carbondale 1956  84 p

## WOODROW WILSON

6829 McCANN William H  Woodrow Wilson as a Man of Letters  MA Boston Univ 1933
6830 MYHR Ivar L  Woodrow Wilson as a Literary Critic  MA George Peabody Coll for Teachers 1928

## OWEN WISTER

6831 BECHARD Eugene E  Social Criticism in the Novels and Short Stories of Owen Wister  MA Washington St Univ at Pullman 1953
6832 McTAGGART Alice C  Owen Wister:  A Study  MA Univ of Kansas 1942
6833 PAST Raymond E  Owen Wister: Critic of America (with Emphasis on Western Writings)  MA Univ of Texas at Austin 1947  152 p
6834 SCHOCK Mary C  The Stories of Owen Wister as Representative of the Rocky Mountain West  MA Univ of Idaho 1931

## THOMAS WOLFE

6835 ADAMS Richard P  Thomas Wolfe and James T Farrell:  A Comparison in the Autobiographical Method  MA Univ of Illinois at Urbana 1940
6836 AKER John E  Thomas Wolfe:  A Study in a Literary Conflict  MA Vanderbilt Univ 1946
6837 BEAVERS Martha E  The Words of Thomas Wolfe  MA Texas Technological Univ 1956  198 p
6838 BELAIR Margaret A  Thomas Wolfe, Romantic Realist:  A Study of His Human Themes and Styles  MA Univ of Montreal (Canada) 1964
6839 BOLEN Frances E  Thomas Wolfe's Homeland:  Certain Aspects of His America  MA Univ of Mississippi 1953  113 p

6840 BORZUMATO Lawrence P  Four Aspects of the Search for Identity in Thomas Wolfe's Novels  MA Univ of Rhode Island nd
6841 BOWLING Cynthia A  Thomas Wolfe's America Theme  MA Colorado St Univ 1967
6842 BROWN L T  A Study of the Works of Thomas Wolfe  MA Wesleyan Univ 1942
6843 BRYANT James D  Thomas Wolfe and the Jew  MA Texas Christian Univ 1967  58 p
6844 BUSH Charles K  A Comparison of the Youths of Thomas Wolfe's Eugene Gant and George Webber  MA Univ of North Carolina at Chapel Hill 1963
6845 CARNER R Charles  A Study of Thomas Wolfe's Vocabulary and Diction  MA Univ of Texas at El Paso 1961  140 p
6846 CLEMENS Edna W  A Study of the Structure of the Narratives in the Short Novels of Thomas Wolfe  MA Univ of North Carolina at Chapel Hill 1964
6847 CLEMENTS Clyde  Symbolic Patterns in *You Can't Go Home Again*  MA Bowling Green St Univ 1961
6848 COLE Joyce M  Thomas Wolfe's Changing Center of Social Consciousness  MA Univ of North Carolina at Chapel Hill 1968
6849 COLONNEL Robert T  Fyodor Dostoyevsky and Thomas Wolfe: A Comparison  MA East Tennessee St Univ 1970
6850 CONE Mary  Thomas Wolfe: The Artist  MA Univ of Mississippi 1953  125 p
6851 CONNOR Fran M  The Isolation of Thomas Wolfe  MA Baylor Univ 1968  71 p
6852 COPENHAVER Carolyn J  The Earthbound Thomas Wolfe: His Rejection of Mysticism  MA Univ of Texas at El Paso 1965  97 p
6853 DAVIS Agnes A  The Modern Confessional Novel: A Brief in the Case of Thomas Wolfe  MA Univ of Tulsa 1969  58 p
6854 DEAN Charles W  Here I Stand: Thomas Wolfe as a Southern Satirist  MA Univ of Massachusetts 1963
6855 DELMARE Maxine L  Thomas Wolfe: Another Estimate  MA Kansas St Teachers Coll at Emporia 1947
6856 DeMERRITT William  A Discussion of the Novels of Thomas Wolfe  BA Rutgers St Univ 1960  75 p
6857 DOGGETT Mary  Themes in the Works of Thomas Wolfe  M Ed Henderson St Coll nd
6858 DONNO Daniel J  The Quest of Thomas Wolfe  MA Miami Univ at Oxford 1947
6859 DOSTER William C  Wolfe and Whitman: A Comparative Study  MA Univ of Florida 1948
6860 DOWDEN William T  Social Classes in the Work of Thomas Wolfe  MA Texas Agricultural and Mechanical Univ 1968  88 p
6861 EHRENHAFT George  Thomas Wolfe and His Relation to Germany  MA Ohio St Univ 1963  64 p
6862 ELLISON Francis E  The Significance of Character Development in Thomas Wolfe's Early Novels  MA Univ of Texas at Austin 1954  191 p
6863 ERSTLING Julius H  Thomas Wolfe's Knowledge and Use of Milton  MA Univ of Florida 1941
6864 FINK Charlotte A  Methods and Devices of Characterization in the Novels of Thomas Wolfe  MA Univ of Tennessee 1945
6865 FORTENBERRY George E  Thomas Wolfe's Fictional Treatment of the Negro  MA Texas Christian Univ 1951  152 p
6866 FOSTER Ruel E  Thomas Wolfe: A Critical Study  MA Univ of Kentucky 1939
6867 FRENCH Alice  The Life and Writing of Thomas Wolfe: A Program for Readers' Theatre  MA Univ of Oklahoma 1969
6868 GEORGE McChesney  Footsteps in the Desert: Thomas Wolfe and the Pre-existence Youth  MA Univ of New Hampshire 1969  47 p
6869 GILBERT John R  Thomas Wolfe: His Development of Social Consciousness  MA Mississippi St Univ 1965  86 p
6870 HALLAHAN Margaret E  Time and Unity in the Novels of Wolfe  MA San Diego St Coll 1968  101 p
6871 HAMILTON Walter L  Thomas Wolfe: Interpreter of America  MA Univ of Kansas 1942
6872 HAMNER Robert D  Thomas Wolfe: A New Appraisal  MA Univ of Texas at

Austin 1966  82 p
6873 HANIG D D  The Comic Element in the Novels of Thomas Wolfe  MA North Texas St Univ 1957
6874 HARRINGTON Evea I  Thomas Wolfe: The Theory and Practice of His Characterization  MA Univ of Idaho 1947
6875 HARRIS W A  The Severed Thread of Gold: The Hero Image in the Works of Thomas Wolfe  MA East Tennessee St Univ 1969
6876 HENSON Darold L  Treatment of the Negro in Wolfe and Faulkner  MS Illinois St Univ at Normal 1969
6877 HERMIZ Thomas  A Critical Analysis of the Ubi Sunt and Loneliness Motifs in Thomas Wolfe's *Look Homeward, Angel* and *Of Time and the River*  MA Univ of Rhode Island nd
6878 HODGE Elizabeth A  A Study of Thomas Wolfe's *Look Homeward, Angel*  MA Univ of Texas at Austin 1949  102 p
6879 HOGAN Frances V  Thomas Wolfe: Whale in a Strait-jacket  MA Columbia Univ 1940
6880 HOLDITCH William K  Of Time and Thomas Wolfe  MA Univ of Mississippi 1957  162 p
6881 HOLLINGSWORTH Marian E  The Search for a Father in the Novels of Thomas Wolfe  MA Univ of North Carolina at Chapel Hill 1957  87 p
6882 HOWELL Betty C  Symbolism in the Works of Thomas Wolfe  MA Florida St Univ 1954
6883 HUME Laura M  Thomas Wolfe's Literary Criteria  MA Univ of Tulsa 1949
6884 JOHNSON George W  Thomas Wolfe: The Groping Weaver  MA Columbia Univ 1953  142 p
6885 JOHNSTON June A  Thomas Wolfe as Lover and Critic of America  MA North Texas St Univ 1965
6886 KAY Barbara R  Thomas Wolfe: The Exile Motif and the Jews  MA McGill Univ (Canada) 1966
6887 KILBURN Pat E  Thomas Wolfe: Critic of America  MA Univ of New Mexico 1947
6888 KINSTLEY Barbara S  Thomas Wolfe's Romantic Affinity for Germany  MA North Texas St Univ 1966
6889 LANCASTER Lyle L  Development of Thomas Wolfe's Socio-political Consciousness as Reflected in His Writings  MA Texas Christian Univ 1969  119 p
6890 LANTOS Carl  Thomas Wolfe: The Struggle for Maturity  MA Univ of Texas at Austin 1948  156 p
6891 LAWLER John J  A Study of Some of the Relations Between the Periodical and Book Publications of Thomas Wolfe  MA Univ of North Carolina at Chapel Hill 1949  98 p
6892 LEHNSTUL A B  A Critical Comment on the Works of Thomas Wolfe  MA New York Univ 1938
6893 LEWIS Norval B  Form and Effectiveness in Thomas Wolfe's Works: A Study in Aesthetics  MA Univ of New Hampshire 1949  60 p
6894 McCLELLAN Robert W  The Literary Reputation of Thomas Wolfe  MA Columbia Univ 1961  139 p
6895 McDONALD Walter R  The Concept of Time in Thomas Wolfe's Fiction  MA Texas Technological Univ 1957  74 p
6896 McNEIL C Craig  Epic Qualities in Thomas Wolfe's *Look Homeward, Angel*  MA Brigham Young Univ 1960  61 p
6897 McNEIL Linda M  Escape Into Life: The Novels of Thomas Wolfe  MA Baylor Univ 1968  105 p
6898 MARTIN Andre A  Thomas Wolfe's Relationship with His Family  MA Midwestern Univ 1955  83 p
6899 MAXWELL Bert H  Thomas Wolfe's *You Can't Go Home Again*: A Critical Study  MA Univ of Texas at Austin 1954  166 p
6900 MILLER John C  Thomas Wolfe as a Novelist  MA Univ of Virginia 1947
6901 MOAKE Frank B  An Evaluation of the Criticism of Thomas Wolfe  MA Southern Illinois Univ at Carbondale 1949  127 p

6902 NELSON John T  Thomas Wolfe: Giant Paradox  MA Colorado St Univ 1962
6903 NEWMAN Carol M Jr  The Symbols of Thomas Wolfe  MA Univ of Virginia 1946
6904 NOLTE William H  The Satire of Thomas Wolfe  MA Univ of Texas at Austin 1952  114 p
6905 O'DELL Carl A  An Analysis of Certain Poetical Devices in the Prose of Thomas Wolfe  MA East Tennessee St Univ 1957
6906 O'HARA Robert C  *Look Homeward, Angel* and *Of Time and the River*: A Bio-critical Study of Three Aspects  MA Univ of Louisville 1953
6907 OLIVER Virginia H  The Theme of Alienation in the Writing of Thomas Wolfe  MA McNeese St Univ 1965
6908 PERREAULT John H  The Relationship Between Technique and Experience in the Novels of Thomas Wolfe  MA Villanova Univ 1965
6909 PHELPS Phil R  The Train as Symbol in the Novels of Thomas Wolfe  MA Univ of Tennessee 1966
6910 PRATER William G  Thomas Wolfe and New York City: A Changing Vision  MA Univ of Tennessee 1964
6911 PRESLAR Robert W  Thomas Wolfe as Novelist-Satirist: An Evaluation  MA Univ of Maryland at College Park 1967  103 p
6912 RANDOLPH E C  Women in the Life and Works of Thomas Wolfe  MA North Texas St Univ 1968
6913 READER Willie D  Thomas Wolfe's Autobiographical Approach  MA Univ of Texas at Austin 1960  89 p
6914 RICE Jerry L  Thomas Wolfe as a Dramatist  MA Ohio St Univ 1959
6915 RICKER Kenneth T  The Theme of Loneliness in Thomas Wolfe  MA Oklahoma St Univ 1952  83 p
6916 RILEY John R  The Structure of the Novels of Thomas Wolfe  MA Univ of Pittsburgh 1950
6917 ROGERS Elizabeth J  An Analysis of Thomas Wolfe's *Look Homeward, Angel* and *Of Time and the River*  MA Ohio St Univ 1944
6918 ROSCHWALB Jerold  The Quest of an American Faust: A Study of Thomas Wolfe  MA Columbia Univ 1960  199 p
6919 ROSS Sue F  A Study of Terry's Edition of *Thomas Wolfe's Letters to His Mother* with Emphasis on Dating Errors  MA Univ of North Carolina at Chapel Hill 1965
6920 SEHON Elizabeth B  The Optimism of Thomas Wolfe  MA Baylor Univ 1951  228 p
6921 SEIB Kenneth A  The Shifting Winds: A Study of the Critical Reaction Toward the Works of Thomas Wolfe  MA Columbia Univ 1961  85 p
6922 SHARPE Lillie L  The Mind and Art of Thomas Wolfe  MA Texas Arts and Industries Univ 1952
6923 SHEALY Ann  Thomas Wolfe: A Critical Study of His Views of the American Scene  MA Univ of South Carolina 1947
6924 SHEFFIELD Jewell F  Female Characters in Thomas Wolfe's Four Major Works: *Look Homeward, Angel*; *Of Time and the River*; *The Web and the Rock* and *You Can't Go Home Again*  MA Texas Agricultural and Mechanical Univ 1968  91 p
6925 SHULFORD Catherine B  Thomas Wolfe and Walt Whitman  MA North Texas St Univ 1941
6926 SIEVERS Margaret W  The Development of Thomas Wolfe's Reputation  MA Western St Coll of Colorado 1949  66 p
6927 SIMONS Helen T  The Pessimism of Thomas Wolfe  MA Univ of Pittsburgh 1947
6928 SIPSEY William J  Thomas Wolfe and the Novel Form  MA Boston Coll 1951
6929 SMITHERMAN Betty J  Thomas Wolfe's Imagery  MA Univ of Texas at Austin 1953  62 p
6930 SPANO Anna  Thomas Wolfe: *Look Homeward, Angel*  MA Ca Foscari (Italy) 1958
6931 STROZIER Robert I  Thomas Wolfe and Death  MA Florida St Univ 1960
6932 SUBERMAN Jack  The Idealism of Thomas Wolfe  MA Univ of Florida 1947
6933 SUTLIFF Harriet J  Thomas Wolfe: American Legend  MA Colorado St

Univ 1942
6934 TAYLOR Douglas C  The Relation Between the Poetic Concept and Autobiographical Memory in the Works of Thomas Wolfe  MA Univ of the Pacific 1949  85 p
6935 TAYLOR P M  Thomas Wolfe: American  MA Boston Univ 1942
6936 THOMPSON B B  "Of Wandering Forever and Earth Again...":  Thomas Wolfe's America  MA Univ of Texas at El Paso 1954  130 p
6937 VALWAY Henry L  Lost and Far from Home: A Study of the Central Theme in Thomas Wolfe's *Look Homeward, Angel*, Its Meaning and Function  MA Boston Coll 1959
6938 VAUSE Edward A  Thomas Wolfe's Narrative Method  MA Univ of North Carolina at Chapel Hill 1949  99 p
6939 VICKERS James E  Theme and Form in *Of Time and the River*  MA Univ of North Carolina at Chapel Hill 1967
6940 WARD William T  The Imagery of Wolfe's *Look Homeward, Angel*  MA Eastern Kentucky Univ 1969  103 p
6941 WEEKS Willis E  Thomas Wolfe's "Images of Strength and Wisdom": Personal Influences on His Literary Practices  MA Oklahoma St Univ 1962  115 p
6942 WEISS Paul  Thomas Wolfe: Far-wanderer; a Biographical Essay  MA Columbia Univ 1941
6943 WEISSER Anne T  The Paradox of the Mountains: A Study of the Influences of Appalachia on Thomas Wolfe  MA West Virginia Univ 1969  163 p
6944 WILEMON Billi M  Thomas Wolfe and His Editors  MA Texas Christian Univ 1964  100 p
6945 WILSON Keith C  The Loneliness of Thomas Wolfe: A Note on Form  MA Univ of New Mexico 1956
6946 WILTGEN Martin C  Existentialism in the Novels of Thomas Wolfe  MA Mankato St Coll 1965  68 p
6947 WINGER William  Thomas Wolfe: God's Lonely Man  MA Columbia Univ 1951
6948 WOODRUFF Lloyd B  A Study of the Structure in the Novels of Thomas Wolfe  MA Univ of Southern California 1948
6949 YONGE Kay N  Thomas Wolfe's Interwoven Themes  MA Hardin-Simmons Univ 1964
See also 213, 214, 3329, 5314, 6543, 6555, 6835

## CONSTANCE FENIMORE WOOLSON

6950 COLBRUNN Ethel B  Regionalism in the Works of Constance Fenimore Woolson  MA Ohio St Univ 1941
6951 TERRY A W  Constance Fenimore Woolson as a Local Color Writer  MA Univ of North Carolina at Chapel Hill 1935

## RICHARD WRIGHT

6952 AMMIRATI Theresa  Wright, Baldwin and Ellison: A Comparative Study of the Negro Novel  MA Lehigh Univ 1966
6953 ANDERSON Jeanette H  A Study of Social Protest of Contemporary Negro Poets (Richard Wright, James Weldon Johnson)  MA Virginia St Coll 1943
6954 BRATZ Gordon T  Art and Experience: The Short Stories of Richard Wright  MA Univ of Massachusetts 1969
6955 BURRELL Evelyn P  Richard Wright: A Tentative Biography  MA Howard Univ 1966  155 p
6956 COLEMAN Virginia B  Art and Propaganda in the Works of Richard Wright  MA Ohio St Univ 1950
6957 CROSSE Charles E  The Novels of Richard Wright: A Study of Major Reactions  MA Univ of Maryland at College Park 1964  120 p

6958  CURRY Constance M  Recurring Themes in the Fiction of Richard Wright  MA Howard Univ 1968  113 p
6959  DILLARD M M  A Survey of the Literary Career of Richard Wright  MA Ohio Univ 1945
6960  FARRELL Dudley E  An Analysis of Richard Wright's Views as Regards Race Relations as Revealed by Selected Novels  MA Mankato St Coll 1969  55 p
6961  GRISSOM Ruby M  Contribution of the Negro to American Literature (Richard Wright, Arna Bontemps, James Weldon Johnson, Booker T Washington)  MA Southwest Texas St Univ 1940
6962  HULL Kenneth G  Prejudice as Depicted by Four Novelists: Richard Wright, Sinclair Lewis, Lillian Smith and Ann Petry  MA Ft Hays Kansas St Coll 1966
6963  JACOBS Connie B  Of Irony in the Fiction of Richard Wright  MA North Carolina Central Univ 1968  92 p
6964  LEWIS Adelene E  The Concept of Freedom in the Negro American Novel, 1865-1941 (Richard Wright, Arna Bontemps, William Wells Brown, Charles Chesnutt, W E B DuBois, George W Henderson, Zora Neale Hurston, James Weldon Johnson, Walter E Turpin, Walter F White)  MA Fisk Univ 1943
6965  LUCAS Portia M  Ethno-centrism in the Poetry and Fiction of Contemporary Negro Authors: A Critical Analysis (Richard Wright, Arna Bontemps, Joseph S Cotter, W E B DuBois, Zora Neale Hurston, James Weldon Johnson, Walter White)  MA Fisk Univ 1939
6966  NEWLON Neil B  *Lawd Today*: An Adaptation of the Novel by Richard Wright  MA Fresno St Coll 1964  79 p
6967  ROBISON Z Catherine  The Color Problem as It Finds Expression in Modern American Negro Literature (Richard Wright, Arna Bontemps, Sterling A Brown, Joseph Seaman Cotter, Georgia Douglas Johnson, James Weldon Johnson, Robert Russa Moton, Walter White)  MA Univ of Utah 1941
6968  ROWE Br Cyprian  Wright's Outsiders: A Study of the Negro in *Native Son* and *The Outsider*  MA Hunter Coll 1963
6969  SPURLOCK Oneada  Naturalistic Techniques in the Fiction of Richard Wright  MA North Carolina Central Univ 1965  43 p
6970  TAYLOR Clyde R  Richard Wright and the Tragic Sense of Life  MA Howard Univ 1959  156 p
6971  WILSON Shirley F  An Examination of Richard Wright's *Uncle Tom's Children: Five Long Stories*  MA Univ of North Carolina at Chapel Hill 1966
See also 1168, 1382, 1547,

## ELINOR WYLIE

6972  CLUCK Julia  The Importance of Shelley in the Prose and Poetry of Elinor Wylie  MA Boston Univ 1939
6973  COGDELL Joy  The Structure and Language of Elinor Wylie's Poetry  MS Auburn Univ 1950  95 p
6974  CORNELL Alice  Study of Elinor Wylie  MA St Univ of New York at Albany 1936
6975  DAVIDSON Dorothy C  The Aestheticism of the Poetry of Elinor Wylie  MA Univ of Texas at Austin 1944
6976  FORD Regina D  Elinor Wylie: The Development of a Metaphysical Style  MA Univ of Louisville 1969  97 p
6977  KELLY Ceil G  The Eternal Pursuit: A Study of the Theme of Death in the Poetry of Elinor Wylie  MA San Diego St Coll 1955  131 p
6978  LENNON John M  The Poetry of Elinor Wylie: An Appraisal  MA Univ of Rhode Island 1969  107 p
6979  McCLAIN Mary M  Elinor Wylie: Tempered Romanticist  MA Florida St Univ 1954
6980  MORTON Margaret S  Elinor Wylie: Her Life and Poetry  MA George Peabody Coll for Teachers 1932
6981  THOMPSON W O  The Use of the Symbol in Elinor Wylie  MA Boston Univ 1941
See also 1030, 2566

## FRANK YERBY

6982 HILL William W  Behind the Magnolia Mask: Frank Yerby as Critic of the South  MA Auburn Univ 1968
6983 VAILS Lavolia  The Literary Reputation of Yerby, 1946-1961  MA North Carolina Central Univ 1963  70 p
6984 YANCEY Sandy Jr  Frank Yerby's Formula for Writing Historical Novels  MA North Carolina Central Univ 1963  81 p

## STARK YOUNG

6985 BOHANNON Alice H  The Influence of Environmental Growth on Texas Verse (Stark Young, Alfred W Arrington, Karle Wilson Baker, Fannie Baker Darden, Molly M Davis, Hilton Ross Greer, Margaret Houston, Mirabeau Bounaparte Lamar, John Avery Lomax, Whitney Montgomery, R M Potter)  MA Univ of Missouri 1941
6986 CLARK Frances E  The New South in Contemporary Fiction (1920-1940) (Stark Young, Erskine Caldwell, Ellen Glasgow, Paul Green, Grace Lumpkin, Elizabeth Madox Roberts, Lyle Saxon, Dorothy Scarborough, T S Stribling, Walter White)  MA Howard Univ 1946
6987 DAVIS Hazel B  Stark Young: His Versatility  MA West Texas St Univ 1948  83 p
6988 DE ROCHE Louis  The Novel of the Civil War (Stark Young, John Esten Cooke, Ellen Glasgow, Thomas Nelson Page)  MA Univ of Georgia 1936
6989 FERGUSON Oliver W  Stark Young and the Southern Tradition  MA Vanderbilt Univ 1948
6990 GREENE Mary E  An Analysis of the Dramatic Criticisms of Stark Young  MA Louisiana St Univ 1941
6991 JOHNSON Willie S  Stark Young: These Constant Things  MA Mississippi St Univ 1956  128 p
6992 LANE Donna D  A Comparative Study of the South as Represented in the Fiction of Stark Young and William Faulkner  MA Univ of Mississippi 1969
6993 LASTER Ann A  Stark Young: A Study of His Interest in Italy and the Influence of Italy on His Life and His Works  MA Univ of Mississippi 1966
6994 McALEXANDER Hubert H Jr  Tradition in the Novels of Stark Young  MA Univ of Mississippi 1966
6995 MARTIN Marco  Some Aspects of the Development of Poetic Drama in America  MA Univ of Cincinnati 1941
6996 NEWMAN Anne E  Contemporary Southern Literature (Stark Young, Karle Wilson Baker, Herschell Brickell, James Branch Cabell, Madison Cawein, Irvin S Cobb, Octavus Roy Cohen, Joseph Wood Krutch, Olive Tilford Dargan, Lucy Furman, Ellen Glasgow, Paul Green, Corra Harris, DuBose Heyward, Hatcher Hughes, James Weldon Johnson, Mary Johnston, Aline Kilmer, Robert Loveman, Walter Malone, Virginia Taylor McCormick, John McLure, John Trotwood Moore, David Morton, Frances Newman, O Henry, William A Percy, Julia Peterkin, John Crowe Ransom, Lizette W Reese, Cale Young Rice, Elizabeth Madox Roberts, Laurence Stallings, Wilbur Daniel Steele, T S Stribling, Charles Hanson Towne, Lula Vollmer, Clement Wood, Martha Young)  MA Univ of Alabama 1926
6997 PLUT Joseph L Jr  Stark Young: A Critical Study  MA Columbia Univ 1961  69 p
6998 RICHARDSON M Moss  Treatment of Christianity by Contemporary Poets  MA Univ of Texas at Austin 1921
6999 SMITH Dorothy E  Attitudes Toward the Civil War and the Reconstruction Period by Southern Novelists (Stark Young, James Lane Allen, James Boyd, George W Cable, John Esten Cooke, Thomas Dixon, Ellen Glasgow, DuBose Heyward, Margaret Mitchell, Thomas Nelson Page,

F Hopkinson Smith, T S Stribling)  MA Univ of Southern California 1939

7000  THORNE Erma C  Stark Young's Novels: A Glimpse of Tradition  MA Univ of Southern Mississippi 1958

See also 4352

GENERAL INDEX

Adamic Myth
    2710, 2972, 3601
Adams, Brooks
    16
Ade, George
    3804
Aeschylus
    3497, 4172, 5812
Africa
    2912
*Alcestis*
    6554
Alegira, Ciro
    5500
Alger, Horatio
    270, 3112
*All Quiet on the Western Front*
    838
*All the Way Home*
    35
*American Mercury, The*
    4222, 4228
American Revolution
    2508, 4717
Anouilh, Jean
    1360
Appollinaire, Guillaume
    884
*April Morning*
    838
Ariosto
    5906
Aristotle
    210, 656, 726, 2748, 4008, 4571
Arnold, Matthew
    1272, 1371, 1507
Arrington Afred W
    6985
Arthurian Legend, The
    3863, 5165, 5166, 5179, 5208, 5222,
    5238, 5240, 5243, 5244, 6744
*Astrophel and Stella*
    5077
*Atlantic Monthly*
    3088, 3101, 4714
Auden, W H
    1289
Baker, Karle Wilson
    6985, 6996
Balzac
    1568, 4787
Bancroft, George
    2508
Barnfield
    6554
Baroja
    2999

Barth, Karl
    6287
Baudelaire, Charles
    1345, 1366, 1378, 4749, 4753, 4780,
    4794, 4910, 4936, 4988, 5005, 5566,
*Becket*
    1360
Beckett, Samuel
    77, 252
Becquer, Gustavo Adolfo
    4939
Benchley, R C
    5833
Benn, Gottfried
    1375
Bennet, Emerson
    4356, 4358
Bennett, Arnold
    3116
Bergson, Henri
    6053
Berkeley, George
    5158
*Bhagavad-Gita, The*
    5768, 6584
Bible, The
    224, 964, 1222, 1233, 1311, 1338,
    2054, 2571, 2745, 3446, 3650, 3742,
    3776, 3778, 3799, 3802, 3815, 4005,
    4101, 4248, 4664, 4725, 5163, 5187,
    5197, 5747, 5914, 6065, 6195, 6237,
    6514, 6524, 6612, 6656, 6676
Blake, William
    4678
Bollingen Prize
    5078
Bontemps, Arna
    6961, 6964, 6965, 6967
Book of Job
    1311, 2054
*Boston Miscellany of Literature and Fashion*
    3855
Botts, John Minor
    3056
Boyd, James
    6999
Brackenridge, Hugh Henry
    687, 2052
Bradley, F H
    1223
Brazil
    6495
Bread and Cheese Club
    666
*Breadwinners, The*
    18

Brickell, Herschell
  6996
Bridge, Horatio
  2696
*Broad and Alien Is the World*
  5500
*Broadway Journal*
  4932
Bromfield, Louis
  6422
Brook Farm
  2671, 2729
*Brothers Karamazov*
  1260
Brown, John
  301, 308, 310, 311
Brown, Sterling
  3161, 6967
Brown, William Wells
  6964
Browne, Ross
  5949
Browne, Thomas
  4023, 4193
Browning, Robert
  1523, 3370, 5082
Brutus
  6323
Bunin, Ivan Alekseevich
  1677
Bunyan, John
  2445, 2562
Burton, W E
  4768
Butor, Michael
  1603
Byron
  4074
Caesar
  6323
Cain
  1773
Calvin, John
  5209, 5911, 6206
Camus, Albert
  252, 1708, 1759, 2861, 2905, 2939
  4201
Canada
  3134
Carleton, Will
  5147
Carlyle, Thomas
  6502
Carroll, Lewis
  4009
Cavalanti
  5083
Cela
  1103

*Century Magazine*
  458
Cervantes, Miguel de
  6127, 6156, 6212
*Charles Auchester*
  3614
Chase, Owen
  4003
Chaucer
  1350
Chayofski
  4539
Chekhov, Anton
  6734
Cherokee Folklore
  2388
China
  410
Chocano, Jose Santos
  6484
*Chung Yung*
  5062
Clark, Badger
  4
Clemens, Henry
  5870
Clemens, Olivia L
  6248
*Code of the Woosters*
  3291
Cohen, Octavus Roy
  6996
Coleridge, Samuel Taylor
  1310, 1433, 1476, 1486, 4999
Confucius
  1392
Conrad, Joseph
  1838
Cooke, John Esten
  6988, 6999
Corbiere, Tristan
  1304
*Cosmopolitan*
  3083
Cotter, Joseph Seaman
  6965, 6967
Cotton, John
  6707, 6709
Coughlin, Father
  3099
Creek Folklore
  2388
Crittenden, John Jordon
  3056
Cronus
  6736
Cullen, Countee
  3537
*Cynthia*
  6554

Dada
    6370
Dana, James
    1189
Dante
    2653
Darden, Fannie Baker
    6985
Dargan, Olive Tilford
    6995, 6996
Darrow, Clarence S
    3067
Darwin, Charles
    1138, 5866
"Daughters of the Late Colonel"
    543
Davidson, John
    1357
Davis, Molly M
    6985
*Deathmakers, The*
    2915
Delta School
    493
Dewey, John
    1895
*Dial, The*
    1397, 2197, 2209
Diaz, Bernal
    3913, 3922
Dickens, Charles
    2403, 3177
Dickinson, Edward
    1068
Dirby, G H
    3804
Donne, John
    987
*Don Quixote*
    6212
*Don Segundo Sombra*
    4
Dostoevsky, Fydor Mikhailovich
    1260, 1707, 1761, 2500, 3991,
    6371, 6849
Dreyfus Case
    5999
Dryden, John
    1279
DuBois, W E B
    6964, 6965
Duncan, Robert
    5083
Dunlap, William
    666
Durand, R S A
    666
Electra Myth
    3497

Eliot, George
    3651
Emerson, Charles Chauncy
    1398
England
    819, 3796
Erdman, L Grace
    5051
*Esquire*
    2895, 2935
Euripides
    3489, 6554, 6732
Europe
    3706, 3784, 6031, 6196, 6250
*Fables*
    2449
Fast, Howard
    838
Faust
    6918
Fichte, Johann Gottlieb
    1519
Field, J M
    4356, 4358
Fitzgerald, Zelda Sayre
    1911, 1959, 1982
Flaubert, Gustave
    520, 592, 3241
Fletcher, John
    3962
Flexner, Hortense
    6995
Fowler
    6648
France
    1584, 3360, 3514, 4777, 4997, 6419
Freud
    3975, 4506, 4695, 5316, 6053
Frisch, Max
    272
Gale, Zona
    503
Galsworthy, John
    3258
Gandhi
    5776
"General Prologue" of *Canterbury Tales*
    1350
*Gentleman's Magazine*
    4768
Germany
    6861, 6888
Gerstaecker, Friedrich
    4903
Gestalt
    1207
*Ghosts*
    4521
Gide, Andre
    3962

God
    968, 1025, 1028, 1071, 1316,
    1495, 1857, 2068, 2113, 2663,
    2976, 3843, 4086, 4197, 4539,
    4658, 4826, 5492, 6522
*Godey's Lady's Book*
    4781
Godkin, Edwin Lawrence
    1102
Goethe
    1426, 1434
Gold, Herbert
    1144
Goodman, Joseph T
    5868
Graham, William Franklin
    1192
Greek Drama
    1271, 1368, 4288, 4643
Greek Mythology
    1427, 1537, 2596
Greer, Hilton Ross
    6985
Griswold, Erwin Nathaniel
    4757
Guiraldes, Ricardo
    4
*Gulliver's Travels*
    5907
Guthrie, A B
    710
Halleck, Fitz-Green
    666
Hamlet
    1830
Hardy, Thomas
    3395
Harris, Mark
    3943
Harvard '47 Workshop
    213, 214
Hawaiian Mythology
    1884
Hay, John
    18
Hegel, Georg Wilhelm Friedrich
    6541, 6588
Henderson, George W
    6964
Henryson
    2449
Herbert, George
    5708
Hernandez, Jose
    4
Hesse, Hermann
    252, 4007

Hillhouse, J A
    666
Hillyer, Robert
    2116
Hoffman, E T A
    2564, 4809, 4998
Hone, Philip
    666
Hopkins, Gerard Manley
    3810, 5736
Horney, Karen
    2640
Houston, Margaret
    6985
*Houston Post*
    4496
Hovey, Richard
    3863, 5179
Howell, Thomas
    2581
Hughes, Hatcher
    6996
Hurston, Zora Neale
    6964, 6965
Ibsen, Henrik
    4263, 4294, 4521, 4548, 6742
Icarus
    4019
*Idiot, The*
    3991
Indians
    1858
Inge, William
    2806
Ingersoll, Robert G
    6004
Ionesco, Eugene
    70, 77
Italy
    3365, 3791, 6412, 6993
Japan
    2766, 2767, 2778, 2780, 2789, 2792,
    2793, 2794, 2796, 2800
Jazz Age
    1913, 1964, 1981
Jeremiah
    1099
Jesus Christ
    1404, 1495, 1573, 1739, 1800, 1823,
    3601, 4050, 5529
Joan of Arc
    5883, 5940, 6037, 6132
Johnson, Georgia Douglas
    2349, 6967
Johnson, Samuel
    1279, 1816
Joseph, Donald
    1085

Joyce, James
 1595, 5322
Jung
 4631
*Kale Vala*
 3801
Kant
 6537
Kastner, Erlich
 3914
Kavaphes, C P
 1312
Kent, James
 666
Killens, John O
 1379
Kilmer, Aline
 6996
Kingsley, Charles
 2437
Kirkland, Joseph
 2023
Koeppen, Wolfgang
 5460
Lamar, Mirabeau Bounaparte
 6985
Lamarline
 3797
Latin America
 4868
*Law of Civilization and Decay*
 16
Lawson, Henry
 4486
Lazarus
 4664
Leacock, Stephen
 3700
Le Conte, Joseph
 4404
Le Fanu, James Sheridan
 4844
Logan, Joshua
 2350
*Lolita*
 4161
Lomax, John Avery
 6985
Lorca, Federico Garcia
 1216, 4585
Lucian
 4841
Lu Hsun
 5060
Lumpkin, Grace
 6986
"Lycidas"
 1816
McCormick, Virginia Taylor
 6996

McKay, Claude
 3537
MacKenzie, Compton
 1967
McLure, John
 6996
Madison, James
 2052
Maecenas, Gaius Cilnius
 5400
Mallarme
 5584
Malory, Thomas
 5235
Malraux, Andre
 2946, 2969
Mann, Thomas
 1707, 4146, 5569
Mansfield, Katherine
 543
*Martin Fierro*
 4
Maturin
 2489
Maupassant, Guy de
 4896, 4920, 4984, 4994
*Medea*
 3489
Menander
 6698
Meredith, George
 3395, 3402
Merton, Thomas
 3810
Mexican War
 3835
Mexico
 5515
Milton, John
 1220, 6863
Mitchell, Margaret
 6999
Mitchell, W O
 4128
*Molloy*
 252
Montaigne
 1518, 1533, 5778
Montgomery, Whitney
 6985
Moore, John Trotwood
 6996
Morris
 258
Morse, S F B
 666
Morton, David
 6996
Mosel, Tad
 35

Moton, Roberta Russa
  6967
Munson
  738
Musaus
  2564
Nabokov, Vladimir
  4161
*Nation, The*
  4328
Newman, Frances
  6996
*News from Nowhere*
  258
New Testament
  5192
New York Wits
  5833
Nietzsche, Friedrich Wilhelm
  1453, 4229, 4577, 4618, 4632
Nye, E W
  3804
*On the Road*
  280
Orestes
  4510
Orin
  4510
Orpheus
  739
Orwell, George
  2969
Osgood, Frances Sargent
  4818
Ostenso, Martha
  4340
Patterson, Norma
  1085
Peabody, Elizabeth Palmer
  2190
Percival, J G
  666
Peterson, Charles Jacobs
  3852
Petry, Ann
  6962
Picasso, Pablo
  2934
Pierce, Franklin
  2516, 2687
*Pilgrim's Progress*
  2562
Pinter, Harold
  54, 77
Piper, Edwin Ford
  5147
Plato
  1420, 1449, 1479
Plinlimmon Pamphlet
  4068

*Poeta en Nueva York*
  1216
Pope, Alexander
  2449
*Portrait of the Artist as a Young Man*
  5322
Potter, R M
  6985
*Prelude*
  5782
Preston, Margaret Junkin
  2762
Prometheus
  2737
*Prometheus Bound*
  5812
*Psychology of the Unconscious*
  4631
Puckler-Muskau, Hermann Ludwig
  4831
Purdy, James
  4020
Quakers
  6517
Rabelais
  5906
*Red and the Black, The*
  4007
Reisman
  35
Remarque, Erich Maria
  838
*Requiem pour une Nonne*
  1759
Revelation of St John the Divine
  964
Richardson, Willis
  2349
Rilke, R M
  5291, 5574
Rimbaud, Arthur
  762, 1304, 4755
Riviere, Jacques
  1227
Rodo, Jose Enrique
  1445
Roman Mythology
  1427, 1537
*Roman Tauben Im Gras*
  5460
Ross, S
  4128
Rousseau
  1479, 3621, 4717
"Ruine the Rewarde of Vice"
  2581
Sacco-Vanzetti Case
  1117
"Sailing to Byzantium"
  2890

St John of the Cross
    1346
Sarrett, Lew
    5147
Satan
    1707, 2663, 4162, 6027
Saxon, Lyle
    6986
Schopenhauer
    1513
Sender, Ramon
    2874
Shakespeare
    3962
Shaw, Henry W
    3804
Sheldon, Edward
    213, 214
Shelley, Percy Bysshe
    6972
Shen, Ts'ung-wen
    5060
Sheppard, Elizabeth Sara
    3614
Sherwood, Robert
    1111
Sidney, Philip
    5077
Silva, Jose Asuncion
    4946
*Sketches by Boz*
    3177
Smith, F Hopkinson
    6999
Smith, Joseph
    4678
Smith, Lillian
    6962
Sophocles
    4571
Southern, Terry
    242
*Southern Literary Magazine*
    4867, 4872, 4933
*Southern Quarterly Review*
    5435
Spain
    2973, 3016
Spanish Civil War
    2828, 2874, 2924, 2969, 2970
Spender, Stephen
    2976
Stafford
    3010
Stallings, Laurence
    6996
Stendahl
    4007
*Steppenwolf*
    252, 4007

Stevenson, Robert Louis
    2513, 5767, 5886
*Stranger, The*
    252, 1708
Strindberg, August
    4541, 4542, 4587, 4641, 4683, 4803, 6737
Suckow, Ruth
    5114
Sullivan, Louis Henri
    6459
*Sunshine Sketches of a Little Town*
    3700
Surrealism
    6370
Swedenborg, Emmanuel
    1467, 1470, 1472, 1496, 3152
Swift, Jonathan
    2449, 5907, 6075, 6269
Switzerland
    686
Tagore, Rabindranath
    6615
*Ta Hio*
    5062
Tahiti
    4128
Taine
    6165
Taoism
    5809, 6571
Teilhard
    4412
Temple, William
    1239
Tennyson, Alfred
    2581
Terence
    6698
Terry, J S
    6919
Thomas, Edward
    2066, 2103
Thomason, John William
    1085
Thompson, William Tappan
    3805
Thorpe, Thomas Bangs
    4356, 4358
"Thyrsis"
    1816
Tieck
    2564
Tolstoy
    3081, 3117
*Tour of a German Prince*
    4831
Towne, Charles Hanson
    6996

Traven, B
  5515
Tristram Legend
  5168, 5214, 5235, 5246
*Trois Contes*
  592
*True History of the Conquest of
  New Spain*
  3913
Tucker, Ellen Louisa
  1528
Turgenev, Ivan
  3235, 3307
Turpin, Walter E
  6964
Unamuno, Miguel de
  4049
Van Buren, Martin
  5080
Venice
  3236
Verplanck, Gulian
  666
*Vienna*
  2976
Vollmer, Lula
  6996
Warner, Charles Dudley
  6230
*Way West*
  710
Webster, Daniel
  1452
Wexley
  4452
White, E B
  5833
White, Walter F
  6964, 6965, 6967, 6986
Whitman, Sarah Helen
  4991
Willis, Nathaniel Parker
  4840
Winters, Yvor
  5102
Wodehouse, P G
  3291
Wood, Clement
  6996
Wordsworth, William
  400, 1266, 2879, 4678, 5782
World War I
  1092
Wright, Frank Lloyd
  5811, 6459
Wyeth, Andrew
  2173
Yeats, William Butler
  2890

Yerkes, Charles Tyson
  1162
Young, Martha
  6996
Zeitgeist
  3376
Zen
  3568, 5317, 5773, 6613
Zeus
  6736
Zola, Emile
  4369, 4370, 4402, 4407

## THESIS AUTHOR INDEX

Aarnes J 158
Aaron C W 4260
Abadie F L 3222
Abbot C S 736
Abbott H P 1555
Abbott P A 1556
Abbott R 500
Abel A R 1387
Abernathy P L 6459
Abernathy R 4700
Abernethy F E 5864
Abolin N 1206
Abrons M G 2053
Abu-Talib M A 5865
Ackerman H C Jr 5562
Ackley R P 5866
Acord J P 2189
Adair M C 4745
Adams B E 2816
Adams C A 3559
Adams E B 5868
Adams E I 4746
Adams E M 5867
Adams G J 5869
Adams H H 3059
Adams H M 501
Adams J F 2055
Adams J G 2054
Adams J M 3223
Adams L 2426
Adams M 347
Adams M J 5442
Adams M J 5727
Adams M S 2190
Adams P 3775
Adams R B 263
Adams R M 502
Adams R P 6835
Adams T S 1905
Adams W C 5348
Adamson J 5870
Adcock M M 5628
Adelman I 1207
Adelsberg L S 5871
Aderholt M 4408
Adkins C A 1906
Adkins D 5872
Adler C H 3963
Adler J 2817
Agler S P 3224
Aglesbee R S 5324
Agte L M 882
Ahearn M L 6290
Aitken J L 3225
Aker J E 6836
Akey J 3810
Akins T W 5873
Albert W W 3668
Alberta R C 3811

Albin J A 5252
Albright T 4747
Albritton S P 1557
Alden E C 2056
Alder P 5874
Alderman T 764
Alderson T R 3226
Aldrich P L 6790
Aldrich T O 242
Aldridge H B 1558
Aldridge M 6390
Aldridge R E 3968
Alexander A S 4748
Alexander D F 3227
Alexander D O 3776
Alexander E M 1559
Alexander G B 6369
Alexander J 4749
Alexander S 3964
Alff J M 2427
Alford W P 3965
Al-Khatib I M 1122
Allan C V 4750
Allard G E 5262
Allbritten G 4701
Allen A 3966
Allen A J 1092
Allen A M 503
Allen B S 1560
Allen C W 1196
Allen C W 2428
Allen D M 5875
Allen E M 3669
Allen F C 2429
Allen G R 1561
Allen H F 5876
Allen I M 3462
Allen J D 1562
Allen J N 4751
Allen J S 3967
Allen M E 5089
Allen Sr M L 32
Allen M W 1208
Allen R A 3928
Allen R C 4752
Alley K D 1896
Allison V M 5877
Allman M H 1907
Allmond N 5325
Allran B M 2818
Almand L C 6791
Alonso J A 5728
Altenbernd A L 4359
Alter L E 765
Altschul D 3803
Altschuler D T 6710
Ambrosetti R J 3969
Amell K 2819
Amend A E 2014

Amini H R 5719
Amlie E 4500
Amman M 4501
Ammirati T 6952
Amorati A 4502
Anastas P N Jr 5729
Andersen M R 264
Anderson A J 3228
Anderson B C 3970
Anderson E C 925
Anderson E E 5878
Anderson E S 1388
Anderson E S 1563
Anderson G 4360
Anderson H M 3229
Anderson J A 2430
Anderson J H 6953
Anderson J M 1564
Anderson J V 159
Anderson L 4753
Anderson L W 1389
Anderson M 3230
Anderson M D 3173
Anderson R 5159
Anderson R G 4361
Anderson R W 2338
Anderson S 5879
Anderson S P 85
Andra C E 4754
Andrew L D 3754
Andrews J L Jr 5880
Andrews P B 3971
Andrews W D 1390
Anger H M 1209
Angrist E P 4715
Ankenbrand H H 504
Annotti E M 5881
Antonin C 2820
Appel A Jr 6341
Applegate B B 3812
Aprad J J 874
Aranovitch L 6270
Arant F 1565
Arbo E A 1908
Archer F B 2821
Archer J H 505
Armstead T J 3161
Armstrong R A 1566
Armstrong S E 766
Arnaud H A 448
Arner R D 6705
Arnett E 6460
Arnett M D 3231
Arnold A J 1123
Arnold H S 767
Arnold J W 3232
Arnold J W 5703
Arnold L F 265
Arnold W W 5449

Arrieta M  2212
Arthur C S  5882
Arthur H  2823
Arthur H M  2822
Arthur R  5563
Arthur R L  5160
Arutunoff A A  1909
Asbahi M  449
Ashburne J G  866
Ashby A L  2057
Ashley O R  2339
Ashley S B  2247
Ashmore D B  5015
Ashworth J D  6461
Askew M W  6391
Aslam J  2824
Aslinger A  665
Asmundsson D R  5883
Aspray R M  2248
Assad T J  2431
Astor S D  2432
Astro R  5469
Atkins D W  2249
Atkinson E M  3583
Atkinson J B  4755
Atkinson J H  506
Atkinson J M  3972
Attane A L  197
Attwood R M  5884
Atwater I M  1890
Atwell Br J S  4217
Aughtry C E  3233
Augur M E  5885
Auld J H  2825
Ault D D  1210
Ausmus M R  3670
Austin A D  2433
Austin L J  2434
Austin Sr M  507
Austin M F  5652
Auvenshine A B  2435
Avanzi W A  666
Avinger J  3973
Ax G  2396
Axtell P M  6462
Axton W F  6
Ayala E  4756
Ayres J B  5090

Babbs J E  4460
Babin J L  3974
Bacoats I B  450
Bacon E  4503
Bacon K H  2058
Baczynski M  5460
Baer R G  5886
Bagley C L  3975
Bailey A L  3234

Bailey C S  2826
Bailey F J  5470
Bailey L  2059
Bailey L  3463
Bailey N I  1910
Bailey P R  4757
Bailey R V  3034
Baily E  875
Bain M J  737
Baird L  3976
Baird R C  4758
Bairrington R E  5326
Baker D C  2043
Baker E  5887
Baker M G  944
Baker M I  5161
Baker M W  5471
Baker R T  3537
Baker W C  6463
Balcer J  4409
Balducci A  3671
Baldwin M E  4504
Baldwin M F  1990
Baldwin W P III  6370
Balkman B A  1567
Ball C D  1180
Ball C R  3977
Ball D  4505
Ball K R  3978
Ball M E  6392
Ball T  3071
Ballard R T  4759
Ballew M  6299
Ballman P G  1911
Baltay V R  1211
Bancroft A D  4760
Banet R A  3979
Bankowsky R J  6300
Banks F W  6464
Bankston D H  1391
Barac V  5564
Barbee P L  508
Barber E M Jr  3584
Barbour B H  1912
Barck M L  5472
Bard E  5461
Barden M L  4261
Barefoot S W  4761
Barfoot A  1568
Barger S F  1569
Baril J R  1093
Barkan C M  1183
Barker J F  5888
Barkley J C  5473
Barkowsky E R  3874
Barksdale H R  3538
Barlow M M  2801
Barnes M S  1124

Barnes M T  2371
Barnet J M  3980
Barnett B M  1570
Barnett G A  3875
Barnett J W  945
Barney D  4362
Barnhill M E  946
Barnier J F  5730
Barre E F  5398
Barrett E T  4262
Barrett T R  3813
Barry D A  3814
Barthen H L  6465
Bartini A G  3981
Bartlett P A  111
Barton C  6711
Barton J F  1913
Barton R A  5399
Baskerville K T  5276
Baskett D L  2213
Bass A L  3072
Bass G R  2763
Bass J N  5889
Bass J W  4506
Bass M  3672
Bass M L  3777
Bassham G H  6371
Bassoff B  5162
Bateman J A  5890
Bates L D  5731
Batten C  1914
Batten C A  3235
Battilana M G  3236
Battistel M L  2436
Batts M G  6393
Bauer S A  5016
Baugh H F III  451
Baugh R M  4315
Bauman E A  6466
Baxter C M  2250
Bay A F  1392
Bay M C  112
Baylor R A  5017
Beach R C  768
Beacom J B  299
Beadle J A  3040
Beal B M  942
Beamer G C  2437
Beams D  3237
Beane M A  2438
Beard A W  5474
Beard C  934
Beard G M  1393
Beard H M  6394
Beard J J  5373
Beardshear W M  4468
Bearzatto G  4762
Beasley A R  4763

Beasley B 5565
Beatty G G 5163
Beauchamp G L 1571
Beaujon R J 509
Beavers M E 6837
Bechard E E 6831
Bechtold I P 5891
Beck B J 266
Beck J P 5732
Beck M F 3514
Beckelman I A 510
Becker J E 2439
Beckum P C 6467
Bedno H M 4363
Beede L E 2397
Beede M F 2060
Beeler A J 5148
Beggs J K 2440
Behar J 3982
Behler V E 2441
Bein M 1094
Beker W G Jr 5400
Bekus A J 2398
Belair M A 6838
Belch G E 3660
Belcher F T 5733
Belgrade H L 5892
Bell B W 1379
Bell C 4507
Bell C P 6468
Bell G E 1394
Bell G H 4508
Bell H H Jr 1572
Bell H L 5893
Bell H M 935
Bell J A 113
Bell J R 1212
Bell M C 5894
Bell R 114
Bell R B 3073
Bell R C 358
Bellamy G C 5895
Bellavia R M 1213
Beller H I 5896
Bellomy J 1573
Belton J E 3585
Beltz G W 2827
Beltz L A 1395
Bendoski L 511
Benedetti R A 5629
Benedikt M J 5566
Benham O J 2251
Benjamin M L 2805
Benner J K 512
Bennett C 4712
Bennett C D 5682
Bennett E E 1915
Bennett E H 5058

Bennett E S 6395
Bennett G M 3983
Bennett G N 2026
Bennett H R 267
Bennett J W 5897
Bennett M A 1574
Bennett W E 1396
Benning R J 3174
Bennington J W 486
Bensten J M 3515
Bentley R H 6469
Benton J 3464
Benton R R Jr 1575
Berces F A 4764
Berdan A 3018
Bere J R 5130
Berg O E 3929
Bergbauer Sr C M 3586
Bergland M 115
Bergquist H E 1916
Bergstrom R F 3984
Berkowitz M S 5704
Berland A 3238
Berlin H R 5734
Berman P I 2828
Berman R H 3239
Bernard E G 390
Bernardin C W 1095
Berneche L 1125
Bernet A M 1900
Bernhardt W F 4218
Bernstein C 6396
Berry M E 5898
Berry W P 4219
Berthelot M C 452
Bertone R E 667
Bertram R M 3240
Bertsch E R 2061
Bervin A E 3876
Bettis L L 6470
Betts R A 5899
Bickley R B 3985
Bickman M E 6792
Bidewell G I 5900
Bier C R 6712
Bigelow M F 738
Biggerstaff D R 3986
Bignell D 2442
Bill J 5901
Billings C 2027
Billings R S 2829
Bills B D 6793
Bilz D 1214
Bingham I D 3567
Bingham R D 3930
Bird A P 2830
Bird R M 883
Birdsong T P 2443

Birky W J 6471
Birney G A 2444
Bishoff R E 6301
Bishop B O 1126
Bishop B S 2062
Bishop M M 5164
Bittinger M S 4702
Black H M 4765
Black J 3722
Black L D 6472
Black M 3175
Black M P 2365
Blackburn A L 3241
Blackburn D W 2831
Blackley C E 5902
Blackman H N 3505
Blackman M 884
Blackmon W F Jr 5121
Blackstock W Jr 2362
Blackwelder J R 1397
Blackwell A L 6342
Blackwell B 947
Blair J W 2214
Blake M M 668
Blakely M L 3673
Blakely P P 3242
Blanchard J A 1576
Blanco Sr M C 2252
Blankenship F 54
Blansett B N 3987
Blau R M 3988
Blay F B 1577
Blaylock J B 1398
Blazek E 769
Blevins C E 5643
Blevins W E Jr 948
Blickman M F 3243
Bliss B M 4364
Blissard T 1578
Blitch L M 3587
Blodgett M H 4238
Blomenkamp A 3516
Blood D B 2445
Bloodworth B E 6473
Bloodworth W A Jr 2832
Blott S G 2833
Blue I J 3162
Blum A M 2063
Blum H 3912
Boake M L 669
Boardman E J 2446
Bobo S B 3074
Bocchieri S 4509
Bockes D T 4766
Bodden L 5903
Bodge R A 1399
Bodin M I 1917
Bodnar C M 6397

Body L M    4767
Boe M A    3244
Boewe C E    3041
Bohannon A H    6985
Boje L M    4768
Bolen F E    6839
Bolin D W    949
Bonander A    1215
Bond R W    739
Bond W D    3778
Bonds G A    5091
Bondurant A M    4769
Bonfoey W L    453
Bongiorno C    867
Bonham R A    1579
Bonham V L    5904
Bonham W D    5905
Bonin J F    1580
Bonner T N    2332
Bontempo C L    885
Bontempo E F    1581
Booker M M    5475
Boone D D    3042
Boone S Z    5349
Booth A D    6713
Booth I L    2447
Booty D V    770
Boozman A P    6474
Borden D M    1582
Boren D J    420
Boroff D    6475
Boros D M    55
Borowsky A G    670
Borsotti C    2448
Borton J C Jr    3989
Borza A M    2449
Borzumato L P    6840
Bose R H    2064
Bost W R    4770
Bostian F F    1583
Boston J    5735
Bothwell E K    2065
Bottoms M R    2028
Boucher J J    3755
Bouit M O    1400
Boulanger F    3674
Boulter J L    1401
Bourke R L    2834
Bourn C E    2066
Bourque J H    116
Bouvier R H    3245
Bowden L    4356
Bowdre P H    4365
Bowen C S    2835
Bower R    1584
Bowerman V L    6271
Bowker A W    1544
Bowker S H    243
Bowles E A    6398

Bowles J C    3953
Bowles L    3176
Bowling C A    6841
Bowers J A    3990
Bowman B F    6476
Bowman M E    3815
Boyd C B    4316
Boyd G W    3075
Boyd J    2450
Boyd J B    6714
Boyd J M    1216
Boyd J T    338
Boyd M A    662
Boyd M C    3991
Boyd M J    1585
Boyd W P    4771
Boyer I    3560
Boykin C    2366
Boyvey M R    4742
Braack G    5092
Brack P L    2215
Brackett D L    5401
Bradbury D L    3732
Braddy H    317
Braddy V    5165
Braden W S    886
Bradfield E    4772
Bradford M J    3465
Bradford R A    6477
Brading E    5402
Bradley C A    4263
Bradley E M    513
Bradley E U    95
Bradley V M    671
Bradley W H    1586
Bradshaw M A    639
Brady M B    4510
Brame W H    2000
Bramlette J M    3816
Bramlette W H    2451
Branam H F    1587
Brand W E    6478
Brandly T O    2452
Brandon B T    359
Brandwein L    454
Branlette G    2399
Brann C B    6272
Brannen A C    2453
Brannon S F    6715
Branom E C    3992
Brashear A F    5906
Brashier M    6332
Braswell J W    4773
Bratz G T    6954
Braum M    4333
Braun M M    4366
Bravo M E    2836
Bray L J Jr    233
Brazeau P A    360

Brazina M L    268
Brean J A    7
Breault Sr M A    2806
Breedlove N E    1096
Breen N E    5736
Breever V M    6479
Breitenberg K    2454
Bremmer J F    1918
Brennan M E    1402
Brennan Sr M T    3993
Bretz L S    3517
Brewer C F    3675
Brewer C W    1217
Brewer E W    6794
Brewer Sr M C    4511
Brewer Sr M P    5392
Brewer N C    771
Brewer W D    1218
Brewington P D    2455
Brick S    4512
Brickman C L    3246
Bridge J    2837
Bridgeforth R E    5737
Bridgers F E Jr    4703
Brier C J    300
Briggs R C    3247
Briggs W M    5907
Briggs W N    5367
Brigham L M    5847
Bright E M    926
Bright M M    1488
Briney J    740
Brining E L    234
Brinkley T E    4367
Brinson L B    3546
Bristow E K    5683
Brittain L C    2044
Britton J S    1127
Broach K    1589
Broad L M    6399
Brobst D E    215
Brock D F    5383
Brockman A A    5848
Brockway P J    3557
Broderick M    5567
Brodie B    4774
Brodie J    1403
Brodsky L D    1590
Brody A    3248
Brody P    4775
Broer L R    2838
Brogunier J E    5568
Broida L K    6480
Brokaw Z S    3579
Brooker J S    950
Brooks A F    2067
Brooks A F    5263
Brooks F J    1991
Brooks I B    415

| | | |
|---|---|---|
| Brooks J 1219 | Bryant D H 5285 | Burns J T Jr 2255 |
| Brooks V F 3076 | Bryant E L 2840 | Burns L S 3163 |
| Brooks V M 318 | Bryant J D 6843 | Burns R A 3996 |
| Brooks W N 5350 | Bryant P T 3251 | Burns R A 5286 |
| Brophy R J 3466 | Bryant R 3519 | Burns R J 1222 |
| Brosius M F 3249 | Bryant S R 887 | Burns R S 5914 |
| Brown A 5127 | Bryant W C 301 | Burnside P 3878 |
| Brown A E 514 | Bryer J R 1920 | Burrell E P 6955 |
| Brown A E 5908 | Bryer J R 4513 | Burrell N P 4310 |
| Brown B I 4220 | Brylawski L B 4236 | Burrow E 515 |
| Brown C F 6795 | Buchanan B 4308 | Burrows D J 5287 |
| Brown C H 4776 | Buchanan L C 772 | Burrum H H 1404 |
| Brown C T 3994 | Buck C C 1221 | Burt D J 4447 |
| Brown D W 4704 | Buckeye R W 5018 | Burtner W T Jr 3997 |
| Brown J L 1220 | Buckley C 3252 | Burton L H 3804 |
| Brown J L 1591 | Buckner R R 3253 | Bush C K 6844 |
| Brown J M 3032 | Budahl L A 5166 | Bush C W 674 |
| Brown J R 1197 | Budd D R 4514 | Bush G D 4411 |
| Brown K K 6372 | Budde N 4782 | Bushman C L 2256 |
| Brown K R 2807 | Buerstetta E A 6680 | Buss J L 1405 |
| Brown L T 6842 | Buffum M S 3467 | Bussola C 951 |
| Brown M 6481 | Bugg V F 3254 | Butcher C P 456 |
| Brown M F 4777 | Buice J C 1592 | Butcher L A 2015 |
| Brown M K 6482 | Buker B V 4515 | Butcher L E 5406 |
| Brown M R 3250 | Bukowsky H S 3255 | Buthod M M 6483 |
| Brown O B 3077 | Bull C E 2216 | Butler D R 3468 |
| Brown P 3877 | Bunch D R 6291 | Butler J 773 |
| Brown P A 1919 | Buncome M H 2253 | Butler J S 5443 |
| Brown P E 3588 | Bunge M 3914 | Butler M J 4329 |
| Brown P J 3056 | Bunn J W 5910 | Butler S P 4785 |
| Brown R 3177 | Burbank B 4783 | Butts B 2257 |
| Brown R 4778 | Burchard R C 6273 | Butturuff D R 1223 |
| Brown R C 5403 | Burchinal K H 3910 | Buxbaum M H 5915 |
| Brown R E 33 | Burd M R 6343 | Buxhaus K L 5916 |
| Brown S L 6400 | Burdeshaw M D 2841 | Buxton T L 3079 |
| Brown T T 5833 | Burdick W M 6681 | Buzby K H 5684 |
| Brown W J 3913 | Burg D F 1128 | Byers M H 1224 |
| Brown W R 6401 | Burge B J 4264 | Bygrave L 3818 |
| Browne M A 5630 | Burgess E L 5911 | Bynum L S 2217 |
| Browne R E 4779 | Burghdurf C J 1593 | Byrd E M 4334 |
| Browning Sr M C 5673 | Burgin C A 2457 | Byrd G D 5917 |
| Browning R L 2210 | Burke M 673 | Byrd J C 6303 |
| Brownlee C G 672 | Burke M M 3995 | Byrd J S 3257 |
| Brownlee M 4780 | Burkett E M 2254 | Byrne Sr M E 1595 |
| Brubaker B R 455 | Burkhardt M 6649 | Byrnes R A 1545 |
| Brubaker D P 6302 | Burkholder C J 5477 | Byrns E I 4516 |
| Bruce C 5476 | Burks J M 5167 | |
| Bruce D F 4410 | Burks S L 1921 | Cabaniss J H 3591 |
| Brumfield B M 2839 | Burks W M 5912 | Cabell L W 5351 |
| Brumleve Sr E M 3817 | Burleson S D 1594 | Cadwell F 952 |
| Brunett R A 5909 | Burnam T B 5913 | Cain R E 1596 |
| Brunton F D 3078 | Burnett A P 5478 | Caire F J 6344 |
| Bryan J F 3518 | Burnett G 3590 | Calabia F 1922 |
| Bryan L H 2456 | Burnette B J 4784 | Calderon P O 6484 |
| Bryan W A 5404 | Burney M A 4732 | Caldwell H H 4786 |
| Bryan W F 3589 | Burns A I 3256 | Caldwell J 2842 |
| Bryant A 4781 | Burns E M 2458 | Caldwell M S 4265 |
| Bryant B R 5405 | Burns H J 5738 | Caldwell S S 6716 |

Calhoun R H   516
Callahan Br F P   3561
Callahan H R   4517
Callahan I B   6823
Callahan M A   2843
Callahan Sr M E   4239
Callard R W   269
Callender N M   3676
Callow J T   391
Caluori M L   5288
Cambron R   1085
Cameron D B   5569
Cameron S D   392
Cameron T D   5918
Camfield G T   3819
Cammack Sr M A   1225
Camp J T   3258
Camp M   5919
Campbell A J   741
Campbell C E   2844
Campbell C E   6485
Campbell D   4266
Campbell D   4518
Campbell D A   6486
Campbell H T   6717
Campbell J G   5570
Campbell J W   2845
Campbell M E   3259
Campbell S   3934
Campenni F J   5920
Canaday D D   6402
Canaday N Jr   3998
Canan J E   953
Candenhead M   517
Cane S   3568
Canfield E C   2846
Cannon E   675
Cannon M H   6718
Cannon W J   361
Cano J M   2847
Cantrell F W   2258
Canzoneri R W   2068
Caplan E D   3080
Capon R L   3592
Capps M L   5921
Carden G J   2459
Carden R   6487
Carey A P   3506
Carey N B   2460
Carey S   1226
Cariou P L   2461
Carleton E L   5093
Carlin J C   3820
Carlitz B B   1129
Carlon W T   6488
Carlson F M   6489
Carlson M J   2029
Carlson P H   3081
Carlton G   2400

Carman J D   319
Carmichael K J   3999
Carmine H   6650
Carnefix V E   3260
Carner R C   6845
Carnes F F   3469
Carpenter F M   4787
Carpenter J A   742
Carpenter J M   4000
Carpenter M C   4001
Carpenter T P   43
Carpenter T W   5087
Carpenter W H   4788
Carr E F   160
Carr E G   3043
Carr H   5168
Carr H M   384
Carr J G   2462
Carr J O   1097
Carroll B H Jr   3261
Carroll C L   6651
Carroll J P   3756
Carroll M E   642
Carroll R T   5922
Carroll R W   2006
Carrow E L   3779
Carruth G V   1227
Carsley A N   3677
Carson D L   5923
Carstensen V R   3044
Carter A B   2259
Carter A B   3935
Carter B B   1597
Carter B W   5393
Carter E H   4469
Carter J L   1923
Carter L L   4727
Carter M   3019
Carter M E   6403
Carter P J   5924
Carter S L   1598
Cartledge M C   4240
Caruthers C M   3661
Carver M C   2069
Carver R P   927
Cary E E   3879
Case G M   5739
Casey L L   6490
Casey M E   3821
Casey M E   4412
Casey W T   4716
Cash T H Jr   2848
Caskey J D   6719
Cassell M H   2849
Castellani Q   4789
Castillo Y Mendoza E   5059
Castillon P S   4790
Castle R G   216
Castro E H   3082

Caswell R W   1599
Cate J O   4791
Cates D G   4002
Cathey B R   4728
Cato H E   5123
Caudill A   5624
Caulkins C M   1406
Cauthen I B Jr   4792
Cavanagh E G   2070
Cavanaugh D E   2463
Cavanaugh J D   3470
Cavarozzi J P   56
Cawley A W   5169
Caylor M   5170
Cebull E A   5407
Cech E J   5019
Cerruti J   1130
Cervantes R S   4327
Cervenka M T   6345
Chabrowe L E   4519
Chaddon M H   646
Chaison S D   244
Chalfant E R   6491
Chalk N E   2260
Chamberlain E E   6720
Chamberlin L E   5149
Chambers A M   5740
Chambers C   2850
Chambers J M   4461
Chambers M L   117
Chambers N J   5925
Champion E L   1600
Champlin S A   6682
Chandler M   3045
Chandler W J   5741
Chaney E B   5742
Chang B S   2851
Chant E R   5171
Chapin H B   44
Chapman G   4267
Chapman M E   1407
Chapman M E   3542
Chappell C M   1601
Chappell M   5408
Charpentier K A   2852
Chase E   4520
Chase M C   118
Chase O S   4003
Chasteen N   1408
Cheeves D   1131
Chelsom E C   518
Chen G   5172
Cheney S A   5844
Chennault H L   1184
Chermside R A   2853
Cherry C L   4413
Cherry K H   4793
Cherry W G   3950
Chesler P   3520

| | | |
|---|---|---|
| Cheung D C 5060 | Clayton M M 5444 | Cole H M 6346 |
| Chiabrandi A P 4794 | Clegg M L 3085 | Cole J M 6848 |
| Chicano P A 1602 | Clegg M P 3086 | Cole M L 1411 |
| Chiesura I 5061 | Clem M D 4522 | Cole R C 5745 |
| Chilcote S M 2854 | Cleman J L 457 | Coleman A C 3264 |
| Childers D M 2464 | Clemens E W 6846 | Coleman B 86 |
| Childers N J 519 | Clemens R A 4009 | Coleman C R 1606 |
| Chirico E M 4004 | Clement M D 4523 | Coleman G 1132 |
| Chisholm Sr J J 4005 | Clement N 5849 | Coleman I W 1607 |
| Chisnell E J 5834 | Clements C 6847 | Coleman T C III 4370 |
| Chisolm M L 1997 | Clements M P 2261 | Coleman T E 6305 |
| Chovanetz M B 3780 | Cleveland G C 3087 | Coleman V B 6956 |
| Christen E L 1603 | Cleveland W H 3733 | Coles V C 4525 |
| Christensen E 5926 | Clift B 3448 | Collette J 4241 |
| Christensen P H 5253 | Cline R A 955 | Colley N M 3757 |
| Christian A D 647 | Cloud G M 5929 | Collier F 2262 |
| Christie M E 5743 | Cluck J 6972 | Collier J 6683 |
| Chun W Y 4006 | Clune Sr M P 1604 | Collier Sr M B 385 |
| Churchill D O 2465 | Coacci R 192 | Collins E A 5097 |
| Churchill J H 2466 | Coates K D 3664 | Collins F 1185 |
| Churchman C J 5927 | Cobb E N 2468 | Collins G B 217 |
| Cicchese Sr L M 1228 | Cobb S S 1410 | Collins H H 2766 |
| Cifelli E M 4368 | Cochran M C 5930 | Collins J K 1229 |
| Claggett F M 5094 | Cockman N R 4010 | Collins M F 3521 |
| Clampitt T F 5020 | Cockran V R 161 | Collins M J 2334 |
| Clanton D D 4795 | Cockrill M H 302 | Collins V A 3872 |
| Clareson T D 320 | Coe B 2340 | Colonnel R T 6849 |
| Clark A F 3083 | Coen M H 4524 | Colson T L 5175 |
| Clark B B 3471 | Coffee J 5931 | Colville D K 2471 |
| Clark B B 5173 | Coffeen R G 6492 | Combs J E 3472 |
| Clark C T 2764 | Coffey J E 3823 | Conboy L J 677 |
| Clark E G 2855 | Coffey T P 4796 | Cone M 6850 |
| Clark F E 6986 | Coffin A B 774 | Conerly M S 775 |
| Clark G G 3178 | Coffman L 6493 | Conklin L M 1412 |
| Clark I H 5143 | Coffman S K Jr 4011 | Conlon M R 956 |
| Clark J 2071 | Cogdell J 6973 | Connally L B 4470 |
| Clark J T 4007 | Cogell E A 5932 | Connally M B 3679 |
| Clark J W 4268 | Coggins P E 4012 | Connell E D 3265 |
| Clark K 4521 | Cognard R A 57 | Connelly M A 45 |
| Clark M J 4008 | Cohen A R 888 | Connor F E 6494 |
| Clark M L 245 | Cohen B B 2469 | Connor F M 6851 |
| Clark M M 3084 | Cohen B K 676 | Connor M 5934 |
| Clark L T 3678 | Cohen C C 520 | Connors G M 1608 |
| Clark P W 3539 | Cohen H J 2470 | Connors J F 4448 |
| Clark R L 3262 | Cohen L W 2191 | Connors M T 5935 |
| Clark R L 5062 | Cohen M D 6721 | Conover C D 6297 |
| Clark W G 5928 | Cohen P E 4369 | Conrad R W 2857 |
| Clarke D L 5095 | Cohen W 3263 | Conrath M C 3594 |
| Clarke M K 5174 | Cohn M 2765 | Conson V J 3543 |
| Clarke P P 321 | Cohn S L 4349 | Constable C R 4269 |
| Clarke S M 5394 | Cohn S M 3931 | Constantinides J C 1186 |
| Claus J A 5744 | Coil K L 5096 | Contey C B 3880 |
| Clay W E 954 | Cok G W 1605 | Conway J D 4797 |
| Clayton D R 1409 | Coker L C 3593 | Conway M L 957 |
| Clayton G N Jr 491 | Colagrossi M 5933 | Coogan J W 5140 |
| Clayton J D 2856 | Colbert Sr M T 1886 | Cook F K 2472 |
| Clayton J U 3822 | Colbert W J 6304 | Cook J E 1924 |
| Clayton L R 2467 | Colbrunn E B 6950 | Cook L W 2072 |

Cook M K        2858
Cook R C        5746
Cooke A L       2473
Cooley J R      1609
Coombs S J      5144
Cooper B        4013
Cooper D M      1925
Cooper G L      4221
Cooper J        362
Cooper J J      3266
Cooper K        4526
Cooper M        4527
Cooper R A      1610
Cooper S T      4222
Copeland M W    2016
Copelin P S     2263
Copenhaver C J  6852
Coplin M K      5936
Coppedge D      3781
Corban E R      3944
Corder J W      1611
Corfield B M    958
Corkrum R E Jr  1133
Cornelius E J   521
Cornelius G D   2859
Cornelius P P   3088
Cornell A       6974
Cornier G       6404
Cornish J I     522
Corsa T K       5937
Corson E W Jr   889
Cortale F       2767
Cosby A         1413
Cosby M A       2474
Cosgrove J D    4528
Cosper V C      3267
Cossaboom B     1612
Costa A M       6495
Costello M      2860
Couch C E       4529
Coulbourn G C   5272
Coulbourn M E   4414
Council M J     5021
Courrieu A      2861
Courtney L F    5938
Cousineau J     959
Cousins P M     4335
Cover J E       3881
Covington S C   4014
Cowan L S       1414
Cowie J E       2045
Cowser R G      3680
Cowsky D L      1380
Cox A B         3595
Cox C M         776
Cox D H         6496
Cox D K         2475
Cox Sr E M      1926

Cox F       4798
Cox H       6497
Cox J F     1546
Cox J L     4799
Cox L H     2341
Cox M E     3089
Cox M H     2004
Cox M M     3473
Cox P       1230
Coxe R W    5631
Craddock W B     722
Craft H M        2862
Crafts H    3179
Craig C A   4015
Craig E J   3180
Craig M     1891
Craig M M   6722
Craig N A   198
Craig P     4016
Craig S H   193
Craig S K   270
Craig V K   2476
Craigie A L      3824
Crain C D   2477
Craine D T  723
Cramer C M  6373
Cramer J M  6306
Crane C C Jr     2401
Crane R     3268
Cranford Sr M E  5939
Crask R M   271
Craven D H  2768
Craver S B  4705
Crawford L H     3540
Crawford M A     4449
Crawford Q  3269
Crawford R W     2478
Crawley Sr M M   777
Crawley T E      6498
Creagh N    46
Credo E     3596
Creech E C  778
Creekmore H 5063
Creighton N E    3035
Creighton R      2342
Cresap P M       5862
Crews H     1415
Crichlow I L     4471
Crick J B   6307
Crider A B  4371
Crigler C A      2863
Crimes M M  5940
Criswell H P     1613
Crockett F Q     876
Cromer V W  3270
Cromwell J  5941
Cronmiller L G   2479
Crookshanks L    1231

Crosby R W   921
Cross A F    2480
Cross R L    4298
Cross R L    6405
Crosse C E   6957
Crouch P V   4530
Crowder A B  4800
Crowder A M  960
Crowe C T    3474
Crowl J R    6499
Crowley S M  2481
Crum C D     6796
Crump Sr A   393
Crymes J A   2218
Cuen G E     6406
Cullen Sr H M    961
Cullinan J T     8
Culver N M   5835
Cunniff A T  5022
Cunningham B E   458
Cunningham I     523
Cunningham J T   5479
Cunningham Sr S A    779
Curley J M   5747
Curran H G   5023
Curran R T   5942
Currie E L   4801
Currier B    6500
Curry C M    6958
Curry G M    524
Curtis A M   352
Curtis J L   4336
Cushing A L  4531
Cuthbert M M     3090
Cvetanovski S    2864
Czaja H M    3271
Czermak H    3475
Cziok V B    6723

Dabala C     3681
Dabney L P   780
Daeschner N  3091
Dagg M H     5943
Daley B J    426
Daley R E    58
Dallamora E L    6724
D'Amato C N  1187
Dambrauskas C K  1927
Dameron J L  781
Damerst W A  363
Dance D C    1614
Dance W L    2372
Daniel E A   1232
Daniel M     2073
Daniel M B   4017
Daniele Rev A J  525
Daniels W C  5277
Danielson J C    5944

Dankertsen E 6298
Dann L M 2264
Dardac J 1233
Darden F E 3272
Darkenwald G G 678
Darnell D G 2017
Darring W L Jr 5691
Dasgupta P 890
Daudet M E 4242
Dauer J E 87
Dauner M L 5176
Davenport A E 3682
Davenport K 162
Davenport M M 2865
Davey F F 3683
Davidson D C 6975
Davidson G A 3449
Davidson I H 4532
Davidson L B 5150
Davidson L K 6501
Davidson W E 5945
Davies C S 3522
Davies H L 2482
Davis A A 6853
Davis B A 5946
Davis B E 2866
Davis B G 6725
Davis C E 3038
Davis C L 427
Davis D H 3882
Davis E A 6308
Davis F J 625
Davis G 3181
Davis G M 4802
Davis H B 6987
Davis J B 2867
Davis J L 3684
Davis J L 5395
Davis J M 724
Davis J M 5098
Davis J R 3597
Davis K J 3883
Davis K W 4233
Davis L G 3273
Davis M 526
Davis M D 2483
Davis M D 3092
Davis M L 2265
Davis M M 4706
Davis N C 4018
Davis P A 3274
Davlin J L 2484
Dawson D L 6502
Dawson V 1098
Day M F 4803
Day R A 5480
Day R K 6274
Daytz P 3093

Deahofe W A 1615
Dean C W 6854
Dean H N 1616
Dean P T 3046
Dean W J 6347
De Angelis V 5445
De Arment W E 6684
D'Easum L 1234
Deaton F W 4804
Deauquier S 1617
DeBard R 256
Debenning E M 936
Deberry M J 3598
De Blasio M A 1235
Decary Y 1416
Decker J P 2485
De Curtis Sr E 3825
Deeman A J 4533
Deen C A 6275
Deeter G D 1618
De Falco J M 5947
DeFato G R 4805
Defoe G M 6276
Defoe J A 164
De France H S 5720
Degenfelder E P 5289
DeGregory J R 5948
DeGruson E H 5571
DeHart V M 218
De Haven R B 6503
Deich F 165
DeKanter C L 4019
Delafield C 4415
Delisle F 1236
Dell W R 782
Delmare M L 6855
Delvental L M 2486
De Maris R E 1619
Dement W P 1417
DeMerritt W 6856
De Motte G M 459
DeMouy J K 4416
Dempsey D P 5748
Dempsey W J 1237
Denboske S 527
Denham A 1238
Dennis E A 6407
Dennis J N 5177
Dennis M J 4243
Denniston C 4020
Denny L J 6652
Denny W L 3275
Denton L W 4021
DeNyse D R 5949
DePasqual J A 2868
De Quesnay M 1239
Deraney B R 4534
De Roche L 6988

DeRose M M 6726
Derrick L E 5950
Derrickson H S 2769
Dervin D A 6727
Desclos Br D 6504
DeShong C T 235
Desmond F J 3685
De Souza A 783
Dessler H 2808
Deval A M 2074
Deveau J H 4022
Devin P L 2343
Devin P L 3723
Devine Sr M E 4535
Devlin M J 528
Dew J V 3734
Dew M N 1620
Dew O E 1621
DeWaide S L 4270
DeWhitt B L 5481
DeWoskin R M 4299
D'Haene Sr H F 1418
Diamond N J 4372
Dibbell A 4023
Dickerson M 2487
Dickey B W 4738
Dickie J A 962
Dickinson G T 963
Dickinson M B 5653
Dickinson W E 1134
Dickstein E L 364
Diehl P H 4806
Diem V T 1135
Dieter J M 4729
Dignam F P 5482
Dijkstra A J 257
Dildy O 2402
Dildy U D 1419
Dillard M M 6959
Dille R G 5836
Dillon M L 6365
Dinwiddie S W 529
Dionne R C 6505
Dirks R A 5951
Di Salvo L P 3276
Dishinger M L 3758
Dismukes J H 2335
Disque J C 88
Distelzweig H L 1622
Dittmer B 5749
Diver S M 5721
Dix W S Jr 4807
Dixon A H 5374
Dixon B L 2344
Dixon B L 2488
Dixon R 5859
Djos M G Jr 2075
Dobbins C 5178

| | | |
|---|---|---|
| Dobbins D R 3094 | Doyle J P 1243 | Dunson D C 2494 |
| Dobbins M H 5483 | Doyle M M 4244 | Dunstan M G 6507 |
| Dobbs L L 2869 | Dozier M D 3759 | Dupuis E 4717 |
| Dodez M L 3476 | Drabik S F 5954 | Duque M R 966 |
| Dodge G H 4024 | Drake C M 6729 | Durr R A 3282 |
| Dodge R K 6338 | Drake J 4536 | Duskis H 5958 |
| Dodge T R 5484 | Drake J A 4450 | Dutton J F 3283 |
| Dodge W S 2870 | Drake M S 5179 | Dwelle R 119 |
| Doerfel H R 2871 | Drake S 5486 | Dwyer Sr M T 2192 |
| Doering A H 4025 | Draper L A 1624 | Dyar P M 3547 |
| Doerry K W 6728 | Drew S H 2077 | Dykes C J 120 |
| Doersam J B 3277 | Drewry G N 3182 | Dykes F T 2266 |
| Doggett I B 5485 | Dreyer L J 4417 | Dynner A J 3169 |
| Doggett M 6857 | Driscoll B G 6277 | Dysinger H H 2080 |
| Doggett M B 5368 | Drucker T 4537 | Dyson J W 3580 |
| Dolan Sr M C 530 | Drugge H 59 | |
| Dolan M F 6685 | Drum C J 784 | Eagan M G 534 |
| Dolan P A 531 | Dry B S 5955 | Eanes E J 4245 |
| Dolbee C E 4808 | Dryden E A 4026 | Earisman D L 3477 |
| Dollard P A 3936 | Dubard L L 2220 | Earle E J 4812 |
| Dombrowski A S 5283 | Dube A 3095 | Early J D 4028 |
| Dominique Br D S 219 | Dubin H N 5956 | Early Sr M N 5409 |
| Donadio S 3278 | Duboise N E 4811 | Earnest E 3599 |
| Donahue M A 3523 | Dubson M 5699 | Earwood O 967 |
| Donaldson J C 303 | DuBuron E V 3911 | Eastburn E W 2875 |
| Donelan S B 1623 | Duckett M 2404 | Eastman J 2495 |
| Donlan A C 5151 | Dudley M D 1625 | Easton P A 221 |
| Donley B L 5952 | Dueck J E 1244 | Eaton C 1420 |
| Donnelly J M 4357 | Duffy D D 5099 | Eaton D J 3478 |
| Donnelly W M 460 | Duffy D D 5957 | Eaton O L 3954 |
| Donno D J 6858 | Duffy J B 2221 | Ebdon P A 1626 |
| Donohue R J 3826 | Duffy M M 5180 | Eberhart J R 5959 |
| Doolan J 1240 | Dufour R E 1099 | Ebersole N A 3096 |
| Dooley D M 6309 | Dugan C W 6686 | Eberwine L A 3284 |
| Doran J P 1241 | Dugan N M 2874 | Echols M M 4472 |
| Dorgan G L 964 | Dugan R J 3279 | Eckhoff E 6508 |
| Dorn D A 2076 | Duggan J E 4027 | Edgar C G 2876 |
| Dorough C D 2770 | Duggar J W 3183 | Edmondson D E 60 |
| Dorough I A 965 | Duke E A 220 | Edwards A L 2267 |
| Dorrington P E 2872 | Duke P R 2490 | Edwards A L 6509 |
| Doss V L 5750 | Dula M A 4418 | Edwards C H 5960 |
| Doster W C 6859 | Dulock J A 2491 | Edwards G T 2222 |
| Dotts G B 2403 | Dummitt C M 1928 | Edwards L D 4246 |
| Doty F M 3782 | Dumbar J R 4373 | Edwards M J 1627 |
| Douglas D M 5953 | Duncan E L 2492 | Edwards M P 5961 |
| Douglas H J 2489 | Duncan J A 2493 | Egan Sr M A 1245 |
| Douglas M C 5751 | Duncan K L 3280 | Egleston L A 3600 |
| Douglass K F 1242 | Duncan S G 3281 | Egner R A 4029 |
| Douthit M H 532 | Dundore I N 6334 | Ehrenhaft G 6861 |
| Dowden W S 4809 | Dunford T A 6506 | Ehrenkranz L 4538 |
| Dowden W T 6860 | Dunham W H 6797 | Eichel S 2877 |
| Dowdle M 2873 | Dunkelberg D S 2078 | Eikleberry D L 4813 |
| Dowdy S 2219 | Dunker J 533 | Eisenman M B 4814 |
| Dowell C R 5752 | Dunlavy M F 6348 | Eisiminger S K 3453 |
| Dowell D F 5290 | Dunn H L 5705 | Ekberg L W 1246 |
| Dowell R B 877 | Dunn Sr M V 679 | Elam J C 2496 |
| Dower J W 4810 | Dunn R E 5487 | Elder O C Jr 785 |
| Downey T H 461 | Dunning S E 2079 | Elenburg M J 2497 |

Eley M   535
Eliason N E   5625
El-Khaldi H B   4815
Elkins D R   6310
Elkins L E   2498
Ellen T H   4030
Ellener L   3686
Ellinger R J   1929
Ellinger R N   5962
Elliott F S   1421
Elliott G D   968
Elliott J K   3097
Elliott L T   1930
Elliott M A   6510
Elliott R   1247
Elliott R A   5488
Elliott W M   3601
Ellis D C   4730
Ellis H J   1422
Ellis J B   1628
Ellis M W   6408
Ellison F E   6862
Ellison J   4539
Ellison R C   2373
Ellsworth M E   2499
Elson J L   1931
Emberson F G   5963
Embry C W   2081
Emerson R L Jr   1248
Emmanuel C   2500
Emmel G J   322
Emmons J L   4540
Emnett R B   5489
Endel P G   6349
Engel F H   2501
England D G   6730
England E K   5964
Engle M S   5024
Englekirk J E   4816
English C N   4817
English D   1629
English N   5632
Englund D L   6374
Enloe H M   3020
Enlow R E   3783
Ennis C A   969
Epperson W R   5753
Epstein A D   3932
Epstein C   6278
Erhard T A   5965
Erickson B A   166
Erickson C A   5352
Erickson G L   5254
Erickson M D   5966
Erickson P B   3285
Erlich M G   5754
Erstling J H   6863
Ertman I P   5967

Erwin M E   680
Erwin M N   4271
Erwin U   3098
Espy G   970
Espy R B   4818
Essary W H   258
Estes E D Jr   2502
Estey H S   4819
Estey R J   3960
Estrin M W   2809
Etheridge B W   4718
Etheridge R J   6731
Ethridge J   1998
Eubanks S W   3507
Eutsler N D   4031
Evans C J   5968
Evans E   4820
Evans F T   4419
Evans M   2503
Evans M E   3735
Evans M K   5181
Evans R A   1932
Evans V   194
Evans W A   1100
Everett G   3827
Everett M S   1630
Everett T E   5255
Evrard I   2504
Ewing L J   4541
Ewing L M   5969
Ewing M D   5025
Ewing V L   421
Exley J E   2878
Eyler C M   3548
Eyler M   4542
Eyring R   2405
Ezch M   1249

Fabian E   4312
Fabian R C   5182
Fachilla L A   1933
Fagan W   5145
Faggett H L   4473
Faggiani L A   928
Fahey J   2879
Faigen A G   4451
Fais M   5860
Faison T C   743
Faith J C   4032
Falen D J   971
Falk S L   4543
Falson M B   786
Fan H   2082
Farber N   6511
Farese J B   2880
Farfworth R M   5572
Farquhar R H   2881
Faris C B   5291

Faris P P   4821
Farish A L   4452
Farmer M J   972
Farnham A Z   5396
Farnum B E   6512
Farr J R   3099
Farragher Mother E   5128
Farrar W H   1631
Farrell D E   6960
Farrell M D   3164
Farrior J E   5410
Fash W G   1901
Faudi S M   3828
Fauer L C   6513
Faught P K   1632
Faulkner C W   5183
Faulkner F K   1633
Faulkner F W   681
Faulkner J E   2882
Faust M   3524
Faust R J   973
Fawcett V E   5755
Fawley J S   5970
Feather G K   725
Feathers S N   6732
Feazel D D   4822
Feeley Br M   323
Feeney Sr M H   868
Feied F J   3760
Fein R J   6514
Feinstein G W   4823
Felder A G   1423
Felder H M   5850
Feldman A   4743
Feldman D E   4544
Feldmann H E   4545
Feley R A   2083
Felker D D   536
Felker V   4474
Fell R D   5633
Felts S S   1424
Fennell C E   487
Fennell E J   4546
Fenner J M   4033
Fenstermaker J J   1634
Ferber D A   2883
Ferguson C E   5100
Ferguson D E   626
Ferguson J A   3687
Ferguson J B   2505
Ferguson J P   5971
Ferguson M G   3220
Ferguson O W   6989
Ferguson S M   5026
Ferguson V L   2268
Ferrell J M   6733
Ferrell M J   2506
Ferrell M J   2507

Feruglio S  3784
Fesler E E  744
Fesmire W S  3602
Ficco D F  6279
Fidelis Sr  5674
Field J T  4034
Field M J  2884
Fields N E  682
Fiene D M  5292
Fife H  3603
Figg R M III  3286
Figgins R H  537
Fill R M  5353
Filler L  2193
Fillmore L M  974
Finck J A  5972
Findley E S  3761
Fink C A  6864
Finkel D  5462
Finken E P  538
Finkle J  3287
Finklestein A D  5027
Finley J H  2084
Finnell F  2269
Finney M C  3288
Fiorelli E A  683
Fireman J K  1635
Fischer D  5973
Fischer H C  272
Fischman B S  1136
Fish M  4547
Fish S L  878
Fishel V R  5124
Fisher A  1636
Fisher A M  2374
Fisher D A  2885
Fisher L H  2810
Fisher L O  394
Fisher N H  9
Fisher W C  4272
Fishlyn S  344
Fisler G W  350
Fitch B A  1637
Fitch M J  4035
Fitchen A N  1250
Fitzgerald J F  203
Fitzgerald M  1425
Fitzgerald P M  1638
Fitzherbert E M  939
Fitzhugh N M  5974
Fitzpatrick D C  2085
Fitzpatrick E  1251
Fitzpatrick G M  3604
Fiveash M S  1639
Fix R J  4548
Flack F M  5975
Flaherty D E  787
Flaig N N  2007

Flanagan V M  2771
Flanigan R C  975
Flannery C B  4273
Flannery P A  4824
Flaxman E  3289
Fleischer C L  1252
Fleishman I P  4036
Fleming D W  1640
Fleming E M  5411
Fleming I R  6734
Fleming J W  745
Fletcher A W  1992
Fletcher E R  976
Fletcher G S  3290
Fletcher M  643
Fletcher W D  61
Fleur L Y  3100
Flibbert J T  4825
Flint J M  2223
Flippen C C Jr  3688
Floerchinger S M  4420
Flomerfelt O  2270
Flood M D  5976
Flory S  231
Flournoy M  2886
Floweday F E  3291
Flowers F C  4826
Fly R D  977
Flynn B F  6515
Flynn C J  3955
Flynn L J  3184
Flynn W J  2087
Fogarty J C  3829
Fogelman F  4350
Foley Sr G  2406
Foley R M  3830
Folsom G R  1641
Folsom S B  348
Folts P A  324
Fondacaro V J  5184
Foote N E  539
Forbis D M  3101
Forbus J K  1642
Ford A L  4731
Ford D L  6516
Ford D W  3746
Ford J M  5977
Ford M A  2086
Ford M J  3831
Ford M M  5978
Ford R D  6976
Ford T W  5979
Forderhase E D  5706
Foreman C G  3832
Foreman H E  4274
Forester W S  1253
Forgey S M  1643
Forman D K  4037

Forrey R J  4038
Forsyth Sr C M  978
Forsythe G M  3605
Fort J C Jr  4827
Fortenberry G E  6865
Fortenberry I  979
Foster C W  5980
Foster E E  2508
Foster E F  5152
Foster E J  5133
Foster E T  1254
Foster M  3915
Foster M J  5756
Foster R E  6866
Foster V N  5981
Foster V W  5185
Fouks T R  4549
Foulon M H  4300
Fourier R G  1644
Fowle P N  540
Fowler A N  4550
Fowler M J  980
Fowler V L  5490
Fowlkes B I  1645
Fowlkes G C  4039
Fox J A  5028
Fox J P  5982
Foys R M  2030
Fraad T J  6409
Frame G A  1646
Francis C N Jr  981
Francis N B  2407
Francis N T  3060
Francke R H  5029
Frandsen C W  2887
Frank K G  1088
Frank W L  2224
Franklin P M  1137
Franklin R F  3292
Franks B L  3916
Franks W M  684
Franz D C  2509
Frazier A H  3884
Frazier A S  1138
Frazier D W  5698
Frazier M E  4040
Fred R M  4828
Fredin R W  4374
Freeman A  2888
Freeman H A  3762
Freeman J  1255
Freeman J Y  4829
Freeman M  4551
Freeman M  5983
Freeman S M  5984
Freeman W E  4421
Freeman W W  4698
Freeze L H  922

Freidel R E    5284
Freling R N    4275
French A    6867
French C A    236
French F    685
French S S    5293
French W G    3171
Fresh L E    6410
Freund Sr M A    4830
Frey E T    1647
Frey G E    4041
Frey S N    492
Frezza L    788
Frick C    4351
Friederich R H    4042
Friedland R L    1648
Friedlander J    1426
Friedli M    62
Friedman H A    3808
Friedman P    3581
Friend R III    1649
Friesen P    5837
Friesen V C    5757
Frigerio E    3293
Frisch R L    5985
Frisk P    5573
Fritz D E    3479
Fritz W F    199
Frizzell J    3525
Frotscher L E    462
Fry A F    6339
Frye M M    200
Fuchs D C    789
Fujii P T    5986
Fujita N    982
Fulboam E G    416
Fulghum W B    6517
Fulkerson S J    1650
Fulkerth R C    3763
Fuller F A    3764
Fuller L B    5987
Fuller L F    4831
Fuller R C    5645
Fulton M F    4043
Fulton R C III    2889
Fultz J R Jr    790
Funk E M    4276
Funk F Z    541
Funk M A    1651
Fussell M B    5758

Gaal M M    3294
Gabbard G N    5064
Gabel S L    5491
Gabrys R E    273
Gaddy C F    3833
Gaetano T A    5988
Gage E M    2088

Gaharan C A    2089
Gainer R J    5989
Gaines B L    4719
Gaither N W    2890
Galbraith E M    3606
Galbraith M E    1652
Gale M H    4832
Gale M S    923
Gallaher M E    542
Galloway N G    2271
Galloway R D    1089
Galvin E H    4422
Galvin J R    4301
Ganim J M    1653
Gannon J A    5759
Garbuio F    3295
Garby H    304
Gardner D R    791
Gardner E    3870
Gardner G C    5990
Gardner H    792
Garig A R    2772
Garner C T    2090
Garner D    5646
Garner M F    5991
Garner N C    6735
Garner R H    10
Garnes D F    983
Garnett A M    3607
Garrett C C    2272
Garrigan K O    3296
Garrison M W    408
Garrow A S    3102
Garry J J    34
Garry Sr M J    5992
Garson H    2273
Gartner D D    1427
Garver J A    2891
Garvin S J    5186
Gaston G M    5760
Gatbonton E S    2892
Gate J E    1654
Gates G H    5446
Gates M H    879
Gatlin J C Jr    5412
Gaulding R G    2773
Gause M J    1428
Gavaghan P F    5993
Gay P M    4833
Gay W T    428
Gear A J    3541
Gearhart E S    4552
Geary Sr M    2031
Gebel G    5838
Geehern R J    2408
Geierman A J    1178
Geiger M L    6677
Genovese C A    5492
Genovese P J    5384

Gentry G E    4277
Gentry R B    2367
George E    2510
George J M    4733
George M    6868
George M R    5692
George S K    2018
Georger A J    1655
Gerber J    2091
Gercin B    5994
Gerety R    493
Gergely E J    5995
Gershgol B    5493
Gessel M A    5030
Getzels J W    3103
Geyer C K    5264
Geyer C W    2511
Gibbons E    543
Gibbs J E Jr    5413
Gibson R V    746
Giffin D A    5065
Gilbert J R    6869
Gilbert M R    4423
Gilborn A C    2274
Giles J R    5494
Gill Sr A B    5707
Gill A L    5626
Gill E L    5414
Gill L A    4834
Gillen M M    4835
Gillespie H R    4453
Gillespie V    5996
Gilliard F W    4278
Gillikin D J    3454
Gillikin S A    4424
Gilliland J D    1656
Gillingham E L    3297
Gillis A    4223
Gilmer H C    5294
Gilmore J    5327
Gimlin J M    5761
Ginkel J    6375
Ginther M L    365
Gipson M R    6411
Gipson P R    3885
Girault E S    1429
Gittings R L    5574
Giuliano G R    5187
Giusti L    1101
Glasgow E A    5851
Glasheen M A    4836
Glasrud B A    1430
Glasser H A    5997
Glendon P E    2275
Glenn B M    1657
Glenn C M    2032
Glenn Sr M C    5675
Glimp I T    4837

Glossup L C   1199
Glover E W   3608
Glover J D   4044
Glueck M W   4045
Gnewuch L   5998
Goad C M   494
Goar T T   35
Goday J M   5762
Godbold M   3736
Goddard M A   5415
Goering M R   5114
Goerlich D S   4734
Goeth R A   793
Goethals T R   5188
Goff I E   5999
Goffe L C   339
Goforth J   3562
Goforth L G   3946
Goldberg B A   6518
Goldberg H W   794
Goldberg M F   6736
Goldman E E   204
Goldman P L   733
Goldsmith O K   2512
Goldstein S   6376
Goldstein S J   5454
Goldzung V J   4838
Gomeau H O   6737
Gonsor R L   984
Gontarski S E   63
Gooch C E   366
Gooch D R   3298
Good R   2276
Goode L B   985
Goodfriend R E   4839
Goodine L O   4046
Goodman G T   1658
Goodman R E   3047
Goodrich R   2513
Goodrich V L   2514
Goodson L   6519
Goodwyn F   4317
Goold E H Jr   2046
Goold L   3886
Goold M L   2409
Goolsby O P   6000
Goran S L   3299
Gordon D W   3480
Gordon R M   5763
Gordon V   4840
Gorecki J E   5101
Goren L   1431
Goren Y N   4047
Gorman Sr M   4553
Gots B A   3300
Gott G E   6520
Gouch R L   2047
Gould A J   2515

Gould W   2516
Gourley D M   1659
Gourley D W   726
Gourley M B   6001
Gower R A   5495
Goyne L   1198
Goza E B   5328
Graber K E   544
Grabois A D   5295
Grace C L   6521
Graff F B   4048
Grafton L R   6377
Gragg P E   2019
Graham D B   5189
Graham E F   2033
Graham K T   1432
Gran C   5031
Granade C J   6522
Grant G G   205
Grant G L   3689
Grant H L   1102
Grant N   3765
Grant R E   1660
Grant R L   2336
Gravely W H Jr   4841
Graves E   121
Graves J A   1661
Graves M M   2517
Gray A A   2518
Gray A E   325
Gray A K   3301
Gray B J   1662
Gray R Jr   4049
Gray R S   1934
Greek B L   2519
Green B J   305
Green C H   206
Green C L   1256
Green F E   2092
Green I E   2774
Green J A   891
Green J E   1103
Green J G   3577
Green L B   986
Green M D   4353
Green M E   5575
Green P D   5066
Green S B   2375
Greene M E   6990
Greene M T   246
Greene N B   4050
Greenhaw C R   3302
Greenough D A   6523
Greenwalt Sr M A   4554
Greenwood J L   367
Greenwood K M   4051
Greer W   1200
Greet T Y   1663

Gregg A L   1664
Gregg D   463
Gregory D L   795
Gregory L B   2277
Grella G   3303
Grenberg B L   4052
Grenthot J S   3887
Gressman M G   3061
Greve F J   3104
Griffin B C   1433
Griffin D W   4302
Griffin E G   1665
Griffin L W   919
Griffin M E   5764
Griffin S   6378
Griffing A H   5622
Griffis M W   2329
Griffith E G   4053
Griffith K S   326
Griggs E L   4842
Grimshaw J A   6311
Grinnage W M   4054
Grinnell J   5496
Grippa E   6412
Grippo H G   4462
Grissom B S   5634
Grissom R M   6961
Griswold F C   3609
Groman G L   1666
Groppe J D   1667
Grosberg C R   2194
Grose C W   5708
Gross D   1935
Gross J R   122
Gross S W   2775
Grossi J L   1668
Grove J L   3105
Grover E B   1669
Grover S   1257
Growe B S   6798
Gruenert C F   2520
Grumet M L   3304
Grunewald W   3834
Gruninger H W   686
Gruver M A   96
Guereschi E F   5576
Guest J W   5153
Guilka Mother T E   4425
Guillory T A   11
Guilmartin A J   2278
Guilmette Rev E   4055
Gulde K   2893
Gulish G   1104
Gullattee L   1670
Gummow W A   3610
Gunderson D V   6002
Gunnell E L   545
Gunning E   2894

Gunter J O 6738
Gunter L B 4056
Gupta R K 4057
Gurian J P 2521
Gurley N W 6524
Gushee A E 2522
Gustafson S 2523
Gutheil R 274

Haas I M 687
Habel H P 6653
Haberstroh C J Jr 1936
Habosian M 1434
Hachadourian S B 4555
Hackett B B 2524
Hackworth R A 4058
Hadas D 2184
Haddad S 6525
Hagen D M 4556
Hagge H P 6739
Haggerty J P 648
Hahamovitch L 5032
Hahn B E 4720
Hahn L E 1435
Haig S L 6003
Haight H R 2525
Hailey V L 1139
Haire Sr M E 3611
Hairston J B 5458
Hairston M C 727
Halbmeier E V 429
Halbrook M S 3612
Hale Sr M F 5676
Haley F R 2034
Halfdon L 3835
Hall A W 5033
Hall B H 2526
Hall C J 2195
Hall D B 929
Hall E P 3048
Hall H M 2279
Hall L H 464
Hall L W 5765
Hall Sr M J 987
Hall P A 1671
Hall R A 6004
Hall R M 3165
Hall T 4843
Hall T H 3575
Hall W I 6526
Hallacy A R 2527
Hallahan M E 6870
Hallauer J W 4557
Haller J M 6005
Halliburton J G 796
Hallisey H A 6654
Hallisey M L 395
Halloran Sr M T 4844

Halpern B R 657
Halpern M 6799
Halpin M C 988
Halsell R J 1672
Halverstadt B H 6312
Halvorson N O 1436
Hamada M 6006
Hamblin B W 1673
Hamblin J B 430
Hamilton J B 5190
Hamilton M H 4059
Hamilton R A 6350
Hamilton W L 6871
Hamilton W T 2895
Hamlin Sr M A 2776
Hammer G W 6379
Hammill M A 2528
Hammock H M Jr 6007
Hammond A L 1674
Hammond C M 546
Hamner R D 6872
Hamon M S 3305
Hampton L H 5134
Hamsher C M 6008
Hanby M L 2529
Hancock A S 1437
Handley R E 2035
Handy D C 5034
Handy W J 1140
Hanes J E 5296
Haniford C M 465
Hanig D D 6873
Hankinson M C 6009
Hanks I M 1897
Hanks L L 4845
Hanley E A 3613
Hanley J L 2530
Hanley J M 3306
Hanlin H M 1258
Hanna W A 3106
Hannah B S 6740
Hannett B A 4279
Hannon E M 797
Hansard J D 4846
Hansen M L 6010
Hanson D N 1898
Hanson W 5451
Harbbell G S 1438
Harbeck C C 3737
Harden E S 547
Hardendorff V H 2756
Hardesty H C 5354
Hardin J B 2531
Hardin J B 6011
Harding A L 3947
Harding B F 5329
Harding W R 5766
Hardwick P A 4426

Hardy E 3021
Hardy T W 1675
Hardyman J W 2896
Hargrove M C 6527
Haring J M 3481
Hark R D 275
Harkey A P 2532
Harkins M E 2533
Harlow A G 5297
Harman W C 1141
Harmon A O 2534
Harmon P M 4331
Harmon W R 5067
Harms T C 688
Harney R 6012
Harold J 5191
Harp J T 5298
Harper B H 2410
Harper E B 3690
Harper I 548
Harper P F 6013
Harper S M 2535
Harrell M S 4475
Harrell R B 2897
Harrell R C 2536
Harrington A P 5693
Harrington E I 6874
Harrington R P 2537
Harris A N 6014
Harris F C 2538
Harris I D 4337
Harris J B 2539
Harris J E 989
Harris J H 5852
Harris J P 5577
Harris K D 892
Harris K E 123
Harris L G 5192
Harris L V 689
Harris M 3691
Harris M J 5578
Harris R 990
Harris W A 6875
Harris W E 1259
Harrison E L 6015
Harrison J P 1439
Harrison L H 6016
Harrison R C 627
Harrison S R 6528
Harrison T D 3563
Harrison W D 2540
Hart B G 2541
Hart C W 4847
Hart G V 4427
Hart W D 3482
Harte M 1260
Hartle A V 6529
Hartley D M 5416

Hartley P E    6017
Hartman J L    2280
Hartmann R A   3888
Hartsell A D   1676
Harvey H A     2281
Harvey J S     2225
Harvey N C     798
Harvey R A     3582
Harvey W M     937
Harvill L O    2093
Harwood M L    2282
Harwood S      4848
Haskel P I     1677
Hasker A K     3555
Haskins A F    1381
Hassinger E C  799
Hassler D B    4224
Hatch S M      89
Hatcher M A    5299
Hatfield F H   4375
Hatfield J F   5300
Hathcock J J   5137
Hatlen B N     6800
Hatley I       3836
Hauber M F     5767
Hauch D C      222
Hauenstein J A 1937
Haun F E       1993
Hauser R P     4330
Hausman S J    6018
Hausmann R D   4376
Hauss M A      2283
Haussman C L   4558
Havel L K      2284
Haverstick I S 4849
Hawkes H S     4850
Hawkins J      2542
Hawkins M M    5154
Hawkins R      3837
Hawkinson B R  4060
Hawthorne M    2543
Hawthorne R J  4061
Hayashi K      991
Hayden P W     1261
Hayes G C      549
Hayes S F      2898
Hayes T        3307
Hayford J H    2094
Hayne K M      36
Haynes A S     167
Haynes J B     6413
Haynes M A     1262
Haynes N B     800
Haywood R S    690
Hazard A M     1440
Hazard F P     3308
Hazlerrig J O  4377
Heady R A      5330

Healy K        5700
Hearn C R      3692
Heartz G W     3838
Heater E K     2008
Heath J H      5331
Heath L L      6019
Heaton C P     5839
Hebaisha H A   1678
Heckert D J    3066
Heckman F J    4851
Heekin R E     5417
Heemann P W    4280
Hefferman T C  5193
Heffernan G D  2544
Hefley A B     4311
Heflin J J Jr  2368
Hefling R J    4303
Hefner L D     1679
Hehl L M       5635
Heiberg A      1382
Heilman E W    3785
Heimer J W     1680
Heimsath C H   3839
Heinemann F J  1681
Heiss R L      4282
Heissenbuttel E G  466
Heitzman M B   2545
Helgeson C M   2546
Hellman D      4378
Helser E R     3062
Hembree C W    3309
Hemke M D      1441
Hempel P A     5301
Hemrich J M    3614
Hench M M      4062
Henchey R F    2899
Henderlite C E 431
Henderson C G  1682
Henderson I S  3615
Henderson M B  5447
Henderson M M  2376
Henderson N G  1263
Hendrick G     5768
Hendricks E    3549
Hendricks R    4559
Hendrickson A  3948
Hendry K       3063
Henn S E       2095
Henning C A    992
Hennis R S Jr  5035
Henry J S      3
Hensgen M D    4379
Hensley D M    4560
Hensley V W    4852
Henson D L     6876
Herlong H K Jr 3553
Herman M M     6801
Hermann L      4063

Hermanson J A    5579
Hermiz T         6877
Hern M A         550
Hernando P M     5497
Herrera V        1442
Herrick G H      6020
Herrin L         2900
Herrin W L       5664
Herring L L      4853
Herschaft P A    2096
Hershow S J      801
Hertz R L        993
Herzog J L       4561
Hess E D         5845
Hessenauer M I   6414
Hesser D C       5636
Hetherington S D 5580
Hewick W E       3766
Hewitt E C       4064
Hewitt R         6415
Hey E W          3693
Heyeck P R       551
Hiatt D F        1683
Hicks A A        4562
Hicks R S        2097
Hicks W J        247
Hiemen W         6741
Higginbotham L A 2547
Higgs R J        168
Highsmith J M    4563
Highsmith J M    6687
Highum C D       4854
Hilberg C K      6021
Hildebrand C J   1938
Hildebrand R P   6655
Hildebrand V O   1443
Hildenbrand C A  5769
Hilfer A C       1684
Hill B           4564
Hill B J         6530
Hill C L         1264
Hill D B Jr      2548
Hill D M         1265
Hill E H         3166
Hill F           5581
Hill G F         6802
Hill H L         1939
Hill J A         1685
Hill J C         4855
Hill J H         930
Hill J K         6531
Hill M A         5770
Hill M F         6313
Hill M V         4380
Hill N G         6351
Hill N M         4856
Hill O A         802
Hill R W         4065

| | | |
|---|---|---|
| Hill S 4066 | Holder K 1267 | Horne M M 3841 |
| Hill W W 6982 | Holder S C 276 | Horovitz S 1142 |
| Hilles O B 4565 | Holditch W K 6880 | Horowitz J A 277 |
| Hilliard L J 1686 | Hole L E 2549 | Horrell J T 3313 |
| Hilliard S R 6532 | Holford C 3840 | Horton A L 3767 |
| Hilt K F 803 | Holladay P 552 | Horwitz D L 3314 |
| Hilton C 1266 | Holland J E 1940 | Hoseman A 5500 |
| Hilton R 3889 | Holland R B 5194 | Hosey A A 6534 |
| Hilton S P 6742 | Holliday H J 1268 | Houghton E A 2286 |
| Hilty J R 4857 | Hollingshead M B 5771 | Houghton R E 1941 |
| Hilty M F 4067 | Hollingsworth M E 6881 | Houlihan E S 804 |
| Hince T E 2901 | Hollins M P 6025 | Housman A B 3618 |
| Hindman I 6743 | Hollister C 3617 | Houston N B 4073 |
| Hindman P K 4566 | Hollman R G 5195 | Houston R H 4567 |
| Hinkle W C 2196 | Holloman C C 2902 | Houtchens W W 5333 |
| Hinrichsen E 90 | Holloway G 2550 | Hovanec E A 3315 |
| Hirsch T 1444 | Holloway P S 4428 | Howard A B 2553 |
| Hitchcock L 4858 | Holman C E 5196 | Howard A B 6380 |
| Hitchens G 4281 | Holman H G 1547 | Howard C J 3619 |
| Hixon C 4476 | Holmes A 2285 | Howard D C 2904 |
| Hnatov F W 5455 | Holmes D 1447 | Howard H E 4707 |
| Hoag L D 5498 | Holmes D B 3558 | Howard I B 4074 |
| Hoar V M 1687 | Holmes D E 2411 | Howard J D 5709 |
| Hobbs D M 6022 | Holmes J W 97 | Howard J K 3316 |
| Hobson H E 124 | Holt B 995 | Howard J M 6744 |
| Hochman S 6314 | Holt E S 4070 | Howard L L 2554 |
| Hock C H 1445 | Holt J G 4860 | Howard W 3805 |
| Hocks R 3310 | Holt J L 6026 | Howard W W 996 |
| Hodge E A 6878 | Holt K C 3312 | Howe H B 3842 |
| Hodge L B 2377 | Holt M E 4713 | Howell B C 6882 |
| Hodge W H 4068 | Holt W A 4071 | Howell D M 4477 |
| Hodgkinson P 4354 | Holtkamp L E 2226 | Howell I R 5661 |
| Hodgson G C 663 | Holub P F 4861 | Howell J R 5256 |
| Hodgson M F 432 | Homan J 4358 | Howell M E 4075 |
| Hoegel R K 6023 | Homan N L 2185 | Howell O 6656 |
| Hoeltje H H 1446 | Homsley B S 6533 | Howze L J 2555 |
| Hoff C H 5332 | Honeycutt A 553 | Hoy J C 4283 |
| Hofferty J S 5701 | Honeycutt I B 3455 | Hoyt C L 6029 |
| Hoffman A R 6280 | Honeycutt J B 4862 | Hoyt G L 691 |
| Hoffman D 6024 | Honor Sr M 554 | Hoyt I S 2101 |
| Hoffman J A 213 | Hood C 2903 | Hubbard E 3695 |
| Hoffman L M 3185 | Hood C G 467 | Hubbard M G 1690 |
| Hoffman M E 3616 | Hoole W S 4863 | Hubbell H B 4864 |
| Hoffman R M 1688 | Hoople R P 3750 | Huber G 278 |
| Hoffman R O 2098 | Hooten M M 5197 | Hubert J M 635 |
| Hofheinz W 3694 | Hoover L 2009 | Hubert T H 997 |
| Hogan F V 6879 | Hoover W B 4072 | Huberth J C 64 |
| Hogan M 5499 | Hopkins A P 2551 | Huckabay E K 4076 |
| Hogan P 4069 | Hopkins D C 1548 | Hudson F 468 |
| Hogan Sr R 994 | Hopkins G M 1689 | Hudson H 6535 |
| Hogg R S 3311 | Hopkins K H 5418 | Hudson W P 396 |
| Hogue D R 5702 | Hopper A B Jr 4454 | Hudspeth R N 3033 |
| Hohl E D 6315 | Hoptiak E 2552 | Huebsch G V 433 |
| Holabach P 3028 | Hord L D 6027 | Huenefeld J 5710 |
| Holbrook T A 893 | Hord M C 5198 | Hueter B A 556 |
| Holden D 2099 | Horn K A 555 | Huff C A 4429 |
| Holden J B 3107 | Hornback W B 2100 | Huff M N 557 |
| Holden R E 4859 | Horne L S 6028 | Hufnell W J 1105 |

Huggins J R 6536
Hughes A J 6416
Hughes B S 3456
Hughes D A 2905
Hughes D F 169
Hughes D M 805
Hughes E E 558
Hughes H J Jr 418
Hughes J M 6657
Hughes J S 5501
Hughes K E 3570
Hughes R L 170
Hughes R N 4247
Hughes W H 1448
Hughey C M 3108
Huguelet J A 6417
Hull A T 3890
Hull D L 1691
Hull K G 6962
Hull M E 4077
Hume L M 6883
Hummel W E 1449
Humpherys A 3317
Humphrey J S 4323
Humphrey M R 4568
Humphrey S O 6030
Humphreys D M 171
Hunt A L 5334
Hunt D A 4569
Hunt H B 2102
Hunter A C 5694
Hunter G D 3318
Hunter H E 5772
Hunter L E 98
Huntington S H 2103
Huntley S M 4478
Huntress K G 5199
Huntsberry W E Jr 5502
Hupp E K 1692
Hurley A H 5582
Hursey R L 559
Hutcheson L 6031
Hutchins M V 1450
Hutchinson A R 1451
Hutter R T 4865
Hutton L 6032
Hyde S J 1181
Hyneman E 4866
Hynes C 4570
Hynes K N 99

Iacono W R 3319
Iga M 5773
Iles R L 259
Illingworth E J 3320
Imbler I I 5200
Imbriano R A 5503
Ing S J 2906
Ingargiola N A 2907
Ingber M R 3321
Ingram B P 1693
Ingram P E 3186
Irby H M 5036
Irby J A 6537
Irby L H 2556
Ireland D B 4078
Ireland H B 6538
Irey E F 1452
Irsfeld J H 3554
Irving D C 1188
Irwin N N 2227
Isenberg B C 728
Ishaq S 4079
Ison D L 1942
Itnyre T F 354
Iverson M 560
Ivey B B 100
Ivey B S 101
Izzard G G 368
Izzo F M 279

Jackson D K Jr 4867
Jackson D S 1453
Jackson F L 4381
Jackson G 4080
Jackson I 561
Jackson J W 2412
Jackson K L 3564
Jackson L B 562
Jackson M A 2908
Jackson M E 3917
Jackson P M 3450
Jackson S L 894
Jackson S W 4248
Jacobowsky N A 1694
Jacobs C B 6963
Jacobs J C 2909
Jacobs L B 1454
Jacobs P E 2287
Jacobs R D 5201
Jacobs T 6033
Jacobs W H 2910
Jacobson H A 2104
Jacoby B P 6034
Jaeger R O 4868
Jaehnig R D 4744
Jaffe M F 692
Jaks Sr M C 5129
James G 3322
James G J 6035
James N 3323
James N E 6688
James S 1695
Jamison R 563
Jancek C 564
Jankowski T A 5711
Jann R 3109
Janney E H 91
Janssen C F 6539
Jarmol H A 1269
Jarrard N E 2911
Jarrett T D 5647
Jaskol H S 3891
Jastremski S L 3571
Jefferies R L 6540
Jemison R K 1696
Jenkin L 4869
Jenkins A 2105
Jenkins J A 65
Jenkins K B 5115
Jennings E L 102
Jensen H 1270
Jensen M D 6541
Jensen V H 1943
Jenson M P 4249
Jernigan J J 434
Jessup W M 5504
Jeter V L 5654
Jetton J K 4571
Jewell P A 4081
Jewell R M 6542
Jewett E 3738
Joannides J M 1549
Jobes L M 1697
Johannsen P R 1944
Johansson J L 6036
John F E 2557
Johns H 6037
Johns R J 6803
Johnsen A 565
Johnsen E A 5505
Johnson A 3508
Johnson A B 806
Johnson A L 3324
Johnson A R 6804
Johnson A S 223
Johnson A W 2363
Johnson B A 1698
Johnson B F 4572
Johnson B M 5202
Johnson B S 2558
Johnson C W 2378
Johnson D C 1902
Johnson D G 5390
Johnson E C 3483
Johnson E G 4338
Johnson E L 5375
Johnson F S 4870
Johnson G 1143
Johnson G S 807
Johnson G W 6884
Johnson J 2559
Johnson J A 172
Johnson J D 6352

Johnson J E 5355
Johnson J K 1455
Johnson J L 1699
Johnson J M 1271
Johnson L 566
Johnson L C 5583
Johnson L E 2560
Johnson M 1700
Johnson M A 2802
Johnson M G 2561
Johnson M K 4573
Johnson N 5302
Johnson N A 6038
Johnson R T 3110
Johnson T O 2757
Johnson W S 2562
Johnson W S 6991
Johnston E B 3111
Johnston F D Jr 998
Johnston J A 6885
Johnston R C 5774
Johnston V L 2912
Johnston W M 2563
Johnston W W 567
Joiner J H 6039
Joiner S B 2288
Jolley H B 6040
Jolly R P 2106
Jones A H 6041
Jones A K 3325
Jones A L 3170
Jones B 5584
Jones B H 2564
Jones C L 4574
Jones D P 4871
Jones D R 369
Jones E 5203
Jones E E 3572
Jones E K 1701
Jones F 6418
Jones F A 5463
Jones F L 660
Jones G E 808
Jones G H 6543
Jones H F 1456
Jones I D 2107
Jones J 5265
Jones J 6419
Jones J A 2913
Jones J B 5356
Jones J H 4382
Jones J M 2565
Jones J W 3112
Jones K K 5506
Jones L A 1272
Jones L B 1273
Jones L C 6042
Jones L C 6043

Jones L L 5204
Jones M B 5419
Jones M D 5205
Jones M G 4575
Jones M J 1702
Jones M M 2566
Jones N E 1457
Jones N J 1458
Jones P J 2567
Jones P M 6044
Jones R H 5206
Jones T 2568
Jones W D 4082
Jones W M 5644
Jones W O 5775
Jons C W 5266
Jordan A G 3326
Jordan C R 3918
Jordan G M 2777
Jordan H H Jr 693
Jordan J W 809
Jordan M M 640
Jordan M R 4740
Jordan M R 5853
Jordan R A 2914
Jordan W D 2569
Jorns E E 694
Joseph E E 999
Joseph V D 4083
Josephs L S 4576
Joss G A 5585
Jost N R 2289
Joyal Sr M R 469
Joyce A B 3113
Joyce D D 630
Joyner N C 5207
Judd D W 2108
Juhan N D 470
Julian E A 2290
Julian H 2570
Julian J L 3327
Julier A L 6045
Junkin L S 1703
Junkin Sr M W 4084
Just E H 2345
Justice M H 1945
Justus J H 5420

Kabelac S L 5586
Kafka K A 4872
Kahn M 6805
Kaimowitz B R 1704
Kalaher L F 2811
Kalmer C A 568
Kalter M H 248
Kalter M J 2803
Kaluzynski T A 2915
Kamei S 6544

Kamins S R 5385
Kane Br A 6046
Kane Sr B 2109
Kannenberg B A 2571
Kaplan R A 5776
Kaplan S 4085
Kapner M R 6281
Karazincir T 12
Kartiganer D M 2572
Kasell W B 1000
Kauffmann L 4577
Kaufman A 3786
Kautz E K 6545
Kavanaugh J M 2346
Kawakubo K 2573
Kawamura K E 2778
Kay B R 6886
Kaye H J 5208
Kaye J 6546
Kays M 3768
Kean W A 3565
Keane J C 2574
Keathley L 4873
Keating E W 6745
Keating Sr M A 2357
Keating W P 66
Keaton E R 2347
Keefe Sr B M 2575
Keefe J C 6047
Keefe Sr M S 3919
Keeling F 6048
Keenan J F 6335
Keetch B 1946
Keeter G B 5507
Keim A M 810
Keleher J 1001
Kelfer G 2110
Keliher A M 2576
Keller M A 5854
Kellet J W 2577
Kelley A W 6547
Kelley C E 3114
Kelley D J 3328
Kelley E G 67
Kelley K M 6049
Kelley Sr M L 5677
Kelley R A 4874
Kelley R J 5777
Kelley W P 6282
Kellogg O L 880
Kelly C G 6977
Kelly H F 6050
Kelly H L 4875
Kelly Sr J 1274
Kelly K E 2379
Kelly Sr M O 4876
Kelly P H 6689
Kelly R 4877

Kelsay A 2578
Kendall D 3892
Kendall E F 2579
Kendall J L 3484
Kendrick J 471
Kendrick J 6051
Kendrick M S 4878
Kennedy B A 4879
Kennedy J H 370
Kennedy M M 2111
Kennedy P B 4086
Kennedy R V 2010
Kennedy S P 2580
Kenworth G E 4087
Kenyon G R 4088
Kephart E H 6052
Kepler L I 5778
Kerich Sr I M 569
Kerr C A 3620
Kerr D 6053
Kestler M 3115
Ketcham J S 5386
Ketterer D A 4089
Kettler S C 6746
Keville P R 5257
Kevordian D M 4090
Keyes C J 1705
Keyes D 3329
Keyser M B 1086
Kher I N 6548
Khiralla G 1459
Khourie J N 5508
Kiber M W 570
Kidd H L 5209
Kidd K H 1002
Kidd W E 2112
Kidder R M 1275
Kikel R J 2581
Kilburn P E 6887
Kiley G B 2779
Kilgore A B 214
Killgallon D A 3457
Killinger J R Jr 811
Kim S H 6690
Kim S J 2916
Kim Y 2582
Kimball J G 4578
Kimball R C 3739
Kimble S B 4304
Kime W R 6292
Kimmell E L 2113
Kimmins P P 2114
Kimzey V D 5335
Kineavy J F 654
King E B 362
King E G 6706
King E M 4318
King F J 6054

King J C 628
King J C 5210
King L F 2115
King M B 3622
King Sr M D 5155
King M P 1106
King M W 4721
King R W 6549
Kinnard K K 931
Kinnard W T 5156
Kinnear V E 5509
Kinnebrew M A 6055
Kinnell G M 747
Kinney F W 4091
Kinney J C 1947
Kinser E A 5037
Kinstley B S 6888
Kintner E 173
Kirby C 1003
Kirby J E 812
Kirby R R 4880
Kirk G C 174
Kirkham E B 5637
Kirkpatrick L F 1887
Kirslis P G 6691
Kirwan P S 6336
Kish D 3526
Kiska P L 3187
Kiss K G 4092
Kitamura T 3167
Klar L A 1550
Klebanow J E 2917
Klein P 5712
Klemas R M 3696
Kligerman J M 2583
Klingbeil E 6337
Klug J B 1948
Kneebone S A 3330
Knies E A 6056
Knight J A 1189
Knight J F 2918
Knight K F 3697
Knight M T 695
Knight W N 3331
Knighton E S 3332
Knival B J 5655
Knoll M F 3623
Knox J 2919
Knox N D 1706
Knox W A 4093
Knudson K D 2228
Ko H 2780
Kobler J F 3458
Koch C 4094
Koch D A 3333
Koch M L 4881
Koch S 6057
Koehler T H Jr 2229

Koehnline P G 696
Koelle K L 6806
Koenig B 4095
Kofosky R N 3937
Kogan R A 2804
Kohlmeyer H B 3116
Kohpay B 4096
Koinm A J 4579
Kolb A 2584
Kolb H H Jr 6550
Kollor D M 4355
Kominars S B 1707
Kompass A M 5840
Kone L R 5376
Koonce P L 6551
Koontz H E 664
Kores M A 1144
Korn T H 6058
Korte A H 5779
Kos S 6059
Kosove J A 729
Kostelanetz A T 5587
Kozloski D P 1708
Kramer E B 4097
Kramer L J 895
Kramer L L 3843
Kramer M H 2585
Kramer R C 3624
Kramer R E 3740
Kramer V A 37
Kramoris I J 4225
Krause D P 4463
Krause S A 1004
Kregor K 4098
Kreisberg M M 5588
Kreisman A 2116
Kremer L 1276
Kretsch C 5627
Krogh L V 5780
Krone G S 1277
Kropp M C 2117
Kruger C F 2781
Krumme E F 6552
Krupat A 280
Krupp K M 4580
Kruse A M 2586
Kruse H M 1709
Kruse M A 1949
Kshemsant S 3787
Kuczkowski R J 5068
Kueker T 2920
Kuhn J G 6553
Kuklis R D 3747
Kurre D L 1460
Kurtz R F 1710
Kurtzman M C 2921
Kuspit J C 6554
Kuyendall T R 2587

Kvasnicka G M Jr   6747
Kwok E G   1005
Kytle J S   6555

Laboon M   2118
LaCasse Sr M S   5589
Lacerva P A   4099
Lacey W R   4100
Lachtman H L   5510
Lackey A D   281
Lackey H G   5038
Lackey J E   1950
Lacy L E   3844
Ladd A M   6353
Ladd H G   3956
Ladd M E   813
Ladu A I   1461
Lagg M G   6556
Lagneau J D   3698
Lagorio V M   571
Lagoudis J A   5590
Laing H W   1278
Laing J   6060
Lakehomer L   2588
Lallamant R J   68
Lally Sr M A   5678
Lally Sr M L   5303
Lamar L W   1734
Lamb J P   3188
Lamb M   2589
Lamb S R   697
Lambert B   4250
Lambert M E   924
Lamun J A   4581
Lan Rev A P   1735
Lancaster L L   6889
Lancaster R H   125
Lanceby J K   1736
Landauer A   126
Landis S E   1006
Landon E G   3334
Landrum L M   2211
Landrum R L   1951
Lane B J   1279
Lane D D   6992
Lane D G   814
Lane M A   3485
Lane M J   1280
Lane T D   472
LaNeve G L   4882
Lang M E   4582
Lang Sr M M   6293
Lang P M   6061
Lang R S   1007
Langford T   4101
Langham M   5211
Lanier M E   6557
Lanigan A M   5722

Lankford W P   6316
Lansford H H   1737
Lantos C   6890
Lanxner W   2590
LaPierre C M   6748
LaPota M E   1952
Lappin C A   435
Larkin B M   1738
Larrabee R   127
Larsen B F   237
Larsen D C   5448
Larsen W W   1739
LaRue C   4583
Laskey H G   1281
Lasser M L   896
Lasseter V K   1740
Laster A A   6993
Latchem D   5212
Lathrop P G   4383
Latta C M   2369
Lauck A B   3117
Lauer C A   2922
Laughlin A T   3527
Laughner C L   4455
Lauter P   6558
Lautermilch S J   1741
Laux M   3335
Lavender T G   3938
Lavi G E   2036
Lavin E I   2380
Lawler J J   6891
Lawrence H W   4584
Laws H L   4251
Lawson D H   1742
Lawson J B   3336
Lawson R N   2591
Lawson V   1176
Lawson W P   4585
Lawton C   5781
Layton J S   1462
Layton P   2119
Lazar B B   4883
Lea M L   5695
Leach C   4234
Leach F H   1743
Leahy A C   2413
Leamon I G   5648
Leary C A   4586
Leathers B M   2592
Leaton A   5591
Leavell F H   6062
Leavitt C L   1
Lebowitz S   4102
LeClair T E   5511
Leddy A F   3509
Ledwell A R   1008
Lee A R   5103
Lee B Y   1744

Lee F B   5685
Lee H   1282
Lee J B   13
Lee J E   2230
Lee J N   3486
Lee L E   6559
Lee P F   572
Lee R B   6063
Lee R E   815
Lee R E   3741
Lee R F   1463
Lee T C   2923
Lee U S Jr   4384
Lee Y G   6560
Leeper H I   2593
Leeper N F   5357
Lees N C   327
Leever R S   6420
Leham A   2414
Lehnstul A B   6892
Lehrenbaum B   5213
Leibel P   3337
Leifeste M M   6561
Leiken H L   3338
Leiris H   1283
Leitz R C   4385
Lemay L   4587
Lembo L J   4588
Lemire B M   3569
Lemley R E   3893
Lemmon M A   1201
Lemon A R   1145
Lemon G   5686
Lennon J M   6978
Lensing W E   6826
Lentz M L   5267
Leonard D R   6749
Leonard J M   2120
Leonard L R   249
Leonard W M   573
LeParte P L   1745
Lerch J H   1953
Lerner C   3742
Lesley B A   4324
Lester F A   6750
Lester W P   1284
Letizia L M   4386
Leuschner G V   5512
Leveroni R   2594
Levin E B   3339
Levine J A   282
Levine J J   6064
Levins L G   1746
Levitt M P   3769
Levret Sr M C   1285
Levy A R   2291
Levy D   4884
Levy N   3049

Lewin L S  175
Lewis A E  6964
Lewis A H  6317
Lewis B  2595
Lewis C A  328
Lewis D  3566
Lewis E C  1009
Lewis J G  6751
Lewis J K  176
Lewis J L  108
Lewis L G  3340
Lewis M C  2924
Lewis M D  1747
Lewis M L  5782
Lewis M P  128
Lewis N B  6893
Lewis R E  1146
Lewis R N  2596
Lewis R P  3845
Lewis R P  4885
Lewis W L  129
Lewis W L  5135
Lewis W R  6752
Lewison N V  5267
L'heureux J C  69
Liang L S  5069
Lichtenstein W  3510
Lickteig Sr M A  4319
Lieberman H E  6065
Liebhafsky H  2121
Liedloff H  5513
Lievens Sr L  6066
Liggera J J  2925
Liggera L D  2926
Liggett W S  5214
Light E M  6421
Light G  2231
Light P  3118
Ligon L C  1748
Lilly P R Jr  5304
Linden P J  5369
Lindenberg J G  1464
Linder R A  2186
Lindley A  4589
Lindley J M  4886
Lindquest R M  816
Lindquist C A  897
Lindquist V R  1465
Lindsay K D  6562
Lindsey L B  5421
Lindstrum J L  698
Lindwall W J  4305
Linehan M W  917
Linger S E  5102
Lingle G H  6067
Link R L  2597
Linker I M  3029
Linkey A  3528

Linney D A  2348
Linton E L  5422
Linville J J  4887
Lipani D J  473
Lipe L C  2598
Lipschitz L  3625
Lipscomb M T  6381
Lipsey A C  5215
Lipson B H  3487
Lipson S  6692
Liptzin S  2782
Little C F Jr  3699
Little M V  5305
Little S V  4888
Littlejohn J J  397
Litz M A  5592
Liu H T  5514
Lively L R  5464
Livingston J T  1286
Lloyd S L  6068
Locher E W  4889
Lockhart M W  2349
Lodewick M S  4890
Loeffler Sr P C  2599
Loesch H G  6422
Loewen E A  5039
Lofton F S Jr  5216
Lofton H J  5783
Logan B L  817
Logan H D  1202
Logsdon K  658
Logue H  398
Logvin R  2037
Lohmann I D  5217
Lokensgard H  3511
Loliva E  5784
LoLordo M W  6423
Lomax K F  3030
Long A G  6069
Long E H  4479
Long P  1749
Long T L  253
Longer R M  5785
Longest G C  371
Longley J L Jr  1750
Longmire K E  5662
Longshore R H  5786
Lorance M  6563
Lorch F W  6070
Lord M F  1751
Lord M J  1954
Lorenzi R  4722
Loughlin J L  4387
Lounsbury M B  4226
Lourie R M  4104
Love A C  1955
Love L E  1466
Lovelace R E  5649

Lovell E S  2783
Lovering J P  1010
Lovering V E  6071
Low D H  6072
Lowderbaugh T E  1752
Lowe L M  5723
Lowe M A  3894
Lowe R H  1467
Lowrey L Y  4105
Lowrey R E  1011
Lowry E J  5040
Lowther A L  409
Loyola Sr M  1287
Luber J F  6073
Lubka B  4891
Lubow D K  5273
Lucas E S  6807
Lucas M F  574
Lucas P M  6965
Lucas W E  6074
Luchtel P M  1956
Luck S G  6075
Ludberg E B  4309
Ludwig A W  4237
Luedeman G  2927
Luke E J  2122
Lukens N  5423
Lunday L M  6658
Lundeen D F  2123
Lundquist R A  2038
Lutz Sr M A  1083
Lyerly R H  2600
Lynch B A  2928
Lynch B V  6076
Lynch J E  3119
Lynch J M  1012
Lynett M J  6077
Lynn J  3488
Lyon A M  2124
Lyon F L  2601
Lyon G M  207
Lyon J C  6078
Lyon J E  4892
Lyon R M  1753
Lyons H G  3895
Lyons J R  575
Lyons L C  6079
Lyons M P  748

Maass H E  5515
Mabbott T O  4893
McAdow M A  2784
McAfee A K  699
McAlester C A  70
McAlexander H H Jr  6994
McAnany E G  4284
McAndrew A J  631
MacAndrew J F  4480

McAndrew W W 4894
McAuley P H 4895
McAuliffe C P 3120
MacBain J A 1013
McBride J M 4285
McBride R H 2602
McBride S 3121
McCabe E J 3788
McCain C 2125
McCall A 6457
McCall D 2603
McCall G M 2126
McCall I S 4896
McCall M S 6458
McCall V 238
McCalman M B 4897
McCann R A 3724
McCann R V 1468
McCann W H 6829
McCarthy A 6080
McCarthy J A 3024
McCarthy L J 3896
McCarthy K M 4106
McCarty M 130
McCarty R E 1014
McCarty R S 5787
McCaskill A S 3626
McCasland E B 6693
McCasland L J 2232
McCausland I R 576
McCay M A 38
McClain E 6564
McClain M M 6979
McClare D A 3341
McClaskey M J 1015
McCleary J M 5516
McClellan R W 6894
McClelland F E 6424
McClimon G L 5855
McClintock P R 4107
McClung D H 6081
McClung J 4108
McCoid C B 208
McCollum N M 2292
McCollum W A 3189
McConn N B 5638
McConnell J C 1147
McCoppin A 4590
McCormick B H 1754
McCorvey E P 3627
McCoy C V 2604
McCraw M H 2605
McCready J D 103
McCrory M D 2606
McCulloh R S 2607
McCutcheon M L 5116
McDaniel A J Jr 3122
McDaniel B A 5517

McDaniel C 4591
McDaniel C Y 3190
McDonald C A 3939
MacDonald E E 6753
McDonald E M 4109
McDonald H S 1016
McDonald J K 6565
McDonald K I 5070
McDonald L C 27
MacDonald R D 4110
McDonald S 2608
McDonald W R 6895
McDonough J W 1182
McDowell A B 3342
McDowell B D 6659
McDowell C B 3489
McDowell J V 1288
McDowell J W 6694
McDowell O C 4111
McEachern M J 4252
McElroy M D 4898
McElroy Sr R M 6425
McEwen R E 422
McFadden L B 3725
McFadden M H 2929
McFadden N 1755
McFadin M A 4708
MacFarland D 71
MacFie A E 3036
McGary Sr M L 1017
McGhee E J 4592
McGinley Sr M W 5125
McGinley W J 1469
McGinn R J 4388
McGinnes J H 577
McGinnis H H 6566
McGlockton Y E 6082
McGoldrick S E 1470
McGoughran J H 4112
McGowan C 1018
McGrath A M 6083
McGrath Sr C M 3628
McGrath N E 3343
McGrath S A 1019
McGraw M H 3050
McGregor M 3573
McGregor M D 1107
MacGregor R R 5306
McGriff R C 730
McGuiggan Sr K L 3897
McGuire E E 6084
McGuire J F 6085
McGuire L S 2187
McGuire W J Jr 5117
Machado J 818
McHaney T L 1756
McHarg C W 6086
McHenry S M 6087

Machin J M 4253
Machin S J 5071
McIlnay P K 5088
McInerney T J 1957
McIntire V S 1020
McIntyre J M 4113
McIver J M 1203
Mack G L 2415
McKay A G 5788
MacKay H H 6567
McKay M B 2197
McKee J 4114
McKee M H 2930
McKee R E 2609
McKeirnan A C 2610
McKeithan D 2611
McKelvain I 5452
MacKendrick L K 5518
MacKenzie E H 4593
McKerahan A L 6568
McKethan F B 5656
McKibben L J 2612
McKinney E L 5657
McKinney V W 201
McKinnon W T 2785
McKitterick T M 283
McKneely L M 2381
McKnight V 5724
McKnight V W 4313
McKoin F 2931
McLain I M 3743
McLain M W 5519
McLane E R 4594
McLaughlin F B Jr 1289
McLaughlin L E 3344
MacLay R F 2932
McLean K R 4115
MacLean M V 6426
MacLean R A 14
McLean R C 819
McLeister W E 940
McLennand M C 2293
McLeod A A 2382
MacLeod N 2933
McMahan E E 6088
McManus M A 3031
McManus M H 4899
McManus P A 6754
McManus P F 6569
McMartin C M 1994
MacMaster J 4116
McMeen M F 5593
MacMillan K D 4117
MacMillan M M 2613
McMullan B L 4595
McMullen M 3345
McNair H 4900
McNamara J W 6089

| | | |
|---|---|---|
| McNamara O 1148 | Mamoli R 1760 | Martin M K 1022 |
| McNames D G 1757 | Mancuso J C 2937 | Martin P 4905 |
| McNeer M W 700 | Maness E M 701 | Martin R T 6827 |
| McNeil C C 6896 | Mangano J V 239 | Martin T J 821 |
| McNeil E S 5424 | Mangano K F 1761 | Martin T K 2040 |
| McNeil K V 6570 | Manly W M 3347 | Martin V A 3898 |
| McNeil L M 6897 | Manning G F 820 | Martinez A M 6575 |
| McNelis Sr M A 1383 | Manning J F 6092 | Martinez I 4122 |
| McNew U H 6755 | Manning W E 4119 | Martyanova O P 2938 |
| McNiff A M 5307 | Mannix E L 6573 | Marx R R 6096 |
| McNille R C 3940 | Mantel M G 72 | Masiuk C A 1023 |
| McNutt A S 6318 | Mantor R 2294 | Mason C R 636 |
| MacPherson D B 2416 | Manuel G E 6093 | Mason D J 3350 |
| McPherson D C 6319 | Manzo F 3666 | Mason I M 6758 |
| McPherson M E 4901 | Marblestone R A 284 | Mason L D 6097 |
| McQuarie E 578 | Marcon A 6094 | Mason M N 4599 |
| McQueen W B Jr 423 | Maresca D G 5595 | Mason W S Jr 4600 |
| McQuilkin R R 4118 | Maria F 3490 | Masse M 6098 |
| McQuiston R 1471 | Marimon R B 2295 | Massello W 4906 |
| McQuitty R A 6090 | Maring A S 1472 | Masters G B 3957 |
| McTaggart A C 6832 | Marino J A 6757 | Masters R W 4601 |
| McTague S H 1149 | Marino P E 4120 | Mastrow W 4602 |
| MacVicar M B 2127 | Mark R N 5790 | Matchette W A 4431 |
| McWhinney N N 4902 | Markey M M 3067 | Matheny C A 6576 |
| McWhirter G E 1150 | Marks A H 6574 | Mather M 92 |
| Madden E M 2614 | Marley M C 133 | Matherne Br A 3789 |
| Madden Sr M R 2615 | Maroney J M 4430 | Matheson T J 898 |
| Magee M K 2616 | Marotte B E 1473 | Mathews A G 5522 |
| Magee M V 4339 | Marple J 3221 | Mathews G S 4907 |
| Magers A J 3700 | Marquardt H L 4903 | Mathews H R 5523 |
| Magginis M A 5218 | Marrin D B 5370 | Mathews R D 3351 |
| Magner J E Jr 1290 | Marsh A M 3629 | Mathias E L 6099 |
| Magowan R A Jr 3529 | Marsh L A 2619 | Matsumoto R 582 |
| Magruder W T 1758 | Marsh M M 580 | Matthews J B 5308 |
| Maguire J L 6756 | Marsh P M 2048 | Matthews R D 1474 |
| Maguire J T 579 | Marshall C E 4904 | Matthews R O 1763 |
| Mahan L W 4596 | Marshall C L 399 | Matthis L C 1475 |
| Mahanay V F 5789 | Marshall D W 5791 | Matzner C 229 |
| Mahar A S 2128 | Marshall I J 5387 | Mauch R C 2131 |
| Maher A M 3846 | Marshall J S 1762 | Maurer B S 1764 |
| Maher M S 2617 | Marshall S S 4597 | Mawer R R 5524 |
| Maher V M 2129 | Marson A 3348 | Maxwell B H 6899 |
| Mahla D K 2130 | Martin A A 6898 | Maxwell E 306 |
| Mahoney C A 5520 | Martin A B 6095 | Maxwell M R 5377 |
| Maier J L 1021 | Martin A H 3349 | May J A 2621 |
| Maik A J 131 | Martin A L 3123 | May S H 3352 |
| Mainord D L 2934 | Martin B 4121 | Mayberry S J 5687 |
| Maixner P R 3346 | Martin C B 5136 | Mayer C W 3124 |
| Major M 2618 | Martin C J 5521 | Mayer N D 1024 |
| Maley D C 6382 | Martin D F 285 | Mayes M A 3125 |
| Malik B A 5594 | Martin H D 2620 | Mayes T R 2622 |
| Malmsheimer L M 2935 | Martin J 1291 | Mayeski Sr M I 1292 |
| Malone F N 2936 | Martin J F 581 | Mayhall F 1151 |
| Malone W K 6571 | Martin J F 4481 | Maynard A J 6577 |
| Maloney F J 6091 | Martin J M 4598 | Maynard Sr A R 3353 |
| Maloney M J 132 | Martin J P 5103 | Mayo E P 6100 |
| Maloney V G 6572 | Martin L J 5792 | Mays J L 73 |
| Maluski A M 1759 | Martin M 3550 | Mays M 3556 |
| Malysz T K 749 | Martin M 6995 | Mazaher K H 4603 |

| | | |
|---|---|---|
| Mazeika E J 2939 | Miller B L 3530 | Mitchell Y G 3057 |
| Mazow J 4908 | Miller D L 1294 | Mitiguy M E 1296 |
| Mazzella A J 3354 | Miller E E 3356 | Mittelstet S R 4286 |
| Meadors O G 4482 | Miller F A 315 | Miura A 825 |
| Meathenia J 5793 | Miller G G 5268 | Miyake A 1297 |
| Meck E C 2623 | Miller G P 2941 | Miyatake T R 1027 |
| Meech L J 1476 | Miller H 5358 | Mizer R E 5425 |
| Meehan F 6101 | Miller J 1025 | Moake F B 6901 |
| Meek P H 1293 | Miller J C 6900 | Moffett A S 4609 |
| Mehlman M H 6102 | Miller J D 2626 | Moffett J L 1712 |
| Mehlman M M 2624 | Miller J L 1152 | Mohrhauser J R 5220 |
| Meier D E 4604 | Miller J L 1153 | Moldenhauer J 6107 |
| Meisel P A 5525 | Miller J A 4456 | Moldenhauer J J 1155 |
| Melrose M M 1765 | Miller L E 1960 | Moldenhauer M L 3128 |
| Meltabarger B A 1766 | Miller M R 2198 | Momberger P 4124 |
| Melvin B W 2940 | Miller M S 4725 | Mongan A 1480 |
| Menefee H H 6354 | Miller N E 4912 | Monherran M 3360 |
| Menke P G 6203 | Miller N G 584 | Monjian M C 3491 |
| Mentin E H 1477 | Miller P A 702 | Mont S 1108 |
| Mentzer E S 5336 | Miller R H 3357 | Montagna A 4610 |
| Mercier J D 822 | Miller R Z 1768 | Montgomery A E 6581 |
| Meredith C 2350 | Miller S 5309 | Montgomery P C 1298 |
| Meredith G 2625 | Miller V 5219 | Moody B D 1481 |
| Merideth R D 4389 | Miller V L 3358 | Mooney D N 705 |
| Merren J J 5526 | Miller W C 6579 | Mooney H F 1961 |
| Merrick A H 3899 | Milligan J P 4607 | Mooney H J Jr 5041 |
| Merriman L 4723 | Milliken E R 329 | Mooney M S 4341 |
| Merritt C S 5665 | Millis W III 2942 | Moor G 4287 |
| Merritt J 583 | Mills E M 4432 | Moore A G 177 |
| Mestayer M 2786 | Mills F H 4340 | Moore C A 6366 |
| Metfessel C S 3790 | Mills J A 254 | Moore C W 2297 |
| Mett M A 5527 | Mills L G 2627 | Moore E L 4709 |
| Metzgar J V 4724 | Mills R B 1026 | Moore G B 6108 |
| Mewshaw N 6104 | Mills R E 5528 | Moore H K 3129 |
| Mexxanotte J J 4909 | Minchew S 2943 | Moore J A 2417 |
| Meyer B R 74 | Minks E W 6105 | Moore J B 6427 |
| Meyer E 3355 | Minniehan H B 6106 | Moore J F 1713 |
| Meyer M G 134 | Minor D E 703 | Moore J K 495 |
| Meyer R A 1767 | Minor O 4714 | Moore J S 1962 |
| Meyerle M H 5666 | Minott A C 4608 | Moore L L 4741 |
| Meyers D 6578 | Minton L 1084 | Moore L S 4433 |
| Miazga R C 1958 | Mintz G K 47 | Moore L Z 3630 |
| Michael C K 2333 | Miranda J C 400 | Moore M M 1028 |
| Michaelson E L 6320 | Mirsky M 1295 | Moore M M 3051 |
| Michelsen C 4605 | Misch T 5713 | Moore Sr M R 1299 |
| Mickleson V 823 | Mishler C W 704 | Moore N 4611 |
| Middlebrook L H 1478 | Miskin R 1711 | Moore P 2049 |
| Middlebrook M A 5378 | Missio R 3359 | Moore R G 5650 |
| Middlebrook M E 4910 | Mitchell A N 1479 | Moore R H 3361 |
| Middleton F S 2351 | Mitchell B L 824 | Moore R H 6109 |
| Miles B L 3900 | Mitchell D P 4123 | Moore R S 2629 |
| Miles E R 3126 | Mitchell E R 4483 | Moore S G 2132 |
| Miles N 2233 | Mitchell J A III 1892 | Moorhead R 3130 |
| Milford N 1959 | Mitchell M 3127 | Moran C R 4913 |
| Milgate E J 1769 | Mitchell M E 2296 | Moran M W 3531 |
| Milicia J Jr 1090 | Mitchell R 1154 | Moran N R 3022 |
| Milkey L M 4606 | Mitchell R E 135 | Moran V A 1482 |
| Millard A E 6660 | Mitchell S L 2628 | Moreland M E 474 |
| Miller A M 4911 | Mitchell W H 6580 | Morelli A 4612 |

| | | |
|---|---|---|
| Morelli M 6582 | Muncy E R 5379 | Nelb B F 1720 |
| Morey F L 1029 | Munitz M K 5359 | Nelms P M 2948 |
| Morey J F 330 | Munk E A 6824 | Nelson A 3701 |
| Morgan A D 6110 | Munoz M E 900 | Nelson A D 6121 |
| Morgan E A 6111 | Murdock M 1718 | Nelson B 2787 |
| Morgan E D 5794 | Murphy A C 6114 | Nelson E J 1303 |
| Morgan J C 3362 | Murphy A F 345 | Nelson F M 3702 |
| Morgan L J Jr 2944 | Murphy B 901 | Nelson G 1304 |
| Morgan M V 3131 | Murphy C 828 | Nelson H S 831 |
| Morgan R A 1963 | Murphy J A 1031 | Nelson J R 832 |
| Moriarty P A 1300 | Murphy Sr M 1301 | Nelson J T 6902 |
| Morillo M 341 | Murphy M W 6430 | Nelson M 2949 |
| Morley I 4434 | Murphy P J 109 | Nelson M S 6294 |
| Morris C M 1030 | Murphy W A 4916 | Nelson P S 5043 |
| Morris E G 4914 | Murray H F 829 | Nelson S A 3367 |
| Morris E V 4390 | Murray H G 706 | Nelson S L 4919 |
| Morris H B 1714 | Murray J 6115 | Nerney J K 15 |
| Morris H H 4391 | Murray M 5795 | Nerone B N 3791 |
| Morris J A 5426 | Murray M F 5260 | Nesbitt I L 5142 |
| Morris M M 372 | Murray P 902 | Ness R W 287 |
| Morrison E V 6428 | Muse J L 6116 | Nesselhof J M 1721 |
| Morrison J T 826 | Mussetter S A 2946 | Netcel T 903 |
| Morrison Sr M K 1715 | Myatt J E 5310 | Nethercutt B G 3191 |
| Morrison N L 2945 | Myer E G 2298 | Neubauer R J 5072 |
| Morrissey W R 827 | Myers A M 286 | Neuman M A 3368 |
| Morrow J L 39 | Myers C 401 | Neumann R 4484 |
| Morse M J 6429 | Myers C R 488 | Neuner M 6122 |
| Morton D B 3363 | Myers M H 1032 | Neuwirth L M 2950 |
| Morton M S 6980 | Myers M O 6117 | Newberry E 4920 |
| Morton P S 6112 | Myers N B 2133 | Newbold M R 2635 |
| Morton W W 4392 | Myers W E 436 | Newcomb M E 3848 |
| Mortus C A 6759 | Myhr I L 6830 | Newell F W 1305 |
| Moseley F S 1716 | Myklebust G 5529 | Newland P D 136 |
| Moseley N L 6113 | | Newlon N B 6966 |
| Moser R E 6583 | Nabers M L 587 | Newman A E 6996 |
| Moses M R 1483 | Nagel J E 4464 | Newman B P 632 |
| Moskowitz A L 5141 | Nagy C E 1719 | Newman C E 4616 |
| Moskowitz M M 4613 | Nahal S 2947 | Newman C M Jr 6903 |
| Moss M C 5596 | Nakamura J 4917 | Newman J 1722 |
| Moss R F 2630 | Nangeroni O M 3365 | Newman M 6123 |
| Moss W H 2631 | Narducci P C 2134 | Newman M B 5221 |
| Motard P P 3364 | Nascimento D C 6431 | Newman P W 6124 |
| Motchenbach F 4915 | Nash A G 3847 | Newman W S 4435 |
| Moudy L F 585 | Nash D J 5530 | Newport V 2636 |
| Mowry V L 734 | Nash E B 5465 | Newton M E 4 |
| Moyer R W 2188 | Nasman D J 6696 | Nichol J W 3770 |
| Moyles R G 1156 | Natterstad J H 1302 | Nicholaides E I 6661 |
| Mukerjee S 6584 | Naugler F W 661 | Nicholas R J 1723 |
| Muldoon M M 5042 | Neal A H 830 | Nichols J 4126 |
| Mulhall Sr M S 4614 | Neal S B 4918 | Nichols G E 2637 |
| Mullady E T 1717 | Neel S E 1157 | Nichols P A 5428 |
| Mullaly G E 4615 | Neel Y L 2633 | Nicholson L L 2135 |
| Mullane Sr M C 2632 | Neeley W A 6118 | Nicholson P J 6321 |
| Mullen J C 5427 | Neff A R 3366 | Nicholson V 707 |
| Mullen P B 899 | Neff E 3726 | Nickless F P Jr 6585 |
| Mullin A B 586 | Neff M L 6119 | Nicoloff P 5796 |
| Mullins P A 4125 | Neidhardt F E 2634 | Nielsen K 4457 |
| Mullins R J 6695 | Neill A B 6120 | Nigliazzo M A 1724 |
| Mumford D 1484 | Neill R E 5597 | Nilsson C M 6125 |

Nisnewitz F  833
Nix R V  475
Nixon N M  5429
Nnolim C E  4127
Noack R B  2136
Noble L  2137
Noble R V  588
Noel P K  6126
Noer P G  232
Nolan C E  2138
Nolan E D  938
Nolan J S  3132
Noland R W  6808
Noll D L  5714
Noll I  2383
Nolte W H  6904
Noonan M A  5222
Nordan L A  5531
Nordin D G  1109
Nordman T H  1306
Nore B  589
Norgress B  137
Norman H M  3703
Norred B A  2299
Norris O W  2788
Norsworthy F  1903
North N C  424
Northcut M N  1307
Norton Sr E  869
Norton S B  1964
Norwood K R  4617
Norwood L R  2384
Norwood V L  5696
Nourse A B  373
Novack A  4921
Novik G M  1308
Nowell R  6127
Nowik N A  6432
Noyes N  3369
Null S  4922
Nunnally E E  6707
Nussbaum J C  1888
Nutter D  2638
Nutter L W  6128
Nyenhuis M E  3370
Nyholm J P  5278
Nyland G C  1033
Nyquist M  6662

Oaks M R  2300
O'Bannon R H  1158
Ober R W  2011
Oberlin B G  3744
Oberparleiter L G  834
O'Brien M  750
O'Brien M C  1725
O'Brien M L  6663
O'Brien W P  5388
O'Bryan P A  5044

Ochiltree R A  6760
O'Connell M C  3371
O'Connell S V  3372
O'Connor J T  4254
O'Connor Sr M C  2639
O'Connor M R  2139
O'Court M E  4128
O'Dell C A  6905
Odell J I  6129
Odle Z R  6130
O'Donnell B N  1485
O'Donnell N F  5797
O'Donnell T F  835
Odum M K  3373
Oehlk R W  4393
Oelke K E  5466
Oetken J  40
Oetting M F  3532
O'Gara E J  1486
Ogden F R  3871
Ogden T H  1309
Ogilvie J T  2140
Ogle G L  4342
Oglesby E A  6131
Ohara D M  5223
O'Hara R C  6906
Ohlin P H  5073
Ohr M E  6664
Ohta K  2141
Oi J T  75
O'Keefe I M  836
Olenick M  476
Olf J M  3025
Olivella T  1159
Oliver C  5532
Oliver E C  3192
Oliver H A  6809
Oliver J C  5311
Oliver J S  5667
Oliver V H  6907
Ollington M H  76
Olmstead P R  5533
Olney C  3374
Olsen F B  1726
Olson C  3901
Olson C J  4129
Olson C R  5598
Olson O J  5224
Olson R H  3631
O'Marra B S  3133
O'Neil Sr M T  3375
O'Neill M M  5045
O'Neill M T  904
Onley G E  3376
Onthank C  4332
Oppenheim A  2301
Ora J P Jr  1160
Oravets A J  1727
Orbison D  905

Ordeman J T  906
Orgain M M  224
Ormsbee E  590
Orozco G H  5225
Orr D B  2951
Orr E E  1728
Orr Sr M S  4923
Orr T J  3492
Orsini D M  1034
Orts D H  5430
Osborne R S  6665
Osburn L  6586
Oscar R E  4255
Oseroff J R  4618
Osikowski J  6587
Ostrander E H  6132
Ostrander J  2640
O'Sullivan R T  2641
Otey R W  1487
Otjen M E  4343
Otness L G  1310
O'Toole A J  4619
Ott C R  4924
Ott E  5431
Ottervik E V  3377
Ottmers B J  6810
Ouellette A J  1110
Ouzts C E  4436
Overpeck E  5651
Overton D  1729
Owen C F  4130
Owen D S  3704
Owen E E  3378
Owen V R  1541
Owens B K  437
Owens L  3193
Owens M  591
Owens S C  708
Owings R S  3632
Owre B M  6811
Oyler M J  5534
Oyzon C K  3379
Ozawa C K  5798
Ozick C  3380

Pace A L  4620
Pack R M  5599
Packenham H E  4925
Packer J E  6133
Pac Urar G  3134
Padden Sr M J  4394
Padgett T E  5639
Page R E  2001
Page R S  1730
Page T M  4926
Page W E  5046
Pagnucco D G  6367
Paine J R  2352
Paine S C  6134

Pak K D  5074
Pak T  1311
Paliez M A  477
Palmer C  4621
Palmer E A  5337
Palmer J H  438
Palmer L H  2642
Palmer M H  6135
Palmer O M  4395
Palmer S G  2199
Palmieri A F  178
Palmquist E  5456
Pandit M  2643
Pappas D M  1312
Pappas G M  4927
Parello S M  1111
Parillard D  4622
Paris M  2050
Park R  837
Park W J  1731
Parker D G  1313
Parker J L  3194
Parker K F  4623
Parker L  1488
Parker M E  5799
Parker M M  1732
Parker P J  3195
Parker R W  5075
Parker T V  4131
Parker T W  4624
Parkinson L F  1899
Parkman M R  1489
Parks A J  592
Parks J S  28
Parks K I  5600
Parks L L  2758
Parks S R  6136
Parkyn S F  5800
Parmantie P A  1551
Parnell H A  1965
Paroissien D  3381
Parr K H  6762
Parrish J A  2812
Parshall R L  4396
Parson S  5801
Parsons H V  3533
Parsons M L  3705
Parsons O W  6588
Parsteck B J  5601
Partridge C E  4928
Pascarelli J T  6812
Pasinetti P  2644
Pasquier-Doumer M C  6137
Past R E  6833
Pastore J M  6368
Patch A  3451
Pates A S  709
Patten L  4929
Patterson D R  3544

Patterson J M  225
Patterson M K  2302
Patterson O M  1035
Patterson V K  2789
Patton F K  6138
Paty S  5856
Paul Br A  4625
Paul C G  2012
Paulin R N  2200
Paulits Br F J  1490
Pavich P N  3578
Paxton P M  138
Payerle C S  5535
Payne D E  4626
Payne D M  907
Payne J P  5536
Payne M B  4465
Payne R D  1904
Payne V  4930
Payton M C  4627
Payzant M  1036
Peabody H W  6139
Peach S  4931
Peacock V S  4306
Pearce E F  3633
Pearce J R  1733
Pearce V R  5725
Pearsall E A  6763
Pearson L M  5688
Pearson L E  5802
Pearson R L  2952
Peck J R II  5118
Peck R W  3706
Peckham B A  2142
Peckler C  5226
Pedersen P  1770
Pelz K L  1037
Pemberton V H  751
Pena J A  731
Pendergraf R C  2143
Pendergraft J H  2144
Pendleton J D  2645
Penner A R  5537
Penner J T  4932
Pennington P G  2145
Pennington R L  5658
Penny B J  2646
Penta C  2201
Pepper G B  6666
Percival M M  4933
Perkins C C  6764
Perkins K  2647
Perkins V L  6295
Perlman H D  4934
Perosa S  1966
Perotti V J  3382
Perreault J H  6908
Perrey R T  4132
Perri J M  6140

Perrin E  4437
Perrin E N  3383
Perrin M L  2953
Perrone M B  179
Perry E B  908
Perry E M  4935
Perry J  4628
Perry J D  1967
Perry M E  3634
Peterie P  307
Peters B L  4629
Peters E R  6283
Peterson C S  195
Peterson J  4133
Peterson J M  6765
Peterson M L  5668
Peterson N A  5227
Petree R L  1038
Petrella M C  1314
Petrick A  2648
Pettie R P  4630
Pettigrew M M  5228
Petty W E  3707
Pfeiffer C G  5726
Pfeiffer J F  1968
Pflugrad G  6766
Pharr M E  4134
Phelps F M  3849
Phelps H C  3493
Phelps M  6589
Phelps P R  6909
Phelps S E  2303
Phillips E  6433
Phillips E L  5803
Phillips J B  1315
Phillips M D  2649
Phillips R C Jr  5804
Phillips R L Jr  4631
Phillips R S  3902
Phillips R V  1771
Phillips S C  6825
Phillipsen E  1316
Phipps M C  1039
Phleger R P  6141
Picard A M  6590
Piccini L  2650
Pichette K H  2146
Pickard C V  3850
Pickard F P  2234
Pickard L D  659
Pickens M  6142
Pickering C  4632
Pierce B M  2790
Pierce C  6383
Pierce F M  1317
Pierce J R  3039
Piercey M A  1995
Pierotti S  5312
Pierson A N  593

Pierson R C    4397
Pietens B G    1112
Piippo L R    5047
Pike C M    4485
Piket D    2651
Pilcher M H    4633
Pilkington J P    1772
Pilkington M A    209
Pilkington W T Jr    4135
Pillai A K    5805
Pinckney E R    139
Pincus H    3384
Piner O    1491
Pines S    4634
Pinkham S V    1087
Pinsky R    1318
Pirozzi J P    6434
Pisk G M    6384
Pitman J    4136
Pitrella M A    4256
Pittman F E    3551
Pittman W L    2954
Pizarro J    4137
Plant J F    4936
Pleasants M G    2791
Ploceinnik E J    3851
Plouffe J B    140
Plut J L Jr    6997
Plyler C A    2759
Pochmann H A    6143
Podolyn J C    2418
Poe J W    6144
Poe M C    1773
Poger S B    5806
Pohler L E    4937
Poindexter J    4938
Poke J O    1774
Polhemus A S    4288
Pollard P H    41
Pollard R A    1775
Pollitt D M    5669
Pollock G W    6145
Polocek J H    5338
Polsgrove C C    1384
Pomidor W J    3196
Pongrace M B    1319
Pool M V Jr    4635
Pope K V    4138
Pope W J    1320
Popp R J    5432
Port R E    2652
Porter D M    2304
Porter J    2955
Porter J L    1040
Porter M D    2305
Porter M G    5313
Porter M M    1321
Porter N W    1492
Porter R J    5076

Porterfield C    1776
Porterfield N    3385
Postell J M    6435
Posten B    1041
Poston C D    4636
Poston T H    1777
Potter D    4139
Potter J L    3920
Potter M L    141
Potter N A    5807
Potter W D    6146
Potts S M    410
Pousson J D    6147
Powell A    1493
Powell D E    6591
Powell D J    3386
Powell F A    5450
Powell W D    649
Power H L    2353
Powers D    870
Powers D A    250
Powers M A    2147
Powers V M    3494
Poxson D M    1778
Pozychki M A    6148
Prang E L    4140
Prater W G    6910
Pratt J C    2956
Prebus H M    2653
Prendergast A F    594
Prengel R D    838
Preslar R W    6911
Presley M C    2957
Pressley R    2654
Presson H    5397
Preston D E    2235
Preston F R    4939
Preston J F    1322
Presturich L A    3852
Prewett J    2958
Price M    6149
Price M M    1323
Price M M    1494
Price N L    6150
Price O R    1042
Price R P    2020
Priddy B H    4289
Priddy J C    3635
Priddy R M    932
Prince F N    4141
Prince P V    6767
Pritchard A S    2354
Pritchard A S    4438
Pritchard O B    3387
Pritchard W L Jr    2959
Proctor I E    5538
Proctor K R    6151
Proper S H    2655
Propst H C    6592

Prosser M H    2656
Proud G F    1495
Prouly J W    710
Prown J D    3197
Prowse W F    355
Pruitt P B    2960
Pruitt V D    6768
Puckett C E    1496
Pugh A E    4940
Pugh G F    5229
Pugh R    6593
Pugh L    3135
Pullen Sr M C    3636
Pullen M G    5453
Pulliam J F    4398
Pulliam R    3136
Pullin Z    2657
Pulvirenti A    2658
Purcell B    6813
Purcell I M    4941
Purvis G G    104
Puryear M J    1542
Putnam R E    752
Puzio E M    1969
Pyland J L    1779

Quaid L D    3949
Quattlebaum M    110
Quayle T D    288
Quesenbery V E    2659
Quick E N    4637
Quigg J M    2961
Quigley M E    2358
Quillen F W    6284
Quillen R C    6761
Quinn F M    1043
Quinn M W    4942
Quint M E    3388

Rabe K G    6667
Rabicot A M    4142
Rabkin G E    1324
Raby T N    226
Rackley B J    5808
Radetsky P H    5809
Radley V L    3792
Radosevic N E    6769
Raffel B    1325
Rager L G    6770
Raisanen E A    5539
Raitt M D    2306
Rakowski L F    1326
Raley Sr A L    871
Ralph E R    6436
Ramee E E    2660
Ramey L O    5659
Ramos D C    6594
Rampersad A    4143
Rampey W L    2307

Ramsey E J    2308
Ramsey E S    839
Ramsey L A    3708
Ramsey V      941
Ramsey W C    1780
Randall E     1781
Randall H L   4170
Randall R B   3198
Randle F A    4943
Randolph E C  6912
Rankin D L    48
Rankin E R    6595
Ranney Z F    2148
Ransom M F    4638
Ransom W S    5122
Ranson R E    289
Rasco E E     4944
Rasco K F     1782
Rasco L       3389
Rasco R C     4639
Raskin J      3390
Ratcliffe R R 6152
Rath S        6596
Rathbun R C   4144
Ratliff S     5048
Rau S G       1783
Ravenel M C   6437
Ravetch P H   2792
Ravn H W      6153
Rawe L R      711
Rawlings M G  2330
Rawlins V M   16
Ray H H       4640
Ray I E       3745
Ray L L       2149
Ray M E       3709
Ray R E       4145
Ray R J       1327
Ray R M       4945
Rayburn H S   2309
Raymond E     308
Reader M      1190
Reader W D    6913
Reading E L   1497
Reagan F C    6154
Reagan R R    1328
Reagan R S    2962
Reardon J D   2963
Reaver J R    4320
Reck T S      6771
Reckford P    6155
Record V S    3199
Redd L M      3255
Redderson T T 2021
Reddy K C     1044
Redekop E H   4146
Redmond J O   2661
Redmond M M   3727
Reed A C      2662

Reed D I      4486
Reed E E      6333
Reed H R      3200
Reed J        3052
Reed J Q      5810
Reed P R      1329
Reed R C      5811
Reeder D C    5360
Reese Sr D    909
Reese O S     2150
Reese R       3903
Reeves E W    840
Reeves R      2310
Reeves R C    2364
Reeves T      1191
Regan J V     5540
Reger L S     6597
Register W R  6598
Reibel D E    3137
Reich R       3391
Reid A        3392
Reid A S      2663
Reid B L      5467
Reid E T      6772
Reid J L      1045
Reid L P      3201
Reid M J      6814
Reif A        1970
Reiff V B     6355
Reiman A E    5602
Reimers F D   2311
Reinke E L    1046
Reirdon S R   1784
Reiss J H     4399
Relkin H J    496
Remaley P P   3495
Renalds B H   180
Reneau P S    5085
Reney Sr M M  1047
Renfrew M     5230
Renzino G     6668
Reser J A     181
Resnick R B   2419
Resnick S     4946
Reumert P     4641
Revelise M    439
Revell P      5146
Rewak W J     1498
Rexroat R     595
Reyer P       4290
Reynolds A    29
Reynolds P    4642
Reynolds V E  210
Rhinesmith S C 182
Rhoades J A   6773
Rhoades N S   5231
Rhodes G M    6815
Rhodes Sr M T 6156
Rhodes R H    4643

Rho-Servi L   6599
Rhyne M R     5603
Riback W H    4235
Ribyn A V     6157
Rice E A      4644
Rice F M      5279
Rice J L      6914
Rice M S      6669
Rice N H      6600
Richard B J   2964
Richard Sr R  596
Richards L R  597
Richards R N  5541
Richardson A  2151
Richardson E A 5258
Richardson J W 2664
Richardson M M 6998
Richardson M S 1785
Richardson R N 349
Richey D J    1786
Richey E B    4947
Richey R D    4458
Richman D J   1330
Richmond L J  3393
Richtel A     3941
Rickels M S   5604
Ricker H      1048
Ricker K T    6915
Ricklefs M C  49
Rickman S M   4466
Riddick R M   6774
Riddle M J    4948
Ridgeway A M  3496
Ridley N      1787
Riedell F     4147
Rieder J E    2152
Riedling G L  2665
Riemer S J    5605
Riesen C F    4148
Riess L P     4949
Riggs J A     1971
Riggs L       1499
Riggs R A     2666
Riker J R     2312
Riley C       3138
Riley C       4149
Riley Br J    374
Riley J R     6916
Riley M       3793
Riley M E     2153
Riley S B     3853
Rindfleisch G 4645
Rindlaub K G  2154
Ringer L K    4290
Ringheim B J  2313
Ringwald G M  6158
Ripper G C    3951
Rismiller A B 2667
Rissover F    2668

Rist R C  1204
Ritch B R  2669
Ritcher G  77
Ritchey L M  3637
Ritter S A  1331
Ritzo B M  5468
Rivera-Pizarro W  5606
Rivera-Rodriquez J  1332
Roach M L  478
Roahen R L  4646
Robb M C  1788
Robbiano H  1789
Robbins B  142
Robbins D  3921
Robbins E L  2965
Robbins O M  5049
Roberson R E  6159
Roberts E  2385
Roberts J L  1049
Roberts M R  479
Roberts W H  4647
Robertson B K  5232
Robertson D E  1500
Robertson H E  2813
Robertson M M  6160
Robertson T L Jr  4150
Robeson H  5104
Robeson J A  6816
Robey A L  1050
Robinson A C  5812
Robinson C R  1972
Robinson D M  143
Robinson D W  6161
Robinson E H  1051
Robinson M L  1501
Robinson P A  309
Robinson V U  6162
Robison J H  6163
Robison Z C  6967
Robyn D J  1052
Rocchio A M  1790
Rocco M L  4151
Rochelle W R  5233
Rochford J J  2966
Rock M H  3873
Rockefeller L  4152
Roddey C  4487
Roden J  6322
Rodenberger M L  3904
Rodewald F A  732
Rodewald F A  2670
Rodgers C D  3394
Rodgers E  2760
Rodgers J  4950
Rodgers R A  1333
Rodman J R  17
Rodman M R  6601
Rodnon S  1791
Roegner J L  2967

Roehl R  650
Roerecke H H  1792
Roeser K M  3395
Roessner W P  1973
Rogers A A  183
Rogers A B  5846
Rogers D M  5105
Rogers E J  6917
Rogers G M  5457
Rogers G P  3053
Rogers H P  4467
Rogers J F  6164
Rogers M A  2314
Rogers M L  340
Rogers R  3396
Rogers R C  6165
Rogers R N  1793
Rogers R R  841
Rohleder P J  78
Rohman D G  5813
Roland A  4951
Roland E E  386
Roller W D  5234
Rollins H B  1502
Romanelli L  196
Roos D F  2968
Ropeter M  3854
Rosa A F  6166
Rosans R  4488
Roschwalb J  6918
Rose A D  375
Rose E  5077
Rose M G  5660
Rose Z  3397
Rosemond L  3398
Rosen N  6167
Rosenblatt P  6602
Rosenblatt W F Jr  4952
Rosenblum H S  2969
Rosener A  842
Rosenfeld N  5078
Rosenheim J  4153
Rosenthal M M  1552
Rosenthal Y C  2315
Roskos N L  4154
Ross B M  3794
Ross F A  843
Ross J M  4325
Ross L H  2039
Ross M  2671
Ross M W  4155
Ross R B  4156
Ross R L  598
Ross S F  6919
Rossard J A  599
Rosselot G S  1113
Rosser D M  2672
Rossi A  872
Rossi D D  2236

Rosso B M  1334
Roth G M  6603
Roth R F  1794
Roth T  3751
Rothe C E  440
Rother C A  1795
Rother J  5607
Rothman A  290
Rothman A B  3497
Rothman J L  441
Rouge J R  5542
Rouillard H L  3399
Roulston C R  2673
Rourke M E  2356
Rousculp C G  5389
Rowan S R  753
Rowe Br C  6968
Rowe M O  2674
Rowland L L  1205
Rowlette R O  6168
Rowley V L  5361
Roy Mother M  844
Royall S L  3855
Royals B J  310
Roye E R  600
Rubin J  376
Rubio M P  1503
Rudnick L P  1796
Rudolph E P  3139
Rudolph J G  5259
Rudzinski J K  5543
Ruedi N P  4648
Ruff P A  1503
Ruffin M S  1161
Ruffin P D  1797
Ruffing A L  2013
Rugg H E  3710
Ruhl U E  2359
Rukas N M  2675
Rumsey A E  2970
Runkel P R  1053
Rupright M P  2971
Rushing L  3202
Rushing L S  845
Ruska M K  4953
Russ C E  79
Russell C S  2793
Russell J G  6169
Russell J J  4157
Russell L A  6170
Russell M F  6356
Russell N K  6604
Rutenber R D Jr  3140
Rutherford B  3942
Ruthledge J W  6775
Ryan A G  2972
Ryan G B  3728
Ryan J P  3141
Ryan Sr M  3203

Ryan M E    5106
Ryberg C L    5841

Sabey F P    1798
Sabukewicz C J    184
Sacks H H    4699
Sadler E L    3711
Sadler G M    1505
Sadler H    6605
Sadler M R    5544
Sadock G J    4954
Sage R L    6678
Sainer S    3400
St Pierre J M    6171
Sakamoto T    2676
Sakowitz N    18
Saks B J    2677
Sala J P    5459
Salatore N T    1162
Salisbury F E    5608
Salisbury N L    6606
Sallee J D    3638
Salmon J C    1091
Salter A B    3748
Saltz K W    601
Sample D J    1799
Sample E J    6172
Samples B T    311
Sampsell P H    1800
Sams O E Jr    4649
Samuels B    4227
Samuels C T    6323
Samuelson J E    4650
Sandberg J S    6173
Sander E E    6607
Sanders E A    3498
Sanders E F    3401
Sanders J P    6285
Sanders M A    3142
Sanders M K    6608
Sanders P R    5362
Sanderson A B    402
Sanderson S D    846
Sandifer H L    5107
Sandsberry J C    1163
Sant T A    2237
Santacroce P J    2973
Santarelli M    411
Santoro W D    3905
Santry A T    4651
Santucho O J    5545
Santuico N V    5814
Sarasohn C L    3143
Sasso L J    2974
Sather M J    1801
Satomi H    602
Sauls B A    19
Saunders J M    4726
Saunders R L    3574

Savage D H    1506
Sawey S C    943
Sawicki R M    1164
Sawyer B D    6174
Sayers D L    2678
Sayre I C    6175
Sayre R W    227
Scales G M    3712
Scales S M    6357
Scalia L F    4439
Scambray T A    4440
Scandrett H V    5640
Scanlan G S    1054
Scanlan J F Jr    5609
Scapin M    712
Scarboro L    480
Scarborough C W    2679
Schaefer Sr M R    603
Schaefle J W    4158
Schaible H    3933
Schaner J E    2680
Schapiro J B    4652
Schaup S M    2681
Schaus H    6176
Schein D E    356
Schemerhorn L H    2814
Schenker S I    6286
Schepers J    5610
Scheuer A    4159
Schick N W    3576
Schiffman M    6177
Schiller J L    1177
Schiller R L    3639
Schiller S M    93
Schindelman L    3402
Schlesinger E K    2682
Schley J B    1893
Schlick C A    1192
Schmalenbeck H    2041
Schmedake D M    3771
Schmerl R B    144
Schmidt B    2975
Schmidt B    6178
Schmidt G    5611
Schmidt G L    1802
Schmidt J E    1507
Schmidt M C    3204
Schmidt P    4653
Schmidt R W    4160
Schmidt S M    4161
Schmitt E L    353
Schmitt M C    604
Schmitt P J    6179
Schmittlein A E    847
Schneider E D    3922
Schneider J M    4955
Schneider S P    3795
Schock M C    6834
Schoen C B    2683

Schoendaller K P    4654
Schofield J B    2202
Scholes J B    3403
Schooley B J    145
Schoppe J L    2316
Schrader C G Jr    644
Schrader E    5546
Schreiber R J    2155
Schroeder L    4162
Schroeder R    1974
Schroeder R U    2156
Schuchard W R    1335
Schueller T G    357
Schuessler L J    1336
Schug C H    3729
Schulz M F    754
Schumacher J F    2684
Schupbach D J    6180
Schwab S V    755
Schwalb S    4291
Schwan F O    4656
Schwartz A H    756
Schwartz E B    1803
Schwartz J C    3404
Schwarz C    6697
Schwegel D M    6609
Schweppe E G    848
Schwertman M P    3405
Schwienher E C    6698
Scoble W F    1553
Scofield S V    3499
Scoles D L    4490
Scott A M    1508
Scott E L    6181
Scott G    442
Scott H T    6340
Scott J H    2685
Scott J M    6699
Scott K K    4163
Scott V J    1337
Scott W B    6324
Scott W D    1509
Scott W H    5547
Scott W P    849
Scrimgeour G J    5079
Seale W A    1804
Seals T D    3640
Seaman G A    4489
Sears Sr C M    3534
Sears Sr M P    1338
Sears V M    4956
Searson M    5314
Seawell E    4957
Seder J M    5612
Seedyke W C    291
Seegers J C    5433
Segal A F    3406
Sehon E B    6920
Seib K A    6921

Seibert R E 2976
Seidel R F 4657
Seigel R K 4400
Seigle N R 5641
Seigler M B 4958
Seiter R D 6610
Selken M A 316
Selzman J 6182
Semmler H C 3205
Senter M L 3407
Senzee N K 6438
Sequeira A A 3856
Serdarevic B 3206
Sereni E 2686
Serpa R L 6817
Serpico L M 2687
Settle E A 2238
Sewell H R 4658
Sewell I 605
Sewell J D 5050
Sewell R 2042
Sexton E 4164
Sexton R J 4959
Seymour B J 1805
Seymour C J 5235
Seymour E 1975
Shafer M J 2977
Shafer M R 6385
Shafer R M 6183
Shah D C 850
Shaheen A A 1339
Shair S N 851
Shands M F 1340
Shane M B 1510
Shankman S R 6358
Shannon R S 3068
Shapiro B H 4165
Shapiro C K 1165
Shapiro J 3857
Sharma J K 1341
Sharp D B 4659
Sharp E R 1806
Sharp H 713
Sharp M P 6184
Sharpe D R 3144
Sharpe J L 6185
Sharpe L L 6922
Sharpe M R 2005
Shavelenko I A 6186
Shaw C E 6670
Shaw D B 4960
Shaw E A 3772
Shaw E P 3641
Shaw J L 606
Shaw M 2157
Shay Sr M I 1055
Shea J P 443
Shea M T 1342
Shealy A 6923

Sheehan Sr H T 1056
Sheehan Sr M 5679
Sheen E D 6187
Sheeran J A 2002
Sheerin W V 4961
Sheffield H M 5236
Sheffield J F 6924
Sheilds J C 146
Shelbourn J A 4326
Sheldon R H 3752
Shell J C 1807
Shell P T 6188
Shelly E W 3408
Shelton F 1808
Shelton J 147
Shelton R W 3923
Shemwell A L Jr 933
Shennum M 2158
Shenstone S L 6287
Sheriff D L 2337
Sherman E F 1809
Sherman E P 6189
Sherman J L 6190
Sherman M C 4344
Sherman W D 3943
Sherwood R 1511
Shields J A 3500
Shields M V 3642
Shields P M 5842
Shin K K 4166
Shipley F C 6191
Shirahama K 3452
Shive F A 5237
Shohan H S 2688
Shook B L 2420
Shore W A 251
Short G M 2159
Short R L 1343
Shropshire A W 2815
Shuck E C 4962
Shuford C E 4228
Shular M 148
Shulford C B 6925
Shumaker H W 1810
Shumaker I C 2689
Shutts J F 1057
Shveiger R 910
Siedlecki P A 4963
Siegel G 149
Sieger M 6192
Siek P P 2690
Sievers M W 6926
Sievert W 1344
Signor L H 607
Silber C A 2160
Silberman D J 4167
Silio T A 2978
Siltzbach M K 4168
Silva J D 1512

Silver J W 5434
Silver R G 2
Silverman D H 3409
Silverman J 3410
Silverman Y 1811
Silvestri E 6439
Silvia B J 4964
Sim L K 2161
Simar A D 5680
Simes M E 3411
Simmen E R 1812
Simmonds R S 6818
Simmons B 3924
Simmons E 5815
Simmons J G 6359
Simmons L W 4660
Simmons M 6440
Simmons S C 645
Simmons T 5126
Simmons V B 4661
Simms K 2162
Simon G J 911
Simoneaux K G 852
Simons H T 6927
Simons M A 1813
Simons M P 6441
Simonton C H 3643
Simpson F W 5435
Simpson H 4965
Simpson H A 1814
Simpson R G 2317
Simpson S K 2979
Simpson S L 6611
Sims L A 5315
Simson G K 4169
Sinclair G 1815
Singleton M K 6193
Sipples H J 2163
Sipsey W J 6928
Sire J W 331
Sissa I 1539
Sitta E 342
Sitton L B 3806
Sitz H A 1058
Skaggs P D 6194
Skates C B 3459
Skeels G 185
Skeels R A 1976
Skey M A 1059
Skov M J 5138
Slack R C 1513
Slade L A 4170
Slagle M L 5119
Slate J E 6819
Slater E 6671
Slaughter C R 1816
Sleeper M E 1166
Slick R D 651
Sloan B L 6195

Sloane D E    4966
Slobbe V E    3958
Slover F   6612
Small E   6196
Small G A   2022
Smalling D   6776
Smart C   2318
Smart F A   918
Smedley E A   346
Smeyak M A   1060
Smigala B L   6197
Smiley C   608
Smith A E   5280
Smith A G   481
Smith A M   1817
Smith B   228
Smith B G   714
Smith B J   2980
Smith B L   1514
Smith C A   2692
Smith C A   6613
Smith C J   6700
Smith C R   2691
Smith C Y   4967
Smith D   6198
Smith D E   6999
Smith D G   6614
Smith E B   1515
Smith E M   4314
Smith Sr G   80
Smith G   5339
Smith G H   1818
Smith G K   6442
Smith H   6615
Smith H J   1345
Smith J A   1346
Smith J A   4491
Smith J D   3644
Smith J D   4257
Smith J E Jr   2693
Smith J H   1819
Smith K A   3906
Smith K I   1820
Smith L   2694
Smith L C   3645
Smith L C   6777
Smith L R   5548
Smith M   5238
Smith M B   656
Smith M E   1821
Smith M E   3961
Smith M E   4968
Smith M E   4969
Smith M H   1347
Smith M H   3412
Smith M I   3501
Smith M J   2695
Smith M M   5
Smith M M   3646

Smith M P   4711
Smith N W   609
Smith P   1822
Smith P A   3207
Smith P D   5120
Smith P D   6616
Smith P S   4293
Smith R A   4171
Smith R A   5670
Smith R B   5816
Smith S F   4970
Smith S H   3858
Smith T J   6199
Smith V   403
Smith W A   260
Smith W C   5549
Smitham S T   5817
Smitherman B J   6929
Smithers B J   1823
Smithline A   1516
Smothers M C   5108
Snell Sr M V   1348
Snipes D M   1517
Snoddy A L   610
Snoddy R L   30
Snoek N   4971
Snook D G   3145
Snow G   6672
Snow J H   4172
Snyder J M   4401
Snyder L E   3413
Snyder L N   4972
Sodergren M F   2696
Sola R   6617
Soland C   1977
Solari R   186
Solderer A E   2981
Solensten J M   1554
Sollers F W   3069
Sollner W J   150
Solomon J L   6386
Solomon L N   1824
Solomon L R   3859
Solomon R H   5316
Solomon R M   3414
Somoza J M   81
Somsen J A   1061
Sorenson E C   2982
Sorrells D J   3809
Soucy A   1349
Sowa E S   332
Sowders B E   377
Spanger J P   6387
Spangler J D   5613
Spangler L   2421
Spano A   6930
Spanos B   3415
Sparks E C   3773
Sparrow M C   4662

Sparrow M S   2697
Spaw G   4402
Speake M M   4973
Spear D A   4974
Spear G E   5715
Spears W   5131
Speck P S   3416
Speegle K S   3417
Speeks I M   6200
Speer M D   1114
Speer M T   5051
Spelman J W   4663
Spence E B   4345
Spencer A   3146
Spencer M   4664
Spencer M   4492
Sphar E A   5689
Spicehandler D   6325
Spiese R D   3502
Spike W S   5818
Spilhaug B   3147
Spillane Sr J M   2698
Spiller E B   4294
Spillman R R   3208
Spitz J D   482
Spivey H E   3647
Spivey S A   312
Sponagle A P   4665
Springer C L   1825
Springman L R   3730
Sproule W J   5550
Sprouse V B   2203
Sprull J C   387
Spurlock J H   5340
Spurlock O   6969
Sroka S G   1518
Stace A C   82
Stack M R   1826
Staehle J T   2699
Stafford E P   2983
Stageberg N C   6618
Staggs B M   2239
Staggs K W   1115
Stahl G   5317
Stahlman L   3209
Stahr A   1827
Staley T F   1978
Stalker J   5671
Stallard C K   187
Stalling D L   5052
Stallings E   611
Stalnaker S L   2319
Stamper J M   3503
Stampleman J R   6201
Standish E Y   3418
Stanley A M   151
Stanley D   1828
Stanley E B   3419
Stanley E E   351

| | | |
|---|---|---|
| Stanley L C 4295 | Stevenson S E 22 | Strange A F 4979 |
| Stanley Sr M C 612 | Stewart A B 5642 | Straub P F 6820 |
| Stansell P A 5436 | Stewart A E 3714 | Straughn L 4672 |
| Stanton B E 1829 | Stewart A F 757 | Strauss L R 5553 |
| Stanton J M 1979 | Stewart D A 2985 | Strauss M T 2709 |
| Stanton R B 2700 | Stewart J E 2370 | Strawn R I 4230 |
| Stappenbeck H L 6202 | Stewart J H 6778 | Streater G L 4673 |
| Stark A W 2701 | Stewart J W 4667 | Strickland A B 3650 |
| Stark H J 4296 | Stewart K K 4976 | Strickler J H 2987 |
| Stark S Jr 4173 | Stewart L M 4258 | Stringer A W 4980 |
| Starosciak K P 2984 | Stewart R A 5239 | Strommer D W 2710 |
| Starr C J 4403 | Stewart S G 4668 | Strommer J P 6821 |
| Startt W 6203 | Stewart W A 3064 | Strongin L 912 |
| Startzman P K 6204 | Stick E 1385 | Strother L M 2387 |
| Stasio M L 3925 | Stienecker W 2240 | Stroup B A 3149 |
| Steadman M S 6333 | Stiff A L 5109 | Strozier R I 6931 |
| Steadmon J D 6326 | Stigdon C F Jr 4459 | Struggles E 4981 |
| Steege M T 1830 | Stilley H M 1834 | Stuart B F 1836 |
| Steele H G 3420 | Stineford R E 5614 | Studer W P 4674 |
| Steele J H 3648 | Stith M E 3945 | Stumbo C 4441 |
| Steele M M 1062 | Stith M E 4977 | Stumbo R R 6209 |
| Steele M T 2702 | Stobart J F 51 | Stump R J 4175 |
| Steele S C 2703 | Stockdale W A 6206 | Sturtevant D F 3460 |
| Steen G E 4975 | Stockstill M A 2986 | Stutman S T 1837 |
| Steen J T 1980 | Stockton E L Jr 5820 | Stutzman D C 4982 |
| Stein W B 2704 | Stockton M 2705 | Suberman J 6932 |
| Steinberg B A 1831 | Stoddart H G 3796 | Suby E H 388 |
| Steingold F S 1350 | Stokes P B 1167 | Suddath J E 6210 |
| Steinhagen C T 613 | Stone A E Jr 853 | Suetterlin E M 483 |
| Steinhagen M J 4174 | Stone E 4229 | Sugarbaker E 4328 |
| Steinmetz E M 240 | Stone F B 3422 | Sugg R E 2711 |
| Steller R E 20 | Stone O 5663 | Suhre M 6622 |
| Stenberg M N 6619 | Stone P M 5843 | Suitor J H 4176 |
| Stenger L 715 | Stone S L 3423 | Sullenberger T E 3425 |
| Stenson M J 4666 | Stone V L 3424 | Sullivan C G 716 |
| Stepaniuk A 3421 | Stoneback H R 1835 | Sullivan E 4231 |
| Stephan E 5819 | Stoner M P 4669 | Sullivan H 1520 |
| Stephens A J 3058 | Stoner P A 4670 | Sullivan J J 3749 |
| Stephens G M 50 | Stordahl L M 6207 | Sullivan J R 2172 |
| Stephens G S 21 | Storey M L 5552 | Sullivan Sr M C 3797 |
| Stephens M M 4321 | Storm D O 1981 | Sullivan M S 3907 |
| Stephens P L 6620 | Storms C B 2165 | Sullivan N C 5241 |
| Stephens R O 6621 | Story A W 5363 | Sullivan N C 5697 |
| Stephenson C C 3713 | Story S 1168 | Sullivan R M 6673 |
| Stephenson E R 5318 | Stott J C 2706 | Sullivan V 1521 |
| Stephenson G D 5551 | Stott N G 652 | Sullivan W J 3426 |
| Stern C S 5341 | Stoufer R 5269 | Sumida A 1522 |
| Stern J H 3148 | Stough P 6360 | Summers H 2204 |
| Stern S 292 | Stout B M 3512 | Sumner R 3150 |
| Sternberg J 2164 | Stout G W 2003 | Surette J E 5364 |
| Stevens A W 2386 | Stout J P 2707 | Sustafson S L 2713 |
| Stevens H F 1540 | Stout N G 4671 | Sutherland H L 4177 |
| Stevens L 2320 | Stout R A 1169 | Sutliff H J 6933 |
| Stevens L R 5080 | Stovall J 4978 | Sutphin K T 489 |
| Stevens P A 1832 | Stovall S S 6208 | Sutrina J J 6211 |
| Stevens S K 1833 | Strain J 3649 | Sutton G W 1351 |
| Stevenson E B 6205 | Strain J H 2051 | Sutton K H 6361 |
| Stevenson F C 1519 | Strain W H 2708 | Sutton L M 6212 |
| Stevenson R M 444 | Straney R M 5240 | Sutton W A 4178 |

Sutton W E   1352
Suzuki K   2794
Svitak V J   23
Swadley D R   854
Swain L H   6213
Swainbank D R   5110
Swallow M R   5554
Swan M B   83
Swank A L   629
Swank D L   2241
Swann W R   6214
Swanson D R   6779
Swanson G N   1353
Swanson K   2795
Swanson M L   5821
Swanson M S   1354
Swanson P L   6215
Swanson R N   4675
Swartz G   5555
Swartz G A   5615
Swearingen J E   3427
Swearingen J H   5365
Swearingen W S   3428
Sweda M K   334
Sweet A C   5242
Sweitzer R H   2988
Sweiven E G   3429
Swigert F H Jr   5822
Swink L H   4346
Swinney D H   3065
Swoboda R J   42
Sykes J T   2714
Sykes M M   6216
Szala A   3430
Szuberla G A   188

Tabb L E   5281
Tadaseo R T   3431
Taffe B J   293
Taggart A E   641
Tagge A W   6443
Taiz N N   5319
Takeshita S   412
Taley S A   2715
Talley M R   4739
Tallman R S   3026
Talman T S   2716
Tal-Mason P   913
Tanasso E M   1355
Tandy K A   5081
Tanguay N J   855
Tanner A B   1063
Tanner H A   4676
Tanner J   6217
Tanner J E   1838
Tanner J E   2989
Tanner J T   6623
Tansel M R   6624
Tanzy C E   1523

Taper P A   3860
Tapley P A   335
Tapp G H   4493
Tarantino F   4677
Tarleton R M   3432
Tart J D   4179
Tate J U   1356
Tatsuguchi E   5274
Taychman M   1357
Tayer D W   4180
Taylor C B   2388
Taylor C R   6970
Taylor C Y   6388
Taylor D C   6934
Taylor F B   2761
Taylor F F   1982
Taylor H   3151
Taylor J   3798
Taylor J R   5716
Taylor J W   3152
Taylor L J   4678
Taylor Sr M C   2389
Taylor P L   1889
Taylor P M   6935
Taylor R L   497
Taylor R M   230
Taylor R M   2205
Taylor S   1064
Taylor T A   6218
Taylor V W   4494
Tedford K S   5437
Teichgraeber S E   6444
Teitz B A   2023
Temple H F   2166
Templin A B   856
Ten Eyck D B   6445
Tenn E E   413
Tenney T A   6219
Tenny M F   5342
Tepley M A   5556
Teplitsky A   2717
Teresa E R   5823
Terrell B L   4735
Terrell B S   3861
Terrell C F   1358
Terris V R   1065
Terry A W   6951
Terry E F   1839
Terry T B   4232
Tetzel G P   24
Tewell D J   4983
Thacher A G Jr   633
Tharp J B   4984
Thayer G R   6220
Thayer H D   2990
Theemler L W   1840
Theiss N L   614
Thel C H   2718
Theriault A A   2719

Therrell K D   6221
Thetford J W Jr   1841
Theurer L A   4985
Thibodeau Mother M H   2167
Thoeni Sr M C   6222
Thomas A G   3433
Thomas B O   6446
Thomas C E   3434
Thomas D A   5824
Thomas E F   5275
Thomas E J   5857
Thomas H K   152
Thomas L   1170
Thomas M A   857
Thomas N B   6223
Thomas N H   1842
Thomas P   2024
Thomas P J   2168
Thomas R B   4679
Thomas R E   1524
Thomas R M   6701
Thompson A   2720
Thompson B B   6936
Thompson C   5672
Thompson D L   6447
Thompson D M   858
Thompson E J   1843
Thompson E J   6224
Thompson G   3153
Thompson H   6780
Thompson J E   6225
Thompson K A   1983
Thompson L C   2991
Thompson L G   1359
Thompson L R   5243
Thompson L S   261
Thompson M B   2992
Thompson M H   2169
Thompson M I   419
Thompson R B   5320
Thompson R F   343
Thompson S M   294
Thompson T M   3715
Thompson W O   6981
Thoms G E   859
Thomson C L   4680
Thomson D T   6226
Thorburn J A   1193
Thorne C D   3753
Thorne E C   7000
Thorne M E   5438
Thornhill E E   3435
Thornton E C   4986
Thornton R M   414
Thorpe B D   5439
Thrift W B   1066
Throckmorton J L   2422
Thurber M S   5139
Thurman K   2206

Thurman L H 2993
Thweatt J K Jr 2170
Tibbetts B H 2994
Tickell J A 5321
Tidwell D 4681
Tidwell L G 153
Tierney Sr M R 4442
Tilford S R 6625
Tillinghast C A 5825
Tillman R J 3651
Tillson M L 1844
Tillson O 2721
Timolin B J 6626
Tinsley B B 6448
Tippetts R H 4181
Tippit G Y 6781
Tipton L 4987
Titchener L F 5082
Tobias R C 5861
Tobiasson L J 3210
Tocchi A 6227
Todd D O 2242
Todd J F 1845
Todd S R Jr 1067
Tolan S S 860
Tolton I 6228
Tomarken C J 1846
Tomei Sr M C 4259
Tomlinson B E 2243
Tomlinson K L 6229
Tommasulo Br A 241
Tommy-Martin Y 1847
Tompkins R D 6708
Tong B L 5717
Toole R W 6230
Toran W B 154
Torrence A 615
Torrents J E 1360
Torres J B 2722
Tosney E M 5371
Toso P 881
Toth B D 6782
Toucheff J R 6702
Tout D J 155
Towers T 445
Towle C K 2723
Townley J F 4495
Townley R D 84
Townsend H W 616
Tracy F X 634
Tracy L G 3211
Trafton B W 3535
Trager T N 4404
Trantham C P 5380
Trapani R M 211
Travis M K 1848
Tray Sr M P 6231
Treadwell P N 1194
Treat A 4988

Treece D Y 2724
Treitel R M 5053
Tremblay W A 1849
Trent L K 2725
Tribble J F 3662
Trilling L R 6232
Trimble L M 4989
Trouy Fr L 4347
Trowbridge C W 4682
Truax E 4683
Truett L J 5381
Truitt D W 6233
Trujillio Br A B 3862
Truscott R B 758
Tschumy R D 2171
Tu H Y 1525
Tua L M 2172
Tubb H 2390
Tuck D J 759
Tucker C H 2726
Tucker C H 6234
Tucker C T 6627
Tucker I W 6235
Tucker P A 6822
Tucker R E 105
Tufts M A 2727
Tulgan G R 6674
Tull M A 2207
Tuohey J P 4684
Turilli E A 6362
Turner B D 717
Turner D A 3436
Turner E H 3799
Turner F W 2728
Turner H 4182
Turner M B 6236
Turner P 3154
Turner T 3667
Turngren J A 1386
Turnipseed J O 3172
Turnquist S E 255
Turrell C R 2729
Tuxbury F K 4685
Tway E 6628
Tyler S L 404
Tyree M I 3863
Tyson B M 2995
Tyson J P 4686

Uka K 4687
Ullrich V 6629
Underwood J K 2391
Underwood M P 4688
Unger L H 1361
Unger W E 6389
Untereiner M A 617
Unthank L T 1984
Updegraff R F 405
Uppman I M 3652

Upton D L 2730
Uzzell M 1850
Uzzle W T Jr 6630

Vails L 6983
Valastro G J 389
Valente F J 5366
Valente J B 4183
Valentine C B 1526
Valentine L B 6631
Valway H L 6937
Van Der Beets R 2025
Vandiver S E 2996
Van Egmond P G 6632
Van Gundy H C 6237
Van Heur M L 6238
Van Loen H R 3212
Van Meter M E 2997
Vann J D 4990
Van Nieumenhuize P F 6783
Van Raes R M 5372
Van Schreeven W J 655
Vardamis A A 3461
Varisco R J 6239
Varner J G 4991
Vathing G S 4184
Vaughn J D 6363
Vaughn S C 1851
Vause E A 6938
Veach J A 1068
Veale T G 618
Vehrs G S 2731
Veit R C 2732
Venable S N 3716
Venettozzi V 295
Vento I D 1171
Verbieren D R 4689
Verduin K 6288
Vernon D 313
Versinger N M 3717
Vest F E 6240
Veters A J 4992
Vetterli C 6241
Vickers J E 6939
Viery Sr E J 5557
Viets M R 1069
Vilas M S 378
Villane M V 2998
Villanueva A 1362
Villarreal J J 446
Vincent J S 914
Vinecour A 4185
Vintschger F E 498
Virsis R A 4690
Vitacco P 296
Viverette J A Jr 1985
Vogel D 1527
Vogel N S 2173
Vogelsang F M 5054

Vogt K M 1852
Vogt M E 760
Vogt W J 5616
Vollman P D 2733
Voltolina A 3800
VonAuw A 1363
Von Doemming J M 1364
Von Maszewski B D 2999
Voorhees V D 4993
Vorsteg R H 5617
Voth R A 1853
Voyles J P 619
Voyles J R 1854
Vreswyk P W 3926

Waddill G W 5147
Wade B G 718
Wade C G 3000
Wafer J W 5826
Wageman J C 4186
Wagener J W 3001
Wages J D 2734
Wagner C A 2321
Wagner D H 6289
Wagner L W 3437
Wagner W D 4405
Wagoner R D 620
Wagstaff L 1855
Wagstaff S D 336
Wahlquist J J 4187
Waiters R C 3002
Wajima S 1070
Wakeland M 6633
Walden M 2322
Waldron R H 2735
Waldrum E 5827
Wales A M 4406
Wales E M 6634
Walford T L 1986
Walker B H 5111
Walker C E 314
Walker D D 3003
Walker D Y 5343
Walker E H 1116
Walker H J 861
Walker J D 3908
Walker J P 6784
Walker L H 5261
Walker L M 5344
Walker M W 1856
Walker R H 4188
Walker R S 5244
Walker V A 4736
Walker W E 637
Wall L F 2174
Wall M G 5270
Wall V C Jr 761
Wallace F M 920
Wallace H J 1528

Wallace J H 4994
Wallace V 52
Wallis K C 2736
Walsh J F 2175
Walsh J M 3004
Walsh Sr M J 2360
Walsh T P 4407
Walters E L 4189
Waltersdorf H L 379
Walton D A 2392
Walton G W 4995
Walton M 3718
Walz L 3005
Walz Sr V 2176
Ward A M 2796
Ward D A 4190
Ward F E 6242
Ward F W III 6327
Ward I M 6243
Ward J C 3864
Ward M 862
Ward M A 3438
Ward Sr M B 4443
Ward W T 6940
Warden Sr L 5690
Warden R W 5558
Warders D F 1857
Ware L 6635
Ware M J 6244
Waring P B 4191
Warmack G 6245
Warner E W 6785
Warner G 2177
Warnick B J 262
Warren C C 499
Warren C L 1987
Warren E 6449
Warren L 2737
Warren N M 4691
Washburn B E 2393
Washburn I A 2738
Washburn M B 4192
Washington J A 4692
Wasserstein A G 1365
Waters C M 4996
Watkins E M 6246
Watkins F C 4737
Watkins H 3653
Watkins J M 189
Watkins R F 6786
Watson A E 1858
Watson B L 1859
Watson C A 6450
Watson G M 4496
Watson R D 6247
Watter I 6636
Watts M E 1543
Weadock V L 1117
Wear C R 2739

Weatherspoon M A 3213
Weaver A K 3054
Weaver B J 4352
Weaver J A 2740
Weaver K R 6248
Weaver L 3654
Webb G P 6249
Webb J W 5282
Webb M A 2208
Webb M H 2423
Webb R W 1529
Webber J M 4193
Weber E 3155
Weber K L 1860
Weber R E 1861
Webner W T 1862
Webster C M 719
Webster V G 3909
Weckerle C W 3663
Weed M 3655
Weed M K 4997
Weeks D S 5245
Weeks F H 3801
Weeks W E 6941
Wegelin C A 6250
Wehrfritz C M 5246
Weinberg K C 1366
Weinman R J 156
Weinsaft M H 2178
Weis T G 6637
Weiskel T F 1367
Weiss D 2797
Weiss I R 3027
Weiss M 2244
Weiss P 6942
Weisser A T 6943
Weisstein U W 4998
Welch B A 6679
Welch E A 5055
Welch E S 3214
Welch J C 1863
Welch L L 5345
Wells A M 5559
Wells B R 6709
Wells C 3865
Wells E E 6638
Wells G 5322
Wells J I 2179
Wells K H 5132
Wells L R 5247
Wells P 106
Wells S M 2741
Welna R D 5056
Welsh C I 4348
Welsh J R 5440
Welsh J W 6251
Wennerberg Sr T A 2361
Wenson C J Jr 5391
Wermers B F 3719

Werner R L 1368
Wertheim F G 6451
Wertheim M H 2798
Weshinsky R K 157
West E L 3215
West E N 5157
West F 621
West J F 3006
West J O 1369
West M V 53
West R 6675
Westall P 5346
Westbrook F L 3439
Westbrook J S Jr 3952
Westbrook M 863
Westbrook R R 5083
Westerbeck C L 5618
Westerman A 406
Wetmore A B 2323
Wexler J S 6252
Weynand I 2180
Whalen A T 6253
Whalen S I 5112
Whaley B P 1530
Whaling A 6254
Wharton M T 6255
Wheeler F 6452
Wheeler H P 3656
Wheeler O B 4194
Wheelock A S 4195
Whichard L R 3023
Whipple A A 2245
Whisenhunt D B 1864
Whitaker D 4693
Whitaker E M 1172
Whitaker G W Jr 3657
Whitaker R 1071
Whitaker T R 25
Whitbeck E C 3216
Whitcomb V R 5382
White B A 5619
White C B 2742
White C C Jr 3866
White C M 720
White D W 5828
White E D 5620
White H H 31
White I R 2324
White J G 5718
White J H 653
White J L 1072
White L 6639
White M E 4999
White M J 1073
White N J 3217
White P F 2181
White P S 6328
White R R 107
White Z B 3007

Whitehead C 4196
Whitehead K 490
Whitehead K B 6256
Whitehouse J H 6453
Whitener C V 6640
Whiteside G A 1865
Whitesides G E 3037
Whitfield J 1173
Whitman M 5000
Whitmore J S 6787
Whitmore S C 1866
Whitnel J F 6454
Whitney R M 735
Whitsell P C 2743
Whitten N M 2394
Whittington J R 1988
Whittle A R 5623
Whitton H F 3867
Whitton W M 3055
Whyte S W 6329
Wickham L R 2744
Widger H D 5001
Wieting M S 297
Wiggins J K 3720
Wilbert C L 4694
Wilbur M A 6364
Wilburn W B 5858
Wilcher O B 1867
Wilcox E J 380
Wilda A R 3440
Wile R L 3536
Wilemon B M 6944
Wiley V 5002
Wiley W J 1868
Wilhelmi N O 1370
Wilkas J J 5003
Wilkerson J C 1174
Wilkerson M J 3008
Wilkes A E 2799
Wilkie B F 1371
Wilkins L W 2424
Wilkins R J 2325
Wilkinson W B 5004
Willard J D 5084
Willcockson R 3658
Willers A C 6641
Williams A E 1074
Williams C M 3731
Williams C S 6455
Williams E F 6788
Williams E M 4695
Williams F M 5829
Williams G V 1894
Williams H S 5005
Williams H W 94
Williams J F 4197
Williams J P Jr 1179
Williams J R 5006
Williams K 1869

Williams M C 1870
Williams M M 1871
Williams O D 721
Williams P A 1075
Williams P A 1531
Williams P A 5441
Williams P E 2745
Williams P F 5323
Williams P W 6257
Williams R E 2762
Williams S J 4198
Williams T J 1372
Williams T W Jr 1989
Williamson D T 4199
Williamson J M 298
Williamson J M 6330
Williamson M 2395
Williamson M W 1373
Willig C L 1118
Willingham J R 6642
Willis L J 3665
Willis L L 5560
Willis S H 2746
Willis V S 1872
Willoughby J D 425
Willowby L 5248
Wills G S 407
Wilsey C M 3659
Wilson B H 3156
Wilson B H 6258
Wilson B M 2747
Wilson C 1873
Wilson C M 202
Wilson D B 1895
Wilson D H 3009
Wilson D W 2748
Wilson E A 638
Wilson F 5249
Wilson F E 864
Wilson F J 5057
Wilson G F 1076
Wilson G R 6331
Wilson J E 2209
Wilson J H 4200
Wilson J M 3441
Wilson J R 1077
Wilson J R 1119
Wilson K C 6945
Wilson K E 5007
Wilson L L 2749
Wilson M B 3157
Wilson M M 6259
Wilson R D 1078
Wilson R L 3158
Wilson R M 6789
Wilson S F 6971
Wilson S W 484
Wilson T H 1532
Wiltgen M C 6946

Wiltshire E 5008
Wimberly J N 1533
Windell V B 5863
Winger W 6947
Wingo E R 485
Winkel C A 1874
Winkelman J 5009
Winks P L 3442
Winn S C 2750
Winner A 1120
Winsor P 3443
Winter F 417
Winters A K 762
Wintroub S Z 6260
Wirth B 2246
Wirtz R S 6261
Wise K K 2331
Wise L F 6643
Wise M E 6676
Wiseman E F 3218
Wiseman W J 4444
Witherington P 1875
Withey L M 3010
Witt R E 337
Witteveld P J 4201
Wold J 3868
Wolf H R 3869
Wolf S R 3959
Wolfe B B 3444
Wolfe D M 1534
Wolfe R H 6456
Wolfrum A L 4322
Wolfsehr C 5347
Wolinski M J 1876
Womack J P 4202
Wood B A 1535
Wood B N 3445
Wood C 4297
Wood C M 5250
Wood D B 763
Wood D C 3721
Wood D F 1877
Wood F L 1079
Wood J W 3552
Wood L 5113
Wood M L 5010
Wood M M 190
Wood M T 2052
Wood N R 4696
Wood P A 5621
Wood P A 5830
Wood R C 4445
Wood R C 6644
Wood S E 4203
Wood T E 1080
Wooddell W C 381
Woodell C H 6645
Wooden W W Jr 4204

Woodfield E E 4205
Woodfin J D 191
Woodham L K 2326
Woodhouse W L 3070
Woodruff L B 6948
Woodrum M 6646
Woods C S 5011
Woods H J Jr 2425
Woods H M 1536
Woods J S 6262
Woodside H C 5158
Woodward C L 1878
Woodward R H 2751
Woodward V S 4497
Woodwell V L 447
Woodworth D W 4206
Woody D D 3219
Workman R F 1121
Worley H C 2327
Worley V 2328
Worline B B 622
Wormell M A 3802
Worrell J E 6263
Worsham M Z 1537
Worst K 1081
Worster D E 1195
Worth D G 1082
Wortham T E 1538
Worthy J 382
Wranek W H Jr 5012
Wright D J 1999
Wright D J 4697
Wright E F 6264
Wright H L 6265
Wright J T 1879
Wright R G 1880
Wright R K 1374
Wright R R 6828
Wright T F 26
Wright V 6647
Wrobel A 6648
Wrubel D 3504
Wulff G E 1375
Wyatt D C 2752
Wyche L M 3011
Wyckoff G J 212
Wylie O G 5831
Wylie R A 4207
Wymer G 3012
Wyndham H P 4307
Wynn L D 1881
Wyss H H 2182

Yancey S Jr 6984
Yang H 4498
Yarbrough S V 5271
Yarup R L 3013
Yates A T 4499
Yates R L 3014

Yeager O S 4208
Yeargin M K 1882
Yehle C F 5832
Yen B Y 1996
Yen M S 4209
Yingling G S 3513
Yoakam W E 4210
Yong E B 3015
Yonge K N 6949
York B M 4446
York D C 3159
York E C 623
York P L 6703
Yoshida M 5561
Young A M 1883
Young C L 4211
Young C R 4212
Young C S 3545
Young D J 3962
Young D T 2800
Young J J 5251
Young L D 4213
Young M 4214
Young M A 6266
Young M O 624
Young N B 865
Young R C 252
Young S H 1884
Young S M 6296
Young S S 5013
Young T D 3774
Youngblood S H 1885
Yount D F 3016
Yuengert J L 383

Zachary R Y 1376
Zagger J A 4215
Zagranski R A 2183
Zalewski Br C 5681
Zara B R 3446
Zauli-Naldi C 1377
Zeady M A 5086
Zehentmayr A 1175
Zeidman N 3168
Zeigler M I 6267
Zelditch B A 2753
Zeller M A 2754
Zerkine A 1378
Zimmerman M P 5014
Zipes J D 4216
Zipse E C 915
Zobarskas N M 2755
Zona Sr M F 3017
Zuanelli E 3447
Zuber L L 3160
Zuck C F 873
Zuckerman F 6268
Zuckerman H S 6704
Zula M I 3807

Zulandt G K   916
Zweig J R   6269